BOOKS BY ALLAN NEVINS
PUBLISHED BY CHARLES SCRIBNER'S SONS

THE DIARY OF JOHN QUINCY ADAMS (*edited by Allan Nevins*)
THE ORDEAL OF THE UNION
ORDEAL OF THE UNION (*two volumes*)
THE EMERGENCE OF LINCOLN (*two volumes*)
THE WAR FOR THE UNION: THE IMPROVISED WAR, 1861–1862
THE WAR FOR THE UNION: WAR BECOMES REVOLUTION, 1862–1863
A CENTURY OF CARTOONS (*in collaboration with Frank Weitenkampf*)
THIS IS ENGLAND TODAY
JOHN D. ROCKEFELLER, THE HEROIC AGE OF AMERICAN ENTERPRISE, 1940
STUDY IN POWER: JOHN D. ROCKEFELLER, INDUSTRIALIST AND PHILANTHROPIST, 1953
FORD: THE TIMES, THE MAN, THE COMPANY
    A History of Henry Ford, The Ford Motor Company, and The Automotive Industry, 1863–1915 (with Frank Ernest Hill)
FORD: EXPANSION AND CHALLENGE: 1915–1933 (*with Frank Ernest Hill*)
JOHN D. ROCKEFELLER
One Volume Condensation by William Greenleaf of STUDY IN POWER

PUBLISHED ELSEWHERE

ILLINOIS (*Oxford Series on American Universities*)
THE AMERICAN STATES DURING AND AFTER THE REVOLUTION
THE EVENING POST, A CENTURY OF JOURNALISM
AMERICAN SOCIAL HISTORY RECORDED BY BRITISH TRAVELLERS
THE EMERGENCE OF MODERN AMERICA, 1865–1877
GROVER CLEVELAND, A STUDY IN COURAGE
HAMILTON FISH, THE INNER HISTORY OF THE GRANT ADMINISTRATION
ABRAM S. HEWITT, WITH SOME ACCOUNT OF PETER COOPER
THE GATEWAY TO HISTORY
FRÉMONT, PATHMAKER OF THE WEST
THE WORLD OF ELI WHITNEY (*with Jeannette Mirsky*)
AMERICA, THE STORY OF A FREE PEOPLE (*with H. S. Commager*)
THE STATESMANSHIP OF THE CIVIL WAR
THE UNITED STATES IN A CHAOTIC WORLD

AS EDITOR

LETTERS OF GROVER CLEVELAND
SELECT WRITINGS OF ABRAM S. HEWITT
THE DIARY OF PHILIP HONE
THE DIARY OF JAMES K. POLK
DIARY OF GEORGE TEMPLETON STRONG (*with M. H. Thomas*)
LETTERS AND JOURNALS OF BRAND WHITLOCK
FRÉMONT'S NARRATIVES OF EXPLORATION
THE HERITAGE OF AMERICA (*with H. S. Commager*)
THE LEATHERSTOCKING SAGA

The War for the Union

GRANT in 1863. This photograph, presented to Grenville M. Dodge during the Vicksburg Campaign, brings out the quiet determination and stern fighting power written in Grant's eyes and jaw. Here is the Grant of whom General David Hunter wrote to Stanton: "He is a hard worker, writes his own dispatches and orders, and does his own thinking. He is modest, quiet, never swears, and seldom drinks, as he took only two drinks during the three weeks I was with him. He listens quietly to the opinions of others and then judges promptly for himself; and he is very prompt to avail himself in the field of all the errors of his enemy." Courtesy of Mr. Fleming Fraker, Jr., and Mr. Claude R. Cook, Curator, Iowa State Department of History and Archives; reproduction by Des Moines *Register and Tribune.*

The War for the Union

VOLUME II...

WAR
BECOMES
REVOLUTION
1862·1863

by ALLAN NEVINS

CHARLES SCRIBNER'S SONS
New York

PREFACE

NO VOLUME, no series of volumes, can do justice to the tremendous story of effort, devotion, and valor North and South, in the war which finally vindicated national unity. A writer can hope but to present a few truthful interpretations of the vast complexity of events and forces. In the first volume of *The War for the Union* I dealt with affairs from the inauguration of Lincoln to his order for a grand Northern advance on February 22, 1862. This was the phase, as the subtitle stated, of "the improvised war." My second volume takes up the narrative as four leaders step forward in powerful roles: Lincoln disclosing his plan for slavery, Stanton taking over the War Office, Grant delivering the first heavy blow in the West, and McClellan preparing to launch his army against Richmond. The book carries the story to the eve of the climactic events at Vicksburg and Gettysburg. Again the subtitle indicates one of the central themes: "war becomes revolution." And again the emphasis falls on the political, administrative, social, and economic developments of the time, though campaigns and battles cannot be neglected.

Far and wide in America, when Chancellorsville was fought in 1863, extended the ice-sheet of the war, seeming to congeal most of the normal activities of men, and still offering no sign of break or thaw; but underneath it the currents of change ran with accelerated force. War partly retards, partly stimulates, the factors of growth in a nation. In the South, with its scanty population and weak economy, the record was of retardation. In the North observers were struck by the ability of twenty-odd millions of energetic people to make use, while lustily fighting, of the new opportunities created by war contracts, tariffs, the great release of capital, and westward expansion. Anthony Trollope, touring the land from Boston to Dubuque, saw that although Illinois had sent one man out of eight to the armies, she choked under the volume of grain and meats she was producing. He saw in New England that the industrialists and traders were neither more covetous nor more generous than those of Britain. "But that which they do, they are more anxious to do thoroughly and quickly. They desire that every turn taken shall be a great turn."

Years of revolution these were on many fronts. Darwin's *Origin of Species* in 1859 had opened a revolution in thought, and given science a far stronger place in the roster of human activities. When Colonel E. L. Drake the same year struck oil in Pennsylvania, he ushered in an energy-revolution. Within a cen-

vii

tury all but one per cent of the labor performed in the United States, some experts have estimated, was to be done by machines, not muscle, and seventy per cent of the machine power was to flow from petroleum; facts which cast an ironic light upon the South's dependence on the muscle-power of four million slaves. If the North was deeply concerned with the idea of national unity, other lands were finding that the same principle loosed revolutionary currents that no man could check. Garibaldi invaded Sicily in the spring of 1860, entered Naples that fall, and soon afterward saw Victor Emmanuel on the throne of an Italy united save for the papal states. Bismarck became prime minister of Prussia in 1862, and with new power moved toward German unification.

The most farreaching change in the United States was organizational. Improvisation of troops, naval forces, munitions, quartermasters' services, chains of command, and modes of attack necessarily gave way to plan and system; the old individualism yielded in a hundred ways to disciplined association. The army with which McClellan began the peninsular campaign represented not only the largest but the best organized deployment of power ever seen in the New World; and behind the carefully planned array of corps, divisions, brigades, regiments, and batteries was a more and more elaborate network of agencies to provide everything the armed forces required, from tent-pins to siege-guns. Factories, machine shops, mercantile offices, and banks operated on a new scale, and in closer relationship with each other and government. The force of a revolutionary shift of commerce from old north-south channels to new east-west highways was illustrated by the prosperity of the trunk-line railways between the Lakes and the Ohio, and the building of a wholly new road, the Atlantic & Great Western. As a country which in Buchanan's time had made Federal expenditures of less than four hundred millions a year began making them in billions, the scale of all enterprises, public and private, was magnified.

In short, pressures of war were compelling the amorphous nation of 1860 to acquire form and structure. The necessity of rallying and concentrating its forces was converting the limp, sprawling North into a coordinated and directed society which set a new value on efficiency. A modern America was being born.

As the war was prolonged, it inevitably accomplished a revolutionary change in the status and outlook of the colored folk who comprised about an eighth of the population. When John Brown was hanged in 1859 slavery had seemed as strongly intrenched as ever. Had fighting ended in the spring of 1862 it might have survived for years. But it suffered shock after shock—the effort of many slaveholders to carry their property into interior fastnesses of the South; the thrusts of Northern columns into Alabama, Mississippi, and Louisiana; the thunder of Northern warships on the rivers and seacoasts; the pervasive propaganda of the grapevine telegraph. By the spring of 1863, with a systematic enlistment of colored troops, the future of the Negro was assured. Much else of the oldtime America died with slavery. E. L. Godkin visited the South just before and just after the war. On the second visit he was conscious of a changed atmosphere, as if the windows of a closed room had been suddenly opened; and when he mentioned the fact, a Southern friend replied, "Yes, sir, we have been brought into intellectual and moral relations with the rest of the world."

As the current of the war flows more strongly its interest deepens. This volume necessarily pays much more attention to the heroic endurance of the South, and the genius of Lee and Jackson. It attempts to do justice to three chief architects of Northern victory, Stanton, Farragut, and Grant; but the one great commanding figure is Lincoln, who grows in stature from crisis to crisis. Some chapters of the war have had to be postponed to later treatment: the blockade, for example, the financial measures, and the intellectual currents of the time. Throughout the book it will be plain that the primary heroes of the struggle are those whom Lincoln called the "plain people," whose belief in national destiny never faltered, and whose capacity for sacrifice knew no limits.

The author is under more obligations to friends than he can fully acknowledge. But he must express special thanks to Bruce Catton, E. B. Long, Henry Steele Commager, Harold Hyman, David Donald, Frank E. Hill, Joseph Rappaport, Ralph Newman, Carl Haverlin, Miss Marian McKenna, and Mrs. Jean Conti. Among librarians he owes a large debt to Dr. John Pomfret and the staff of the Huntington, Drs. Carl White, Richard Logsdon, and Roland Baughman of Columbia University, Stanley Pargellis of the Newberry, Paul M. Angle of the Chicago Historical Society, Clyde C. Walton and Miss Margaret Flint of the Illinois State Historical Library, and Dr. David Mearns and the staff of the Congressional Library. He must thank Mr. S. L. M. Barlow for allowing him to see a portion of the Barlow Papers before their transfer to the Huntington. The patience of Charles Scribner and Dr. Wayne Andrews in helping the book through the press has been invaluable. For constant encouragement he owes much to the late Dr. Abraham Flexner, and for material aid he is under obligation to Mr. Lessing Rosenwald, the late Mrs. David Levy, the Carnegie Corporation, and its able head, John W. Gardner.

A final word should be said about the spelling of proper names. I have followed the form used in the Dictionary of American Biography in identifying E. Kirby-Smith, who himself did not use the hyphen. I have also followed DAB usage with the name Fitz-John Porter, who sometimes used the hyphen and sometimes did not. I have preferred Savanna to Savannah for the Tennessee River town to avoid any possible confusion, among foreign readers, with the Atlantic port. In naming battles I have taken what seems the most familiar usage, and hope in a later volume to insert a table giving variant appellations.

Allan Nevins
The Huntington Library

CONTENTS

ILLUSTRATIONS

xiii

The War for the Union

1

Lincoln and Grant Launch
Two Thrusts

AS THE chill dawn of New Year's Day in 1862 broke over Provincetown on Cape Cod, townspeople flocked to the shore to see a British sloop of war, the *Rinaldo*, drop anchor in the harbor immortalized by the *Mayflower*. Curious Yankees in small boats, hailing her, got no information from the officers. But when the New York pilot who had brought her in came ashore with a cipher message to Lord Lyons in Washington, he divulged the news that James M. Mason and John Slidell were to be put aboard and taken to Halifax. Excitement mounted in the little town when word came by telegraph that the two Confederates had left Fort Warren in Boston harbor at eleven. About four the smoke of another steamer rose over Long Point, and a few minutes later the tug *Starlight* rounded it. Soon Mason, portly, bald, and pompous, and Slidell, a dapper man with a sulky air, clambered up the side of the British ship; their luggage followed; and the *Rinaldo* steamed smartly to sea. The American surrender of the envoys, managed tactfully in this quiet port, gave anguish to Southerners who had hoped for a collision between the North and Britain. Their chagrin would have been greater had they known of the talk at an evening dinner party at Secretary Cameron's two days earlier, when Lincoln had unceremoniously joined a group comprising Seward, Chase, and Sumner. After Seward had remarked that he gave up Mason and Slidell without the least rancor, the President made some statements which Sumner summarized in a sentence: "He covets kindly relations with all the world, especially England."

The termination of this anxious crisis was a gleam of sunshine. So, as the new year began, was the Senate's confirmation of Edwin M. Stanton as the new Secretary of War with but two dissenting votes, for faith in Stanton was prodigious. So was the intelligence that George H. Thomas had taken some prisoners, twelve guns, and large stores in what Stanton hailed as a brilliant

I

victory at Mill Springs in Kentucky. A few such gleams had been badly needed.

For in most respects the year 1862 opened grimly. Both East and West, the war that had been so full of ardor seven months earlier seemed chilled into torpidity. McClellan in his Washington headquarters merely extended his inaction into a new phase when he fell ill of typhoid. Halleck in St. Louis was awkwardly clutching the reins in a scene of angry confusion left by Frémont's removal, and Buell in Louisville appeared unwilling to move forward. The North had seized the advantage in the Border States, planted outposts on the Southern coast, and begun a blockade, but the real work of reducing the Confederacy had scarcely begun. Behind lay a year of frustration; ahead clearly stretched another year of upheaval, effort, and perhaps graver reverses. The gaunt President, pacing between White House and War Office, could not escape an agonizing question. Was the Union really the land of the heroic old-time warriors, explorers, and state builders, of John Smith and William Bradford, of Washington, Hamilton, and Madison, of Jackson and Webster? Or was it the irresolute land of Pierce and Buchanan, of doughface Whigs and proslavery Democrats, of compromisers, time-servers, and outright traitors?

He never lost faith. And if the first ardent passion of war was gone, a better spirit was taking its place, and calling for fiercer resolution and sterner measures. A new year, a new War Department head, new troops and new generals—these, men hoped, would bring victory within grasp. This changed temper dictated a set of harsh orders by Halleck in Missouri. All secessionists who loitered near camps to gain information or who conveyed it to the enemy would be arrested, tried, and shot. The St. Louis authorities were empowered to aid the host of destitute refugees from the southwestern counties by quartering them in the houses of Southern sympathizers, while a commission in the city levied upon rich disloyalists for contributions running up to $10,000 apiece—resistance to this levy being punishable by death. In Kentucky, meanwhile, arrests of alleged traitors were filling the military prisons.

Congress had no sooner met in December than Senator Lyman Trumbull offered a radical measure for the confiscation of rebel property. The House by a party vote refused to reaffirm the moderate Crittenden resolution that the war was being waged for the Union alone; plainly, the Republican majority expected to cripple or extinguish slavery. Some members were declaring that all war costs should be paid out of Southern wealth. The Senate expelled John C. Breckinridge, the former Vice-President now in the Confederate army, and Jesse D. Bright of Indiana, who had written an improper letter to Jefferson Davis. Before Christmas the Committee on the Conduct of the War met in threatening mood and prepared to question a list of generals.

But it fell to a woman, a figure in letters and not war, to catch most memorably the spirit of the hour. The nation already had some stirring war songs, and George F. Root's "Battle Cry of Freedom" would soon resound on the Chickahominy. But it had no song of moral passion until Julia Ward Howe, a forty-two-year-old descendant of Cromwellian and Revolutionary fighters, appeared this winter in Washington. As her train entered the city at nightfall she had thrilled to the watchfires of a hundred circling camps; her hotel was bathed by the distant low thunder of cannon and the notes of drum, fife, and bugle. One evening as she returned from a review her carriage was blocked by columns of troops, and her party and the soldiers joined in "John Brown's Body." What a pity, she said, that the air had no better words. Before dawn next morning she was sitting in her nightdress scribbling the lines of "The Battle Hymn of the Republic." They soon appeared in the *Atlantic*. Wedded to the thudding folk tune, for the John Brown song was essentially a popular creation, her majestic stanzas caught the nation's ear and strengthened its heart.

Some manifestations of the growing Northern rigor were unfortunate. Halleck's orders could be so regarded.[1] William H. Russell, the London *Times* correspondent, had given offense by his graphically truthful description of the Bull Run panic. In vain did honest officers endorse his account, Sherman declaring every word of it true, and Keyes commenting, "I don't think you made it half bad enough." James Gordon Bennett of the *Herald* denounced him, a drunken Senator insulted him, and a German recruit leveled a cocked rifle at his head. Early in the new year he had prepared, with McClellan's full approval, to cover the advance into Virginia. But Secretary Stanton interposed with an order excluding him from the army, and no plea could modify it. The episode had larger consequences than appeared on its face. Not merely was Russell fair and expert, the ablest reporter the war had found, but he leaned to the Union side. His successor took the opposite attitude and abetted the *Times* in its unfriendly policy. Returning to London, Russell published *My Diary North and South*, so illuminating a record that all students of the war must regret that he could not continue it to the end.[2]

1 O. R., I, viii, 405–529, covers Halleck's decrees. His order barring fugitives from his lines aroused Northern wrath over its cruelty to helpless Negroes; his property levy on St. Louis sympathizers with the South was denounced throughout the border region and termed inhuman by the Unionist leader Senator John B. Henderson of Missouri. See *Cong. Globe*, 37th Cong., 2d Sess., 3348–3350, July 15, 1862. Coulter, *Ky. in the Civil War*, 147–150, treats arrests of disloyalists there.

2 Sam Ward saw Russell off in the *China* and set down some tart words on Stanton's tendency to "tomahawk" anybody he disliked; to Seward, April 9, 1862, Barlow Papers.

[I]

"For months past (and lately more pressingly)," wrote Attorney-General Bates on New Year's Eve, "I have urged upon the President to have some military organization about his own person. . . . I insisted that, being 'commander in chief' by law, he *must* command—especially in such a war as this." Other advisers thought that the President should organize a staff, require regular reports from each army, and direct large movements; and Lincoln did not wholly reject the suggestion. He continued to study manuals of war. To Buell on January 13, 1862, he sent a memorandum embodying shrewd thought. He wished Halleck to advance from St. Louis along the Mississippi line while Buell from Louisville pushed into East Tennessee. His general idea of the war, he continued, was that as the North had the greater numbers and the South the greater facility of concentration on points of collision, the proper strategy was to menace the enemy with superior forces at different points; so that if he weakened one to strengthen another, the Union could strike against the more defenseless front.

The President fixed a critical eye on the Western as well as Eastern theater, as he revealed in telegrams to Buell and Halleck inquiring whether they were acting in liaison. These generals were in fact not merely uncooperative but mutually jealous, each hoping to get the chief command in the West. Lincoln bluntly rebuked another jealous brigadier, who grumbled that he was being kept at Leavenworth with three thousand men while Buell had a hundred thousand. "He who does *something* at the head of one regiment will eclipse him who does *nothing* at the head of a hundred," commented the President.[3]

While watching the fronts, urging army ordnance to make proper use of mortars, and helping Seward draft some foreign dispatches, Lincoln showed his resourcefulness by a special approach to his principal problem: slavery. He had pondered the subject for years. With great uncertainty, with protestations that he would not know what to do with the institution if given absolute power, he had long before concluded that some system of gradual emancipation at national expense, coupled with an effort to colonize the freed people abroad, would offer the best solution. Now public and Congressional pressure compelled him to act, and before New Year's he had hammered into rough form a project which represented as bold a step as Jefferson had made in the purchase of Louisiana. Although the war was but nine months old, it was high time he grappled with the issue. A hundred Northern communities

3 *Works,* V, 84, 85 (to Hunter), 98, 99 (to Buell).

were circulating petitions for emancipation; anger over the annulment of Frémont's proclamation lingered, for Frémont, said *Harper's Weekly*, "undoubtedly touched the mainspring of the rebellion." [4]

"The nigger's in the Congressional woodpile," grumbled W. H. Wadsworth, a conservative Kentucky Congressman. "Abolition in the District— abolition in the insurrectionary States or districts—and general emancipation —this is their purpose, and it will blow them up." He meant that the radicals would be hoisted by their own petard.[5]

When in the previous summer John J. Crittenden had asserted in the House that the government possessed no power to meddle with slavery in the States, Thaddeus Stevens, recalling J. Q. Adams' prediction that a Southern rebellion would sweep away all barriers to emancipation, had scornfully replied: "Mr. Speaker, I thought the time had come when the laws of war were to govern our action; when constitutions, if they stood in the way of the laws of war in dealing with the enemy, had no right to intervene." Joshua Giddings held that *all* slaves might be freed under the war power, for even those who worked at home grew bread for Southern troops.[6] Sumner, Wendell Phillips, Owen Lovejoy, and Beecher with their voices, and Bryant, Whittier, George William Curtis, and Lowell with their pens, pleaded for lifting the war to a higher, bolder plane.

Lincoln was quite ready to elevate the objects of the war. Like nearly everyone, he cherished a hope that powerful advances in Virginia and down the Mississippi would end the fighting in 1862. During these advances, he expected to see slavery shaken and eroded. At the same time, however, he shrunk from antagonizing loyal Kentuckians, Marylanders, and Missourians by abrupt measures. A scheme of compensated emancipation in the Border States, he decided, could arrest heedless Congressional action, facilitate the surrender of the Confederacy, and give notice that slavery everywhere must be regarded as a temporary and not a permanent institution.

"Well, Mr. Sumner," Lincoln told the Massachusetts Senator early in December, "the only difference between you and me on this subject of emancipation is a difference of a month or six weeks in time." He asked for patience until he could disclose his plan of action, and Sumner promised to say nothing more for at least six weeks.[7]

Lincoln detested slavery for moral, economic, and democratic reasons alike; he had hated it ever since he told the Illinois legislature in 1837 that it

4 Lincoln to Hunter, *Works*, V, 84, 85, to Buell, 98, 99, *Harper's Weekly*, November 30, 1861.
5 To S. L. M. Barlow, Dec. 6, 1861, Barlow Papers.
6 Joshua Giddings, Washington, Dec. 19, 1861, Giddings Papers, Ohio Hist. Society.
7 E. E. Hale, memorandum of April, 1862, in *Memories*, II, 189-196.

represented both social injustice and bad policy. He regarded it as the principal root of the war. It had divided the national house. While at home it had negated and crippled the American ideals of freedom and equality, abroad it had sullied the principles which, as he said in his Independence Hall speech, gave hope to the world for all future time. The South *must* be made to join in laying plans for its extirpation. But his hostility to the institution never carried him beyond a deep-seated belief that so disruptive a change should be effected gradually in order to minimize its hardships, and that the results of extirpation would be more wholesome if it were coupled with at least a partial removal of the colored people to another land. Like most other white men of the time in Europe and America, he at first believed that inherent racial differences made it undesirable for Negro and Caucasian to dwell together. The stronger race would oppress the weaker group, and thus retarded, the colored man would pull down the white competitor to his own level. Some system for colonizing the freedmen abroad should therefore be attempted. But Lincoln had no fixed prejudices. As the war progressed, and as Negroes proved themselves brave fighters, industrious workers, and people of character, he began to discard the idea of inherent racial inequalities [8]; while he simultaneously realized that large-scale colonization was impracticable. At the beginning of 1862, however, he still clung to his old preconceptions.

[II]

When Lincoln talked with Sumner, he had already taken secret action. Early in November he had called Representative George P. Fisher of Delaware to the White House to discuss compensated emancipation in that little State, where the last census had enumerated only 587 slaveholders, holding fewer than 1,800 slaves. An open-minded slave owner, at Lincoln's instance, was soon brought into the talks. The President asked the two men to ascertain whether the legislature could be persuaded to free the slaves if the government paid for them at local and individual appraisals. "I am satisfied," he said, "that this is the cheapest and most humane way of ending the war." The cost, after all, would be trifling; the bill for a single half-day of hostilities would pay for all Delaware's slaves, with enough left over to colonize them abroad. Once the plan was proved feasible in Delaware, he hoped he might persuade the other Border States to adopt it. Delaware would be bellwether of the flock.

When Fisher, who had been elected on a Constitutional Union platform, broached the proposal to friends, he met with some encouragement. The op-

8 See his tribute to the Negro in his letter to J. C. Conkling, Aug. 26, 1863.

position came chiefly from Southern sympathizers—though a few antislavery Republicans thought that the State should emancipate without compensation, and some conservatives feared that the freedmen would become a burden. With advice from Lincoln, Fisher helped draw up a bill to be presented to the legislature when it met late in December. It provided that when the national government had appropriated money to pay an average of $500 each for the slaves, emancipation should go into effect. As soon as it was made public, this measure provoked an acrimonious debate, the Wilmington *Journal* supporting it while the Wilmington *Gazette* led the attack.[9]

Meanwhile, Lincoln clung to the idea that, as he had said years before in a tribute to Henry Clay, there was "a moral fitness in returning to Africa her children, whose ancestors have been torn away from her by the ruthless hand of fraud and violence"; or, if Africa offered no refuge, in sending them to another tropical land. He talked with Ambrose W. Thompson, a Philadelphian who had grown rich in coastal shipping. With some associates, Thompson had obtained control of several hundred thousand acres in Panama, and had devised a plan for opening coal mines in the Chiriqui district there and bringing in liberated Negroes as labor. He proposed to sell his coal to the Navy Department at half the price the government had been paying, and to use the revenue in sustaining his colored colony while it developed plantations of cotton, sugar, and coffee. Lincoln had the matter investigated. His brother-in-law, Ninian W. Edwards, a special commission, and Francis P. Blair, Sr., all in time made enthusiastic reports. At the very time that the President was secretly talking with the Delawareans, Thompson was pressing his proposal eagerly. "I am very anxious to have this contract closed immediately," he wrote the elder Blair in mid-November.[10]

For a time Lincoln felt hopeful of progress with his broad plan, which he still kept confidential. He thought that border slaveholders must see the inevitability of emancipation, for the grapevine telegraph rapidly diffused the idea of

9 H. C. Reed, "Lincoln's Compensated Emancipation Plan," *Del. Notes,* 1931, pp. 27 ff.; *Cong. Globe,* 37th Cong., 2d Sess., 1175, 1176 (Fisher's speech, March 11, 1862). There should have been no prejudice in Delaware against free Negroes, who were as sober, industrious, and thrifty as the poorer whites. When Senator Saulsbury talked about their laziness and vice, informed observers indignantly contradicted him. W. M. Connolly, Wilmington, July 5, 1862, to Fessenden; Palmer Coll., Western Reserve Hist. Soc. J. T. Scharf, *Delaware,* I, 345, 346, gives a dubious report of Lincoln's first talk with Fisher.

Lincoln's plan was of course not original, but could be traced back for years. Before he was inaugurated the New York *Tribune* had discussed the gradual compensated emancipation of 600,000 slaves in the Borderland, Texas, Arkansas, and Louisiana, saying that at $400 apiece the costs would approximately equal those of Buchanan's proposed purchase of Cuba; Jan. 30, 1861.

10 See letters of Thompson, Nov.-Dec., 1861, in Blair-Lee Papers, Princeton; and W. A. Beck, "Lincoln and Negro Colonization," *Abraham Lincoln Quarterly,* VI (September, 1950), 162–168.

freedom among the slaves, and they flocked eagerly to every Union standard in secession territory.[11] He found another favoring circumstance in Confederate efforts to stop cotton production, a blow at one of the principal economic foundations of slavery. To George Bancroft, calling at the White House in December, the President declared that the leviathan had already been harpooned near the heart, and that he was pondering what course he should take if slave insurrections broke out. At the same time he told Sumner how fervently he hoped he could soon announce a broad program of recompensed emancipation. Meanwhile, he directed Henry T. Blow, the capitalist and former protector of Dred Scott who was now minister to Venezuela, to investigate all the possibilities of the Chiriqui area: the lands, harbors, potential railway routes, and facilities for defense.[12]

But Delaware, alas! failed to come up to the mark. Party rancor conspired with proslavery sentiment and other motives to defeat the proposal. Our main work is to save the Union and not to meddle with slavery, declared the Democrats. Defiantly, they drew up resolutions that Congress had no right to buy slaves, that the State could not guarantee any debt depending on a mere pledge of Federal faith, and that when Delawareans wished to abolish slavery, they would do it in their own way. Early in 1862 the friends of Fisher's bill abandoned it as hopeless. They could have obtained a narrow majority in the Senate, but would have met defeat in the House. A quixotic opposition thus blocked Lincoln's plan; fundamentally, no doubt, because many Delaware voters could imagine no feasible mode of controlling race relations without slavery.[13]

Still, Lincoln had to do something, and do it immediately. The radical demand for drastic measures of emancipation mounted ever higher. The legislation which Lyman Trumbull had so promptly introduced provided for the forfeiture of every species of property belonging to those who in any way aided or abetted the rebellion. Lincoln just after New Year's paid Horace Greeley the compliment of attending a lyceum lecture given at the Smithsonian as part of an antislavery series arranged by the Washington Lecture Association. As the band played "Hail to the Chief," the President, Secretary Chase, Senators Preston King and Henry Wilson, and Speaker Galusha Grow

11   The governor of Kansas estimated that during 1861, 5,000 fugitive slaves came in from various areas; and a great efflux of Missouri slaves also took place to Illinois and Iowa. Washington *National Republican*, Jan. 22, 1862.

12   Some free Negroes in parts of the North early in 1862 were circulating a petition asking Congress to buy a tract in Central America for colonization, and Anna Ella Carroll, who favored the project, was writing letters to the press to support it; Washington *National Republican*, April 23, 1862. For Lincoln's statement to Bancroft see M. A. DeWolfe Howe, *Bancroft*, II, 147.

13   The one Lincoln Republican in the House was opposed; Conrad, *Delaware*, I, 205.

filed upon the platform. They heard Greeley's squeaky voice deliver sentiments as unflinching as Cato's. It was time to look the archenemy in the eye,
he said; slavery had been the aggressor, and had earned a traitor's doom. Conservatives had at first stood aghast at Butler's contraband order, he continued,
but soon endorsed it; they had condemned Frémont's order of liberation, but
had learned to accept the idea; and every Union man would yet agree with
Andrew Johnson that "no traitor has any right to own anything." [14] Explosive
applause followed Greeley's denunciation of compromise: "My motto is, the
Union forever as our fathers made it; but Liberty forever, with or without the
Union!"

Though Lincoln could not have joined in that applause, the occasion must
have impressed him with the force of emancipationist feeling. He knew that a
great part of the Northern press was as extreme on the subject as Medill's
Chicago *Tribune,* or Bryant's *Evening Post.*[15] The Harrisburg *Telegraph* was
asserting that the people called for general abolition; the Portsmouth (N. H.)
Journal pronounced any lasting peace impossible until Congress used the war
power, so far as it could, to exterminate slavery from the land. The principal
governors, from Andrew to Yates, were as emphatic as Wade, Bingham, Thaddeus Stevens, and other Congressional radicals. And Sumner, despite his promised
patience, continued to press Lincoln. At various periods, and this was one, his
influence in the White House was great. During the crisis of the *Trent* affair
he had told Lincoln that it would have caused much less trouble had he done
his duty against slavery, for he would have possessed stancher friends in Britain.[16] When the dispute was settled on December 26, he pressed Lincoln
again: "I want you to make Congress a New Year's present of your plan"—
the nature of which he did not know.

Lincoln, however, discouraged by Delaware's rebuff, absorbed by military
problems, and wrung by the mortal illness of his son Willie, put the subject
aside in February—to wait.

Yet he had adumbrated the boldest movement in the history of the

14 George Weston, editor of the Washington *National Republican,* declared that anything short of unconditional emancipation of all slaves of rebels was useless; Jan. 8, 13, 16,
1862. Later lecturers in the series mentioned, all strongly antislavery, included Emerson,
George William Curtis, and John Jay.

15 Medill was privately more radical than his paper. He wrote Elihu Washburne, January
13, 1862: "I guess between the doctors—i.e., West Point proslavery generals, a rotten Cabinet,
and a blind cowardly Congress, the public patient is done for and will soon require the
services of the undertaker." Washburne Papers, LC.

16 T. C. Grattan, recently British consul in Boston, thought this was true. In a
pamphlet published in England late in 1861 he wrote: "Terrible as would be the results of
a servile war, there is great likelihood that the inconsiderate shout for immediate abolition
would ring in the ears of all England like an alarm bell, and stir the depths of popular
feeling with the fervor of the Reformation, or the fanaticism of the Crusades."

Presidency. His conception ran beyond the mere liberation of four million colored folk; it implied a far-reaching alteration of American society, industry, and government. A gradual planned emancipation, a concomitant transportation of hundreds of thousands and perhaps even millions of people overseas, a careful governmental nursing of the new colonies, and a payment of unprecedented sums to the section thus deprived of its old labor supply— this scheme carried unprecedented implications. To put it into effect would immensely increase the power of the national government and widen its activities. If even partially practicable, it would mean a long step toward rendering the American people homogeneous in color and race, a rapid stimulation of immigration to replace the workers thus exported, a greater world position for the republic, and a pervasive change in popular outlook and ideas. The attempt would do more to convert the unorganized country into an organized nation than anything yet planned. Impossible, and undesirable even if possible?—probably; but Lincoln continued to hold his vision.

Such bold action would lie open, however, only to a government which won victories and became able to impose its will on its enemies. From Lincoln's West now came the first substantial augury of success in the war.

[III]

The Administration, hoping that the impending thrust in Virginia and the march down the Mississippi would quickly succeed, and that together with the blockade they would bring the Confederacy to its knees, had hardly paused to consider whether the Eastern or Western theater was the more important. Because of the sense of peril to Washington, it had given precedence to the East. This was a grave error. The severest single stroke that could be dealt the Confederacy would be the seizure of the Mississippi Valley, separating Louisiana, Texas, and Arkansas from the rest of the South, and giving the Union the important railroad ganglia of Corinth, Jackson, and Nashville. By comparison, a victory of McClellan in Virginia was unlikely to accomplish decisive results.

During most of 1861 the West had thus been given stepchild treatment. Weak officers were made brigadiers; Frémont was stinted in troops, arms, and intelligent support; and any man who complained of shortages as vehemently as W. T. Sherman did ran the risk of being pronounced insane —as Sherman was. Scott, McClellan, and Cameron all had difficulty in seeing over the Alleghenies. But Westerners had felt high hopes of a more dynamic attention to their needs when on November 9 Henry W. Halleck was appointed head of the new Department of Missouri, which included Arkansas and western Kentucky, and on the 15th Don Carlos Buell took command of the Department of the Ohio. The situation inevitably made the two men rivals. While Halleck was to direct the southward advance along the Mississippi, Lincoln expected Buell to liberate eastern Tennessee, rescue its Unionist population, and cut the vital railway linking Virginia with Chattanooga and the Southwestern Confederacy. Which would evince the greater capacity and achieve the larger results?

Buell's assignment was particularly promising at a distance, and particularly difficult at near view. Lincoln in his "Plan of Campaign" written about October first had declared that he wished troops sent to seize a point on the Virginia & Tennessee Railroad near Cumberland Gap, then guarded by F. K. Zollicoffer with 6,000 to 8,000 Confederates. McClellan all winter was equally anxious, for the sake of his Richmond campaign, that Western troops occupy East Tennessee and cut its railway lines north, so that the Confederates in Virginia would be isolated. "My own advance," he wrote Buell on January 6, 1861, "cannot, according to my present view, be made until your troops are soundly established in the eastern portion of Tennessee." That is, *he* could not move forward, but Buell could and must.[17] Lincoln was eager to aid the sorely harried Unionists who might make northern Georgia, eastern Tennessee, and western North Carolina a free mountain domain, a cancer in the Confederate vitals. This area, which could be regarded as the back door of Virginia, held a situation which looked with menacing adaptability on other Atlantic and Gulf States. If only a strong Union army could be planted and supported there! With Andrew Johnson pressing for action, Lincoln fretted over lost opportunities. Of 45,000 adult males in East Tennessee, it was later said that 35,000 enlisted in the Union service; but just now they were cut off.

But Buell knew that the crow-flight distance from Lexington to Cumberland Gap is 110 miles, and that only crows can fly over mountains. In eastern Kentucky lie four ranges, the Pine Mountain, Little and Big Black, and Cumberland; one peak rises well over 4,000 feet. The few dirt roads wound through tortuous creek or river valleys, lined much of the way by steep mountainsides to which clung cabins where a hardy folk tilled patches of corn. This forested country produced little surplus food or forage. In winter rains even the road from Frankfort to Shelbyville in the rich center of the State was sometimes impassable. Rebel bushwhackers were active in the area. The general feared that problems of communication and supply would prove insurmountable. He went so far as to promise to send 12,000 men and three batteries toward East Tennessee as soon as possible, but that was all. His

17 O. R., I, vii, 531.

stubborn impassivity in maintaining that the true route of advance was up the Cumberland to Nashville gave Lincoln an accurate impression that he was slow, and he certainly exaggerated enemy numbers in informing Washington just before Christmas that while he could muster only 50,000 effectives, the Confederates had fully that number at Columbus and at least 30,000 more at Bowling Green, on his flank. But he had a clearer grasp of the situation than far-off Washington. Thomas, even after defeating G. B. Crittenden at Mill Springs on January 19, 1862, also thought that the terrible roads and lack of subsistence barred any extended advance.[18]

Halleck meanwhile remained in St. Louis, trying to cope with the murder, arson, and pillage committed by guerrillas, answering querulous letters from his subordinate John Pope, and complaining to Washington of the lack of proper men, officers, and arms. But his strength grew rapidly. General Samuel R. Curtis was soon to lead part of his forces into northwestern Arkansas, while Pope was to march other troops against New Madrid and Island No. 10.[19]

Neither of the two generals in top Western command was as yet well known to the country. Halleck, with bulbous brow, large staring eyes, pursed lips, and short dimpled chin, had a schoolmasterish face. He looked like a college professor about to open chapel with a learned discourse. His heavy cheeks, sagging into the short gray sideburns that clothed them, and his heavy-set, dumpish figure gave him an ineffectual aspect. His career—he was not yet fifty—seemed, however, to offer an earnest of ability. A Phi Beta Kappa student at Union College, third in his class at West Point, author of the best American treatise on the art of war, which he had revised to include data on the Mexican and Crimean conflicts, translator of Jomini, a sufficiently good engineer to be offered the chair in that subject at the Lawrence Scientific School of Harvard, the head of a prominent law firm in San Francisco—so the record ran. He had impressed Scott so much that he was made major-general in 1861. Numerous officers shared the opinion which Grant expressed: "He is a man of gigantic intellect and well studied in the profession of arms." But this awkward pedant, slow of speech and gait, who dressed shabbily, picked his teeth as he strolled after dinner, and scratched his elbows as he talked prosily in his office, had weaknesses of irresolution, confusion, and timidity which events shortly proved serious.[20]

The stiffly erect Buell, full-bearded and stern-eyed, looked more the

18 On Kentucky conditions see the WPA *Guide* to the State; Thomas D. Clark, *Hist. of Kentucky*, 261 ff.; F. Winston Coleman, *Stage Coach Days in the Blue Grass;* and F. G. Davenport, *Ante-Bellum Kentucky.* The Seward Papers for January, 1862, show how Senator Andrew Johnson and Representative Horace Maynard pressed Lincoln. W. R. Carter, *Hist. 1st Tenn. Cavalry*, pictures the tremendous war effort of Tennessee.

19 O. R., I, viii, 33 ff., 189 ff., 367–577.

20 See the characterization in Fuller, *Generalship of U. S. Grant*, 79.

military man. While this short, slight, hawk-nosed professional soldier, a graduate of West Point in 1841 and a veteran of the Seminole and Mexican Wars, was so chill and taciturn that he repelled casual observers, intimates thought well of him.[21] He was a firm disciplinarian, nearly the equal of McClellan in the organization and drill of troops, and despite his besetting fault of slowness, an officer of some imagination. Possibly he could have done more to help the harassed Unionists in the mountains southeast of him. But he saw how risky a large movement toward East Tennessee would be without well-coordinated operations in western Kentucky; as early as November 27, 1861, he recommended that two flotilla columns should move up the Tennessee and Cumberland, and that an advance should be launched against Nashville. In one respect Buell was Halleck's exact opposite, for he was happiest when fighting in the field. Both, but especially Buell, were blind to the political factors in the war, and both were deeply hostile to "political generals," meaning men who never saw West Point.

Buell took vigilant care of his command, selecting camps cautiously, insisting on proper sanitary measures, providing decent commissary service, and punishing desertion and drunkenness. One of his shortcomings was that in his emphasis on discipline, he did not sufficiently distinguish between the plodding regular soldier of the old army, and the high-spirited volunteer of the new, so that his harshness made him generally disliked. A graver fault was his lack of initiative. He hesitated when action was called for, and when committed to action he still hesitated. "I don't believe the general is capable of a decision!" wrote one incensed subordinate. In the end his want of aggressive vigor was to ruin him. But before this happened his clear-sighted activities did the Union great service.[22]

Grant, who was Halleck's principal advanced commander at Cairo as Thomas was Buell's advanced commander at Lebanon, Kentucky, was steadily growing into his responsibilities. At Belmont he had mismanaged his two brigades so that part of his troops became a rabble of looters and then a panicky mob, and he had almost lost the 27th Illinois. After Belmont he failed to organize an adequate staff, or give his officers and men really tough training. The fact was that like everybody else he knew little about large-scale war and had to learn step by step. This short, black-haired man with close-cut black-and-gray beard and small, keen gray eyes wore a look at once determined and thoughtful. Those about him were still uncertain

---

21 T. C. Smith, *James A. Garfield*, I, 181. Grant declared after the war: "Buell had genius enough for the highest commands"; *Memoirs*, I, 318, 319, 344 ff. See also the Comte de Paris, *Civil War*, I, 522 ff.; Freeman Cleaves, *Rock of Chickamauga*, 92 ff.

22 T. A. Mitchel, January 25, 1889, Hay Papers, Ill. State Hist. Lib., gives Ormsby Mitchel's opinion of Buell; Foulke, *Morton*, I, 197, 198.

whether he had sufficient foresight to plan a campaign or enough intellectual agility to handle complicated troop movements. But intimates knew he did possess invaluable qualities: integrity, singleness of purpose, hard common sense, industry, and above all an instinct for the enemy's jugular. He never lost his self-command or his cool combativeness. His taciturn inscrutability and his mixture of simplicity and strength threw an aura of mystery about him. He was a strange character, declared W. T. Sherman long after the war; stranger than any in Plutarch. "I knew him as a cadet at West Point, as a lieutenant of the Fourth Infantry, as a citizen of St. Louis, and as a growing general all through a bloody civil war. Yet to me he is a mystery, and I believe he is a mystery to himself." [23]

The vital word in Sherman's characterization is "growing," for as much as Lincoln did, Grant *grew*. And though he lacked the intellectual power of a Moltke, Foch, or Bradley, he possessed the faculty of sorting out from many facts the few that were critically significant. He was growing also in that asset which the Anglo-Saxon world has always esteemed most, strength of character. That is, he was growing in promptness, for once he made up his mind, he moved; in nerve, for in tight squeezes he kept his head; and in stubborn grit, for he never knew when he was beaten, and so could lose every battle till the last one. Modesty and magnanimity were inborn traits; the modesty that saved him from a single touch of brag, the magnanimity that was later to infuse his letter explaining why he treated his Vicksburg prisoners generously. From Alfred and Cromwell to Washington, Grant, and Lee, elemental strength of character has been held the prime requisite of leadership. Quick, clever men may supply the ideas, but it is the rarer man of character whose integrity, resolution, and clarity of view make them count.

[IV]

It was one of the weaknesses of the Confederacy in the West that two rivers, the Tennessee and Cumberland, reached inland from the North toward its center. The Cumberland, the less important, did not penetrate far. Nashville marked its southernmost navigable point. But the Tennessee bent a great arc deep into Confederate territory, giving a short northeastern boundary to Mississippi and traversing all northern Alabama before it drained the Great Smokies of North Carolina. Troops ascending it could thrust between Memphis and Nashville, outflanking both, could gain the railway centers of Corinth, Mississippi, and Decatur, Alabama, and farther upstream, if they had

23 Sherman, Nov. 18, 1879, in *Century Magazine*, LIII (April, 1897), 821. "Not a brilliant man," Sherman wrote his wife in 1862, but brave, sober, hardworking, and kind; *Home Letters*, 228.

high water at Muscle Shoals, could reach the vital railroad junction of Chattanooga, Tennessee.

The Tennessee River, moreover, intersected the most important communication line between the Eastern and Western Confederacy, the Memphis & Charleston Railroad. This primary artery for traffic between the Mississippi and South Atlantic coast, running from Memphis east through southern Tennessee and northern Alabama, was cut or touched by the meandering river at several points. Gunboats with a few troops could disrupt it. They could also seal off Nashville, which lay on the Cumberland and was connected with the Memphis & Charleston by two railroads and a macadamized highway. A sufficiently large force on the Cumberland, in fact, could seize Nashville —a rich provision depot for the Confederacy, now rapidly being made into a busy manufactory of arms, munitions, and general stores.

A mere glance at the map would seem to reveal that the Tennessee-Cumberland river system offered the North a heaven-sent opportunity to thrust a harpoon into the very bowels of the Confederacy; but it did not. We have no more telling indication of the planless improvisation of this war than the fact that not until late in 1861 did Union commanders think of attacking along this line.

One retired naval officer did grasp the idea as early as June, 1861. We do not know his name; we know only that he approached a Unionist in Nashville, and proposed that the North should invade central Tennessee by the two rivers, capture Nashville, and at a single bound carry the war into northern Georgia. The rivers were then unfortified, and the rebel troops assembling in the region were unorganized, ill armed, and badly officered. The naval officer believed that a swift force could take Nashville, draw volunteers from that area and East Tennessee, and push on into northern Alabama, where several counties teemed with Federal sympathizers. But obviously he took no account of Kentucky's neutrality or of Northern military weakness, and his suggestion was not even considered.[24]

Not until autumn did others show equal prescience. Then various people saw the possibilities of the situation almost simultaneously. One was an experienced steamboatman of St. Louis, Charles M. Scott; one a strong-minded young woman, Anna Ella Carroll, daughter of a former governor of Maryland, who visited the Western theater and talked with Scott. Still another was Charles Whittlesey, chief engineer on the staff of General Ormsby M. Mitchel, who wrote Halleck on November 20, 1861, proposing the movement. Frémont during the summer and fall had a spy, Captain Charles D'Arnaud, make two trips within Confederate lines to map highways, bridges, and forts in

24 See letters signed "Tennesseean" in N. Y. *Times*, Nov. 17, Dec. 21, 1861.

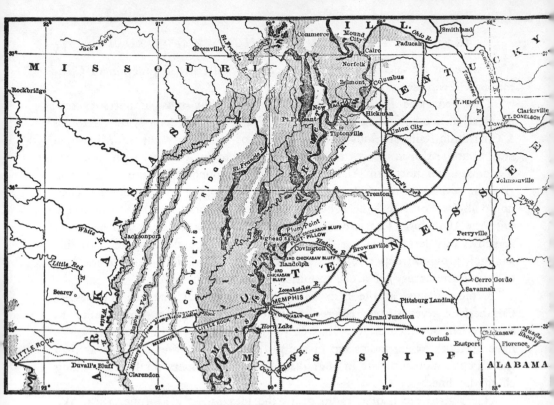

THE MISSISSIPPI–TENNESSEE–CUMBERLAND CAMPAIGNS

Kentucky and western Tennessee, and report on enemy movements. Among the materials he brought back were maps showing the positions of Forts Henry and Donelson. It is certain, however, that nobody in Washington caught the early inspiration. McClellan thought of using gunboats and troops either on the Mississippi or the Cumberland-Tennessee system simply as a diversionary action to aid Buell in descending upon East Tennessee, just as Buell's first idea seems to have been to coordinate a flotilla movement on the two rivers with land operations against Nashville.[25]

25 For Colonel Whittlesey's plan see O. R., I, vii, 440; M. F. Force, *From Fort Henry to Corinth*, 25. Senator B. F. Wade in 1872 credited the conception to Miss Carroll, saying that Lincoln and Stanton had done so. No evidence exists that she submitted a matured plan to the War Department, or that Lincoln and the Department suggested her idea to any general in the field. She did, however, place a paper on the possibilities of a Tennessee River campaign, with a map, in the hands of the Assistant Secretary of War, Thomas A. Scott, on Nov. 30, 1861. Charles M. Scott drafted a plan which he sent Miss Carroll in Washington; and he says he gave a copy of it, with other information, to Grant, apparently on or about Dec. 15, 1861. Both Grant and Adam Badeau deny that Grant received any prompting from either Captain Scott or Miss Carroll. Grant wrote Washburne March 22, 1862, that no general could claim credit for so obvious a move, for gunboats had been running up the rivers all fall and winter, looking at Forts Henry and Donelson, **and it is true**

But as the year closed, light dawned on so many people that experts could hardly believe, later, that the idea had ever been ignored. Thus Lew Wallace, with perfect hindsight, declared that the true strategy had been too plain to miss; that the trend of the two rivers, their navigability by steamboats, their secure road to the rear of the Confederate forces in Kentucky and Tennessee, and their large advantages as a supply line, were visible to all. Late in December, Halleck conferred with W. T. Sherman in St. Louis. Sherman explained that the enemy's main line of defense ran from Columbus east to Bowling Green. Thereupon Halleck took a ruler, drew a line on the map well north of these two points, and drew another line perpendicular to the center. This second line roughly coincided with the Tennessee River, and he announced that it was to be the main route of attack.[26] Buell's ideas also had been maturing. On December 29 he wrote McClellan that all possible force should be brought to bear on the Columbus-Bowling Green front, for "the center, that is the Cumberland and Tennessee where the railroad crosses them, is now the most vulnerable point"; to penetrate it would unseat the enemy, "and give access through the two rivers to the very center of their power." He also wrote Halleck on January 3, 1862, urging that a Tennessee-Cumberland expedition be launched with all possible speed. Meanwhile Lincoln continued to reiterate that he wished Halleck to push down the Mississippi while Buell threatened East Tennessee, and said nothing of the two lesser rivers.[27]

Prime responsibility for deciding the direction of the great initial thrust in the West lay with Halleck, who on January 20, 1861, made up his mind. "This line of the Cumberland or Tennessee is the great central line of the Western theatre of war," he wrote McClellan.

Grant's shrewd view of strategy buttressed this decision, for thinking quite independently, he had decided that he should attack one of the river forts. He sent Brigadier-General C. F. Smith, whom he had placed in charge of Paducah, on a reconnaissance up the Tennessee, and Smith returned with word that the river defenses could be captured. Thus encouraged, Grant

that the *Conestoga* ran upstream and inspected Fort Henry on Oct. 18. Confederate defensive preparations alone would have indicated the plan. See Badeau, *Mil. Hist. of U. S. Grant*, I, 22 ff.; Lew Wallace, *Autobiography*, I, 333 ff.; Sydney and Marjorie Greenbie, *Anna Ella Carroll and Abraham Lincoln*, Ch. XXIII; Sarah Ellen Blackwell, *A Military Genius, Anna Ella Carroll*, Ch. IV, and Kenneth Williams, "The Tennessee River Campaign and Anna Ella Carroll," *Indiana Magazine of History*, XLVI, No. 3 (Sept., 1950), 221-248.
26 Sherman, *Memoirs*, I, 248.
27 Lincoln's exchanges with Halleck and Buell, Jan. 1-15, 1862, are illuminating. Lincoln wanted action; he was "deeply distressed that our friends in East Tennessee are being hanged and driven to despair"; but he did not see the true strategy of the hour. Halleck wrote Jan. 5 arguing against operations on an exterior as opposed to an interior line. Lincoln, *Works*, V, 87-100; O. R., I, vii, 533.

went to St. Louis January 23 to explain his ambition to Halleck. He met a frigid reception, for Halleck shared the regular-army prejudice against Grant as a drinker, and the resentment of many regular officers that he outranked C. F. Smith, an older, more experienced, and widely beloved officer. Embarrassed, Grant stumbled in his speech. "I had not uttered many sentences," he wrote later, "before I was cut short as if my plan was preposterous." He returned to Cairo crestfallen, and talked over his plans with Flag-Officer Andrew H. Foote, commanding the gunboats. Always stubborn in his purposes, he waited only a few days; then on January 28 he and Foote together telegraphed Halleck of their urgent wish to attack. This time he met better fortune. Halleck had changed his mind, and without authorization from Washington, wired Grant to prepare for his expedition.[28] That telegram loosed a wild scene of jubilation at Grant's headquarters.

Of course no amphibious assault was possible until gunboats and transports were ready. All fall, against legions of difficulties, Foote had been struggling in St. Louis, Cairo, and other river towns to complete a flotilla. Not until mid-January were his vessels finished. On the 15th he gave a trial trip to the *Benton*, a powerful iron-plated boat, carrying a large battery. He simultaneously put into commission the seven gunboats which had been built to fill James B. Eads's contract. Even yet, the gunboat fleet was hampered by want of gunners and deck hands, and the army had to press volunteers into the service.[29] But Foote, a shrewd Connecticut Yankee who had helped suppress the slave trade on the African coast, was indomitable. At one point he was shrewder than Grant, whose original idea had been to ascend the Cumberland against Fort Donelson. Foote convinced him that the initial blow should be leveled against Fort Henry on the Tennessee.[30]

The impatient general got his orders from Halleck on February 1, and the very next day he and Foote set out—three weeks before the date set by Lincoln for a general advance.

[V]

While the Union leaders in the West stumbled toward their proper strategy with little help from Lincoln and none from McClellan or the War

---

28 Grant, *Memoirs*, I, 286; O. R., I, vii, 120, 121, 930. Perhaps Halleck swung about because his slow mind took several days to grasp Grant's plan. Perhaps he did so because, jealous over the triumph which Buell shared with Thomas in the victory of Mill Springs, he saw that the Tennessee-Cumberland move would give him a counter victory; J. F. C. Fuller, *Generalship of U. S. Grant*, 82.

29 James M. Hoppin, *Life of Admiral Foote*, 154–190; Grant, *Memoirs*, Ch. VIII; Naval O. R., I, xxii, 502–506.

30 Secretary of the Navy, *Annual Report*, 1862; Hoppin, *Foote*, 194, 195.

Department, Confederate leaders had stumbled toward an inadequate defense with even less help from Richmond. Albert Sidney Johnston, to many the knightliest of Southern officers, to some the brightest hope of the Confederacy, had been put in command. A Kentuckian by birth, a graduate of Transylvania and West Point, the leader of the national troops in Buchanan's ill-conceived and bungled Mormon expedition,[31] he was now fifty-eight. Tall, handsome, magnetic, he had great prestige—but in resources little else. At the outset he possessed about 23,000 men to hold a line 430 miles long, running from Columbus on the west to Cumberland Gap on the east, against nearly 40,000 Union troops.

The day he took command he implored the governor of Georgia to furnish every possible assistance, for he desperately needed arms and supplies, and sent a copy of this letter to Jefferson Davis. Simultaneously, ex-Governor Neill S. Brown of Tennessee laid before Davis a piteous plea for the protection of the whole central section of the State. This district, Brown wrote, needed a gunboat each on the Tennessee and the Cumberland, a brigadier-general to attend to a thousand details which Johnston could not oversee, and a heavy enlistment of troops based on the fact that family men were willing to serve for one year, but not three. He pointed out that on the undefended Cumberland stood the largest iron mill of the Southwest, indispensable to gunshops and cannon foundries, and near it was a large powder mill, State owned but about to be transferred to the Confederacy.[32]

"Ill armed"—"ill armed"—that plaint rings a doleful refrain through the letters of all the Confederate commanders in the West: Leonidas Polk, Gideon J. Pillow, F. K. Zollicoffer, and the others who were attempting to thrust sandbags into a leaky dike. Ill trained, ill officered, ill clothed, ill fed might well be added. "The Army of Missouri," wrote Secretary of War Benjamin to Braxton Bragg as 1861 ended, "is represented to be a mere gathering of brave but undisciplined partisan troops, coming and going at pleasure, and needing a master mind to control and reduce it into order and to convert it into a *real* army." Other forces were not in much better condition. Polk had his headquarters at Columbus; Pillow, intently watching Grant, was at New Madrid with about 10,000 men; Zollicoffer, a former newspaper editor and politician, had a wretchedly inadequate array to protect the Cumberland Gap and Knoxville area. Pillow informed Richmond that to get his forces even partially equipped he had to make stupendous exertions, and that nearly all

31 The bungling was mainly by the War Department under Floyd, and by other officers in Washington, and none of it reflected on Johnston.

32 Johnston, Sept. 15, 1861, to J. E. Brown, in Davis Papers, Duke Univ.; N. S. Brown, Nashville, Sept. 22, 1861, to Davis, *ibid.*

the arms and munitions held by the State had been gathered by himself at an expense of $200,000.[33]

It seems almost incredible that in the West, as in Virginia, Union commanders quaked for fear of attack by these new, ill-conditioned levies. When A. S. Johnston sent the capable Simon Buckner with 5,000 men to occupy Bowling Green, panic seized Louisville. Its home guard hurriedly mobilized, Governor Morton of Indiana rushed several regiments to the city, and other forces were mustered. Under W. T. Sherman, they took a defensive position at the Lebanon railroad southeast of the city. Here it was that Sherman's evidences of nervous strain—his appearance in uniform with a stovepipe hat, his borrowing from a sergeant a fresh cigar to light his own cheroot, after which he threw the cigar into the mud—first gave rise to rumors that he was insane; and his apprehensions of rebel attack helped inspire his demand for 200,000 men. It was a mystery to Sherman then and later why Johnston did not advance on ill-defended Louisville. The mystery was not very deep. In mid-October Johnston, talking with his aide, said crisply: "There will be this winter, on this line, no military operations that I can prevent. We have no powder." [34]

As his son later wrote, Johnston lacked everything that winter: men, munitions, supplies, and the means of obtaining them. He had the right to ask for anything, and the governors had an equal right to refuse. The onset of the winter found fewer than 22,000 men at Bowling Green, not half of them really furnished with weapons. Even then public opinion had not awakened to the imminent crisis. On Christmas Day, Johnston beseeched Governor Harris to arouse the people to the danger, or the whole Mississippi Valley would be lost: "Ten or fifteen thousand additional troops would make me feel assured of victory. With this additional force I could avail myself of every fault of their movements. Without them, I must be a spectator without power to seize the opportunities." [35] All fall he had masked the weakness of his forces by a series of pinprick raids along his entire front, especially on the east, while he strove to create a real army behind this screen. By this con-

33 Benjamin, Richmond, Dec. 27, 1861, to Bragg, in Civil War Coll., Mo. Hist. Soc.; Pillow, New Madrid, n.d., to L. P. Walker, extra-illustrated *Battles and Leaders*, HL; Pettus Corr., Alabama State Archives. Polk, immediately after invading Kentucky and seizing Columbus, had been succeeded by Johnston, who assigned him to the defense of the Mississippi. Pillow, a quarrelsome, shallow strutter, who had been the senior major-general of Tennessee's provisional army, became a brigadier-general in the Confederate forces, repining because his Napoleonic genius was so ill recognized. Simon Buckner, a leader of fine spirit, whom Lincoln had personally offered a commission as brigadier-general, was sent with that Confederate rank to Bowling Green, Ky.

34 Col. R. M. Kelly, *Battles and Leaders,* I, 379–385; memorandum by Thos. C. Reynolds, Johnston's aide, Reynolds Papers, Mo. Hist. Soc.; Col. Wm. Preston Johnston, "Albert Sidney Johnston at Shiloh," *Battles and Leaders,* I, 542; Peter F. Walker, "Building a Tennessee Army, 1861," *Tenn. Hist. Quarterly,* XVI, 99–116 (June, 1957).

35 Johnston, Bowling Green, Dec. 25, 1861, to Isham G. Harris, Brock Coll., HL.

tinuous activity he did succeed in bluffing some of the Union commanders.

Johnston did something—perhaps as much as he could—to fortify the rivers. Fort Henry was the Achilles' heel of his defenses. The first gun had been installed there in July, and by fall a considerable work had been erected; but a young captain who arrived in September to command the artillery concluded that the men who had selected the site were guilty either of preposterous folly or outright treachery. The engineers had placed it on the east bank of the Tennessee, on low land commanded within rifle range by high hills. It was so low, indeed, that the ordinary February rise would put the highest interior point under two feet of water. The armament was with difficulty increased to seventeen effective guns, all but one smoothbores, and the ammunition was so poor that some quick-burning powder had to be added to each charge, a dangerous expedient. Reiterated complaints about the position caused Johnston to dispatch a competent engineer, who made an unavailing effort to improve matters by fortifying some heights on the opposite bank. General Lloyd Tilghman collected a garrison of about 4,000 men, armed chiefly with shotguns and hunting rifles—one of his best-equipped contingents carrying flintlock Tower muskets used in the War of 1812! [36]

Fort Donelson on the west bank of the Cumberland, ten miles away, was a far stronger post, which some Federal officers thought really formidable. Built on a bluff nearly a hundred feet above the water, it was covered on the north by Hickman's Creek, deep and wide in the high water of winter, and on the south by Indian Creek. In a half circle around the fort ran a crescent line of rifle pits, largely following a ridge and protected by felled trees which formed an abattis. Two water batteries sunk in the northern face of the bluff, thirty feet above the river, held twelve guns and a ten-inch Columbiad. The fort seemed well adapted to the height which it crowned. Attacking infantry would find Hickman's Creek almost impassable, and to reach the rifle pits they would have to struggle at most points up hillsides some seventy feet high. [37]

Yet actually Donelson was full of weaknesses. The yellow-clay rifle pits were shallow, and where they reached Indian Creek could be penetrated without scaling any slope. The garrison, some 18,000 ill-trained, ill-armed, ill-provisioned recruits, lacked spirit. These and other defects were summed up in a colonel's roughly eloquent letter to Governor Harris:

We have no preparations for defense comparatively speaking. The guns command the river tolerably well, though we have no practised companies to serve them. The line of fortifications is not complete, or closed, and our

---

36 Jesse Taylor, "The Defense of Fort Henry," *Battles and Leaders*, I, 368 ff. The engineers were hampered in choosing the sites for defense by Kentucky's neutrality.

37 Grant, *Memoirs*, Ch. VIII; Lew Wallace, *Battles and Leaders*, I, 398 ff.

force can be attacked in the rear coming up the river, from below us. There are three hills, which, if the enemy gets possession of, will command our fortifications. There is a high hill in the rear that entirely commands our camp, and if the enemy gets possession of it we will be unable to hold our position. . . .

All our provisions are in Dover—we have no well-drilled troops here and very inferior arms—and badly supplied with ammunition—our caps are defective—the cartridges are made of coarse powder and will not suit our sporting guns—we have none of the sporting caps. The men generally have but little confidence in their guns. . . .[38]

Could the Confederates, thus holding almost untenable forts, save the situation? The boldest course would have been the best: Johnston should have marched in person to reinforce the garrisons and take command against the Union assailants. His will, courage, and reputation would have been invaluable. It is true that he had never commanded troops on the battlefield. But his keen intellect, sustained by his imposing presence, made him a force on any scene. The troops which he kept with him at Bowling Green could better have been employed at the critical point. They would have been invaluable at Fort Donelson. He knew how much the loss of the forts would cost the Confederacy. Later his aide wrote that a few weeks before Grant moved, Johnston had remarked that he expected to see Union armies ascend the river and break the line there, and realized that Buell would never attack him in his strong fortifications at Bowling Green; he only wished he would! [39]

This, in fact, was the first of Johnston's two great lost opportunities. The generals he had sent to Donelson were, with one exception, mediocre or worse. John B. Floyd, the ranking officer, was the same muddleheaded incompetent who had been Secretary of War under Buchanan; the vain, hot-tempered Pillow fancied that his reputation as lawyer, planter, and politician, with two Mexican War wounds, made him a general; and Buckner alone, a West Point graduate of ability, could be taken seriously. Grant later remarked caustically that he had known Pillow in Mexico, and judged that with any force, however small, he could move unmolested within gunshot range of any position Pillow was holding. Johnston knew how weak his subordinates were. Particularly when he was so ill served, it was his duty to be at the critical point of the contest.[40]

[VI]

Landing his 17,000 troops just below Fort Henry on February 5–6, 1862, Grant ordered an advance at 11 A.M. on the 6th. But Foote was before him.

38 Col. J. M. Head, Jan. 26, 1862; Palmer Coll., Western Reserve.
39 Statement by Col. Mumford of Johnston's staff in W. P. Johnston, *Life of A. S. Johnston,* 491. Fuller thinks that Johnston was bewildered.
40 *Memoirs,* Ch. VIII.

He had seven gunboats, including the *Essex* under Commodore William D. Porter. Tilghman had wisely sent practically all the garrison of 2,800 overland to Donelson. By a severe fire of an hour and a quarter the boats took the almost unmanned fort, which could train only eleven of its twenty pieces on the river. Seven of these eleven guns were knocked out by about four hundred gunboat shots. When Tilghman rowed out to Foote's flagship to ask for terms, the commodore made curt reply: "No, sir! Your surrender will be unconditional!" But hardly a hundred officers and men laid down their arms.

On February 12–13, Grant slowly moved his army across the frozen fields to throw a three-mile line around the outworks of Donelson. Here the gunboat attack failed, nearly all of Foote's vessels being crippled in a hot action lasting little more than an hour. Some infantry fighting began the first day. It grew more intense on the 13th, as Grant tightened his hold, and fiercer still on the 15th as the Confederates tried to cut their way out. The weather enhanced the cruelty of the struggle. Thursday the 13th grew very cold, the thermometer dropping to ten above zero; Thursday night it sleeted and snowed; Friday it froze all day, and Friday night more snow fell. The lines were so close neither side could build fires, and the troops lacked shelter tents. Wet uniforms quickly became as stiff as boards, and many of the wounded froze to death. The neighboring village of Dover was choked by dead and maimed, surgeons operating in nearly every house. Men could not open a door without hearing groans. On both sides the volunteers fought as fiercely as veterans, and officers distinguished themselves by heroism. Lincoln's friend Richard Oglesby, a Decatur lawyer who had been defeated for the House the year that Lincoln met defeat for the Senate, led his regiment with great gallantry. The South had to mourn Dabney Carr Harrison, a young man of fine talent who died shouting, "Rally to the charge!" [41]

In the end, the battle at Donelson was decided by three factors. One was Grant's quick grasp of the situation when he returned from a conference with Foote on his flagship to find that Pillow had tried to force his way through the Union lines, and had scattered John A. McClernand's division; a second was the spirited counterassault on the Confederate works which Grant ordered C. F. Smith to launch immediately with Iowa and Indiana troops; and the third was the elan with which Illinois and Ohio infantry recovered their positions. Though sixty, Smith spent the bitter ensuing night without shelter on a captured ridge—the greatest night in the career of that rough-mannered, warmhearted, and thoroughly dedicated soldier.

On both sides the brightest laurels of Donelson belonged to the rank-and-file, for the generalship had distinct flaws. Had the garrison launched its

41 Description by Cairo corr., N. Y. *Tribune*, Feb. 27, 1861. A Confederate Tract Society Pamphlet No. 57, "The Confederate Hero and His Heroic Father," eulogizes Harrison.

FORT DONELSON

attack at the moment when Grant moved with inescapable confusion from Henry to Donelson, it might have smashed his column. Later, Pillow's attempted escape from the fort was tardy, and he halted it just short of success. As for Grant, he had distributed his forces defectively. He should have anticipated a sortie by arranging for deployment in depth, with skirmishers, a strong firing line, and adequate reserves to reinforce any attacked sector. C. F. Smith, a master of tactics, did try to maintain a reserve brigade, but McClernand's division was strung out in a long thin line, all too vulnerable.

However, Grant's decision to counterattack was a master stroke. Hearing that the Confederates had swarmed out with haversacks and knapsacks, he eagerly demanded, "Are the knapsacks filled?" Opening the captured knapsacks to find several days' rations, he saw how desperate was the Southern movement, and his order magnificiently seized the opportunity. Smith, too, realized that swift counterattack would bring victory, and his division poured over the rifle pits with such impetuosity that another half-hour of daylight would have put him inside the fort.[42]

Saturday night the 15th, while Smith's men huddled in the cold, a remarkable scene was enacted inside the fort. Buckner spurned a proposal by Pillow for another sortie, saying that it would cost three-fourths of their men, and Floyd assented: "We shall have to capitulate." Though it was Floyd's duty to share the fate of his troops, he knew that capture would mean trial in Washington for the theft of public funds when he was Secretary of War, if not for treason. Pillow declared that he and his men would die before surrendering. Buckner therefore assumed command, saying: "Give me pen, ink, and paper, and send for a bugler." To his note asking for a parley Grant sent one of the famous replies of military history: "No terms except unconditional and immediate surrender can be accepted. I propose to move immediately upon your works."

With Donelson, Grant took more than 14,000 prisoners, 40-odd pieces of artillery, and some stores. Though Pillow estimated the Confederate casualties at 2,000, Union officers put the total much higher. While on paper the captures of material seemed impressive, men who looked about the fort were struck by Confederate destitution. Most of the firearms were pitiable, the ammunition was wretched, and the two-wheeled ambulances were mere rough carts covered with white cloth. When the people of Chicago saw thousands of Confederate prisoners marching through muddy streets to Camp Douglas, they were struck by the gauntness of the privates, dressed in coarse butternut, with no trace of a uniform except perhaps a stripe on the trousers; carrying tattered blankets and a spoon, tin cup, or frying pan. They went to a new destitution, for the Federal ration cost eleven cents a day.[43]

The results of these river conquests were far-reaching. Albert Sidney Johnston, who knew that the chief blame for the Southern defeat ought to fall on public inertia, pronounced Donelson a disaster almost without remedy.

42 On Donelson, see Grant, *Memoirs*, Ch. VIII; Badeau, *Grant*, I, Ch. II; Lew Wallace, *Battles and Leaders*, I, 398–428, a stirring account but not wholly dependable; A. L. Conger, "The Military Education of Grant as a General," *Wis. Mag. of Hist.*, IV (March, 1921), 239–262, an indictment of Grant's tactics, but with credit for his crucial decision to assault; and Kenneth P. Williams, *Lincoln Finds a General*, III, 229–259, the best study, and one very favorable to Grant.

43 Chicago corr., N. Y. *Tribune*, Feb. 27, 1862.

Aware that silence would best serve his cause, he wrote a report which offered no explanations and delivered no judgments. Floyd and Pillow he reassigned to duty, while he stoically accepted the storm of censure which rained upon him. "The test of merit, in my profession, with the people, is success," he wrote President Davis. "It is a hard rule, but I think it right." [44]

The seizure of the forts at once smashed the Confederate line from Columbus to Bowling Green, compelled the evacuation of these posts, and made Nashville, a city of about 18,000, indefensible. Alarm bells called people into the streets. A special train was hurriedly made up to carry citizens southward. Buggies, carriages, and wagons, crammed with movables, blackened every road leading out of town. Officers hurriedly removed about 800 wagon-loads of pork, clothing, and fixed ammunition. On February 17–18 Johnston marched his main force out of Nashville to Murfreesboro, thirty-one miles away, and on the 23rd his rear guard left the city, which Buell's forces entered next day. In the forward swing of Northern forces, Foote felt chagrined that the naval elements were shouldered aside. "An army major told me," he shortly wrote in his report on operations, "that we were purposely held back from Nashville that General Buell might take it, although that officer sent for a gunboat, which went to Nashville before he entered the city."

All Kentucky now seemed safe in Union hands, the Mississippi was open as far as Island No. 10 on the Kentucky-Tennessee border, and strong Union forces stood in central Tennessee. They held not only the rich manufacturing center of Nashville, with its flour mills, foundries, leather tannery, powder mill, and field-gun shop, but most of the Memphis branch of the Louisville & Nashville Railroad—a line which ran from Bowling Green southwest through Clarksville, Tennessee, to Memphis. Washington's Birthday found C. F. Smith's troops busy listing the commissary stores, ammunition, and artillery which they had taken in Clarksville, and Grant joined them there on February 25. [45]

No wonder that Washington was elated, and Richmond correspondingly depressed! At the White House as late as the morning of February 17 Lincoln still felt great anxiety, for the previous day had brought news of the repulse

44　Johnston, Decatur, Ala., March 18, 1862; *Battles and Leaders*, I, 399. Peter F. Walker, "Failure in Command: Forts Henry and Donelson," *Tenn. Hist. Quarterly*, XVI, December, 1957, accepts the double condemnation of Johnston, first for not choosing abler commanders at the forts, and second for not taking charge there himself when the critical hour struck.

45　Foote's complaint, April 23, 1862, is in Naval O. R., I, xxiii, 10, 11. Nashville was making about 3,000 pounds of powder daily for the Confederacy, 6 good field guns a week, and large quantities of caps and fixed ammunition, while it had a plant for the conversion of flintlock muskets to percussion. James D. Porter, *Confederate Military History,* Vol. VIII (Tennessee), p. 8; Henry McRaven, *Nashville,* 93; Nashville Directory, 1860-61.

of Foote's gunboats, and the evening only some vague accounts of the land fighting, with a dispatch that Union forces had taken the "upper fort." Not knowing what the upper fort was, he could make no estimate of the situation. He feared that the Confederate forces at Bowling Green might suddenly be thrown upon Grant! The whole East lay in the same depressed fog. Then suddenly came Grant's announcement of the capture of the forts, throwing Lincoln's secretaries into transports of joy, and filling the streets of New York and Philadelphia with jubilant men.

"The effect was electrical," states Charles A. Dana. "It was the first significant victory over the rebellion, and filled the country as well as the army which gained it with confidence and enthusiasm; yet the Government and its military chiefs were amazed. They could hardly understand that this unknown man and undisciplined army had gained such an advantage over the public enemy, while the Army of the Potomac, with its perfect equipment and organization, its large number of trained officers and its enormous preponderance of force, had not yet begun its forward movement." [46]

And immediately afterward came another Western victory. The Missouri army under Major-General Samuel R. Curtis, 11,000 strong, pressing into northwest Arkansas, met the troops of Ben McCulloch and Sterling Price at Pea Ridge or Elkhorn Tavern. The supreme Confederate command lay with a dashing harum-scarum West Pointer, Major-General Earl Van Dorn, whose 14,000 men included 3,500 Indian warriors. The Missouri and Arkansas troops, both ill armed, failed to coordinate their movements, while the Indians broke in panic under artillery fire. Van Dorn reorganized the Confederate remnants at Van Buren, for Halleck ordered Curtis not to push far into Arkansas.[47]

Grant found the Donelson campaign a personal triumph, for his energy and judgment were primary elements in its success; and he sent an unwontedly jubilant letter to Congressman Washburne. Our volunteers, he wrote, "fought a battle that would figure well with many of those fought in Europe where large standing armies are maintained. I feel very greatful [sic] to you for having placed me in the position to have had the honor of commanding such an army and at such a time. I only trust that I have not nor will not disappoint you." [48] His unconditional-surrender dispatch to Buckner caught the imagination of the North. Millions applauded a man who could write: "I propose to move immediately on your works." The foundation stone was laid for the fame of a national hero. For the moment, Grant found but one bitter drop in his cup, the jealous pique of Halleck. He resented

46 Nicolay, February 17, 1862, to his wife, *Nicolay Papers*, LC; Dana in N. Y. *Sun*, July 24, 1885.
47 For Pea Ridge, see *Battles and Leaders*, I, 289–334; it was fought March 7–8.
48 To Elihu Washburne, February 21, 1862, Grant-Washburne Papers, Ill. State Lib.

to the end of his life the telegram Halleck sent Washington on the 19th awarding the victory to another, and by implication censuring Grant's leadership: "Smith, by his coolness and bravery at Fort Donelson, when the battle was against us, turned the tide and carried the enemy's outworks. Make him a major-general. You cannot get a better one. Honor him for his victory, and the whole country will applaud." [49] This was the old-army prejudice against Grant and admiration of Smith, along with a vein of petty jealousy that was Halleck's own.

For Halleck lost no time in arrogating the chief glory of the victory to himself and seizing precedence of Buell. The day after Buckner's surrender he telegraphed McClellan: "Make Buell, Grant, and Pope major-generals of volunteers, and give me the command in the West. I ask this in return for Donelson and Henry." Three days later he added: "I must have command of the armies in the West. Hesitation and delay are losing us the golden opportunities. Lay this before the President and Secretary of War. May I assume the command? Answer quickly." [50]

Golden opportunities! Halleck was the last man in the army with a right to talk of them. A fumbling leader before battle, he was always at his worst after one. He could exhibit sheer genius in making a victory less profitable than a sharp defeat. Beyond question, had he now vigorously pressed a Union advance all along the line, the richest fruits might have been garnered. Grant's army had been reinforced at Donelson to 27,000. Buell in Nashville had 15,000 to 20,000. Additional troops could be brought in from Ohio, Indiana, Illinois, and Iowa. For the time being the Confederate armies were disorganized, demoralized, and separated. The Union thrust into central Tennessee had cut squarely between Johnston's force, which fell back to Murfreesboro, and Beauregard's army at Jackson, Tennessee.[51] Grant, drawing on Pope in Missouri for troops, might march westward at once against the Confederates at Hickman on the Mississippi; or might join Buell at Nashville and enable that general to push Johnston back into northern Alabama.

If Grant did march west to the Mississippi, he might cut off the retreat of the Confederates who were evacuating Columbus, for Leonidas Polk, commanding there, had fewer than 15,000 badly armed, badly officered men. Even greater possibilities existed. While Buell immobilized Johnston at Murfreesboro, Grant might rapidly push on up the Tennessee River to northern Mississippi, seize the Memphis & Charleston Railroad there, and march west along the line to take Memphis itself. All the points on the

49 O. R., I, vii, 637; M. F. Force, *From Fort Henry to Corinth*, 64, 65. Halleck, graduating at West Point in 1839, with Smith a favorite instructor, had taught several years under Smith as head of the Academy.
50 O. R., I, vii, 628, 641.
51 Roman, *Beauregard*, I, 233.

Mississippi north of Memphis—Fort Pillow, Hickman, Island No. 10, Columbus, New Madrid—would at once fall. Polk's 15,000 troops would join their Donelson comrades in Northern prison camps. As Vicksburg was still hardly fortified, even that city might lie open to capture.[52]

Indeed, Grant declared later that by swift steps the whole West might have been subjugated. In his opinion, a determined leader, using all the troops west of the Alleghenies, could have captured Memphis, Corinth, and Chattanooga, and have taken Vicksburg. Volunteers were coming forward steadily in the Northwest. These wide seizures of Confederate territory would have stimulated enlistment, and prevented the recruiting of tens of thousands of able-bodied young men into the Southern ranks. "Providence ruled differently," wrote Grant long afterward. "Time was given the enemy to collect armies and fortify his new positions; and twice afterwards he came near forcing the northwestern front up to the Ohio River."[53] But for a brief hour Northerners who saw what *might* be done believed the end near. "After this, it certainly cannot be materially postponed," declared the New York *Times* of February 14, 1862. "The monster is already clutched and in his death struggle." Alas, that hope faded.

Why did it fade? For one reason, because for three critical weeks the high Western command remained divided between Halleck in St. Louis and Buell in his new post at Nashville, making unitary action practically impossible. For another reason, because Buell showed excessive caution. He no sooner arrived in Nashville than he indulged in McClellanesque exaggerations of enemy strength. He sent C. F. Smith a panicky telegram on February 25: "If the enemy should assume the offensive . . . my force at present is altogether inadequate." Smith justly termed this nonsense. Grant, who immediately visited Nashville, found it impossible to persuade Buell that he was in no danger. The enemy, Grant said, is retreating as fast as his legs can carry him. When Buell denied this, asserting that the enemy were fighting only ten or twelve miles southeast of Nashville, as if they meant to return, Grant rejoined sharply: "Quite probably; Nashville contained valuable stores of arms, ammunition, and provisions, and the enemy is probably trying to carry away all he can. The fighting is doubtless with the rear guard who are trying to protect the trains they are getting away with."[54]

The principal reason why the chance of overrunning the whole Western

52 So says Beauregard, who knew the situation; Roman, I, 234. The head of the Vicksburg police, M. Emmanuel, wrote the governor Nov. 27, 1861, that the city was "defenceless" against an invasion; Pettus Corr., Alabama State Archives. Grenville M. Dodge wrote Horace White, Aug. 5, 1909: "There is no question but if Grant's advice had been followed right after Donelson and Buell's army had joined him and without halting marched to Vicksburg, they would have taken it"; White Papers, Ill. State Lib.
53 Grant, *Memoirs*, Ch. II.
54 Grant, *Memoirs*, Ch. IX.

theater slipped away, however, was that Halleck never perceived it. The day before Donelson capitulated he had written McClellan: "I have no definite plan beyond the taking of Fort Donelson and Clarksville." [55] Before March ended, Grant, Buell, Pope, C. F. Smith, and Lew Wallace all received major-generalcies. On March 11, meanwhile, Halleck obtained command of the Department of the Mississippi. The whole valley was his; he could move the generals like knights on a board stretching from Arkansas to Chattanooga and Atlanta. But he had no program whatever for moving them and never held a serious consultation with any of them. Though it was his business to look far ahead, neither to the War Department nor to his subordinates did he specify what steps were to be taken. With the gates to the heart of the South thrown ajar, he paused outside.

"Transports will be sent you as soon as possible," he telegraphed Grant on March 1, "to move your column up the Tennessee River." But for what? Grant was merely to destroy by swift dashes a railroad bridge near Eastport, Mississippi, and rail connections at Corinth, Mississippi, and Jackson, Tennessee, and then fall back. "Avoid any general engagements with strong forces," enjoined Halleck. "It will be better to retreat than to risk a general battle. This should be strongly impressed upon the officers sent with expedition from the river."

And Halleck and McClellan between them came near dismissing the general with ignominy. "I have had no communication with General Grant for more than a week," Halleck informed McClellan March 3. "He left his command without my authority and went to Nashville." He added that Grant's army seemed demoralized. "I can get no returns, no reports, no information of any kind from him. Satisfied with his victory, he sits down and enjoys it without any regard to the future. I am worn out and tired with this neglect and inefficiency." McClellan telegraphed in reply: "Do not hesitate to arrest Grant at once if the good of the service requires it, and place C. F. Smith in command." On the 4th Halleck told McClellan he had heard "a rumor" that since Donelson, Grant had resumed drinking. He simultaneously placed C. F. Smith in command of the Tennessee River expedition, ordered Grant to remain at Fort Henry, where he was kept almost a week under virtual arrest, and sharply rebuked him. The difficulty actually lay with communications. Grant had written the chief of staff every day, reported every move, and gone to Nashville solely for the good of the service. "If my course is not satisfactory," he telegraphed Halleck, "remove me at once." [56]

Halleck continued to nag Grant and to caution him and Smith against any general battle. The expedition up the Tennessee, crippled by his orders, accomplished nothing. It is difficult to avoid the suspicion that Halleck was jealous of Grant's achievements. Well might he be! Long afterward, one of the wisest Confederate soldiers was to write: "To my mind the Southern Confederacy died at Donelson." [57]

[VII]

During the four weeks in which his eleven-year-old son Willie sickened and died Lincoln was increasingly distraught and unnerved. The bright, gentle boy had been a ray of sunshine in the White House. When the ordeal ended on February 20, the President, who for some days had been almost incommunicado, resumed sorrowfully his postponed undertakings, of which the compensated emancipation scheme was chief.

In a message on March 6 he asked Congress to adopt a joint resolution: "Resolved, that the United States ought to cooperate with any State which may adopt gradual abolishment of slavery, giving to such State pecuniary aid, to be used by such State in its discretion, to compensate for the inconveniences, public and private, produced by such change of system." [58] He argued that the mere initiation of a gradual scheme in some or all of the Border States would do much to shorten the struggle, for it would cut off from Confederate leaders the hope that they could ever win that area. Other considerations played a part in his stroke. It enabled him to test the sentiment of slaveholders from the Chesapeake to the Missouri; it would temporarily quiet the radicals; and it advertised to the country two of his basic principles—that while the eventual extinction of slavery must be accepted, the work should be gradual, and the whole nation should bear the cost.

Lincoln sent his secretaries to fetch Charles Sumner to the White House early on March 6. "I want to read you my message," he told the Senator. "I want to know how you like it." As he finished, Sumner seized the paper to con it closely. He did not like the word "abolishment"—which is good English—and objected to one sentence bearing on reconstruction, which Lincoln struck out. When he asked what the Cabinet thought, Lincoln told him that they had all heard it read the previous evening, and all, including Seward, Bates, and even Caleb Smith, liked it. Sumner related later: "Well, I sat with it in my hands, reading it over and not bearing to give it up, but

57   John A. Wyeth, N. Y., Nov. 14, 1905, to J. W. DuBose, DuBose Papers, Ala. State Archives.
58   *Cong. Globe*, 37th Cong., 2d Sess., 1102, 1103.

he said, 'There, now, you've read it enough, run away. I must send it in today.' " [59] His secretaries took it at once to the Capitol.

The message pleased all but the most indurated conservatives and fanatic radicals.[60] Most of the press and pulpit gave it hearty praise. If Congress approved the resolution, said the New York *Times*, it would loom up as a landmark in American history, for the government would have declared in favor of freedom and of the use of national funds to promote it; Lincoln had hit "the happy mean." The *Evening Post* was delighted; so was the *Tribune;* and so, measurably, was the eccentric *Herald*. Greeley in an article in the *Independent* declared that the step placed Lincoln at the head of the nation, and would deter foreign powers from intervention. The *World* published a long editorial commending Lincoln's moderation and foresight. The Washington *National Republican* gave him full support. It is evidence of Lincoln's earnestness that he placed copies of these comments in these papers; and he furnished additional evidence when, replying to some doubts by Henry J. Raymond over the cost, he pointed out that charges for eighty-seven days of war would pay for all the slaves in Maryland, Delaware, Kentucky, Missouri, and the District at $400 each.[61]

Thaddeus Stevens summed up the bitter condemnation of the plan by abolitionists: "the most diluted, milk-and-water gruel proposition that was ever given to the American nation." [62] On the other side, reactionaries were hoarse with denunciation. They opposed it as vehemently as the confiscation bill. Democratic opponents quickly adopted the argument of the Cincinnati *Enquirer*, which asserted that after the President spent a billion dollars to buy freedom for the slaves, a great part of the freed Negroes would then come North, to be supported as paupers at public expense, or to compete with white laborers and thus take the bread from white children's mouths. Frank P. Blair, Jr., made a speech in the House April 11 which, aimed at border sentiment, angered great elements in the North. He denied that the war was a slaveholders' rebellion, and declared that emancipation would be a terrible mistake until arrangements could be made to colonize the Negroes abroad; they could not be sent back to Africa, but they could be shipped to areas south of the Rio Grande and settled under Federal protection. His indiscreet action did

59 E. E. Hale, *Memories of a Hundred Years*, II, 189–196.
60 T. D. Woolsey, president of Yale, wrote that Lincoln had acted gloriously in bringing slavery before the country in a way to allay agitation by both extremes; April 12, 1862, Lieber Papers, HL.
61 The N. Y. *Evening Post* published a full compendium of opinion in an article, "The Emancipation Movement: Its Progress in the Border Slave States," May 16, 1862. The Phila. *Evening Journal*, a moderate Democratic sheet, and the Wash. *National Intelligencer* were warm in praise.
62 *Cong. Globe*, 37th Cong., 2d Sess., 1154.

the Administration real harm in all circles friendly to the Negro and his early liberation. Both at home and abroad, many people agreed with the London *Times* of May 7, 1862, that the idea of forcible colonization was immoral.

The real test of the plan, it was evident, would come in the Border States, where its fate was doubtful. A Republican Congress could not fail to toe the mark; on March 11 the House passed Lincoln's resolution 97 to 36, and on April 2 the Senate followed, 32 to 10. The contest was on party lines, all but two Democratic Senators and four Democratic Representatives voting no. But while it was easy for Congress to act, in the Border States a battle royal lay ahead. While that struggle began, all eyes were turned to the battlefront in Virginia.

2

Stanton, McClellan, and the Virginia Front

VICTORY in the Virginia theater depended on three men: Lincoln, Stanton, and McClellan. The first two were eager to see the third give battle. "Now, gentlemen," said Stanton at his first reception to officers, "we will, if you please, have some fighting. It is my business to furnish the means, it is yours to use them. I leave the fighting to you, but the fighting we must have." [1]

Stanton's accession had been almost as unexpected by him as it was sudden. He had not spoken to Lincoln between the inauguration and the day the President handed him his commission. That the labors of his office would crush him he well understood. "I knew that everything I cherish and hold dear would be sacrificed," he wrote a friend four months later. "But I thought I might help to save the country, and for that I was willing to perish." [2]

Visitors at the War Department saw a short, sturdily built man whose broad shoulders bore a massive head, looking bigger still because of his heavy black beard and flowing dark hair. His full face, large, brilliant eyes, and flattish nose gave him a Socratic aspect. His forehead was broad though not high, his mouth firm and tightly compressed, and his general expression intensely serious. He exhaled an air of vigor, earnestness, and sternness. No other member of the Cabinet was so severely impressive. From his deep chest came a voice not only resonant but surprisingly musical. Though on occasion his gray eyes twinkled behind his large round spectacles, and his lips softened into an engaging smile, he was usually so intensely absorbed in his work that he bore a fiercely imperious aspect. When angered, his eyes blazed as he jerked out a harsh retort or a rebuke that made subordinates quail. He antagonized most of the people who did business with him. Don't

1 Donn Piatt, *Men Who Saved the Union*, 61.
2 To the Rev. Heman Dyer, May 18, 1862, Stanton Papers; N. Y. *Sun*, Dec. 25, 1869. McClellan, soon to change his mind, was delighted by the event, writing S. L. M. Barlow, "Stanton's appointment was a most unexpected piece of good fortune, and I hope it will produce a good effect in the North"; Barlow Papers, Jan. 18, 1862.

send me to Stanton to ask favors, John Hay once begged Nicolay: "I would rather make a tour of a smallpox hospital." [3] But he could inspire as well as terrify associates, and the affluent beauty of his language when he was moved would delight all hearers. It was no accident that perhaps the two most memorable sentences ever uttered upon Lincoln came from Stanton's lips.[4]

A dictatorial, arbitrary quality so consistently ruled Stanton that most men thought him a tyrant. He loved power, seldom brooked opposition, and showed an enjoyment of authority that struck—and offended—all who came in his path. The result was that Grant, Sherman, Gideon Welles, Seward, Lincoln's secretaries, and others have etched the lines of a caustic portrait. His arbitrary temper was accentuated by his tendency to jump to conclusions. He would impetuously take a stand just to prove his authority, as he did early in the war in trying to destroy the invaluable Sanitary Commission. It was accentuated also by his intolerant, vindictive nursing of prejudices and grudges. He almost never admitted himself wrong, tried to see a situation from an antagonist's eye, or showed generosity to a foe either victorious or defeated.

Few acts of the war were more outrageous than his treatment of General Charles P. Stone after Ball's Bluff, ordering the arrest, prejudging the case, delaying justice, and offering no regrets. He sometimes showed the capricious malignity of other despotic-tempered autocrats: Frederick the Great, Napoleon III, Stalin. His harsh treatment of unprotected men was the more glaring because he cautiously gauged the strength of those whose power and prestige surpassed his own. He took good care not to assail Congressional leaders like Wade, Stevens, and Sumner, treated powerful governors like Morton or Andrew respectfully, and was scrupulous not to press the patient Lincoln too far. Once he refused to obey an order of Lincoln's. "Mr. Secretary, I reckon you'll have to obey it," said Lincoln—and he did.[5]

At times an apparent duplicity seemed to actuate this fierce, ill-governed, dynamic executive. He burned with envy of his peers, for his thirst for authority, as James G. Blaine writes, was subject to its counterpart of jealousy. Gideon Welles never regarded him as trustworthy. Not merely did Welles shrink from a man who could be rude and domineering toward subordinates,

3 Helen Nicolay, "Lincoln's Cabinet," *Abraham Lincoln Quarterly*, V (March, 1949), 282; sketch in Fanny Seward's MS Diary, April 5, 1862; A. E. H. Johnson, "Rems. of Stanton," *Columbia Hist. Soc. Records*, XIII, 69–97 (1910).

4 Late in the Administration, "There goes the greatest ruler of men who ever lived"; at the deathbed, "Now he belongs to the ages." But while still uninformed, Stanton wrote Buchanan of Lincoln's "painful imbecility."

5 Provost-Marshal Fry has preserved the whole colloquy about this order, which related to prisoners of war; A. K. McClure, *Lincoln and Men of War-Times*, 185. McClure describes Stanton's brutally senseless imprisonment of a Pittsburgher; 177-181 (edition pages vary).

while a sycophantic dissembler with those he feared; the Secretary of the Navy thought him a two-faced intriguer. That view was shortly taken also by McClellan, who became convinced that Stanton was worse than Judas Iscariot. It was taken by many more, down to the time when President Andrew Johnson dismissed him for what he held to be barefaced treachery. General Ethan Allen Hitchcock, however, a close observer inside the War Department, and a man who detested his brutality and violence, declared that Stanton was not a man of reason.[6] "He decides a point one day in one way; and a week after (forgetting his decision and having no principle) he will decide the same point in another way. [Then] he flies into a passion with someone for having followed his first decision; and his fits of passion almost always break out upon a few individuals, against whom, without any cause, he has conceived some prejudice."

A. K. McClure of Pennsylvania, who admired him greatly, declared that he was capable of the grandest and basest actions alike. In this he was almost another Bacon, "the wisest, noblest, meanest of mankind." Only a psychoanalyst possessing the fullest data could really explain his combination of glaring weaknesses and brilliant virtues. A vein of hysteria amounting to partial insanity had repeatedly appeared in his early career. After his brother's suicide he had to be guarded against the same act; the loss of his baby daughter had thrown him into a frenzy; and the death of his first wife so prostrated him that for a month he could hardly be dragged from her grave. Even in 1862 he was still easily overwrought. Numerous military men, including Grant, believed that he was both morally and physically timid in the hour of danger. Grant bluntly declares that, conscious of Union weakness but ignoring that of the Confederates, he wished to keep protective armies much nearer Washington than was proper. It is not strange that observers, seeing him in one of his sudden rages, hearing him sputter insults or launch unfounded accusations, or watching him in a brief access of panic, concluded that he was partially demented.[7]

One almost lifelong intimate, Donn Piatt, writes of him as rendered fiercely aggressive by "disease that overwhelmed his nervous system," and this same

---

6 Blaine, *Twenty Years*, I, 563; Welles, *Diary*, I, 129; McClellan, *Own Story*, 137; Diary of E. A. Hitchcock, W. A. Croffut Papers, LC. Hitchcock wrote Henry H. Hitchcock, April 25, 1862: "He is coarse in the use of language and insulting in the mode of address towards those he dislikes, and his dislikes are mere prejudices. . . ."; Hitchcock Papers, Mo. Hist. Soc. But Horace White, who served in the War Department, states in an undated memorandum: "During all the time I was in Mr. Stanton's office I was never subjected to any ill treatment, roughness, or even impatience at his hands, although I witnessed such treatment visited by him upon others more than once."

7 See Burton J. Hendrick, *Lincoln's War Cabinet*, 241 ff., for material on Stanton's private life; Welles, *Diary*, I, 64–66, for Stanton's behavior during the *Merrimac* scare; Grant, *Memoirs*, II, 537, for his timidity.

observer speaks of Stanton as "furious almost to insanity over the failures of his generals."[8] Two heads of the Sanitary Commission, Henry W. Bellows and George Templeton Strong, concluded that he suffered from cerebral disease. Admiral D. D. Porter received the same impression when, after the capture of Fort Fisher, Stanton kissed him! Generals, Cabinet members, newspapermen, disliked or detested him. Why, then, must he be called one of the chief architects of victory?

His abilities were great and they were combative abilities. Whether because of his timidity, his ambition, or his fierce nervous ardor, he battled savagely. In his career at the bar he had played the part not of an interpreter of legal principles but of a courtroom fighter, using every weapon within reach. He had achieved his widest popular fame when he got Daniel Sickles acquitted of the murder of Philip Barton Key on the ground of temporary insanity. Becoming Attorney-General just before Christmas in 1860, he had done the country unforgettable service in his adamant stand against the disunionist plotters in Buchanan's cabinet; he had written the resolution authorizing a House committee that winter to investigate clandestine plots against the government; and he had kept Seward informed of everything that went on in Buchanan's circle. In short, he had been a stubborn champion of the Union in the darkest months of its history. He had dealt with treason and stratagem without mercy. His patriotism was of the most unflinching kind. Now in 1862 he found joy in fighting both the Confederates and the sinister men who stalked in the shadowy byways of Washington. The battle he was waging was demanded, he felt, by every interest of the nation, of civilization, and of God. "I believe that God Almighty founded the government, and for my acts in the effort to maintain it I expect to stand before Him in judgment."

This was no pretense, for he was fervently religious. An associate, entering his office unexpectedly, found him with head bowed on his desk, in a passion of tears, muttering over and over: "God help me to do my duty! God help me to do my duty!" Nevertheless, he loved battle for its own sake. He liked to deal blows and see their effect. And he never lost courage, for he never doubted the end.[9]

This faith steeled him, while suffering paroxysms of asthma, to endure more grueling labor than perhaps any other leader, North or South, put into the conflict. As an attorney he had become famous for his tremendous industry in mastering the law and facts, and in marshaling his arguments.

8 Piatt, *Men Who Saved the Union*, 88 ff.; Strong, *Diary*, III, 226, May 15, 1862; Porter, *Incidents and Anecdotes*, 279.

9 Dana, *Recs. of the Civil War*, 161 ff.; Henry Wilson, "E. M. Stanton," *Atlantic*, xxv (February, 1870), 234–246.

Investigating California land titles for the government, he had carried his search of Mexican archives and other sources to the deepest level. In the War Department he now toiled day and night mastering the details of business. His carriage would come in the small hours, but he still kept it waiting. Often he stayed the entire night at his post; "receiving reports, requests, information, and suggestions by telegraph and mail," writes Henry Wilson, "holding personal consultations with military and civil officers of the government, and others having business, and issuing orders." As he expected bureau heads to keep pace, his department became a center of such unceasing, anxious labor that those who did not possess his physical endurance, powers of concentration, and iron will sank under the strain. Peter H. Watson, his best Assistant Secretary, a strong man, soon quit office quite worn out; his successor Walcott shortly went home to die; and Charles A. Dana, who followed, held on only because his eyes would not let him work at night, while the appointment of a solicitor to the department reduced his labors.

Like Lincoln, he never took a vacation, and unlike the President, never relaxed in informal talk or over a humorous book.

Stanton's industry was matched by executive genius. His decisions were rapid, his purposes inflexible, and his readiness to take the largest responsibilities unhesitating. When Morton of Indiana required more than $250,000 for war purposes which the legislature failed to appropriate, Stanton grasped the situation instantly and drew his warrant on the Treasury for the sum. If the cause fails, warned Morton, we shall land in jail. "If the cause fails," responded Stanton, "I do not wish to live." His instinct for system, method, and orderliness amounted to a passion. Finding the basic military arrangements of the nation in a clutter, he gave them pattern and harmony. His consolidation of regiments irritated State and local pride; no matter, it was sternly directed. His sweeping military censorship stung the press to violent protest; with scathing words on editors who would ruin an army to print a good news story, he maintained it. He gave the War Department practical control over the whole telegraph system of the country, Thomas T. Eckert, David Homer Bates, and other able young men manning the instruments in a room adjoining his own day and night. In that nerve center of the North, Lincoln spent much time. Stanton's rule that every military or political telegram on all the various wires, even a message from Lincoln, even a general's communication to his wife, must be read there, angered many leaders. Grant, deeming the delay intolerable, ultimately circumvented the rule. On the whole, however, it promoted efficiency.[10]

10 Dana, Wilson, ut sup.; W. D. Foulke, Morton, I, 260–261; A. E. H. Johnson, Stanton's confidential clerk, Wash. Post, July 14, 1891, in McClure, op. cit., 176; D. H. Bates, Lincoln in the Telegraph Office, Chs. VIII–XVII.

His courage, which did much to earn him his reputation for cantankerous ill temper, was unflinching. He met politicians, generals, and businessmen in the open, rapping out his answers for all to hear. One reporter saw him dispatch man after man, more than two hundred in a five-hour period. More than once he literally shoved a rascal out of his office. His stern sudden judgments were sometimes wrong; his rule that his desk must be cleared every night meant rough surgery on complex problems; he could be outrageously unjust to other strong men who rasped him, like Surgeon-General Hammond. But, meeting slovenliness, stupidity, and dishonesty on every hand, he was like a powerful swimmer tangled in marsh grass; he had to lash out or be drowned. His blazes of anger were particularly fierce when he suspected selfishness or crookedness. In a nation of improvisation, of rule-of-thumb, Stanton thought of himself as conducting a one-man war for plan and foresight. With the country's life in the balance, slackness and clumsiness became crimes. He rapidly developed a scathing contempt for the cautious McClellan, the dilatory Buell, and the hesitant Rosecrans.[11] The arrogant ways of Little Mac grated upon his sense that the cause was everything, the individual nothing. Soon after he took office he called unexpectedly at McClellan's headquarters, and the general kept him waiting. His secretary, A. E. H. Johnson, reports his furious comment: "That will be the last time General McClellan will give either myself or the President the waiting snub."

All his virtues of industry, system, and courage would have availed nothing without sound judgment; and unquestionably he stood pre-eminent in Lincoln's cabinet for his sturdy common-sense sagacity. He quickly divined the weaknesses of generals who had been his personal friends. He just as quickly grasped the strength of two of the indispensable generals, Grant and Thomas, and gave them support in hours bright and dark. From Donelson to the end of the war his faith in Grant, bolstered by Dana's shrewd report of the man, never wavered; and he pushed the general steadily up the ladder, keeping him in charge of Vicksburg operations when the clamor for removal ran high, giving him Rosecrans' place at Chattanooga with enlarged authority, and urging through Congress the measure which made him head of the armies with the rank of lieutenant-general. His admiration for Thomas was unbounded. He stood by the calm Virginian when, just before the battle of Nashville, many wished to displace him, and he exulted when Thomas vindicated this confidence by one of the most crushing victories of the war.

11 Stanton was capable of fine generosity. Piatt, 90, 91, saw him brush aside high military officers to speak to a ragged private, obviously ill, who came to his office. The lad gave him a letter from Ormsby M. Mitchel stating that he was the sole survivor of a heroic band sent south to burn railway bridges. Stanton read it aloud, held it aloft, and exclaimed with emotion: "I would rather be worthy of this letter than have the highest commission in the army of the United States." He promised to make the boy an officer.

But the greatest proof of Stanton's judgment was his perception of the importance of the Western theater, which Cameron had slighted. As quickly as Lincoln, he saw that there the war was destined to be won.[12]

It should be added that Stanton always commanded the confidence of those men whose confidence was indispensable. Watson, Dana, and other office intimates were staunch adherents and admirers. The Congressional military committees always met his wishes and gave his measures firm support. Senator Henry Wilson later counted among his most cherished recollections the fact that no misunderstanding or unkindness ever marred his relations with the Secretary. Grant, while resenting Stanton's interferences with his generals, acknowledged his great powers; the sensitive Thomas, while conscious of some buffets, pronounced him a just man. Above all, the Secretary gained and held the faith of Lincoln, who, late in his Administration, said with feeling: "You have been our main reliance." [13] Indeed, the President spent more time with him than with any other Cabinet member, often stepping from the telegraph room at the War Department to Stanton's adjacent office, and sometimes driving with him to or from their neighboring cottages at the Soldiers' Home near Washington.

The popular supposition at the time that Stanton complemented Lincoln, supplying a firmness and decision which the President lacked, was untrue, for Lincoln needed no complement. But it is true that Lincoln's strength did not lie in careful planning and systematic administration—and Stanton's did. The two sometimes clashed. Stanton not only said cutting things of Lincoln but indulged in contemptuous gestures, as when he tore up a memorandum and tossed it into the wastebasket. But Lincoln was always the master. When he restored McClellan to command after Second Manassas, Stanton made his resentment as plain as did Chase. "No order came from the War Department," he said. "No," replied Lincoln, "I gave the order." That Lincoln soon learned to deem the Secretary indispensable we have ample testimony. He firmly repelled all proposals that Stanton should give way to N. P. Banks, Ben Butler, or some other favorite of the radicals. The two stood firmly together on critical issues. Once a talebearer reported that Stanton had said the President was a fool. "Indeed!" Lincoln replied, "then it must be true, for Stanton is usually right." [14] In general, however, Stanton was wise enough to deal with

12 For Stanton's unfailing support of Grant see Badeau, *Military Hist.*, II, 13 ff. The Secretary did not approve of Sherman's march to the sea, which was open to grave strategic objections, nor did he like Sherman.

13 Flower, *Stanton*, 311. Once when a friend protested against Stanton's brutality of speech, Lincoln replied that they might have to deal with him as some Westerners once dealt with a too-fervent Methodist exhorter, putting bricks in his pockets. "But I guess we'll let him jump awhile first." Mrs. H. B. Stowe, *Men of Our Times*, 370.

14 Julian, *Political Recs.*, 212.

Lincoln tactfully. He thought the President too slow in proclaiming emancipation and arming the Negroes.[15] But his method was to express his opinion forcibly, and leave the rest to time.

"Nor was it his practice," recalled Dana, "pertinaciously to urge upon the President the removal of a general in whom he had confidence no longer. Having fully expressed his opinion to Mr. Lincoln, he would wait until the President had himself come to the same conclusion."

[I]

We have said that Lincoln's Special Order No. 1, directing McClellan to lead his army by February 22 in a flanking movement southwest of Manassas, was meant to force the general to disclose his plans. That was precisely its result. Immediately on receiving it, McClellan wrote Stanton a twenty-two-page letter which for the first time revealed his hand.

Lincoln's proposal was essentially for a movement upon Joseph E. Johnston's army through Manassas, with Washington as base; it was for a direct overland attack. McClellan preferred to move the Union army down the Potomac and up the Rappahannock to a point opposite Richmond, a hamlet called Urbana. His base would be served from Chesapeake Bay. He argued that this course would place the army on the shortest feasible land route to Richmond, and would possess other advantages. The roads on the Urbana-Richmond line were passable at all seasons; the country, being sandy with sparse woods, and enjoying an early spring, was specially favorable to offensive operations; while a march in force southwest from Urbana would cut off Magruder's troops on the Peninsula, compel a quick evacuation of Manassas, and enable him to reach Richmond before it was reinforced. Failing that, he could, with the aid of the Navy, cross the James and attack Richmond from the rear. "Worst coming to worst," he could take Fort Monroe as base, and "operate with complete security," though with less brilliancy of result, up the Peninsula. He specially stressed the superior celerity of his plan. If the army used Washington as a base to advance through Manassas, it would have to wait until the roads, as yet sloughs of mud, dried, but if it moved by the roads of the lower Chesapeake area, it could calculate its march "almost to a day, and with but little regard to the season." [16]

This letter possibly still lay on Stanton's desk, but had more probably been shown to Lincoln, when the President on February 3 sent McClellan

---

15 Cf. Eaton, *Grant, Lincoln, and the Freedmen*, 179.
16 McClellan's long letter bears date Feb. 3, 1862; text in O. R., I, v, 41 ff.; with previously unpublished passages, Lincoln, *Works*, V, 119 ff.

some piercing inquiries. In a few lines he went to the heart of the issue between them. He would gladly yield his plan for an advance based on Washington and accept McClellan's if he could get five questions satisfactorily answered:

1st. Does not your plan involve a greatly larger expenditure of *time*, and *money*, than mine?
2nd. Wherein is a victory *more certain* by your plan than mine?
3rd. Wherein is a victory *more valuable* by your plan than mine?
4th. In fact, would it not be *less* valuable, in this, that it would break no great line of the enemy's communications, while mine would?
5th. In case of disaster, would not a safe retreat be more difficult by your plan than mine?

The point as to breaking the enemy's communications deserves emphasis. Johnston's army had two main railroad lines connecting it with the body of the Confederacy: one from Richmond southeast to Wilmington, one southwest to Lynchburg; the first of limited use for military operations, the second almost indispensable. The mere capture of Richmond would effect little except the seizure of some valuable works, notably the Tredegar iron mills, and a blow to Confederate morale at home and prestige abroad. Lincoln proposed a movement from the northwest on Richmond which would cut the lifeline to Lynchburg; McClellan, a campaign from the east which would leave the western escape route open.

The reasons why Lincoln demurred to McClellan's plan actually ran beyond the queries here stated. He and Stanton naturally accepted the general's estimates of formidable enemy strength. Pinkerton, chief of McClellan's intelligence service, placed the Confederate force in northern Virginia at 115,500 men, with 300 field guns and 26 to 30 siege guns.[17] They were reluctant to leave Washington unprotected by the departure of the main Union army while Johnston lay near with such great numbers. Lincoln had the support of McDowell for his plan. McClellan made no written response to his queries, and it is possible that he replied orally in a personal conference with the President; it is also possible that he did not, for Lincoln remained anxiously perplexed.

Unfortunately, Lincoln's three possible courses really boiled down to one. He could force McClellan to adopt a plan which the general believed might prove disastrous; he could remove McClellan while as yet he had no successor available; or he could yield. In deep distress, he gave way. On February 14 the War Department called for proposals to furnish transports,

17 Pinkerton's report of March 8, 1862; Greeley, *Amer. Conflict*, II, 129. Actually Confederate reports for the Potomac district Jan. 22 show the aggregate present as 24,882— though other forces lay in the Shenandoah and at Aquia; O. R. I, v, 1040.

and on the 27th ordered its agents to begin buying steamers and sailing ships. Lincoln told McClellan that his plan had been accepted, with its details still to be fixed.[18]

Stanton and other Cabinet members, in talking with Lincoln, saw how apprehensive he was over the removal of the great army which shielded Washington. The President suggested minor movements which would make the capital safer, such as the sending of N. P. Banks's division in Maryland across the Potomac against Winchester to open the Baltimore & Ohio. McClellan went up to Harpers Ferry to superintend Banks's stroke. His plan was to bring canal boats through the Chesapeake & Ohio Canal locks to that point, and use them for a pontoon bridge. But on the night of February 27 Stanton came to Lincoln's office with a dispatch from the general. The canal boats had been found six inches too wide to pass the locks! McClellan sent word that he could not build the bridge before Winchester was reinforced.

"What does this mean?" demanded Lincoln.

"It means," said Stanton, "that it is a damned fizzle. It means that he doesn't intend to do anything."

Lincoln was deeply dejected. Seward arrived, and the three held a long conference. They sent for Marcy, McClellan's chief of staff. The President addressed him with manifest anger.

"Why in the nation, General Marcy," he demanded, "couldn't the general have known whether a boat would go through that lock before spending a million dollars getting them there? I am no engineer, but it seems to me that if I wished to know whether a boat would go through a hole or lock, common sense would teach me to go and measure it. I am almost despairing at these results. Everything seems to fail. The impression is daily gaining ground that the general does not intend to do anything." As Marcy expostulated, Lincoln abruptly ended the interview. Marcy telegraphed McClellan that the President "was in a hell of a rage." [19] Perhaps Chase's thrust, "The expedition died of lockjaw," best summarized the episode.

It is plain that early in March, Lincoln and Stanton actually feared that some ulterior motive might lie behind McClellan's delays. Radical editors and Congressmen were intimating a sinister purpose. The general did not wish the South severely defeated, they said; he wanted the Union restored without emancipation, and without centralization of national power. When As-

18 Ropes, *Civil War*, I, 233; Nicolay, *Lincoln's Secretary*, Ch. XII. McClellan says in *My Own Story*, 237, that he held many conferences with Lincoln at this time. But since the evening when he went to bed leaving the President waiting downstairs, Lincoln required him to come to the White House.

19 Nicolay, *Lincoln's Secretary*, 142–144, for the Lincoln-Stanton-Marcy meeting; Horace White to Medill, March 3, 1862, on Marcy's telegram, C. H. Ray Papers, HL. The WPA *Washington Guide*, 486, gives a photograph of Lock No. 5.

sistant Secretary Watson had told him the previous November that un-
restricted war was a necessity and the South must be subjugated, McClellan
dissented, declaring that the North must avoid harshness and give the South
as little offense as possible. "If I felt as you do," he informed Watson, "I
would lay down my arms!"

Greeley was now accusing the McClellanites of seeking a compromise
solution. By a war all expense and little fighting, they would make the exhausted, discouraged North "ready to buy a peace of Jeff Davis by almost
any possible surrender." Congressman Gurley told Washington dinner parties
that McClellan was a traitor, and Ben Wade went almost as far. Count
Gurowski was writing Governor Andrew that if McClellan won a victory he
would "throw off the mask and become champion of the preservation of
slavery and of general amnesty to the traitors." Radical wrath rose when
McClellan barred the Hutchinson Family singers from the army camps because their repertoire included such material as Whittier's "Hymn of Liberty,"
declaring that slavery whetted the knife for the nation's life. It was heightened
when on Washington's Birthday the general appeared before the House to
receive strong Democratic applause. Even the mild Seward was so disgusted
with McClellan that after the canal boat episode he thought Lincoln generous
in keeping him in command.[20]

As for Stanton, he had rapidly lost all confidence in McClellan. In a letter
to Dana he spoke resentfully of the recent "ridiculous and impertinent effort"
of S. L. M. Barlow at a railroad convention in the capital "to puff the General
by a false publication of words I never uttered." He was irritated because
a coterie of newspapermen representing the Associated Press, the *Herald*, and
other agencies were magnifying McClellan. Still more was he outraged by
the general's efforts to claim Grant's Western laurels. "Was it not a funny
sight to see a certain military hero in the telegraph office at Washington last
Sunday organizing victory, and by sublime military combinations capturing
Fort Donelson *six hours after* Grant and Smith had taken it sword in hand and
had victorious possession!" He, too, thought Lincoln generous in allowing
McClellan to keep his command. As a matter of fact, Lincoln called the
general to the White House on March 8 to rebuke his negligence and explain
some new orders. During their talk he referred to McClellan's Chesapeake

---

20 N. Y. *Tribune*, Jan. 18, 1862, for Greeley's comment; Bates's *Diary*, 253, on Gurley and
Wade; *Battles and Leaders*, II, 122, for McClellan before the House; Chase, *Diary and Corr.*,
50, 51, for McClellan's statement to Watson; Gurowski, March 1, 1862, Andrew Papers.
    Seward never accepted McClellan's estimates of enemy strength. He told Sam Ward on
March 26 that he did not believe the South had as many men in Virginia and thereabouts as
New York had, or that there had been more than 30,000 at any time during the past three
months. Ward, March 27, 1862, to S. L. M. Barlow, Barlow Papers.

plan as suggesting a "traitorous" intention of leaving Washington open to the foe. When McClellan quite properly resented the word, Lincoln explained that he did not use it himself, but that the circumstances wore a dark look, and others placed an ugly interpretation on them.[21]

This meeting, of which McClellan gives us all too brief a record, was a curious—and an ominous—episode. We may be sure that Lincoln measured his words carefully. Knowing how often McClellan had expressed the characteristic contempt of the military mind for politicians, he doubtless meant to remind him of the paramount rights of the civil authority, and of the fact that politicians also have their prejudices and suspicions. It is also probable that, suspecting that McClellan might really intend to strike cushioned blows, he wished to clear the air between them and make sure of his purposes. But his candor evoked no response. The two men parted without any enlargement of mutual confidence.

While acceding to McClellan's Chesapeake plan, Lincoln felt a lingering mistrust, and was determined to keep vigilant watch over the general's actions. Stanton, who made a similar resolve, told the Cabinet that McClellan as general-in-chief had required all army reports to be made to him, and then had kept the War Department in the dark, giving it neither information nor plans. It was partly for this reason that the Secretary insisted on the transmission of all telegrams through the War Department.[22] Still tormented by doubt, Lincoln directed McClellan to hold a conference of division commanders on the Chesapeake plan. Four generals, McDowell, Heintzelman, Sumner, and Barnard, voted against it, and eight supported it, though Keyes did so on condition that the Potomac batteries be first reduced. This was decisive, and Lincoln tacitly admitted as much.

But the President nevertheless restricted McClellan's execution of his plan by three orders of March 8. The first directed that the Army of the Potomac be divided into four corps, and nominated to their command Generals McDowell, Heintzelman, Sumner, and Keyes. Three of these men had

21   Memorandum by McClellan, W. S. Myers, *McClellan*, 245, 246.
22   The able Gen. James S. Wadsworth wrote Bryant that it was outrageous that McClellan with 135,000 men and 43 batteries had not advanced against the far weaker enemy; that the dreary inaction had dispirited the army; that the general never consulted any division commanders south of the Potomac save Fitz-John Porter; and that it was as impossible to move the army without dividing it into corps as it was impossible to move divisions without dividing them into regiments. McClellan seemed to think they were facing an army of British or French veterans instead of a hastily trained, inadequately equipped enemy. "Is it possible to account for all these errors on the theory of incompetence alone? Is there not in some high quarters a plan for putting down this Rebellion by some other means than by whipping the Rebels?" Upton Hill, Va., Feb. 3, 1862, Bryant-Godwin Coll., NYPL. Wadsworth probably found means of getting these views before Stanton and Lincoln. The conference of division commanders met March 8.

opposed McClellan's strategy, and the fourth had approved it only conditionally! The second order directed that the army should not move from the Washington base without leaving such a force as McClellan and the corps commanders deemed entirely adequate to its protection, that no more than two corps should be moved until the Potomac was cleared of enemy batteries, and that the movement must begin not later than March 18.

Most important of all was Lincoln's third order, which divested McClellan of the command of other departments than that of the Potomac. No longer was he general-in-chief. All the principal Cabinet officers approved this step, and Stanton urged it strongly. Seward spoke of the "imbecility" of McClellan's recent operations, and Bates said the general was "fumbling and plunging in confusion." Despite the wisdom of the decision, for not even a Napoleon could command the Army of the Potomac in an active campaign and oversee all other military operations, McClellan resented it. He always believed that it tied his hands so that he would have to fight in eastern Virginia without being sure of cooperative action elsewhere, while he found affront in the fact that it first reached him by a newspaper. It is not recorded that he came to the White House before leaving for the Chesapeake, and Lincoln certainly never revisited his headquarters before he went.

[II]

The campaign could now begin—and it began with an anticlimax. McClellan had predicted that by placing his base on the Rappahannock he would compel the evacuation of Centreville; on March 9, before he ordered a platoon to march, the Confederates left the place. Jefferson Davis, the Cabinet, and Joseph E. Johnston had agreed on this step in February.

So effective were Johnston's preparations and so weak was the Northern intelligence service that the Confederates were able to remove most of their stores without exciting any suspicion. Not until the torch was applied to huts and stores was the movement discovered. It was easily made, because the Southern forces actually numbered only 50,000 or 55,000 effectives. McClellan said later that the enemy retreated safely because information leaked out to them while he was discussing his plans with the Administration. This excuse is contradicted by two facts: the Confederates began preparations before his plans were settled, and their general gives an entirely different explanation. Johnston regarded one avenue of Union attack as so much more dangerous than any other that he was sure McClellan would adopt it. The Northern army could make a concealed march along the Maryland shore of the Potomac, swiftly cross near Aquia Creek, and occupy Fredericksburg.

Unless anticipated, they would then be two days nearer Richmond than his own army; and Johnston fell back to forestall this possible movement.[23]

McClellan at once broke camp and advanced toward Centreville. He hoped to strike a blow at the rear guard. He also wished to shake his troops free of camp habits, and get rid of useless baggage.[24] His cavalry shortly discovered the Confederates in force at Warrenton Junction, where he left them severely alone; but he did remain long enough in the area to stage a revealing performance.

Leaving the main force at Centreville, he, McDowell, and their staffs, with 2,000 cavalry, rode to the old Bull Run battlefield. It was a beautiful day. They inspected the Confederate debris—skeletons of burned machine shops, wrecked locomotives and cars, and broken weapons. McClellan then halted the cavalcade where the hardest fighting of 1861 had taken place, and the two generals, with the cavalry a blue wall behind them, took places in front of their staffs. All eyes were fixed on the handsome young leaders, seated on magnificent steeds. McClellan insisted that McDowell rehearse the story of Bull Run, pointing out troop positions, battle corners, and the scenes of flight. Telling the whole tale with no attempt at self-vindication, the humiliated McDowell could not restrain his tears over the whitened bones that illustrated the terrible reverse. When he had finished, McClellan wheeled with the curt words: "Gentlemen, we will now return to quarters." All observers noted the deep humiliation of McDowell, intensified by McClellan's frigid demeanor, without a single consoling word.[25]

The Confederates having dislocated his initial scheme, McClellan turned to his alternative plan for an advance up the peninsula between the York and James Rivers. This decision was confirmed at a council of high officers at Fairfax Court House March 13. In his long letter to Stanton he had written that if the Urbana plan were frustrated, he could make Fort Monroe his base and operate along the Yorktown-Williamsburg road to Richmond, "although with less celerity and brilliancy of results." It was unquestionably a

---

23 Johnston in his *Narrative*, 98–106, dilates on the unnecessary destruction of many stores at Manassas, against which he protested, and the loss of a large meat-curing plant there. He thought that, moving behind the Potomac shield, McClellan would cross slightly downstream from Aquia Creek. Comte de Paris, *Battles and Leaders*, II, 121, rejects McClellan's idea of a leak. Almost incredibly, McClellan had the effrontery to claim the unexpected evacuation as his own great victory. He wrote S. L. M. Barlow: "My movements gave us Manassas with the loss of one life—a gallant cavalry officer—history will, when I am in my grave, record it as the brightest passage of my life that I accomplished so much at so small a cost." Barlow Papers.

24 T. Jefferson Coolidge, *Autobiography*, 40, reports McClellan saying this in 1863.

25 Prince de Joinville, *Campagne de l'Armée du Potomac*, 1862, p. 14; T. B. Gates, *Ulster Guard*, 172–178. McDowell and McClellan had clashed on the wisdom of the Chesapeake plan.

sound plan. The council of war unanimously approved it on two fundamental conditions: that the safety of transports and communications be assured, and that the force left to cover Washington "shall be such as to give an entire feeling of security for its safety from menace." Lincoln also gave his approval, emphasizing that Manassas be held and Washington left safe.[26]

Off for the Peninsula! The movement of 130,000 men, with horses, wagons, and artillery, was a great adventure in logistics. Since late February the Assistant Secretary of War, John Tucker, had been busy chartering a fleet of nearly 300 steamers, schooners, and barges, including river, lake, and ocean vessels of almost every size.

A singularly impressive movement it was.[27] The flotilla, scurrying to and fro in the waters about Washington, filled the air with smoke, fluttering flags, and deep bass whistles. For three weeks the dingy streets of Alexandria were clangorous with military bands and the tread of marching boots. Lines of bayonets gleamed alongside rivulets of white-topped wagons, ambulances, and artillery caissons, all moving to the waterfront. With endless profanity, straining, and whipcracking, nearly 15,000 horses and mules, more than 1,100 wagons, and 44 batteries were loaded aboard. With them went rolls of telegraph wire, timbers for pontoons, forges for repairs, boxes of medicine for field hospitals, and an endless variety of stores. Throughout fickle March the transfer went on—in bright sunlight and driving rain, under star-bespangled skies and in murky nights of storm. Down the Potomac fell the craft, down the Chesapeake, past the mouths of the Rappahannock and York, and on to Fort Monroe and Hampton Roads. Richmond no longer lay to the south. Suddenly it was west—even a little northwest. On the map it seemed astonishingly close.[28]

A picturesque movement this was, but time-consuming. Though Tucker boasted that for speed it was without parallel in history, and a European observer termed it the stride of a giant, some officers thought it was badly handled. As troops passed through Alexandria many bought liquor from the crowds, and got drunk; the command failed to put enough vehicles ashore at the Hampton–Newport News landing places; shelter and rations there were scarce. It was on February 14 that Stanton advertised for vessels, and on the 28th that Tucker was told the movement was fixed. Yet not until April 2 did McClellan himself reach Fort Monroe, and not until the 5th was the transfer fully effected.

26 Webb, *The Peninsula*, 28, 29.
27 The N. Y. *Weekly Tribune* gives a good description, April 12, 1862.
28 Swinton, *Army of the Potomac*, 100; MS diary of David F. Ritchie, of the 14th N. Y. Vols., in private hands. This regiment, beset by mud, drunkenness, and other delays, took ten hours to cover six and a half miles from its camp to Alexandria.

While it was being completed, the atmosphere in Washington improved. A measure of confidence was restored between Lincoln and McClellan, for the fact that the army was at last moving heartened the President. Moreover, he saw that, the die once cast, he must give the general proper support. McClellan wrote Barlow on March 18 that the attack of the abolitionists did not bother him: *"The President is all right—he is my friend."* And Benjamin Stark assured Barlow that Lincoln was facing the radical pack courageously: "He has declared so emphatically that he will not back down on Mac that the hounds in and out of Congress have ceased their yelpings; but it is only for a time." [29]

At no point had Lincoln let the public or the Congressional leaders know about his doubts respecting McClellan. Instead, he told a group that probably the only man in the country more anxious for a battle than himself was McClellan. "He repudiated in words of withering rebuke," wrote Representative A. S. Diven, "those who make the charge that he or Mr. Seward or General McClellan were temporizing or delaying out of any consideration for rebels or rebel institutions." Lincoln knew the vital importance of an appearance of unity even when the reality was imperfect. And he certainly had much more faith in the general than Stanton had. He told his close friend Senator O. H. Browning that he was sure of the man's fidelity; but Stanton on the same day expressed a deep distrust to the Senator.

By the first days of April, troops of Heintzelman's, Sumner's, and Keyes's corps had occupied the plateau behind Hampton and moved inland. Union forces were pushing toward Big Bethel of unhappy memory. The low, flat, partly marshy, and well-wooded tongue between the York and James, ten to fifteen miles wide, lay before them. Here Captain John Smith had landed, and here Cornwallis had surrendered. Here Confederate forces had now gathered. Only seventy-five miles from Fort Monroe lay Richmond. On the road thither the army expected to inscribe a resplendent new chapter of history.[30]

29 Stark to S. L. M. Barlow, March 20, 1862, Barlow Papers.
30 For Diven, see Columbia, Mo., *Statesman*, Feb. 14, 1862. Representative P. B. Fouke of Illinois wrote Feb. 15 that he had talked with McClellan and learned "the President has justly unlimited confidence in his capacity to manage the greatest army ever known"; Gillespie Papers, Chicago Hist. Soc. Joseph E. Johnston, fearing the Union numbers, had wished to defer Confederate resistance until McClellan approached Richmond, but Davis, on the advice of Robert E. Lee and Secretary of War Randolph, decided to make a stand on the Peninsula; Johnston, *Narrative*, 114, 115.

[III]

Already, in fact, a memorable page had been written in Hampton Roads. The day Lincoln signed the three orders to McClellan, Saturday, March 8, the Confederate *Merrimac* made its dramatic appearance; the day Johnston's troops evacuated Manassas, March 9, the *Monitor* grappled with the Southern giant. Had McClellan made a determined attack on Norfolk the previous winter, this encounter would never have been necessary.

The *Merrimac*, a 40-gun frigate of 3,200 tons, left a ruined hulk at Norfolk, was now a formidable monument to Confederate industry and ingenuity. Her scuttled hull had been cut down almost to the water line, pumped clean, floated, and repaired. Lieutenant John M. Brooke and J. L. Porter had shielded the top and sides with heavy timbers, plated with railroad iron; had installed 10 guns, 4 of them rifled and 6 of them 9-inch smoothbores; and had fixed a powerful iron beak to the prow. The cost was trifling, the result astounding. When the ship suddenly lumbered out of Norfolk into Hampton Roads to meet the Union frigates, it looked like a huge floating fort, its black iron sides sloping up from the water, its guns protruding from small square portholes, and its flat deck topped by a flagstaff and one great funnel spouting smoke and cinders. With a length of 262 feet 9 inches, and a breadth of just over 51 feet, the *Merrimac* (which the Confederates called the *Virginia*) bore a complete cuirass of three inches of armor.

No naval encounter of the war, perhaps of all history, was more picturesque than this. Hampton Roads, a calm sheet about seven miles long and four wide, opening into the Chesapeake by a narrow channel past Old Point Comfort, is like a large inland lake, fed by three rivers: the Elizabeth, the Nansemond, and the wide James. On the northwestern side of the Roads, at the entrance from the Chesapeake, loomed the Union stronghold Fort Monroe; on the eastern and southern sides, protecting Norfolk, stood Confederate ramparts and batteries. As the sinister *Merrimac* moved into open waters, the battlements of Fort Monroe and the island post called the Rip-Raps were crowded with men in blue, leveling their glasses on the ship. The opposite shores were full of Southerners brought to the scene by rumors of the attack. Before the majestic progress of the ironclad, dozens of small vessels —transports, sloops, schooners, tugs—began to scatter and scurry like chickens before a swooping hawk. Beneath a bright sun, with a crisp breeze whitening the sea, these craft, from double-decked steamers to sailboats, hurried to shelter, while their protectors, the *Minnesota, Congress, Cumberland, Roanoke,* and others, moved in to engage. The combatants came steadily closer, till spectators on the distant strands thought them almost touching. Then a fierce puff of smoke shot out from the *Merrimac*; an instant later, jets of flame and rolls of smoke burst from the Northern warships.

The daylong battle which followed was a complete victory for the *Merrimac*. Her first task was to dispose of the old twenty-four gun sailing sloop *Cumberland*; putting on all steam, she twice sent her double beak into the very entrails of the ship, and left her sinking. Then she turned her cannon on the fifty-gun frigate *Congress*, covered her decks with dead and dying, and was ready to ram her when she surrendered. The *Roanoke, Minnesota*, and *St. Lawrence*, helpless to aid their comrades, would all have been destroyed had they not taken refuge in shoal water where the *Merrimac* dared not follow. As night approached Confederates on shore could see the debris marking the grave of the *Cumberland*. They could see the western sky reddened by the flaming *Congress*, hopelessly aground, her guns going off as they became heated, until at midnight the five tons of powder in her magazines blew up with a sullen roar. Not far away the *Minnesota*, badly crippled, quivered fast on the shoals.[31]

Captain Franklin Buchanan of the *Merrimac* had been wounded, and was succeeded by Lieutenant Catesby Ap. R. Jones. This officer expected to make the next morning one of the darkest in Union records. He did not know that at ten that night the ironclad *Monitor*, an experimental turreted two-gun ship just completed, had reached Fort Monroe, and immediately taken her station by the wounded *Minnesota*. Not until daybreak did the general body of Confederates espy this reinforcement, and then they took it for an odd floating battery.

Brilliant Confederate improvisation had been met by shrewd Union planning—last-minute planning. "We ask," Senator Ten Eyck of New Jersey had declaimed in the Senate as the summer session of 1861 drew near an end, "that we shall have an engine that we need for the protection of our coasts hundreds of miles in length, and our harbors, and the great harbor of New York." He was speaking for a bill authorizing a naval board to examine the so-called Stevens Battery and similar devices, and appropriating $1,500,000 for one or more armored craft. The debate showed that French and British experiments with ironclads had attracted world-wide attention,

---

31 J. L. Porter in the Charleston *Courier*, March 19, 1862, describes the rebuilding of the *Merrimac*; John S. Wise, *End of an Era*, 196-200, offers a superior eyewitness account of the battle. See also Church's *Ericsson*, I, 280 ff., and C. L. Lewis, *Admiral Franklin Buchanan*, Ch. XIII. Hawthorne, seeing the *Monitor* later, wrote that it was not a ship, but a machine, and that the wooden walls of Old England were no more. He rightly declared that nothing finer had been said in the war than the words of Commodore Smith, father of the commander of the *Congress*, when he heard that his son's ship had capitulated. He knew that his boy would never haul down the flag. "Then Joe's dead!" said he. And he was.

and that the French ship *La Gloire* and the British *Warrior*, both armored, were regarded as potential threats to American ports. It showed that while naval experts were uncertain of the value of such ships as cruisers—the *La Gloire* had never been tested outside the Mediterranean, and carried only five days' supply of coal—they agreed on their importance for harbor defense.

Out of that debate, and out of the able planning and indomitable energy of the Swedish-American engineer John Ericsson, had sprung the *Monitor*. Various members of Congress talked of "jobs," and some naval men expressed horror. There are experts, said Senator McDougall, who oppose everything that is more destructive than the ancient galley. But Welles had appointed a board immediately after the passage of the appropriation; Ericsson presented his plan, and spent two hours before the board explaining it; and that body, encouraged by Lincoln himself, made a swift decision. On October 25 the *Monitor* was begun in Brooklyn, and on January 30, 1862, was launched. Ericsson's basic ideas were that she should be of light draught for coastal work, with a hull submerged for protection, so that seen from below she looked like a ship-bottom fixed to a raft. On this deck stood a single small revolving turret, only 20 feet in diameter and 9 feet high, with two 11-inch smoothbore guns; well forward was a tiny square pilothouse, hardly big enough for three men. The craft was 179 feet long and 41.5 feet wide; her deck was just awash, and she drew only 10.5 feet. The sides of the turret were protected by eight layers of one-inch iron plate. Built in 118 days, she was ready in the very nick of time. Lieutenant John L. Worden took command, and she set out southward. On her way to Hampton Roads March 6–8, she was twice almost swamped in high seas.[32]

The battle of the second day was gripping, for the closely matched antagonists struggled for hours without result. Running slowly down on the *Minnesota*, the *Merrimac* resumed her shattering fire, when suddenly the iron battery swung out from behind the Union warship, and advanced like some cocky champion entering feudal lists. At first sight she seemed hopelessly outmatched. From the shore she looked a little shoe-polish tin on a shingle. A single shell from the bulky dark *Merrimac*, a single square blow by the iron beak, would apparently shatter her.

32 For the debate on armored ships see *Cong. Globe*, 37th Cong., 1st Sess., 345, July 30, 1861. The ironclad vessel called the Stevens Battery lay incomplete at Hoboken, N. J., with $12,000 needed to finish her. R. L. Stevens had built it. For a review of the building of the *Monitor* see speech by Rep. C. B. Sedgwick of New York, April 28, 1862, *Cong. Globe*, 37th Cong., 2d Sess., Appendix 124 ff. Material of value may also be found in *Century Magazine*, XXXIX (March, 1890), 798 ff. The fullest books are a standard British work, H. W. Wilson, *Ironclads in Action*, I, 1–36, and Robert S. McCordock, *The Yankee Cheese Box*, *passim*. For years the expert engineer Charles Ellet had been vainly urging the government to build rams; had he succeeded, his boats might have stopped the *Merrimac*.

But bold Worden ran alongside his enemy like a skillful boxer attacking a heavy lout. The *Merrimac's* first shot missed, and other shots glanced off the smooth armor of the tin can. Meanwhile, an eleven-inch missile from the *Monitor*, whanging against the *Merrimac* casemates with a tremendous blow, flung her crew to the floor with bleeding noses and ringing ears, and showed that the little craft bore stout guns. Two hours of grim tussle followed, amply proving that neither vessel could penetrate the other's armor. A shell bursting just outside the *Monitor's* pilothouse filled Worden's eyes with powder and dust, temporarily blinding him and forcing him to relinquish the command, but that was all. Their efforts at ramming each other were equally futile. The light-draft *Monitor* easily escaped into shoal water, while the *Merrimac* was too massive to be hurt by her frail enemy. Later the *Merrimac*, suddenly plunging at the *Monitor*, strained her machinery and broke her huge iron beak as it grated over the enemy's shallow deck.

"Thousands have this day blessed you," the engineer of the *Monitor* wrote Ericsson that night. "I have heard whole crews cheer you." The North boasted a new war hero. As the *Merrimac* retired to Norfolk, David had the better of Goliath. The loss of Union sailors stood at about 400; two Union warships were gone; Worden was wounded; the *Monitor* had been hit twenty-two times, and its pilothouse had proved vulnerable. But the Confederates had failed of their main goal, and acknowledged a final checkmate.[33]

The officers who had rebuilt the *Merrimac* had done well, but not well enough. As they designed the ship, it drew too much water. Then after she was launched, the base of the sloping armor-clad roof was found to be several feet above waterline, and she had to be ballasted so heavily that the draught was increased to eighteen feet. The beak was crudely attached, and the engines were weak. Worse still, the ironclad proved too cumbersome, slow, and ill fueled to cover long distances, leave deep waters, or maneuver smartly. She was useful only for defensive operations. The popular view that if unchecked she might have brought Washington, New York, and Boston under her guns was wide of the mark, for she could never have tubbed her way very far from Norfolk. The *Monitor*, on the other hand, proved the value of the most important innovation in the duel, the revolving armored turret. As her engineers wrote, this was "a splendid structure," destined to a great future in naval development.[34]

33 Alban C. Stimers, Hampton Roads, March 9, 1862, to Ericsson, *National Intelligencer*, March 15. "I consider that both ships were well fought," he wrote. The Confederacy thrilled to the exploits of what it called "the iron diadem of the South," the North to the feat of "the little bumblebee."
34 Ericsson's turret revolved on a central spindle; the British engineer Stines devised a safer system of roller bearings.

When the news reached Washington on Sunday, March 9, of the destruction the previous day, Cabinet members hastened to the White House—Stanton overwrought, Seward despondent, Welles worried but self-possessed. The President got neither comfort nor counsel from them. In a quick visit he found Dahlgren at the Navy Yard equally unable to suggest expedients, and even the resourceful Meigs offered no help. The frantic Stanton paced up and down the President's office painting frightful visions of the *Merrimac* shelling the capital, laying New York in ashes, and levying on the whole seaboard for money to continue the war. He even rushed off panicky telegrams to Northern governors and mayors. Alternately sneering at Welles and denouncing him, he showed a bitter malevolence. When Welles explained that the *Merrimac* could never leave the Chesapeake and that the *Monitor* was at hand, Stanton's scorn became volcanic. "You rely on that craft with *two guns?*" he thundered incredulously.

Indeed, the battle between the Secretaries of War and the Navy that day rivaled the battle of the *Merrimac* and *Monitor*. Welles met his assailant with icy contempt. At one point Stanton wildly besought Lincoln and Dahlgren to order a half hundred canal boats laden with stone sunk in the Potomac channel. Welles protested. "For six months," he told Stanton, "the Navy Department has argued and implored to get McClellan and the War Department to help us open the Potomac. And now that the rebels are leaving it, the War Department wants to block it with stone!" Lincoln forbade any closing of the channel unless it became certain the *Merrimac* was coming up the river. Gradually the mood of alarm, with Stanton pacing to the window to look for the smoke of the Confederate giant downstream, subsided. And when that evening news of the *Monitor's* successful resistance and the victory at Pea Ridge reached the White House almost simultaneously, the President indulged in some happy jubilation. A few weeks later, descending the Potomac and passing the unused canal boats, he jested about "Stanton's navy." [35] Lincoln showed the depth of his feelings when Henry A. Wise brought the wounded Lieutenant Worden up to Washington, put him to bed in Wise's own room, and went to the White House. Worden relates:

Wise found the President in counsel with his Cabinet, to whom he recounted the fight as he saw it, and when he finished President Lincoln got up and said, Well gentlemen, I am going to see that *feller*, he accordingly came to Wise's house where I was in bed and as Wise opened the door of my room he said, Jack, here is the President who has come to see you. I raised up and the President took my hand and I said, You do me great honor, Mr. President, by this visit, and for a moment he did not reply (and Wise said tears were in his

35 Welles' *Diary*, I, 63–67; G. T. Strong's *Diary*, III, 210, March 16, 1862; Worden's undated narrative, Lincoln Memorial Univ. Lib.; Ruth White, *Yankee From Sweden: John Ericsson*, 210–227.

eyes) and then he said, No, sir, you have done me and your country honor and I shall promote you. My eyes were filled with powder and much swollen, face lacerated, and hair burned and was a sad looking object which seemed to touch his feelings greatly. . . .

The battle marked a revolution in naval warfare, but its exact character and extent are often misstated. The fate of the *Congress* and *Cumberland* showed decisively that the day of wooden frigates was ended. The London *Times* declared that whereas before Hampton Roads the British navy had possessed 149 first-class warships, after that battle only two were available, the ironclads *Warrior* and *Ironside*. The naval revolution had actually begun during the Crimean War. While during that conflict the Russian guns at Fort Constantine, before Sebastopol, had badly damaged a wooden fleet of the Allies, at Kinburn some hastily built armored warships had smashed the Russian batteries with trifling loss. The French admiral had written afterward that "everything may be expected from these formidable engines of war," and France and Britain had undertaken ironclad ships. Ericsson was quick to boast that his *Monitor* outmatched anything in the European navies. But the *Warrior*, a seagoing ship of fourteen knots with 4.5-inch solid rolled plates, would have been a far more doughty antagonist than the *Merrimac*. The American navy could be content to emphasize coast-defense vessels, but British warships had to be able to keep the high seas.

The most significant feature of the *Monitor*, as we have said, was her turret system of mounting guns. The armor could thus be concentrated, instead of being distributed, as on the *Merrimac*, along a great casemate; and a revolving turret enabled the guns to reach every point of the compass. The success of the *Monitor* immediately inspired the United States to begin building other ironclads, some for ocean service and some for harbor defense, so that when the year ended about thirty were under way. "They are a vast improvement over the *Monitor*," Worden wrote Fox. Those which approximated the original Ericsson lines became unpopular with naval officers, who called them floating prisons, or after the *Monitor* foundered off Cape Hatteras during a storm, airtight coffins. Sailors complained that they were slow, that they carried only a small quantity of ammunition, that although the turret itself might be invulnerable, repeated concussions would disable the pivot, and that the rivet heads flew about like bullets. But Ericsson had done the country an unforgettable service.[36]

The sudden threat to Washington from an unexpected quarter, mean-

---

36 See report of Vice-Admiral Alex Milne, British Naval Command-in-Chief in North America, Bermuda, May 22, 1863, Admiralty Papers, Public Record Office; reports of Capt. S. Kennedy, H. M. S. *Challenger*, July 13, 1863, and Capt. R. V. Hamilton, H. M. S. *Vesuvius*, Dec. 3, 1863, *ibid.*; Church, *Ericsson*, II, 23 ff.; N. Y. *Tribune*, Jan. 27, 1863; Worden Papers, LMU.

while, enhanced Lincoln's conviction that the capital must not be left un-covered for an hour. And the *Merrimac* remained an embarrassment to Mc-Clellan's campaign, for Lincoln ordered the *Monitor* to take no risks in attack-ing her, and she could not be enticed into a disadvantageous position. Lying at Norfolk, she made it impossible for Northern ships to enter the James. When the fleet area commander was asked to aid McClellan in his attack on Yorktown, he refused on the ground that his first duty was to watch the *Merrimac*. So skittish were the Union warships that on April 11 they let her capture three Union steamers without molestation, and on May 8 broke off an attack on Sewell's Point as soon as she approached. Thus she played her part in the defense of Richmond.

[IV]

McClellan, who had represented that the movement by the Chesapeake and the York River would be quick and certain, soon discovered that he had miscalculated. At Fort Monroe he possessed 58,000 men and 100 guns ready to move. Somewhere before him lay J. B. Magruder's small Army of the Peninsula. His plan, simple and sound, was to march a right column directly on Yorktown while a left column thrust toward Williamsburg. If Confederate fortifications at either place offered stubborn resistance, Mc-Dowell's corps should be brought from Washington to Gloucester Point opposite Yorktown, so as to turn the two strongholds—"to take in reverse whatever force the enemy might have on the Peninsula," as McClellan later put it. A price would have to be paid. Soldiers about Fort Monroe noted the many signs of undertakers: corpses embalmed and boxed, $50.

The march began on April 4. Yankees unfamiliar with the Southern land-scape gazed wonderingly at snake fences, deserted houses, Negro huts, and tangled pine woods. Occasional orchards were bright with apple and peach blossoms. But as blue squads scrambled over the broken breastworks of Big Bethel in triumph, the weather changed. Cold rain turned McClellan's as-surances of dry sandy roads into mockery. The long lines of wagons, guns, and ambulances constantly mired down; men in mud to their knees lashed at mules and pushed at wheels; a thousand axes rang to cut logs for corduroy-ing the quagmire; progress became snail-slow. In the marshy fields along-side, soldiers leaped from one hill of rotting cornstalks to another. Many slept that night in puddles.[37]

On the 5th the march was resumed with more cold rain, and more splash-

37 Ritchie, MS Reminiscences; Webb, *The Peninsula*, 43, 44; O. O. Howard's letters to his wife, Howard Papers, Bowdoin.

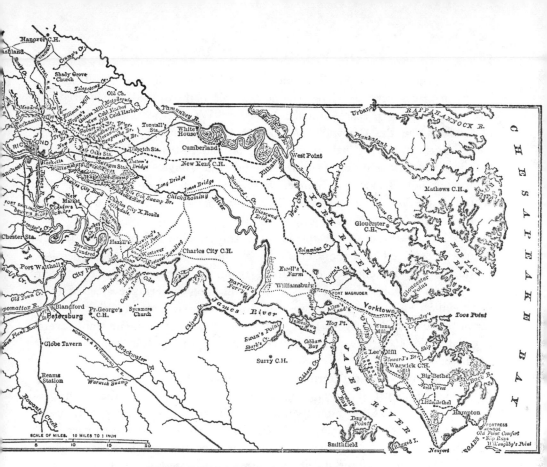

THE PENINSULAR CAMPAIGN

ing, swearing, and hauling. Colonel H. Berdan's sharpshooters deployed in front of the right wing, where fighting was sure to begin. Before long, as Confederate shots whizzed overhead, they saw looming through the mist and rain high earthworks, with barbettes protecting thirty-two-pounders. The first Union field guns came into play, while behind them began massing dense bodies of Northern troops. Southern engineers had utilized swamps and boggy streams to protect their positions, and around Yorktown had deepened some of the old British trenches. The twelve-mile front was soon ablaze; but when dusk shut down, the stars and bars floated over undented lines, and Southern bands gaily played "Dixie" and the "Marseillaise." The siege of Yorktown had begun.

McClellan had not expected to find Confederate fortifications extending wholly across the Peninsula, from the York to the James. His maps, like his intelligence services, were inaccurate. The one he trusted, made by an engineer aide to General Wool at Fort Monroe, failed to show that the Warwick River, in places very wide, barred most of his path; instead, it pictured the stream as running parallel with the James! [38] "We did not know of the line of works along the Warwick," McClellan later admitted. Expecting to surround Yorktown with little impediment, he had instructed Keyes to march to the Half-way House, six miles behind and above Yorktown, and encamp; but now Keyes and Sumner were brought up short by well-manned works on the Warwick River line. The army that McClellan had expected to swing around Yorktown was at a standstill.[39]

And now McClellan's temperament betrayed him. After being too sanguine, he reverted to a more characteristic mood of excessive apprehension. Finding his troops checked on a broad front, he jumped to the conclusion that Joseph E. Johnston had arrived with most of the army evacuated from Centreville. This was a delusion, for Johnston's advance division did not reach the line until April 10, and other divisions did not come up until several days later. For six or seven days McClellan's strength was fully four times that of the enemy.

During this week a determined thrust would have broken the defenses. Magruder on April 5 had only 11,000 men, of whom more than half garrisoned Yorktown, Gloucester Point, and Mulberry Island, leaving only about 5,000 to defend the remaining ten miles. The Confederates were so certain of an imminent assault that they slept in the trenches beside their muskets. But to Magruder's astonshiment, day after day passed without any test of his strength. The explanation was soon evident: in every direction picks flashed as Union troops dug trenches across fields, woodland, and swamp. While they dug, Richmond poured reinforcements forward, until, Magruder writes, "anxiety passed from my mind as to the result of an attack upon us." [40]

Why did McClellan not attack? Partly because he exaggerated the enemy strength. Partly because before leaving Washington he had fixed his mind on a siege of Yorktown, where the enemy was to be shut up in his fortifications, and captured by the most deliberate operations. Constructing batteries and parallels opposite the Yorktown redoubts, McClellan installed nearly a hundred heavy pieces—mortars, howitzers, Parrott guns—to bombard the defenses. This *idée fixe* of a siege indisposed him to rapid field maneuvering.

38 N. Y. *Weekly Tribune*, April 12, 1862.
39 Webb, 53, 54.
40 Magruder's *Official Report*, O. R., I, xi, pt. 1, pp. 405–411; *Battles and Leaders*, II, 160 ff. O. O. Howard thought it would have been far better to attack Yorktown the day after arrival there, and wrote his wife that McClellan "inclines too much to *engineering*"; May 7, 1862, O. O. Howard Papers. Three British officers who made a report to London declared that Yorktown might easily have been taken the first few days; War Office, Confidential File, Aug. 1, 1862.

Finally, he believed that Lincoln had unduly weakened his force by holding McDowell's corps in the Washington area, for the very day that his army reached Magruder's lines, he learned that Lincoln had ordered that it or Sumner's command must stay to protect the capital.

He immediately protested against this order, telegraphing Lincoln that he would now have to fight the whole Confederate forces at or near York-town, and needed his army intact. Though Lincoln did not know that Mc-Clellan had greatly outnumbered Magruder, he suspected some such state of affairs and sent a crisp reply:

You now have over one hundred thousand troops with you independent of General Wool's command. I think you better break the enemies' line from Yorktown to Warwick River, at once. They will probably use time, as advantageously as you can. A. LINCOLN.[41]

[V]

Behind Lincoln's order lay some simple logic. He had stipulated, in approving of the Peninsula strategy, that Manassas should be held in force and Washington kept entirely safe. On April 2 General James S. Wadsworth reported to Stanton that his force of 19,022 ill-disciplined men was entirely inadequate for the defense of Washington. Stanton immediately asked Adjutant-General Lorenzo Thomas and Major-General Ethan Allen Hitchcock to inquire, and they at once declared that Lincoln's order on the safety of the capital had not been obeyed. The President knew that the council of corps commanders had asserted that 55,000 men were necessary. He knew that the capture of Washington might be fatal, for foreign recognition of the Confederacy would doubtless follow, while half of the North would deem the war lost. As he could afford no risks, and as public feeling was very sensitive about Washington, it *seemed* essential to keep McDowell's corps at hand. Actually, as McClellan's defenders contend, it was not; the best defense was the offense. Under political pressure, Lincoln had already (March 31) detached Louis Blenker's division from McClellan to go to Frémont's new Mountain Department. Whether these steps were errors is a debatable matter —and it has been endlessly debated.[42]

41 R. T. Lincoln Papers for McClellan's dispatch, May 5; Lincoln, *Works*, V, 182.
42 O. R., I, xi, pt. 3, pp. 60–62. Wadsworth's veracity was later impeached by the N. Y. *World*, and he replied in a letter to the N. Y. *Times* (in *Tribune*, May 21, 1863). He stated that on March 31, 1862, the troops he commanded in and about Washington numbered 19,591 present for duty; on April 3, they were 19,045; on April 30, they were 19,475. But the low numerical strength was not the chief element of weakness. Many of the regiments were new; some had just received their arms; they were crippled by incompetent and drunken officers; they had poor liaison. McClellan ordered him to detail from this force four good regiments to Richardson's, Heintzelman's, and Hooker's divisions.

The amazing fact is that the President and the general had reached no clear understanding on this subject before McClellan left Washington. It seems almost incredible that room should have been left for a misunderstanding. McClellan, before going to Fort Monroe, should have obtained clear directions from the President; Lincoln, for his part, should have demanded a full statement, and made still plainer his intention of safeguarding Washington beyond mischance. This want of liaison was a terrible misfortune. Had McClellan and Lincoln discussed face to face the proper division of troops to defend Washington and troops to move against Richmond, and come to an explicit agreement, the expedition would have begun under a far brighter star.

It was McClellan who was chiefly in the wrong. Lincoln had been frank about his fears, even mentioning the talk of "traitorous" action, but McClellan had never been equally frank about his plans. McClellan knew that the corps commanders had declared on March 13 that Washington must have such force "as to give an entire feeling of security for its safety from menace." Yet he had made no such provision. "After you left here," Lincoln now wrote him, "I ascertained that less than 20,000 unorganized men, with a single field battery, were all you designed to be left for the defense of Washington and Manassas; and part of this even was to go to General Hooker's old position." While Lincoln was aware that public sentiment demanded above all else the security of the seat of government, McClellan was ignorant of and indifferent to public sentiment. The President had to think daily of the Committee on the Conduct of the War, of Congress, and of the great uneasy masses. If he allowed Washington to fall into perils like those of April, 1861, an angry Congress might impeach and remove him. It is true that in desperate emergencies a national chieftain may denude home defenses to strengthen some vital outer point, as Churchill in 1940 stripped England of essential materials to save North Africa and Suez, the backbone of Empire. But this situation was entirely different. Washington was the vital point, McClellan had an army far exceeding his foe's, and he could much better afford to take risks than the Union government could.

The spirit in which McClellan received Lincoln's order did him no credit. Regarding Washington as a "sink of iniquity," he now felt himself the victim of a conspiracy. His staff agreed that McDowell had taken advantage of his absence to play a "scurvy trick" in getting his corps withheld from the critical field of operations, and talked of foul play. General T. F. Meagher reported to Democratic leaders in New York that according to regular-army officers, although McClellan was as cool, determined, and active as ever, "it was his determination after the siege and battle of Yorktown to resign his command." [43]

Actually, McClellan's operations were not impeded by the retention of one corps in the Washington area. When he asked Stanton to spare two of McDowell's divisions for attacking Gloucester Point from the rear, the War Department cheerfully released them under a general specially congenial to him, Franklin. But preposterous delays occurred. Franklin's troops did not reach the Gloucester area until April 20, and then the mere preparations to disembark them consumed two weeks! In the end they were not used against Gloucester at all, for it was too strong to be taken from the rear. At no time, moreover, did McClellan lack enough men; what he lacked was promptness in using them.

For the Yorktown siege was doggedly prosecuted on classic lines. "I do believe that I am avoiding the faults of the Allies at Sebastopol, and quietly preparing the way for great success," wrote McClellan on April 23. Yorktown a Sebastopol! He installed his heavy guns and mortar batteries, built redoubts to protect his parallels, and exulted over successful reconnaissances. As he sat still and poured rockets, bombs, and solid shot at the Confederate lines, the impatience of Washington grew. Stanton even thought of handing the command over to Ethan Allen Hitchcock.[44] Lincoln sent an exasperated dispatch to the general: "Your call for Parrott guns alarms me—chiefly because it argues indefinite procrastination. Is anything to be done?" This was somewhat unjust, for McClellan, as he courteously explained, had been expecting the guns for two weeks, and was trying to hurry, not procrastinate; but he never properly explained his delays or his objects to the President or the War Department. He put his main dependence, as his opponent Johnston wrote Richmond, upon artillery and engineering. But he was now perfecting plans for a grand final assault which would probably have involved heavy bloodshed.[45]

Then, as all was ready for this climax, the Confederates at dawn on May

43 Meagher to S. L. M. Barlow, Yorktown headquarters, April 24, 1862, Barlow Papers. McClellan wrote privately, April 18: "No general ever labored under greater disadvantages," *Own Story*, 311. Franklin's letter of explanation is in *Own Story*, 335, 336; cf. Webb, 61, 62.

44 Hitchcock, grandson of Ethan Allen and veteran of the Mexican War, could hardly be seriously considered, for he was sixty-four this year. But he states in his Diary, April 13, 1865, that Stanton, who used him in an advisory capacity, became so irritated by the slow siege that he asked Hitchcock to accept an order giving him immediate command of McClellan's army. Stanton added that the President wished it, and that if Hitchcock said the word, he could have the order in two minutes. "I at once refused," writes Hitchcock. Hitchcock Papers, LC.

45 Lincoln, *Works*, V, 203. For an able defense of McClellan see W. W. Hassler, Jr., *McClellan, Shield of the Union*. We should remember that McClellan never had the time to grow that Grant had; both needed it.

4 deserted their works. They left behind some seventy cannon, with small quantities of ammunition and stores, but Union efforts at pursuit were futile, and not until nightfall did Northern troops regain contact with the Confederates at Williamsburg.

Here next day partial Union forces fought a pitched battle. This savage, confused combat, waged in heavy rain driven by an icy wind, and ending inconclusively, offered several points of interest. The soldiers, plastered with Virginia clay, struggled among trees, stumps, and interlaced bushes. The principal hero was a Pennsylvania brigadier, a West Point graduate named Winfield Scott Hancock, who showed true generalship in the most responsible movements of the day. He won the praise of his superior, William F. Smith, for "the brilliancy of the plan of battle, the coolness of its execution, the seizing of the proper instant for changing from the defensive to the offensive, the steadiness of the troops engaged, and the completeness of the victory." If he was the best figure of the day, General Sumner was the sorriest. This *vieux sabreur*, whose fire and dash were never matched by his judgment, proved unequal to the strategic demands of battle. As for McClellan, he was so busy at Yorktown helping Franklin embark his men to ascend the York River that he did not reach the field until late afternoon. Though when darkness fell the Confederates still held their key position, Fort Magruder, during the night they retired.[46]

McClellan made the most of his capture of Yorktown and Williamsburg. Of the former he telegraphed Stanton: "The success is brilliant, and you may rest assured that its effects will be of the greatest importance." He reported the Confederate works "most formidable," and British officers with him agree that they were. After Williamsburg he was similarly exultant—"a brilliant victory." But even in the hour of triumph he was certain he needed far more troops. Joe Johnston stood before him with an army "probably greater a good deal than my own," he telegraphed Stanton, adding: "My entire force is undoubtedly inferior to that of the Rebels. . . . but I will do all I can. . . ."

The national outlook at the moment seemed hopeful. McClellan by his own statement had 85,000 effective men, and by the adjutant-general's returns 105,000; Johnston in February had given his own force as 60,062 men, of whom 42,860 were effectives.[47] McClellan had now brought his army to a position where he could thrust directly at Richmond, upon which Johnston rapidly retreated. In the West the military and naval commanders had scored

46 Swinton, 115–118; Webb, 73–81. Heintzelman's MS Diary, LC, is explicit on Sumner's bad showing.
47 O. R., I, v, 1086; K. P. Williams, *Lincoln Finds a General*, I, 154–165.

success after success. The eastern navy had not merely stopped the South's greatest warship, but had broken through old rules of design to a wide new future. Foreign intervention, as C. F. Adams and John Bigelow labored astutely in Europe, seemed less likely than ever. The acutest problems of finance and supply had been met. All waited to see McClellen deliver his final blow.

[VI]

While they waited, Stanton took an unfortunate step. He had capably organized his department and stopped the incessant drain of politicians and officers on his time. As he put it, he had his machinery working, the rats cleared out, the ratholes stopped, and the champagne roisters on the Potomac ended. "God helping me I shall prevail," he wrote Charles A. Dana of the *Tribune*. "I feel a deep *earnest* feeling growing up around us." [48] Then on April 3, 1862, he suddenly closed the recruiting service throughout the North. Bryant's newspaper declared next day: "The Secretary of War cries out 'enough.' The Union armies are full."

With the war at its crisis, why this step? Though it was one of the principal blunders of the conflict, no satisfactory explanation has ever been offered. We can only say that it reflected the general mismanagement of recruiting, which in turn reflected the basic want of organization in the nation. McClellan by General Order No. 105, effective January 1, had given the War Department practical control of the field, decreeing that no more regiments or other units should be raised by the government except on its authority. The Department appointed superintendents for each State, under whom recruiting for all regiments old and new was to be conducted by specially detailed officers. Cameron had interpreted McClellan's order as meaning that enough troops had been raised to quell the rebellion, and that the only further need was for machinery to maintain the existing regiments. A steady flow of replacements was wanted—that was all. Congressional penny-pinching also played an unfortunate role in the situation. Economy-minded Senators declared early in the year that the government had more men than the law allowed, and that the costs of maintenance and recruiting were excessive.

Pressed by Congress, Stanton reported that he could not ascertain the exact size of the volunteer army raised by the States, but estimated it between 700,000 and 800,000 men. On March 28 Henry Wilson, head of the Senate Military Affairs Committee, declared that the government ought im-

48   Feb. 1, 1862, Dana Papers, LC.

mediately to stop enlistments. Stanton's discontinuance of the volunteer recruiting service followed within the week. He told Halleck that he had
stopped it for the purpose of forcing the governors to make accurate returns.
Henry Wilson said later that the step was taken to compel fragmentary
regiments to coalesce, and to clear the way for a better enlistment service.
The one fact certain is that it cut off the flow of replacements at the very
time the spring campaigns made them most needed, and threw recruiting
into a confusion from which it did not recover for months. It is also certain
that just as disease and battle losses began to reduce regiments at an alarming rate, full reports showed that the government had fewer troops by
150,000 or 200,000 than had been represented. Within a month the Administration and public began to realize what a fearful error had been made. A large
section of the press became clamorous for more troops, and May 19 found
Stanton frantically telegraphing the governors for as many regiments as
they could raise.[49]

But the war happily had its brighter pages. Suspense in the East was
coupled with achievement in the West, and to that theater we may now
return.

49 See Wilson's long review, *Cong. Globe*, 38th Cong., 1st Sess., 58 ff., Dec. 21, 1863;
Stanton, May 1, 1862. O. R., III, ii, 29; Phila. *North American*, April 22, *et seq.*; N. Y.
World, Times, May 23, *et seq.*; L. L. Lerwell, *The Personnel Replacement System in the
U. S. Army*, 86–88.

3

Shiloh

THE FACT that half of the Confederacy lay in the wide Mississippi Valley was always in men's minds. The same newspaper issues which described the occupation of Manassas detailed the grapple at Pea Ridge. McClellan's march on Yorktown had to share headlines with the jubilant return of Andrew Johnson and other Unionists to Nashville, the siege of Island No. 10 on the Mississippi, and Grant's push southward along the Tennessee. After all, Louisiana and Texas had a combined population exceeding that of Confederate Virginia, and greater wealth; Mississippi was richer and more populous than South Carolina. By far the largest port of the Confederacy was New Orleans.

After Donelson and Pea Ridge, March witnessed an extension of Union control over most of Arkansas and Tennessee, raising hopes for a rapid conquest of that area. On an April morning Island No. 10 surrendered to John Pope with artillery, small arms, 6,000 prisoners, and 3 generals. As Grant reached Savanna, Tennessee, people scanning their maps saw that this was close to the southern boundary of the State, close even to Florence, Alabama. Buell's troops were marching south from Nashville to join Grant.

[I]

These rapid advances were possible because American organizing talent, concentrated upon the transportation revolution, had achieved a substantial mastery of water commerce. The fact leaped from the newspapers as men read how Grant had put 15,000 men on transports at Cairo, and then within three days he and the gunboats had taken Fort Henry. As an example of engineering ingenuity the river steamboat was remarkable; as illustrations of business enterprise, the river packet lines were equally striking. These facts robbed the problems of Western logistics of half their difficulty. No British engineer, wrote Norman S. Russell, could visit America without perceiving "that a vast system, combining great engineering talent with dexterous naval architecture, is exhibited on the noble rivers of America." [1] Wherever navigable streams ran, armies could be carried swiftly and easily. While McClellan's host, under dripping skies, dragged a few weary miles through viscid Virginia clay, Western forces moved over the waters faster than any legion ever traversed a Roman road. And the Mississippi, Tennessee, and Cumberland led into the heart of Western rebeldom.

How was it done? A typical story is told by the historian of a Western regiment. His command had hardly averaged fifteen miles daily through the winter mud of Kentucky, leaving some wagons completely bemired. Then one night they reached the banks of the Ohio, and dawn revealed sixteen steamboats waiting in the stream. The sight of their comfortable decks intoxicated the tired soldiers. The brigadier in charge quickly issued his orders. The Thirty-sixth Indiana would board the *Woodford;* the Michigan Engineers the *Golden State;* the Sixth Kentucky, the *Switzerland* and *City of Madison;* the Forty-first Ohio, the *Silver Moon* and *Lady Jackson;* and so on. Embarkation proved a lark. Dense smoke rolled from the tall stacks of the sixteen craft, whistles boomed deep bass roars, steam exhausts contributed treble notes, and paddle wheels splashed musically. Down the river they went in two columns. The *Diana,* crammed with the general, his staff, a thousand Ohio and Indiana troops, a cavalry detachment, and mules, horses and wagons, led one line, the *Autocrat* the other. Playing cards, chatting, joking, singing, the troops watched the wooded shores drop effortlessly behind. Cannelton hove in sight. Then suddenly the general was on the hurricane deck reading the news of Donelson, and bands were striking up "The Star-Spangled Banner." [2]

Five decades of hard planning—of continuous steamboat development, engine improvement, river harnessing, and mastery of the techniques of operation—lay behind such smooth voyages. These decades had brought the art of steam navigation to a high level. In the years 1851–60 no fewer than 1,346 steamboats, of well over 300,000 tonnage, had been built in the West. During the period 1811–70, a total of 4,688 had been launched—a tremendous fleet.[3] It was on the thousand available vessels that Union armies rode into the Western Confederacy.

Steamboat design was governed by certain principles of which Henry M. Shreve was traditionally the discoverer, but which grew naturally out of basic river conditions.[4] A shallow, lightly built hull, one step above a raft,

1 Russell, "On American River Steamers," *Trans. Institution of Naval Architects,* II (1861), 105, quoted by Louis C. Hunter, *Steamboats on the Western River,* 61.
2 E. Hannaford, *The Story of a Regiment,* 195–198.
3 Louis C. Hunter, 105 ff.
4 A. B. Hulbert, *Paths of Inland Commerce,* 175; but see Hunter, 75, 76, 89, 90. Shreve,

was needed to run in low water. A wide, low main deck was required for cargo room and ease in handling freight, and this deck also accommodated the boilers and machinery. An upper cabin, which might be as plain as that of a canalboat or as palatial with crystal, polished woodwork, rugs, and snowy paint as that of the *Grand Republic*, gave passengers ample room. Above it rose the hurricane deck, which bore the pilothouse, and after the mid-forties perhaps also offered a row of luxurious staterooms on the texas. With their three decks and superstructure the big steamboats of the fifties, even after their length reached 200 or 250 feet, looked bulky and topheavy. Running without cargo, a fine Cincinnati packet might be submerged only four feet while its pilothouse towered forty-five feet above the water. But the broad low main deck, made wider still by the guards or extensions beyond the hull line at the sides, rendered them admirable freight carriers, rapidly filled or emptied by gangplanks. They had great stability, for most of the machinery and cargo was on or below this lower deck. Two ingenious devices, bow frames or longitudinal trusses arching through the superdecks on each side of the vessel, and hog chains or heavy iron rods rising from the hull timbers into these decks, helped to brace the construction.

Mark Twain, in his pages on the antebellum St. Louis–New Orleans boat which gave him a berth as a cub pilot, has drawn the portrait of the Mississippi packet at its shining best. The long gilded cabin, glittering with prism-fringed chandeliers and dainty as a drawing room; the boiler deck spacious as a church; the fires glaring fiercely from a wide row of furnaces under eight boilers; the big glass-enclosed pilothouse with red window curtains, sofa, leather cushions, and a costly inlaid wheel; the regiment of servants; the lordly pilot, master of commerce on the four-thousand-mile water system—all this was imposing, convenient, and sumptuous. American steamboat architecture, wrote a traveler, "is not only original . . . but it is sometimes splendid in appearance." [5] Such a boat could be quickly jammed with troops, guns, horses, and stores. So could a dingy old river tub, or any of the countless craft of intervening quality. And they could be handled as dashingly, as recklessly as men handled old wagons and muskets, for the steamboat tradition stood for a short life and cheap replacement.

The engine used on Western waters was a high-pressure, noncondensing device which conservative critics abused as wasteful, inefficient, and dangerous,

---

son of a New Jersey Quaker, had helped Jackson at New Orleans, built a new type of river boat, the *Washington*, and as superintendent of Federal river improvements designed the steam snagboats called "Uncle Sam's Toothpullers."

5 *Life on the Mississippi*, Ch. VI. Mark Twain noted the rapidity of loading: "You should be on board when they take a couple of those wood-boats in tow and turn a swarm of men into each; by the time you have wiped your glasses and put them on, you will be wondering what has become of that wood."

but which for good reason held its place. Why was it not replaced by the low-pressure engines of the East? Ocean seamen declared that ignorance, stubbornness, and crazy recklessness supplied the answer. But engineers who were really familiar with the demands of midland river navigation knew that the time-honored steamboat engine admirably met them. Shallow Western waters compelled steamboatmen to reduce the weight to the lowest feasible point. A high-pressure engine, using what the pioneer engine builder George Evans called "strong steam," was substantially lighter than its low-pressure counterpart.[6] It cost far less money; in 1861 a 180-ton low-pressure engine required an outlay of $50,000, but the smaller high-pressure engine of equal power only $20,000. The Western type of motive power, less ponderous and bulky, and more cheaply repaired, provided speed. By the later 1850's the typical time for a trip from Cincinnati to St. Louis was two days, twenty-two hours, and from Cincinnati to New Orleans eight days. In 1853 the *Eclipse* ran upstream from New Orleans to Cairo in three days and just over three hours.[7]

It needs spunk to run a river boat, said one fireman. A lake steamer doesn't burst her boiler once in five years. "But I tell you, stranger, it takes a man to ride one of these boats, head on a snag, high pressure, valve soldered down, six hundred souls on board and all in danger of going to the devil." In wartime, men had to make the most of high pressure and face the perils imperturbably.

As steamboat design was improved, so were the rivers. A canal was built around the rock ledges which created twenty-two-foot falls at Louisville. Army engineers, initially under Robert E. Lee, widened and deepened the channel at the Des Moines rapids. The Federal government year by year from 1824 expended large sums in bettering navigation not only on the Ohio and Mississippi, but on their major tributaries: the Wabash, Missouri, Cumberland, Arkansas, and Red. Competent engineers, using special boats, removed snags, boulders, logs, hidden wrecks, and other menaces from the channels. They dug away sand and gravel bars, and blew up rock reefs.[8] Thus was the river system tidied in preparation for the day when continuous improvement, patrolling, and beacon placement would make the Mississippi, in Mark Twain's words, a sort of 2,000-mile torchlight procession [9]—improved, also, for the day of war. At the height of the antebellum work, in thirty-one months in 1842–45, the government took from the lower Ohio, Mississippi, Missouri, and Arkansas 21,681 snags, 36,840 roots, logs,

6 Hunter, Ch. III, deals fully with mechanical development.
7 See tables of speed in Hunter, 490; *Life on the Mississippi*, Ch. XVI.
8 Hunter ably covers this subject in Ch. IV, pp. 181–215.
9 *Life on the Mississippi*, Ch. XXVIII.

and stumps, and 74,810 trees likely to topple into the water. The 700-mile Cumberland became a busy artery as far as Nashville, 200 miles, and in high water took steamboats on to Burnside, 200 miles farther. The Tennessee, meandering through three States, carried large boats 260 miles to Florence, Alabama, and small ones 650 miles to Knoxville.

Commercially, the railroads when the war opened were strangling the river trade. Their network served a far larger territory; they moved freight with greater celerity; they could send it by spurs and sidings to the factory door; they ran their carriers on frequent and regular schedules. But from the military standpoint, in enemy or disputed territory a river offered a far safer invasion road than a railway. Union commanders found that it was impossible to guard rail facilities over wide distances; guerrilla bands, organized cavalry detachments, or even single fearless men could spring from the woods to saw trestles, fire bridges, or tear up iron. Grant learned this lesson at heavy cost. Of course river vessels were also molested. But they could scatter the guerrillas by charges of grape, fight off larger forces, and sweep with little hurt past strong fortifications. The river lines could not be cut.[10]

Command of the Western rivers was held from the outset by the Union for the simple reason that the North owned most of the steamboats, produced a great majority of the trained rivermen, and had nearly all the facilities for building, fortifying, and repairing vessels. Pittsburgh, Cincinnati, Louisville, and St. Louis were in that order the important centers for steamboat construction in the 1850's. Conceivably New Orleans might have developed shipyards despite its lack of rolling mills and good machine shops, but it never did. The brave little start it made in the times of Madison and Monroe withered away. A search for steamboat builders along the whole lower Mississippi in 1861 would have turned up only a few craftsmen who made tiny boats for the bayous and lesser rivers. The small number of bottoms available at Memphis, Vicksburg, Port Hudson, and other places were soon crippled, sunk, or captured, so that Foote and Porter lorded it over the river world.[11]

One long-forgotten hero of the war, Colonel Lewis B. Parsons, took charge of Western army transport in St. Louis, where his foresight, vigilance, and energy made the most of water facilities in Western logistics. A single fact illustrates the thesis that in this theater of advance, as distinguished from the Eastern scene, rivers held a place more significant than rails: in the fiscal

10 Sherman wrote in the fall of 1863 that a railroad took a whole army to guard, "each foot of rail being essential to the whole; whereas they can't stop the Tennessee, and each boat can make its own game." Oct. 2, 1863, Naval O. R., I, xxv, 474.
11 Hunter, 106, 107; Hoppin, *Foote*, 154–168.

year 1862–63, almost 338,000,000 pounds of military stores were hauled by river as against 153,100,000 by cars.

Combined operations by land and water gave the conflict, especially in the West, what a European critic termed "an entirely distinctive character among all modern wars." A House committee later made a boast which was little exaggerated. "It is now practicable," it declared, "on twenty-four hours' notice, to embark at Boston or Baltimore a larger army than those with which Napoleon won some of his most decisive victories, and landing within three days at Cairo, twelve hundred miles distant, there embark it on transports, and within four days' more time disembark it at New Orleans, a thousand miles further, or two thousand two hundred miles from the point of departure." [12] The most strategic points of the war included those at which lines of rail touched a navigable river, for there huge supply depots were most useful.

[II]

The gunboat and mortar fleets embodied very special skills and enterprise.

When the war began James B. Eads, who as a poor boy had peddled apples on the streets of St. Louis, was at forty-one independently rich. By salvaging wrecked steamboats with a specially invented diving bell, he had become more expertly familiar with the Mississippi and its tributaries than any other man. When Lincoln called him to Washington to give advice, he proposed to the War Department a fleet of armored river gunboats. [13] As soon as the government asked for bids, he submitted plans for building 7 of 600 tons each, mobilized 4,000 men within a fortnight to speed the task, launched his first vessel in forty-five days, and had the others under way soon after. He proved a dynamo of well-directed energy.

Meanwhile the mariner Andrew H. Foote, whose short beard, tousled hair, mastiff jaw, and resolute look made him the image of an old sea dog, had arrived August 26, 1861, to take charge of Upper Mississippi operations with the rank of flag officer. He loved blue waves and a cloud of sail over his head. The "hybrid service" of the West, partly water, partly swamp, partly land, was utterly strange to him. But the officer who had led a stubborn crusade to abolish grog in the Navy was not daunted by his many difficulties. He found that his force consisted of three Ohio freight-and-passenger steamers recently altered and armed at Cincinnati and brought downstream,

12 Comte de Paris, *Civil War*, I, 215, 216; 39th Cong., 1st Sess., House Exec. Doc., I, 216, 217.
13 Nicolay and Hay, V, 118.

the *Conestoga, Tyler,* and *Lexington,* protected only by oak bulwarks; two vessels converted into gunboats by Frémont; the seven gunboats being built by Eads; and thirty-eight mortar boats constructed under Frémont's orders. Foote also found that because Washington had denied the Western Department money, credit, and materials, neither the gunboats nor mortar boats could be finished at the time stated by contract. If they *had* been finished only two months earlier, one of Foote's officers later wrote, no fighting at Columbus, Island No. 10, Memphis, and Vicksburg would have been necessary, and the Western forces might have been sent East.

"Our difficulties have been legion," Foote wrote Meigs October 29. He was still not certain of a successful result; "that is, of having guns and mortar-boats in efficient condition for going down the river in December." Like others, he complained of the Western propensity to grab contracts and then cheat in fulfilling them.[14] But by frenzied effort Eads and Foote met the demands thrown upon them. No chapter of hasty improvisation in the war is more striking than that which they wrote. They made and remade designs, solving many fresh problems—that of adequate clearance for the paddle wheel of an armor-weighted vessel in shallow water, for example. They built new yards and docks, invented new machinery, spurred rolling mills, machine shops, sawmills, and foundries to make the parts they needed, and kept the telegraph wires hot with demands for ordinance. When Eads and Foote began, "the timber to form the hulls of the vessels was as yet uncut in the forest, and the engines to drive them were unbuilt." They toiled incredible hours, seven days a week. The launch of Eads's earliest ship—the first armored river boat in American history—took place on October 12, at Carondelet, Missouri. The vessel, which had her boilers and engines in place, was named first the *St. Louis,* later the *De Kalb.* Then came the others, bearing the names of river places: *Pittsburgh, Cincinnati, Cairo, Mound City, Carondelet,* and *Louisville.*

Eads's gunboats, 175 feet long and 55.5 wide, had wooden hulls plated with iron two-and-a-half inches thick, and mounted thirteen guns, three in the bow, four on each side, and two at the stern. The largest of the early vessels added to this fleet was the *Benton,* of about 1,000 tons, a well-armored snagboat; but some boats of 1,200 tons soon came into service. Before the end of 1862 the Western Flotilla numbered 55 warships in all, of a great variety of sizes and types. Some were stern-wheelers. These had exceptional power and speed, but were difficult to manage in currents and headwinds. The

14 O. R., I, viii, 77–674, contains much about naval work on Western waters; so does Naval O. R., I, xxiii, *passim;* and see Gideon Welles, *Annual Report,* December 1, 1862. Foote was a captain until November 13, when his rank as flag-officer became effective; Hoppin, 184.

side-wheelers were more easily directed, better protected, and fast enough for most purposes. The counter-wheel boats, converted from ferries, were found too slow. For several reasons it was impossible to use propellers: the water was often too shoal to give them purchase, and they were easily broken by snags and floating timber. Eads's boats could make nine miles an hour under perfect conditions, but the others were slower. The most vulnerable elements were the boilers—a single penetrating shot might explode them, parboiling the crew—and the paddle wheels. In default of better plating, railroad irons and chains were used.[15]

The flotilla, manned largely by volunteer drafts, and subject to over-all army command, offered an arduous service. In summer, night and day, the cabins, wardrooms, and gun rooms were hot and stifling. Sharpshooters lurking on shore were ready to pick off any unwary man on deck. Hostile boats, batteries, and fire ships were a peril. But the fleet was endlessly useful. It carried troops, stores, wounded, mules—everything. Its fifty-pounder rifled guns, able to reach targets nearly five miles away, could disperse enemy columns, frighten guerrillas, and protect landing parties. From the low chimneys dense smoke advertised the imminence of the boats long before they rounded a distant bend, and the mere sight of this smoke and the hollow thud of the guns inspired terror. Even Eads's well-armored boats drew only six feet, while lighter craft among "Uncle Sam's web feet" carried deadly cannon up shallow creeks and bayous. No command gave better service for the money. "Our gunboat flotilla has not cost, including the building of the gunboats, $3,000,000 to date," wrote the fleet quartermaster to Foote late in May, 1862. Yet, he added, see what it has done.

The mortar boats which Frémont had commissioned were both a special asset and a difficult problem. The design was bad. Flat-bottomed, rectangular, with pointed bows and sterns, and vertical sides, a sort of scow, they offered great resistance to the water when towed—for they had no motive power of their own. In the center a structure of logs laid at right angles to each other supported the mortar beds and mortars, the whole weighing about thirteen tons. The recoil whenever a mortar was fired added about twenty tons to this vertical weight; and this soon sprung the seams, so that the boats had to be pumped. They had no conveniences to enable crews to live aboard. The novelty of the fittings made it hard to equip them. By herculean effort Abram S. Hewitt, stepping into the breach, got a number of mortar beds completed in his Trenton ironworks and sped them westward, earning the special thanks

15 Boynton, *Navy During the Rebellion*, I, 501; Hoppin, *Foote*, Ch. XIII; Report of Commander W. D. Porter, St. Louis, May 6, 1862, Naval O. R., I, xxiii, 82, 83; description of flotilla life in N. Y. *Weekly Tribune*, April 19, 1862.

of the War Department. The much-distrusted mortars soon proved useful against a variety of fortified strongholds.[16]

Another example of effective improvised effort was furnished by Charles Ellet, Jr., and his rams. A leading civil engineer, Ellet had long before the war conceived the idea of destroying enemy warships by ramming them with heavy steamers. He wrote the government. Stanton, in late March, 1862, when the *Merrimac* had demonstrated the power of a ram, ordered him west to buy and refit the boats immediately. He took old steamers, stiffened them by bulkheads of heavy timbers running through the hulls from head to stern, properly braced, strengthened the structure with tiebolts, and filled the bow with solid timbers. Within about forty days after quitting Washington, he had thus made seven rams and two consorts. The entire fleet, with its equipment and with coal and provisions for eighty days, cost less than $300,000. Ably commanded by Ellet himself, who was responsible to Secretary Stanton alone, it was destined to perform a spectacular feat at Memphis.[17]

Altogether, the building and mobilization of the river navy, first advertised to the world by the capture of Henry and Donelson, was one of the great initial achievements of the North. Along with the making of the new volunteer army of half a million men, it may be called the first impressive demonstration of the nation's war power. In a sense it was improvisation: the hurried, scrambling utilization of whatever came to hand in old boats, old ideas, and old methods, along with new machines, new conceptions, and new designs. But out of the improvisation came planned organization. Here at least, applied to war, was the peculiar American genius that had vanquished the greatest enemy of the pioneer—distance—by the Concord coach and Conestoga wagon, Fulton's steamboat, Baldwin's light basket locomotives, and Ellet's daring railway curves. Here was the quick energetic use of the trained expert, for Eads, Foote, and Ellet had three different varieties of proficiency.

Historians have written of the capture of Donelson as a turning point in the Western war effort. Not so; it was this capture together with the forging of the river fleets which was the turning point. The Confederates, who had a keen appreciation of the importance of the Mississippi and its tributaries, but who were poor in boats, yards, and pilots, were staggered by the sudden emergence of Foote's and Ellet's flotillas. General Pillow in August had dropped his projected attack on Cairo when he learned that Frémont had

16 Quartermaster George D. Wise, St. Louis, May 25, 1862, Naval O. R., I, xxiii, 105–107; Hoppin, 193, 194; Nevins, *Frémont*, 484, 492; *Rebellion Record*, III, 434, 435; Fox Corr., NYHS; Nevins, *Hewitt*, 199–204.
17 Ellet got his orders to build March 27, 1862. He reconstructed three of his boats at Pittsburgh, three at Cincinnati, and one at New Albany, Ind. Each had three heavy, solid bulkheads of timber 12–18 inches thick stretching fore and aft. Naval O. R., I, xxiii, 65–66, 274–277.

brought nearly 4,000 troops down from St. Louis by boat in 26 hours, and that the three steamers armed at Cincinnati had passed the New Albany bar downstream. From that hour the amphibious Union advance was sometimes delayed, but never stopped.

[III]

Organization and mechanization could solve the problems of logistics. But inexperience, rashness, and improvisation could bring any army to the brink of ruin once it was placed and supplied.

At Donelson the first Confederate line of defense in the West had been not merely pierced but shattered. The troops holding it sagged back toward the southern boundary of Tennessee, leaving Memphis on the west and Knoxville on the east in a precarious situation. Albert Sidney Johnston was temporarily stunned. A clamor for his dismissal arose; but Jefferson Davis told a complaining Tennessee delegation, "If Sidney Johnston is not a general, the South has none to give you." [18]

We have seen that one of the vital communication lines of the Confederacy connected Memphis and Chattanooga along the southern boundary of Tennessee: the Memphis & Charleston, which ran from the Mississippi River almost due east through Corinth and Huntsville to Chattanooga, whence it sent one fork northeast into Virginia and another southeast into South Carolina. Just after Donelson, Judah P. Benjamin wrote Lee that this lifeline "must be defended at all hazards." [19] It was so important that the Confederate Cabinet even discussed the possibility of abandoning the Virginia capital to defend it. Obviously, as much Tennessee territory as possible ought to be saved to the South, for every new Union advance sheared away more of the Confederacy's iron resources. The State, with 17 furnaces smelting some 22,000 tons in 1860, was the largest Southern producer of pig iron. Yet the Tennessee River, now that the forts had fallen, opened a broad avenue of invasion. [20]

When Albert Sidney Johnston left Nashville with about 10,000 discouraged, disorderly, ill-armed troops, he realized that he must retreat into Northern Mississippi, concentrate, and augment his forces. A powerful Confederate army must be assembled at some single point to block the pursuing Union cohorts. This principle of concentration was strongly espoused by Beauregard, who had succeeded to the command at Columbus, and by Bragg at Pensacola. The week after Donelson saw messengers scurrying about and detachments march-

18 Fiske, *Miss. Valley*, 70.
19 O. R., I, vi, 398, 828.
20 Eaton, *Confederacy*, 175, 176.

ing forward in a frenzied attempt to create a strong force while there was yet time. Although Johnston was chief in command, Beauregard was probably the prime mover.

Strenuous effort gave the undertaking success. Bragg brought up about 10,000 men from the Pensacola-Mobile area; Leonidas Polk helped gather together all the effectives scattered along the river at New Madrid, Columbus, and Fort Pillow; and Johnston besought the governors of Tennessee, Louisiana, and Alabama for at least 5,000 men apiece. West of the river Earl Van Dorn had a small force in Arkansas. Beauregard called on him to assist in forming a joint command of fully 40,000: "We must do something or die in the attempt, otherwise all will shortly be lost." The exuberant Creole spoke of launching a northward sweep, aided by twelve gunboats from New Orleans, to retake all the ground surrendered. To Corinth, a junction on the Memphis & Charleston, designated as the central rendezvous, Johnston on March 25 marched his own army. Unit after unit then came in, until 40,000 men were really assembled. The high officers, including not only Johnston, Beauregard, Polk, and Bragg, but Hardee, Breckinridge, and shoals of brigadiers, overawed ordinary soldiers who had never dreamed of seeing so much top brass.[21]

Considering the recent defeats and the poverty of the area, this force had been gathered with astonishing promptness. The sight of strong new levies and detachments from the Gulf filled veterans of Donelson with angry regret. "Why couldn't this help have come in January?" they demanded. "We begged for it; we foretold the disasters which lack of it entailed; and now that so much has been lost, the help arrives!" [22]

Before the concentration at Corinth was completed, Beauregard sent two regiments and some field guns to hold a bluff on the west bank of the Tennessee called Pittsburg Landing, where peacetime steamboats had unloaded cargoes for the neighboring countryside. Behind the abrupt red clay bluff lay a wide, roughly seamed plateau, stretching along the river about four miles, and at the highest point a hundred feet above the water. A small Methodist meetinghouse called Shiloh Chapel, log-built, was the principal landmark. On the south, northwest, and north, this tableland was bounded

21 Johnston's report on the loss of Nashville, O. R., I, vii, 426, 427; Roman, *Beauregard*, I, 367 ff.; A. P. James, "Strategy of Concentration of the Confd. Forces," Am. Hist. Assn. *Annual Report* (1919), 365–374; Beauregard to Van Dorn, Feb. 1, 1862, Brock Coll., HL. The State of Mississippi called for 10,000 men. But James Burnet of West Point, Miss., wrote that many were sneaking into the ranks of companies whose terms were soon to expire, while some who anticipated a draft were writing favorite commanders to find places. Feb. 18, 1862, to John J. Pettus, Miss. State Archives.
22 Polk, *Polk*, II, 87 ff. Beauregard wrote Van Dorn that by rapid marches of a large army they might "take Cairo, Paducah, the mouths of the Tennessee and Cumberland and most probably be able to take St. Louis by the river. What say you to this brilliant program?"

by deep creeks, while it was cut with minor ravines and hollows, and in part covered by a thick growth of oak, hickory, locust, sycamore, and other trees, interlaced with bushes and briars. The main road from Corinth, twenty miles away, entered it from the southwest, well masked by woods. But the Southern regiments did not long hold the place, for Foote's gunboats on the Tennessee soon made it untenable. Then General C. F. Smith, bringing up troops at the suggestion of Sherman, chose the Landing as the spot where Grant and Buell should unite their armies. Grant, on reaching Savanna farther down the river, at once ratified the choice without even inspecting it.

It was imperative for the Confederates to strike before Grant and Buell joined forces. From the moment he reached Corinth, Johnston was impatient to finish organizing his four corps and advance; but he labored under a great impediment in the woebegone state of his army. Bragg wrote on March 18 that he felt deep concern over their "disorganized and demoralized condition," and one soldier thought that May might approach before they could be whipped into shape.[23] The first days of April, however, found the men fairly ready, and the situation favorable for dealing a blow. Johnston knew that while Grant's main force had spread its camps over Pittsburg Landing, Buell's men had not arrived. He heard that Lew Wallace's division had appeared at Bethel Station, about twenty-odd miles north of Corinth and that far west of the Tennessee; if this were true, Wallace could give no aid to Grant. Johnston and Beauregard gave orders to the corps commanders to be ready to march at six the next morning, April 3.

The curtain was about to rise on Shiloh.

[IV]

While the Confederates were concentrating, the Northerners should have been doing the same, and planning their own swift offensive. But overconfidence, imperfect training for battle, the obtuseness of Halleck, and the carelessness of Grant placed the recent victors in a position of the utmost peril.

The overconfidence had some excuse, for Union leaders knew that the Confederate retreat southward from Nashville had been almost a rout. They were told that the ragged, hungry columns covered a line of twenty miles, that stragglers numbered thousands, and that at every crossroads soldiers deserted by squads. Military men concluded that the Army of the West was helpless to check Grant and Buell. The imperfect Union training was also a fact. All the Western forces had a dismaying proportion of inefficient, untrustworthy junior officers. Resignations and dismissals were getting rid of

23 O. R., I, x, pt. 2, p. 340; C. J. Johnson, March 23, 1862, to family, C. J. J. Papers, LSU.

many, but more remained. The troops, especially in Buell's Army of the Tennessee, included dozens of raw and undisciplined regiments who needed stern drill like that given in the Potomac camps. The quartermaster and commissary departments also required drastic reform. Rations, for example, were to a great extent dealt out to be miscooked by the soldiers individually or in squads, although in camp it would have been easy to establish company kitchens.

As for Halleck, he had hesitated in a complete muddle, and finally had directed Grant, as we have noted, to execute what was hardly more than a raid southward, for Halleck wished to be on hand when a great engagement was fought.[24] He had therefore ordered Grant to steam up the Tennessee and cut the Memphis & Charleston by penetrating into northern Mississippi, destroying a key bridge, and tearing up parts of the line. But he was to avoid a general battle, retreating rather than fight one; and it was under these limitations that his army on March 17 had reached Savanna. Here Grant had established his headquarters.[25] He had five divisions present or not far distant, commanded by Sherman, McClernand, Hurlbut, Lew Wallace, and C. F. Smith; reinforcements were arriving daily, and as they came in were organized first into brigades and then into a sixth division under Benjamin M. Prentiss. On the very day that Grant set up headquarters, Buell with 35,000 men began his overland march to join him. Grant, who despised Halleck's order against battle, later wrote: "When all reinforcements should have arrived, I expected to take the initiative by marching on Corinth." [26] He thought that might be soon, for on March 19 Buell was only 90 miles from Savanna.

It was thus to prepare for striking a blow that Grant accepted Pittsburg Landing as the spot for gathering the Union forces. Sherman had fallen in love with the place. "The ground itself admits of easy defense by a small command," he wrote Grant, "and yet affords admirable camping-ground for a hundred thousand men." [27] C. F. Smith was equally enthusiastic. The last ten days of March saw the plateau whitened by tents as unit after unit took station there. Sixty-nine puffing transports unloaded men and materials. Though the elderly Smith had nominal charge of dispositions, he was so ailing that Sherman took field control, pointing out to each division the ground it was to occupy. McClernand came in on the 27th, and Lew Wallace brought his division ashore at Crump's Landing, about halfway between Savanna

24 O. R., I, vii, 674; Fuller, *Grant*, 95 ff.
25 See Mil. Hist. Soc. Mass., *Campaigns in Ky. and Tenn.*, 104–109; O. R., I, x, pt. 2, pp. 32–43.
26 *Memoirs*, I, 332.
27 O. R., I, x, pt. 1, p. 27; cf. Greeley, *Amer. Conflict*, II, 58. Sherman comments in his *Memoirs*, I, 228, that "at a later period of the war, we could have rendered this position impregnable in a night."

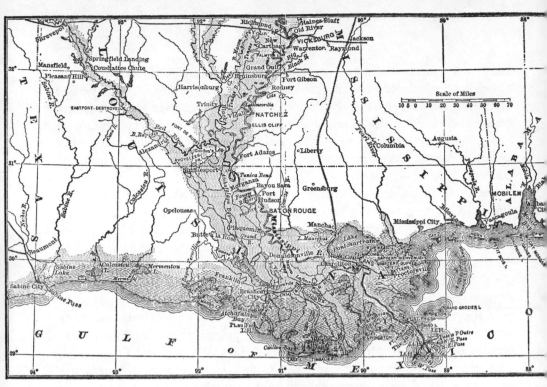

THE LOWER MISSISSIPPI

and Pittsburg Landing; not so far away from the main force as the false report heard by Johnston had placed him, but too far for a rapid junction.

By April 1 a great army was comfortably settling at Pittsburg Landing. All too comfortably settled, all too negligently ensconced! The very choice of campsite had been characteristically casual, for Grant had accepted the recommendations of Smith and other officers without making any personal investigation. As the army settled in, Johnston was marching. At dawn on the 6th he attacked.

The most arresting aspects of Shiloh are not its charges, panics, and rallies, but its evidences that both sides were still waging war with impromptu confusion, inexperience, and planlessness. No battle of the war does more to justify Moltke's sneer at the American fighting as a struggle of two armed mobs. Everyone knows the outlines of the conflict: how the Confederate attack completely surprised the Union camp, how Grant's troops were forced back far toward the river, where 10,000 fugitives soon huddled under the bluff, how when utter defeat stared the Northerners in the face Albert Sidney Johnston was mortally wounded and the first detachments of Buell's army arrived on the field, how that night more of Buell's forces came into position, and how on the second day the Confederates were driven back and forced to retreat to Corinth. The battle abounds in controversial questions. Was Grant completely overwhelmed the first day, so that only Buell's arrival retrieved the field, or had he stopped the Confederates before Buell's first detachment appeared? Was the transfer of the Confederate command from Johnston to Beauregard, followed as it was by Beauregard's immediate order to halt, the fatal blow to the Confederates?

What is far more important is the fact that the battle illustrates as do few others the want of organization, plan, vigilance, and discipline which crippled both sections in waging war; defects connected, of course, with the whole character of American society.[28]

Grant was still learning his trade as soldier; his staff was still but partly filled and imperfectly trained. With him was John A. Rawlins, his assistant adjutant-general since the previous August, a grim, hard-jawed young attorney in his early thirties, with stiff black hair, a dark complexion, a gruff low voice, and brusque manners. Some said he was Grant's brains, and no question existed about his quick, razor-edged intellect; but he was more than that—he was Grant's conscience. From his lawyer days in Galena he knew that one of his responsibilities was to keep Grant away from drink. He stood no nonsense from anybody, his chief least of all. "Insubordination twenty times a day," commented one officer. Theodore S. Bowers, another Illinoisan, born in poverty, a printer who had become country editor, not yet thirty, was a faithful, efficient secretarial aide; "gallant little Bowers," an officer called him for his loyal courage. But the strong responsible figures of Grant's subsequent staff—the engineers, C. B. Comstock and W. F. Smith, the Mexican War veteran F. T. Dent, the Indian Ely S. Parker, the quick Adam Badeau, the skillful young West Pointer Orville E. Babcock—were still to be added. He had few capable helpers and lacked what he needed most, an intelligence officer.[29]

Overwork may explain why Grant paid no personal visit to Pittsburg Landing until April 1, but proofs that he had much to learn abound. Still insensitive to the need for an efficient intelligence service—spies, scouts, patrols —he knew practically nothing of Johnston's position, strength, and intentions. Sherman on April 1 made a mere steamboat reconnaissance from the Landing,

28 Good accounts of the battle are available in Military Hist. Soc. Mass., *Campaigns in Ky. and Tenn.*; 101–254; *Battles and Leaders*, I, 465–610; M. F. Force, *From Fort Henry to Corinth*, 91–182; A. L. Conger, *Rise of U. S. Grant*, 238–275; and Kenneth P. Williams, *Lincoln finds a General*, III, Ch. XIV.

29 On Grant's staff see Williams, III, 181 ff. Captain A. S. Baxter was quartermaster-general, and W. R. Rowley, W. S. Hillyer, and Clark B. Lagow were aides. Sherman wrote in 1885 that "his staff at Shiloh was very inferior, Rawlins, Lagow, Hillyer, etc."; to W. J. Eliot, Sept. 12, 1885, Sherman Papers, LC.

thirty miles up the river, and on April 3 sent the Fifth Ohio Cavalry on a nine-mile push west which discovered nothing; that was all. It was negligent of Grant to let Lew Wallace's Second Division be posted near Crump's, six or seven miles above Pittsburg Landing, and cut off from it by Snake Creek, a stream out of its banks with two dismantled bridges to mock at the troops. It was negligent of him not to hurry Buell along in his snail-slow advance from Nashville.[30]

These lapses intermeshed, obviously, with those of other Union commanders. Why did Buell take more than a fortnight to march his 30,000 men 90 miles from Columbia to Pittsburg Landing? Partly because this able soldier was deficient in stern energy. Lincoln's secretaries have endorsed General Ormsby Mitchel's verdict: "He lacked decision." Partly because nobody told him to hurry; Halleck, indeed, advised him on April 3 to concentrate his troops at Waynesboro, where they would have been useless, while Grant on the 4th suggested that he take his time, since it would be impossible to give him water transportation from Savanna to Pittsburg Landing before the 7th! He allowed a burned bridge at Duck River on his line of advance to delay him ten days, while he languidly built another. The imperious General William Nelson finally lost patience, obtained permission to lead the way, and found that with care a ford was feasible; and thus on the 29th McCook's division got across. Had it not been for Nelson's tremendous will and energy, Buell might never have arrived at Shiloh until too late.[31] An entry in Colonel Jacob Ammen's diary is illuminating:

March 27—Late in the evening General Nelson, in returning from General Buell's headquarters, informed me that he had General Buell's permission to take the advance, and gave me a verbal order to cross Duck River at daylight the 29th. I inquired if the bridge would be done. He answered, "No." "Are there any boats?" He said, "No; but the river is falling; and damn you, get over, for we must have the advance and get the glory." He enjoined secrecy, lest we should be prevented from taking the advance. March 28—Went to Duck River to examine the fords; sent some of my cavalry in; river 200 yards or more wide; fords crooked. Fortunately, some army wagons return with forage and ford the river; the water just touches the beds of the wagons; current strong; water above and below, deep; no boats. . . . March 29—Reveille at 3 A.M., breakfast, wagons loaded, column formed. . . . The Tenth Brigade, infantry and artillery and train, crossed Duck River this cold and disagreeable day without accident.

Worst of all was the failure of Sherman, despite ample warning of the enemy advance, to take precautions to meet it. Halleck had emphasized the

30 Conger, *op. cit.*, Chs. XVII, XVIII.
31 O. R., I, x, pt. 1, pp. 329-330.

importance of entrenching in the vicinity of the enemy, and Grant and Sherman knew well that Johnston at Corinth was but twenty miles away. But the West Point, regular-army theory was that field works made the troops cowardly, for they should be made to "stand up and fight man-fashion." Sherman later wrote that they did not fortify "because we had no orders to do so, and because such a course would have made men timid." [32] This was absurd; an obvious precaution can be taken without orders—and Halleck did instruct Grant to entrench. Moreover, far from dispiriting the troops, entrenchments with openings at intervals give special confidence to raw soldiers. One of the great lessons of the war was to be the power of the bullet as delivered by rifled breechloaders; but a still greater lesson was to be the power of the defensive once infantrymen learned to dig trenches and erect breastworks.

The Confederate army from Corinth, approaching Pittsburg Landing along two roads on April 5, was not in a position for attack until midafternoon. The previous day an advance force had come into collision with some Union troops who were busy drilling, and after a little fighting had retired; then that night some Confederate buglers had recklessly sounded calls. It seemed to Beauregard that all opportunity of surprise and hence success had been lost, and he advised a retreat; but Johnston insisted that they go ahead. "I would fight them if they were a million," he told a staff officer. The Southern army was then deployed in three parallel lines along the Union front, Hardee commanding the first, Bragg the second, and Polk and Breckinridge the third; and they were put in readiness to make their onslaught at dawn.[33]

Seldom in war has a surprise been more complete. It is true that Sherman sent out daily reconnaissances, but he made little use of the data gained. On the 5th, with Johnston two miles distant, he wrote Grant: "I have no doubt that nothing will occur today more than some picket firing. The enemy is saucy, but got the worst of it yesterday, and will not press our pickets far. I will not be drawn out far unless with certainty of advantage, and I do not apprehend anything like an attack on our position." In another note to Grant he wrote: "All is quiet along my lines now." He knew that some cavalry was on his front, and he thought that probably two infantry regiments and a battery were a couple of miles away. "I will send you 10 prisoners of war and a report of last night's affair in a few minutes." Several of the prisoners

---

32 Cortissoz, *Whitelaw Reid*, II, 336, 337.
33 *Battles and Leaders*, I, 495; T. Harry Williams, *Beauregard*, 133 ff.; Johnston, *A. S. Johnston*, 484-522; Jordan and Pryor, *Forrest*, 117 ff. Beauregard had hoped to attack on the morning of the 5th of April and was horrified by the delays. Johnston showed much greater firmness and courage. But Beauregard recovered his spirits when Hardee asked him to ride down the front of his men to encourage them.

boasted they were the advance guard of an army which within twenty-four hours would throw the whole Union army into the Tennessee. This talk might have been taken for loose vaporing, but one mortally wounded Confederate, when told he could not live, sent for a colonel whose relatives he knew, and warned him that a Confederate host of 50,000 was about to smash against the Northern lines. When the colonel sent word to Sherman, the general refused to believe the story.[34]

It is clear that Sherman had the *idée fixe* that no danger of attack existed. A man of nervous, excitable temperament, he was never lethargic, for his perceptions were acute and his mind incessantly active. But he sometimes lacked balance and judgment. As an admiring friend once said, his intellect was a beautifully intricate piece of machinery, with all the screws a little loose.[35] When on the afternoon of the 5th a sergeant brought word that Ohio pickets had noted rabbits and other small animals scurrying out of the woods, and had seen enemy cavalry, while one outlying soldier had descried infantry in line, Sherman actually ordered the sergeant put in confinement for circulating a false report. Additional reports he waved aside. "Oh, it is only a reconnoitering party," he said complacently.[36]

A few Union officers were alert for the Southern onset. Under orders from General Prentiss the advance guard on the Corinth road had been strengthened, and at 3 A.M. on April 6 five companies of Colonel David Moore's Twenty-first Missouri were nearly two miles out from the Union camp. Here at daybreak fighting began. But elsewhere the surprise was general. Many troops at the point of impact were first alarmed when soldiers of the advance guard stumbled out of the woods, shouting: "The rebels are coming! Get into line." Men just beginning to cook breakfast were startled by pealing orders and the long roll of drums. As they caught up their muskets messengers galloped off to notify brigade and division headquarters, and neighboring regiments sprang confusedly to arms. Firing all along the picket lines redoubled, and companies hurried forward to reinforce them. Everywhere coffee pots were being kicked over, sleepy officers were jerking on their trousers, and soldiers were loading their guns. "The searching bullet," wrote Major George Mason later, "found many an unfortunate in his bed." As one company which had rushed to reinforce the pickets fled back through

---

34 O. R., I, x, pt. 2, pp. 93–94; Grant, *Memoirs*, I, 334 ff.; Mil. Hist. Soc. Mass., *op. cit.*, 115 ff., 134 ff. Grant had shown uneasiness over the danger of attack by a considerable enemy force, but the blow he feared was one on Wallace's force at Crump's Landing, not an assault by the whole Confederate array on his own army.

35 See the perceptive article on Sherman's *Memoirs* in *Galaxy*, XX (1875), 325 ff., 450 ff.

36 T. Harry Williams, *Beauregard*, 132; Mil. Hist. Soc. Mass., *op. cit.*, 115–117; Fuller, *Grant*, 106 ff.

the brush in hot retreat, its captain yelled to the camp: "The rebels up there are thicker than fleas on a dog's back." [37]

A brilliant sun was beginning to mount in a cloudless sky. The bright green foliage, flecked by dogwood and redbud blossoms, half hid the advancing Southerners, but the barrels of new Enfield muskets carried by the Confederate battle line gleamed through the leaves, and puffs of smoke curled over the trees. The Southern battlefront suddenly emerged on J. J. Appler's flank within easy musket shot, and the colonel began to shift front to meet the attack. He hurried his sick, nearly a third of his whole command, out of their tents to the rear. Some cowards joined the fleeing invalids, and most of the remainder, who had never held a battalion drill, milled about in utter confusion. Sherman rode up with an orderly. At first he turned his field glasses to the empty woods in front, ignoring the advancing lines on the flank. "Look out, General!" cried Union soldiers. "You'll be shot! Look to the right!" As the Confederates loosed a new volley, the orderly fell dead. "My God, we're attacked!" cried Sherman. "Appler, hold your position— I'll support you!" He rode off for reinforcements. And Appler, seeing the Confederates advance amid the smoke and flame of their discharges, took to his heels with a shout to his men: "Retreat! Save yourselves!" [38]

Johnston and Beauregard had achieved their object of taking Grant's army unaware. The attack had begun at five. Johnston, mounting, told his aides: "Tonight we will water our horses in the Tennessee River." [39]

The surprise was not merely tactical, but represented strategic blindness of an unforgivable kind. The New York *Tribune*, reading the weather signs (including Southern journals), had concluded that an important movement was afoot. An editorial of April 2, "The Expected Blow," declared that no Eastern stroke seemed likely. "On the other hand, we see much that indicates a determination on the part of the Secession chiefs to strike a sudden and heavy blow in the Southwest. They are evidently concentrating their forces at Corinth or some other point near the south line of Tennessee, with intent to hurl the great mass of them suddenly on an exposed detachment of ours, thus repeating the lesson of Bull Run, Wilson's Creek, and Lexington. We trust they are to be baffled in this game by the cautious energy of General Halleck." If newspapermen on Park Row saw this, why did not

37 *Ibid.*, 117. The surprise and recovery are described in detail by Albert Dillahunty, *Shiloh*; Otto Eisenschiml, *The Story of Shiloh*; and *Battles and Leaders*, I, 558 ff. A mass of letters and reports may be found in O. R., I, x, pt. 2, pp. 93–627.
38 Lloyd Lewis, *Sherman*, 220, 221; Williams, *Lincoln Finds a General*, III, 356, 357. Useful papers may be found in Illinois Commandery Loyal Legion, *Essays and Recs.*, I, 9–124. Col. Jesse J. Appler commanded the Fifty-third Ohio.
39 Whitelaw Reid's comprehensive account of Shiloh in the Cincinnati *Gazette* of April 14, twelve close columns of more than 19,000 words, was exaggerated in some details, but in general surprisingly accurate; Cortissoz, *Reid*, I, 86, 87.

Grant see it? Or since he was harassed by a thousand details, why did not Halleck in St. Louis and Stanton at the War Department see it?

The failure of the Union commanders to raise any field works stupefied Beauregard, who had said after the clash on April 4, "Now they will be intrenched to the eyes." [40] A decent intelligence system and a service of advanced sentries would have been equally valuable. Colonel G. F. R. Henderson points out in a classic military text that throughout the war the armies never made laborious use of outposts and pickets. Surprises were frequent. More than one great battle opened with a sudden attack on sleeping men, and sometimes when two armies were in close proximity, one withdrew in the night leaving the other unaware. He contrasts this with the vigilance of the German armies in 1870–71, when surprises were unknown. "After a forced march or a hard day's fighting, no relaxation was allowed. Before the fires of the bivouac were lighted, scouts were moving far to the front. Through the night watches every road and path was traversed at short intervals by patrols; and the earliest light saw stronger parties pushing toward the enemy's lines." [41] American individualism had bred an ungirt lack of method.

Grant, Sherman, and others were learning their trade. Many a brave Illinois and Ohio youth died in agony that spring Sunday because generals learn by trial and error. Later Sherman would blush to remember he had written that "I think" two enemy regiments and a battery are "about two miles out," and Grant would blush to recall the letter he had sent Halleck just before the storm: "I have scarcely the faintest idea of an attack (general one) being made upon us. . . ." [42]

The generals erred because they underestimated not only the speed with which the Confederates recovered from their disasters, but the whole power and determination of the Confederacy. They lay under McClellan's illusion in the East, that one strong thrust would win the war. "Up to the battle of Shiloh," writes Grant, "I . . . believed that the rebellion against the Government would collapse suddenly, and soon, if a decisive victory could be gained over any of its armies." The fall of Donelson, Bowling Green, and Nash-

---

40   T. Harry Williams, *Beauregard*, 132.
41   *Science of War*, 208.
42   O. R., I, x, pt. 1, p. 89. Many Union officers criticized Grant and Sherman angrily. The saddest day of Illinois history, wrote John M. Palmer, was that melancholy Sunday when the flower of her troops were slaughtered at Shiloh; unless the day Grant was made a general might be regarded as sadder still. To Trumbull, April 24, 1862, Trumbull Papers, LC. After Washburne delivered a flamboyant defense of Grant in Congress, where Sherman of Ohio and Harlan of Iowa attacked him, Joseph Medill of the Chicago *Tribune* wrote it was no use—Grant "is played out. The soldiers are down on him."; May 24, 1862, Washburne Papers, LC.

ville had buttressed the view that the Confederacy was fast staggering to its doom. Both Grant and McClellan thought that the Confederates would retreat until cornered like Cornwallis; then, the capitulation. "I had no expectation of needing fortifications," Grant writes.[43]

By their courage and sacrifice the 80,000 men who struggled at Shiloh, in the bloodiest contest thus far fought on the continent, consecrated one of the greatest battlefields of the war. Here visitors may see the bluff below which the terrorized fugitives of Grant's most demoralized regiments took shelter, a mob which horrified Buell when he saw it. They may see the ground on Grant's left flank called the Hornet's Nest, where the Confederate losses were particularly staggering. They may find the spot where Albert Sidney Johnston, trying to put fresh nerve into a shaken Tennessee regiment, received his mortal wound. On one part of the battlefield is the Bloody Pond where many fell dying, and to which men of both armies crawled for their last taste of water. On another runs the sunken road where some of Prentiss' men, taking shelter, fought with indomitable devotion until the remnants of his surrounded division were forced to surrender. The Union losses were officially reported as 13,047 men; the Confederate, 10,699. "We can never forget what they did here"—but it is not a field on which qualities of generalship earned laurels for either section.

At the end, the lack of bold Union generalship made the battle far less decisive than it might have been. The Confederates, decimated, wearied, and in part almost famished, had become badly shattered by the end of the second day. "The fire and animation had left our troops," wrote one Southern leader of the last hours of fighting. Grant at nightfall intended to follow up his success with fresh troops and cavalry; and his failure to execute this intention, when the combined strength of his and Buell's armies so heavily overweighed the foe, excites wonderment. Confederate commanders expressed surprise over the lack of pursuit. Could Grant not have scattered Beauregard's forces to the wind, taken multitudes of prisoners, seized Corinth at once, and all but put an end to the war in the West? The best military historians think so.[44]

Some psychological deterrent, some half-hearted unwillingness to risk freshly won laurels, to push tired troops into desperate new exertions, and to stake all on a final cast, seems involved in the frequent Union failure during the war to follow a success by grasping complete victory. Grant makes three excuses: the Confederate retreat churned the muddy roads into morasses; he had not the heart to order wornout men to pursue; and his sen-

---

43 *Memoirs*, I, 332, 368.
44 Reports of Jacob Thompson and others, O. R., I, x, pt. 1, pp. 400 ff., treat Confederate demoralization. John Codman Ropes, *Civil War*, II, 90–92, and Fuller, *Grant*, 114, 115, emphatically condemn Grant's failure to pursue.

iority in rank over Buell was so recent that he hesitated to give him positive orders.[45] These excuses are fragile. If the Confederates could drag wagons, artillery, and wounded back over the roads, he could march over them; Buell's troops and Lew Wallace's division were comparatively fresh; and he had every right as chief commander to give Buell peremptory instructions. Sherman's explanation is still flimsier. Questioned by John Fiske, he jauntily remarked of the Confederates: "I assure you, my dear fellow, that we had quite enough of their society for two whole days, and were only too glad to be rid of them on any terms." Buell, who was anxious to pursue, is frankest of all. Everybody in Grant's army, he writes, "appeared to have thought that the object of the battle was sufficiently accomplished when they were reinstated in their camps." [46]

Once more Grant's lack of a good intelligence service crippled him, for he believed that the Confederate army, far from defeated, remained near his front ready for stubborn renewal of the battle. For a time he thought he could not safely remain west of the Tennessee much longer without large reinforcements. Yet in actual fact, the Confederates were broken.

Bragg wrote April 8, halfway back to Corinth: "Our condition is horrible. Troops utterly disorganized and demoralized. Road almost impassable. No provision and no forage. . . ." Breckinridge, whose force was to furnish a covering rear guard, declared: "My troops are worn out and I don't think can be relied on after the first volley." [47] The starved horses were dropping by the roadside; guns had to be abandoned. The sufferings of the wounded were indescribable. An observer who rode alongside the retreating columns the first night wrote that he saw more human agony and despair than he had dreamed possible. The army wound along a narrow, bottomless road in cold, drizzling rain which fell ever harder till it turned into hail. In the long lines of wagons the moaning casualties were piled like bags of grain, most of them without even a blanket. As hundreds died, they were thrown out to make room for the men who walked alongside with broken arms or fearful wounds. Several thousand men deserted on the retreat, while more arrived at Corinth sick of the war. They had lost irreplaceable arms, ammunition, blankets, and knapsacks. [48]

But in spite of their hopeless inferiority, their griefs and despairs, the

45 See Grant's report, O. R., I, x, pt. 1, pp. 108–111; *Memoirs*, I, 354, 355.
46 Fiske, *Miss. Valley in Civil War*, 99; *Battles and Leaders*, I, 534; and see Grant's letter to Buell, April 7, 1862, *ibid.*, I, 532, 533.
47 Bragg to Beauregard O. R., I, x, pt. 2, pp. 398, 399. Reports of Union officers on the battle (Sherman, Buell, Nelson, Wallace, and others) are in O. R., I, x, pt. 1, pp. 93–381; of Hardee, Breckinridge, and other Confederate officers in O. R., I, x, pt. 1, pp. 382–627.
48 An Impressed New Yorker, *Thirteen Months in the Confederate Army*.

heroic Confederates did return safe to camp. The Union troops were not in a much happier frame of mind. Burying the dead, picking up the battle-field debris, discussing the blunders of their officers, they were surly victors. Grant's and Buell's men exchanged recriminations which created a morose animosity outlasting the war. Meanwhile, the advent of the bumbling Halleck to take charge aroused general discontent among intelligent officers.

4

Springtide of Northern Hope

FOR THE three months from February to June, 1862, after their winter of discouragement, the Northern people plucked up hope. Stanton's vigor gave heart to everybody. After all his delays, McClellan did besiege Yorktown, and did fight a successful battle at Williamsburg. Meanwhile, the thrusts by Grant and Buell cheered the West, the blockade began to take a real grip, and those who kept an eye on the navy rubbed their hands over its energetic operations in the Gulf. People began to remember the twittering voices of autumn, when McClellan had told a Philadelphia committee that the war could not endure long, Robert J. Walker had predicted that the conflict would not outlast the spring campaigns, and Cameron had closed a description of the government's martial preparations with the words: "Therefore I say to you, our day of trouble has gone by." [1]

The gloom of the South matched the cheerfulness of the North. As the installation of the permanent Confederate Government in Richmond had been fixed for Washington's Birthday, it took place under the unhappiest circumstances. Donelson was less than a week old, Roanoke Island had just been lost to an amphibious Union expedition, and McClellan was imminently expected to deliver a series of sledgehammer blows. Under black skies, in cascades of rain, a dense crowd gathered before the Virginia capitol to hear Davis' inaugural. It departed chilled, for his speech was as limp as the wet flags. An appeal to the people to accept their meed of blood, sweat, and tears, a robust call to battle, might have set the South ablaze with new ardor. The Virginia press, much of it always critical of the cotton-kingdom leaders, loosed an avalanche of criticism on the despondent President. He is fainthearted, men said, he is trying to do too much and doing it badly, and he plays favorites in both civil and military affairs; he should summon abler lieutenants to his side. Davis was in fact one of those romantics who stand up to the realism of adversity badly.

1 Phila. *Evening Journal*, Nov. 5, 1861. "The backbone of the rebellion is already broken," said the Lexington, Ky., *Observer and Reporter*, Feb. 19, 1861, "and its utter annihilation cannot but follow."

"I have understood (from Judge Campbell)," wrote Kean of the War Department later,[2] "that in February 1862 just after his inauguration the President talked seriously of resigning, in consequence of the opposition in the Congress and his unpopularity in the country."

Yet the Davis Administration, grappling with crises that never ended and trying to surmount difficulties that were often insuperable, had gained in strength, and showed commendable ability, courage, and devotion. With all his faults and shortcomings—his physical frailty, his hypersensitive temperament, his tactlessness, his want of eloquence and magnetism—the President himself showed an energy, determination, and administrative dispatch that proved him the best leader the South could have found. He gave his principal attention to military affairs, and dealt with them capably. His problem here was very different from Lincoln's. The South did magnificently with its Eastern commanders and badly with its Western; the North did splendidly with Grant, Sherman, and Thomas in the West, but poorly in the East. This fact should be remembered in appraising the familiar criticism of Davis as neglectful of the Western theatre. A more valid charge was that he sometimes failed to protect his Cabinet members properly from attacks in Congress—but so did Lincoln; neither could do the impossible. The State Department had passed in the summer of 1861 from the sulky, intractable Robert Toombs to the sane, coolheaded R. M. T. Hunter, who in March, 1862, gave way to the brilliant Judah P. Benjamin— each change being for the better. In the War Department the highminded but feeble Leroy P. Walker, who lacked administrative capacity, had been ousted by Davis in September, 1861. After a brief interim service by Benjamin, his place was taken by George Wythe Randolph, grandson of Jefferson, who deserves credit for his stern attempts to enforce conscription in the face of State Rights opposition. Randolph was to hold office until the fall of 1862, when in November James A. Seddon would succeed. Stephen R. Mallory in the Navy Department, and Christopher G. Memminger in the Treasury, wrestled heroically with impossibilities.

The new Confederate Congress, an abler body than the old, showed less resolution than the critical situation demanded, but it did pass a series of stern acts. The most important was the draft law of April 16, 1862, a more Spartan measure than any other English-speaking land had ever enacted. Though Congress immediately weakened it by allowing many exemptions, it was a bolder law than the North dared make for nearly another year, or than Britain was able to put on her statute books until deep in the First World War. It withdrew every white male between 18 and 35 from State jurisdiction, placing him at the disposal of the President as commander-in-

2 Kean, MS Diary, July 27, 1863, Univ. of Va. Lib.; Pollard, *Lost Cause*, 215 ff.

chief, and extended all short-term enlistments by two years or, if less, the duration. It established in every State a training camp with a national commandant to take charge of organizing and instructing the new levies. All this awakened the wrath of State Rights men, so that Governor Joseph E. Brown was soon serving notice on Davis that the Georgians "will refuse to yield their sovereignty to usurpation." [3] Another drastic measure passed by Congress required the destruction of all cotton and tobacco likely to fall into Union hands.

The loss of Roanoke Island and subsequent capture of New Bern and Fort Macon, all on the North Carolina coast, were staggering blows to the South. Late in 1861 the Rhode Island brigadier Ambrose E. Burnside, a West Point graduate who had gone into arms manufacture, and was best known for the breech-loading rifled carbine he had devised, proposed to McClellan a plan for seizing historic Roanoke, the site of Raleigh's lost colony. It was accepted, and he was made head of the expedition early in the new year.

The South should have been ready to meet him, for the island, as its defender Henry A. Wise declared, was the key to the rear defenses of Norfolk, and unlocked Albermarle and Currituck Sounds with their half dozen rivers reaching into coastal Virginia and Carolina. But with McClellan about to launch his thunderbolt, Judah P. Benjamin in the War Department protested that he could furnish neither troops nor cannon powder. He refused even to order Benjamin Huger, who had 13,000 men at or near Norfolk, to reinforce Wise's little garrison of 2,500 on Roanoke. The consequence was that when Burnside's expedition steamed inside Hatteras Inlet and reached the southern tip of Roanoke Island on February 7, it went through Confederate defenses like a battering ram through pasteboard. The 20 Union gunboats with their 64 guns brushed away the 7 rickety Confederate vessels of only one gun each; the 13,000 Federal troops jamming the transports smashed the shore defenses, and took all Wise's force prisoners. That general made his escape, declaring that Roanoke had fallen because Benjamin had provided "Nothing! Nothing! Nothing!" [4]

Burnside at once directed his expedition against the useful little port of New Bern. Undergoing more fatigue from bottomless roads than peril from Confederate troops, he quickly took the town with guns, stores, and prisoners. Control of the entire North Carolina coast was now within grasp of the Yankees, and they achieved it when a Union attack on April 25 reduced Fort Macon at the entrance of Beaufort Harbor. This opened one of the best anchorages of the South to Union vessels. The occupation of the coast

3 O. R., IV, ii, 131.
4 Wise, *End of an Era*, Ch. XII; Shelby Foote, *Civil War*, 227–235.

brought large numbers of slaves flocking into the national lines. While these losses, coinciding with Donelson, shook the whole Confederacy, naturally Virginia showed special bitterness. As a public funeral was held in Richmond for Wise's brilliant young son Jennings, killed on Roanoke,[5] spokesmen for the State accused the Confederacy of sacrificing its interests, and demanded an investigation of Secretary Benjamin. He had blundered in underrating the Union peril, and although he had shown an industry and organizing capacity from which his successors profited, Davis had to transfer him, as we have seen, to the State Department. Actually the largest responsibility for the Confederate disaster rested upon the inert Huger.[6]

The North rejoiced over these spectacular gains, which by outflanking Norfolk helped force its evacuation on May 10. Stanton devised a quick plan for an amphibious attack on that city; he, Lincoln, Chase, and Egbert L. Viele descended the Potomac to put it into effect; and after running the perils of seasickness and sharpshooters, the President had the satisfaction of seeing the force they landed make an almost bloodless conquest of the port. "Every blow tells fearfully against the rebellion," exulted Greeley, adding: "It now requires no very far-reaching prophet to predict the end of the struggle." [7] The capture of Norfolk had the effect of gaining full and free entry for the Union forces into the James River, which they could ascend to the defences of Richmond. It was an exciting little operation—the only one in our history personally supervised by the President of the United States as commander-in-chief.

[I]

In Washington, meanwhile, Lincoln urged the borderland to agree to his project for compensated emancipation. From Delaware to Missouri the outlook for acceptance was dubious. Much of the inarticulate laboring population was hostile; white workers felt a deep antipathy toward Negro competitors, and the entry of colored hands into Baltimore shipyards as

5 A Norfolk correspondent of the Richmond *Dispatch* gives us a pathetic glimpse of Wise's grief: "Last night, when the steamer arrived at Currituck, Gen. Wise directed that the coffin containing the remains of his son should be opened. Then, I learn from those who were present, the old hero bent over the body of his son, on whose pale face the full moon threw its light, kissed the pale brow many times, and exclaimed in an agony of emotion, 'Oh, my brave boy, you have died for me, you have died for me.'" Quoted in Phila. *Evening Journal*, March 4, 1862.

6 R. W. Patrick, *President Davis and His Cabinet*, 162–183; R. D. Meade, *Benjamin*, 219–230; Jones, *Rebel War Clerk*, I, 118.

7 N. Y. *Tribune*, May 23, 1862; Viele, "A Trip With Lincoln. . . . ," Scribner's, XVI (Oct., 1878), 813–822, writes that Stanton felt such bitter prejudice against McClellan he could not bear to hear his name mentioned.

caulkers had recently caused a bitter strike. Most conservatives also remained adamant, asserting that discussion of emancipation would arouse public resentment, impair property values, and hinder the Union cause. The best policy, said Senator Saulsbury of Delaware, would be to assure citizens of all loyal States that property and business would be protected; the worst policy would be to nourish the incendiarism of abolitionists in slaveholding areas.[8]

Yet as Lincoln was not the man to bring forward his scheme without solid prior assurances of support, no little approbation also came from the border zone. First and last, he had talked with a good many slaveholders, some of whom had gladly endorsed the plan. When the first flurry of dismay died away, it was evident that many plain citizens stood with him. In Kentucky the eastern mountain folk were reinforced by bluegrass moderates who had been critical of slavery since the days of Henry Clay. The yeomanry of western Maryland took the same stand. In Delaware half of the citizens were on Lincoln's side. As for Missouri, all sensible men knew that emancipation in some form would soon be adopted in that State.

Indeed, a hasty observer might have wondered that Lincoln's plan was not immediately victorious. What had the borderland to lose? The novelist Trollope, after visiting Missouri, pronounced slavery so unpopular there that it would soon die out. As he wrote, even conservative slaveowners recognized that their property was of dubious value, prone to run away at the first opportunity, for Negroes dribbled into Kansas, Iowa, and Illinois by thousands. Missouri stood in a happy position, with a problem much simpler than that in the cotton kingdom, for she had only to get rid of slavery; she did not need to worry about a substitute labor system, nor would her 115,000 slaves, which were only about a tenth of the population, offer any complex problem of race adjustment. This spring some Missourians formed a powerful Emancipation Society.[9]

To Marylanders, who seemed about equally divided, antislavery editors appealed with pragmatic arguments. "We advise the people to take the money if they can get it," declared the Cecil County *Whig*, "for their negroes are running away as fast as they can. All of the slaveholders we have heard speak of the project are in favor of it." In Baltimore the *American* crisply declared: "The revolution has commenced, and must go on." [10]

While discussion thus raged in the borderland, Congress was abolishing

8 N. Y. *Evening Post*, April 2, 1862, for Maryland; *Cong. Globe*, 37th Cong., 2d Sess., 1357, 1358.
9 Trollope, *Travels*, II, 24 (1862 edition). See the excellent summary of border opinion in N. Y. *Evg. Post*, May 16, 1862.
10 All quotations are from the N. Y. *Evg. Post* article.

slavery in the Territories and the District of Columbia. Inasmuch as Republicans held that the natural condition of the Territories was one of freedom, the first measure had only a limited significance. The more important District bill, introduced by Henry Wilson early in the session, appropriated a million dollars to compensate slaveholders, the total sum paid not to exceed an average of $300. Slavery was a dying institution in the District, where in 1860 only 2 per cent of the white residents owned the 3,185 slaves (a drop of 500 in the decade), with a total value of two millions at most. A brisk antislavery agitation had enlisted many of the new politicians, contractors, lobbyists, and reformers who had swarmed into the capital. Within Washington most citizens realized that slavery was doomed and did not regret its passing.

In the acrid debate on the District bill Congressional radicals treated emancipation as a matter of fundamental right and Christian duty. "What God and Nature decree," blazed Sumner, "Rebellion cannot arrest." Other advocates declared that emancipation was an experiment, and the District was a good place to test it. Certain border members, however, took the stubborn stand expected. The venerable Crittenden stigmatized emancipation as inexpedient, unconstitutional, a threat to border institutions, and potentially a major impediment to restoration of the Union. Senator Garrett Davis tried to hamstring the bill by an amendment making foreign colonization of freedmen mandatory. After much oratory, moderate Republicans finally effected a compromise agreement that the released slaves might be colonized in Liberia, Haiti, or other places with their own consent. In the House, Thaddeus Stevens forced emancipation to a vote by ruthless tactics. The majority was more than two-thirds in each chamber, and it was significant of changing public sentiment that among 38 Democrats from free States, only 21 voted *No.*

When the measure reached Lincoln's desk April 14, some doubt existed whether he would sign it. His stand on the principle was of course clear, for as a Congressman in 1849 he had offered his own plan of District emancipation. He knew, however, of the feeling in the Border States that $300 was too low, that the price should be fixed by the courts and not by Congress, and that Maryland's consent should have been obtained; and he was above all anxious that the measure should not jeopardize his larger plan. For two days he kept the bill on his desk, while Sumner told him reproachfully that he was "the largest slaveholder in the country." Then on the 16th he signed it, assuring Congress that he had never doubted its constitutionality nor wavered in his wish to see Washington cleansed of the blot; but he retained his doubts about some details, and by recommendations for supplementary legislation showed that he was determined to assert his leadership in this field.[11]

"I am gratified," he noted, "that the two principles of compensation, and colonization, are both recognized, and practically applied in the act." Full civil rights, except that of jury service, were almost immediately granted all Negroes.[12]

The formal abolition of slavery in the Territories by the Lovejoy bill carried no compensation, for it was Republican doctrine that no valid title to slave property had ever existed there. This measure passed the House 85 to 50 by nearly a straight party vote, Republicans for it, Democrats and border men against it.[13] Conservative members of Congress, much alarmed by the rising tide of emancipationist feeling, held the first of two meetings in the House on May 10, with Crittenden presiding, S. S. Cox as secretary, and Garrett Davis a prominent speaker, in a hopeless effort to stem the swift-running current. Here, too, was a front on which most Northerners could feel that progress was being made.

[II]

As Lincoln was trying to move the Border States, as Grant was recovering from Shiloh, and McClellan was looking beyond Williamsburg toward Richmond, the navy was dealing the Confederacy the heaviest blow of all. When the previous November S. F. DuPont drove the Confederate garrisons out of the two forts protecting Port Royal on the South Carolina coast, Union leaders had realized that greater prizes might be taken in the same way. On November 15 a conference under Lincoln had decided to make the effort to seize New Orleans.

With this decision, the last of the half dozen greatest fighters of the war stepped upon the stage—David Glasgow Farragut.[14] Gideon Welles, Gustavus V. Fox, and Montgomery Blair were primarily responsible for selecting him to take command. During the Mexican War, Welles as head of a Navy

11 For summaries of the debate on the bill see Blaine, *Twenty Years*, I, 369, 370, and *Ann. Cyc.*, 1862, pp. 333-344. The N. Y. *Tribune*, April 16, 1862, carried an illuminating article, "Slavery in the District."

12 *Works*, V, 192; W. B. Bryan, *Hist. Nat. Capital*, 513, 516, 521-523; *National Intelligencer*, April 5, 12, 1862.

13 N. Y. *Tribune*, May 13, 1862.

14 The other five were Lee, Stonewall Jackson, Grant, Sherman, and Thomas. Farragut alone in this group was not of pure British ancestry. His father was a Spaniard, born under the British flag in Minorca in 1755; his mother a North Carolinian, Elizabeth Shine. He had passed his early boyhood in New Orleans and both his marriages were to Virginians, but he never hesitated in choosing the Northern side.

Department bureau had been present when an officer laid before Secretary Bancroft a plan for seizing the castle St. Juan d'Ulloa at Veracruz. Struck by its system and daring, he took pains to learn that the author was named Farragut. Indeed, boldness, decision, and ability to plan were among Farragut's primary traits. This Tennessee-born officer was now sixty, and since entering the navy in 1810 as midshipman had found scant opportunity to show his talents. While peace reigned he was a dignified gentleman, thoroughly alert but conspicuous for his serenity and cheerful talkativeness; once the bugle sounded he was an aroused lion. His spare, erect figure, his intent, determined bearing, at all times revealed the underlying force of his strong personality and dynamic temperament, and in action he could be overwhelming.

Like Grant, Farragut was made eminent by force of character rather than of intellect. Without brilliance, eloquence, or marked originality, he had three other qualities which rendered him a leader of power. He was intensely combative, always eager to attack; he was a stern disciplinarian, who made his subordinates see that every weapon was ready for action, every precaution taken, every sailor vigilant; and true to his motto of "Audacity, still more audacity, always audacity," he was fearless in seizing any opening. He kept constantly busy, made decisions quickly, and enforced them with a natural port of command. All the old tars recognized his fighting qualities. A veteran quartermaster urged that the government pick him for the Gulf Squadron: "If Davy Farragut came down thar, it wouldn't be long till the fur was flying."

Yet with all his driving power, his natural tact and courtesy enabled him to inspire his fleet as well as control it. It was his rule to familiarize himself with the duties of all his officers so that he could understand their special problems. His large brow, covered with curling black hair, his long face, keen hazel eyes, and tremendous jaw made him look the leader he was— "Old Heart of Oak"; but his face usually bore a genial smile. A man of great sensitiveness, himself easily hurt, he was considerate of the feelings of others; a simple-hearted Christian, who liked to hear his wife or flag-lieutenant read the Bible, he had a keen sense of justice. His pride in the service made him emphasize prolonged training: "You can no more make a sailor out of a land-lubber by dressing him up in sea-toggery and putting a commission in his pocket than you could make a shoemaker of him by filling him up with sherry cobblers." He was as devoid of mannerisms, guile, or vanity as Grant, and like Grant he had but one passion in war—to find the enemy, attack him, and hold on until victory was won.[15]

15 See C. L. Lewis, *Farragut, passim;* W. T. Meredith in *Battles and Leaders,* II, 70 ff.; W. S. Schley, *Forty-five Years Under the Old Flag,* 50 ff.; Stolzman, *Stormy Ben Butler,*

Though the strategic move against New Orleans was as obvious as that against Donelson, it was almost as tardily grasped. At first, the whole hope of seizing the city had rested on a combined army and gunboat expedition from Cairo. But in June, 1861, Commander D. D. Porter of the *Powhatan*, blockading the mouth of the Mississippi, had conceived the idea of a thrust *up* the river. Late that summer the Navy Department hammered out a definite scheme. Gustavus V. Fox, familiar with the lower Mississippi, believed that warships could pass the two forts below New Orleans, Jackson and St. Philip, without military assistance, and after Port Royal he converted the dubious Lincoln. McClellan agreed to the effort once he was assured that only about 10,000 troops would be needed—that the fleet would *take* the city and the troops simply hold it. Work then started in November on a tripartite expedition embracing a naval squadron, a mortar-boat flotilla under Commander Porter, and a small infantry force. Near the end of the year troops under Ben Butler were designated to go to Ship Island in the Gulf. Stanton sped the effort as soon as he took office.

When informed of his appointment, Farragut had flushed with elation. With even two-thirds of the forces proposed, he assured Fox, he would take New Orleans and the whole Confederate navy to boot! From that moment he acted with characteristic energy. The prevailing belief was that well-armed shore works could defeat wooden ships, as at Sebastopol; but he was confident that if the navy moved speedily, he could push his squadron past the forts below New Orleans and any other defenses the Confederates could make ready. Though Welles had ordered the expedition to *reduce* the defenses, Farragut determined upon the sounder plan of pushing past them, capturing New Orleans while it was still practically undefended, and leaving the forts below to wither upon the vine. Porter, who had personally explained to Gideon Welles and Lincoln his plans for taking the city, was equally elated. This black-bearded sea-dog, now nearly fifty, who had made his first cruise with his famous naval father, David Porter of War of 1812 renown, at the age of ten, and who had fought at Veracruz, was as combative as his chief. With high approval, he had heard Lincoln tell Welles a characteristic anecdote about an Illinois farmer and his shotgun—a story with a point: "Now, Mr. Secretary, the navy has been hunting pet rabbits long enough; suppose you send them after skunks." Behind Porter's heavy beard and weatherbeaten countenance lurked a spirit fiery, determined, optimistic, and erratic. Farragut would

---

57 ff. Few Civil War leaders had Farragut's breadth of interests, embracing art, literature, science, religion, and natural history; see the dedication in H. H. Brownell's *War Lyrics and Other Poems*. His letters in the *Correspondence of G. V. Fox*, I, 297-353, well express his personality.

gladly have left the mortar-boats behind, but the energy with which Porter had pushed his plans made their inclusion necessary.

Once more the naval forces demonstrated the value of that careful planning and preparation which the military arm too often neglected. Sailing from Hampton Roads in his trim flagship *Hartford* on February 2, 1862, Farragut reached Ship Island on the 20th, and took command of the blockading squadron on the Gulf Coast. Other vessels rapidly arrived until his force included 17 ships of 154 guns, 4 of them splendid new additions to the navy. Porter commanded a supplementary force of 20 schooners carrying one 13-inch mortar apiece, and 6 gunboats. Late in March the heavy ships were gotten across the bar at Southwest Pass into the Mississippi, where they joined Porter's command, which had entered from Pass à l'Outre.[16]

Farragut made certain of ample ammunition, drilled his crews interminably, and perfected their marksmanship. He neglected no detail in readying the fleet for battle. All spars and rigging that could be spared were stripped down, hulls were smeared with river mud to reduce their visibility, and decks were painted white to facilitate night work. All seagoing gear was sent ashore, even chronometers being temporarily discarded. Every aperture that could show light was darkened. When Porter brought his mortar boats into position near the riverbanks just below the two forts he carried camouflage a step further by dressing the masts with bushes to imitate trees.

[III]

Coast Survey officers piloted the fleet up its winding reaches to Forts Jackson and St. Philip, where on April 16 it anchored just below the point chosen for Porter's bombardment. At ten on the morning of the 18th the mortar boats opened a fire that continued until nightfall on the 23rd. They were not much more than platforms for their big black kettlelike pieces, one to each boat. The mortars let go with a terrific blast of flame and smoke, through which the bomb could be seen rising in a graceful parabola. Altogether, 7,500 bombs and shells were fired at the forts in these six days, some bursting in air with a flash and roar, some raising a heavy splash of brown water in the marshes, and some exploding in the rebel works amid flying debris. But beyond burning the wooden casemates, dismounting four guns, and injuring eleven carriages, the bombardment accomplished so little that

16 The beginnings of the New Orleans expedition are discussed by Montgomery Blair in the *United Service Magazine*, IV (Jan., 1881), 33–41; by Gideon Welles in the *Galaxy*, XII (Nov.-Dec., 1871), 669–683, 817–832, and in his *Diary*, I, 60, 61; and by Lewis, *Farragut*, II, 5 ff. See also Mahan, *The Gulf and Inland Waters*, 54–59. Porter's garrulous *Incidents and Anecdotes of the Civil War*, 63–81, is interesting but sometimes undependable.

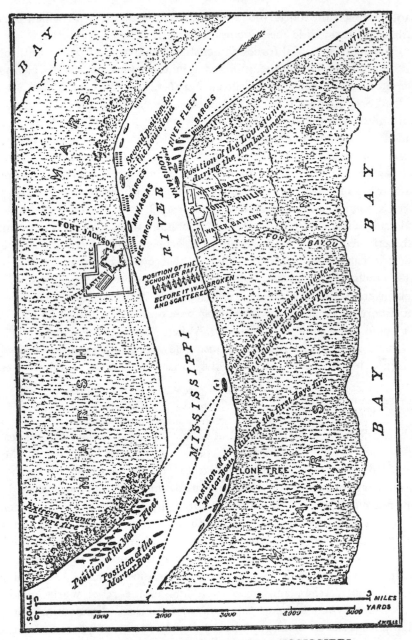

THE DEFENSES OF THE MISSISSIPPI

Ben Butler termed it superbly useless. Gustavus V. Fox suspected later that Porter's squadron had actually been advantageous to the enemy in giving them time to augment their defenses.[17]

Fortunately for the expedition, victory did not depend on smashing the forts. As Farragut was intent on passing them, the greatest potential danger lay in the naval vessels which Confederate leaders had made a tardy, ill-coordinated effort to muster at the river barrier. Fortunately for the Union, both the naval and military auxiliaries were weak. In all their work of defense the Southerners had been hampered by poverty, disorganization, lack of skilled engineers and craftsmen, friction between State authorities and Richmond, and want of foresight.[18] Most of the perhaps 150 guns which the forts mounted were too small to be effective, many being mere twenty-four-pounders. The heavy boom stretched across the river was easily broken. Men of the *Itasca* on the night of the 20th made fast to the mooring hulk directly under Fort Jackson, and with sledgehammers and chisels intrepidly cut the chain, so that the hulk was swept down against the bank. The current rapidly enlarged the breach until the river was partially free.

On the evening of April 23 the Union ships took position for their effort, "What do you estimate our casualties will be?" Farragut asked his clerk. "We shall lose one hundred," was the answer. Startled by the low estimate, Farragut rejoined sadly: "I wish I could think so."

The risks might well have daunted him. To breast the current of three and a half miles an hour, run the gantlet of fire rafts, forts, and ships, and then encounter batteries of unknown strength above, seemed a foolhardy venture to some of his men. But the commander was serenely confident. At one o'clock on the morning of the 24th, officers quietly awoke the crews, an hour later two red lanterns on the flagship signaled anchors aweigh, and before three the advance division was moving upstream. Farragut clambered into the rigging of the *Hartford* to watch the action. At 3:40 St. Philip opened fire, and soon the guns of both forts enveloped the vessels with bursting shells and low-hanging smoke, but he leaned against the shrouds as calmly as if watching a beautiful sunrise.[19]

17 Porter in *Battles and Leaders*, II, 22–54, describes the bombardment as highly effective; Butler in his *Book*, 358, and C. L. Lewis in *Farragut*, II, 44–54, support Fox's view.

18 General Bragg had written Governor Moore from Pensacola when Lovell was appointed: "The command at New Orleans was rightly mine. I feel myself degraded by the action of the government and shall take care that they know my sentiments. I am not surprised at the President, who, in his feeble condition, is entirely under the control of a miserable *petticoat* government as tyrannical as Lincoln's despotism. But from Benjamin I expected better things." Later he could thank his stars that he had not been placed in so precarious a situation. Oct 31, 1861, Moore Papers, LSU Archives.

19 Later, yielding to his officers, Farragut returned to the poop deck.

For an hour and a half, as the Union ships forged upstream, the most exciting panorama of the war unrolled itself. The great turgid river, black and swollen, stretching in places so far inland that Fort St. Philip looked as if it had gone to sea; the two lines of Farragut's divisions, lighted up by fire rafts, shells bursting over ships and forts, and the lightning of their own guns; the *Richmond* blazing, heavily hit, in midstream; the forts bellowing in cross fire at each other, the flame of their guns reddening the smoke clouds of their previous discharges; the hissing round shot plunging into the water; far beyond the bend in the rear the red shimmer of the mortar boats, and high in the velvet sky the blazing crisscross of their bombs—it was a superb spectacle. A square mile of water seemed in conflagration.

One Confederate ship placed at the forts, the *Governor Moore*, fought valiantly until she sank the Union vessel *Varuna*. A well-aimed shot from Fort Jackson hit the boiler of the *Itasca* and disabled her. When the *Hartford* grounded, the Confederates immediately pushed a fire raft against her side, and flames leaped halfway to the mizzen tops. For a second Farragut thought his flagship doomed. "My God, is it to end this way?" he exclaimed. As some sailors flinched, he shouted: "There's a hotter fire than that for those who don't do their duty!" Then his quick-witted clerk uncapped three thirteen-inch shells, rolled them over the side upon the burning raft, and blew it apart. The *Hartford* backed off and continued on her way. Meanwhile the side-wheeler *Mississippi*, piloted by young George Dewey, sustained a hard blow from a Confederate ram, but went on. So did the *Cayuga*, hit forty-two times.[20]

The issue was quickly decided. The battle had but fairly opened, later wrote a Confederate naval officer, before the Union ships were standing up-stream—"and the Uncle Sam of my earlier days had the key to the valley of the Mississippi again safely in his pocket." With casualties of only 37 slain and 149 wounded, Farragut's main fleet swept up the river and anchored at quarantine, seven miles above the forts, for breakfast. Before ten that morning New Orleans learned that the warships had run the gantlet. Business houses clapped their doors shut, steamboats puffed northward to safety, churchbells rang a summons to all military organizations, and dejected troops prepared to evacuate the city with their supplies. Before noon the cloudy skies were lighted by blazing stores of cotton and tobacco. The people, still heartsick over the long daily lists of men dying from their wounds at Shiloh, were in despair, and under a dismal rain, some joined in a stampede to the country.

---

20 The Confederates had a half dozen so-called rams, wooden tugboats with reinforced stems, at the first bend above the forts; they displaced only 900 tons and were so weak that some sensibly ran away.

That morning seventeen-year-old George W. Cable, standing in the doorway of the Canal Street store which his employers had abandoned to his charge, saw the masts of a Confederate vessel in the river tipping, sinking, and finally disappearing. He ran to the levee. About him the riffraff of the city were staving in boxes of sugar and rice, and barrels of molasses. "Are the Yankee ships in sight?" he asked a bystander. A gesture was the reply, and Cable saw their mast tops across the wide riverbend where they were silencing the Chalmette batteries. The firing soon ended, and then

Ah, me! I see them now as they come slowly round Slaughterhouse Point into full view, silent, grim, and terrible; black with men, heavy with deadly portent; the long-banished Stars and Stripes flying against the frowning sky. Oh, for the *Mississippi!* the *Mississippi!* Just then she came down upon them. But how? Drifting helplessly, a mass of flames.

And presently two officers, walking abreast, unguarded, impassive, never frowning nor flinching while a yelling mob cursed them and threatened them with knives and pistols, strode along Common Street to City Hall to demand the surrender. The mayor and council, advised by that fiery Southern leader Pierre Soulé, refused to lower the State flag over the city hall; whereupon a naval detachment, protected from the angry crowd by shotted cannon, did it. A young man named William B. Mumford who recklessly assisted in hauling down a United States flag raised over the mint was in due course executed for the offense. Farragut immediately handed the custody of the city over to Ben Butler and his 15,000 troops; and that general, making his headquarters at the St. Charles Hotel, agreed with the municipal authorities that they should retain power in all matters unconnected with military affairs. The transfer of the city to the Union, though a source of intense chagrin and resentment to most of the high-spirited population, was therefore accompanied with less friction than might have been anticipated.[21]

The Confederacy had lost its greatest city with scarcely a real battle. The main reasons, apart from confusion, myopia, and tardiness in high Southern circles—"too little and too late"—lay in better Northern power and leadership. Superior Northern engineering, constructive skill, and well-mobilized resources made the Union naval forces irresistible. The disparity of power was symbolized by the contrast between the best Confederate ship, the hastily converted *Manassas*, and Farragut's *Hartford*. The one excited derision; the other

---

21 *Battles and Leaders*, II, 20. The builders of the ironclad *Mississippi*, in which the Louisianians had placed such faith, Nelson and Asa F. Tift of Florida, failed to complete it in time because they were ignorant of the foundries, machine shops, lumber yards, and labor sources of the area. H. A. Trexler, "The Confed. Navy Dept. and the Fall of New Orleans," *Southwest Review*, XIX (Autumn, 1933), 88-102. When the Tifts went to Vicksburg they were almost lynched by a mob.

was an almost new, finely finished Boston-built vessel of 2,900 tons, 225 feet in length, 44 feet in beam, and 16 to 17 feet in draft. The *Manassas*, proudly called a ram, was actually a tiny tugboat roofed over with a half-inch of iron, and armed with a 32-pound carronade of antique vintage pointing straight ahead. She looked like a hump of a black whale with a smokestack in its center, and shot went through her thin sides as through paper. The *Hartford*, armed with twenty-five guns, including 9-inch Dahlgren shell pieces and three rifled 30-pounders, had been built to match the best British warships in her wooden category. Her engines made eight knots, while sails brought her speed to a maximum of thirteen or more. All the Confederate ships were badly officered and manned, for Southerners had shown little taste for the sea. The *Hartford*, on the other hand, had a superb crew and experienced officers, led by one of the great admirals of history.[22]

For Farragut's leadership was the other primary element in the victory. His care in preparations, skill in fleet management, and courage in battle served his decision that the best strategy was to run past the forts. He knew that the city would be helpless under his guns. On the Confederate side Commodore George N. Hollins, who knew the New Orleans situation thoroughly and wished to launch a naval attack on Farragut's fleet below the forts, was transferred just as his plans neared maturity, and his place given to Captain John K. Mitchell, who had never commanded on the Mississippi before. Hollins might have done much better. After the city was lost, Louisianians complained bitterly that two strangers, Lovell and Mitchell, had held its fate in their untried hands. The remark of one Southern historian that "as a military leader Lovell was a fine horseman" is hardly too scornful. And while Farragut gripped the reins of his force tightly, the Confederate command had been hopelessly divided. Lovell's 8,000 or 9,000 troops, who would have been far more useful with Johnston at Shiloh, were disconnected from the river forces; each fort had its own commander; and each ship fought without reference to the other ships or the forts. Unified plans under an energetic unified leadership might well have saved the city to the South.[23]

News of the victory had to reach the North through the Confederacy. People had passed a quiet Sunday on April 27, 1862, for little of note seemed to be occurring. Union blockaders had captured some Confederate correspondence from the ship *Calhoun*, but even an impudent letter from T. Butler King of Georgia to Lord John Russell, suggesting a man to be the first British minister to the Confederacy, aroused no great interest. Next morning, how-

22 Lewis, *Farragut*, II, 15, 16; Naval O. R., II, i, 99.
23 *Corr. Between the War Dept., and Gen. Lovell; Corr. Between the President, War Dept., and Gov. T. O. Moore*, Richmond, 1863; Harold Sinclair, *Port of New Orleans*, 227-241; Alcée Fortier, *Hist. La.*, IV, 13-20.

ever, the sudden shouts of newsboys in Northern streets brought citizens to their doors. They read flaring headlines: "Fall of New Orleans." Flags began fluttering from every staff, steeple, and window. Crowds gathered in every square. Mobile had telegraphed Richmond that on the afternoon of April 25 all communication with New Orleans had ceased, and the news had rapidly percolated from Confederate picket lines into Northern camps.

With New Orleans the South lost a great deal of wealth, manpower, and manufacturing capacity, for its energetic people were already making an impressive amount of war material. It had opened machine shops and iron foundries, and had pressed its shipbuilding plans. Still more important was the fact that the lower segment of the Mississippi was gone. Because the river was the greatest single communication line tying the republic together—a bond which had kept alive, if latent, a strong Union feeling in New Orleans itself—a special moral value attached to its mastery. Thomas Hart Benton had called the Mississippi–Missouri–Ohio river system *Mare Nostrum,* our sea; to change the image, it had been the backbone of the nation. Men reared on its Northern waters now felt a new confidence. The capture of its lower extremity gave the Western armies both heart and help in the stubborn struggle for the remaining river strongholds, Port Hudson and Vicksburg, while it lessened the disloyal sentiment that smoldered under the surface in parts of Illinois, Indiana, and Ohio.

And the 145,000 proud people of New Orleans, conscious of their rich history and cultural heritage, now entered upon their most tragic years. A swarm of profiteers flocked in, with Ben Butler's approval and perhaps in some instances his secret and indirect partnership, to seize the many opportunities for making a fortune. Turpentine was $3 a barrel in New Orleans and $38 in New York; flour was $6 a barrel in New York and $25 in New Orleans; many other commodities showed a comparable spread in prices. The greedy activities of some Yankee traders, vividly pictured later by the Northern soldier-novelist J. W. DeForest in *Miss Ravenel's Conversion,* became in time one of the most poignant Southern legends. Butler stole no silver spoons, but he protected an unhappy amount of legal plundering of needy people—as well as much quite healthful trade.[24]

One additional river triumph remained to be scored, this time by forces coming down from the north. "Memphis may be taken," a Southern newspaper had said, "for even Saragossa was taken." It fell at the first stroke. A smart action, to be sure, was fought, but the Union won it with astonishingly

24 Butler's autobiography, *Butler's Book,* and James Parton's graphic *General Butler in New Orleans,* defend the general; Robert S. Holzman, *Stormy Ben Butler,* and Thomas E. Dabney, "The Butler Regime in La.," *La. Hist. Quarterly,* XXVII, 487–526 (April, 1944), present a more critical view. Butler's *Private and Official Correspondence,* arranged by Jessie Ames Marshall in five volumes (1917), amply proves his energy and decision.

little loss. On June 6 a flotilla of gunboats under Flag-Officer C. H. Davis came into collision, off the city, with the river fleet of the Confederates, the Southerners having the larger number of ships but weaker array of guns. When the engagement had raged for a half hour in full view of thousands of spectators on the Memphis shore, two of the rams which Charles Ellet had persuaded Secretary Welles to let him prepare and which lay upstream heard the rumble of the fray. Ellet on the *Queen of the West* waved his hat to his son on the *Monarch* and shouted: "The guns of the enemy! Round out and follow me! Now is our chance!" Churning through the line of Union gunboats, the two rams delivered an effective assault, instantly putting two enemy ships out of action. The running encounter lasted another hour, and carried the contending vessels ten miles below the city; when it ended, seven of the eight Confederate ships were sunk, aground, or captured—"totally destroyed," said the Southern commander Jeff Thompson.[25]

The battle was a memorable triumph for the river navy, a deep humiliation to the Tennesseeans, and a stroke pregnant with large economic results. Memphis had been a busy center of the sugar and cotton trade, and the metropolis of a wealthy slaveholding section. Under the Confederate regime it was as dead as Herculaneum. But immediately after the Union occupation an influx of merchants from Chicago, St. Louis, and Cincinnati crammed the hotels, the sound of saw and hammer filled the air, and packet boats lined the wharves to discharge goods and pick up Southern products. Cotton buyers, licensed and unlicensed, scattered into the interior as far as Forrest's cavalry would let them, and a brisk contraband traffic in medicines, percussion caps, shoes, and clothing began to nourish the Southern army. The gambling dens, saloons, and bawdy houses for which Memphis had been famous once more sprang to life.[26]

"On Tuesday of this week," the correspondent of the London *Daily News* wrote in mid-June, "3,000 bales of cotton, 5,000 full barrels and 3,000 half-barrels of molasses, and 6,000 barrels of sugar, were shipped to the North, and more, it was reported, would follow next day." The first day the post

25 Herbert P. Gambrell, "Rams Vs. Gunboats," *Southwest Review*, XXIII (Oct., 1937), 46–78; A. W. Ellet, "Ellet and his Steam-Rams at Memphis," *Battles and Leaders*, I, 453–459; Henry Walke, "The Western Flotilla," *Ibid.*, 449–452; Naval O. R., I, xxiii, 118–140. Ellet's papers are at the Univ. of Michigan. The only Union man injured in the action, this inventor, constructor, and independent commander of the rams died as his boat reached Cairo June 21.

26 N. Y. *Tribune*, Chicago *Morning Post*, June 11, 1862, *et seq.*; Knox, *Camp-Fire and Cotton-Field*, 179–196; Lew Wallace, *Autobiography*, II, 581–588; Capers, *Biog. of a River Town*, 146–155; Shields McIlwaine, *Memphis*, 124. Zack Chandler estimated the trade at 20 to 30 millions; *Cong. Globe*, 38th Cong., 1st Sess., 3324. One Northern cavalryman records that the colored women "felt loving towards us because they thought we were bringing them freedom, and they wouldn't charge us a cent."

office reopened, a thousand letters were mailed, mostly on business to Northern cities. Memphis swiftly became the chief depot for contraband trade between North and South, within two years sending an estimated $20,000,000 worth of supplies, or more, into the Confederacy. It also became a great and troublesome rallying point for Negro refugees. All in all, for the rest of the war it was probably the most picturesque city on the continent.

[IV]

As Yorktown fell, as the Union won at Williamsburg, and as McClellan on May 8 set his army moving toward Richmond, hopes ran high. It was in this context that Stanton issued the unhappy order to discontinue recruiting. Public sentiment greatly influenced him. Henry Wilson, in a letter in the N. Y. *Herald*, Aug. 8, 1862, explained the discontinuance on the ground that Cameron, Meigs, and the paymaster-general had reported that the Union possessed between 700 and 800 regiments, with at least 700,000 under arms; that hundreds of recruiting stations, supported at great cost, were doing little to fill the hundred or more partially organized regiments scattered over the land; *and that the recent victories had created an excessive optimism.* Congress had authorized the raising of 500,000 men for the new army, but it was supposed that the States might have enlisted altogether as many as 750,000, half again the number proposed. Unhappily, as we have seen, Stanton's order to stop recruiting was based on misinformation. When the War Department obtained exact figures on the forces, it learned that they aggregated not more than 500,000 to 550,000. But this was not known in May, when people supposed the armed forces ample for their task.

If now McClellan would but strike the decisive blow! It was a bold plan which he had made for placing a great army at the gates of Richmond, but success depended upon three vital elements: rapidity, strategic skill, and complete mutual confidence between the government and the general. Already, taking a month to seize Yorktown, he had sacrificed valuable time, and opened a door to strategic complications. Would he now show enough skill and energy to win the full trust of Lincoln and Stanton?

The troops who marched from Williamsburg up the peninsula, although it was only forty miles to the battle lines before Richmond, never forgot the experience. McClellan's promise of easy sandy roads and open country stood exposed in all its hollowness.

The weather had a New England fickleness, now lovely May brilliance, now broiling heat, now streaming rain. Two days of hot sun would make the dust intolerable; then downpours would leave the roads bottomless. On narrow ways under lashing sheets some columns took a day to traverse two or three miles. Wagons, ambulances, caissons, and guns filled the road, at times laboring forward, at times bogged down. Drivers lashed and swore, horses and mules plunged, and details of privates with arms slung pushed at the miry wheels, or in lines of thirty or forty tugged at ropes attached to fieldpieces. As the day closed in misty gloom, troops would crawl exhausted into dog-tents and brush shelters. Toiling in this world of mud and water, they thought of their former existence of dry clothes, warm houses, and good food as a Sybaris of luxury. "Yet would not swop!" exclaimed one soldier.

Till they reached the Pamunkey the country they traversed was almost deserted. Many farmers had razed their houses and filled their wells, or let Southern troops do it for them. Hardly a cow, horse, or cart was to be seen. At the few occupied dwellings only women, children, and old men were in evidence. Most of the slaves had been taken inland. Here and there patches of woods had caught fire and burned to piles of smoldering ashes.

But when finally the rear units emerged at the cluster of huts called Cumberland, on the crooked little Pamunkey River five miles from McClellan's base at the old mansion called the White House, they saw a magnificent sight. Covering the plain before them was an army of 80,000 men. By day columns drilled; by night innumerable campfires glowed and twinkled. When on May 15 McClellan held a review, the panoply of marching regiments, glistening cannon, and waving flags impressed every beholder. By May 21 the whole army was fairly in line seven to twelve miles from Richmond, and full of confidence.

For at last the antagonists seemed at close grips, with every prospect favoring the Union. When all of McClellan's force had come up he possessed about 115,000 men, much the largest and best-equipped army ever assembled in the New World. Facing him, Joseph E. Johnston had about 70,000 Confederates, far worse provided. In any battle in the open field McClellan should have a decided advantage. He would lose it only if he mismanaged his forces, or assaulted the enemy within their works, for as Union troops learned later, well-entrenched lines could repel twice their numbers. McClellan's strategy was entirely sound; he had taken a good road to Richmond. Yet he could now see the wisdom of Lincoln's warning that going down the bay instead of advancing through Manassas was only shifting a difficulty, for he would find the same enemy and equal entrenchments at either place. He was confident, however, that he could tempt or compel the enemy to fight outside their works.

Actually, on three battle grounds in the next three weeks McClellan was to have a full opportunity of defeating Johnston or Lee in the open field. He had looked forward to delivering *one* crushing blow. On March 19 he had written Stanton that it was important to make his base on the upper reaches of the York–Pamunkey River as soon as possible, and then "we shall fight a decisive battle between West Point and Richmond." He assured his wife on May 18 that he would close up on the Chickahominy to find out what Secesh was doing: "I think he will fight us there, or between there and Richmond." He kept protesting to Washington, however, that he needed reinforcements—more reinforcements. Under pressure of his entreaties, Lincoln on May 17 ordered McDowell to march down the Fredericksburg–Richmond railway to furnish the needed cooperation, with the vital condition that he should not uncover Washington. McDowell was to begin moving as soon as Shields's division joined him, about May 26. If and when he thus stood at McClellan's side, the Union array would reach 150,000 men, a more than satisfactory strength.

Lincoln by this time comprehended that he had in McClellan a complex psychological problem. He must prod the general into energetic action, yet treat him with sufficient tact not to arouse his latent insubordination. We have noted the crisp rebuke he had sent the general May 1 at Yorktown: "Your call for Parrott guns from Washington alarms me—chiefly because it argues indefinite procrastination. Is anything to be done?" Some days later he got a dispatch from McClellan complaining again of the organization of the army into corps. Already this had cost a thousand lives and a near rout, whined the commander. Lincoln replied bluntly but mildly:

I wish to say a few words privately to you on this subject. I ordered the Army Corps organization not only on the unanimous opinion of the twelve Generals whom you had selected and assigned as Generals of Division, but also on the unanimous opinion of every military man I could get an opinion from, and every modern military book, yourself only excepted. Of course I did not, on my own judgment, pretend to understand the subject. I now think it indispensable for you to know how your struggle against it is received in quarters which we cannot entirely disregard. It is looked upon as merely an effort to pamper one or two pets, and to persecute and degrade their supposed rivals. I have had no word from Sumner, Heintzelman, or Keyes. . . . but I am constantly told that . . . you consult and communicate with nobody but General FitzJohn Porter, and perhaps General Franklin. I do not say these complaints are true or just; but at all events it is proper you should know of their existence.

The corps organization was kept, but Fitz-John Porter and Franklin were advanced on May 18 to the grade of provisional corps commanders. However, in mid-May McClellan was irascibly telegraphing Lincoln again. He could get no replies from Stanton, he grumbled. He had only 80,000 effectives to fight a much larger force, perhaps double his own. He must be reinforced without delay, and to get help he would waive some personal objections he had stated against McDowell. Lincoln could not gainsay McClellan's guess of an enemy force of perhaps 160,000, for McClellan was supposed to know. He could only move McDowell forward to add 41,000 men to the 115,000 men whom, on paper, McClellan already had.

On the Southern side, the necessity of facing this powerful concentration daunted the Confederate leaders. The prospect of a hurried evacuation of Richmond seemed so imminent that preparations were made to ship the military papers and government archives to Columbia, South Carolina. Members of Congress had gone home in late April amid the jeers of the Richmond *Whig* and the laments of the *Examiner*. Now Mrs. Davis, after seeing her husband privately baptized in the Episcopal Church, left with her children for Raleigh. The Treasury gold was packed ready to be loaded aboard a special train. Virginia legislators voted to put the city to the torch rather than surrender it to the Yankees. While rockets by night and the growl of guns by day warned of the near approach of the enemy, officers on leave from the Confederate lines told of seeing Union tents, artillery parks, and wagon trains cover the whole landscape in front of them. The *Merrimac* had been scuttled on May 11, and after that date nobody was sure that gunboats would not suddenly steam up the James, leveling their cannon on the city. The fortifications on Drewry's Bluff might or might not hold.

To make the Confederate position more desperate, many Southern troops were badly disciplined and despondent. In the trenches on the Yorktown line they had suffered from cold, rain, poor food, and bad water. Some had been stricken by malaria. After Williamsburg, clumps of wounded saddened the Richmond streets, and a host of stragglers, mud-bedaubed and exhausted, slept in doorways and sheds. "The men are full of spirits when near the enemy," Johnston wrote Lee on May 9, "but at other times, to avoid restraint, leave their regiments in crowds. To enable us to gather the whole army for battle would require a notice of several days."

The war seemed at its climax. The advances for which Lincoln longed had taken place, and those anaconda pressures on all the fronts which might yet crush every bone of rebellion were growing tighter and more powerful. But people who looked with high hope to the future little realized how swiftly incompetent generalship and ill fortune could change the scene.

5

McClellan Comes a Cropper

HIGH AS the hopes of Lincoln and the North had risen, the crucial tests still lay ahead. With well over half a million men under arms, with New Orleans, Roanoke Island, and Port Royal in Union hands, with powerful armies far up the Tennessee and on the outskirts of Richmond, could Northern leadership use its great opportunities?

The battle of Shiloh, and the immediate sequels in that quarter, seemed for a time to disappear into a dense cloud. For days all kinds of reports about the encounter circulated in New York and other cities; newspaper accounts conflicted, and the War Department was silent as the grave. All that people knew was that the Confederates had been repulsed, but had retired unmolested to their positions at Corinth, and that some Ohio regiments were uttering loud criminations. One Senator complained on April 13 that not a syllable had been communicated officially.[1] Four weeks after the battle Greeley pointed out that no official report had been given the North except the totally inadequate one which Grant had written while the guns were still warm. This omitted the fact of the surprise, understated the losses as merely 1,500 killed and 3,500 wounded, and left the panic, the captures of Union cannon, and other important facts in a fog.[2]

As we have said, the leaders of neither side had much to boast about in Shiloh. No great encounter of the war showed less prevision, science, or imagination. For both armies it had been simply a slugging match, marred by the bad discipline of two large elements, the Union troops who fled and the Confederates who stopped to plunder, and redeemed by splendid heroism. Northern troops blurted out a good deal of truth in their letters home. We were "more than surprised," one officer of the Forty-fifth Illinois wrote; "we

1 Benjamin Shanks of Oregon, April 13, 1862, Barlow Papers.
2 N. Y. *Tribune*, May 6, 1862. According to Phisterer, 213, the Union loss was 13,573, of whom 9,617 were killed or wounded, and 3,956 missing—mainly prisoners; the Confederate loss was 10,699. Greeley correctly declared that nearly all that people knew about the battle they gained from press correspondents, whom Stanton barely tolerated and Sherman treated like vermin. It was time for a reform. "The millions of anxious, aching hearts are not to be lightly trifled with."

were astonished." It is not strange that stories of Grant's intemperance again circulated freely. When Elihu Washburne defended him in the House, Medill of the Chicago *Tribune* wrote that such loyalty was admirable, but that his star seemed sinking, for the Western soldiers condemned him.[3] Grant did himself no credit when he sent Washburne a letter which misrepresented the battle, the subsequent criticism, and the motives of his assailants.[4]

Generals who were so painfully learning their job could not be expected to exhibit signal skill in garnering the fruits of victory. The main lesson of Shiloh, wrote Bragg later, was speed: "never on a battlefield to lose a moment's time, but leaving the killed, wounded, and spoils to those whose special business it was to care for them, to press on with every available man, giving a panic-stricken and defeated foe no time to rally." In saying this he was criticizing Beauregard's action just after Johnston's death in halting the Confederate onslaught; but his words were still more applicable to Grant's failure to pursue. The failure is only slightly palliated by the fact that when Northern troops recovered the battlefield, they had to treat thousands of casualties, reunite regiments and brigades, and restore morale, under conditions still highly chaotic.

The 8,000 wounded were a particularly grave problem. Theoretically, Grant's army had brigade field hospitals and ambulance trains; actually, only regimental medical units were available. Volunteer women nurses labored on the field as fighting raged, tearing up their petticoats or using leaves and grass for bandages. On Tuesday nine-tenths of the wounded still lay where they had fallen, some of them untouched since Sunday. Ambulances brought many to the shelter of tents, but others were dumped in rows outside. The scene about the rough surgical centers was sickening: mangled bodies of dead and dying, amputated limbs in piles, gouts of flesh, and puddles of blood, with a horrible stench. Grant telegraphed for hospital boats, most of which were furnished him by the United States and Western Sanitary Commissions; and a large

3 J. E. Smith, May 16, 1862, to Elihu Washburne, Washburne Papers, LC; Joseph Medill to Washburne, May 24, *Ibid*. W. R. Rowley wrote Washburne from Grant's headquarters April 19 denying the charge of intemperance as an unmitigated slander. Union authorities were sensitive about drunkenness in the army. "At this moment," wrote the N. Y. correspondent of the London *Times* on April 29, "common rumour and the newspapers accuse no less than six of the most prominent men of the country of habitual intoxication." The cheapness of whisky and prevalence of frontier manners had made drink a terrible evil in mid-century America.

4 In this letter of May 14 Grant covered up. He wrote that his critics expected the battlefield "to be maintained, for a whole day, with about 30,000 troops, most of them entirely raw, against 70,000"; actually his army had the advantage of numbers, arms, and natural position. He wrote that "looking back at the past I cannot see for the life of me any important point that could be corrected"; he had not taken obvious and cardinal precautions. He wrote that his critics "may have felt disappointed that they were not permitted to carry off horses, firearms, and other valuable trophies"; his important critics were honest men.

squadron soon evacuated many sufferers to the North. One striking innovation was born of the chaos. Military thinking of the period was antagonistic to large hospitals, for it was supposed that they favored mysterious concentrations of poisonous "effluvia," and all authorities distrusted open-air treatment. But under pressure of necessity Dr. B. J. D. Irwin of Buell's army commandeered enough infantry tents for a roomy field hospital, where casualties could be segregated according to needs, the medical staff could be given specialized functions, and a central administration of drugs, diet, laundry, and other functions would be possible. This, accommodating 2,500 patients, was the first hospital of the war entirely under canvas, and the fresh air made it both comfortable and salubrious.[5]

As the armies sent out their casualty lists, the shock of the battle spread up and down the Mississippi Valley in pulsations of anguish. Tens of thousands of families in the Northwest waited in dread; then as the names of dead, wounded, and missing were published, thousands of homes were prostrated with grief. For the first time the meaning of war struck home. Sorrow struggled with anger when war correspondents reported that on the fifth day after the battle began, untended casualties were still being brought in, and that hundreds had perished needlessly. In the South the shock was still greater. Throughout all the lower Valley the death lists, the return of the blind or limbless, and worst of all, the harrowing silences of those never again seen, knelled the end of the period when war had seemed a romantic experience.

The conflict was becoming implacable. But each side showed a chastened temper, for it had learned at last how dangerous the other could be. An exaggerated sense of this power of the enemy to sting and crush explained the bizarre performance now staged by Halleck. He had arrived at Shiloh with his dislike and distrust of Grant unabated. Taking command of the joint forces of Grant, Buell, and Pope—the armies of the Tennessee, the Ohio, and the Mississippi—he set out three weeks after the battle to march on Corinth. He had only twenty miles to traverse, without high ridges or deep streams, and his well-equipped army outnumbered the wretchedly armed Confederates more than two to one. The question whether Beauregard would venture a battle might have been resolved by a quick thrust or intelligent use of scouts. But Halleck, whose sobriquet should have been Old Pedantry instead of Old Brains, took no chances. He divided his army into a right corps under Thomas, a left corps under Pope, and a center corps under Buell, with McClernand commanding the reserve, and began an elaborate crawl forward. The humiliated Grant,

5 Adams, *Doctors in Blue*, 81, 82; Hannaford, *Story of a Regiment*, 286; N. Y. *Weekly Tribune*, May 10, 1862. The British in the Crimea had seen the death rate in the hospitals drop spectacularly as soon as they were opened to free ventilation, while the French losses in tightly closed wards were appalling.

nominally second in command, he ignored, sending orders directly to the four other subordinates without showing them to him.

Halleck marched his overwhelming force forward at an average rate of a mile a day, entrenching every night. When he had crept within five miles of Corinth he paused to erect double breastworks, put siege guns in position, and take additional precautions. For a week thereafter the ground gained daily was measured in hundreds of yards. He shelled every patch of woods before an advance. On May 30 he prepared for battle—and next day found that Beauregard had completely evacuated Corinth by rail. Halleck had ordered press correspondents ("unauthorized hangers-on") to quit his camps. But one man managed to inform the North from Corinth that the roads had been hard and unobstructed, the town's fortifications worthless, and the noise of the evacuating railroad trains unmistakable. It was clear that the foe had never for a moment intended any resistance.[6] Grant and Sherman agreed that the proper course was to march rapidly on Corinth and storm any works there. "Corinth was conquered at Shiloh," said Grant. But Halleck made Logan entrench to the end, so that his men were actually using shovels while Union cavalry were scouring the deserted Corinth streets. "My men'll never dig another ditch for Halleck except to bury him," exclaimed the wrathful Logan.

Generalship indeed! Halleck had thrown away a month, until the heat of summer shut down on operations. Once in Corinth, instead of using his irresistible concentrated force to seize a key position of the enemy, like Vicksburg, he dissipated it, sending Buell on a slow march toward Chattanooga, Pope in another direction, and Grant to Memphis, while he himself kept a large force inert.[7]

[I]

Equally unhappy was the anticlimax which followed Farragut's victory. Northern elation over the seizure of New Orleans gave birth to clamor for a victorious advance up the Mississippi, and Lincoln, Stanton, and Welles unwisely bowed to it. The river could be partly used, but not held, by naval forces alone. At most points along it, to be sure, warships could drive Confederate troops out of range; but the moment the ships steamed away, the troops would come back. Nothing but a powerful amphibious expedition,

6 Dispatch, April 23, in N. Y. *Weekly Tribune*, May 10, 1862. See also the scornful letters of C. C. Washburne and A. L. Chetlain on Halleck's march in Washburne Papers, LC.

7 William Wood, *Captains of the Civil War*, 105 ff., analyzes this well. For the expulsion of the correspondents and Halleck's combination of arbitrariness and shiftiness in the matter, see J. Cutler Andrews, *The North Reports the Civil War*, 182–188. Reporters for the Chicago *Tribune* and Cincinnati *Commercial* ridiculed the march into Corinth, and the Associated Press told the truth about it.

with enough infantry to capture and hold the principal strategic points on the banks, could accomplish effective results. So long as no Union army was available to co-operate with Farragut in an attack on Vicksburg, any naval attack would prove abortive.

It would have been wiser for the government to send Farragut eastward against Mobile, then still weakly fortified. From the beginning, however, its orders had been that he push upstream: "If the Mississippi expedition from Cairo shall not have descended the river, you will take advantage of the panic to push a strong force up the river to take all their defenses in the rear." This was a relic of Scott's idea that a joint army-navy expedition could rapidly traverse the whole artery. Farragut had hardly taken New Orleans when he was prodded again: "The only anxiety we feel is to know if you have followed up your instructions and pushed a strong force up the river to meet the Western flotilla." With but 1500 troops as a landing force, he had to undertake this preposterous campaign. After capturing Baton Rouge, he steamed on up to Vicksburg, 500 miles from the Gulf, fighting the current, dodging snags, bars, and shore snipers, and running a constant danger of going aground.

The result was inevitably disappointment and loss. When he and the able troop commander with him, General Thomas Williams, reached Vicksburg, they found 30,000 Confederate troops in that fortified town or within a day's march. To throw the small land force ashore would have been to court disaster. With stores running short, for his communications were precarious, Farragut had to return downstream. He arrived in New Orleans with less than a week's provisions, much loss of equipment, and a bad temper. "They will keep us in this river," he grumbled in a private letter home, "till the vessels break down and all the little reputation we have made had evaporated. The Government appears to think that we can do anything. They expect me to navigate the Mississippi nine hundred miles in the face of batteries, ironclad rams, etc.; and yet with all the ironclad vessels they have North they could not get to Norfolk or Richmond." [8]

Once more he was ordered up the river, on the ground that it was imperative to join hands with the upper Mississippi flotilla which Flag-Officer Charles H. Davis was bringing down to Vicksburg. Again he reached that city. With the aid of Porter's mortar boats, he ran past the fortifications on June 28th and joined Davis three days later. There he stayed uselessly waiting until mid-July, while the slow Northern military campaign against Vicksburg was beginning to take shape. When a dangerous ironclad Confederate ram, the *Arkansas*, appeared, he remained still longer in the hope of destroying her. Lying under the Vicksburg bluffs, she survived his forays, only to become

8 Lewis, *Farragut, Our First Admiral*, Chs. IX-XI; Naval O. R., I, xviii. 473 ff.

helpless when her engines failed and to be blown up by her crew. Finally, as the Confederates threatened an attack on Baton Rouge, he returned to the New Orleans area. Three of his gunboats helped to beat off this attack when it took place at the beginning of August. Then, his duty done, Farragut joined the blockading forces in the Gulf; two months of arduous labor had accomplished nothing, for Baton Rouge had immediately to be evacuated.

[II]

If the sequels of Shiloh and New Orleans were a disappointment, so on the political front were the results of Lincoln's effort to deal in a large-minded way with slavery. His appeal to the borderland met in the end a chilly response. We have seen that although Congress passed his resolution for compensated emancipation combined with an effort at colonization, the border members offered an almost solid phalanx of opposition.

Throughout May, throughout June, the months when Lincoln deemed action urgent, most border leaders continued to oppose his plan. The influential Crittenden hung back, while others denounced the measure. One adverse argument was that Congress lacked constitutional authority to spend national funds to compensate slaveholders within selected States. Lincoln's supporters of course replied that such expenditures were justifiable under the war-making power. Opponents also argued that even if Congress did possess the power, it would never exercise it, but after cajoling the States into emancipation, would leave them in the lurch. Was the government about to become a huge Negro-trader? demanded Saulsbury of Delaware incredulously. Above all, border members repudiated the President's proffer as a gross invasion of State sovereignty, and an interference with their domestic institutions. This interpretation did wrong to Lincoln, who intended his plan not as an interference in State affairs, but as a system of cooperation between State and nation, with the States holding the decisive voice. But it appealed to a deep sense of pride.

Behind these superficial arguments lurked the main obstacle, the perplexity of borderland leaders over the problem of post-emancipation adjustment. Like other Southerners, they knew how to manage Negroes as slaves; they did not know how to manage them as freedmen. Certain emotional factors also counted heavily. Abolitionism was detested all along the border, where even moderate men placed it among the virulent causes of the war, and it was easy to give Lincoln's plan a Garrisonian coloration. The President's suggestion that border emancipation was needed to deprive the Confederacy of all hope of gaining the border slave States offended Crittenden, who called it an insult;

Kentucky would never leave the Union, and the South knew it. Crisfield of Maryland believed that unless colonization abroad was total in scope, emancipation would prove inhuman: "We must either keep them as they are, or turn them off to be brutalized, and after a season of degradation and suffering to become extinct." [9] Altogether, a majority of leaders disliked the plan, even if they did not accept Powell's characterization of it as "a pill of arsenic, sugar-coated."

Kentucky first wavered, and then turned back. Its people were attached to the traditions of Virginia and North Carolina; they feared that since one-fifth of the population were slaves the problem of race adjustment would prove fearfully difficult, and they believed that in abandoning State neutrality for the North they had received a moral guarantee of their property. The legislature had declared the previous November that slavery was untouchable save by the States themselves, had demanded Cameron's dismissal for proposing to arm the Negro, and had forbidden the military liberation of any slave. Thus State pride was deeply involved in a firm stand. Lincoln's proposals received no real consideration from half the Kentuckians, who had already made up their minds.[10] Even stout Leslie Combs, the general and legislative leader who had fought secession, was certain that the plan would hinder Federal enlistments and endanger the Union party in elections.

In Missouri the situation was better, for hardly one citizen in fifty had any direct interest in slaves, while the emancipationist trend was clear. Late in the summer the people were to elect a governor, legislature, and Congressmen; emancipation was certain to be the central issue, and unless the legislature adopted a counter plan, the emancipationists would strive to write a liberating clause into the State constitution, without any Federal compensation. Bates, the Blairs, and J. B. Henderson exercised real influence, and all three called for a tender of support to Lincoln on his efforts to protect the border States.

9 When Seward, at Lincoln's instigation, explored the idea of an extensive colonization of freedmen abroad, he met a chill reception. The chief European nations wanted no concern with the matter. The minister of Guatemala and Salvador, A. J. de Yrisarri, called attention to the fact that those two republics allowed no colonization of foreigners without special permission. The American envoy to Nicaragua reported that the people there had a deep-rooted and strong opposition to the scheme, and the minister to Costa Rica called attention to "the excitement prevailing over Nicaragua and Honduras on account of a dreaded deluge" of American Negroes. See 37th Cong., 3rd Sess., House Exec. Doc. No. 1, pp. 881–910; Nicolay and Hay, *Lincoln*, VI, 357 ff.; L. C. Hill, *Dip. Rels. Between the U. S. and Brazil*, 158–162; N. A. N. Cleven, *Journal of Negro Hist.*, XI (Jan., 1926), 41–49.

10 Adoption of the plan, many Kentuckians believed, would increase a disorganization and unrest among the slave population which threatened to deprive agriculture of its labor. Already many slaves had become boisterous and disorderly, and some were escaping to the North. This was natural, but it was equally natural that many Kentuckians should want no talk of emancipation whatever. Coulter, *Kentucky*, 247.

"He should . . . in his oft-manifested determination to see that they shall not be wronged," wrote Henderson, "be met with a word of approbation." [11] The question in Missouri would soon be one not of slavery vs. abolition, but of gradual vs. immediate emancipation.

Even in Missouri, however, inertia, Democratic rancor, jealousy for State rights, and suspicion of the radicals in Congress all counted and all helped the opposition to magnify the practical obstacles. Nobody knew just how many slaves were left, for many had fled to freedom, and many had been dragged south into the Confederacy. Estimates of the remainder ranged from 70,000 to 100,000. Even at a low valuation, the cost of purchasing them would run from $28,000,000 to $40,000,000, and valuation was a sore point, for as soon as Missourians began discussing it their estimates of what they should be paid rose. An additional difficulty was the question of dealing with the slaves of Confederates and Southern sympathizers. As the State had no power to discriminate between loyal and disloyal owners, Congress would have to solve that problem. On all such points opponents found it easy to raise objections and throw up clouds of dust.

With the border leaders so largely recalcitrant, Lincoln doubtless felt great discouragement, but was too shrewd to show it. In March, General David Hunter had taken charge of the Department of the South, embracing coastal parts of South Carolina, Georgia, and Florida; and on April 11 troops under his command captured the old national post near the mouth of the Savannah River, Fort Pulaski. His abrupt issuance of two orders, the first on April 12 liberating the slaves in Union hands and the second on May 9 freeing all slaves in the department, gave the President opportunity for a fresh appeal, embodying the first full burst of Lincolnian eloquence the country had yet heard.

Hunter, who though morose and ambitious was devoted to Lincoln, had acted to meet what he thought a plain necessity. He had found the coast and sea islands in social chaos, the slaves abandoned by their masters to destitution and fear. Neither the Treasury Department nor philanthropic agencies could give adequate help. Believing that Negro recruits would be useful in garrisoning posts in malarial districts, he forthwith sanctioned the enlistment of a Negro regiment, the First South Carolina. He also held that since slavery existed only under civil law, it died whenever the slaveowner placed himself beyond the pale of such law. His assertion that slavery and martial law were "incompatible" exposed him to much ridicule, for Lincoln had insisted that

11 June 16, 1862, Gamble Papers, Mo. Hist. Soc. But Henderson hedged his support of Lincoln's plan about with conditions, such as a firm guarantee of the colonization of the freedmen, and an immediate appropriation of money by Congress to be deposited to Missouri's account. See the pamphlet version of his Hannibal speech, no date, NYPL.

generals had no right to free slaves under martial law, but this was only a soldier's verbal maladroitness. Hunter had meant well in a difficult situation —nearly as difficult as Frémont's.

The fact remained that in freeing *all* slaves he had gone much further than Frémont, and that he had meddled with a subject which the President was determined to keep in his own hands. While Bryant's *Evening Post* praised the general, such moderate organs as the Philadelphia *North American*, New York *Times*, and Boston *Morning Journal* condemned his action. Not only had he usurped improper powers; his hasty liberation without preparatory steps was a cruelty to colored people, and if it encouraged servile revolts it might lead to the slaughter of thousands. Though Lincoln was not angry with Hunter, he had to annul the order, and a Cabinet meeting on May 17 found all in agreement with him. Afterwards, the President tactfully met with leading members of Congress to tell them of his decision, and describe the pressure placed on him by border men. On May 20 he issued his revoking proclamation, a brief, emphatic document.

As men read it, against a background of news of heavy fighting in Virginia, they saw how skillfully the President had converted his annulment into a platform from which to exhort the Borderland once more. Asserting that emancipation under the war power was a responsibility which he reserved to himself, he pointed out that the offer of gradual compensated emancipation still held open a door. With heartfelt fervor, touching the high chord which was to make some later utterances immortal, he urged the border to pass through it. "I do not argue. I beseech you to make the arguments for yourselves. You can not if you would be blind to the signs of the times. I beg of you a calm and enlarged consideration of them, ranging, it may be, far above personal and partisan politics. This proposal makes common cause for a common object, casting no reproaches upon any. It acts not the pharisee. The change it contemplates would come gently as the dews of heaven, not rending or wrecking anything. Will you not embrace it? So much good has not been done, by one effort, in all past time, as in the providence of God, it is now your high privilege to do. May the vast future not have to lament that you have neglected it." [12]

12 The Washington correspondent of the N. Y. *Evening Post* suggests that Chase demurred; May 18–21, 1862. Lincoln's paper was dated May 19; *Collected Works*, V, 222, 223. Stanton helped Lincoln draft the proclamation of annulment, the two working in complete harmony. Chase doubtless assented to the revocation, but at heart he approved of Hunter's orders. "I think like orders should be promulgated in all the Gulf States at least," he wrote Murat Halstead; May 24, Chase Collection, Pa. Hist. Soc. At most points on the slavery issue Chase disagreed with Lincoln. He objected to compensated emancipation on the general abolitionist ground that slaves and slave labor were stolen property, to be released without payment. He thought colonization wrong.

This was Lincoln's first but not last reminder to the nation that man's "vast future" waited upon its decisions. But no answering voice came from the border. The giants Partisanship, Inertia, and Racial Intolerance still barred the way—or perhaps, rather, these were seneschals of the real fortress: "A castle, called Doubting-Castle, the owner whereof was Giant Despair." Slavery, by the year A.D. 1862, was synonymous with Despair.

Lincoln was resolved to make yet another effort to win the Borderland. He knew that appreciation of his high intentions was widespread. To be sure, few men believed in either the wisdom or practicability of colonizing the colored folk abroad; even Seward was against it, saying that he wished to bring men into the Union, not send them out. But gradual compensated emancipation did seem to offer a hopeful new path. Lincoln also knew that every obstacle only damned back forces that before long would become irresistible. Perspicacious men now saw that the problem of racial readjustment was impossible of quick solution, and that every step would be painful.[13] As with so much else in this horrible war, one exhausting effort but led to another. And how much would depend on the fate of McClellan's great stroke in Virginia!

[III]

On that campaign the North, as May passed into June, pinned its fairest hopes. The Virginia thrust was its supreme bid for a short war. In mid-May numerous observers thought that the great army just outside Richmond would prove irresistible. Then two unexpected elements altered the outlines of the situation: the Chickahominy River, and the strategy of Stonewall Jackson.

Few Northerners, unless they had read Captain John Smith's travels, had ever heard of the swamp-bordered Chickahominy. The first mentions by war correspondents described it as a narrow, shallow stream, said to be partly dry in summer. Yet it was potentially formidable. Rising in the hills northwest of Richmond, it flows east and south, describing the quadrant of a circle around the city, and emptying into the James about fifty miles below it. Although the main channel was easily passable, all the timbered bottom lands were low, and it was belted in places by actual bogs. Even in dry weather the swampy margins and the bottom lands, varying from three quarters of a mile to a mile in width, were too spongy for cavalry and artillery. If rain raised the river two feet above normal level, it would spread in channels through the

13 Bancroft, *Seward*, II, 346. The London *Daily News* and the Church of England daily, the *Record*, strong adherents of the Union, joined many Northern papers and the great body of Negroes in condemning the "deportation" of freedmen. It looks too absurd a plan in European eyes, said the *Daily News*, to be treated as real; Sept. 24, 1862.

bogs, while if continued storms lifted it three or four feet, it would over-flow the whole low area. Even light infantry would then find the Chickahominy impracticable.

To add to its dangers, the woods made examination of the terrain difficult. Tall trees rose to a height level with the bluffs rimming the valley, so that unwary troops might think themselves safe until they found the ground abruptly dropping away and their advance files floundering in a morass. A Union private told a tearful woman who had a son in the Confederate army that he expected to get into Richmond without much fighting. "No!" she stormed, forgetting her fears, "you-all will drink hot blood before you git thar." [14] It was certain that the river would run red.

That the army command was astonished by the suddenly disclosed perils of the Chickahominy was not its fault. Scientific mapmaking in the United States was yet in its swaddling clothes, and those who wanted detailed knowl-edge of any district usually groped in vain; they were lucky if they could get anything better than a page from a school geography! Here and there a sharp ray of light fell upon a special area. The Army engineers had mapped some points of defense, while the topographical corps had prepared maps of rivers and harbors, of certain roads, and of routes of exploration. But as late as 1872, Captain M. Wheeler of the topographical engineers could declare: "The United States has thus far organized no systematic topographical survey of any portion of its territory." Not until four years later was the Geological Survey authorized. Virginia fell behind most of her sisters in the preparation of maps, and the counties of Hanover, King William, and Henrico, which the Chickahominy drains, fell behind sister counties with mining interests. Neither the Union nor Confederate forces had adequate maps of the country environing Richmond; nothing better than some old railroad surveys. [15]

McClellan's first dispatches exhibited a blithe contempt of the river. He examined the bridge which carried the Williamsburg–Richmond road over the stream, and on May 21 telegraphed Stanton that he would have it repaired by the morrow and would at once construct others. He was pleased by his base at the White House landing on the Pamunkey. The handsome two-story mansion of this name, recently held by W. H. F. ("Rooney") Lee, second son of the general and a colonel in Stuart's cavalry, was busy with officers coming and going. Along the Pamunkey stretched offices and warehouses of the quartermaster's department, and the roadways littered by boxes, bar-rels, hay bales, wandering Negroes, and mules; the stream was crammed with

14 W. L. Goss, *Battles and Leaders*, II, 130, 131.
15 L. A. Brown, *The Story of Maps*, 276; P. L. Phillips, *Virginia Cartography, A Bib-liographical Description*. The Atlas volume of O. R. and the Coast Survey map of the Potomac (1862) indicate that real Virginia mapmaking began with the war, not before.

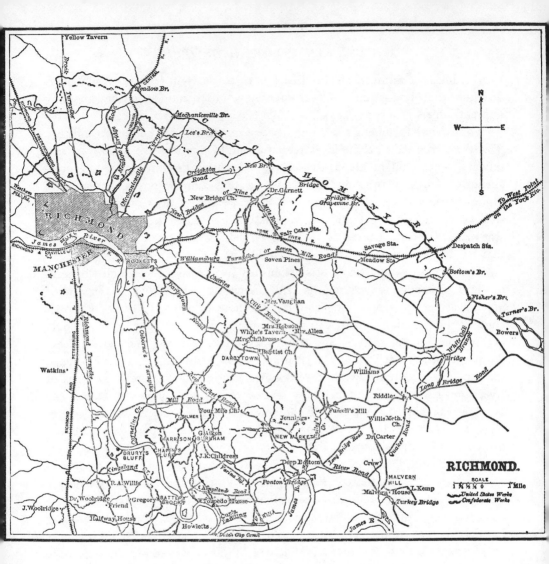

RICHMOND AND ITS DEFENSES

rows of vessels of every description, unloading at floating wharves their supplies of salt meat, biscuit, clothing, and ammunition. Moored apart were huge floating hospitals bearing the flag of the Sanitary Commission, their decks piled with boxes. Some large stores sold general goods, the biggest offering a miscellany from potted lobster and shoeblacking to toothbrushes and straw hats. From this base the Richmond & York River Railroad was swiftly put in running order up to the banks of the Chickahominy.[16]

16 See description in the London *Times*, July 10, 1862. Soldiers had trampled down the shrubbery and made the banks of the streamlets quagmires. The correspondent found the

As long as the army used this base it was able to maintain close liaison with Washington by telegraph. A curiously roundabout single-wire line had been carried from Washington by way of Wilmington and the eastern shore of Maryland and Virginia to Fort Monroe, about two hundred miles in length. The telegraphers worked under fire in the trenches before Yorktown, keeping McClellan in touch with his generals and the War Department. After the battle of Williamsburg the courageous construction party kept the main line up with the advance of the troops, and at every halt strung branches to corps headquarters. The Comte de Paris describes the surprise and delight of the generals at finding the telegraph always at hand. All the urgent orders for supplies and reinforcements, all the critical instructions, all the news of battle and lists of killed, passed over the one throbbing wire. Sometimes the telegraph was of vital importance; at Gaines's Mill, Fitz-John Porter was to obtain reinforcements at a critical moment through the prompt service of his operator. For important messages a simple cipher, frequently changed, was used.

Yet in reality the White House was a defective base for operations. The Pamunkey was too small to afford proper naval protection. Much more importantly, any army advancing on Richmond from the White House would have to push part of its force across the Chickahominy while keeping another part on the near side. That is, one section would have to remain on the north bank to hold the communications with White House Landing while the other crossed to the south bank to attack the Southern capital. Such a division of the army would be safe if the weather proved dry or the engineers erected numerous good bridges. It would be highly unsafe if storms raised the river, flooded the lowlands, and swept away jerry-built crossings. McClellan had not advanced far before his staff realized that the Chickahominy was no trifle. Prisoners dropped references to the great swamp, and a deserter told how apprehensive Magruder's forces retreating from Williamsburg had been lest the Union army should catch them before they crossed the stream.[17] But McClellan, following the plan he had made before he learned that McDowell would advance overland upon Richmond rather than by the Potomac and York Rivers, quickly put his army astride the Chickahominy.

That is, during May 20–25, the two corps of Keyes and Heintzelman were thrown across to the south bank to maneuver against Richmond, while the three corps of Sumner, Fitz-John Porter, and Franklin were kept on the north bank. This offered Joseph E. Johnston an opportunity he was quick to seize. He saw that if he could mass superior strength against McClellan's exposed

---

camps covering the countryside filthy, disorderly places, made worse by whole Negro families that had established themselves in tents and huts among the troops.
17 N. Y. *Tribune*, May 23, 1862.

wing under Heintzelman and Keyes, he might crush them before other troops could cross to their aid. On the morning of May 27 he received news that McDowell was advancing from Fredericksburg with his 41,000 men; and although a scouting movement by J. E. B. Stuart's cavalry quickly proved the report false, he concluded he must act before these reinforcements reached McClellan. "We could not afford to wait," writes General Gustavus W. Smith.[18]

The Confederate blow, ably conceived, was aided by good fortune. Johnston was able to attack at a time when the river had just flooded. On Sunday, May 25, the Keyes-Heintzelman forces, well across the stream, had strolled about the area of Fair Oaks or Seven Pines under a warm sun, listening to the church bells of Richmond seven miles away. Three bridges crossed the Chickahominy at their rear, two of them rough new structures. But Monday evening brought a drenching rain, which continued for much of the 27th. Troops gathered in dripping, gloomy groups about the smoking fires, on short rations. "The army is morose and savage this morning," wrote a correspondent, "and worse than all, the begging and borrowing of bread has begun." The river rose, and the narrow, tortuous roads became execrable. By the 30th Johnston's dispositions were completed. Late that afternoon nature renewed her alliance with the Confederacy, for a heavy thunderstorm began and continued all night.

"The face of the country was literally flooded," writes a Confederate general. "At daybreak on the 31st the Chickahominy was booming, passable only at the bridges, and it continued to rise during the day, although it had ceased to rain."

At daybreak Johnston expected his troops to attack like wolves; and indeed, only a combination of Confederate delays and Northern gallantry saved McClellan's forward wing from being torn to pieces at Fair Oaks. "My attempt," Johnston later wrote, "would have been a *full* success but for the sloth of a new division, which delayed Longstreet's attack six hours, which did not leave us time to complete the destruction of Keyes' corps." He himself was partly to blame. His plan required careful timing, for columns separated by forest and swamp had to be brought together; the commanders were novices in such coordinated movements; and Johnston erred in not giving his generals written orders defining their authority and tasks. Even so, his troops struck with crushing force before noon of the 31st. Silas Casey's division of Keyes's corps recoiled in hopeless disarray. By five in the afternoon it seemed that the Union forces would be cut into ribbons. But at that hour brave old Sumner, who had

18 Johnston had been so anxious to strike before the junction of McClellan and McDowell that he had contemplated delivering a blow from the still intact bridges downstream; letter to Wigfall, Nov. 12, 1863, Wigfall Papers, Univ. of Texas; cf. G. W. Smith, *Battles and Leaders*, II, 223.

put his corps in readiness, began moving across the river, and came on the field with almost the impact of Blücher at Waterloo.

No episode of McClellan's campaign was more creditable to Northern arms than this emergency crossing of swamp and swollen river by the Massachusetts veteran. Only one half-wrecked bridge was available. The log approaches were afloat, held by their fastenings to tree stumps, and the bridge itself was precariously kept in place by ropes. Many officers had doubted the feasibility of passage. As the solid infantry column came forward the structure swayed to and fro in the angry flood, settling down safely only when filled with men; and after they had crossed it quickly became worthless. Although Sumner expected to be wiped out along with Keyes and Heintzelman, he meant to exact a price. He told a division commander, John Sedgwick: "The enemy may win a victory, but we must make it a victory that will ruin him." [19]

In the end the Union lines held. The Confederate loss, about 6,150, materially exceeded the Northern loss of 5,000, while Johnston was severely wounded. Both sides, however, were so severely shaken that they were immobilized; and worst shaken of all was McClellan's reputation as a strategist. He had committed a terrible error in throwing his army astraddle a dangerous river and in leaving Keyes's corps standing isolated for several days within reach of a crushing blow from Johnston. Indeed, he was lucky to escape so easily. Johnston always believed that a vigorous renewal of the battle on June 1 would have destroyed Keyes and totally crippled McClellan.[20]

In a single week, the situation of the Union army had totally changed.

[IV]

Meanwhile, the second unexpected obstacle made itself felt: Stonewall Jackson's bold Shenandoah campaign, and its effect in exciting the deepest apprehension in Washington. To the campaign itself, a classic feat of modern warfare, we need yield little space. Lincoln and Stanton should have given the command of all Virginia operations, apart from McClellan's, to a single able general, and should have kept the forces west of the Blue Ridge well concentrated. Instead, they had offered the enemy a rich opportunity by dividing the leadership and troops among three generals; Banks with 19,000 men in the heart of the Shenandoah Valley, Frémont with 15,000 partly in the Alleghenies

19 A. S. Webb, *The Peninsula*, Ch. VI; Smith, *Battles and Leaders*, II, 225 ff.; N. Y. *Tribune, Times*, May 31, June 2, 3. Much ink was spent on the poor behavior of Casey's division in Keyes's corps. Sumner brought over 20,000 fresh men.
20 Johnston, *Narrative*, 141.

and partly in the Valley, and McDowell with 41,000 far to the east of Fredericksburg. Supreme command was retained by Lincoln and Stanton, who knew just enough about maneuvering to be dangerous practitioners.

For a fast-moving, hard-hitting leader like Jackson this presented an ideal situation. Lee in a historic dispatch of April 21 had submitted to Jackson three plans of action against Banks and his associates, writing: "I have hoped in the present divided condition of the enemy's forces that a successful blow may be dealt them by a rapid combination of our troops before they can be strengthened themselves either in position or by reinforcements." And never did a general use his opportunities more brilliantly. On May 21 Jackson suddenly smashed a small Union force at Front Royal. During the next five days —the days in which McClellan put two corps across the Chickahominy and that river rose in flood—Stonewall with 16,000 men drove Banks's troops up the Valley. By swift blows he pushed the Union forces out of Strasburg, out of Middleton, and out of Winchester, sending them flying on north to Martinsburg. Banks's shattered command, throwing away arms and covering more than thirty miles in one day, did not pause until it was safe behind the Potomac.

When he did stop, while Jackson's troops gleefully packed up the huge quantity of munitions and supplies taken at Winchester, Washington was in a state of wild alarm. The War Department in particular gave way on Sunday the 25th to what some Northerners later termed "the great scare." When Cabinet and Congressmen learned that day that Banks was fleeing helter-skelter, they leaped at the conclusion that Jackson might suddenly invade Maryland, or by a march through Harpers Ferry hurl himself on Washington. Senators Fessenden and Grimes jocularly assured Sumner that he would be among the first men executed. Stanton was as much alarmed as when the *Merrimac* had emerged; so frightened, in fact, that with the full concurrence of Lincoln, the Cabinet, and various generals he telegraphed the Northern governors for troops. John A. Andrew and others hastily began assembling militia. From the White House, Nicolay wrote his wife: "We have been 'stampeded' all day with news from Gen. Banks's army." The whole city was convulsed, he added, and a frightened woman had just rushed in to ask if she should leave immediately. To Sumner, Seward, and some military men that evening Lincoln gave a vivid description of the rout.[21]

Great excitement seized the North. Governors Curtin in Pennsylvania and Sprague in Rhode Island took steps to hurry off troops that they possessed ready for service. In Boston Governor Andrew, his adjutant-general, and their

21 Nicolay Papers; Sumner to R. H. Dana, Jr., May 31, 1862, Dana Papers. The Valley campaign is covered in O. R., I., xii, pt. 1, pp. 3–818; Freeman, *Lee*, Ch. IV; *Lee's Lieutenants*, Chs. XXIV–XXVI; Henderson, *Jackson*, Chs. IX–XII. See also the vivid record in Henry Kyd Douglas, *I Rode With Stonewall*, 68–94.

aides toiled all Sunday night, and at dawn on Monday, May 26, the news-papers were carrying his alarmed proclamation to the people. A barbarous horde of traitors, he wrote, had routed Banks and were marching on Washington. To arms! Let Massachusetts rise! By nightfall 2,000 militia had gathered on Boston Common and started to the capital. "Our people are rushing in as in April, 1861," Andrew telegraphed Stanton.

This sudden change in the situation disrupted the machinery in motion for taking Richmond. As Banks fled on the 24th, Lincoln and Stanton ordered McDowell to drop the march on that city fixed for the 26th, and put 20,000 men in motion toward the Shenandoah. They hoped to stop Stonewall and trap him in the Valley. McDowell telegraphed back that the order was a "crushing blow," and Lincoln replied: "The change was as painful to me as it can possibly be to you or anyone." His denial of aid to McClellan was a momentous decision, but it was not taken without careful thought of the consequences. The possible gains seemed to justify the risk. The President and Secretary were motivated partly by apprehension over the safety of Washington, and partly by a desire to use converging columns to cut off Jackson when he turned back toward Richmond. That they made a mistake time soon proved.

Actually, the Administration had no reason for its alarm over Washington. Troops could be and were rapidly brought in from Baltimore and other neighboring points for its defense. The march of Frémont alone into the Valley would compel Jackson's rapid withdrawal from his exposed position near the Potomac. No consideration of safety required a change in Mc-Dowell's destination. And when the President and Secretary planned to outwit Jackson and "bag" his force by using the telegraph office to move the separate armies in the Valley, they based their impromptu strategy on very dubious chances. The distances Frémont and McDowell had to cover in order to close the gate behind Jackson were excessive; the muddy, rocky roads were atrocious; and while McDowell's troops were well equipped, Frémont's had been shockingly neglected by the government. As Carl Schurz certified to Lincoln, they were largely destitute of clothing, tents, and even shoes, many marching barefoot. Their pioneer companies in this mountain country had no axes, picks, or saws; their horses were barely able to drag the artillery. Banks's troops were disheartened by defeat, Frémont's by repeated slights, and McDowell's by the unwelcome change in orders. Nor could these separated armies be maneuvered properly by telegraph.[22]

The three commanders did their best, and for a brief hour it seemed that they might actually cut off bold Jackson. McDowell's vanguard under

22 Schurz, *Reminiscences*, II, 344-347; Nevins, *Frémont*, II, 636-639.

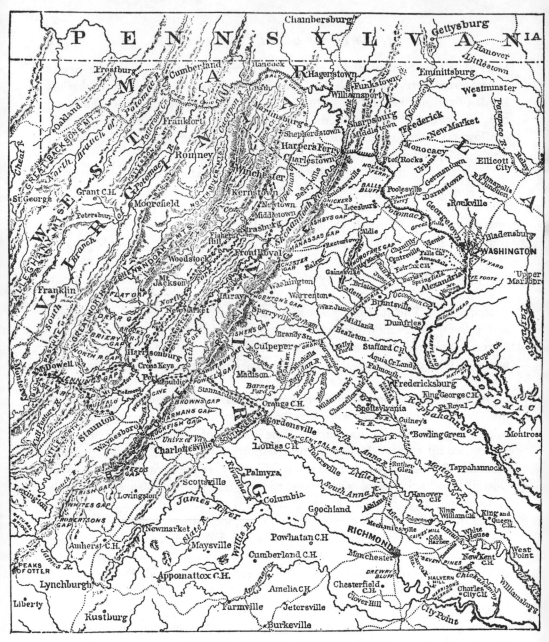

THE VIRGINIA CAMPAIGNS

Shields on May 30 reached a point twelve miles from Strasburg on the east, and Frémont a village twenty miles on the west, while Jackson was still eighteen miles to the north. Woe to the Confederacy if they closed the pincers![23]

23 Ropes, *Civil War*, II, 129, 130; Freeman, *Lee's Lieutenants*, II, Chs. XXVII, XXVIII. Kenneth P. Williams, *Lincoln Finds A General*, I, 187–213, strains the evidence to defend

But the trap remained unsprung. Shields, though a natural fighter, took a defensive attitude just when he should have moved forward. Frémont, after first misunderstanding his orders, was impeded by storms, the worsening of the mountain roads, and the fatigue of men and steeds. The upshot was that Jackson, taking the splendid Valley turnpike and exhibiting characteristic skill, slipped between the Union armies and escaped. When pursued, he used Turner Ashby's cavalry to check his assailants, and fought two effective rear-guard actions, one with Frémont at Cross Keys June 8, and one next day with Shields at Port Republic. He paused for a time to rest his army, and then quietly rejoined the main Confederate force. The detachment of McDowell had thus accomplished nothing in the Valley, while it gravely weakened the campaign against Richmond. Indeed, this detachment had been precisely what the Confederate leaders wished to effect!

Both McDowell and McClellan regarded the Administration's recall of McDowell's troops as a horrible mistake, and McClellan's bitterness intensified all his sullenness of attitude thereafter. He had reached the Richmond front deeply distrustful of the Administration. "Those hounds in Washington are after me again," he had written his wife on May 18. "Stanton is without exception the vilest man I ever knew or heard of!" He received Lincoln's telegram of May 24 announcing the suspension of McDowell's junction with his army just as he was putting his two corps in peril across the river. Next day brought a much more alarmed message from the President, declaring that the enemy seemed to be making a general movement northward: "I think the time is near when you must either attack Richmond or give up the job and come to the defense of Washington." [24] This expressed Lincoln's apprehensions over Banks's retreat and also his irritation over McClellan's long delays on the Peninsula. But, reaching the general at a moment of deep anxiety, it exploded all his pent-up anger. "Heaven save a country governed by such counsels!" he wrote his wife, and after reassuring Lincoln that the mass of Southern troops were still in Richmond, he burst out: "It is perfectly sickening to deal with such people and you may rest assured that I will lose as little time as possible in breaking off all connection with them." [25] McClellan believed that the best defense of Washington was an all-out attack on Richmond, and he was entirely right—though he himself failed to make it.

Once more he suspected McDowell of treachery—of conniving at the detachment of his force. The fact was that McDowell had protested sharply, writing Lincoln that he could not possibly rescue Banks, and that the change

Lincoln's leadership in the Valley campaign, quoting with approval Shields's statement, "The plan for Jackson's destruction was perfect."
24 *Works*, V, 235, 236.
25 Myers, *McClellan*, 291–293; Hassler, *McClellan*, 114 ff., a careful account.

of plan would paralyze the main Union activities north of Richmond.[26] He shortly sent a New York friend a letter of angry frustration:

It is now the middle of the third week since I was at Fredericksburg with a splendid little army of 41,000 men, 100 pieces of artillery, and 14,000 horse —fully equipped, admirably organized, and as a general thing well disciplined and well officered! We were all in high spirits. For this army which had been assembled quietly, was the *next morning* to march down and join the army before Richmond under McClellan. I had been held back by peremptory written orders from the President not to cross the Rappahannock. And not even for a while, to make the bridges over the River!! But he had given his consent, had issued his orders that I might go as soon as Shields' division should join. It had joined. The wagons were all loaded, the orders given, and we were to march the next day! When came the orders breaking us up and sending us over to the valley after Jackson!

I telegraphed the President that the order was a crushing blow to us all. That I could not get to the valley in time to affect Banks' position. His case would be disposed of one way or the other before I could arrive! . . .

But they were alarmed over the safety of Washington! Then came this extraordinary forced march over the Piedmont and Blue Ridge mountains to Front Royal, in which I estimate that we had 4,000 men broken down.[27]

When this letter was sent, Lincoln had just ruefully informed McClellan that Shields's division was so terribly out at elbows and toes that it would take a long time to get it in shape again. Except for McCall's division, McDowell's army never did join the resentful McClellan before Richmond.[28]

From the Valley campaign suddenly emerged one momentous fact: a military genius had appeared on the Southern side. The gifts of a surpassing commander were united in Stonewall Jackson: imagination, boldness, determination, vigilance, and rapidity. The least eloquent of men, he had no superior in holding the devotion of his troops. Of all Confederate officers the most careful in his precautions, he could be the most adventurous.

He had three cardinal rules. One was always to mystify the enemy; one

---

26   May 24; O. R., I, xii, pt. 3, pp. 220, 221.
27   To C. A. Hecksher, June 17, 1862, Barlow Papers.
28   McClellan still cherished the idea of a conspiracy. He said in Boston in February, 1863, that the cabal against him had gained great strength when he lay ill of fever. He thought that the fears of the President for Washington had been adroitly excited by men who knew the city was really safe, and who did not wish the Peninsular campaign to succeed, for that would mean the end of the influence of ultra-radical Republicans. McClellan said he knew the war had given a deathblow to slavery, but he did not want the property of innocent men a thousand miles away to be confiscated. T. Jefferson Coolidge, *Autobiography*, 41. On the other hand, McClellan should have realized that some radicals honestly doubted that his heart was in defeating the South, while his needless delays had discouraged Lincoln; and he should have seen that the supreme risk which the President could not afford to take was that of the capture of Washington.

was to maneuver his troops until he could throw his main force upon a weak part of his antagonist's army and crush it; and the third was to be utterly relentless in pursuit of a stricken foe. "Such tactics will win every time," he told a subordinate. The Spartan characteristics of this gentle-voiced, imperturbable, alert man stamped him as a soldier born, and he subordinated all his thought and activity to war. To start at dawn, to pray, to fight, to suck lemons, to live on hardtack and water, to look after his troops' welfare, to ponder long and hard—this was all his creed. He could be harsh, for he hated weakness. He was always ready to exact the last ounce of effort from his columns. His supply trains might be left behind, but his ammunition wagons had to get through. After this spring campaign the legend of his ways—his insistence on action, movement, quick-step, "bay'nets and grape" always characteristic, but so too his rocklike firmness in defense—possessed the South, and helped animate her soldiers:

> We see him now—the queer slouched hat
> Cocked o'er his eye askew;
> The shrewd dry smile; the speech so pat
> So calm, so blunt, so true.

The bloody, indecisive battle of Fair Oaks was followed by more than three weeks of waiting which sorely tried the patience of watchers North and South. Both sides in the interval had an opportunity to weigh the sad costs of battle. "Our loss is heavy," McClellan had telegraphed Stanton, "but that of the enemy must be enormous." In fact, all the carriages of Richmond were impressed to bring dead and wounded into the city, hotels were turned into hospitals, and the need for additional shelters evoked a bitter outcry against the churches for keeping their doors closed. A German-born officer in Confederate ranks who had seen the battlefields of Hungary and Italy wrote in the *Kölnische Zeitung* that he had never beheld such a butchery as that at Fair Oaks. He helped organize a midnight convoy of sixty wagons bearing two hundred gravely wounded. Reaching the first hospital in the city, he met a refusal. "All full!" was the reply to his inquiry. "Forward to the next hospital," he commanded, only to receive the same response: "All full!" At last a tobacco warehouse was thrown open and men with ghastly wounds were laid on hard planks in a stifling loft, without windows, in the June heat.[29] On the Union side, meanwhile, the casualties were in an even worse situation. Wrote one correspondent:

The wounded! It is now fifty-six hours since they received their injuries. Those away from water—oh, how they suffer! those in the wet—how they

29 Translated in N. Y. *Herald*, Dec. 25, 1862. This officer writes that after Johnston fell, Lee made preparations for 10,000 wounded in the hospitals.

contract new diseases, and how they undergo wintry torments from the night cold! I dread to go upon that battleground. For forty-eight hours I have worked, and slept, and ate, and served among a thousand wounded soldiers—wounded in every possible degree of severity. The screaming of stout men under surgeons' knives—the groaning everywhere over three acres of lawn—the piteous cries for drink, for help, for shade—the delirium of the dying—the blood and discoloration and disfigurement and dirt and wretchedness of the unfortunates who are brought in an uninterrupted stream of tardy discovery and lie under foot everywhere, waiting surgical help—the ceaseless labors on the operating table in the great hospital tent—the use of knife and probe by lantern light all around this country-seat, and the dressing of ghastly wounds all night and all day, and all day and all night—'tis a memory that shall make the Seven Pines painful till I die.[30]

Throughout the three weeks following the battle McClellan's inaction, reflecting his chronic indecision and the atrocious weather, was complete. He beguiled the North by day-to-day promises. On June 2, sending news that Hooker had led a reconnaissance within four miles of Richmond, he added: "I only wait for the river to fall to cross with the rest of the force and make a general attack." The army was still dangerously astraddle the Chickahominy, but the larger part of it was now south of that stream. The 75,000 men who had entrenched beyond the river reached the Mechanicsville Bridge, bearing a signpost reading "To Richmond, 4½ miles," and on still nights the city clocks chiming the hours could be heard within the Union camps. But the weather again interposed, for on June 4 it poured for hours, until the river reached its highest level in twenty years and its current swept men off their feet. And McClellan was writing confidentially: "I dare not risk this army. . . . I must make a sure thing of it"—as if anything were sure in war![31]

Lincoln sent him troops from Washington and from Fort Monroe, which with McCall's division from McDowell's army made 20,000 in all. McClellan announced June 7: "I shall be in perfect readiness to move forward and take Richmond the moment McCall reaches here, and the ground will admit the

30 Letter by N. Y. *Tribune* reporter dated Monday morning, June 2, in issue June 6. The first day's fighting was usually called Fair Oaks, and the second day's Seven Pines.
31 The London *Times* correspondent admired the patience of the volunteers under hardships which they did not realize were avoidable. They were often paid only after long delays. They had filthy water to drink. Whole divisions for days on end got no food but poor biscuits and wretched coffee, and when they did receive meat it was salt beef as hard as sole leather. "Nowhere is to be seen more military stupidity and more dishonesty than in this brave American army. You must not wonder if I get warm and bitter." Amid general muddle, the troops were exhausted by needless marches through swamp and mud. McClellan would not risk a battle, "and therefore he lets the volunteers die in the swamps." Embalmers did a large business in fever-killed soldiers, charging $25 for privates, $50 for officers, and shipping the corpses home in zinc-lined pine boxes by Adams's Express. One embalmer said that 2,000 corpses had thus been shipped since the war began. London *Times*, July 10, 1862. For the weather see O. R., I, xi, pt. 1, p. 31; pt. 3, p. 193.

passage of artillery." Five days later McCall's division was paraded at the White
House. The North eagerly awaited word of the taking of Richmond. It knew
that Jackson had not yet rejoined Lee, and saw no reason why the Union
army should not advance. But McClellan had telegraphed on the 10th: "I am
completely checked by the weather. The Chickahominy is in a dreadful state:
we have another rainstorm on our hands." He was nervously asking Stanton
to consider the propriety of bringing east a large section of Halleck's Western army to reinforce him. When Stanton assured him on the 12th that Mc-
Dowell's full independent force would soon arrive to cooperate, he flared up
angrily: "If I cannot control all the troops I want none of them, and would
prefer to fight the battle with what I have, and let others be responsible for
the result." Yet he certainly did not lack for men, for on June 20 his returns
showed an army of 156,838, of whom 115,102 were present for duty.[32]

While McClellan waited, the enemy resolved to strike, for the Southern army
was now headed by a man of lionhearted qualities. If the emergence of Jackson
was one of the memorable developments of the war, the replacement of Johnston
by Robert E. Lee signalized a quite new phase of the conflict. Since April 23,
1861, by State appointment, Lee had been major-general and commander of
the Virginia forces, and since May 10, 1861, he had also held supreme control
of all the Confederate forces in Virginia. Primarily concerned with organizing State forces, fortifying Virginia rivers, and (during the winter) improving
the defenses of the South Atlantic coast, he had also been Jefferson Davis' military adviser. He kept aloof from the dispute between Davis and Johnston
over the latter's rank. By common consent he was easily the ablest man to
take Johnston's place, although he had never directed a battle. In the prime of
life—fifty-five years old, powerfully built, in superb health—he was glad to
exchange his empty if honorable desk eminence for a field command. On
June 1 he took charge of the force he named The Army of Northern Virginia, and promptly began planning an offensive.[33]

Lee saw that he could not wait. If McClellan marshaled his hosts and
brought his powerful siege guns to bear, Richmond would be lost. Nothing
but fierce lunging blows could extricate the Confederacy from its disadvantages
of inferior strength. Like Jackson, he was a thinker. Although his symmetry of
character was so noble, and his reticence so complete, that many have credited
him with greatness of personality rather than intellect, the fact was that he
possessed both. In quickness of perception, subtlety of thought, and power
of devising complicated operations, he equaled Marlborough or Frederick, as

32 Ropes, *Civil War*, II, 159, gives the figure 105,445 men on June 20; Webb, *The Peninsula*, 120, estimates the effective force at 92,500.
33 See the clear statement on Lee's official status 1861–62 in the *Nation*, Dec. 23, 1897,
and in Freeman's *Lee*, II, Ch. VIII.

in coolness he surpassed them. He knew that a general must always take chances, that the leader with inferior forces must move swiftly and shrewdly to make his chances better than even, and that he must realistically equate the power to act with the power to imagine.[34]

If in many ways Lee seemed limited, it was intensity of purpose that limited him. All his thoughts, apart from religion and family, were centered on the profession of arms. He did almost no general reading; he never accumulated a library, never gave a leisure hour to literature, and never once in his letters refers to Shakespeare or Milton, to Dickens or Thackeray. The great scientific advance of the age of Darwin, Huxley, and Spencer made no appeal to him. Even in religion he paid no attention to austere theological thought; the Bible was enough for him. But in strategy and tactics, in engineering, and in what we now call logistics, he made himself proficient by hard study. Nobody in America knew military science so well.

War was in fact a passion with him, and as befitted a son of "Light-Horse Harry" Lee, he delighted in martial problems and exercises. A merciful man, he was sensitively aware of the suffering which war imposes. "You have no idea what a horrible sight a battlefield is," he wrote his family from Mexico. The knightliest of commanders, he set his face sternly, in his invasion of the North, against any retaliation for the devastation and plundering of which many Union forces had been guilty. But his energetic nature, which comprehended a taste for excitement and a delight in seeing intricate mental combinations translated into army evolutions, made conflict a congenial element. Remembering well what his father's unresting activity had accomplished at Stony Point, Paulus Hook, and in the long Southern campaign, he drew a special pleasure from swift movement and battles against odds.[35] When told after the war that such daring decisions as the splitting of his army at Second Manassas had risked the utter ruin of the Confederacy, he replied that this was obvious, "but the disparity of force between the contending forces rendered the risks unavoidable."

Yet he did his best to minimize the risks to be taken. While still in the Lower South, he had appealed to the governor of Virginia for more men, with the result that the legislature in February had provided for enrolling all citizens between eighteen and forty-five, and that Letcher the following month had called 40,000 men to the colors. It was Lee who had inspired the Confederate conscription law of April, Major Charles Marshall of his staff drawing up the main features of the bill, and Lee himself taking it to Jefferson Davis for introduction in Congress. Thus the peril of a disorganization of Con-

34 Cf. Henderson, *Jackson*, II, 4–7; Hendrick, *Lees of Va.*, 412 ff.; Freeman, *Lee, passim.*
35 See his edition of his father's *Memoirs*, with biographical essay (1869).

federate defense by the expiration of the terms of nearly 150 regiments was averted. Laboring in May to hurry troops up from the Carolinas and other points, he was hopeful that the arrival of Huger, Holmes, and Ripley would give the Confederate defenders of Richmond 80,000 or even 85,000 men.[36]

As yet untried, he did not command enthusiasm when appointed; the troops cheered tepidly, and the newspapers expressed little more than a belief that he would prove competent. But his qualities quickly impressed his army. He had a deep faith in his troops, and would have echoed Stonewall Jackson's exclamation as his lines swung past: "Who could fail to win battles with such men as these?" Such a faith was sure to be repaid. Another element of strength lay in his remarkable capacity for judging his antagonists. Whether they were formidable like Grant or contemptible like Pope, he keenly appraised their traits. He was wont to refer scornfully to Hooker as "Mr. F. J. Hooker," the initials being his abbreviation for "Fighting Joe," and he remarked that he could forgive his nephew for fighting on the Union side, but never for joining John Pope's staff. He deemed Ben Butler beneath contempt. Liking Burnside as a man, he was quick to take his short measure. "We always understood each other," he said regretfully when McClellan was displaced. "I fear they may contrive to make these changes until they find someone I don't understand." For all his modesty, he knew that the fighting power of his army was doubled by his and Jackson's talents.[37]

McClellan he now understood particularly well, for they had served on the same staff in the Mexican War. He had hardly been astonished by Mc-Clellan's strange winter inaction, his month-long pause before Yorktown, and his slow creep to White House Landing, for he knew that McClellan's taste was for a war of position. Invariably, in McClellan's strategy, boldness in conception was fettered by an appalling slowness in execution. Though Lee respected McClellan's abilities, he knew that his operations were always half defensive; that he never caught at a military opportunity without saying to himself, "Suppose the enemy has hidden reserves?" And Lee realized that the timidities of his opponent opened the way for operations impossible in the face of a more resolute foe.

[V]

McClellan's golden opportunity, unperceived and unused, came between the 18th and 25th of June. Jackson in the Valley was still distant from Lee. The Confederate works around Richmond remained weak. Although Lee had

36 Freeman, *Lee*, II, Chs. III, IV, V.
37 Allen, *The Army of Northern Va.*, 200; Swinton, *Army of the Potomac*, Ch. IV; Freeman, *Lee*, Chs. VII, VIII.

frantically called for troops from every quarter, his forces were still much under the Union strength. But while McClellan waited, Lee matured a daring plan. A magnificent cavalry raid by Jeb Stuart all the way around McClellan's army gave him full information on the Union dispositions. He decided to bring Jackson stealthily down from the Valley, so that the two commands could suddenly strike McClellan's right wing, one in the rear and one in front, crushing it as in a vise. He gave the proper orders. On June 25 Jackson reached Ashland, seventeen miles north of Richmond. A council of generals that day decided to begin the pincers attack at three the next morning.[38]

Would this new operation succeed? The attacker had become the attacked; would McClellan, who so recently had expected to seize Richmond, himself be destroyed? The answer was given in the Seven Days' Battles that followed; an answer that comforted neither side.

Lee's first heavy stroke at Mechanicsville on June 26 failed partly because a reconnaissance in force by McClellan the previous day had altered his plans, and partly because of poor staff work and poor coordination of forces; but it resulted in a Union retreat to Gaines's Mill. Here a renewed attack next day smashed the Union right wing under FitzJohn Porter with heavy losses. McClellan, now in real peril, concluded that the only way to foil Lee was to shift his base from the shallow Pamunkey to the deep James, where he might find full naval protection. On the night of the 27th he began the agonizing march. His retreat across country was a masterly operation, executed despite heat, thirst, hunger, and fatigue. When Lee discovered it he delivered sharp intercepting strokes in White Oak Swamp and at Frayser's Farm. The fighting at the second point was so fierce that Union soldiers thrust their ramrods against trees to force the charges into the hot barrels.[39] Then the retreat went on:

> The spires of Richmond, late beheld
> Through rifts in musket haze,
> Were closed from view in clouds of dust
> On leaf-walled ways.

Exhaustion and discouragement dogged the Union troops to the last. Finally the movement ended at Malvern Hill on July 1 in a memorably spectacular battle.

McClellan had gained refuge on a high, broad plateau, reaching to the James on one side, and protected at the back by creek and ravine. On this plateau he posted a major part of his army, with massed artillery in front, cavalry in the rear, and gunboats protecting his flank. The Confederate host,

38 O. R., I, xi, pt. 2, p. 489 ff.
39 F. W. Palfrey in Mil. Hist. Soc. Mass., *Campaigns in Va.*, 219–251.

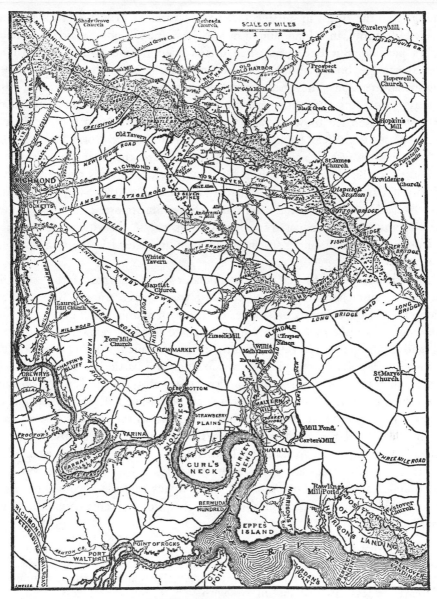

THE SEVEN DAYS

issuing from the forest in pursuit, faced tier on tier of grim batteries rising, as D. H. Hill wrote, in a huge amphitheater. It seemed almost suicidal to attack such a position. But Lee's army had passed over ground strewn with Union rifles, cartridge boxes, and knapsacks, amid a roadside litter of abandoned wagons and caissons; they had picked up scores of groaning wounded. Mistakenly concluding that Northern morale had sunk to a low ebb, Lee hoped that by one frenzied blow he might yet annihilate the Union forces. His decision to use his artillery to silence the Union batteries and storm Malvern Hill by mass assault was in some respects a rehearsal of the attack on Cemetery Ridge. When he found that only a small number of his guns could be forced up through swamps and brush, he tried to cancel the attack—but it was too late. At half past five in the afternoon, 10,500 unsupported men swept forward against the Union panoply, marching up the slope with the orderliness of columns in review; and a storm of grape and canister laid them in writhing swaths.[40]

Participants never forgot the magnificence or the horror of the scene. In the bright summer evening not a breath of wind stirred the air. From the artillery rose black columns of smoke, towering in stately columns to the sky. The crash of musketry and the deeper roar and thud of cannon were deafening and continuous. As one Southern brigade recoiled, another pushed forward with desperate courage. By seven o'clock the battle had reached its climax, with a mass of fresh troops under Stonewall Jackson fiercely pressing Fitz-John Porter and Couch, while Sickles' and Meagher's brigades hurried forward to help hold the Northern line. By eight, as the sun cast its last rays on the smoky crest of Malvern and on the green treetops below, the Confederate columns were breaking back to the shelter of ravine and swamp. As the artillery poured its last shells after them, from the river came the flash and thunder of the gunboat mortars, their bombs curving through the dusk in fiery golden lines. This closing scene, wrote a Pennsylvania captain, was indescribably picturesque:

The cavalry on either flank, galloping in haste to harass the retreating foe; the foaming, panting horses flying from point to point with aides or orderlies carrying dispatches; the stretcher bearers tenderly carrying the wounded to the rear; the less disabled limping in with gun for crutch or supported by a comrade, and, as the darkness gathered, the various colored signal lights advancing and waving and flashing back their messages, all served to impress the beholder with the pride, pomp, and circumstance of glorious war.[41]

40 Descriptions of the battle in Lossing, *Civil War*, II, 431–435; Comte de Paris, *Civil War*, II, 900; and *Battles and Leaders*, II, 406–427, have not been bettered by subsequent accounts.
41 MS Diary of Captain Robert Taggard, Pa. State Hist. Society.

But it was not all glory. While the troops on both sides sank exhausted on their arms, the moans, cries, and shrieks of the wounded on the field were heartrending, and little could be done to succor them. The sky grew overcast and inky darkness shut down. Toward dawn came a heavy downpour. "Such rain, and such howling set up by the wounded," wrote a Confederate soldier; "such ugly wounds, sickening to the sight even of the most hardened as the rain beat upon them, washing them to a pale purple; such long-fingered corpses, and in piles, too, like cordwood—may I never see the like again." [42]

The Confederate loss exceeded five thousand, nearly thrice that of the North, and the fourteen of Lee's brigades that had been repulsed were sadly demoralized. Many Union officers, elated by victory, felt that it was not yet too late to turn on the foe and attempt a new advance upon Richmond. But McClellan had the *idée fixe* that the army must establish a safe base of supplies, and early in the morning ordered the retreat to continue to Harrison's Landing. The angriest grumbling ensued. Fitz-John Porter, devoted as he was to his commander, urged him to turn about and attack. Hooker took the same view; they should be pursuing the enemy, not flying from him. Phil Kearny asserted that they could easily take the Confederate capital. "And I say to you all," he told a knot of fuming officers, "such an order can only be prompted by cowardice or treason." A bolder general would have renewed the struggle. [43] To McClellan, however, the first necessity was safety. Independence Day found the army occupying a broad level tract on the James, shielded by streams flowing through swamp and woodland, and protected by guns of the navy.

[VI]

It also found the nation facing the fact that every one of the luminous hopes of spring had been quenched. Halleck had thrown away the happy possibilities after Shiloh; worse still, he had frittered away the powerful army which had won it, scattering the forces in every direction. Farragut's campaign up the river had resulted in total frustration. Lincoln's effort to make the Borderland a constructive demonstration ground for the gradual elimination of slavery had broken down. Worst of all, the second invasion of Virginia had ended in

42 MS Autobiography of James Hewes, Palmer Coll., Western Reserve Hist. Soc.
43 Ropes, *Civil War*, II, 204-207, and *Battles and Leaders*, II, 423 ff., discuss McClellan's refusal to counterattack with a fair estimate of pros and cons. Some Southern officers expected McClellan to take the offensive, and declared later that their troops could not have stopped him. Ropes believed that he could at the very least have held the Malvern lines, nearer Richmond than Harrison's Landing.

failure; a failure that was one long tale of delays and defeats, that had called into play Southern generalship of the most formidable kind, and that ended in the deepest distrust between the chief field commander and the Washington Administration.

Before the North stretched the prospect of a prolonged war, with all its implications: dismaying financial problems, the necessity of conscription, a harsher scrutiny of Administration shortcomings, a deeper schism on war aims between moderates and radicals, rising discontent and disloyalty, a starker danger of foreign intervention. Until thus suddenly ringed by failure, most Northerners had hoped to see the insurrection suppressed without a profound national upheaval. Now revolution faced them on every hand: a party revolution as factional strife boiled up, an economic revolution as war contracts, tariffs, and inflation spurred industry forward, a social revolution, even an intellectual revolution as millions began to think more responsibly and more nationally. From the beginning it had seemed likely that the war would mean the extirpation of slavery, the subordination of the South to the North and West, and a business domination of government; now this was certainty. Transcending all other changes was the fact that every new day of war demanded a larger mobilization of national energies, and that under this demand an organized nation was taking shape, as different from the old as Hector from a babe.

After the Seven Days: Lincoln's Decisions

THE COLLAPSE of McClellan's thrust from the Peninsula made trying demands on Lincoln's patient resolution and resourcefulness. Haunting the War Department and often holding consultations far into the night, he passed some of the most anxious days of his life. When the combined onslaught of Lee and Jackson on McClellan cut off his communications with White House Landing, he sent a series of frantic messages to Burnside at New Bern, John A. Dix at Fort Monroe, and Hunter at Port Royal, urging them to hurry any reinforcements they could spare to the general. He telegraphed Flag-Officer Goldsborough to do what he could with the gunboats. He attempted to borrow some troops, even 10,000, from Halleck in the West. Finding that he could muster not more than 25,000 in all, he telegraphed McClellan on July 4: "Under these circumstances the defensive, for the present, must be your only care. Save the army—first, where you *are*, if you can; and secondly, by removal, if you must." [1]

The great fear, once McClellan was safe, was that Lee might turn northward and attack Washington before a large defensive army could be assembled. McClellan feared it; the enemy, he informed Lincoln on July 4, might prefer an advance upon the capital over an attack on his own force. Seward feared it; the Confederates, he wrote Thurlow Weed, might hold McClellan with a small force and immediately strike northward. General Keyes of McClellan's army feared it; shortly questioned by Lincoln, he said he thought that Lee had withdrawn and was preparing "to go to Washington." Most Northern editors, as the public mourned the hosts of slain and mutilated at Fair Oaks, Gaines's Mill, and Malvern Hill, thought the situation extremely grave. Greeley reproached the government for not telling the nation candidly that the army had been decimated and threatened with extinction, and calling every regiment of militia to Washington. "Men in authority!" he exclaimed. "We entreat you to lean upon the great heart of the people!" [2]

1 Lincoln, *Works*, V, 288, 289.
2 O. R., I, xi, pt. 3, 294; Seward, *Seward in Washington*, 114; Lincoln, *Works*, V, 311; N. Y. *Tribune*, July 5, 1862.

The nation had indeed been ill informed, but not by Lincoln's fault. On June 25, as the Seven Days began, McClellan had ordered all reporters excluded from the front lines. Nothing but rumors and overoptimistic reports got through in the next week. Not until July 3, when the New York *Times* scooped the other papers by a full account of the recent battles, did the North learn that the army had met severe reverses and was in a position of great peril. Next day the *Herald* partially relieved the country's anxiety by dispatches which included the Malvern Hill victory. But still gloom persisted, deepened by reports like that of the Chicago *Tribune* on a "stunning disaster."

The press was soon full of stories that aroused the most poignant emotion. Northerners read of the wounded lying untended for days, while every wagon shed, barn, and Negro cabin was turned into a hospital.[3] They read of the steam coffin factory working night and day on the Chickahominy to make thousands of pine boxes; the vulturelike embalmers with their engines, tubes, and chemicals; the burial parties who shoveled gashed corpses into trenches three feet deep. Battles were inevitable in war. But was it necessary to let pestilence slay more than rifle or cannon, and permit the "Chickahominy fever" to take the army by the throat? People read how the soldiers sickened by platoons: how their eyes brightened, their cheeks flushed, and then they shriveled as their vitality drained away, until their faces grew mummified in death. Southerners, meanwhile, read of a Virginia countryside as wasted as if Tamerlane had passed over it.

Northern feeling was deepened by the steady arrival, train after train, boat after boat, of the human wreckage of the battlefield. The press printed long columns of names with a single word: "J. Eaton, F, Ist N. Y., thigh; F. E. Gass, C, 5th N. H., kdy; T. Scott, G, 18th Ill., dead." Every large city had its tale of young wives searching for wounded husbands, themselves ill, destitute, and half crazed with anxiety. Convalescents were hurried forward as rapidly as possible to their home towns and villages, where their faded uniforms, thin sunburnt faces, and empty sleeves brought home to multitudes the brutality of war. Grief was edged by hatred as atrocity stories studded the press: the bayoneting of wounded, the murder of prisoners. Though mainly baseless, they were believed, and were repeated in the first report of the Committee on the Conduct of the War. Parson Brownlow was doing his utmost to stir up anger over the "fiendish outrages" reported from East Tennessee. Some Southern newspapers meanwhile shrieked for vengeance on despoilers and assassins. It was becoming an ugly-tempered war.

3 Lee wrote D. H. Hill on July 4 to continue the work of burying the dead and picking up the wounded. "I understand that many of the enemy's wounded on Monday's fight are still on the field, they must have suffered greatly, every effort should be made to remove all of them where they will be comfortable." D. H. Hill Papers, Va. State Library.

The two armies before Richmond settled down to recuperate. Lee wrote his wife on July 9: "Our success has not been as great or complete as we could have desired, but God knows what is best for us." Yet the victory was so signal that the spirits of his troops and of the Southern people rose to new heights. His losses totaled more than 19,000, as against 15,250 on the Union side, and in future campaigns he would sadly miss the brave men forever gone. This, however, seemed a small price to pay for the salvation of Richmond and the defeat of the enemy, and Jefferson Davis proclaimed a general thanksgiving. From abandoned Union stores the Confederates took a rich profit, for all along the roads the litter of materials enabled the troops to replenish their arms and supplies. Shoes were stripped from the Union dead. Rifles and cartridges were substituted for wornout powder-and-ball muskets. At Savage Station, Jackson captured not only the huge field hospital of the North, with 2,500 wounded, but ammunition, wagons, pontoon trains, mules, a war balloon, camp utensils, barrels of beef and pork, and what one rebel called a very Eden of other foods. For the first time in months many Southerners tasted butter and coffee, and slept under woolen blankets.

The morale of McClellan's army was now difficult to assess. Fighting magnificently, it had won victories at Glendale and Malvern Hill in the last days of the change of base; and though it had lost much of the pride and confidence with which it had entered on the campaign, to an astonishing degree the troops kept their faith in their leader and themselves. For this faith the army could offer two main reasons. First, it shared McClellan's conviction that it had been beset by superior forces, and that selfish politicians had denied it proper reinforcements. Frederick Law Olmsted of the Sanitary Commission wrote of the overpowering enemy array, which Union men thought more than double their own, and told how anxiously the Northern army had looked over its shoulders in every battle to see if reinforcements were coming. The rank and file at Malvern Hill believed, just as much as McClellan, that they had 200,000 Confederates facing them. And in the second place, the troops appreciated the care McClellan had taken to spare life and limb. Privates appalled by wholesale death and amputation were content that he had besieged, not assaulted, Yorktown, and that after Fair Oaks he had entrenched for a gradual advance instead of making frontal assults. During the perilous retreat to the James they were thankful for McClellan's cautious movements and foresight in providing so large an artillery park.[4]

4 See Olmsted Papers, July 8–20. Against excessive amputations a thousand voices were raised. "A cry comes up from our hospitals, and its echo is heard all over the land," said the N. Y. *Tribune*, July 30, 1862, "against the free use of the surgeon's knife and saw on the legs and arms of our wounded soldiers. That there is just cause for complaint we have the assurance of medical men. . . . Young aspirants for distinction in the profession of

Most soldiers blamed Northern radicals for not giving them sufficient force; few blamed their leader.

McClellan's own attitude united his faith in a providential mission with his conviction that treacherous men and stupid policies had ruined all his labors. At the beginning of the Seven Days he telegraphed his wife: "I am confident that God will smile upon my efforts and give our arms success." Just after the struggle he assured her that the power of the Almighty "has saved me and my army." [5] Positive that, outnumbered almost two to one, betrayed by the jealous McDowell, and stabbed in the back by Stanton, he had brought the nation through the storm, on June 28 he sent Stanton a hysterical dispatch that did him no credit. He had just fought the most desperate battle of the war, he wrote (though Gaines's Mill did not compare with Shiloh). He had lost it because his force was too small (though he had 20,000 more men than the Confederates, much better armed). With even 10,000 fresh troops next day, he would take Richmond, but he had no reserves whatever (though two of his corps commanders could have sent in more than that number of fresh men). He was not at fault—it was Washington!

"I have seen too many dead and wounded comrades," he concluded, "to feel otherwise than that the Government has not sustained this army. If you do not do so now the game is lost. If I save this army now, I tell you plainly that I owe no thanks to you or to any other person in Washington. You have done your best to sacrifice this army." The supervisor of telegraphs struck the two last sentences from the copy given Stanton, so that neither he nor Lincoln saw it. Happily for the national morale, no part of the dispatch was published till seven eventful months had elapsed. Stanton carried the telegram to Lincoln in the deepest agitation, saying, "You know, Mr. President, that all I have done was by your authority"; and Lincoln shared his resentment.[6]

Most of the Northern public took a realistic view of McClellan's record, for with few exceptions, the press gave an accurate report of the disasters to the army. Interpretation was naturally colored by party feeling. The Chicago Tribune, like other radical organs, began calling for his dismissal on June 20; the Cincinnati Commercial, with most conservative Democratic journals, placed the blame for his failure squarely on Stanton. While Bryant's Evening Post regarded the general's leadership as imbecile throughout, the National Intelli-

surgery easily persuade themselves that the wounded or shattered limb of a soldier is a proper subject on which to practise the science of amputation."

5 Quotations from My Own Story, 441, 445; on July 17, McClellan wrote of the Seven Days that "I stood alone without any one to help me." See also Browning, Diary, I, 559.

6 The dispatch without the two last sentences appeared in the Report, Committee on Conduct of War, I, 339, 340, published in the press April 6, 1863. The two offensive sentences were included by McClellan in his Report, published in book form in 1864; pp. 257, 258.

gencer pronounced the march to the James a masterly movement. However, although the *World* assailed Lincoln in a way which grieved its correspondent Edmund Clarence Stedman, and the *Herald* attacked the War Department, it was McClellan who suffered most. Great numbers of intelligent observers agreed that no faith could now be placed in this "hero of a hundred ungained victories." [7]

[I]

Lincoln was indeed ready to lean on the great heart of the nation, but not to issue appeals that would provoke a panic, to yield an iota of his due powers to Congress, or to foment sectional hatreds. On the date Lee began the Seven Days, June 26, Lincoln had consolidated the scattered forces of Banks, Frémont, and McDowell into one new command, the Army of Virginia, under Major-General John Pope. He had made a flying visit to New York for a five-hour consultation with Winfield Scott, who apparently recommended calling Halleck to the East. Stanton had just previously telegraphed the governors, on June 18: "We are in pressing need of troops. How many can you send on immediately?" Their replies had been most discouraging. Illinois alone could send troops at once, a regiment of infantry and cavalry apiece; Ohio could forward a regiment of ninety-day men within a fortnight; New Hampshire and Vermont could each supply a regiment in July—but the others pleaded helplessness. The fact was that at that date, as a news dispatch in the Springfield *Republican* asserted, most Northerners still believed the Union had troops enough if only they were properly distributed. It had taken a thunderclap of defeat to awaken the nation. Now that the blow had fallen, Seward proposed to hurry North to arouse popular determination, and arrange for raising new armies. Lincoln and Stanton approved the step, giving the Secretary their fullest encouragement.

Seward at once departed (June 28) to confer with Governors Morgan and Curtin, bearing a letter in which Lincoln declared that 100,000 new troops were imperatively needed. "I expect to maintain this contest," wrote the President, "until successful or till I die, or am conquered, or my term expires, or Congress or the country forsakes me; and I would publicly appeal to the country for this new force, were it not that I fear a general panic and stampede would follow. . . ." The situation clearly required a larger body than the number named, and the press was demanding it. "We have foolishly under-

---

7 The Chicago *Morning Post*, July 6, 10, and the N. Y. *Times*, July 7, published surveys of press opinion. Stanton was deeply hurt by the abuse showered upon him, and wrote a long letter to a friend defending himself, but made no public reply; Gorham, *Stanton*, II, 426–432. He refused to risk injury to the cause by an open quarrel.

rated the strength and pluck of the rebels," said the *World;* "we foolishly stopped recruiting." Out of Seward's New York conferences came a proposal that the governors should unite in asking Lincoln for a great new levy, and that the President should respond. Some of the governors thought that half a million men were needed, and Lincoln, after considering 200,000, telegraphed John A. Andrew that it seemed safest to set the figure high: "It is 300,000." On July 11 he called on the States for that number of additional men, chiefly infantry, who should serve for three years.[8]

The President's last hope that the war would be short expired in these bitter days. He wrote Governor Morgan on July 3 that time was everything, and that if he had 50,000 additional troops "here *now,* I believe I could substantially close the war in two weeks." But at this very moment the arrival in Washington of Marcy, McClellan's father-in-law and chief of staff, with a gloomy report of the army's situation, gave the President a bad shock. Furnishing Stanton his own and McClellan's views, Marcy said he would not be astonished if the army were obliged to capitulate. In angry consternation, Stanton flew to the White House with this statement, and Lincoln, equally incensed, at once summoned Marcy. "General," he said sternly, "I understand you have used the word 'capitulate'; that is a word not to be used in connection with our army." Capitulation would be precisely the treason of which many radicals suspected McClellan! As Lincoln proceeded with his reprimand, Marcy blundered out a lame apology, while later he returned to the War Department to make peace with Stanton. But it had been an ugly moment, and never after digesting the news of McClellan's failure did Lincoln make another statement like that to Morgan. He saw that two years was a likelier measure of the continuance of the war. He was now ready for a pragmatic experimentalism with commanders; he would take the best he could get, East and West, try them thoroughly, discard the unfit, and promote the able. This gaunt Illinois frontiersman, still mild, still patient, had developed a greater sternness than Andrew Jackson ever showed.

Lincoln needed steel traits to deal not only with the South, but with Congress. Some Republican leaders inevitably seized upon the opportunity for striking at McClellan, at Seward, and indirectly at the President; for emphasizing their own powers and setting a chisel to Lincoln's. They were abetted by the Democrats, who commenced a pitiless assault on Stanton as the real culprit in McClellan's reverses. But this Democratic attack, while irritating,

8 Frémont promptly resigned because he believed that Pope had deliberately frustrated him in the Missouri campaign, and could not bear to serve under Pope's orders. For Lincoln's call, see *Works,* V, 296, 297. The *World* followed its demand for more troops (June 21) with repeated editorials asking Stanton's dismissal. Seward, *Seward in Washington,* 100–124, presents full detail on the Northern trip of the Secretary.

was not really important. It scored just one heavy blow against Lincoln—the revelation that he and nobody else had been responsible for the order stopping the march of McDowell to reinforce McClellan; for in the light of subsequent events, this order appeared most unfortunate.[9] But Lincoln had no desire to conceal it, and no great fear of Democrats. The Republicans controlled Congress, and their maneuvers gave Lincoln his principal anxiety.

The chorus in denunciation of McClellan was led by Zach Chandler, who defended Stanton, and pointed out that the Democratic diatribes against the Secretary of War were really aimed at Lincoln. The President's hold upon public esteem was such that few had the hardihood to indict him, and Democrats therefore invented the fiction that Stanton really ruled the government in military matters. This fable the Republicans easily exploded. Chandler's indictment of McClellan's campaign was echoed by the Chicago and New York *Tribunes*. Congress meanwhile set up a renewed outcry for making the South feel the full edge of the sword; for waging war at rebel expense, on rebel property, and with rebel slaves and supplies. Numerous voices took up the exhortation. Lew Wallace told a crowd of serenaders in Washington that he favored putting a black regiment into every white brigade for digging trenches and driving teams, and that he would never again lead a column through a Southern countryside without seizing all that it offered. "Oh, if I could get a little backbone into those who are governing us!" The lieutenant-governor of Ohio proclaimed that he would enlist Negroes, confiscate property, and if necessary lay the South as waste as the Mojave desert.[10] Even Thurlow Weed, just back from a useful propagandist sojourn in England which had taught him a good deal, believed the military should accept and employ every slave it could get.

But nowhere did the cry for stopping "kid-glove warfare" ring louder than in the Senate. Henry Wilson of Massachusetts and Henry M. Rice of Minnesota solemnly avowed that the choice lay between harsher measures and a recognition of Southern independence. Wilson knew that Stanton was with them. A bill amending the Militia Act was before Congress, and many members favored enrolling large numbers of Negroes "for any war service for which they may be found competent," as a clause read. We need less tenderness toward traitors and murderers, asserted Fessenden of Maine, and John Sherman agreed.

As part of this Spartan severity, members swiftly resuscitated the confiscation bill lying in conference committee. Reported to the House with stiffened terms, it passed that body 82 to 42. Its direct provisions on confiscation were

9 Browning, *Diary*, I, 559, for the Marcy incident.
10 The N. Y. *Tribune*, July 11, 1862, gives these speeches in full.

much less important than its frontal attack upon slavery. To be sure, the bill declared it the duty of the President to cause the seizure of all property of long categories of Southerners, and made all other persons who abetted the rebellion, sixty days after he gave public warning, equally liable to loss of their estates; Federal courts being empowered to dispose of forfeited property for the benefit of the Treasury. Obviously, the effectiveness of these clauses depended on Presidential cooperation. But much more important were the provisions that the slaves of all who supported the rebellion should be deemed legitimate war seizures, "forever free"; that the President might employ as many Negroes as he saw fit, and in such tasks as he deemed best; and that he might also colonize freedmen abroad.[11] The Senate, passing the bill July 12 by a vote of 28 to 13, sent it to the uneasy President—for Lincoln saw how frontally it challenged his intention to keep the slavery question in his own hands.

During the debate Lincoln had tried to modify this legislation, talking with Fessenden and other callers at the White House, and even threatening a veto. Wade of Ohio angrily characterized his activities as illegitimate and unconstitutional, "the most unfortunate thing during the whole war," and Lane of Indiana was equally wrathful against what he called legislation under duress.[12] The President had his way, for Congress at the last moment averted the veto message he had prepared by passing an explanatory resolution which removed most of his objections. At heart, radical members and editors were apprehensive that he would not enforce the law with drastic vigor—and hence their outcries. They were quite right. He signed the Second Confiscation Act, for he saw that public sentiment demanded something of the kind; but he never wavered in his belief that such vindictive measures should be avoided, for the nation must in time be restored as a truly fraternal union, a union of hearts, and he never abated his determination to keep the handling of slavery, which would lie at the core of national reconstruction, under his own control.[13]

[II]

Yet the President could not stand still. Time, as July advanced, pressed him hard in the management of opinion no less than of the armies. He read snatches from the more extreme newspapers, in which Bryant, Greeley, and Medill were

11 *Cong. Globe*, 37th Cong., 2d Sess., 3197–3207; 3266–3268.
12 *Cong. Globe*, 37th Cong., 2d Sess., 3376 ff. for this debate. Chandler of Michigan continued pressing a motion to obtain the correspondence between the executive department and McClellan, obviously for the purpose of making trouble for both. Moderate opinion deplored both the motion and his speeches; N. Y. *Times*, July 10, 1862.
13 For Lincoln's views on the importance of a truly fraternal reunion, see Nevins, *Papers of the Abraham Lincoln Association* (1930), 51–92. The explanatory resolution of Congress, relieving the bill of all taint of ex post facto or attainder implications, is in *Works*, V, 328–331, along with Lincoln's draft of a veto message.

ever more clamorous against slavery; watched the closing Congressional debates, in which Sumner, Thaddeus Stevens, Trumbull, and other men he respected were nearly as outspoken as Wade and Chandler; heard echoes of the utterances of Owen Lovejoy, Parson Brownlow, and Henry Ward Beecher; talked with Congressional leaders; and in short, felt the quickening of the national pulse. Meanwhile, he devoted his own anxious thought to the Negro. Hating slavery, he was more intent on its ultimate eradication than ever.

Sumner had called at the White House twice on July 4 to plead that the President reconsecrate the day by a decree of emancipation. The first time Lincoln protested that while he might take such a step for eastern Virginia, a proclamation for the entire South was "too big a lick now." Sumner replied that the nation needed big licks. The second time Lincoln offered a detailed argument for delay, as if he might be weakening.[14] On July 11 Governor Yates exploded in a fierce dispatch to the White House. He telegraphed that "the time has come for the adoption of more decisive measures," that "blows must be struck at the vital parts of the rebellion," that loyal Negroes who offered to serve the Union should be accepted, and that Union armies should forage on the enemy. Lincoln knew that the governor spoke for general Republican sentiment in Illinois. On the 12th, the day the confiscation bill passed, he telegraphed his old Illinois friend: "Dick, hold still and see the salvation of God." [15]

It was plain to him that if he did not keep his leadership of the movement against slavery, Congress would wrest it from him. The true title of the confiscation act, as his secretaries later wrote, should have been: "An act to destroy slavery under the powers of war." The new law proposed freeing all slaves of all rebels wherever reached. It did not touch the slaves of loyal persons. But how many citizens in Missouri or South Carolina could prove their loyalty? Lincoln acknowledged that the Act was constitutional, and that Congress could free a slave if that slave had been forfeited to the government by a traitor. But he believed that as commander-in-chief he possessed larger powers than Congress over slavery. He also believed that, as President of the whole people, he possessed broader views and a more moderate temper than the extremists in Congress.

As the crowded first fortnight of July drew to a close, he therefore made a final plea for cooperation by the Border States. Calling their members in Con-

14 Sumner had taken steps to see that other men reinforced his arguments. "Won't you come here to help?" he wrote Carl Schurz July 5. "By voice and presence you can do much—very, very much. God bless you!" Schurz Papers, LC. What Lincoln and Sumner said to each other was reported by A. S. Hill, July 9, 1862, to S. H. Gay; Gay Papers. Sumner records that Lincoln told him July 4: "I would do it if I were not afraid that half the officers would fling down their arms and three more States would rise." *Works*, VII, 215.

15 Lincoln's reply to Yates is not in the *Works*. Yates later quoted it in a speech to a New York meeting; N. Y. *Tribune*, October 30, 1863.

gress to the White House on the 12th, he read a careful argument. He assured them of his conviction that if they had supported his gradual emancipation plan in March, the war by summer would have been substantially ended. He again promised an effort toward colonization, and spoke of ample room in Latin America. He described the tremendous outcry which had followed his annulment of Hunter's liberation order: "I gave dissatisfaction, if not offense, to many whose support the country cannot afford to lose. And this is not the end of it. The pressure is still upon me and is increasing." He appealed to self-interest, saying that if the war continued long slavery would be extinguished by mere friction and abrasion. "It will be gone and you will have nothing in lieu of it. Much of its value is gone already! How much better for you, and for your people, to take the step which, at once, shortens the war, and secures substantial compensation for that which is sure to be wholly lost in any other event." They could save the nation "the money which else we sink forever."

When next day two Illinois Representatives, Isaac N. Arnold and Owen Lovejoy, called on him at the Soldiers' Home, he showed an unwonted intensity of emotion. "Oh," he said, "how I wish the border States would accept my proposition. Then you, Lovejoy, and you, Arnold, and all of us, would not have lived in vain!" So Arnold later recalled his words, though we know that his thoughts were already turning in an alternative direction.[16]

While utterly sincere in this appeal, Lincoln was sadly aware that it would meet no response. Without delay a majority reply signed by Crittenden, Garrett Davis, and eighteen other border members reiterated the old objections. They protested that the original Northern policy was simply to restore the Union, that State Rights and a sacred domestic institution were at stake, that Congress had paid an average of only $300 for District slaves and would haggle over the costs, and that the step would not reduce but augment Confederate defiance. George P. Fisher and six others signed a statement, drafted by Neill of Missouri, promising to entreat the people to consider the proposal, while Henderson of Missouri and Maynard of Tennessee made the same declaration separately. The

---

16 Nicolay and Hay, *Lincoln*, VI, 111, 112; *Works*, V, 317-319; Arnold, *Lincoln*, 251; N. Y. *Times, Tribune*, July 19, 1862. Secretary Caleb Smith had informed the President that District of Columbia freedmen were unwilling to go to Liberia and that Haiti was objectionable, but that New Granada (Colombia) offered favorable conditions. J. Watson Webb, minister to Brazil, believed that the Brazilian plethora of land and shortage of labor would make colonization feasible there. For Smith's letter of May 9, 1862, to Lincoln, see Department of the Interior, Division of Slave Trade Suppression, National Archives. Panama and Chiriqui were part of New Granada. Webb suggested that the United States ship its freed Negroes to Brazil at its own expense, and that Brazil provide wild lands free of cost and guarantee eventual citizenship. When he asked for power to negotiate a treaty with Brazil covering this scheme, Seward, who had encountered such violent objections from Costa Rica, Nicaragua, and Honduras to any colonization there, replied that the whole subject was under discussion and until the public mind evolved some decision, the question must remain in abeyance. Webb's plan thus died. *Dip. Corr. U. S., 1862*, pp. 712-715.

response thus stood 20 to 9 against Lincoln.[17] His earnestly-pressed plan received its deathblow.

Did it ever really have a chance of success? Despite all appearances to the contrary, we may believe that the President's sagacity had not failed him. If Delaware had promptly accepted his proposal, selling her slaves for the $500,000 that Congress would have gladly distributed in bonds, the movement might have swept Missouri and Maryland along with it. Delaware refused by a close margin. Missouri sentiment was steadily ripening. Though a special convention which the governor had called for various purposes was unwilling to take action on Lincoln's proposal, antislavery feeling was crystallizing with such energy that abolitionists were forming local societies at many points, and met in convention on June 16 to call for gradual emancipation. The radical leader B. Gratz Brown elatedly proclaimed: "This is Transition, This is Progress, This is Revolution." [18] Certainly three-fourths of the people of West Virginia, as of western Maryland, were anxious to rid themselves of slavery. With more vision and nerve among border leaders, with less stiffnecked pride, these States might have trodden Lincoln's path.

Anticipating rejection, the President had now almost taken a great resolve. He knew that the nation, after its military humiliation, needed a fresh inspiration. He knew that liberal opinion overseas could not understand his delay in striking at slavery. It was difficult to give up his plan. Sumner was impressed by his earnestness. "His whole soul was occupied. . . . In familiar intercourse with him, I remember nothing more touching than the earnestness and completeness with which he embraced this idea." But as he had to give it up, one alternative alone was feasible.

Part of the morrow of the futile conference, Sunday, the 13th, Lincoln occupied in driving with Seward, Welles, and Mrs. Frederick Seward to the funeral of Stanton's infant child. His companions were struck by his gravity. The government had reached a crisis, he remarked; it must make new military arrangements to meet the astonishing strength of the Confederacy, find a fresh inspiration to stimulate volunteering, and tap the reservoir of slave power. For the first time in Welles's hearing he spoke of emancipation as a war weapon. It was a grave step, but he had "about come to the conclusion" that it was essential;

17 The division was actually closer than this figure indicates, for three out-of-town members, Whaley of Virginia, Leary of Maryland, and Blair of Missouri, would have signed the assenting paper. The N. Y. *Tribune*, July 16, 1862, believed that several who voted no were at heart in favor of Lincoln's plan.

18 F. A. Culmer, *A New History of Missouri*, 428 ff. Local emancipation societies were being formed in Missouri as branches of the General Emancipation Society in the State, and displayed enthusiasm in their call for gradual abolition. A bill to appropriate ten millions (amended to twenty) to pay for Missouri slaves was introduced in Congress. Trexler, *Slavery in Mo.*, 233 ff.

they must free the slaves or be subdued. When he asked Seward and Welles how the proposal struck them, Seward hesitated. "Emancipation involves consequences so momentous that I wish time for mature reflection before giving an answer," he said in effect. "But my present opinion inclines to the measure as justifiable, and I might say expedient and necessary." Welles agreed. After the funeral they reverted to the subject. Lincoln entreated them to give the question earnest thought, for "I am fixed in the conviction that something must be done." [19]

[III]

At this moment he was drastically reorganizing the structure of military command. On July 11 he appointed Henry Wager Halleck general-in-chief of the Union armies. The press reported on the 14th that Lincoln had the appointment in mind, and on the 16th that Halleck was about to reach Washington. On the 22nd he arrived, and next day Lincoln published the order giving him control of all the land forces of the nation. Obviously he would keep his headquarters in the capital and would not exercise a field command. This fact did not reconcile McClellan, who had no advance intimation of the step from either Lincoln or Stanton, for he found it grating to serve under the authority of a man "whom I know to be my inferior." He instantly wrote a friend that Halleck's appointment was intended as a slap in his face, and told his wife that he would be inexpressibly happy to resign: "I am weary, very weary, submitting to the whims of such 'things' as those now over me." [20]

Lincoln had made two new selections of the highest importance, and both Pope and Halleck were in different ways to prove weak appointments. It is natural to ask whether he had shown proper circumspection in his choices. Defective as the intelligence service of the Union armies was, that of the White House and War Department was worse. Had Lincoln possessed the means of gathering full, astute, and candid information, he would not have chosen such a swaggering, muddleheaded egotist as Pope to direct a critical army, and would have hesitated longer in designating such a myopic, indecisive pedant as Halleck to govern all the military forces. Here, as never before, he needed an industrious, tough-minded adviser on personnel.

The public knew John Pope as a West Pointer who had served capably in the Mexican War, accompanied Lincoln's party to the inauguration, and won a reverberant success at Island No. 10. Apart from his Illinois background, Lincoln

19 Welles, *Diary*, I, 70, 71, offers the only record of this drive. See also Browning, *Diary*, I, 553-559.
20 McClellan's *Own Story*, 450-453; McClellan to S. L. M. Barlow, July 23, 1862, Barlow Papers.

did not know much more. But a shrewd White House aide could have found out a good deal. Gustav Koerner could have told him that Pope was disliked by comrades in the regular army, and that as division commander in Missouri his tactlessness, aggressiveness, and braggadocio had made him unpopular with officers and men.[21] Frémont could have furnished clear evidence of insubordination. Journalists would have scored Pope for his false claim that he had taken 10,000 prisoners in the mopping-up operations after Corinth, when he had only a tenth of that number, while others would have assured Lincoln that he was an untruthful, undependable, and unintelligent Captain Bobadil. Dark, martial-looking, and handsome with his flowing hair, full beard, and flashing black eyes, he was too florid, too obese, and too loose in ideas and manners to be a good commander. Reporters were struck by his incessant smoking, garrulous story-telling, and shallow vanity.[22]

For Halleck much more could be said, and to many Lincoln's elevation of the man, recommended by Winfield Scott and accepted without enthusiasm by Stanton, appeared sound. We have rehearsed the impressive facts of his career, and army officers in general would have joined Joseph Hooker in pronouncing him a man of ability and expert military knowledge.

Nevertheless, he had received laurels which he had not earned. He had been credited with clearing up "abuses" in Missouri which were partly imaginary; with the movement against Donelson, which he did not conceive; and with the victories of Pea Ridge and Island No. 10, to which he had made but minor contributions. What was more significant, he had escaped blame for serious blunders. On the day of Grant's first great victory he had cautioned him not to be "too rash," while he was responsible for the costly delay after Donelson in moving on Nashville. His suspicions had almost robbed the army of Grant's talents. He had taken a month to get to Corinth when a week should have sufficed, and had given a misleading impression of the march that had deceived Stanton and half the country. Capping all this was the aplomb with which he flung away his opportunities after Corinth.

Before the war ended numerous men were to set down their judgment of Halleck in terms only less scathing than McClellan's. Actually he meant well, worked hard, had sound general views, and stood loyally by his superiors. But, fussy, pedantic, and plodding, he lacked grasp and imagination. General Ormsby

21 Koerner, *Memoirs*, II, 235.
22 He was temporarily a pet of Chase's, and Chase's diary is revealing. See also G. A. Townsend, *Campaigns of a Non-Combatant*, 218; Welles, *Diary*, I, 221; and Schofield's derisive statement in *Forty-Six Years*, 358, 359. For the false claim of 10,000 prisoners after Corinth see Villard, *Memoirs*, I, 279-281. Pope maintained that Halleck was responsible for this fabrication, and that he evaded admitting the fact. It involved both men in great ridicule, but when Pope later visited Congress he bragged that altogether he had taken 30,000 prisoners! Interesting Pope letters may be found in the Hay Papers, Ill. State Hist. Lib.

Mitchel, coming to discuss a critical problem, found him willing to talk only of his hay fever. "When the enemy are thundering at the gates," exclaimed Mitchel, "hay fever!" Sanitary Commission leaders, calling on him in Washington, retired in despair. "God help the country!" exclaimed one. W. T. Sherman came to detest him. He did not know the meaning of energy and foresight; new problems worried his legalistic mind, and new enterprises irritated him. "He sits and smokes and swears and scratches his arms," wrote Gideon Welles. Attorney-General Bates decided that he was "both knave and fool."

The harshest verdicts, however, were unfair. His letters in the *Official Records* prove his industry, understanding of general principles, and scholarly insight. He stood like an iron barricade against placing various unfit men in high commands, and bore the brunt of attacks for some unpopular acts that were really Lincoln's or Stanton's. Welles came closest to the truth when, making a valid distinction, he declared that Halleck was a good scholarly critic of other men's deeds and ideas, but was incapable of originating or directing military operations himself. Excellent in grasp of theory, he was inert, muddy-headed, and erratic in action. He had an unmilitary cast of mind, and recoiled from direct control of armies.[23]

It was unfortunate that the signal demonstration he had just given of his limitations as a field commander was not yet properly understood. At the beginning of June, as we have seen, he had possessed at or near Corinth an army of 128,315, of whom 108,538 were fit for duty. Their generals included Grant, Sherman, Thomas, Sheridan. After the capture of Memphis on June 6, this array, eager for action, was capable, as Grant later said, of rolling up half the Confederate map in the West. It might have taken the remaining river strongholds of Port Hudson and Vicksburg; it might then have marched to the mountain stronghold of Chattanooga, the gateway through which armies from the central Confederacy would have to advance if they ever tried to recover important parts of Tennessee and Kentucky. At the very least, one of these great Union objectives could have been secured before September browned cornfield and meadow.

23 A study of Halleck has been much needed. Badeau, *Mil. Hist. U. S. Grant*, is a treasury of information on his merits and defects; see index. Lincoln at first, with little real information, thought well of him, but in the summer of 1862 realized that he totally lacked nerve in critical situations, and let him become a colorless office general who deputed real authority to others. Hay, *Diaries*, (Dennett ed.), 176; J. D. Cox, *Rems.*, I, 254–262; G. T. Strong, *Diary*, III, 258 (Sept. 24, 1862). Ropes declared (*Civil War*, II, 234, 235, 285) that neither the Administration nor public can be criticized for calling Halleck to his high post, for his qualifications seemed great; and Ropes then concurs in Welles's balanced estimate. Grant's statement on Halleck's "gigantic intellect" is the more notable because made in a private letter; Grant to E. Washburne, July 22, 1862, Washburne Papers, LC. But then Grant was often overgenerous in estimates of other generals. For Sherman's views, see *The Sherman Letters*, 345.

But Halleck lost all the rich opportunities before him by dispersing his army in fragments of ineffective size. It is true that extenuating circumstances existed. He later told Sherman that he had been hampered by orders from Washington, and an abler general than he might have felt confused by the real difficulties before him. They included the great distances for offensive operations—some 200 miles from Corinth to Chattanooga, some 240 to Vicksburg; the problem of supplying more than 100,000 men at Corinth while the Tennessee River was steadily falling; the strength of the enemy, for Beauregard had nearly 60,000 effectives, and other commanders 30,000 in the Jackson-Vicksburg area, while considerable forces lay in Tennessee and Arkansas; and the possibility that McClellan's demands would force Stanton to withdraw troops from the West. But the sad fact was that he advanced against neither Vicksburg nor Chattanooga. To be sure, he moved Buell *toward* Chattanooga, but with inadequate strength and with unwise orders to repair and hold the railroad as he went.[24]

Official dispatches put the general in a dubious light. Lincoln on June 5 sent him a message from McClellan beseeching him to occupy Chattanooga and Dalton—"the importance of this move . . . cannot be exaggerated." Halleck was able to report that Buell's troops had already moved in that direction, but not that they were making any progress. He notified Stanton that Pope's force had met great impediments in its chase of Beauregard's army retreating from Corinth. "I do not propose pursuing him any farther, but to send all forces not required to hold the Memphis & Charleston to the relief of Curtis in Arkansas and to East Tennessee. . . ." Stanton approved of this, but added: "I suppose you contemplate the occupation of Vicksburg and clearing out the Mississippi to New Orleans." Halleck did *not* contemplate it, for he replied that he would send an expedition against Vicksburg only if Farragut and Davis could not take it, and only after reinforcing Curtis. When the heat and anxiety of the Seven Days came on, Lincoln had Stanton ask Halleck to spare 25,000 troops, unless their dispatch would endanger the Chattanooga movement. But as Halleck expostulated that the departure of this force *would* ruin it, Lincoln bade Stanton re-emphasize this insistence that the Chattanooga expedition must not be abandoned on any account.[25]

The upshot was that Bragg's Confederates got to Chattanooga first, and

24 The older treatments of Halleck's Western command range from the sweeping indictments by John Fiske, Ropes, and Adam Badeau to the more sober criticism of F. V. Greene; but practically all are condemnatory. Kenneth P. Williams, *Lincoln Finds a General*, III, 428–436, gives a moderate view, but on the whole is adverse.

25 O. R., I, x, pt. 1, pp. 668–671; 1, xvi, pt. 2, pp. 8, 62–82. Halleck was disgusted by the call for 25,000 of his troops, happily at once revoked. He informed McClernand at Jackson, Tenn., on June 30: "The defeat of General McClellan near Richmond has produced another stampede at Washington," adding, "The entire campaign in the West is broken up by these orders and we shall very probably lose all we have gained."

Vicksburg remained unthreatened. Halleck had directed Grant, Buell, and Pope (later Rosecrans) to resume command of their armies of the Tennessee, Ohio, and Mississippi. He sent McClernand and Lew Wallace to Bolivar, Tennessee, northwest of Corinth; Pope to Rienzi, Mississippi, due south; Grant and Sherman to Memphis on the west; and Buell northeast. Ormsby Mitchel, who had a small force at Huntsville, Alabama, had shown what celerity could accomplish by a dash early in June to the very portals of Chattanooga, culminating in his erection of batteries on the north bank of the Tennessee opposite the town. Halleck, however, made no effort to hurry Buell to his assistance, and he had to fall back. At Vicksburg, meanwhile, the Confederates were toiling night and day to augment their fortifications, and were soon bringing in large reinforcements. Farragut in breaking off his river offensive made a statement on which Union leaders could soon reflect ruefully. "I am satisfied," he reported, "that it is not possible to take Vicksburg without an army of 12,000 to 15,000 men." Halleck could have spared twice that number without great difficulty; and in the end, five times as many would be needed.

One great gain from Halleck's transfer to Washington was that Grant obtained a fuller freedom of command and a larger field. From his Memphis headquarters he controlled all the troops in Tennessee west of the Cumberland, and in Mississippi so far as he could conquer that State. Halleck's first instructions to him from Washington began (July 31): "You must judge for yourself the best use to be made of your troops." Grant's advancement was to prove one of the momentous events of the war.

As for John Pope, on reaching the East he began working hard to put his troops in better condition. On July 14 he issued to his army a deplorable address. He saw fit, on the heels of McClellan's retreat to the James, to boast that Western troops had always seen the backs of *their* enemies. "I hear constantly of taking strong positions and holding them—of lines of retreat—and of bases of supplies. Let us discard such ideas." Foolish at any time, such an address at this moment rubbed salt in all McClellan's wounds, angered Fitz-John Porter and other corps commanders, and antagonized the troops on whom Pope must depend for cooperation. While his own men laughed at it, McClellan's men thought it outrageous. Its worst aspect was its suggestion that Pope expected to lead his army to separate and speedy victory, when if any need was paramount it was for unity of effort.[26]

However, Pope quickly did worse. On July 18 he issued a set of general orders which, inspired by Stanton, stained the whole Northern war effort. They were intended to show that Pope, unlike McClellan, had a mailed fist. Order No. 5 directed that his Army of the Potomac should subsist, as far as practicable,

[26] For troop attitudes see N. Y. *Tribune*, Aug. 1, 1862.

on the country, giving vouchers for supplies taken; the vouchers to be payable at the end of the war, and then only if the owners proved they had been consistently loyal since the date of receipt. Order No. 6 declared that cavalry should dispense with supply trains and levy on the localities traversed for their needs. Order No. 7 notified the people of Northern Virginia that they would be held responsible for guerrilla outrages. If any railways, roads, or telegraphs were damaged, the inhabitants within a radius of five miles should be turned out to repair them, while any person detected in firing on Union soldiers from a house should be shot without civil process. Five days later Pope issued his still more Draconian General Order No. 11. This required officers to arrest immediately all disloyal citizens of Virginia within reach, to give them a choice of taking the oath of allegiance or accepting deportation to the South, to treat all who returned across the line as spies subject to the death penalty, and to shoot all who violated their oaths of allegiance.[27]

These orders had much better never been written. Those for subsistence on the country inspired an appetite for looting which responsible officers found it difficult to check. As for No. 7, President Davis immediately let it be known that the Confederacy would retaliate if anyone were put to death, and it remained empty bombast. Had it been enforced, it would merely have sent more men across the lines to strengthen Lee's army. But however ineffective, Pope's harsh edicts worsened the moral climate of the war, for troops East and West long remembered them and were influenced by their tone. They angered McClellan, and steeled Southerners to a more bitter resistance. Halleck, to his credit, pronounced them injudicious.[28]

It is true that Pope found much provocation in the fact that guerrillas had been picking off isolated soldiers. The marching troops, writes one regimental historian, occasionally saw a grizzled man hoeing vegetables near his cabin, oblivious to the passing column. But when the main body had passed and some footsore boy came limping along, the man had dropped his hoe. He was crouching with his rifle in the bushes—and at company roll call next morning another soldier was reported missing.[29] Some papers of Colonel John D. Imboden, which were captured in July, showed that members of his First Partisan Rangers were expected to stay home part of the time as noncombatants, and rove the countryside at others. "My purpose," wrote Imboden, "is to wage the most active war against our brutal invaders, and their domestic allies; to hang about their camps and shoot down every sentinel, picket, courier, and wagon driver we can find; to watch opportunities for attacking convoys and wagon

27 O. R., I, xii, pt. 2, pp. 50 ff.
28 O. R., I, xi, pt. 3, p. 359; I, xii, pt. 3, pp. 500, 501; Rhodes, IV, 101, 102.
29 Alfred Davenport, *Fifth New York*, 175, 176.

trains." [30] But such facts do not excuse Pope's orders to regularly organized troops.

It seems astonishing that Lincoln, who had so quickly annulled a milder order by Frémont, should have read all four edicts without objection. They contravened his characteristic spirit of magnanimity, and Order No. 11 violated the recognized rules of war. Doubtless he knew that Stanton was their real author; perhaps he did not wish to chastise Pope just as he took command; he had to consider the popular temper, and he was wrestling with many other problems. Still, he should have interfered.[31]

[IV]

The principal question before Lincoln, Halleck, and Stanton was what to do with McClellan. Should he be reinforced at Harrison's Landing, so close to Richmond, and encouraged to make a fresh movement against Lee, or should he be brought back to unite his army with Pope's in northern Virginia, or should he be dismissed? Montgomery C. Meigs thought he should be ousted, and his army combined with Pope's. Two members of the Cabinet favored an equally drastic course. Stanton and Chase urged the President to dismiss McClellan, send Pope to take his place on the James, and put Ormsby M. Mitchel in command of the forces covering Washington.

Lincoln's dejection as he considered this problem was plain to all. Throughout McClellan's campaign he had hoped as earnestly as the myriad anxious mothers of the North for an early end of the war. The Seven Days during which the army seemed battling frenziedly to extricate itself were a Gethsemane to him. He had felt the deepest relief when McClellan telegraphed that the withdrawal was completed, and had returned fervent thanks. "Be assured the heroism of yourself, officers, and men, are and will forever be appreciated. If you can hold your present position, we shall '*hive*' the enemy yet." [32] Anguish and frustration were still written upon his countenance when just after the Fourth he journeyed by the steamer *Ariel* to Harrison's Landing to talk with McClellan and review the troops.[33]

Lincoln arrived on July 8 accompanied by Assistant Secretary of War Peter H. Watson and Frank Blair. The terrible fatigue of the troops after three months of marching, entrenching, and fighting impressed every visitor;

---

30 W. H. Beach, *First New York Cavalry*, 182.
31 Cf. K. P. Williams, *Lincoln Finds a General*, II, 252–254.
32 *Works*, V, 307.
33 One soldier thought he resembled Don Quixote, The Knight of the Rueful Countenance, for he was "drooping, woeful, wan, like one forlorn, or crazed with care." Col. Wm. Kreutzer, *Four Years With the 98th New York Vols.*, 102.

fatigue was a disease, and a chronic disease, wrote one. But, bathing in the James, donning new uniforms, and parading to the bands, the men were recovering. Though the sick rate continued high, they shook off part of the malaria and diarrhea which had wasted thousands. The President, addressing the troops, said he knew they would never give up without going into Richmond. "He had been unable to sleep from anxiety, but after what he had seen and heard, he would go back to Washington, satisfied that it was all right with the army of the Potomac."

He indeed found the situation of the army better than he had dared hope. Its losses during the Seven Days, most stragglers having returned, were now officially put at only 10,400. The reports of desertion had been exaggerated, its spirit was good, and its position on the James was the best that it had held since the campaign began. In front, the wide river was busy with supply ships and transports. The camp was protected there by gunboats; on the west by a series of almost impassable ravines; on the northeast by the morasses of Herring Run Creek; and beyond the creek by the Heights of Eglington. This country of the lower James was reckoned the very garden of Virginia. Harrison's Landing, open, level, and dry, with abundant water and bathing facilities, and material to build arbors against the fierce sun where trees were lacking, gave the tired soldiers repose and security. "I feel as though I'd worked my passage through hell and come out in paradise," said one.

The troops lay amid historic surroundings. In the Harrison home, "Berkeley," a fine brick mansion, had dwelt Benjamin Harrison the Signer, and here William Henry Harrison had been born. Near at hand was the "Westover" of the Byrds, beautifully situated on the James. Not one Union soldier in a thousand had heard of William Byrd of *Dividing Line* fame, but the fine house and rich land were admired by all. A mile and a half back from the river lay the long, irregular house of ex-President Tyler, set in an 1,100-acre plantation somewhat more than half cleared of woods; and across the James was the plantation home of Edmund Ruffin, Jr., eighty feet above the water on a bluff. All these seats suffered heavily from the Union occupation. Fine mantelpieces that had cost £600 apiece in colonial days, furniture that was a triumph of British cabinetmakers, handsome rugs and old paintings, meant little to war-worn privates.[34]

---

34 The elder Ruffin has left a shocking picture of the destruction at his son's place. The yard was strewn with smashed chairs and other furniture, broken china and glassware, and feathers emptied from mattresses. Many windows were broken. Inside, every movable article had been broken or defaced. His papers, and some thousands of his and his son's books, had all been carried off. His harmonium had been ruined. The hand-molded plaster of the walls had been smeared with tobacco juice and covered with insulting charcoal inscriptions. Nearly all the livestock had been taken. Many trees had been cut down, and a large and

Lincoln had probing questions to ask of the outwardly polite, inwardly sulky McClellan, especially upon the evident wastage of manpower. On paper, the general had received 160,000 men. The President learned at Harrison's Landing that he had 86,500 remaining; where were the other 73,500? Assuming that 23,500 had been killed, wounded, or captured, and 5,000 had died of disease, 45,000 were absent—fully half of them, Lincoln believed, fit for duty. If McClellan regained these 22,500 troops, he could march into Richmond within three days. How could they be rounded up? McClellan's figures were different, but eloquent of bad army management. He counted 34,500 absent with leave, many of them sick or wounded, 3,800 absent without leave, and 16,600 present and sick; yet he himself believed that more than 20,000 absentees were probably fit for duty. If he could get these men and cure most of his sick, on his own statements he would have enough to take Richmond.[35] Still, of course, he demanded reinforcements—always reinforcements.

Other questions by Lincoln referred to the best use of McClellan's army. Certainly it would be worthless at Harrison's Landing unless it attacked soon and determinedly. McClellan was ready to attack—but only if he got additional troops. On the day of Malvern Hill he had telegraphed that he needed 50,000 more, and he still thought so. Altogether, Lincoln knew that only a miracle could make McClellan turn about promptly and fight; meanwhile, might not Washington be placed in real peril?

A fear that Lee's army of 200,000 (accepting McClellan's estimates) might use 50,000 men to hold McClellan immobile and the other 150,000 to execute a swift northward march on Washington, haunted many breasts. McClellan himself entertained the idea, for he had telegraphed Lincoln on July 4 that the enemy might prefer to advance on Washington instead of attacking his forces. Seward feared it, writing Thurlow Weed on July 7 that Lee might immediately organize a campaign against the national capital.[36] Quartermaster-General Meigs feared it; he had ridden out to the Soldier's Home just before Lincoln left to argue vehemently for bringing the army back, and had found Lincoln's noncommittal attitude disappointing. "How long," he wrote in his diary next day, "before he comes to my opinion to withdraw the army from a dangerous and useless position, and use it to defend the free states and as a nucleus for new armies?" [37] Stanton, naturally apprehensive and prone to sudden panic, feared it.

---

beautiful oak had been wantonly girdled. Ruffin noted that all but one of the thirty-one names he copied from the walls belonged to Pennsylvania regiments. MS Diary, LC.
35 See Lincoln, *Works*, V, 322–323.
36 For McClellan's views see O. R., I, xi, pt. 3, p. 294; for Seward's see his *Works*, III, 114.
37 For opinions of corps commanders, see Lincoln, *Works*, V, 309–312. For Meigs's opinions see his pocket diaries, entries July 4, 5, 1862, Meigs Papers, LC.

On the other hand, the new base so near Richmond had manifest advantages if aggressively used. Three corps commanders were sharply averse to removal of the army. Sumner told Lincoln that it would be equivalent to giving up the cause, Heintzelman thought that it would be ruinous, and Fitz-John Porter used the same language—"move the army and ruin the country." Keyes, however, told Lincoln that the army could safely be shifted by rapid action, and Franklin declared that it ought to be moved, for the Rappahannock was the true line. The President may have learned that General J. C. Barnard, McClellan's chief of engineers, was also strongly for withdrawal, for he had always opposed using the Peninsula as a base.

In the back of everybody's mind lay the question whether McClellan should be retained. Confidence between him and the Administration was not eased by Lincoln's flying visit. The commander wrote disdainfully to his wife that His Excellency had come and gone, but had, he feared, profited little from his visit. As for Stanton, McClellan lacked vituperative talent to characterize this Judas; he hated to think that "humanity could sink so low." The general's anger as recently conveyed to Stanton in Washington by his chief-of-staff Marcy, and his apparent threat that he might surrender if he were not better supported had so shaken the Secretary, who was overwrought by the mortal illness of a child, that he wrote affirming his friendship and his readiness to offer any assistance within his power. McClellan replied with cool courtesy; but as the two men shook hands, each held a dirk behind his back. Writing S. L. M. Barlow on July 15, the general expressed sadness that so many brave men "have fallen victims to the stupidity and wickedness at Washington which have done their best to sacrifice as noble an army as ever marched," and made another veiled threat.[38]

"I do not care," he wrote, "if they remove me from this army—except on account of the army itself. I have lost all regard and respect for the majority of the Administration, and doubt the propriety of my brave men's blood being spilled to further the designs of such a set of heartless villains."

Lincoln was trying to remain patient with McClellan, though he knew how powerful a body of Northern opinion demanded the general's dismissal. At Harrison's Landing he was politely considerate. But McClellan put an intolerable tax on his forbearance when he handed the President a letter, dated July 7, expressing all his innate arrogance. It was time, he informed Lincoln, that the government determined on a civil and military policy which covered the whole ground of the national troubles; and he would kindly instruct the President of the United States on what it should and should not do. Lincoln silently read the paper. This was no longer rebellion, but war, McClellan wrote, and should

38 Barlow Papers.

be treated as such. But it should be waged mildly. Such orders as Pope's, such legislation as Trumbull's confiscation bill, such ideas upon reconstruction as Charles Sumner was enunciating, should—he implied—be repudiated: "It should not be a war looking to the subjugation of the people of any State in any event. It should not be at all a war upon population, but against armed forces and political organization. Neither confiscation of property, political executions of persons, territorial organizations of States, or forcible abolition of slavery, should be contemplated for a moment." [39]

We can well understand why Lincoln vouchsafed no comment to the waiting McClellan; why, as the general says in his memoirs, he coldly refrained from alluding to the letter during his visit, or at any time thereafter. No seizure of property for war uses, no subjugation of the enemy, no shooting even of red-handed assassins, no attack upon slavery! He even presumed to meddle with reconstruction; no territorial reorganization of the States! The grossness of this military intrusion into the political sphere matched the revelation that the commander believed in a limited, moderate, indecisive kind of fighting. All this was much worse for coming from a general whose chief of staff had just talked of capitulation. When Lincoln returned to Washington, he had not yet finally decided on the disposition of the army or of McClellan, but he must have moved close to a conclusion.

His next step, immediately after Halleck reached Washington, was to send that general to the James. As head of all the armies, Halleck's conclusions should be final.

And Halleck lost no time in deciding for a withdrawal. McClellan, in great agitation, pleaded for massing all available Eastern forces on the James for an attack. When Halleck told him that 20,000 men were all he could get, he said he would try an offensive with that number. His well-conceived plan was to cross the James, seize the still unfortified town of Petersburg, cut the railways to Lynchburg and Wilmington, and so take the rebel capital. But he and his officers showed so much hesitancy and such conviction of Lee's numerical superiority that Halleck emerged from his talks hostile and distrustful. Back in Washington he told Chase that he thought McClellan a poor general. His distrust was fortified when McClellan wrote him that fresh troops were pouring into Richmond, and that to meet them he wanted Burnside's men, Hunter's men, other units, and if possible 20,000 Western troops to boot. "The true defense of Washington consists in a rapid and heavy blow given by this army

39 McClellan, *Own Story*, 487–489. The letter, given in Nicolay and Hay, *Lincoln*, V, 447–449, contained one specially offensive sentence: "A declaration of radical views, especially upon slavery, will rapidly disintegrate our present armies." As Nicolay and Hay say, it had probably been prepared weeks before, and marked the beginning of McClellan's distinctively political career.

upon Richmond," he wrote. True enough; but if he got all these troops, would
he not still demand more? Lincoln in profound discouragement told Attorney-
General Bates that if he gave McClellan 200,000 men, the general would promise
an instant forward movement, but would telegraph next day that he had proof
of 400,000 in Lee's ranks, and could not possibly advance.[40]

By this time a decision had become urgent. Lincoln had two widely separated armies, not in communication, with a doughty foe lying between them
ready to strike at either. They *must* be concentrated on the James, or on the
Rappahannock. Had Lincoln known that Lee's forces did not reach 80,000
men, and had he possessed a firm faith in McClellan, he would have decided on
the James. By straining every resource, he could have added 50,000 fresh troops
to McClellan's 90,000; and this army of 140,000, moved into Petersburg, could
have forced the evacuation of Richmond. But Lincoln had to give weight to
McClellan's continued estimate of 200,000. One man alone, the astute Meigs, by
careful study of Southern newspapers concluded that Lee possessed not more
than 105,00 troops, and he was not credited. Lee, in fact, had encountered formidable obstacles in trying to bring his muster rolls back to the strength shown
just before the Seven Days. After making the most of new conscripts, the return
of the slightly wounded, and the elimination of unnecessary absences, and after
receiving two new brigades from Charleston (July 28), he still had only 74,000
men.[41] So great was now Lee's prestige with the troops and public that he was
an army in himself. The Richmond press lauded him deliriously, the *Enquirer*
comparing his recent strategy with Austerlitz, and the *Dispatch* asserting that
he must be enrolled with Hannibal, Caesar, Frederick, and Napoleon. Nevertheless, the vital fact was that his force remained what it had always been, much
weaker in numbers and arms than McClellan's. Had Lincoln guessed this, his
course would have been bolder.

Believing in the superior strength of the Confederate armies in the Richmond
area, hopeful of Pope, and distrustful of McClellan, the President and Halleck
determined to concentrate the two armies at a point where they could best
cover Washington. Various engineer officers agreed with Barnard that this was
the best strategy. Medical officers also predicted that the army, which had
from 12,000 to 17,000 men sick, would suffer grave losses if kept on the malarial
James in August and September. Already a plague of vicious horseflies made life
a burden to men and animals.[42] On August 1 the die was cast: Halleck ordered

40 Welles, *Diary*, I, 221, 226; *Report, Committee on Conduct of War*, I, 437, 438;
Shuckers, *Chase*, 448.
41 Meigs gave his figures to Halleck, O. R., I, xi, pt. 3, pp. 340, 341. Gen. Keyes contro-
verted this; 200,000 was correct, he wrote. Meanwhile, Lee's army was troubled by internal
divisions, revealed when Longstreet put A. P. Hill under arrest; Freeman, *Lee*, II, 256-258.
42 "The Peninsula is sickly here, as it was at the White House," wrote McClellan's aide

Burnside's force, balanced at Newport News halfway between the James and Washington, to join Pope on the Rappahannock. Two days later he telegraphed McClellan to take immediate measures to withdraw his army, of which he would keep command, from the Peninsula to Aquia Creek.

McClellan expostulated in great anguish, begging Halleck to rescind his order, which he characterized as ruinous. His army, now in splendid condition, could resume the offensive as soon as it was reinforced—the old condition! He pleaded eloquently. "Here, directly in front of this army, is the heart of the rebellion. It is here that all our resources should be collected to strike the blow which will determine the fate of the nation. All points of secondary importance elsewhere should be abandoned. . . . It is here on the banks of the James that the fate of the Union should be decided." [43] This was partly true. In the end the decision was to be reached in the James valley—but only when the Union army was commanded by an indomitable fighter in whom the Administration had perfect confidence.

Halleck, aided by Burnside, did his utmost to cushion the blow to McClellan and keep him in good heart for further service to the Union. They wrote arguing that he must forget his personal disappointments, suppress his irritation, and work valiantly for the cause. But would he? In a resentful letter to his wife McClellan actually intimated a hope that disasters to the army under its new leaders might prove him right. "Their game is to force me to resign; mine will be to force them to place me on leave of absence, so that when they begin to reap the whirlwind they have sown I may still be in a position to do something to save my country." Halleck had urged him to move his troops promptly; would a general animated by this spirit do so? [44]

Once the decision was made to move the army, speed was vital. Lee, taking the short chord of an arc, might reach the Rappahannock before McClellan's troops joined Pope. If McClellan, never a marvel of celerity, dragged his feet, the result would be disaster.

[V]

Meanwhile, ever since the carriage ride with Seward and Welles on July 13, Lincoln had stood by his determination to issue an emancipation proclamation. It

Rufus Ingalls, July 18; O. R., I, xi, pt. 3, pp. 326, 327. On the sick see O. R., I, xi, pt. 3, p. 341. Edmund Ruffin, who visited the Harrison's Landing vicinity just after McClellan left, pungently describes the unsanitary litter and the maddening clouds of flies; MS Diary, July–August, 1862, LC.

43　The full correspondence between Halleck and McClellan is in O. R., I, xi, pt. 1, pp. 75–105.

44　Olmsted, James River, July 13, 1862, to Bellows, Olmsted Papers, LC, reflects McClellan's hatred of Stanton as a "liar, hypocrite, and knave."

had become essential as a political measure, to keep the Republican Party behind him; a war measure, to cripple the South; a foreign policy measure, to align the humanitarian sentiment of the world, and especially Great Britain, with the North; and a measure to lift national morale.[45] Lincoln had begun to draft his proclamation. Going to the telegraph office at the War Department, where he could work with little interruption, he would seat himself in the cipher room and write deliberately on long foolscap sheets. The telegrapher Thomas T. Eckert records that he would set down a sentence or two, ruminate deeply as he stared out the window, and write again. When called away he would lock up the draft in the office. This continued for several weeks prior to July 22, when he had finished.[46]

The languor with which the army grew made it plain that a new inspiration was needed. Under Lincoln's call for 300,000 volunteers, the War Department fixed State quotas according to population, New York heading the list with 59,705 men. For a time a general bustle and enthusiasm presaged adequate results. The governors appointed field officers for the new regiments. Indiana and Illinois, competing to fill their quotas first, promised to put half their recruits in camp within a few days. The financial editor of Bryant's *Evening Post*, John S. Gibbons, published his stirring verses: "We are coming, Father Abraham, three hundred thousand more."

Vociferous war meetings were held all over the North, at which orators sounded a new note of anger, denouncing traitors and threatening condign punishment to the South. Towns, counties, and cities, aided by business firms and wealthy individuals, offered generous bounties to recruits. During July a group of New York businessmen subscribed $8,000 for the Produce Exchange Regiment. Northampton, Massachusetts, appropriated $30,000 for its volunteers, and many other towns and cities pledged payments of $100 to $300 a man. In a few places the total, added to the Federal bounty of $100, reached $500. Central squares in Chicago, Cleveland, Pittsburgh, and other cities once more took on the aspect of army camps. City Hall Park in New York was resonant with drums and bugles as twenty-five tents enlisted volunteers for the Halleck Guard, Stanton Legion, Pope Rifles, Doubleday Artillery, and other outfits.

The results, however, were disappointing. Government confusion once more interfered with systematic recruiting. For example, the War Department directed governors to organize *new* regiments, and they issued appropriate orders;

45 Much of the Northern press, led by Bryant and Greeley, was now stressing two contentions: that no foreign land but Dahomey would dare side with the South once the North made its antislavery position clear, and that public opinion was crystallizing that a permanent settlement with the South must include general emancipation. See N. Y. *Tribune*, August 13, 1862.
46 Bates, *Lincoln in the Telegraph Office*, 138–141.

but Lincoln told a New York deputation that 100,000 soldiers enlisted in depleted old regiments would be worth 300,000 in the new ones, and the press
set up a clamor for sending volunteers only to units already in the field. Under
War Department regulations, however, recruiting for the old regiments was
controlled exclusively by Federal authorities, and State action was restricted to
new formations. And recruits lagged anyway. Anxious citizens began writing to
the newspapers urging universal conscription as the nation's only salvation.[47]
Greeley's *Tribune* sent a correspondent on a wide tour to report on the situation. "The difficulty seems to be with the large cities," he wrote, "where most
of the able-bodied young men enlisted and marched out with the first levies of
the war." [48]

Finally, on August 4, Lincoln took a drastic step. He ordered that any State
which had not raised its quota of the 300,000 new volunteers by August 15
should make up the deficiency at once by special draft; and at the same time, to
lift the army to a round million, he called out 300,000 nine-months' men to be
drafted from the militia. These approaches toward conscription electrified the
North, which had dreaded it. Governor C. S. Olden of New Jersey, for example,
had written that while the rebels filled their waning ranks by compulsory service, "let it be our boast that we defend the nation by the heroic volunteer." The
Federal bounty and advance pay were limited to volunteers, and Lincoln's
orders were intended primarily to stimulate volunteering. Unfortunately,
drafted men were allowed to hire substitutes, and companies both private and
public were immediately formed to obtain them; they sent out agents who
scoured towns and countrysides, offering larger sums than the aggregate bounties in some places, and thus put a brake on volunteering. The effective way of
meeting this evil, said Greeley, would be for the authorities to fix a sum of
money which they would accept in place of a substitute, thus driving the companies out of business. Various modes of draft dodging appeared. The simplest
was to sneak off to Canada; the most expensive was to bribe a doctor to give a
certificate of physical disability; the most profitable and dangerous was to enlist,
take the bounty, and desert.[49]

47 N. Y. *Tribune*, July 28, 1862, for Lincoln's statement. In the end, the call of July 1
brought in 421,465 men, but only after intensive prodding, and fewer than 50,000 of them
were assigned to old regiments; L. L. Lerwill, *Personnel Replacement System in the U. S.
Army*, 90.
48 See analyses in N. Y. *Tribune*, Aug. 13, 15, 1862.
49 Lerwill, *Personnel Replacement*, 90 ff.; N. Y. *Tribune*, Aug. 15, 1862; Croffut and
Morris, *Connecticut*, 242-245. The London *Daily News*, Aug. 18, 1862, noted the results of
the bounty system in stimulating mercenary impulses and numbing patriotism, and the London *Illustrated News*, Dec. 27, 1862, commented on the "large enrolment of Irishmen and
Germans, to whom the bounty-money was the attraction rather than love of the cause."
(Both papers strongly favored the Union.) The fluctuating price of substitutes gave rise to
speculation; a Wesleyan College student sold himself for $300, found another man for $200,

In these weary weeks some dramatic step to lift men's hearts was needed. "You used to maul rails," Representative I. N. Arnold, preparing to return to Chicago at the end of the session, told Lincoln; "now you must maul rebels." "Tell the people of Illinois that I'll do it," responded the President.[50] Four days after Congress adjourned he told the Cabinet that commanders in all parts of the Confederacy had been ordered to subsist their troops in hostile territory, and to employ as paid laborers as many Negroes as were useful.

Then on August 22, in the most historic of Cabinet meetings, he made the momentous announcement that he had drafted an emancipation proclamation. Seward and Welles were of course prepared, but the others were taken aback. The apparent suddenness of the step bewildered one or two, and its boldness startled others. Even Stanton had never proposed going as far as a *general* emancipation in rebellious territory. He and Welles rallied to the defense of the proposal. Chase promised to give the measure cordial support; but as he was fearful of slave insurrections, he thought that emancipation could be accomplished more safely by directing the commanders of departments to proclaim it as soon as feasible, and allowing generals in the field to arm and organize slaves.[51] Montgomery Blair, coming in late, gave a response characteristic of his political-minded family: he apprehended that the proclamation would have a bad effect on the fall elections. No objection, however, moved Lincoln until Seward spoke up. The President later told the painter Carpenter just what Seward had said:

He said in substance, "Mr. President, I approve of the proclamation, but I question the expediency of its issue at this juncture. The depression of the public mind, consequent upon our repeated reverses, is so great that I fear the effect of so important a step. It may be viewed as the last measure of an exhausted Government, a cry for help; the Government stretching forth its hands to Ethiopia, instead of Ethiopia stretching forth her hands to the Government." His idea . . . was that it would be considered our last shriek on the retreat. . . . "Now," continued Mr. Seward, "while I approve the measure, I suggest, sir, that you postpone its issue until you can give it to the country supported by military success, instead of issuing it, as would be the case now, upon the greatest disasters of the war." [52]

---

and pocketed the difference; Middletown, Conn., *Sentinel*, Nov. 24, 1862. Harold Frederic's story *The Deserter* (1898) poignantly sets forth the situation of a New York State private who deserted to look after his dying father.

50 Wash. corr., N. Y. *Tribune*, July 31, 1862.

51 The treatment of the Cabinet meeting in Nicolay and Hay, VI, 125–130, is somewhat misleading. As Welles was previously committed, no emphatic statement from him was needed; he had a gift for self-effacement. Chase strongly favored both emancipating and arming the Negroes, but feared "depredation and massacre" if emancipation were not accompanied by military restraints. The intimation by Nicolay and Hay that these men refused support is unjustified. See Chase's not wholly candid statement of his views in Donald, ed., *Inside Lincoln's Cabinet*, 99, 100.

52 Carpenter, *Six Months in the White House*, 22. Obviously Carpenter is a secondhand authority, but we must take his record in default of a better.

It is curious that Lincoln did not himself think of Seward's demurrer, which was strongly stated by some newspapers when the proclamation later appeared. Seeing the wisdom of the view, and given pause by Chase's objections, he laid the paper aside for an hour of victory. "From time to time I added or changed a line," he tells us, "touching it up here and there, anxiously watching the progress of events."

Meanwhile, he dealt shrewdly with public opinion. As premature disclosure would have done great harm, he deliberately obscured his purpose, talking to different men in different veins. He often dissented from visitors anyway, just to excite them to a more vigorous statement of their reasons. To radicals, such as a deputation of ministers, he now argued reasons for delay; to conservatives like his old Maryland friend Reverdy Johnson he offered reasons for acting. He gave Chase the impression that he would let the field commanders arm Negroes for defensive action; Leonard Swett, however, departed with the impression that he was adamant against both emancipation and the use of freedmen as soldiers.[53] The last thing he could afford at the moment was to speak out. Nevertheless, he did drop some pregnant hints. He must save the government, he assured Reverdy Johnson, "and it may as well be understood, once for all, that I shall not surrender this game leaving any card unplayed." More caustically, he informed August Belmont that the nation would no longer play a game in which it staked everything and its opponents nothing. "These enemies must understand that they cannot experiment ten years trying to destroy the government, and if they fail still come back into the Union unhurt."

The general public guessed nothing. But the great decision had been taken; the most revolutionary stroke, in a war which had now become revolution in the broadest sense, hung poised for delivery.

53 Swett's curious record of his interview with Lincoln, sent to his wife Aug. 10, 1862, is in the David Davis Papers, Ill. State Hist. Library. As he was conservative, wishful thinking doubtless entered into his report that Lincoln would issue no emancipation proclamation; that Lincoln thought Union troops in Kentucky and Tennessee would go over to the enemy if he did; and that the President had no confidence in Negroes as fighting men. Like Hamlet with Polonius, Lincoln could fool some men to the top of their bent.

7

John Pope and Second Manassas

FOR HALF a dozen reasons, in these midsummer days of 1862, Lincoln and the Union needed a victory more urgently than ever before; reasons military, political, diplomatic, and financial. But victory depended on the generals, and some of the generals were aptly characterized by Attorney-General Bates: "The thing I complain of is a criminal tardiness, a fatuous apathy, a captious bickering rivalry, among our commanders—who . . . overlook the lives of their people and the necessities of their country." [1]

It was largely for lack of victory that recruiting for the new army of 300,000 men moved slowly. To be sure, high wages and abundant employment helped slow enlistment, but the London *Times* correspondent in New York had warrant for reporting that the people seemed to be losing faith in their generals.[2] In the end the State quotas were obtained; Illinois filled her ranks by mid-August, and New York eventually surpassed the levy made upon her. In many States the annual increase in the number of men reaching the age of enlistment more than met the new levy. But the spirit of the population, facing an obstinate war, was very different from that after Bull Run.[3]

The new recruits had to be armed; and where, asked the New York *Times*, were they to get their guns? Although part of the forces in the field were still equipped with smoothbores, the government could as yet make only 13,000 Springfields a month, and private contractors were hardly producing a thousand monthly.[4] The situation was rendered more difficult by the fact that great stocks of weapons had been worn out in the Virginia battles, captured by the Confederates, or destroyed during McClellan's retreat. To meet the emergency, the War Department had to turn to Europe. Stanton resolved to send a new agent abroad, and Governor E. D. Morgan and Robert Dale Owen,

---

1 Bates to Lieber, Sept. 3, 1862, Lieber Papers, HL.
2 London *Times*, July 26, 1862, with editorial comment.
3 The N. Y. quota was nearly 60,000, but under the call the State eventually supplied 86,097 men; *Annual Reports State Adjutant General*, 1862, 1863.
4 N. Y. *Times*, July 17, 1862; H. J. Raymond, like other editors, assailed Ripley, Chief of Ordnance.

deputed to make a choice, selected the sagacious New York merchant Marcellus Hartley. Before July ended he arrived in Birmingham with large credits on Baring Brothers, and instructions to buy all the good available firearms in Britain.

Hartley encountered a difficult situation. While McClellan threatened Richmond, rifles were a drug on the British market, and manufacturers were taking contracts at low prices to work up their materials. But immediately after the call for 300,000 fresh troops, speculators rushed out to buy all the ready-made guns. Large purchases were also being made for China, where the Tai-Ping rebellion was raging. The Birmingham combination of manufacturers called the Small Arms Company had given an option to a New York house which hoped to get a Federal contract at $17 a rifle, but Hartley was determined not to pay more than fifty shillings or $12, while he also insisted that the makers improve the quality of their weapons. Such was the dearth of available arms that he had to inform Stanton on August 30 that he would not be able to get more than 70,000 Enfields by November. He urged the bold step of taking the whole Enfield market.[5] Hartley's haunting fear in these weeks was that a sudden decision by the British government to recognize the Confederacy might cut off all further arms supplies. In the area of foreign relations the lack of Northern victory was as keenly felt as at home.

Financial circles, and above all the Treasury Department, also had reasons to long for victory. McClellan's reverses, combined with the steady expansion of the paper currency and the demands of European trade for exchange, precipitated an approach to panic in the New York money market. Early in July the premium on gold shot up in two days from 10 per cent to 17 per cent, and the premium on silver to 8 per cent, while demand notes commanded 8 or 9 per cent premium.[6]

Congress by this time had authorized the issuance of $300,000,000 in legal-tender notes or greenbacks, and Secretary Chase was trying hard to induce the public to use them and other media to buy a half-billion dollars worth of so-called five-twenties; that is, 6 per cent bonds redeemable in five years, and payable twenty years after the date of issue. Despite the government's dire need for ready cash, the average daily sale when the Peninsular campaign bogged down was a mere trifle, only about $150,000, and the reluctance of the public to take these attractive securities greatly distressed the Secretary.

5 Anon., *Marcellus Hartley; A Brief Memoir*, privately printed, 1903. In the end Hartley's mission was eminently successful, and he obtained 200,000 rifles before he returned home early in 1863; but for these critical months the stringency was acute.

6 N. Y. *Shipping and Commercial List*, July 13, 1862, describes the panic, which gave a pronounced impulse to inflation, particularly in costs of imported goods.

People were not merely unused to bonds; they needed reassurance as to the future of the republic. Another fact which had to be considered was that a comprehensive new tax law, including an income tax, had just been put on the statute books, and nothing would so much encourage the public to meet its burdens as a decisive victory.[7]

It was meanwhile clear that, in view of the approaching Congressional elections, the Administration would be assailed with equal venom by conservative Democrats and radical Republicans. On the evening of July 1, the day of Malvern Hill, a mass meeting of discontented New Yorkers gathered at Cooper Union to listen to ex-Mayor Fernando Wood, Representative James Brooks, and the jurist William A. Duer, son of a former president of Columbia, as they denounced the government in the most waspish Democratic style. Duer declared that if traitors were hanged in the order of their guilt, the next man who marched upon the scaffold after Jefferson Davis would be Charles Sumner.[8] At about the same time Byrant's *Evening Post*, voice of radical Republicanism, indicted the Administration for shameful inefficiency, asking why enlistments had been stopped that spring, why the militia had not been armed, drilled, and organized for instant service, why depots had not been filled with munitions.[9] Wendell Phillips assured an audience filling Boston Music Hall that Lincoln was a second-rate man, whose slackness was doing more than the malice of Conferates to break up the Union.

In vain did Lincoln look to the West, for the situation there had deteriorated with startling rapidity. Hardly had Halleck left for the East than Braxton Bragg executed the most masterly movement of his career. He saw that Buell, compelled by Halleck's fatuous orders to repair and garrison a long railroad as he marched against Chattanooga, was moving at snail's pace. Leaving 15,000 men as part of his army to guard Vicksburg, he marched his remaining 35,000 to Mobile, and as we have noted, hurried them by rail to Chattanooga. It was one of the most spectacular railway operations of a war in which rails for the first time played a critical part.

Safe in Chattanooga on July 29, Bragg held a vantage point from which he could seriously threaten Buell. At once Grant had to take steps to reinforce Buell's Army of the Ohio, weakening his own force until it was in danger from a sudden attack by Van Dorn. And when Bragg had saved Chattanooga, he could meditate bolder undertakings. By striking into the heart of Kentucky, even as far north as Louisville, might he not loosen the Union grip on that

7 The London *Economist*, Feb. 22, 1862, had published an editorial, "Will the State of the Federal Finances Bring the American Civil War to an End?"
8 Quoted in the *Atlantic*, "The New Opposition Party," X (Sept., 1862), 377.
9 Quoted in Chicago *Morning Post*, July 12, 1862.

commonwealth and on all middle Tennessee? Using their daring cavalrymen, Nathan Bedford Forrest and John Hunt Morgan, the Confederates began to harry Union detachments in two States.

[I]

As we have seen, Halleck's order to McClellan on August 3 to transfer his 88,000 men from the James to the Potomac emphasized speed. Lee, who had a good intelligence service, would infallibly hear of the movement as soon as it began and move to attack Pope before a concentration could be effected. When McClellan protested, Halleck wrote that this order must be obeyed "with all possible promptness." On August 7 he struck the note again: "I beg of you, general, to hurry along this movement; your reputation as well as mine may be involved in its rapid execution. I cannot regard Pope and Burnside as safe until you reinforce them. Moreover, I wish them under your immediate command, for reasons which it is not necessary to specify."

The irate McClellan, however, did not hurry. Three days after Halleck penned this anxious letter, he was still planning to redeem his badly smutched record by action on the James front. "I hope to be ready tomorrow afternoon," he wrote his wife August 10, "to move forward in the direction of Richmond. I will try to catch or thrash Longstreet, and then, if the chance offers, follow in to Richmond while they are lamming away at Pope." He did not care what happened to Pope! McClellan would never have dared to inform Halleck on the 10th that he proposed to move upon Richmond. He had received a dispatch from that general on the 9th that "you must send reinforcements instantly to Aquia Creek," and that "your delay is not satisfactory." But he unbosomed himself to his wife, adding that he was certain "the dolts in Washington" were bent on his destruction. Once more he was playing the spoiled child.[10] Ordered in one direction, he planned to move in another.

Pope's army, even when he had united the forces of McDowell, Sigel, and Banks, was small—only 43,000 men—compared with McClellan's, but on paper a fair match for any army Lee could bring against him without badly weakening Richmond. He took the field July 29, and under Halleck's orders moved forward swiftly to the Rapidan, so that he could occupy enough Confederate troops to enable McClellan to evacuate the Peninsula with safety. Unhappily, one of his three corps suffered a bloody defeat in this advance. Banks, attacking Stonewall Jackson's superior force at Cedar Mountain on August 9, was soundly trounced; after which the North had to watch a sorry

10 For these Halleck-McClellan exchanges see O. R., I, xii, pt. 2, pp. 4 ff.; McClellan Papers, LC; *Own Story*, 460 ff. (home letters), 490 ff. (official dispatches).

wrangle between him and Pope over the responsibility. By mid-August, Pope was at the Rapidan, Jackson was near Gordonsville—and Lee was on the move. For the Confederate commander, confident that McClellan was at last withdrawing, elated by Jackson's victory, and angered by Pope's harsh general orders, decided on the 14th to take advantage of his interior lines, and attack directly north. Leaving only three divisions to hold Richmond, he would join Jackson in an effort to crush Pope before material reinforcements from the James reached him.[11]

The Confederates held the trump cards. They could move across country, using the railroad much of the way, with a rapidity and secrecy impossible to Union forces moving down the Peninsula to Newport News, and ascending the Potomac to Aquia Creek. McClellan on the 12th was still arguing with Halleck. On the 15th, at 1:30 in the morning, Halleck was still imploring him to send up his troops "with all possible rapidity." [12] Meanwhile, from the 14th onward Lee was moving north with decision and vigor.

Out of the acrid exchanges then and later between Halleck and McClellan, out of the investigation presently made by a Congressional committee, out of a mass of collateral evidence, emerges one unquestionable fact: McClellan was inexcusably late and reluctant in his withdrawal. He pleaded a deficiency of transports and wharf space, and the necessity of providing for his sick. Nevertheless, energy and address could have mastered these shortages. He had complete control over a great flotilla of transports in the James, Hampton Roads, and Potomac. To shorten the journey, he could have begun just after August 1 marching his troops quietly by land to Yorktown, Newport News, and Fort Monroe instead of proceeding as if he expected to embark them all at Harrison's Landing. A capable observer, General Victor Le Duc, wrote that but for gross mismanagement, the whole army could have been transferred to Aquia within two weeks.[13] By August 10 at latest the movement should have been well under way. Actually, the evacuation did not really begin till four days afterward, only the sick, some batteries, and some cavalry being moved earlier. To hasten the movement of the force, Halleck had finally sent Burnside, a close friend of McClellan's stationed at Fredericksburg, to argue him into greater energy. And after talking with Burnside, the general belatedly promised his "full cooperation."

"On Thursday [14th August]," wrote a New York *Tribune* correspondent, "the army commenced evacuating in earnest. All the siege guns were removed from the front and safely embarked on Thursday and yesterday [Friday,

11 Freeman, *Lee*, II, 272-278. At Cedar Mountain, Banks had 2,353 losses; Jackson, 1,338.
12 *American Conflict*, II, 171. Williams, *Lincoln Finds a General*, II, 273-290.
13 General S. M. Quincy in *The Va. Campaign of 1862 under Pope* (Mil. Hist. Soc. Mass.), 24-26, condemns McClellan for making mountains out of molehills in the evacuation.

the 15th] on board barges and schooners. Porter's corps led the van of the overland portion of the army on Thursday night. On Friday morning every tent was struck, and then, for the first time, it was generally known that the *whole* army was about evacuating Harrison's Landing." [14] The last sick and wounded were carried into boats; Negroes, with much hilarity and shouting, struggled aboard a variety of craft; huge bonfires consumed tents, barrels, and all stores that might be of use to the Confederates. McClellan, taking pride in being the last to go, rode with his staff to Yorktown, whence on August 21 he embarked—ten days late.

He, his staff, and his favorite corps officers went in surly temper. They looked to the past with anger, and to the future with foreboding. The Administration, they reasoned, dared not remove McClellan for political reasons, but was determined that he should no longer be chief general. What could it do? It had brought Halleck east, but that was the smaller half of its plan. The larger scheme was that Pope should be helped to make so brilliant a record that all difficulty would disappear; parts of McClellan's army could be added to Pope's from time to time, until this force became the center of the war. As Pope rose, McClellan would be sidetracked. This was the opinion of Fitz-John Porter, who had been writing truculent letters criticizing the abolitionists, the government, and above all Stanton. It was the view taken by McClellan himself. The general's loyal lieutenants were as likely to abet this program as a proud church leader would be to abet heresy.

As McClellan's army tardily moved back toward Washington, the clouds began to lower blackly over Pope's forces. Lee's array, pushing toward the Rapidan fords some 54,000 strong, faced what was now a larger number, for Burnside had reinforced Pope; but the Southerners were full of confidence and the Union troops dispirited, the Confederate leadership superb and the Federal generalship mediocre. [15] Pope fell back to Culpeper, for he wished to get behind the Rappahannock. The general who never turned his back on the enemy was retreating. Could he get behind the river in time? Would he meet adequate reinforcements? By August 22 Pope's Army of Virginia had completed its retirement to the north bank of the Rappahannock and held every ford between Fredericksburg and Warrenton Springs. Falling back eighteen miles, they had gained positions of marked strength. But who could predict what Lee and Jackson, supposed to have such superior strength, would do?

14 Harrison's Landing corr., N. Y. *Tribune*, Aug. 19, 1862.
15 Longstreet later wrote D. H. Hill giving Lee's strength Aug. 29, 1862, as Longstreet 30,000; Jackson, 20,000; artillery for both, 4,000; total, 54,000. These figures were based on Col. Charles Marshall's testimony in the Fitz-John Porter Case. Hill adds that R. H. Anderson came up on Aug. 30 with 5,000 more. D. H. Hill Papers, Va. State Lib. Livermore in *Numbers and Losses*, 88, 89, gives Lee's strength at Second Manassas and Chantilly as 48,527; Pope's strength as 75,696.

At that critical moment McClellan's army hung suspended, like Mahomet's coffin, between heaven and earth. Though it had ceased to threaten Richmond, it had not begun to sustain Pope. A great part of it that day was afloat on the Potomac, and another great part trudging overland to ports of debarcation. Nor was the army in a mood for fighting. Thousands had broken away from their regiments and were wandering aimlessly without rations or shelter. Temporarily the Army of the Potomac, on which the order to return had fallen like a thunderbolt, was limp, grumbling, disheartened; it was shrunken, homesick, tired.[16] The decay of morale had begun among officers, whose desperation to get home, applications in shoals for furloughs, and readiness to invoke political pull had disgusted Frederick Law Olmsted. It had spread among soldiers who felt that after they had undergone an Iliad of woes which entitled them to return as heroes, they had been called back with the stigma of defeat.

Some high officers were in the worst possible frame of mind. McClellan in private letters wrote that he expected to see Pope "badly thrashed." He was sure the government would "throw upon me the blame of their own delays and blunders"; he was bitter over the failure of Washington to keep him informed—"they may go to the deuce in their own way"; and he expected to be traduced and shelved, unless Pope was defeated, "in which case they will want me to save Washington again." [17] Fitz-John Porter not only used scorching language about the Administration, but expressed the sharpest hostility toward abolitionist tendencies in the war. He wrote Manton Marble of the *World* that Stanton was an "ass"; that the President was "controlled" by this incompetent Secretary; and that the *World* ought to raise the question whether the Administration had a covert purpose in crippling McClellan— whether it wished "to cause defeat here for the purpose of prolonging the war." Such a prolongation would of course serve the interests of the abolitionists, whom Fitz-John Porter despised and hated as "our enemies in rear." But Stanton, "poor fool," wished to deprive McClellan of the credit of victory,

---

16 The N. Y. *Times, Tribune,* and *Herald,* and Phila. *Press,* Aug. 12-18, give full details.
17 McClellan could justly complain of want of information, for Lincoln and Halleck should have taken greater pains to inform him of their own and Pope's military plans. McClellan's spy, Allan Pinkerton, strolled into the White House August 22, first making sure that Lincoln was out, to pump Nicolay for information which he at once sent the general. Nicolay told him that the President believed McClellan an able and safe general, but like the country was impatient for action, and wanted vigorous compaigning. He added that McClellan's enemies constantly warned Lincoln that he would never fight unless sure he would win—he would take no risks. Even so, Nicolay felt sure that Lincoln would not supersede McClellan until the general had another chance. For one reason, sentiment favorable to Pope in his army had ebbed away, and apart from Halleck, Pope now had few friends. Pinkerton, August 23, 1862, to McClellan; Pinkerton Papers. McClellan wrote home August 21; "I do not know what they intend doing with me." Halleck should have told him.

and of the means of reconquering the South "in a manner that will develop Union feeling." [18]

Seldom has a stage been more elaborately set for a debacle. Lincoln, watching haggardly at the War Department from dawn to midnight, had dark forebodings of the tragedy to be played. As Lee moved forward, suddenly communications with Pope's menaced army were severed. "What news from the front?" the President telegraphed McClellan, who had just arrived at Alexandria, on the afternoon of August 27. "Any news from General Pope?" he telegraphed Burnside on the 28th. "What news from Manassas? What generally?" he telegraphed Herman Haupt on the 29th.

[II]

Throughout much of the North, men were aware on Thursday, Friday, and Saturday, August 28–30, that a terrible battle was raging in Virginia. For the first two days, because Halleck had barred reporters from the area,[19] the agonized public caught at a hundred rumors. On Friday came fragmentary intelligence that Jeb Stuart with 2,000 men had descended on Manassas Junction, taken trains, prisoners, and stores, and cut the only railroad between Pope's headquarters and Washington. Later that day the War Department released a dispatch from Pope which was boastful yet alarming. Stonewall Jackson and Stuart by a flanking march had gotten to his rear, he admitted, but he was moving to overwhelm them: "I do not see how the enemy is to escape without heavy loss." On Saturday morning the public read this dispatch in the press with a mixture of hope and apprehension. No more word came. Toward evening, in Washington, knots clustering atop public buildings distinctly heard the roar of cannon. Seeming to drag slowly nearer, its fury never slackened until nightfall. Still no authentic news came, and none next day. Not for nearly a week did the North realize that Saturday had witnessed one of the bloodiest defeats of the war.

What had happened? In a sentence, Lee had thrown a powerful force under Jackson around Pope's western flank to his rear; Pope had attempted to surround and crush this force, but his dispositions were blundering, while some of his generals were dilatory; Lee and Longstreet meanwhile broke through with the other part of the Confederate army to reinforce Jackson; and in the end a united, determined Southern host, rejoicing in unmatched

18 Porter, May 21, June 20, etc., Manton Marble Papers; Patrick, MS Diary, July 18, Aug. 4, 1862, LC.
19 Halleck gave his fatuous order Aug. 19 because intercepted Confederate letters spoke of information gained from Northern papers, because he mistakenly supposed that the Confederates had gotten word of McClellan's withdrawal from the James out of the N. Y. *Tribune*, and because he never understood the right of the public to full news. Starr, *Bohemian Brigade*, 130–132; A. S. Hill, Aug. 22, 1862, Gay Papers.

leaders and a proud record of victory, had crumpled up the disunited and dispirited Army of Virginia, forcing it back to the old field of Bull Run.

Lee had known from the beginning of the campaign that he would have to move rapidly if he hoped to crush Pope before McClellan's forces reached that general. He and President Davis showed great courage in stripping Richmond of all but two defensive brigades to permit of a northward thrust. It was the courage of desperation, for only by audacious strokes could the South snatch victory from the odds against it, but it nevertheless revealed leonine daring. Lee pushed the movement hard despite his grave lack of wagons and horses. When Pope in alarm retired behind the Rappahannock, and that stream and the Rapidan rose, the Confederate leader not only persisted, but resolved on a still more intrepid move. He detached Jackson with 20,000 men to make a long forced march, cross the upper Rappahannock, swing to Pope's rear, and sever the railroad to Alexandria. Thus to divide his inferior army of 54,000 men in the very face of his opponent's 65,000 troops defied all military maxims.[20] While Longstreet held the attention of Union commanders by some desultory fighting, Jackson would execute his march, strike at Pope's communications, and compel the Northern army to accept all the confusions and chagrins of retreat.

On the evening of August 24 Jackson's three divisions assembled. They put three days' rations in their haversacks; they caught a few hours' sleep. Under the morning stars, as the men struggled into line, they heard an unexpected order: "Unsling knapsacks!" With dubious faces, they laid them on the grass. "Left face! Forward, march!"—and they never saw the knapsacks again. A herd of cattle provided their only stock of food; a few frying pans, tin cans, and forks were their only impediments. As they turned northwest, away from Longstreet's guns thudding on the Rappahannock, their fast-moving columns caught a sense of exhilaration. The men could have echoed Stonewall's own exclamation: "Delicious excitement!" They guessed that their mysterious errand was taking them around Pope's army. With jest and hilarity, amid glad greetings from farm folk who brought out milk, water, biscuits, and ham, they swept across the river, marching twenty-six miles before the midnight halt. One later wrote:

Swiftly along the high country roads, day long and far into the night, through the fields to make short cuts, letting down the bars here, or pulling down a panel of fence there, along byways and farm roads, we pushed, unencumbered

20 See note 15 above. Col. Wm. Allen in Mil. Hist. Soc. Mass., *Va. Campaign of 1862*, 195 ff., puts Pope's army at 70,000, Lee's at 49,000; in *Battles and Leaders*, II, 500, Pope is credited with at least 63,000 and Lee with 54,000. But for three reasons Lee's army was much the stronger. He had in Jackson an incomparable lieutenant; the morale of his troops was superb; and he held them well in hand, while Pope's demoralized, badly led army lost men in large numbers by straggling.

by wagons—glad to rest and sleep when the night's halt was made—no rations issued, faring on green corn and apples from the fields, helped out by such bread and butter and milk as we had money to buy from the people, or they would give—so "Jackson's foot cavalry" went hurrying northward.

Or, as a Southern poet still more stirringly put it:

> Steady! the whole brigade!
> What matter if our shoes are worn?
> What matter if our feet are torn?
> "Quick-step! We're with him before morn!"
> That's "Stonewall Jackson's way." [21]

Pope's right wing extended to the Bull Run Mountains, a long ridge running from near Warrenton north to the Potomac. Moving under the western lee of this ridge, Jackson's swift columns swept upward until they reached Thoroughfare Gap, well northwest of Pope's lines. Through this winding gorge, the high forested hills about it all unguarded, the Confederates marched until at its eastern margin they could look down on the countryside from Fairfax Courthouse to the Rappahannock. Descrying the highway which ran southeast from the Gap, they could see it intersected at Gainesville by another road extending from Warrenton to the high-seated town of Centreville. Empty, unpatrolled, both roads stretched into the distance. No tower of dust, no glisten of bayonets heralded a Union movement to intercept Jackson's stroke. Instead, the way lay open to the Southerners to cut the principal highway between Pope's army and Washington. Then, pressing beyond it, they could seize the Alexandria line, his sole rail artery, at Bristoe Station or Manassas.[22]

Why Pope allowed himself to be thus outflanked he never explained.[23] The chief of railway transportation, Herman Haupt, declares that as early as the 22nd he had warned Pope of a possible flanking movement, and ascertained that he did not have his scouting parties well up on the headwaters of the Rappahannock. "Is that far enough?" inquired Haupt. "What is to prevent the enemy from going even as far as Thoroughfare Gap and getting behind you?" The general shrugged: "There is no danger."

Union headquarters were thus asleep to the situation when the gray columns poured into Bristoe Station as the sun sank on the 26th. They captured most of the garrison, smashed the bridge over Broad Run, tore up the tracks, and wrecked two trains. Other trains escaped, one north to Alexandria, one

---

21 MS Recollections of H. G. Benson, Southern Coll., Univ. of N. C.; John W. Palmer, "Stonewall Jackson's Way."
22 Henderson, II, 148.
23 He slips over the subject in *Battles and Leaders*, II, 460, 461, but made some excuses in *Supplemental Report, Committee on Conduct of the War*, Pt. II, 141, 142.

south to Warrenton, to give the alarm. With not a moment to lose, Jackson thrust two regiments of tired men up the railroad in utter darkness, and at midnight Manassas Junction was theirs. He himself followed with two full divisions, reaching that place the morning of the 27th.

Well might Halleck hide these events from public view! At Manassas, Jackson was only thirty miles from Washington, one long day's march; he was almost squarely behind Pope's main army; and he counted on Longstreet, with the other part of Lee's host, to follow and reinforce him! The Confederates in their midnight seizure of the Junction had captured 300 men, miles of freight cars, streets of bulging warehouses, and whole fields of barrels, boxes, and piled munitions. For a few brief hours Jackson's ragged, famished divisions held revelry amid the richest body of stores ever brought into the field, a prodigal variety of materials to feed, clothe, and arm the Union troops. After rations had been issued, and liquor locked up, officers threw open these treasures. Here men seized on toothbrushes, candles, coffee, and tea; here they choked down lobster salad, potted game, and jellies. From piles of new clothing the naked took blue uniforms, from heaps of shoes the barefoot carried off new boots, from stacks of rifled muskets the ill-armed drew burnished pieces. For sick comrades they pocketed delicacies and medicines. Then Jackson, aware that strong forces were moving up from Warrenton to attack him, put the torch to the remaining stores, and under cover of flame and smoke withdrew his rear guard before Pope's first units appeared.[24]

Jackson now had to join hands with the main body under Lee and Longstreet, which also had made for Thoroughfare Gap, before the aroused swarms of Northern troops could pounce on his 20,000 men and sting them to death. He knew that Pope might even block Thoroughfare Gap before the two Confederate armies could unite. He knew that some forward elements of McClellan's army were moving west from Aquia Creek. Indeed, on the afternoon of the 27th, Hooker's division, 5,500 strong, emerged near Bristoe Station and deployed for action, driving back small Confederate forces under Ewell. A cordon might yet be thrown around Stonewall's bold men. On the night of August 27-28, therefore, while burning stores lighted the skies above Manassas, Jackson hurried north and northwest by three roads, and by morning had his whole command hidden in the woods beyond Groveton, within reach of the Gap. Here he bivouacked to let his troops recover from their fatigues.[25]

The rest of the story presents a picture of Pope's complete miscalculation

24 Gordon, "Army of Virginia," in Henderson, II, 133, 134; A. C. Redwood in *Battles and Leaders*, II, 532, 533.
25 Ropes, *Civil War*, II, 266; O. R., l, xii, pt. 2, p. 644. Ropes remarks of Jackson that "no one could have displayed sounder judgment or acted with greater promptness." O. R., I, xii, pt. 2, contains a mass of relevant material.

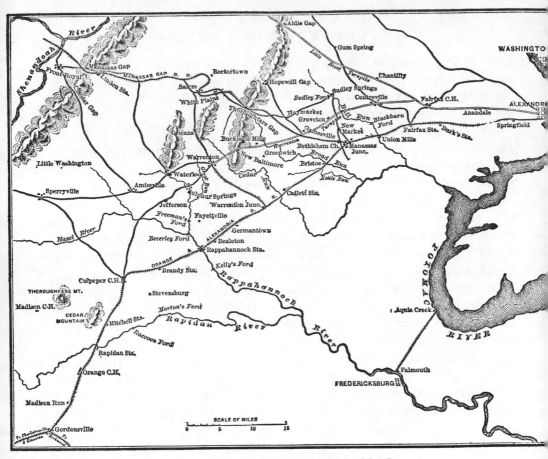

POPE'S SECOND MANASSAS

projected against the screen of Lee's luminous mastery of the situation. Had
Pope comprehended that as he had swung his main army back toward Gainesville, his forces stood between Jackson's and Longstreet's corps, and that by
blocking Thoroughfare Gap, within easy reach, he could keep the two parts
of the Confederate army divided, he might have won a tremendous victory.
But erroneously thinking that Jackson was immobilized in the Manassas area
and must entrench himself there, he decided to use all his forces to surround
him. Instead of closing the Gap, he would move the army in three columns
upon Manassas. "We shall bag the whole crowd, if they are prompt and ex-
peditious," he crowed to Halleck.

When at noon on the 28th the first Union troops reached Manassas and
halted amid the embers of the yet burning stores, they found it deserted.
Whither had Stonewall fled? Pope was completely mystified. While he sought
for intelligence, a report came that the Confederates were far north at Centre-

ville, where they had cut the railroad to Alexandria. The army at once pushed on to Centreville, with Hooker and Heintzelman on the right, Sigel and Reynolds in the center, and McDowell on the left. Hooker reached the town late in the afternoon to find it deserted save for a few cavalry patrols. But suddenly the roar of cannon to the westward indicated that the left wing had found the Confederates. Around Groveton and toward Thoroughfare Gap, the flash and thud of artillery, rattle of musketry, and drift of smoke from distant woods indicated a fast-developing battle between McDowell and Jackson.

It was when he heard the news of this battle, shortly before 10 P.M., that Pope penned his last boastful dispatch. He thought that McDowell had intercepted the enemy retreat and that Jackson was at last trapped. Once more he miscalculated.[26] Jackson had no idea of retreating westward through the Gap; at that very moment Lee and Longstreet were moving through it eastward. As the bright sun of the 29th rose, the advance guard emerged well beyond the portal. Not only were all Pope's brilliant hopes dashed; he was put in the greatest danger, for while Longstreet thus broke through, fresh Union forces were slow in coming up, and were so ill coordinated that at the points of battle the Southern strength was superior.

Before noon on the 29th the whole Confederate panoply was on the field, with Lee, Jackson, and Longstreet now confident of victory. The Union army, on the other hand, was but half embattled, its brigades and divisions reaching the scene in hit or miss fashion, the generals in imperfect touch, most officers and men distrustful of Pope's capacity, and Fitz-John Porter's all-important corps not getting into action at all. As darkness fell, Pope had to confess that his efforts to crush Jackson had totally failed. Five successive assaults had broken down, with 8,000 Union soldiers killed or wounded. Not only had the Union army been worsted, but the stage had been set—though Pope did not realize it, for he did not even know that Lee had joined Jackson—for a greater defeat on the morrow.

At 2:30 that afternoon Lincoln had telegraphed McClellan another agonized appeal for news. From his safe coign at Alexandria, McClellan had returned the callous reply: "I am clear that one of two courses should be adopted. First to concentrate all our available forces to open communication with Pope. Second to leave Pope to get out of his scrape and at once use all our means to make the capital perfectly safe." [27] For himself, he favored the second course.

26 His staff and perhaps subordinate generals share the blame; K. P. Williams conjectures in *Lincoln Finds a General*, I, 320, 321, that inaccurate reports had reached him.
27 Lincoln, *Works*, V, 399.

Again on the 30th the fighting was terrible. Pope's half-shattered army badly needed rations, and his horses forage; he had both telegraphed and written urgently for them; but on this morning he got only a curt letter written by General Franklin at McClellan's order stating that goods would be loaded on wagons and cars at the Alexandria base if he sent back a cavalry escort to guard the train! [28] Still under the hallucination that he might crush a divided enemy, Pope ordered his hungry forces forward to the attack. Once more they made assault after assault until every division on the field had fought, and every division had been beaten back. The main reason for his failure was that his piecemeal deployment of his infantry never brought more than 20,000 into battle at once. As the last valiant charge broke down, Lee ordered his whole army to advance. Wave after wave of bayonets beat against the Northern positions, and as the Southerners came on like demons, the Union divisions stubbornly fell back.[29]

It was this Confederate advance amid the thundering guns which men standing on the Washington housetops divined; an advance which carried the surge of battle up to Henry Hill on the old Bull Run grounds. Here the Northern lines held, and as darkness fell Second Manassas ended in mutual exhaustion.

On Sunday, under a cold, drizzling rain, Pope's dejected troops filed into the old Confederate defenses about Centreville. Behind them they left more than mounds of slain and wounded; they left all the bright hopes with which the Union forces five months earlier had begun their advance on Richmond. All the fatigue, the sickness in malarial swamps, the toils under burning Virginia suns, the endless fighting, the mutilations, the deaths of hosts of comrades, were in vain. They were back just where they had started, discouraged, cynical, resentful. They knew that they had been betrayed; they looked to the future with dark foreboding. At the best a deep melancholy, at the worst a bitter hatred of their incompetent leaders, possessed them; but their determination to fight on never flagged.

[III]

Once more endless lists of the slain and wounded filled pages of the Northern dailies at a time. Some casualties had been brought off the field by

---

28 Pope said in his official report of the McClellan-Franklin message: "All hope of being able to maintain my position, whether victorious or not vanished with this letter. My cavalry was utterly broken down. . . . At the time this letter was written, Alexandria was swarming with troops, and my whole army was interposed between that place and the enemy." McClellan deliberately and brutally sacrificed him.

29 Henderson, II, 161–176, is supplemented by K. P. Williams, II, 320 ff.

the retreating Union forces. Long trains rolled into Alexandria and Washington with them, and meanwhile, trains of surgeons and nurses—one of them carried a thousand—crept south to Centreville. Pope's forces had of necessity left multitudes on the battleground, where Confederate surgeons were at first too busy with their own men to care for many Northern wounded. Later Lee had allowed Union ambulances on the field. Only sixty were sent, and they brought in but a small part of the stricken. The surgeons had neither time nor means to look after thousands who, with unstanched wounds, mortifying limbs, and severe shock, were dying by inches. Descriptions of that field offer as classic an indictment of the horrors of war as Henri Dunant's picture of Solferino. Over an extent five miles in length and three in width it was strewn with dead and wounded, lying sometimes in thick windrows. As late as Thursday, September 4, a week after the battle began, the *National Intelligencer* reported the estimate of one surgeon that 2,000 wounded had as yet received no succor.[30] One of the earliest workers on the scene was a devoted woman of Massachusetts birth, now resident in Washington, who had thrown all other activities aside to help organize the movement of supplies to wounded soldiers, and who later became first head of the American branch of the Red Cross which Dunant founded.

Clara Barton, heroically busy distributing supplies to the troops, went out the day after the battle ended to Fairfax, where the wounded were being brought down in ambulances and laid on the ground till they covered acres. Bales of hay for horses were broken apart to cover the wet earth. When night shut down with utter darkness Miss Barton's party had only one lantern. She obtained some candles, but the wind put them out every few minutes, and the wounded lay so thick—by midnight 3,000 of them, she thought—that she and her aides hardly dared take a step. "We had two water buckets, five dippers, the stores which we carried to eat, besides hard crackers, [and] my one stew pan which I remembered to take, and this made coffee for them. All night we made up compresses and slings, and bound up and wet wounds, when we could get water, fed what we could, travelled miles in the dark over those poor helpless creatures, in terror lest someone's candle fall into the hay and consume them all. Still the ambulances came down." They broke their bread into wine and water to help sinking wretches as the stretcher-bearers brought them in. "Oh," writes Miss Barton, "how I needed stores on that field." [31]

Louder than the cry of anguish in the North was the cry of anger; anger at the Administration for not uniting the armies in Virginia more swiftly;

30 This surgeon had left the battlefield Wednesday, Sept. 3. Confederates had done what they could to distribute hardtack and water.
31 Washington, Sept. 4, 1862, to John Shaver; extra-illustrated *Battles and Leaders*, HL.

anger at McClellan and his subordinates, especially Fitz-John Porter and Franklin, for not moving more promptly to Pope's aid; anger at Pope and McDowell for their incompetence. Ever since Cedar Mountain, Banks's men had cherished a fierce animosity toward Pope for pushing them into a trap. Other units were now equally angry. Reporters who talked with officers of all ranks in all corps found them unanimous in asserting that they must have a new commander. The army, they said—and so wrote home—demands a general. During the battle, McDowell at Groveton had ordered a brigade to advance to a position commanded on one side by woods swarming with the enemy. The incredulous brigadier made him repeat the order. A private blurted out in McDowell's face: "Don't the damned fool see that the Johnnies will flank us?" Inevitably, the brigade was flung back with heavy losses.[32] After the battle troops openly jeered McDowell. Whenever Pope appeared, a menacing rumble ran along the ranks. "I have lost a thousand men," said Carl Schurz, "and I dare not go into the hospital and look in the faces of those wounded, who, I know, have shed their blood bravely and in vain."

The troops, we repeat, wrote the facts home in letters which were passed from family to family, read aloud in country stores, and printed in local newspapers. Meanwhile, the press published home truths in scorching language. Ridiculing McClellan's idea that Lee had a magnificently equipped army of 200,000, the correspondents now had facts to show that all along he had really possessed fewer troops, with less artillery, arms, provisions, and transport, than the Union side. The unvarnished truth, wrote a *Tribune* reporter, is this: "We have been whipped by an inferior force of inferior men, better handled than ours." [33]

What particularly incensed Northern opinion, however, was not Pope's incompetence, but the willful limpness if not outright treachery of other officers. They would rather lose battles and sacrifice troops than abandon their jealousies. This was a portentous development, suggesting something rotten at the heart of American democracy, and raising question of a fatal flaw in the national character.

What was the evidence? Even after McClellan's late start, the earliest corps of the Army of the Potomac, under Fitz-John Porter, had reached Aquia in fairly good season. Burnside, who had come thither from Fort Monroe, ordered it forward to join Pope. Other troops in the Army of the Potomac, except for Keyes's corps, which was left to garrison Yorktown, came slowly up the

32 MS Diary, Capt. Robert Taggard, Ninth Pa. Reserve Infantry, Pa. State Hist. Lib.
33 Schurz to a war correspondent in camp near the Chain Bridge, N. Y. *Tribune*, Sept. 5, 1862; Bragg, Sept. 13, 1862, Bragg Papers, Wis. State Hist. Lib.; N. Y. *Tribune* reporter, Sept. 7; Ropes, *Civil War*, II, 276–338, and K. P. Williams, *op. cit.* I, Ch. XII, cover Pope's confusions in detail.

Potomac to Alexandria, and Halleck at first sent them to Pope's aid by direct orders to the corps commanders. But after McClellan arrived on August 26 at Alexandria, Halleck gave orders through him; and glass could not have stopped electricity more effectively than McClellan stopped some of Halleck's most pressing demands. A sequence of messages will demonstrate the fact:

Halleck by telegraph to McClellan 10 A.M. August 27: "Franklin's corps should march in that direction [Manassas] as soon as possible."

McClellan at 1:15 P.M. August 27 to Halleck: "Franklin's artillery has no horses, except for four guns without caissons. I can pick up no cavalry. . . . Can Franklin, without his artillery or cavalry, effect any useful purpose in front? Should not Burnside at once take steps to evacuate Falmouth and Aquia, at the same time covering the retreat of any of Pope's troops who may fall back in that direction? I do not see that we have force enough on hand to form a connection with Pope, whose exact position we do not know. Are we safe in the direction of the Valley?"

Halleck on the morning of August 28 to General Franklin: "On parting with Gen. McClellan, about two o'clock this morning, it was understood that you were to move with your corps today toward Manassas Junction, to drive the enemy from the railroad. I have just learned that the General has not returned to Alexandria. If you have not received his order, act on this."

McClellan at 1:05 on August 28 to Halleck: "Your dispatch to Franklin received. I have been doing all possible to hurry artillery and cavalry. The moment Franklin can be started with a reasonable amount of artillery he shall go."

Halleck at 3:30 P.M. August 28 to McClellan: "Not a moment must be lost in pushing as large a force as possible toward Manassas, so as to communicate with Pope before the enemy is reinforced."

McClellan at 4:45 P.M. on August 28 to Halleck: "Neither Franklin's nor Sumner's corps is now in condition to move out and fight a battle. It would be a sacrifice to send them out now. . . . I still think that a premature movement in small force will accomplish nothing but the destruction of the troops sent out." [34]

In the end Franklin and his corps got only as far as Annandale, a mere start toward Manassas. And Fitz-John Porter, if Pope's charges were to be believed, delayed shamefully the first day of battle, mishandled his men, and let one brigade at the crisis of the conflict avoid any fighting whatever. Later he offered a defence based largely on a conflict of opinion over orders; but was it valid? [35]

No wonder that Lincoln that black Saturday night, August 30, let his

---

[34] Dispatches from which these excerpts are taken were first printed, with others of the same purport, in *Report, Committee on Conduct of War*, I, 456–470.

[35] Jacob D. Cox, *Second Battle of Bull Run as Connected with the Porter Case;* Otto Eisenschiml, *The Celebrated Case of Fitz-John Porter*, take opposed views. Porter has left a MS defense in his papers.

wrath against McClellan blaze forth. No wonder that Pope next day, watching his exhausted ranks limp through the rain into the works at Bull Run, winced at sight of the spruce figure of General Samuel D. Sturgis, of Franklin's corps, his uniform unstained by battle. They were old Missouri rivals. "Too late, Sammy, too late!" called Pope in a voice of despair. And from Sturgis came an expression of McClellan's own malevolence: "I always told you that if they gave you rope enough you would hang yourself!" [36]

Why these attitudes? Fundamentally, because of that want of discipline, deeply felt patriotism, and selfless dedication to great causes which was an unmistakable canker in the overhasty, overmaterialistic growth of the country. Some of the jealousies had begun at West Point, but most of them had origi-nated in the war. McClellan knew well that if Pope won a dramatic victory, then Pope might be given command of the combined armies in Virginia. The idea was intolerable to him. Just before the battle, on the 24th, he had written his wife: "I don't see how I can remain in the service if placed under Pope; it would be too great a disgrace. . . ." If he did not consciously wish Pope to fail so that he might emerge as the rescuer of the nation, subconsciously that was his desire, and he acted throughout on the callous principle of letting Pope, as he put it, get out of his scrape as best he could. Later that same day he sent his wife more of his wishful thinking: "They will suffer a terrible defeat if the present state of affairs continues. I *know* that with God's help I can save them. . . ." Porter shared his views, felt a passionate hatred of abolitionists, and longed for the humiliation of Stanton.[37]

[IV]

In this war, however, some of the greatest battles were fought not on hill or plain, but in cabinet chamber and government offices. While the dead of Second Manassas still lay unburied, and while Lee was swinging his victorious legions toward the invasion of Maryland, Lincoln won a moral victory so far-reaching that history should not fail to take due account of it. Against the somber stormclouds of vanity, selfishness, and malice raised by military leaders, the President gave the nation a lightning flash of magnanimity, patriotism, and courage so swift that the rush of events obscured it.

As the streets of Washington filled with ambulances bearing wounded, and as the press began publishing dispatches and editorials condemning the army

36 Jacob Piccard, MS Life of Sigel.
37 McCleilan, *Own Story*, 472–521, covers this lamentable chapter. See also Peter S. Michie's indictment in *General McClellan*, 381–392, written by an officer and military expert who knew the general well. McDowell's condemnation of both McClellan and Porter may be found in Warden, *Chase*, 460.

leaders, Cabinet sentiment against McClellan boiled over. Stanton declared to his colleagues that he could no longer bear his intolerable burdens if he had to struggle against the general; that he could not and would not endure him; that Lincoln must dismiss him forthwith. He wrote a memorandum embodying these ideas which he showed to Chase, who was equally incensed, and who besought Gideon Welles to sign. "McClellan ought to be shot!" exclaimed Chase. Welles refused, primarily on the ground that the procedure seemed discourteous to the President. Thereupon Attorney-General Bates revised the protest against continuing McClellan in command, and in its softened form he, Stanton, Smith, and Chase all signed it. Though Welles still abstained he was sympathetic, and promised that when he conferred with Lincoln he would endorse the main sentiments of the paper.[38]

That Lincoln's anger burned deeply is unquestionable. He told the Cabinet just after the battle that McClellan's conduct had been "shocking" and "atrocious." The general, he remarked to John Hay, *wanted* Pope to fail: "This is unpardonable." He appreciated the desire of most Administration supporters, as of the Cabinet, to see McClellan sent home in disgrace.[39]

But Lincoln faced a crisis. The Union troops simply would not follow Pope or McDowell. Scattered, in part exhausted, bitterly discouraged, they could not be pulled together and reanimated by a Burnside or Franklin, a Sumner or Heintzelman. And the army must have a leader instantly, for the continuing emergency brooked no delay. Union generals might doze between battles, but Lee was an unsleeping tiger. While Second Manassas still reeked of blood and smoke, he launched his new stroke. Determined to keep the initiative, hopeful that Union disorganization would give him opportunity for another brilliant strategic stroke, cherishing the belief that large Maryland elements were ready to spring to his side, and realizing that he dared not attack Washington, he resolved to turn westward, open a new base in the Shenandoah Valley, and cross the Mason and Dixon Line. Ill prepared as he was, he lost not a single day.

To meet him, to strike back, to save the North, Lincoln put aside all animosities and resentments; his one thought was for the Union, and to save it he would make any sacrifice. "If McClellan will win victories," he had told Hay long before, "I will hold his stirrup." Only McClellan now could recall stragglers, reorganize the divided forces, and restore morale—for most of the men trusted him. The Army of the Potomac had never lost faith, and a majority of Pope's Army of Virginia were eager to turn to a commander who, whatever

38 Welles, *Diary*, I, 92–106.
39 Cabinet feeling is treated in Welles, *ut sup.*; Seward, *Seward at Washington*, 126–127; Hay, *Letters and Diaries*, 49; Chase, *Inside Lincoln's Cabinet*, 116–119; and Flower, *Stanton*, 178–181.

his lack of fighting edge, was always considerate of his troops. A passionate President, an Andrew Jackson, would have given way to his personal anger; a weak President, a James Buchanan, would have bent to Congressional and Cabinet pressure. Lincoln rose above such frailty to answer the nation's need.

When the first Cabinet meeting after Second Manassas took place September 2, with Seward absent, it was electric with tensions. As the members gathered before Lincoln came in, Stanton announced in a voice choked with emotion that the President had just notified McClellan to take command of all the forces about Washington. No formal reappointment as head of the Army of the Potomac was needed, for he had never lost this command. He had re-established himself at his old quarters on Pennsylvania Avenue. General astonishment greeted the news. Amid dismayed murmurs, Lincoln seated himself, and began sadly to explain his action. He knew how culpable McClellan was, he said, but the general was needed: he was good at defense, he was an expert engineer, and he excelled in organizing capacity. Halleck had approved of the step.

Stanton's angry dismay was patent. Chase stormily declared that he was certain McClellan's retention would prove a national calamity. "Much was said," records Welles. "There was a more disturbed and desponding feeling than I have ever witnessed in council; the President was greatly distressed." No doubt Lincoln was distressed beyond measure. But in this decision he proved how completely he could rise above past resentments. He proved that he was determined to be commander-in-chief, and would not let Stanton usurp that position. He proved that he would not let Congressional radicals dictate war policy. Above all, he proved that in everything he would act with single-minded devotion to the best interests of the republic.

Pope was immediately informed that, his army having been consolidated with the Army of the Potomac, he should report to the War Department for orders; and he was soon bound for a routine post in the Northwest. He departed burning with hatred of the man who, he believed, had ruined him. "The greatest criminal," he wrote Halleck, "is McClellan." One of his staff published in the New York *Herald* of September 7 a defense of his commander combined with an attack on others unnamed. All Pope's movements, he wrote, had been dependent on support and reinforcements at fixed times and places—and again and again the support had failed. The country eagerly read the official report which Pope published four days later, reflecting severely on McClellan and most of his corps commanders. All these generals except Sumner, wrote Pope, had hung back, insisting that their commands were too dispirited since they left Harrison's Landing to fight; though events showed that the rank and file, when put to the test, fought with energy. Pope

The undersigned, who have been honored with your selection, as a part of your confidential advisers, deeply impressed with our great responsibility in the present crisis, do but perform a painful duty in declaring to you our deliberate opinion that, at this time, it is not safe to entrust to Major General McClellan the command of any Army of the United States.

And, we hold ourselves ready, at any time, to explain to you in detail, the reasons upon which this opinion is founded.

To the President.

Edwin M Stanton
Secretary of War

S. P. Chase
Secy. of the Treasury

Caleb B Smith
Secy. Interior

Edw Bates.
Atty Genl.

UNDATED LETTER BY STANTON, CHASE, BATES, AND CALEB B. SMITH, IN THE STANTON COLLECTION, LIBRARY OF CONGRESS

leveled his gravest accusations against Fitz-John Porter. That leader, he stated, had been given written orders to attack the Confederates in flank; had he obeyed them the Union army would have destroyed Jackson; but after merely touching the enemy flank, he remained inert. Thus was launched a famous controversy that was to occupy public attention for decades. Much has been said in Porter's defence, and part of it is valid. Much of the evidence, however, strongly suggests that he felt at least a subconscious wish to serve McClellan before he served Pope or the country: McClellan of dark impulses and dark delays.

But Lincoln knew that he had done right. He summed up the situation in a single sentence to John Hay: "McClellan has acted badly in this matter, but we must use what tools we have." The country's great need remained just what it had been—a victory. But the underlying strategic situation had dramatically changed since May; instead of hoping for victory in a great offensive, men now had to hope for victory in a desperate defensive.

40 Pope had grounds for his hostility toward McClellan and Fitz-John Porter, but he had no basis for the rancorous feeling he later expressed toward Lincoln. The essential littleness of the man appears in the expressions of antagonism he sent his father-in-law V. B. Horton, a Representative in Congress; see especially a bitter letter of March 9, 1863, N. Y. Hist. Soc., accusing Lincoln of letting him be traduced and maligned while "the very men who betrayed their country and produced the disasters for which the country was denouncing me, were rewarded with the very object for which they perpetrated their treachery."

8

On Capitol Hill

THROUGHOUT spring and summer the news of battle had held every eye, so that people paid scant attention to civil affairs. Yet Congress was hard at work, and it ended one of the most constructive sessions of its history on July 17, 1862. The session had begun in angry gloom as the two chambers acted to expel disloyal members and inquire into the disaster at Ball's Bluff; it ended in gloomy anger as Zack Chandler made the Senate ring with his arguments laying the recent defeats at McClellan's tent door. Its own record, however, was brilliant, for it had opened a new chapter of national affairs by a dozen enactments of far-reaching social and economic import. It was the first Congress, as an Ohio Representative said, whose vision embraced the entire continent. Sumner, sending the Duchess of Argyll a list of the achievements, pronounced them sufficient to mark an epoch.[1]

The Republican majority, which had restricted itself to imperative war measures in the brief session of Bull Run days, now became a harvest force garnering the sheaves of party victory. Measure after measure that had been unattainable so long as Southerners held their seats went on the statute books. Land for the landless, higher tariffs, a national foundation for colleges of agriculture and the mechanic arts, the Pacific railroad, and an agricultural bureau or department were gains securely seized; and meanwhile blow after blow was leveled at slavery. The steps taken ranged from the establishment of a new arsenal at Rock Island to recognition of the black republics of Haiti and Liberia. The mood underlying Congressional action was sometimes sternly realistic, sometimes idealistic, sometimes both. It was realism to issue $300,-000,000 in greenbacks and make them legal tender;[2] it was idealism to create schools for colored children in Washington and Georgetown; while the Pacific railway was romance and realism combined.

Direct leadership in Congress was furnished not by the President in any such degree as Polk had exercised it in his littler war, but by the principal

---

1 A. G. Riddle, *Recs. of War Times*, 69 ff.; Sumner, Boston, Aug. 11, 1862, HL.
2 Congress did this in two steps, February and July; cf. Blaine, *Twenty Years*, I, Ch. XX.

committees and their chairmen—with whom he kept in rapport. The most powerful Senators remained Sumner, Fessenden, Trumbull, John P. Hale, and Henry Wilson, heads respectively of the committees on foreign relations, finance, judiciary, naval affairs, and military affairs; the most powerful Representatives were Speaker Galusha M. Grow, Thaddeus Stevens, John J. Crittenden, F. P. Blair, Jr., and Charles R. Sedgwick, the last four being heads of the ways and means, foreign affairs, military affairs, and naval affairs committees. With them should be named the men who gave a stern assessment to military operations—Senators Ben Wade and Zack Chandler, and Representatives John Covode and George W. Julian of the Committee on the Conduct of the War. Of the fourteen named, one was crooked, half were timeservers, and fully half were mediocrities; but four, Sumner, Trumbull, Crittenden, and Thaddeus Stevens were leaders of principle and of some statesmanlike vision, while Grow, Fessenden, and Henry Wilson, all earnest, capable, and honest-hearted, held highly creditable places. Wilson, in fact, was endlessly useful.[3]

Parties were in chaos when Congress met, and the session did little to fix firm lines. Radical Republicans, conservative Republicans, War Democrats, Peace Democrats, Lincoln-haters and Lincoln-defenders, made up an assemblage defying clear analysis. At the outset Joshua Speed, Lincoln's intimate friend, was fearful that a large party of Republican extremists was being organized to combat the President, and urged Joseph Holt to help form a coalition of conservative Republicans and War Democrats to resist them. This fear proved exaggerated, for the Congressional radicals never had enough public support to control the government, and they knew it. However abusive of Lincoln such men as Chandler and Thaddeus Stevens might be in private talk, they did not yet dare an open encounter with him. The caustic Stevens, in fact, served Lincoln well on many issues. His hardworking partnership with Chase in dealing with unprecedented financial problems was invaluable, and his rough treatment of Peace Democrats and Border obstructionists on the House floor sometimes gave the President satisfaction. Speed's suggested coalition was unworkable and unnecessary. On the main party program, apart from slavery issues, the conservative and radical Republicans labored well in harness. Lincoln never put either group into a position where it had to choose between fighting him or surrendering its vital principles, and hence neither was tempted to join hands with an undependable Democratic faction.

For "undependable" best characterized the Democratic membership of

3   E. H. Stiles, *Public Men of Early Iowa*, quotes Senator James W. Grimes of Iowa as saying that Fessenden was the greatest man in the Senate; he was certainly indispensable in financial affairs. Hale of New Hampshire took a large fee from a contractor who was later convicted of defrauding the government. He had sold his influence; but it should not be forgotten that he was the Senator who had flogging abolished in the navy.

Congress. Had Douglas survived, his skill, determination, and forensic power, his devotion to the Union, and his personal respect for Lincoln, would have given the minority party a constructive role it never played. Since his death no Democrat possessed sufficient foresight and ability to recall his fellows to Jacksonian principles. George H. Pendleton of Cincinnati, one of Douglas' best aides in the battle against Lecompton, a finely educated man now in his third term, rejected the opportunity; resenting the defeat of the Crittenden Compromise and the refusal to let the Southern sisters go in peace, he became a mere obstructionist. The witty S. S. Cox of Columbus in the same State followed a more positive path, steadily voting for supplies of men and money, but he lacked force, was anxious to end the war on any basis maintaining the Union, and kept on cordial personal terms with the egregious Clement L. Vallandigham of the Dayton district. Though able and useful in marshalling the War Democrats, and witty in debate, he could not be called a commanding leader. In the Senate, Crittenden was too old to be effective, James A. Bayard opposed every important war measure, and Garrett Davis of Kentucky showed a weathercock changeability which robbed him of all influence.[4]

The most irresponsible of the Democrats, Vallandigham, made personal capital of his party's confusion. A handsome, fluent exhibitionist, and a lifelong dissenter on all kinds of questions, he was swayed more by Southern sympathies and love of notoriety than by any patriotic considerations. All his views were short-term views. He saw that by adoption of a firm support of Lincoln's war measures the party would suffer temporary eclipse. He did not realize that a strong body of War Democrats would be able by 1864 to compel Lincoln and his associates to accept a Union Party in place of the Republican Party—as Lincoln tried to do anyhow; he did not see that while War Democrats would have a good chance of recapturing the government soon after the inevitable Northern victory, the discredited Peace Democrats would wander in the wilderness for twenty years. In February he brought forward a scheme of reconstruction so absurdly unworkable and so patently designed to protect slavery that it met universal derision. He also arranged a House caucus in which thirty-one Democrats, by signing a compact to act together, bartered away their individual freedom for a worthless show of party unity. This group was thereafter an impediment, not an asset, to the nation.[5]

4 A vehement Unionist for a time, Davis was later the subject of a motion for expulsion because of alleged disloyalty; Coulter, *Kentucky*, 209.

5 Riddle, *Recs.*, Ch. XX. The wealthy, aristocratic Bayard would gladly have made peace on the basis of Confederate independence.

[I]

While Lincoln, endlessly occupied with the war, offered meager direct leadership on any subject but compensated emancipation, he did furnish general guidance, letting the influential men of Congress know by tactful pressure what he desired. He had been a Congressman himself, and knew their hopes and fears. In the control of government patronage he had a large source of strength. He took time month by month to study appointments in relation to the desires of members of the House and Senate; and by choosing a minister from one area, a postmaster elsewhere, a marshal or collector in another place, he bulwarked his own position as head of the party. It became more and more a national Lincoln party and less a federation of State organizations. However unsavory the work, he would not commit J. Q. Adams' error of neglecting it. He welcomed calls by men on the Hill, and if some came as seldom as Thad Stevens, others were as frequent visitors as Sumner. Contrary to a general view, he showed quite as much skilled leadership in cooperating with organization men as in direct addresses to Congress and people.[6]

He spoke consistently for moderate policies, following the principle which he stated to Zach Chandler: "I hope to 'stand firm' enough not to go backward, and yet not go forward fast enough to wreck the country's cause." He tried always to be reasonable. It is not strange that even amid recurrent disasters his prestige with other reasonable men steadily mounted; rather, it would have been marvelous had it not. Conservatives valued his moderation in proportion as they feared the incendiaries, while radicals valued it in proportion as they feared the diehards. He disliked flamboyant measures—and so did the country. When George W. Julian urged him to "stir" advanced groups by giving Frémont another command, he dryly remarked that this would irritate large conservative groups, and that his own emancipation proclamation had proved less "stirring" than many had hoped. In perilous times a democracy best trusts the cautious statesman.

Another element in Lincoln's popular strength was his manifest devotion to all his duties. He toiled nearly to exhaustion, giving an average of not less than fourteen hours a day, as Greeley recorded, to his public functions—not including state dinners. It was said that he entered the White House conservatory only once in his four years. His life, as John Hay testifies, was

6 Harry J. Carman and Reinhard H. Luthin, *Lincoln and the Patronage*, describe Lincoln's adroit use of patronage throughout the war; William B. Hesseltine, *Lincoln and the War Governors*, deals with his construction of a national party organization independent of State machines. David Donald in *Lincoln Reconsidered* calls him a politicians' politician, and this view is emphasized in Richard N. Current's *The Lincoln Nobody Knows*.

almost devoid of recreation, and most evenings he spent in his office, working or conferring with business callers. With difficulty his wife would sometimes carry him to Shakespeare or a concert. He felt keenly his responsibility as military commander-in-chief as well as head of the civil government, studying military treatises, scrutinizing every important dispatch from the field to the War Department, talking with generals, and making himself almost a one-man bureau for the examination of new weapons which offered some promise of shortening the contest. Endorsements on papers of the quartermaster bureau, some never published, show his interest in the flow of supplies. He was not a talented administrator, deputed labor poorly, and never organized the office of the President as it needed to be organized for war; but his vigilant attention to business was untiring.

His happiest moments were the rare occasions when a few intimates gathered after dinner in his office and he relaxed in political gossip and general talk, telling stories and giving his humor and surprisingly ready wit—for he spoke of himself as a slow thinker—free scope. In such a group he would talk of critical military and political affairs with complete candor, stating his opinion of men and events in plain prairie language, and it speaks well for his judgment of friends that his confidence was never abused. Sometimes he was glad to be repeated. When he told a correspondent of S. L. M. Barlow, "My idea of this war is that it should always have a peace in its belly," he knew that the statement would soon be circulated in the Barlow-Manton Marble-Samuel J. Tilden circle.[7] It amounted to a declaration that, once assured of maintenance of the Union, he would gladly consider a negotiated peace.

As he had faith in the people, so the people gathered faith in him. "This is essentially a people's war," he had told Congress when it first met after Sumter. It was a contest, he went on, for that form of government which would elevate the condition of all men—and he was "most happy to believe that the plain people understand and appreciate this." [8] He kept the White House doors excessively open to the people. At any time he could have lightened his burden by a simple refusal to see callers except at certain hours and upon business of public importance, but as fast as his secretaries tried to erect barriers he himself broke them down. Once when Henry Wilson remonstrated, he replied: "They don't want much; they get but little, and I must see them."

7 Julian in A. T. Rice, ed., *Rems. of Lincoln*, Ch. IX; Robert V. Bruce, *Lincoln and the Tools of War;* Greeley in N. Y. *Tribune,* Sept. 28, 1863; Hay in *Century Magazine,* XLI (Nov., 1890), 33–37. Carl Sandburg's *Lincoln: The War Years, passim,* is a rich treasury of material.
8 *Works,* VI, 320.

He even saw men who came to beg trifling positions as messengers, watch-men, and clerks, and devised his own plan for getting rid of them without ill-feeling. Assistant Secretary Harrington in the Treasury Department found squads of them descending upon him with Presidential chits. One day at the White House he expostulated, saying that Lincoln ought not to spend time on such matters, and that he had no more places. "Why, bless you," said the President, with a twinkle. "Did you suppose I expected you to appoint every-one bringing you a note? Why, but for you and General Ramsey at the Arsenal I should die. One week I send all such applicants to you, and the next to General Ramsey."

Although Hay thought that the swarms of visitors wore upon him and aged him before his time, it seems perfectly clear that they more often re-freshed him. He liked the chance of hearing about some old friend, as when one caller proved to be a daughter of Henry M. Luckett, who used to preach in Springfield; "a tall angular man like I am," said Lincoln, "and I used to be mistaken for him in the streets." He liked the opportunity for a merry quip. Once a solemn Buffalo citizen in the reception line ejaculated, "Up my way we believe in God and President Lincoln," to which Lincoln responded: "My friend, you are more than half right." On another occasion, at a time when the army complained of financial delays, a paymaster in major's regalia appeared in the reception line. "Being in Washington," he explained, "I have called to pay my respects." "From what I hear," rejoined Lincoln, "I guess that's all any of you do pay." He liked sometimes to cross his legs and have his talk out, as when he kept Governor Buckingham of Connecticut waiting more than a half hour so that he could enjoy his chat with that interesting Negro, Frederick Douglass. What aged him more than his burdens was such harsh talk as he heard from General Butler:

I said [writes Butler]: "Yes, Mr. President, the bounties which are now being paid to new recruits cause very large desertions. Men desert and go home, and get the bounties and enlist in other regiments." "That is too true," he replied, "but how can we prevent it?" "By vigorously shooting every man who is caught as a deserter until it is found to be a dangerous business." A saddened, weary look came over his face which I had never seen before, and he slowly replied, "You may be right—probably are so; but God help me, how can I have a butcher's day every Friday in the Army of the Potomac?" [9]

Above all, the clear logic and even temper of Lincoln's state papers and letters, his elevation, magnanimity, and kindliness, and his evident desire not

9 Quotations from Daniel W. Voorhees, Frederick Douglass, and Butler in Rice, ed., *Rems. of Abraham Lincoln.* Hay, *ut sup.*, admits that Lincoln listened with the eagerness of a fascinated child to Garfield's graphic account of Chickamauga, and always delighted in the wise and witty talk of three tars, Dahlgren, Gustavus V. Fox, and Henry A. Wise. The papers of George Harrington, HL, contain his story.

to make smart points or win rhetorical triumphs, but to reason with fair-minded people and convince them, steadily won sensible men to his side. "If ever there could be a proper time for mere catch arguments, that time is surely not now," he wrote in his December message of 1862. "In times like the present, men should utter nothing for which they would not willingly be responsible through time and eternity." His letter to Greeley this summer assuring the editor that his overriding purpose was to save the Union, and that he would free none of the slaves, or part of them, or all of them, as his action might best serve that purpose, was memorable not only in its immediate logic, but in its demonstration of power to pierce to the heart of national perplexities, and resolution to cling to his purpose. He was always ready to admit his fallibility. In this same letter he told the editor: "I shall correct errors when shown to be errors, and I shall adopt new views so fast as they shall appear to be true views." His frequent references to God, or to the will of the Almighty, were coupled with an admission that no man could grasp the divine intent. "In the present war," he wrote in a scrap of religious meditation dated September 30, 1862, a prelude to the Second Inaugural, "it is quite possible that God's purpose is something different from the purpose of either party; and yet the human instrumentalities, working just as they do, are the best adaptation to effect his purpose." [10]

He occasionally expressed his profound sense of duty, avowing that he could never betray "so vast and so sacred a trust as these free people have confided to me." But he never thought that this gave him license to abuse honest opponents. He had only one political test: let men help carry the war for the Union to success, and they might quarrel with him on any other issue whatever. If they would only vote supplies of men and money, discourage desertions, and encourage enlistments, he would admit their right to support slavery, defend State rights, oppose tariff changes, and denounce the homestead bill. Party differences were to him not merely permissible, but a necessity. "We cannot have free government without elections," he said; nor, he would have added, without Congressional battles. If dangerous men spoke up in debate, everyone would soon know their badness: "What kills the skunk is the publicity it gives itself." [11]

And the country chuckled over the sayings with which he spiced his large purposefulness. Men repeated appreciatively his remark that if McClellan was not going to use the army, he would like to borrow it a while. They relished his comment to a gentleman requesting a pass to Richmond: he had given McClellan more than 200,000 men with passes to the city, but

10   Lapsley, *Collected Works*, V, 535; Nicolay and Hay, *Complete Works*, VIII, 52.
11   Sandburg, *War Years*, II, 186.

not one had yet got there. They appreciated such fair hits as his statement to Montgomery Blair about his irascible brother Frank: "He has abundant talent —quite enough to occupy all his time without devoting any to temper." It was an equally fair hit to tell the unco-guid people who warned him about Grant's drinking: "If I knew what brand of whisky he drinks I would send a barrel or so to some other generals." This had the more force because it came from a rigid abstainer. "I am not a temperance man," he said, "but I am temperate to this extent: I don't drink." He remarked of the Congressional scolds and newspaper termagants who abused him only to a safe point: "Mrs. Grundy will talk, but she knows enough not to scald her bottom in her own pot." How apt, too, his little stories were! The one he told when, to his great relief, heavy firing was heard from Burnside's beleaguered army in Knoxville, had perhaps been related earlier of other imperiled forces. "A neighbor of mine in Menard Country," it ran, "named Sally Ward, had a very large family of children that she took very little care of. Whenever she heard one of them yelling in some out-of-the-way place she would say, 'Thank the Lord! there's one of my young ones not dead yet.' " [12]

While partisan haters of Lincoln abounded, and innumerable denunciatory or disparaging remarks might be quoted from editorials, speeches, and letters, two cardinal facts steadily added to his strength. The first was that close associates almost universally recognized his superiority. "He is the best of us all," Seward wrote, and the Secretary's biographer records: "The President was the only member of the administration whom Seward praised often." Welles could be critical, but was certain that the future would recognize his greatness: "The Cabinet, if a little discordant in some of its elements, has been united as regards him." Chase alone thought that *he* would make a better President. The other fact was that a tide of growing popular regard set in his favor. In general, to see him was to like him. Now and then a man took from his presence an unhappy impression. Henry Lee of Boston, for example, Governor Andrew's military aide, wrote his wife in the fall of 1861:

Then to the President's, where I waited in his room for one hour and a half while he slowly disposed of one caller after another.

He is enormously tall and bent and slab-sided and ungainly, his eyes are dead, his cheeks hollow, his skin gummy and sallow, his beard thin, and that and his hair dyed apparently.

His talk is shrewd and vulgar (not profane but uneducated) and as I sat there

12 For the comment on McClellan see Barton, *Lincoln*, II, 394; on Frank Blair, *Works*, VI, 555; on Grant, Nicolay and Hay, *History*, VII, 154; on temperance, B. A. Ulrich, *Abraham Lincoln*, 7; on Mrs. Grundy, Barlow Papers; on Sally Ward, Nicolay and Hay, *Lincoln*, VIII, 178.

I grew more and more cross to think that this Western mummy of a railsplitter should sit in Washington's chair. He seems like a perfectly honest and quite intelligent man.[13]

The highly perceptive attorney and diarist of New York, George Templeton Strong, saw the President far more clearly. He and other Sanitary Commission executives had an hour's relaxed talk in the White House at the end of January, 1862. Lincoln, manifestly enjoying it, stopped several movements of the group toward an exit by a little incident he recalled, or an anecdote he had "heered" in Illinois. He had little outward polish, spoke of "humans," and even used Sangamon Valley grammar. But Strong pronounced him "a most sensible, straightforward, honest old codger," "the best President we have had since Andrew Jackson at least," and a man whose evident integrity and simplicity of purpose would compensate for any amount of rusticity. He quoted the President: "I hain't been caught lying yet, and I don't mean to be." A bright young friend of Strong's who some months earlier had called Lincoln a "gorilla ape" had now learned enough to praise him as the most honest and patriotic man in the Administration.[14] Personal documents of the time, in fact, are studded with expressions of a growing faith. Josephine Shaw wrote in her diary May 22, 1862:

Yesterday we had a beautiful and touching proclamation from Lincoln, rendering Gen. Hunter's order freeing the slaves in North Carolina, South Carolina, and Georgia, null and void. One of the most extraordinary things that has happened for a long time was the calmness with which the order was received. We have certainly advanced in the year. The confidence in the President was shown by the entire acquiescence in everything he does. We feel that he is earnest and means to do right. A unique man. . . . As mother says, if his luck proves equal to his goodness, he's a paragon.

And John M. Palmer wrote a friend from Huntsville, Alabama, July 4, 1862:

I fully agree with you in regard to President Lincoln. I do not believe on the whole we could have a better man for the crisis. A brilliant man would have ruined the country long ago. On thinking over the list of Presidents our nation has had since its birthday, I cannot think of one with qualities better suited, all things considered, for the helm than Old Abe.[15]

"He never rubbed Congress the wrong way," Speaker Grow remarked of Lincoln. "He was masterful in diplomacy as in politics." Of course he repeatedly did rub Congress the wrong way, but never in such wise as to

13 Seward's opinion, Bancroft, *Seward*, II, 358; Welles's opinion, *Diary*, I, 500; Henry Lee, Washington, Nov. 2, 1861, to his wife, Henry Lee Papers, MHS.
14 Strong, *Diary*, III, 204, 218, 243.
15 Palmer Papers, Ill. State Hist. Lib.

leave any deep rancor. While in vital matters he had his way, he forced no humiliating capitulations; as he put it, he never planted a thorn in another man's pillow.

Yet his outward suavity was controlled by an iron resolution, and he was capable of bolder action than a Cromwell. Underneath half the debates of the session ran an implied discussion of the basic question: Where did the Constitution place the ultimate sovereignty in waging war and controlling reconstruction? On this subject Lincoln was granite. Final powers lay in the Presidency. Thad Stevens, applying to the suppression of rebellion the clause which authorized Congress to make all laws necessary and proper for carrying into execution its stated authority, declared that the two houses "possess all the powers now claimed under the Constitution, even the tremendous power of dictatorship." Sumner made the same sweeping assertion. "I claim for Congress all that belongs to any government in the exercise of the right of war," he said, adding, "it is by an act of Congress that the war powers are set in motion. When once in motion the President must execute them. But he is only the instrument of Congress under the Constitution of the United States." This went further than Henry Wilson's declaration that Congress was to make the laws defining policy, and the Executive was simply to administer them: "I had rather give a policy to the President of the United States than to take a policy from the President of the United States." But it was no more drastic than the statement by Lyman Trumbull that inasmuch as the President was a mere executor of Congressional law, "He is just as subject to our control as if we appointed him, except that we cannot remove him and appoint another in his place." [16]

These arrogant declarations in Congress presaged an opening of the conflict that was not to close until Cleveland successfully defied the Tenure of Office Act. Lincoln intended to resist such views to the bitter end. But he provoked no immediate collision. Instead, he at first merely inspired his warm friend Orville H. Browning, repeatedly his Senate spokesman, to make a speech defining his position. War, Browning said, vastly enlarged the powers of government. [17] "But is Congress the government?" It was not. "All the powers that Congress possess are those granted in the Constitution." He denied Fessenden's assertion that Congress held unlimited authority, for "it is invested with the absolute power of war." This, he commented, "is as broad and deep a foundation for absolute despotism as was ever laid." If the President ever abused the war powers, Browning pointed out, he was

16 *Cong. Globe*, 37th Cong., 2d Sess., 440 (Stevens); 2972 (Sumner); 2734 (Wilson); 2973 (Trumbull).
17 *Ibid.*, 1136.

answerable, when peace returned, to the civil authority for his excesses. But if Congress "usurps and prostitutes them the liberty of the citizen is overthrown, and he is helpless, without remedy for his grievances."

And soon afterward, Browning delivered an even more direct statement of Lincoln's views. He declared: "When the Constitution made the President commander-in-chief of the army and navy of the United States, it clothed him with the incidental powers necessary to a full, faithful, and forceful performance of the duties of that high office; and to decide what are military necessities, and to devise and to execute the requisite measures to meet them, is one of these incidents. It is not legislative, but an executive function, and Congress has nothing to do with it." [18]

In this conflict between Congress and the Executive, however, Lincoln was more interested in acts than in words. While Sumner and Stevens were dreaming of dictatorial powers, he was ready to checkmate them with the astuteness of a consummate master of the political chessboard. He was determined to keep the vital questions of slavery and reconstruction—questions affecting the whole future of the republic—in his hands and beyond the grip of the radicals. In March, 1862, he appointed Andrew Johnson military governor of Tennessee, instructing him to bring as much of the State as possible under Union authority; and at the same time he named similar governors for Louisiana, Arkansas, and North Carolina. In the Senate, Sumner offered a resolution demanding that the President revoke this action. [19] While Lincoln's friends blocked Sumner, the President was pressing his plan for ending slavery in the borderland; and when that failed, he took the breath of Congress away with his message of July 14 offering a draft bill for compensated emancipation in *all* slave States. Some Senators at once raised a question of the President's right to introduce a bill.

His boldest assertion of Presidential power against Congress, however, lay in his handling of the confiscation bill. By preparing a veto message and letting members know that he was ready to use it, he compelled a removal of the features that he found objectionable. This, said the radical Senators, was coercion. Then when he signed the bill, he advertised his leadership by giving Congress and the press the veto message he had prepared. Even Jackson would not have shown such audacity. The rage of Trumbull, Chandler, and other

---

18 *Ibid.*, 2922.

19 Sumner's resolution was offered June 6, 1862; see his *Works*, VII, 119. Lincoln also gave support to Francis H. Pierpont as provisional governor of Virginia. Pierpont converted the Unionist members of the old Virginia legislature, from the western counties, into a new legislature. This body adopted a constitution, and created the State of West Virginia, which chose a new governor. Pierpont meanwhile was given a four-year term as governor of the "restored" Virginia, a handful of counties under Union control.

Jacobins approached hysteria. "No one at a distance," states George W. Julian, "could form any conception of the hostility of the Republican members to Lincoln at the time of final adjournment, while it was the belief of many that our last session of Congress had been held in Washington. Senator Wade said that the country was going to hell, and that the scenes witnessed in the French Revolution were nothing in comparison with what we should see here." Their anger measured their chagrin in finding themselves over-mastered.[20]

The President, however affable, tactful, and gentle, was resolved to maintain his own supremacy in waging war and shaping the peace. This was what mattered to him most of all. On broad measures of mobilization and national development, meanwhile, he was a willing partner of Congress.

Did Lincoln comprehend, as he signed these successive measures, what a drastic economic and social revolution was transforming the nation? Did he grasp the fact that large-scale capitalism was taking control of the land, and that war contracts, tariffs, greenback issues, the expanded credit system, and railroad subsidies were helping defeat not only the South, but the old Jeffersonian ideals which he had shared? Did he see how portentously big business was looming on the horizon? No sure answer can be given, for he was too much engrossed in the conflict to discuss these matters.

We can only say that Lincoln was better equipped than most other leaders to understand both the good and bad aspects of the great changes accelerated by the war. By temperament he was a Jeffersonian. He disliked goals that represented a crass materialism; he did not wish to see America worshiping what William James later called the bitch-goddess success. His idea of social democracy was best represented by the contemplative, friendly life of the countryside or small city, and on one of his last drives with Mrs. Lincoln he spoke of returning to Springfield and its 12,000 people, and resuming his practice with Billy Herndon. But although in temper he belonged to the passing age, his political education had given him a clear appreciation of the new forces of the time. He had been a firm believer in Clay's American system, which derived partly from the politico-economic program of Alexander Hamilton. In the Illinois legislature he had contended for a rather reckless internal improvement system, and later had been attorney for the Illinois Central. As a matter of principle he supported all the measures fostering the new industrial order: tariff protection, a national banking system, railway subsidies, port improvements, and a strong national government. It is illuminating to find that after the Pacific railroad legislation passed, Lincoln called the engineer Grenville M. Dodge to Washington to discuss the point of

20 W. E. Binkley, *President and Congress*, 116–120; Julian, *Political Recs.*, 220.

commencement. Dodge found him much in earnest. "He took out the map and discussed with me for quite a long time the different lines and different views. I saw that he was very thoroughly posted in the demands of the different places." He leaned toward Omaha and Council Bluffs as the eastern terminus, and it was shortly so designated. He also believed that the promoters of the road could not raise capital unless their bonds were made the first mortgage, and the government's loan the second—a concession that was eventually granted.[21]

But Lincoln would have tried to reconcile the Hamiltonian transformation with the old Jeffersonian idealism and humanism of the early republic.

[II]

Congress deliberated in a city that had improved during the first year of conflict. It was less of a camp and more of a capital. The chief thoroughfares were better cleaned and policed, and street railways were being brought into operation. Of course the war atmosphere remained pervasive: endless lines of army wagons and ambulances, groups of spruce officers, knots of sick and wounded with white faces and weak steps or crutches, processions of dirty, ragged, yet unmistakably manly rebel prisoners, their heads held high even when they were shoeless and hatless, and galloping squads of cavalry. Throughout the year work was pressed on the Capitol dome so that the colossal figure of Liberty might be in place before Christmas, and presently the statue was there, with cape, shield, and sword, shining—as Walt Whitman noted on his visits to hospitals—like a star against the sky every bright morning and evening. The city grew in population, bustle, and affluence.[22] The chain of forts about the city had been strengthened until a complete line, connected by rifle pits, glowered down every road—about forty in all. Their clay sides were innocent of grass, and the fields around them showed by long vistas of tree stumps and sodden brush piles the sites of noble forests, now gone forever.

Nathaniel Hawthorne, visiting Washington in early spring, looked curiously at troops, generals, and legislators, at the tavern in Alexandria where Ellsworth had been killed, at Harpers Ferry, which reminded him of some Apennine village set beside a rushing stream, and at Fort Monroe, where old

21 J. R. Perkins, *Trails, Rails, and War*, Ch. IX, describes the meeting of Lincoln and Dodge. Every center from St. Louis (through Kansas City) to Sioux City asked to be made the terminus. Lincoln showed familiarity with railroad projectors in Illinois and sympathy with their struggles. See E. R. Richardson and A. W. Farley, *John P. Usher, passim.*
22 Noah Brooks, *Wash. in Lincoln's Time*, Chs. I and II; Bryan, *The National Capital*, II, *passim; Walt Whitman and the Civil War*, 163. Senator S. G. Arnold of Rhode Island ascribed the improvements to Yankee enterprise; to Manton Marble, Nov. 24, 1862, Marble Papers.

frigates like the *Minnesota* were now as obsolete as the Armada. He reflected that whether the war ended soon or late, the nation was in for a long domination by bullet-headed generals. A rainy day in Willard's Hotel gave him the impression that it could more justly be called the center of Washington and the Union than either the Capitol or White House. Among the crowd were office hunters, wire pullers, editors, army correspondents, inventors, artists, and railroad directors, mostly waiting for some favor, and meanwhile consuming whisky skins, gin cocktails, brandy smashes, and rum cobblers in an atmosphere of cigar smoke. [23] But the novelist was mistaken: the true centers of power remained the White House and Capitol, though the pressure of lobbyists was more fearful than ever before.

Pressures, indeed, accounted for much of what Congress did or refrained from doing. Members were not radicals or conservatives through innate wickedness, but rather because constituents made them so. George Pendleton represented the solid, conservative Ohio Valley citizens of Virginia or Carolina blood; Ben Wade and Elihu Washburne the Yankee stock of the Western Reserve and Chicago, with their economic interests.

"We are growing more radical every day," one citizen wrote Lyman Trumbull, who was well aware that many plain voters of Illinois were just as vehement in condemning McClellan as Medill's *Tribune*. "If things had not turned more favorable," one Rockford journalist assured Washburne just after Donelson, "I believe the people would have rebelled, they were becoming *desperate*." An Ohioan was warning Ben Wade that true men were distressed to find so many of those charged with the war more intent upon robbing the treasury than upon subduing the rebellion. "The people of the West are becoming disgusted by these delays, and beginning to inquire into the [real] cause. Our commerce is nearly prostrated by the closing of its natural channel, and the artificial ones Eastward are taxing our products beyond endurance. The Eastern capitalists may be suited with the delays of the war, but the yeomen of the *West* demand action, and they must soon be listened to." The audacious Zach Chandler, his temper alternating between jaundice and jocularity, but fierce as a panther for his opinions, precisely reflected the money-and-morality outlook of Detroiters.[24]

The ultraconservatives equally represented a great body of plain Americans. Some were men with Southern friends and relatives who would be ruined if Trumbull and Thad Stevens carried out their harsh measures; some were attached on principle to strict-construction ideas of the Constitution;

23   "Chiefly About War Matters, by a Peaceable Man," *Atlantic*, July, 1862, 43–61.
24   White, *Trumbull*, 171, 172; H. P. Sloan, Jan. 29, 1862, Washburne Papers, LC; Timothy C. Day, Cincinnati, Feb. 2, 1862, Wade Papers, LC.

some were agrarians who perceived that the new tariff and tax system would enrich industry at the expense of the farming interest. Less adept than the radicals in drawing a cloak of patriotism about their shoulders, these people had a case and needed spokesmen.

It was not Sumner or Wade, Chandler or Washburne who wrote and carried the truly important measures of the session. These men, indeed, were regarded as impracticable even by their own faction. "He originates no measures," Senator Grimes said of Sumner, "but simply makes two or three rather sophomorical set speeches." W. H. Russell had correctly remarked that Sumner was as ignorant of realities in the South as of the politics of Timbuctoo. Many thought that the Boston Senator had just one great aim beyond Union victory, an aim which Lincoln near the end summed up in a single sentence: "He hopes to succeed in beating the President, so as to change this government from its original form, and make it a strong centralized power." Charles Francis Adams, Jr., who knew Sumner intimately, enumerated the faults which disabled him from constructive action.[25] He was a theorist, agitator, and rhetorician, a doctrinaire who lacked insight into the men he attacked and the measures he discussed, and an egotist who let vanity override common sense. He was so intolerant that he regarded a difference of opinion on any subject as a moral delinquency. Once he let his emotions seize control of him, his voice vibrated in a tremulous rumble, he coined magniloquent phrases, he laid down the law, and he made opponents instead of friends. Of course he had great virtues, battling indefatigably for abolition, Negro rights, and honest government, but most Republican associates never really trusted him as a lawmaker.

Even in legislation touching race and slavery the real leaders were found elsewhere. It was Henry Wilson, hardworking, genial, shrewd, who did most to carry the bill for District emancipation, and Henry L. Dawes of the Berkshire district who stood foremost in the House for that measure. Wilson again, with Grimes in the Senate and Lovejoy in the House, provided for the schooling of the District freedmen. Arnold of Illinois, a close friend of Lincoln, introduced the bill which made freedom the rule in all Territories. While Trumbull was author of the confiscation measure, Collamer of Vermont gave it acceptable form. Early in the debate he expressed the opinion that private property could not be confiscated without judicial action, and offered an amendment to substitute due process for legislative seizure; and he with Fessenden and others hammered the legislation into such form that Lincoln could approve it.[26]

25 Stiles, *op. cit.*, 60, 61; Russell, *My Diary*, II, 121; C. F. Adams, Jr., *Autobiography*, 83–90.
26 *Cong. Globe*, 37th Cong., 2d Sess., *passim*; cf. Anna L. Dawes, *Sumner*, 171.

The debate on confiscation brought out the angriest exhibition of party feeling on both sides. "Sir, pass this bill," Saulsbury of Delaware told the Senate, "and if there ever was a hope of the reunion of these States, it is balanced upon this point." Thaddeus Stevens used still hotter language on the other side: "I am for inflicting all the consequences of defeat on a fallen foe in an unjust war. I am for confiscating the property of the rebels, and making it pay the cost of this rebellion." [27] When the bill finally became law, it seemed that the adverse arguments of reasonable men had been in vain. Radical members congratulated themselves upon the provisions for liberating all the slaves of those who aided the rebellion; for halting the return of fugitive slaves; and for the military employment of Africans in any manner the President might deem advantageous. They were delighted by the section which punished participation in or encouragement of rebellion by imprisonment up to ten years, or a fine not exceeding ten thousand dollars, or both, at the discretion of the courts. They rejoiced over other vindictive sections which made the property of designated categories of "rebels" subject to forfeiture.[28] Yet in the long run the views of moderates substantially prevailed. President Lincoln and Attorney-General Bates had such large powers to delay or restrict action, and most courts were so reluctant to press cases, that the Act remained almost a dead letter. Though hundreds were indicted for treason, not one was punished; though many confiscation actions were begun, little property was taken. The whole amount placed in the Treasury under the law was $129,680.67. Nobody was terrified, and almost nobody hurt.[29]

On the great constructive measures, meanwhile, party rancor was limited. Repeatedly members broke across old lines to unite in action for the nation's long-term growth.

[III]

Free homesteads—for whom, and how free? No man had earned a better right to answer these queries than Horace Greeley. When Speaker Grow on May 16, 1862, signed the engrossed copy of the Homestead Act, he congratulated the editor, recalling that the battle had been waged for more than ten years. "Its friends are more indebted for success to the unwavering support given it by the New York *Tribune* than to aught else." [30] Theretofore,

27 The hottest House debate occurred May 4 and 5, 1862.
28 See J. W. Grisfield's speech in *Cong. Globe*, 37th Cong., 2d Sess., 2129–2134; Greeley's editorial in N. Y. *Tribune*, June 19, 1862.
29 J. G. Randall's *Const. Problems under Lincoln* covers the subject in detail. See also A. C. Cole, "President Lincoln and the Illinois Radical Republicans," *Miss. Valley Hist. Rev.*, IV (March, 1918), 417–436.
30 N. Y. *Tribune*, May 22, 1862. It passed the House 82 to 42, and the Senate 27 to 12.

public lands had been open to private entry at a minimum price of $1.25 an
acre, or, if they lay within a few miles of one of the land-grant railroads,
$2.50 an acre. Advocates of the new law believed that it would offer the
country two major benefits. It would drive from the field the pernicious
speculators who, clutching large tracts, had compelled the actual settler to
pay from $5 to $30 an acre for an unimproved quarter section, unless he took
the risk of plunging into the wilderness long weary miles from churches,
schools, mills, stores, and doctors. Now, since the nation's lands were thrown
open to hardy colonizers without charge, dealers would see that it was a losing
business to buy thousands of acres to hold for a rise. The second gain would
be the laborer's; any workingman who felt cramped or maltreated could gather
his possessions together and remove to the boundless frontier.[31]

The provisions of the law encouraged these hopes. After January 1, 1863,
any citizen or intended citizen, male or female, over twenty-one, could file
for title to any quarter section of the public lands. So could any citizen under
twenty-one who was head of a family, or who had spent fourteen days or more
in the military service of the government. For the land thus taken, the settler
must pay $10, with some trifling legal fees. To perfect his title, he must then
spend five years in actual residence and cultivation. Where would he find the
fertile acres? Ten thousand railroad agents, editors, politicians, and emigrant
outfitters pointed to the great Northwest, from Michigan to Dakota and from
Missouri to Minnesota, as a region full of rich farming land subject to entry.

But the Americans were a nation of land-jobbers, and speculation did *not*
stop; particularly as successive enactments opened wide gates to it. The new
law was thrust into an older land system which clashed with and resisted it,
so that it failed to operate as intended. Greeley himself was by no means
unrealistic in his attitude toward homesteading. He urged people not to go
West without careful thought. He pointed out that the law did not *give*
people farms; on the contrary, those who paid for the land by $10 cash,
legal fees, transportation costs, equipment costs, and years of rugged toil,
commonly paid all it was worth. He recommended planned community settlement as far wiser than individual action. Let two or three hundred poor men
contribute a dollar each to send an agent to find a promising township;
then let each pre-empt his quarter section, and a well-rounded community,
like those of Puritan New England, Mormon Utah, or New Zealand, would
spring up, with its own grist-mill, sawmill, physician, clergyman, stores, and
schools. Such a settlement would attract railroads. If people acted sensibly,

31 The homestead bill was impeded by efforts to combine with it a sentimental grant of a
bounty to soldiers. Grow, who guided it in the House, struggled against this, and obtained
the assistance of Wade in the Senate. Lincoln signed the Act May 20, 1862; *Cong. Globe*,
37th Cong., 2d Sess., 39 ff.; DuBois and Mathews, *Grow*, Ch. XIV.

Greeley saw great hope in the law: "Young men! Poor men! Widows! Resolve to have a home of your own! If you are able to buy and pay for one in the East, very well; if not, make one in the broad and fertile West!" [32]

A brief trial of the new Act, however, proved that few laborers indeed would benefit from it, and not many farmers. The average workingman, toiling for a meager wage, could not save money to buy railway tickets, horses, plows, and other tools, and if he went into debt for them, found that he must work several years before his farm became profitable. He lacked experience, and in most instances taste, for country life. It was farmers' sons, or other young farmers looking for a better chance, who filled the ranks of the homesteaders. Even they, however, found that land speculation and land monopoly remained lions in their path. Capitalists who were looking for 20 per cent on their money obtained a great part of the areas granted to railroads, canal companies, and builders of wagon roads. They alone were able to pay the high prices asked for the most desirable lands granted to certain States. Rich timber, cattle, and mining interests soon found means, by bribing local land officers, making false oaths, and using dummy entrymen, to lay their hands on broad areas. One of the few really vigilant heads of the General Land Office was presently reporting that the vast machinery of his department had been perverted to permit the alienation of the public domain by a bad construction of loose regulations. [33]

Nevertheless, the popular belief in 1862 and later that the Homestead Act was a landmark in the history of the farmer and the West had genuine validity. Driving home the fact that the government possessed nearly two billion acres of land, it helped advertise the nation's boundless trans-Mississippi resources. It gave multitudes who never used it a sense of potential freedom, of escape, of spaciousness. And it has been estimated that perhaps one acre in nine of the remaining public lands did go to true small pioneers!

Quite as important in the long run was the College Land Grant Act which, with Justin S. Morrill of Vermont—a largely self-schooled lover of books, travel, and art—in charge, offered the republic an endowment of higher education such as no other country could match. The bill gave the States of the Union, including those of the South once they returned, the right to select 30,000 acres for each Senator and Representative. This was 10,000 more than under the bill which Buchanan had vetoed. Men broke over party lines to support the measure. "To many Democratic leaders of Congress,

32 N. Y. *Tribune*, June 6, 1862.
33 See Paul W. Gates, "The Homestead Law in an Incongruous Land System," *Am. Hist. Review*, XLI (July, 1936), 652–681; J. B. Sanborn, "Some Political Aspects of Homestead Legislation," *ibid.*, VI (Oct., 1900), 19–37; and Ray Allen Billington, *Westward Expansion*, 698, 699.

and more outside, I am much indebted for kindly sympathy and cooperation," wrote Morrill later.[34] Some Western Republicans, led by Jim Lane of Kansas, fought the measure because they believed that the land properly belonged to their States, and saw no reason to make gifts to the Eastern sisters; while a few members feared that it would seriously diminish the national revenue. All Kansas, said Lane, will be lost to its people—nothing will remain!

Fortunately, believers in elevating agriculture and the mechanic arts had aroused an immense popular sentiment behind the bill, so that newspapers, pulpits, and farm organizations all battled for it. Their aims were more practical than intellectual, but that fact made success all the easier. Since 1850 Jonathan B. Turner, a high-minded Yankee settled in one of the little Athenses of the West, Jacksonville, Illinois, had campaigned for nationally endowed universities serving the "industrial classes." Greeley and others had meanwhile advocated a system of People's Colleges, and an institution of that name had reached puny infancy in upper New York. The primary strength of the movement was a farm strength, and the principal aim a greater dignity and larger success for agriculture. However, many well-informed men, including college presidents, shared the democratic sentiment which Ezra Cornell expressed to Andrew D. White: "I would found an institution where any person can find instruction in any study." Year by year the impulse had gained vigor. It borrowed part of its strength from a parallel British movement, and such passionate pleas for the education of ambitious artisans as Kingsley's *Alton Locke*. A number of legislatures instructed their senators to vote for the bill.[35]

When the measure came to final passage in June, the Senate approved it 32 to 7, the House 90 to 25; a rainbow of hope bent against the murky battlefields of Virginia. Lincoln signed it on July 2, 1862. Senator Timothy O. Howe of Wisconsin as debate closed painted a melancholy vision. He saw the States putting their land scrip up to raffle, greedy investors buying it as they might buy gaudy jewelry, and a national treasure frittered away without enough return to keep a professor alive for a year.[36] In actual fact, some States did dissipate their grants. New York, with the largest land endowment of all, would have done so but for the stout fight waged by Andrew D. White and especially by Ezra Cornell, who when urged to sell some of the acres at a sacrifice answered: "No, I will wear my old hat and

34 Parker, *Morrill*, 272. Morrill attended a Vermont academy.
35 *Cong. Globe*, 37th Cong., 2d Sess., 2275–2277, for a typical exchange of views; White, *Autobiography*, I, 300; W. E. Sawyer, "The Evolution of the Morrill Act of 1862," Ph. D. dissertation, Boston Univ., 1948; Paul W. Gates, "Western Opposition to the Agricultural College Act," *Indiana Mag. of Hist.*, XXXVII (March, 1941), 103–136.
36 *Cong. Globe, ut sup.*, 2634, 2770.

coat a little longer and let you have a little more money from my pocket."[37] But others in Congress had a truer vision than Howe—a vision of crowded lecture halls, rich libraries, and laboratories full of eager experimenters, a vision of hundreds of thousands of lawyers, doctors, engineers, farm experts, and other professional men scattering fruitfully over the land. Some of those who gave the bill its overwhelming majority lived to see the new seats in Ithaca, Urbana, Madison, Minneapolis, and Berkeley take places among the important universities of the world.

At long last, too, agriculture won a place in the national government. Lincoln had pointed out in his annual message that the farming and stock-growing interests possessed no department, bureau, or office—only a clerkship; and he had suggested that Congress consider the matter. No Niagara of support met this common-sense proposal, for this was precisely the area in which American individualism was most rugged. Members expatiated upon the sturdy independence of the yeoman, who wanted neither favors nor interference, and wished to lean on his plow handles, not on Washington. The National Agricultural Society, wary of politicians, favored the establishment not of a non-Cabinet department, but of a mere bureau. Fessenden declared that not one farmer in a hundred wanted even a bureau. But after much discussion Congress decided in May for a so-called department, headed by a $3,000-a-year commissioner charged with diffusing useful information, procuring and distributing new plants and seeds, keeping statistical records, and making whatever special reports were requested by the President or Congress. It was natural for Lincoln to promote to the new position the Patent Office clerk who had looked after agricultural matters, Isaac Newton —a Quaker with a farm of his own in Pennsylvania. Newton soon had a chemist, an entomologist, a statistician, and most important of all, the versatile Scottish-born botanist William Saunders, working beside him.[38]

One other great constructive measure, the Pacific railroad bill, passed with little opposition. Since the Southerners had left Congress, almost everyone agreed on the central route for the road, a line equally fair to St. Louis and Chicago, and to all trunk lines connecting the East with those cities. Most people believed that within the lifetime of mature men the Pacific slope would have at least ten million people, who must be tied by iron strands to the Union. Great Britain had set an example of large-scale railroad-building in India and Australia; Russia had employed the American engineer

---

37 White, *Autobiography*, 318.
38 See *Cong. Globe*, 37th Cong., 2d Sess., 2013–2017, for debate. Fessenden grumbled that government was getting too big and too expensive; seed appropriations had risen in a decade from $1,000 to $60,000. Newton's career is treated in *Lincoln Lore*, No. 1441, March, 1958, pp. 1–3.

G. W. Whistler, father of the artist, in building the 420-mile double track railway from St. Petersburg to Moscow, and had undertaken still larger projects. Anyone with pad and pencil could compute the sums which might be saved by a pair of iron rails. Senator J. A. McDougall of California, for example, estimated that the cost of hauling men and goods between Eastern ports and San Francisco approached $76,000,000 a year, and that a railroad could furnish the same service for less than $23,000,000. Of course the inconvenience was worse than the annual loss of some fifty millions.

How long, Senators asked, would it take to construct the transcontinental line? On the basis of information furnished by Theodore D. Judah, the enthusiastic engineer whom Collis P. Huntington, Leland Stanford, Mark Hopkins, and Charles Crocker had sent to Washington to lobby for an endowment of the Central Pacific, McDougall declared that he expected to cross the continent by through train as early as the year 1870.

The debate showed a singular confusion in Congress about Western topography, about costs of railroad construction, about modes of railway operation, and about the best means of protecting the national investment. Some thought that $16,000 a mile would be a reasonable average cost, some much less. Some regarded a uniform gauge to the Pacific of the utmost importance; but McDougall declared that it did not matter, for merchandise and passengers should be shifted to new trains every thousand miles, or less —"Everybody knows that the engine, the locomotive, cannot run safely more than a thousand miles." Some believed that the government, in giving the Union Pacific and Central Pacific companies a specified land subsidy, was driving a rather hard bargain, but Howe of Wisconsin said that on the contrary Washington was supplying "a most ample, I was about to say a most profligate, bounty." Plainly, Congress was legislating in the dark; but amid many tokens of popular approval, the Senate passed the bill 35 to 5, and the House 104 to 21.[39]

Under this measure, the Union Pacific was authorized to build westward from the 100th meridian across the Rockies, and the Central Pacific eastward from San Francisco and Sacramento across the Sierra Nevada, meeting at the California-Nevada line. Five branch roads at the eastern end would connect the Union Pacific with Omaha, Sioux City, St. Joseph, Leavenworth, and Kansas City. Each of the lines received a 400-foot right of way, with necessary ground for stations, shops, and switches, and five alternate sections of land on each side of the railway as fast as it was built. The government agreed, moreover, to lend the companies $16,000 in United States 6 per cent

39 *Cong. Globe*, 37th Cong., 2d Sess., Appendix, 381 ff., offers the text of the bill; *ibid.*, 307 ff., McDougall's speech; 2804–2840, the best part of the debate.

bonds for every mile of track laid on the plains, $32,000 a mile in hilly country, and $48,000 a mile in the mountains, this loan to be a first mortgage on the roads. The President was to appoint two directors of the Union Pacific, and to fix a uniform width of track for all the lines. Telegraph lines were to accompany the railroads. If the roads did not finish building across the continent from the Missouri to the Sacramento by the middle of 1876, they and all their properties were to be forfeited to the government.

Without delay, the Central Pacific was off in the race. Judah, the son of an Episcopal clergyman of Connecticut, trained at Rensselaer Polytechnic, found his brightest dreams realized when on July 1 Lincoln signed the act. For years he had spoken and written on the necessity of a transcontinental line; he had done more than anybody else to agitate the subject in Washington during Buchanan's Administration, had discovered a practicable route across the Sierra, and had brought Huntington and Stanford into the organization of the company. While the Union Pacific marked time, for the government inducements did not at first call forth sufficient private capital, the Central Pacific obtained a loan of $1,660,000 from the State of California, and an opinion from Lincoln that the Sierra Nevada extended well down into the Sacramento Valley. The first rails were hammered fast in 1863. That same year John A. Dix was elected president of the freshly-organized Union Pacific. In due course Lincoln, after a premature decision in favor of a broad gauge, took the advice of experienced railroad executives, and set the width of the transcontinental at four feet, eight and one half inches, thus fixing a standard for the whole United States. During 1864 the Union Pacific, with enlarged aids from the government, also began construction.[40]

That is, to facilitate the raising of capital, Congress—with Lincoln approving—made the government loan a second and not a first lien on the railroad. The 100th meridian runs through the center of Nebraska, but the building of the road got under hesitant way at the then dismal hamlet of Omaha, fronting Council Bluffs across the muddy Missouri. It made scanty progress until the managers almost forcibly haled from the army General Grenville M. Dodge, who had learned some theoretical engineering at Norwich College in Vermont, and a great deal more of practical surveying and construction first with the Mississippi & Missouri in Iowa during the 1850s, and later in the rebuilding and equipping of wrecked lines for Grant's army. He knew Lincoln, and the President trusted him. The engineering work of the transcontinental road was to be as creditable as the financial record was to be dishonorable. Dramatic clashes

40 Stuart Daggett, *The Southern Pacific, passim;* Judah quarreled with Huntington and others the year of his death, 1863. Dix, *Dix,* II, 127, emphasizes the faith of the general in the Union Pacific.

had attended the controversy over the proper gauge. The Central Pacific had chosen a five-foot width, and Kansas railway projectors favored that type of line. But the Iowa-Nebraska branch, and most Easterners, insisted on four feet eight and a half inches, and after Senator Harlan of Iowa introduced a bill designating that gauge, Lincoln yielded.

The rattle of sledge hammers was drama to the world, as Jules Verne's *Eighty Days* attests, and music to the West. A terrible war had not numbed the constructive enterprise of the republic. Actually in many ways the time was propitious. The West was bulging with foodstuffs that had once gone down the Mississippi and could now be sent out to supply the construction gangs. The depressed iron industry was anxious to furnish rails, spikes, cars, and locomotives. While some of the Negro refugees from Missouri and Kentucky acted as navvies, paroled or discharged soldiers could fight off the Indians. Many people held an exaggerated idea of the trans-Mississippi region as a vast treasure house, which would yield everything from buffalo robes to gold bars; tap its wealth by railways, as Grant later said, and it might pay the costs of the war. At any rate, the North was showing its ability to wage a great conflict with one hand, and build up the West with the other.[41]

[IV]

The Confederates might fight without money, as various men said, for they had no national credit to protect; but the Union had to provide means for the war effort while avoiding a ruinous bankruptcy. Congress had failed, in its midsummer session of 1861, to use the taxing power energetically. When it met again in the winter of 1861–62, it found the country's financial needs instant and exigent; they would not wait for the slow institution of a machinery of taxes, assessment, and collection. A very limited stock of gold and silver was available. The Treasury notes which Chase had issued to help meet the emergency were not being paid in coin on demand, and had fallen into such disrepute that leading commercial banks refused to accept them as money of account, taking them only as a special deposit. They were therefore ceasing to circulate. The Eastern banks suspended specie payment as 1861 ended, and this left the country in a situation where its many reckless speculative bankers might fill the land with worthless paper.

41 It must be remembered that the country, despite some grumbling by agrarian elements, was still in a generous mood toward railways. And benefits were being reaped from earlier railway land grants. The Illinois Central hauled thousands of troops and huge quantities of supplies for the Union. Thomas A. Scott and Montgomery C. Meigs decided that the government was entitled under law to free use of the road, but should pay for use of locomotives and cars, and hence fixed freight rates one-third below the charges of other lines.

A dependable currency was desperately needed to pay the soldiers, buy supplies, and keep business active. It seemed to many that the only feasible course was to have the government take bold control, issue its own circulating medium, and give it credit by pronouncing it legal tender for debts. This step would be so unprecedented, so momentous, and so full of risks that many recoiled from it. Secretary Chase, who felt great aversion to making anything but coin a legal tender, was himself reluctant. But the House Ways and Means Committee, led by E. G. Spaulding, an experienced Buffalo banker, had the courage of desperation; and on January 22, 1862, it submitted a legal-tender bill which at once provoked a violent debate. It provided for the issue of $150,000,000 in legal-tender paper.

A powerful group of Republicans at once joined the Democrats in opposition. Justin S. Morrill, hopeful that the war could be ended by midsummer, assured the House that the measure would make the enemy grin with delight. V. B. Horton of Ohio declared it unnecessary, for an appeal to moneyed men would bring out an abundance of gold. Owen Lovejoy of Illinois proposed to tax the country at the rate of 200 millions a year, if necessary, to sell interest-bearing government bonds, and to compel the banks to return to a specie basis; thus the nation could avoid a bottomless abyss. Roscoe Conkling of New York also used the word "abyss." The bill was a legislative declaration of national bankruptcy, he said, for after the first issue of legal-tender bills another, and another, and another would follow. In the Senate, Collamer of Vermont and Preston King of New York threw their weight against the measure, the former arguing that it was unconstitutional. Opponents naturally made much of the fate of the American continentals and the French assignats. Even Sumner was deeply troubled by the apparent necessity of incurring all the evils of an inconvertible currency, forced into circulation by act of Congress.

But the argument of necessity could not be gainsaid. As members pointed out, the Ways and Means Committee estimated that the government must pay nearly $350,000,000 before July, and of this $100,000,000 was already due to soldiers, contractors, and other creditors. The aggregate capital of the banks of the three principal cities of the country hardly exceeded this latter sum. Secretary Chase, at first hesitant, came out for the bill in a letter which Spaulding read to the House on February 4, and which probably had decisive influence. The chambers of commerce in New York, Philadelphia, and Boston endorsed it. Particularly effective was the advocacy of Thad Stevens in the House, and of John Sherman in the Senate. In the end it passed the House by 93 yeas, all Republican, to 59 nays; and the Senate, after approving the legal tender clause by the close vote of 23 to 17, accepted the measure 30 to 7. The Rubicon was crossed! [42] The printing presses were put in operation, and greenbacks soon rustled in every hand.

This legal-tender legislation, passed in the nick of time, gave wide benefits to both the Administration and the nation. No doubt stringent taxation and the maintenance of a metallic currency, had they been practicable, would have reduced the costs of the war. But the nation's stock of hard money was quite inadequate to the needs of business, which the greenbacks helped revive; and heavier taxes would have excited grave popular discontent. Added to the gloom caused by military reverses, such discontent might have made Lincoln's prospects in the fall elections discouraging indeed. The nation was to pay a heavy penalty for its resort to paper money in the inflation, speculation, and widespread financial demoralization of the next ten years. But a different course might have cost it still worse disasters.

Along with its resort to greenbacks, the government of course had to raise large new revenues by taxation. The tariff had been increased in 1861 by placing tea and coffee on the dutiable list, and raising the average ad valorem rates from 18.8 per cent (under the very low tariff of 1857) to 36.2 per cent. Even so, the duties collected in the fiscal year 1862 fell short of fifty millions; they were obviously limited by the capacity of the people to consume foreign goods. The government therefore turned to excise taxes. It was a special felicity of Americans that for a long generation—since 1821 —they had been practically unknown. Now a comprehensive and heavy system of excise taxes was framed by Congress; a law so thorough that it took 30 royal octavo pages and more than 20,000 words to list its provisions.

Every manufacturing interest, every branch of commerce, and every profession save the ministry felt the weight of the new enactment. Liquor and tobacco were of course taxed; so were such luxuries as carriages, billiard tables, yachts, gold and silver plate, and confectionery. Manufacturers of textiles, iron, steel, and wood paid a tax of 3 per cent. Physicians, bankers, brokers, lawyers, livestock dealers, and even street jugglers paid their share. Butchers paid thirty cents for every beeve slaughtered, and ten cents for every hog. Men ruefully recalled Sydney Smith's lament over the British taxes entailed by the Napoleonic wars: "taxes on everything which it is pleasant to see, hear, feel, smell, or taste; taxes . . . on the sauce which pampers man's appetite and on the drug that restores him to health; on the ermine which decorates the judge and the rope which hangs the criminal; on the poor man's sauce and the rich man's spice; on the brass nails of the coffin and the ribbons of the bride."

42 Besides the *Cong. Globe*, 37th Cong., 2d Sess., Jan.–Feb., 1862, *passim*, see the interpretive narrative in Cox, *Three Decades*, 126–144, and Blaine, *Twenty Years*, 409–429.

In the summer session of 1861 Congress had provided for an income tax of 3 per cent on all incomes exceeding $800 a year, but had postponed the appointment of assessors and collectors to the following spring. Now the income tax was fixed at 3 per cent on incomes between $600 and 10,000 and 5 per cent (later 10) on incomes above $10,000. It was thought wonderful when A. T. Stewart of New York paid by one check $400,000 on an income of four millions.[43] The burdens which the excise and income taxes laid on manufacturers mainfestly handicapped them in competition with foreign exporters, and a general revision of the tariff was therefore carried through in June, 1862. This raised the rates on practically the whole range of imports, producing bitter complaints abroad, and much criticism in the West. But the effect of this second Morrill Tariff can best be considered when we turn to a study of wartime industrialism.

[V]

Congress in its seven and a half months of effort had written one of the most important parts of the Administration's record for 1862. The army and navy gained ground, but met defeat after defeat in the process; the departments managed their activities with increasing vigor and skill, but committed blunders like Stanton's interruption of recruiting; the President gained in strength, but failed to carry his great plan of compensated border emancipation. Congress marched steadily forward. In easy control of both Houses, the Republicans redeemed every important promise they had made to Northern voters. Such measures as the Homestead Act, the Pacific Railroad, the Morrill Tariff, and the expansion of the currency by legal-tender paper would shape the growth of the nation for decades to come. It was largely on the basis of this record that the party would face the electorate in the fall elections.

43 Sidney Ratner, *American Taxation*, 57–93.

9

Antietam and Emancipation

IN THE dark hours before dawn on September 4, Lee's veterans began splashing through the shallow fords of the Potomac midway between Harpers Ferry and Washington. He had chosen a point near the capital so that his invasion of Maryland might menace both Baltimore and Washington, and draw the Union army after him until he could fight it somewhere distant from its base. Thousands of his troops were barefoot, and nearly all tattered, darkly sunburnt, lean, and hungry-looking. Though a Union battery banged away with some effect near Edwards's Ferry, elsewhere they swarmed across with little opposition. D. H. Hill's fresh division had reinforced Lee, giving him in theory nearly 70,000 men, but he took only about 60,000 into Maryland and his ranks continued thinning.[1] On the morning of the 7th the Confederates marched into Frederick, where Lee issued a proclamation declaring that they had come to liberate Maryland, not harm it. As foraging groups scoured the country for livestock, paying partly in greenbacks, partly in Confederate paper, his major forces concentrated about the town. Here he could threaten even Philadelphia, and menace the communications of the capital with the North and West.

A tremor ran through the Union. Boston on the 9th gave a frantic ovation to the Sixth Massachusetts, leaving for the front once more. The New York

1 John Esten Cooke, himself in the army, writes: "All the roads of northern Virginia were lined with soldiers, comprehensively denominated 'stragglers'; but the great majority of these men had fallen out from the advancing column from physical inability to keep up with it; thousands were not with General Lee because they had no shoes, and their bleeding feet would carry them no farther, or the heavy march without rations had broken them down. This great crowd toiled on painfully in the wake of the army, dragging themselves five or six miles a day; and when they came to the Potomac, near Leesburg, it was only to find that General Lee had swept on, that General McClellan's column was between him and them, and that they could not rejoin their commands." He estimates that 20,000 or 30,000 thus failed to reach the Maryland battlefields. *Stonewall Jackson*, 341. Lee's numbers have been the subject of much dispute. O. R., I, xix, pt. 2, p. 639, gives a field return Sept. 30 of 62,713 present and 52,990 present for duty. Longstreet estimated after the war that the army should have numbered 63,000 at the passage of the Potomac; letter July 15, 1885, to D. H. Hill, Hill Papers, Va. State Library. A careful military critic in the N. Y. *Nation*, Dec. 20, 1894, computed that Lee had 60,000 in the campaign.

press declared that the hour of opportunity had at last struck, for Lee might be defeated so decisively as to crush the rebellion. Throughout New England and the Middle States enlistments, lagging again since Pope's defeat, showed tokens of a revival. In Philadelphia, as long troop trains of replacements began passing through the city, the armories were thrown open for volunteering, and green recruits were hastily drilled. In Scranton cannon and bells summoned the adult males for training; in Harrisburg, Governor Curtin conferred with Thomas A. Scott on emergency measures. Deepest of all was the alarm in Baltimore, where merchants, knowing what wholesale seizures of goods the Southern host would make, and Unionists, well aware that the "Secesh" element in the city was growing dangerous, looked to their defenses.

Lee's hazardous movement was not difficult to explain, for politically and militarily it was almost a necessity. His army was so ill equipped and so inferior in numbers to the growing Northern forces that he could not afford to stand still. As he had to move aggressively, he shared the view of most Southern officers and editors that it should fight on enemy soil, and there make the war support itself. Jackson was particularly anxious to invade. Some of the troops told Frederick citizens that to them the movement was a question of food or starvation—for three days they had lived on green corn, apples, and little else. The effort to buy out shops in Frederick and other towns disclosed other necessities. Lee wrote Davis that the army lacked shoes, lacked clothes, lacked transport animals, and lacked "much of the material of war." He knew with Napoleon that an army marches on both its shoe leather and its belly.[2]

The political motives were equally important. A victory beyond the Potomac not only offered the best hope of gaining Anglo-French intervention, but also presented the largest chance of raising Northern war weariness to the point of negotiations for peace. "There is but one method of putting an end to the war," declared the Richmond *Examiner*, "and that is by destroying the Federal credit"; in other words, financial pressures would compel a new attitude.[3] As soon as Southern legions made good their stand on Maryland soil, Colonel J. F. Marshall of South Carolina prophesied to Davis, the North would lose heart. "The tone of the Masses, the Press, and the Legislatures will all

2 Lee had information that Washington had already received 60,000 replacements who would soon be embodied in the army. Freeman, *Lee*, II, 350. McClellan actually had a mobile force of nearly 100,000 in addition to the troops about Washington and Harpers Ferry. The North continued to overestimate Southern force in the grossest manner; thus the N. Y. *Herald* on September 9 declared that Lee's army was "at least 150,000 strong."

The sad outward appearance of the Confederates led some observers to form hasty judgments. "They are the dirtiest, lousiest, filthiest, piratical-looking cut-throats white man ever saw," wrote Edward S. Bragg to his wife, Sept. 21, 1862, Bragg Papers; but they were gentlemen compared with some marauding troops under Pope and Grant.

3 July 21, 1862.

change from a thirst for our blood and property to that for peace." [4] And Lee no sooner reached Frederick than he wrote Davis that the time had come for the Confederacy to propose to the North a recognition of its independence, for it would obviously be negotiating from strength, not from weakness.[5]

Because Lee hoped to win both recruits and friends in Maryland, his army behaved with exemplary restraint. No citizen was maltreated, no goods were taken without payment, and no offensive display of Southern sentiment was permitted. General Bradley T. Johnson, the provost-marshal charged with enlisting as many men as possible, rode up to a soldier cheering in the Frederick streets for Davis, and smashed him over the head with his revolver. "There, you damned blankety-blank," he said, "see if you disobey orders again!" [6] The army brought with it a civil commissioner, E. Loring Lowe, a friend of Herschel V. Johnson, with authority from Jefferson Davis as well as General Lee to undertake any political mission for which victory might clear the way. Lee's proclamation in Frederick assured Marylanders that they would once more enjoy their ancient freedoms, and could freely decide their own destiny. One Union officer paid tribute to the conduct of the hungry, dysentery-weakened rebels as they marched through the Maryland towns. Though they looked haggard, their clothes were often mere bundles of rags, and many were so unkempt and unwashed that they stank, yet in discipline they surpassed the well-fed, well-clothed, Union forces.

"No one," wrote this officer, "can point to a single act of vandalism perpetrated by the rebel soldiery during their occupation of Frederick, while even now a countless host of stragglers are crawling after our army devouring, destroying, and wasting all that falls in their devious line of march." [7]

[I]

Lee had to open his campaign with a hazardous blow to maintain his communications. His hope that Marylanders would rally to his banner proved unfounded, for they remained timid or hostile. While Eastern Maryland, which held the great body of Southern sympathizers, was dominated by the Union forces, the invaded heart of the State stood mainly with the North.[8] Although

4 July 11, 1862, Davis Papers, Duke Univ.
5 See O. R., I, xix, pt. 2, p. 600, for evidence that he expected Maryland to rise.
6 Baltimore corr. dated Sept. 11 in N. Y. *Tribune,* Sept. 13, 1862.
7 MS letter of James Gillette, commissary officer, to mother, Sept. 13.
8 As the Barbara Frietchie legend, immortalized by Whittier, suggests. This legend has no basis in fact. Mrs. Frietchie, then ninety-six, waved a Union flag from her porch when Union troops passed through Frederick later, not when the Confederates passed, and she and Jackson never saw each other; *Battles and Leaders,* II, 618, 622. But it possesses poetic truth, for many Maryland women had the defiant valor imputed to Mrs. Frietchie, and Jackson had the chivalry. Cf. Lenoir Chambers, *Stonewall Jackson,* II, 192, 193.

some hundreds of young men did flock in, most of them soon flocked back, explaining that after "seeing and smelling" the rebel host, they had decided to stand aloof. It was a most heroic army, but its life was all too heroically arduous. Realizing that he could not rely for communications on the Leesburg-Manassas line close to Washington, Lee had to make sure of the Shenandoah Valley instead. He had supposed that his penetration of Maryland would compel the Union forces to evacuate Harpers Ferry and Martinsburg, and McClellan in fact urged their removal; but bad policy kept them there. He therefore determined to send Stonewall Jackson to take Harpers Ferry and open the Valley line while the rest of the army continued operating in Maryland.

This division of his tired, ill-equipped force was perilous, as Longstreet pointed out in a protest. But Lee knew McClellan well enough to be sure he would move slowly; he was aware how wretched a commander the North often put at places like Harpers Ferry, and he never forgot that the South had to take desperate chances. Before Little Mac rouses himself to active operations, he told one of his brigadiers, "I hope to be on the Susquehanna." He outlined the proposed operation with care in Special Order No. 191.

If Lee were to succeed—not only dividing his army in the presence of superior enemy forces, but placing a river between the two parts—he required complete secrecy, and he counted on the abysmal inefficiency of McClellan's intelligence service. Fortune, however, betrayed him. At this time his general orders were frequently transmitted by headquarters direct to each division commander; that is, the staff took Lee's instructions, wrote them down, entered one copy in the "confidential book" or held it to be copied later into the general order book, and sent another copy by orderly to the commander addressed. Sometimes the orderly was told to bring back a receipt, sometimes not.[9] This time Jackson, seeing the importance of a clear understanding of Special Order No. 191, wrote out a copy in his own hand and sent it to General D. H. Hill, of his command. It directed that part of the army was to march northwest on the morrow to Hagerstown and Boonesborough. The divisions of McLaws, Anderson, and Walker were to turn south, however, and seize Maryland Heights, Loudoun Heights, and Harpers Ferry, while Jackson by the longest march of all was to recross the Potomac, cut the Baltimore & Ohio, take Martinsburg, and pick up any fugitives from Harpers Ferry. All these detached forces, their mission accomplished, were to rejoin the main army at Hagerstown or Boonesborough.

This vital order some Union troops, entering Frederick on Lee's heels, found

9 Charles Marshall, Nov. 11, 1867, to D. H. Hill on procedure; Hill Papers, Va. State Lib. Lenoir Chambers, Stonewall Jackson, II, 188-191, 200-202, supplies details.

wrapped around three cigars in a field outside Frederick, and they sent it to Mc-Clellan on September 13! D. H. Hill has usually been held responsible for losing it, for though he later denied culpability, Charles Marshall, Lee's aide and military secretary, holds him to blame.[10] Whatever the circumstances, McClellan had early notice of the division of the Confederate army; the troops of Jackson and Walker had hardly recrossed the Potomac before he knew they were south of the river.

The forces which Lee sent on this daring mission moved with characteristic rapidity. By afternoon of the 13th they had taken Martinsburg and the two eminences overlooking Harpers Ferry, and held the Union garrison there at their mercy. The commander, D. H. Miles, should either have abandoned the trap in time or posted all his troops on one of the strong heights; he did nothing. The Confederate batteries were soon shelling him heavily, and at dawn on the 13th he surrendered his 11,500 men, with 73 guns, 13,000 small arms, 200 wagons, and much camp equipment.

Jackson as usual wasted not a moment. Astride his horse in the early sunlight, he received the Union officer sent to offer unconditional surrender, and penned a dispatch to Lee. Then he rode into Harpers Ferry past dejected Union troops, many of whom uncovered. "Boys," said one, "he's not much for looks, but if we had him we wouldn't have been caught in this trap." [11] Late that afternoon, the 15th, his forces were on their way to rejoin Lee. It was high time, for the main Confederate army by that hour was in a dangerous predicament. Stonewall and his fellow commanders in their brilliant two-day coup had taken a larger army than those of Burgoyne or Cornwallis, well armed, well provisioned, and established near highly defensible heights; as Northern newspapers said, Hull's surrender was nothing to that of Miles.[12] The guns, small arms, and wagons that the Confederates had seized were of inestimable value to them. Nevertheless, the South would have paid too high a price if Lee had been smashed before Jackson could get back to him.

10 Hill's denial is explicit. He declares no such order came to him from Lee, but that an identical one did arrive from Jackson, which he kept; "The Lost Dispatch," in *The Land We Love*, February, 1868. Colonel Marshall could not conjecture just what had happened, but admitted later that the loss of the order might have occurred in many ways. Randolph B. Marcy and S. W. Crawford, in affidavits written May 5 and Aug. 22, 1868, state reasons for believing that the order was found in the tracks of A. P. Hill, not D. H. Hill; D. H. Hill to Marshall, Nov. 11, 1867, Hill Papers. See also Hal Bridges, "A Lee Letter," *Va. Mag. of Hist. and Biog.*, LXVI (April, 1958), 161–166.

D. H. Hill had been accused of losing an important order during the Seven Days, which was recaptured on the person of a Union soldier before it got to headquarters; Fitzgerald Ross, *Cities and Camps*, 45, 46.

11 *Battles and Leaders*, II, 625–627.

12 Miles had been prominent in the Bull Run disaster, and critics demanded why he had been given such an important command; N. Y. *Tribune* editorial, Sept. 20, 1862. A chance shot as the white flag was raised mortally wounded him.

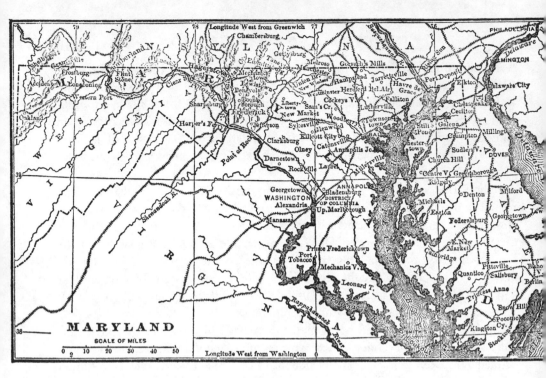

MARYLAND WITH HARPERS FERRY AND ANTIETAM CREEK

Indeed, Lee might have been crushed by the 16th but for McClellan's delays. The statement that he was warned in time that McClellan had obtained the lost order seems untrue. But McClellan had been displaying his characteristic defects and virtues. He had capably reorganized his forces, putting Banks in charge of the Washington fortifications, replacing McDowell (who now disappears from active duty) by Hooker as a corps commander, and keeping Burnside, Sumner, Franklin, and Fitz-John Porter in command of their old corps. But as Lee had anticipated, his movements were dilatory. In the six days from September 7, when he took the field in Maryland, to the 13th, he advanced barely thirty miles. Certain as usual that Lee outnumbered him, on the 11th he demanded reinforcements of 25,000. Halleck shared his nervousness.

Lee was thus able to bring his troops into good defensive position on the eastern slopes of South Mountain, the long irregular range of hills which continues the Blue Ridge into Maryland. Longstreet, Stuart, and D. H. Hill took their stand in the area of Crampton's and Turner's Gaps, passes from 400 to 600 feet high which pierce the thousand-foot ridge. Here on September 14, Confederate officers, peering through field glasses from the heights, descried an advance division of Jacob D. Cox's force on the turnpike to the southeast;

and soon they could see the blue uniforms and glittering bayonets of almost the whole Army of the Potomac swarming down from the far-off Catoctin Ridge near Frederick, and crossing the intervening valley. By noon that hot day the battle was raging violently. Along a wide stretch of South Mountain the Union troops performed astonishing feats in surmounting steep hills, penetrating dense woods, and scrambling over jagged rocks. The Northern artillery outranged the Confederate guns, while superior infantry strength permitted outflanking operations. By five in the afternoon Franklin had pushed his way through Crampton's Gap.

The day's fighting along South Mountain might be called a drawn battle. To be sure, it left the Confederates in a position of great peril. With one gap forced and the other rendered untenable, Longstreet and D. H. Hill at nightfall had to retreat. But the anxious Lee could take pride in the stubborn courage with which 18,000 Southerners had held the front against 30,000 Union troops. While the Northern volunteers displayed steady valor—"not a man fell back or straggled," wrote one reporter—the Confederates had fought with almost unmatchable devotion. And Lee had after all gained what was really important to him—time; time for Jackson to come up. He had in fact gained the whole twenty-four hours beginning at dawn of the 14th. His men fell back in exemplary order. At Keedysville, on the road to Sharpsburg, citizens later testified that the half-starved troops took nothing unless people were willing to sell. One miller, asked to dispose of grain and flour, refused, saying they could have nothing without breaking his lock. "We break no locks, sir," was the reply, and the hungry column marched on.[13] As Lee's forces crossed Antietam Creek he learned by a courier from Jackson that Harpers Ferry had surrendered, and he then disposed his troops on the hills about Sharpsburg.

McClellan next day indulged in exultant boasts. At 8 A.M. he telegraphed Halleck: "I have just learned from General Hooker, in the advance . . . that the enemy is making for Shepherdstown in a perfect panic; and that General Lee last night stated publicly that he must admit that they had been shockingly whipped." Two hours later he reported that the rout had been confirmed. "It is stated that Lee gives his losses as 15,000." [14] Actually Lee's losses had been only 3,400, and his retreat was effected without panic. Moreover, as he formed his lines in the new position near Sharpsburg, he had the comfort of knowing that Jackson was on the way. By a "severe" march after midnight, Stonewall reached Lee's lines early on the 16th.[15]

13 N. Y. *Tribune*, Sept. 19, 1862.
14 O. R., I, xix, pt. 2, pp. 294, 295.
15 Henderson, II, 226, 227; Freeman, *Lee*, II, 381, 382.

[II]

Although the Confederates had escaped a hammer blow while still divided, their position remained dangerous. At Sharpsburg, a hamlet only three miles from the Potomac, they lay behind the crooked Antietam Creek, which wriggles its way down to the river above Harpers Ferry. They had the advantage of holding a low crescent-shaped ridge, their right flank resting on the Antietam, and their left making some use of stone walls, limestone ledges, and thicketed woodlands. Perhaps because they lacked tools, they dug no entrenchments, though they could have strengthened their lines greatly at various points by hasty field works. With but 50,000 men at most, they faced McClellan's well-armed force half again as large. They were more tired, hungry, and ragged than ever, and their spirits had suffered by the retreat from South Mountain while those of the Federal army had risen. "The *morale* of our men is now restored," McClellan informed Halleck.

Lee's daring resolution was never better exhibited than in his decision to stand and fight. Longstreet, always cautious, advised retreat, and some military critics have regarded Lee's choice as a cardinal mistake. But Jackson, when he arrived, approved a decision that for several reasons was almost inevitable. The invasion of Maryland was a desperate effort to end the war at one stroke by laying a foundation for foreign intervention, and spreading discouragement throughout the North; luck, strategy, and heroism could yet win a victory, and if it were half as signal as Second Manassas it might achieve the object. McClellan exaggerated when he wrote later: "One victory lost almost all would have been lost. Lee's army might have marched as it pleased on Washington, Baltimore, Philadelphia, or New York . . . nowhere east of the Alleghenies was there another organized force to avert its march." This was McClellan's self-glorification as the savior of the Union. The Northern forces were now too numerous to be scattered by one blow, and each of the four cities would have remained well defended. Nevertheless, the effect of a Union defeat on foreign opinion and the autumn elections might have been disastrous. With so much to gain, Lee could only play his hand out to the end.

By retreating, Lee would put his army on the defensive for months to come. That no army fighting a defensive campaign with smaller numbers ever wins a decisive battle is a well-tested maxim of war; Hannibal, Marlborough, Frederick, Washington, Napoleon, Wellington, all won their victories when they took the offensive.[16] Moreover, if Lee fell back he could augment his forces but slowly while the Union army would grow rapidly in strength. Under

16 Sir Frederick Maurice, *Lee*, 151, 152.

recent calls, the North was putting 600,000 more men under arms; it was at last manufacturing artillery, small arms, ammunition, and camp supplies in almost adequate quantity; it was finding better brigadiers and colonels. As Herschel V. Johnson was writing A. H. Stephens, a protracted war must close in combatant exhaustion—and the South would be exhausted first.[17] If Lee waited, he would soon find that the North had trained its raw recruits and gained an overwhelming field superiority. McClellan could then enjoy just what he desired; a campaign of movement after full ranks, improved administration, and an overhauled supply system put his army in shape to prosecute the war without intermission to a successful end.

It was a remarkable battlefield that Lee had chosen, so compact that from some vantage points observers could witness the struggle in its entire length and breadth. The crescent-shaped ridge which furnished the main Confederate line was backed by a broad tableland of woods and ravines, offering cover for troops everywhere. Lee had two good highways, the Shepherdstown Road and the Williamsport Road, open at his rear for possible retreat to the Potomac. The sluggish Antietam flowed in front of the Confederate position, too deep for passage by artillery and well guarded at its three stone bridges. But in view of the heavy superiority of the national troops and of the guns which McClellan massed at the center, the Confederates needed every aid they could draw from the terrain.[18]

[III]

McClellan was as usual open to criticism. He had delayed in thrusting his columns forward on September 13 to reach South Mountain before the Confederates could establish themselves on its slopes, and he had then made a faulty use of his forces in attacking the Southern positions on that ridge.[19] He delayed again in pushing forward after the retreating Lee. He knew early on the morning of the 15th, when he telegraphed Halleck, that D. H. Hill and Longstreet had evacuated Turner's Gap, and he declared that "our troops are now advancing in pursuit of them." But they were not advancing.[20] A swift forward movement would have caught Lee off balance before he could con-

17 Johnson to Stephens, Sept. 28, 1862, Johnson Papers, Duke University. At the moment, the disparity in size between the two armies, while great, was not overwhelming. Livermore in *Numbers and Losses,* 92, 93, concludes that at Antietam, Lee had 51,844 men engaged, and McClellan 75,316 effectives.

18 The N. Y. *Tribune* of Sept. 20 has a graphic description sent from Sharpsburg.

19 Cf. Henderson, II, 226.

20 O. R., I, xix, pt. 2, pp. 294, 295. Some Union services were poorly organized, as usual. Lossing writes, II, 476: "There was found to be a lack of ammunition and rations, and these had to be supplied from tardily approaching supply trains."

centrate behind Antietam Creek. Instead, orders to move were inexcusably
delayed. Some units, like the Ninth Corps under Cox, did not receive them
until late afternoon. A correspondent posted near the Confederate lines wrote
the evening of the 15th that Union troops had been slowly coming up all day:

> Sumner arrived about three o'clock and took command, but his troops were
> mostly far back on the road. Very little artillery came, and altogether the
> whole movement was unaccountably slow. The road was good, and the ground
> on both sides favorable for parallel columns, but yet no considerable force
> arrived until nearly dark. Burnside emerged from the lower gap about five
> o'clock, but Hooker's own troops were not within a mile of the front at
> seven o'clock. . . .[21]

The Union army might, as many officers expected, have attacked on the
16th. McClellan, however, spent most of the day reconnoitering Lee's lines, and
fixing an exact position for not only every corps, but every division and
brigade. This annoyed subordinates. His battle plan, as he explained it, was
simple. His right wing under Hooker and Sumner, already partly across the
Antietam, would swing around to force the Confederate left back on the
center, while cutting off the roads to Hagerstown and Williamsport. His left
under Burnside would meanwhile force the Antietam at a stone bridge a mile
below the central turnpike, and crumple the Confederate right into Sharpsburg. This would pinch Lee in a vise, and bar his retreat towards the fords of
the Potomac. For any emergency, Fitz-John Porter's force at the center would
act as a reserve.[22]

At daybreak on the 17th desultory infantry firing began. As the sun rose
the musketry deepened to a roar, and before the mists lifted from wood and
field Hooker was hotly engaged with the veterans of Stonewall Jackson and
Hood. On the Confederate side the story was one of stubborn resistance, varied
by one magnificent charge—that of A. P. Hill's division, which, ordered up
from Harpers Ferry at dawn, after marching seventeen miles without rest, fell
with tigerish ferocity on the Union left. These roadworn troops flung an
advancing corps in confusion back down the ridge toward the Antietam. On
the Union side equal leadership was displayed by one corps commander,
Hooker, whose impetuous vigor fairly earned him his sobriquet of "Fighting
Joe"; but two others, Sumner and Burnside, failed to seize opportunities that
might have led to complete victory. Here McClellan's overall strategy was
chiefly at fault, for he had ordered piecemeal attacks instead of simultaneous
assaults along the whole front.[23]

21 N. Y. *Tribune,* Sept. 19, 1862; W. C. Cochran, "Political Experiences of Jacob D. Cox,"
MS, Western Reserve Hist. Soc., I, 669–671.
22 "Personal Recs. of the War," by a Virginian, *Harper's Magazine,* XXXVI (February,
1868), 281.
23 Ropes believes that if Burnside had attacked early and furiously, he might have gained
the victory before A. P. Hill's troops came up; Kenneth P. Williams indicts McClellan's

At Antietam the sun looked down on some of the bloodiest close-order fighting of the war. Where Hooker's men fought with Jackson's in a corn-field smitten by artillery on both sides, the losses were murderous. Thirty acres of grain, reported Hooker, were cut as close as by a scythe, and on the stubble Northern and Southern dead lay in heaps. Later, when two Union brigades struck Hood's Texan command, the blue and gray seemed like duelists who had lashed themselves together. They stood loading, firing, and reloading at fifty to eighty paces, determined to kill before being killed. In another area the slain lay in rows precisely as they had stood in their ranks a few moments before. Francis M. Palfrey commanded the Twentieth Massachusetts when Sumner marched a division into an ambush where ten Confederate brigades took three Union brigades in front, flank, and rear. "Change of front was impossible," wrote Palfrey later.[24] "In less time than it takes to tell it, the ground was strewn with the bodies of the dead and wounded. . . . Nearly two thousand were disabled in a moment."

The day closed on an undecided field. The Confederates had been forced back on their left by more than a mile, and on their right by half that distance. However, they still held a strong continuous line passing through Sharpsburg, and affording about as many natural advantages as that first chosen. On the field lay a multitude of dead and dying, for of the 130,000 men in the two armies, at least 21,000 or 16 per cent had been slain or wounded. "Who can tell, who can even imagine," wrote the colonel of the Twentieth Massachusetts long after, "the horrors of such a night, while the unconscious stars shone down, and the unconscious river went rippling by?" McClellan stated—or more probably understated—the Union loss as 2,010 killed, 9,416 wounded, and 1,043 missing. The Confederate casualties were fully as great; McClellan reported that, after the rebels themselves had buried many, 2,700 were counted and buried by the Northern forces.[25]

Lee and Jackson knew that although the army had fought magnificently, their gamble had failed. Nevertheless, Lee was unwilling to acknowledge defeat. Early that night the Confederate generals rode up, one by one, to report. They found Lee seated on his horse beside the highway. He asked each commander in turn, "What of your part of the line?" Each reported heavy losses, deadly

---

whole management of Burnside and others. Ropes, *Civil War*, II, 373–375; Williams, II, 450–458. A. D. Richardson wrote his managing editor Sept. 27: "The feeling with some of Burnside's staff officers (and I infer, with him also) is very bitter. They swear that Mc-Clellan tried to ruin him in the battle, by putting him where, with the force he had, he was sure to fail. They attribute it to jealousy of Burnside's reputation; Burnside *is* a great favorite with the troops." McClellan knew that Burnside earlier had been offered the command in his place, but we can agree with Richardson that he was above such an act. Gay Papers.
24 Palfrey, *Antietam and Fredericksburg*, 86, 87.
25 See map of the field, *American Conflict*, II, 205; Henderson, II, 261; Palfrey, *op. cit.*

fatigue, and a dismaying Federal superiority in numbers; the consensus favored retreat across the Potomac before daybreak. Even Jackson betrayed discouragement. He had never before met such odds, he said, and many of his best officers were dead. Hood was still more dejected, declaring that he had no men left. "Great God!" exclaimed Lee, "Where is the splendid division you had this morning?" "They are lying on the field where you sent them," responded Hood. "Few have straggled. My division has been almost wiped out."

Lee remained undaunted. He did not say, as a subsequent fable stated, that he was ready to give battle again in the morning; but he was confident that if McClellan delivered an attack, the Confederate lines would bloodily repulse it. At his back he had only one good ford over the Potomac, and in front a much stronger army, much of which McClellan had never used, for he had deliberately declined to throw in his reserves. No matter; with serene determination Lee posted artillery, distributed rations, and sent out guards to collect stragglers. He was ready for any eventuality except immediate retreat.[26]

Why did not McClellan hold a council of *his* lieutenants? Late in the afternoon he had met one of his division commanders, an old and trusted friend, who reported that his troops had done well but were somewhat scattered. "Collect them at once," said McClellan. "Fifteen thousand fresh troops have come up; more will arrive during the night. Tell your men that! We must fight tonight and tomorrow. If we cannot whip the enemy now, we may as well die upon the field. If we succeed we end the war." But he did not stick to this resolution.[27]

Lee counted on the cautious Union commander to lie still next morning— as he did. The long lines of troops faced each other, as the sun rose, with rifles and muskets loaded; the batteries stood unlimbered for instant action; pickets fingered their triggers nervously. While hour after hour ticked by, McClellan made no use of his overwhelming superiority in men and materials. Lee was encouraged by this quiescence to think of delivering an attack, but a brief inquiry showed it out of the question. He reluctantly admitted that it would be folly to attempt, as he momentarily thought of doing, to break the Northern right wing under Hooker. This was the unanimous judgment of his officers. When Jackson bade an able chief of artillery, Colonel Stephen D. Lee, to inspect the Union lines and ascertain positively whether with fifty guns and the available men he could smash the Union position, the report was unequivocal:

26 Henderson, II, 262, 263, Freeman, *Lee*, II, 403, 404. Longstreet wrote General E. A. Carman, Feb. 11, 1897, that the assemblage was not a council of war, but "the usual meeting of leading officers at night after battle to make their reports"; extra-illustrated *Battles and Leaders*, HL.

27 So reports A. D. Richardson, N. Y. *Tribune*, Sept. 29. McClellan also received large supplies of ammunition from Baltimore, while thousands of Pennsylvania militia had reached the Maryland boundary.

"General, it cannot be done." With evident dejection, Robert E. Lee accepted the verdict.[28]

All day September 18 the Confederate army waited in battle array. But its position grew more untenable every hour, for large national reinforcements were coming up. Late in the afternoon Lee decided upon retreat, and that night the Southern units, one by one, moved down to Boteler's Ford, two miles from Sharpsburg, and recrossed the Potomac. McClellan made no effort to molest them. Indeed, not until dawn of September 19 did reconnoitering Union detachments discover that Sharpsburg had been deserted, and by eight that morning the last Confederates were crossing the river.

[IV]

Of all McClellan's errors this failure to pursue was one of the most inexcusable. Had he pushed the national forces forward in a night attack, he might have thrown Lee's army into confusion. Rain fell throughout the night, roads and fields turned into pasty mire, and the single lane which led from the Shepherdstown highway to the ford was dangerously narrow. An enterprising commander would have inflicted heavy losses. As it was, the Union forces took not a single gun or wagon. "We were the conquerors," wrote one Northern reporter, "and yet our property—small arms and accoutrements by the hundred —was the only property thrown away to waste upon the field." [29] When McClellan on the 20th tardily ordered Fitz-John Porter to exploit the enemy retreat, he still had an opportunity to achieve a striking success. Union troops had now taken the ford, so that Porter easily crossed to the south bank:

The Confederates [writes Henderson] were in no condition to resist an attack in force. The army was not concentrated. The cavalry was absent. No reconnaissances had been made either of lines of march or of positions. The roads were still blocked by the trains. The men were exhausted by their late exertions, and depressed by their retreat, and the straggling was terrible. The only chance of safety lay in driving back the enemy's advanced-guard across the river before it could be reinforced; and the chance was seized without an instant's hesitation.[30]

So before Porter's force, inadequately sustained, could move a mile and a half beyond the Potomac, Jackson struck him and drove him back with a loss of 340 men. McClellan was so easily discouraged that he made no further effort to follow Lee, though he had received the quite fresh divisions of Humphrey

28 Henderson, II, 264–267, based on a letter by Gen. Stephen D. Lee; Freeman, *Lee*, II, 405.
29 N. Y. *Tribune*, Sept. 23, 1862.
30 Henderson, II, 269.

and Couch, and Washington made it plain that it expected pursuit and battle. Once more the Union intelligence service proved wretched. When a great cloud of dust had been espied in Virginia on September 18, one Union general demonstrated that it was Confederate reinforcements coming up. The morrow showed that the dust had been stirred by retreating rebel trains. It is very strange, commented one correspondent, that our generals, with their elaborate and expensive detective work, get such poor information. "The enemy outwit us under our very noses." [31] Lee's army, physically exhausted, disorganized by losses, and bereft of some of its ablest officers, was in sad estate. He informed President Davis that his force was too far diminished in numbers, and worse still, too much shaken in fighting spirit, to permit of a renewal of the offensive: "the hazard would be great and a reverse disastrous." [32] It was highly vulnerable to attack, but no attack came.

While Lincoln, Stanton, and the whole North waited for news of rapid movement and repeated blows, McClellan was writing Halleck: "This army is not now in condition to undertake another campaign nor to bring on another battle, unless great advantages are offered by some mistake of the enemy or pressing military exigencies render it necessary." He actually feared "a renewal of the attempt in Maryland"; he demanded every possible reinforcement.[33] The fact was that McClellan, as his letters to his wife show, had no thought of *destroying* Lee, for to check him seemed enough. "I feel some little pride," he wrote, "in having, with a beaten and demoralized army, defeated Lee so utterly and saved the North so completely." And again: "I feel that I have done all that can be asked in twice saving the country." [34] Not to conquer the South, but save the North—this was the object!

Lee's failure in his throw for high stakes was complete. The handful of recruits gained in Maryland did not equal his desertions; the captures of shoes, clothing, and other stores did not offset the loss of material by wear and tear; the gaps torn in Confederate ranks could never be repaired, for the men slain, disabled, and captured were among the best veterans of the army. But at any rate he had exerted himself to the utmost.

No such claim could be made for McClellan. Given a rare opportunity of overwhelming victory by his discovery, from the lost Confederate order, that Lee had divided his army, he had moved his troops at least twelve hours too late. Had he thrown the heavy bulk of his army through Crampton's Gap in South Mountain, he would probably have saved Harpers Ferry and would almost certainly have severed Jackson from Lee. Thereafter he moved so slowly

31 N. P. in N. Y. *Tribune*, Sept. 23, 1862.
32 O. R., I, xix, pt. 2, p. 627; Sept. 25, 1862.
33 *Ibid.*, pt. 1, pp. 70, 71.
34 *Own Story*, 613, 614.

that at Antietam, too, he fought his battle at least a day late—perhaps, says his subordinate Francis W. Palfrey, two days late.[35] Not only that, but his movements the evening before the battle advertised to the enemy his intention of using Hooker's right wing in the initial attack. His subsequent orders were of mediocre quality. He made practically no use at all of two corps, the Fifth and Sixth; permitted Burnside to delay his movement until six or seven hours after he had been ordered to seize a vital bridge and move forward; and failed properly to coordinate the action of the first, ninth, and twelfth corps, which should have moved forward in unison.

Lee, falling back to the area of Winchester and Bunker Hill, where the Shenandoah Valley afforded ample supplies, indulged his troops in much-needed rest while he made every effort to refill his ranks. The Richmond authorities so effectively assisted him that by October he had almost 68,000 officers and men. Though shoes and weapons were at first much needed, the government gradually supplied them. McClellan reoccupied Harpers Ferry as a safe bridgehead on the south side of the Potomac, placing Sumner with two corps in possession of it and the fortified heights. While he had just boasted that "our victory was complete," he was still not quite certain as to Sumner's safety, writing: "I think he will be able to hold his position until reinforcements arrive." His own strength was fully half again as large as Lee's. But believing that the Confederate army still outnumbered his own, he did not think it "safe" to go beyond Harpers Ferry, for it would not do to provoke this overwhelming Confederate host. Not until October 26th did the main national army, 110,665 strong (not counting the corps which was kept at Harpers Ferry under Henry W. Slocum and 4,500 troops guarding the upper Potomac) begin crossing the river.[36]

In the aftermath of the battle a telling illustration of the reliance Americans still placed upon improvisation was furnished by Oliver Wendell Holmes in his long-famous "hunt after the captain"—the captain being the future Justice Holmes. The night after Antietam the Autocrat of the Breakfast Table received from some unknown source a curt telegram: "Capt. Holmes wounded through the neck thought not mortal at Keedysville." He at once set off southward. After two days of travel he reached Frederick, where he heard a rumor that his boy was killed. Hiring a wagon, he began ransacking hospitals in all the towns about Sharpsburg—in Middletown, Boonsborough, Keedysville. It

35 Palfrey, who fought on the field, is explicit also in censuring McClellan for not doing more to inspire the troops by his active presence on the field once the battle was joined: "He passed the whole day, till toward the middle of the afternoon, when all the fighting was over, on the high ground near Fry's house, where he had some glasses strapped to a fence. . . ." *Antietam and Fredericksburg,* 119.
36 O. R., I, xix, pt. 1, p. 70; Ropes, *Civil War,* II, 440, 441.

would seem that colonels should have been able to report their dead and wounded; that hospitals could have made up central lists in each town; that nurses could have kept records to show when and where the wounded were forwarded to new destinations. But Holmes groped in the dark for his son. Finally he heard that the captain had set off north, not badly hurt, in a milk cart. Hotly pursuing this scent, at Harrisburg he learned that his son had taken the train to Philadelphia; but then came word that he had not appeared at the house of some Philadelphia friends whom he would naturally seek. Another frantic search of Harrisburg hospitals still disclosed no son. Finally, almost by accident, he lighted on the wounded captain in a train.

How many thousands of parents thus searched for their sons? How many wives waited weeks in anguish for news of a husband's fate? With no proper record of casualties by officers, no proper hospital lists, no burial records or graves registration, a darkness settled down on every great battlefield.

The dreary story of McClellan's complaints, delays, and excuses, which had so long irritated Lincoln and enraged the radicals who insisted on a vigorous war effort, was being resumed. Disappointment in the army itself over McClellan's failure to follow up Antietam was intense. Some soldiers read his excuse of "fatigue and exhaustion" with incredulity. "To us of the Thirteenth [Massachusetts]," wrote one "it seemed just possible that the enemy might be equally tired and a good deal more discomfited. . . . When men are stimulated by success in battle they forget everything but pushing their good fortune to a complete triumph." Many intelligent volunteers agreed with A. D. Richardson: "If McClellan had only attacked again early Thursday morning, we could have driven them into the river or captured them. . . . It was one of the supreme moments when by daring something, the destiny of the nation might have been changed." [37]

The anger of even moderate men in Washington when they saw that no effort was being made to press Lee's forces was emphatic. T. J. Barnett of the Interior Department talked at length on September 23 with both Lincoln and Caleb Smith. "I am convinced," he wrote S. L. M. Barlow, "that the government, if they dared, would supersede Mac." Why did they not dare? Because of apprehension that much of the army would be resentful, fear of a violent reaction in the North, and inability to find anyone to put in his place. But, records Barnett, Lincoln's praise for the victor of Antietam was very chilly: he felt "great confidence" in McClellan, he thought the general "well educated but very cautious," and altogether damned him with faint praise. In high circles, since Lee's escape, Barnett found men again whispering that McClellan was of a

37 C. E. Davis, Jr., *The Thirteenth Mass. Volunteers*, 142, 143; Richardson to S. H. Gay, Sharpsburg, Sept. 19, 1862, Gay Papers.

school and party which wished to exhaust the two sections, with a view to reconstructing the Union along conservative lines. This story had many variations and many believers.[38]

But if Northern discouragement after Antietam was keen, that of many Southern leaders was greater. The defeatism of Herschel V. Johnson and Alexander H. Stephens deepened. Jefferson Davis, subject to alternate waves of optimism and depression, was so hard hit that he again talked of resigning. "Our maximum strength has been mobilized," he told the Secretary of War, "while the enemy is just beginning to put forth his might." [39]

[V]

If McClellan could not use victory to convert the defensive into an offensive, Lincoln could. He had to deal with moral and political forces as powerful for harm as Lee's army, with Democrats hoping to use victory in the fall elections to save the South from utter revolution, selfish moneyed men whining about bankruptcy, and foreign haters of the United States who, encouraged by Confederate agents, hoped to use intervention to cripple the republic. But he knew how to strike promptly and effectively. As he said later, he did not wait for crushing victory; he waited only until Lee was driven from Maryland. That gave him sufficient vantage ground for the offensive he intended to launch.

Lincoln saw it was important, while waiting, to prepare the public mind for his decision to use emancipation as a war measure. Horace Greeley fortunately offered an opportunity. When readers opened the *Tribune* of August 20, 1862, they found the editorial page blazing with an open letter by Greeley headed "The Prayer of Twenty Millions," addressed to Lincoln. The editor

38 Barnett to Barlow, Sept. 23, 1862, Barlow Papers. Judge Thomas M. Key of Cincinnati, an Ohio legislative leader who became aide and acting judge-advocate on McClellan's staff, gave Nathaniel Paige, a well-known Washington lawyer serving as war correspondent of the N. Y. *Tribune*, just three days before Antietam, a remarkable story. "He told me," later stated Paige, "that a plan to countermarch to Washington and intimidate the President had been seriously discussed the night before by the members of McClellan's staff, and his opposition to it [that is, Key's opposition] had, he thought, caused its abandonment." McClellan himself did not know about it. These staff officers wished to make Lincoln abandon his interferences with slavery, in the hope that thus the war could be stopped. Eighteen years later a writer for the Washington *Capitol*, who had known Paige, gave some corroboration. He declared that these staff officers used to call Lincoln, Halleck, and Stanton "the old women at Washington"; that they regarded Lincoln with contempt and Stanton with hatred; that it was their fixed belief that the war was folly, and bound to end in failure; and that they were really fighting for a boundary line, and not for the Union. Paige's statement, clipped from the *Tribune* without date, is in Hay Papers, Ill. State Hist. Library; Washington *Capitol*, March 21, 1880.

39 Edward Younger, *Inside the Confederate Govt.*, 28, 86; Strode, *Davis*, 307 ff.

stated at length what the twenty millions complained of, what they had a right to expect, and what they required.

They demanded, he wrote, that Lincoln execute the laws, and especially the provisions of the new Confiscation Act liberating the slaves of rebels. They insisted that he cease giving undue weight to the counsels of fossil politicians in the Border States, and recognize that whatever fortified slavery in this area also fortified treason. They wished the government to show more energy, opposing force to force in an undaunted spirit. They asked that he give up his mistaken deference to slavery in the South, and called on him to rebuke the army officers, including prominent generals, who showed greater regard for slavery than freedom. Finally, they demanded that he turn to the Negroes for aid. "We cannot conquer Ten Millions of People united in a solid phalanx against us, powerfully aided by Northern sympathizers and European allies. We must have scouts, guides, spies, cooks, teamsters, diggers and choppers. . . ."

This letter, with what Lincoln called its erroneous statements, false inferences, and impatient dictatorial tone, had to be answered. It gave him so perfect an opportunity for an explanation paving the way to his proclamation that Greeley three years later expressed the belief that the President had his statement ready written, and seized the occasion to promulgate it.[40] Lincoln saw that he must make his position entirely clear without prematurely betraying his decision on emancipation, and Greeley gave him a sounding board. He was President of the whole nation, Democrats and Republicans, conservatives, radicals, and moderates; he was not the tool of border reactionaries as Greeley intimated, or of Senate abolitionists as some Democrats said, but his own master, prosecuting the war with a single eye to maintenance of the Union. He sat down to produce one of his most memorable state papers—a paper that, published everywhere within the week, was worth a battle gained:

I would save the Union. I would save it the shortest way under the Constitution. The sooner the national authority can be restored, the nearer the Union will be to "the Union as it was." If there be those who would not save the Union, unless they could at the same time *save* slavery, I do not agree with them. If there be those who would not save the Union unless they could at the same time *destroy* slavery, I do not agree with them. My paramount object in this struggle *is* to save the Union, and is not either to save or to destroy slavery. If I could save the Union without freeing *any* slave I would do it, and if I could save the Union by freeing some and leaving others alone I would also do that. What I do about slavery, and the colored race, I do because I believe it helps to save the Union; and what I forbear, I forbear because I do *not* believe it would help to save the Union. I shall do *less* whenever I shall believe what I am doing hurts the cause, and I shall do *more* whenever I shall believe that doing more

40 Greeley's MS lecture on Lincoln, HL, published in *Century Magazine*, XX (July, 1891), 371 ff.; he was mistaken.

will help the cause. I shall try to correct errors when shown to be errors; and I shall adopt new views so soon as they shall appear to be true views.[41]

The applause given Lincoln's reply in moderate circles far outweighed the dissent from extremists on both sides. Greeley attempted a rebuttal; but Raymond's *Times*, the Douglasite *Morning Post* in Chicago, the Springfield *Republican*, the Cincinnati *Commercial*, and the influential Presbyterian *Observer* agreed on the President's cool sagacity. News was spreading around Washington (for the Cabinet had leaked it) that he had an emancipation proclamation ready, but that Seward and Blair wished it withheld.[42] Reports also spread of a colloquy between Lincoln and a Western delegation, including a couple of Senators, who had called to offer two Negro regiments—which under the new confiscation law he was empowered to accept. The President told them that he was ready to employ Negro teamsters, cooks, pioneers, and the like, but not soldiers. A warm discussion followed, which Lincoln was said to have closed with the words: "Gentlemen, you have my decision. It embodies my best judgment, and if the people are dissatisfied, I will resign and let Mr. Hamlin try it." Such heat had been generated that one caller exclaimed: "I hope, in God's name, Mr. President, you will!" [43]

Lee's retreat across the Potomac brought Lincoln the opening for which he had waited. At noon on Monday, September 21, occurred the famous Cabinet meeting at which he announced his final action. The members, summoned by messenger, were portentously solemn; and Lincoln, who did not like portentous solemnity, broke the spell by taking up a newly received copy of Artemus Ward's latest book, and reading aloud with happy enjoyment the chapter "Hihanded Outrage at Utica." Everybody except Stanton shared his laugh. Then the President also became solemn, and recalled their previous consultation on emancipation. Chase reports his speech:

"I think the time has come now. I wish it were a better time. I wish that we were in a better condition. The action of the army against the rebels has not been quite what I should have best liked. But they have been driven out of

41 Dated Aug. 22 and published in the *Tribune* Aug. 25, 1862; *Works*, V, 388, 389.
42 A few days before Greeley published "The Prayer of Twenty Millions," his reporter Adam S. Hill had written S. H. Gay, the managing editor, that Summer and Gurowski both possessed inside knowledge of the emancipation proclamation, and the fact that it had been temporarily suspended at the suggestion of Seward, Blair, and Thurlow Weed. Hill also wrote Gay that Senator S. C. Pomeroy gave him to understand that Lincoln would issue the proclamation as soon as he had assurance that his colonization project would succeed; Pomeroy being much interested in the Chiriqui plan. Greeley must therefore have known that the proclamation was impending when he brought out his letter of minatory tone. Perhaps he hoped to end all hesitations. See Hill's letters, Aug. 21, 25, 1862, Gay Papers.
43 The Chicago *Morning Post* and Chicago *Tribune*, Aug. 6, 1862, both carry accounts of this scene from their Washington correspondents.

Maryland, and Pennsylvania is no longer in danger of invasion." When they were at Frederick, he said, he had promised himself and God that he would issue his proclamation as soon as they were driven out. "I am going to fulfill that promise. I have got you together to hear what I have written down. I do not wish your advice about the main matter—for that I have determined for myself." But he would be glad to accept suggestions about phraseology or other minor points.

Lincoln added that he knew that various men in this and other transactions would do better than he, and if satisfied that another leader had a fuller measure of public confidence, he would—were it constitutionally possible—yield to him. "But though I believe that I have not so much of the confidence of the people as I had some time since, I do not know that, all things considered, any other person has more. . . . I must do the best I can, and bear the responsibility. . . ."[44]

All the Cabinet members acquiesced. Chase said he would have taken a somewhat different course, Blair reiterated his old fears as to the effect of the proclamation on the border and the army, and Seward suggested some verbal changes, but they were obviously pleased. Executed that day, the proclamation appeared in the morning newspapers September 23. Its essence lay in the third paragraph:

That on the first day of January in the year of our Lord, one thousand eight hundred and sixty-three, all persons held as slaves within any State, or designated part of a State, the people whereof shall then be in rebellion against the United States, shall be then, thenceforward, and forever free; and the executive government of the United States, including the military and naval authority thereof, will recognize and maintain the freedom of such persons, and will do no act or acts to repress such persons, or any of them, in any efforts they may make for their actual freedom.

Lincoln's sagacity did not fail him in the form of the document. It was an exercise of war powers; its main intent was not the liberation of a race (though he was fully conscious of this aspect) but the furtherance of the war effort and the preservation of the Union; and he did well to couch it in cold legal phraseology, direct and deadly as a bullet. Sumner and Greeley regretted the absence of rhetorical flourishes; "a poor document, but a mighty act," was John A. Andrew's verdict. But its moral import spoke for itself, and Lincoln, as Lowell remarked in the *Atlantic*, would have weakened it by an attempt at misplaced eloquence.[45]

44 Donald, ed., *Inside Lincoln's Cabinet*, 149, 150.
45 The proclamation did not embrace Tennessee, but in all of eight other States, and in the greater parts of Virginia and Louisiana, it did proclaim freedom. "We shall drive the conservatives of proslavery hunkerism into the very caves and holes of the earth," wrote Governor Andrew to Col. A. G. Brown, Sept. 23, 1862; Carnegie Bookshop Catalogue, N. Y.

That the proclamation was indeed "a mighty act" nobody could deny; but what were its precise results? To answer this question we must examine two entirely different subjects: first, its direct pragmatic effects in turning slaves into freedmen, and second, its impact upon public sentiment—the sentiment of the North, of the army, of the South, and by no means least, of Britain and the overseas world.

It is quite true that the popular picture of Lincoln using a stroke of the pen to lift the shackles from the limbs of four million slaves is ludicrously false. Since the proclamation was an exercise of the war powers, what its legal effect would be after the war ceased was uncertain. As the President could issue a proclamation, so he, or a successor, could revoke it. It did not apply to those districts which the Union armies held on the date Lincoln designated, January 1, 1863; could not be enforced in those districts which they did not hold; and had no application whatever to the four border slave States. To this extent it is a fact that, as Seward said, the proclamation emancipated slaves where it could not reach them, and left them in bondage where it could have set them free.[46] Lincoln himself continued to believe gradual emancipation better than summary liberation, and to cherish his plan for thus freeing the Negro in loyal areas. His friend David Davis, visiting him two months after the proclamation, found his ideas unchanged. Wrote Davis: "Mr. Lincoln's whole soul is absorbed in his plan of remunerative emancipation and he thinks if Congress don't fail him, that the problem is solved. He believes that if Congress will pass a law authorizing the issuance of bonds for the payment of emancipated negroes in the border States that Delaware, Maryland, Kentucky and Mo. will accept the terms. He takes great encouragement from the vote in Mo." [47]

But the proclamation had three immediate, positive, and visible effects. First, every forward step the Union armies took after January 1, 1863, now became a liberating step. Every county in Mississippi, Alabama, Virginia, and the Carolinas that passed under military control was thenceforth legally a free-soil county, the army bound to "recognize and maintain" emancipation.

In the second place, the percolating news of the proclamation encouraged slaves to escape, bringing them first in trickles and then rivulets within army

46 Greeley fiercely attacked Lincoln for not at once decreeing the liberation of all slaves in Louisiana and Tennessee; two States, he wrote, which "have more than One Hundred Thousand of their citizens in arms to destroy the Union." N. Y. *Tribune*, Jan. 3, 1863.

47 Davis found Lincoln weary, careworn, and heavily burdened with preparations for the imminent Congressional session. "It is a good thing he is fond of anecdotes and telling them," commented Davis, "for it relieves his spirits very much." To Leonard Swett, Nov. 26, 1862; David Davis Papers, Ill. State Hist. Lib. Missouri sentiment on slavery was changing fast, largely because of Lincoln's offer of reimbursement. Two months after Davis' letter the legislature was to pass a resolution declaring that $25,000,000 would be needed to carry out emancipation in the State, and asking Congress for that amount. H. A. Trexler, *Slavery in Missouri, 1804–1865*, p. 233 ff.

lines. How did it percolate? By grapevine telegraph, by the overheard discussions of masters, by glimpses of newspapers, by a new tension in the air. The idea that nearly all slaves wished to cling to their masters, a staple of Southern white folklore, did not fit the facts, for whenever escape became feasible, most of them were ready to embrace the opportunity. Edmund Ruffin, prominent among those who defended slavery as a positive good, must have been shocked when after McClellan's invasion nearly the whole work force decamped from his "Marlbourne" plantation in Princess Anne County. A few days later he wrote in his diary: "The fleeing of slaves from this neighborhood, which seemed to have ceased, has begun again. Mr. J. B. Bland lost 17 more a few nights ago, making his whole loss 27—though 5 were recaptured." [48]

The eminent cleric James Freeman Clarke, visiting a contraband camp in Washington early in 1863, asked one Negro just from Virginia whether the slaves down there had heard of the proclamation. "Oh yes, massa! We-all knows about it; only we darsen't let on. We pretends not to know. I said to my ole massa, 'What's this Marse Lincoln is going to do to the poor nigger? I hear he is going to cut 'em up awful bad. How is it, massa?' I just pretended foolish, sort of." [49] In the West the story was the same. The Cairo levees were black with fleeing slaves; Sherman wrote from Memphis that he had a thousand at work on the Memphis fortifications, and could send any number to St. Louis. Peter Cooper reported:

I learn direct from Mr. Dean, the provost-marshal of St. Louis, that the Proclamation of Freedom has done more to weaken the rebellion . . . than any other measure that could have been adopted. On his late visit to my house he informed me that he had brought on a large number of rebel officers and men to be exchanged at Fortress Monroe. During their passage he took the opportunity to ask the officers in a body what effect the President's Proclamation of Freedom had produced in the South. They reply was . . . that "it had played hell with them." Mr. Dean then asked them how that could be possible, since the negroes cannot read. To which one of them replied that one of his negroes had told him of the proclamation five days before he heard it in any other way. Others said their negroes gave them their first information of the proclamation.[50]

And in the third place, the proclamation irrevocably committed the United States, before the gaze of the whole world, to the early eradication of slavery

48 Ruffin MS Diary, July, 1862, LC.
49 *Autobiography*, 286.
50 Letter to Horatio Seymour, Sept. 28, 1863, Seymour Papers, LC. Sherman was using about 600 additional Negroes as stevedores, teamsters, cooks, and the like. More Negro men would have fled but for the fact they could not bring wives and children along. Sherman, Aug. 30, 1862, to Capt. Lewis B. Parsons, Parsons Papers. Herbert Aptheker in *Negro Slave Revolts* offers illuminating data on the readiness of slaves to escape.

from those wide regions where it was most deeply rooted; after which, all men knew, it could never survive on the borders. There could be no turning back! The government had dedicated itself to the termination of the inherited anachronism that had so long retarded the nation's progress, and crippled its pretensions to the leadership of the liberal forces of the globe. What was more, Lincoln had converted the war into a struggle for the rights of labor in the broadest sense.

[VI]

The reception given the proclamation ran the gamut from Greeley's paean of joy to Southern denunciations of it as a malignant effort to excite a servile revolt. The radical carping at Lincoln temporarily ceased. He had not merely pledged freedom to four million blacks, wrote Greeley; he was freeing twenty millions of whites from an ancient thralldom. For the moment Wade, Sumner, Chandler, Thad Stevens, Ashley, and their associates were transported. Charles Eliot Norton could scarcely see to pen a letter for his tears. "The President may be a fool," wrote George William Curtis to Frederick Law Olmsted, a stubborn critic. "But see what he has done. He may have no policy. But he has given us one." Among temperate free-soilers a great body undoubtedly took the view indicated by David Davis. "The people," he wrote an Illinois friend, "are fast getting into the belief that as quiet and moderate war measures have accomplished no good, severe measures are now necessary, and if the rebels will not lay down their arms, that is the duty of the Govt. to smite them hip and thigh." [51]

The highest note was struck by those who viewed the proclamation in the light of its liberating power: Whittier, Bryant, Lowell, all using pens tipped with flame. Most eloquently of all rose the voice of Emerson, declaring in the *Atlantic* that the force of the act was its commitment of the republic to justice. Doing this, it proved that the Northern soldiers had not died in vain; it made a victory of the sad defeats; it repaired the health of the nation. It was by no means necessary, he went on, that it should produce any sudden or signal results in the ranks of either the slaves or the slavemasters; indeed, the final redemption of the black race must lie with the blacks. Still, this ill-fated, much injured people would benefit at once. They will "lose somewhat of the dejection sculptured for ages in their bronzed countenances, and uttered in the wailing of their plaintive music"—a race naturally benevolent, joyous, and in-

51 Greeley in N. Y. *Tribune*, Sept. 23, 24, 1862; Curtis, Sept. 29, 1862, Olmsted Papers; Davis, Nov. 26, 1862, David Davis Papers.

dustrious, whose very miseries sprang from their talent for usefulness, "which in a more moral age, will not only defend their independence, but will give them a rank among nations." [52]

The jeers of the South were echoed by hisses and groans from the copperhead press of the North. The New York *Express* declared that this foolscap thunder would add 300,000 men to the rebel armies, and bring 30,000 Kentuckians to the side of Bragg. It was grand-scale bunkum, swaggering bravado, which, alas! converted a war for the Constitution into a war against Southern rights and liberties.[53] The Chicago *Times* took the same position. Two chords on which Northern objectors harped were that the proclamation altered the objects of the war, and that its direct result would be a heavy influx of Negroes into the free States. Indiana and Illinois already barred Negro immigrants. S. S. Cox of Ohio, a State which had no bar but repeatedly considered raising one, had already dwelt in his House speeches on Northern fears of a flood of freedmen. Could anyone be sure that Ohio troops would continue fighting if the fruit of their sacrifices was a northward flow of "millions of blacks?" [54] It saddened Lincoln to find his friend Orville H. Browning, his helper in revising the inaugural address, and an able exponent of his Borderland policy, taking the same Negrophobe stand.

In private utterances, few Northern critics were harsher than McClellan, who was aware that Democrats spoke of him as their next Presidential nominee. The ink was hardly dry on the newspaper headlines before he was sounding out the merchant William H. Aspinwall; "I am very anxious to learn how you and the men like you regard the recent Proclamation of the Presdt inaugurating servile war, emancipating the slaves, and at one stroke of the pen changing our free institutions into a despotism—for such I regard as the natural effect of the last Proclamation suspending the habeas corpus throughout the land." [55] His ideas were shared by Fitz-John Porter, who maliciously reported to Manton Marble of the *World:* "The Proclamation was ridiculed in the army—causing disgust, discontent, and expressions of disloyalty to the views of the administration, amounting I have heard, to insubordination, and for this reason—All such bulletins tend only to prolong the war by rousing the bitter feelings of the South—and causing unity of action among them—while the reverse with us. Those who fight the battles of the country are tired of the war and wish to see

52 *Atlantic Monthly,* X (Nov., 1862), 638–642; a forecast of free Ethiopia, Ghana, Liberia, Nigeria, and all the rest. Whittier's "Laus Deo" and Bryant's "The Death of Slavery" in due course fittingly commemorated the great step. "Great is the virtue of the Proclamation," wrote Emerson in his journals. "It works when men are sleeping, when the army goes into winter quarters, when generals are treacherous or imbecile."
53 Oct. 20, 22, 1862.
54 *Cong. Globe,* 37th Cong., 2d Sess., 2501–2503, June 3, 1862.
55 Sept. 26, 1862, extra-illustrated *Battles and Leaders,* HL.

it ended soon and honorably—by a restoration of the union—not merely a suppression of the rebellion." [56]

The question of the real attitude of the troops toward the document is too complex, and the evidence too conflicting, for easy summarization. The army was a reflection of the nation, possessing its radical and conservative wings. But certainly Fitz-John Porter misstated the attitude. The safest generalization is this: that most Northern soldiers approved of the proclamation, but did so not so much from humanitarian motives as because their blood was now up, they wanted to win a decisive victory, and Lincoln's edict seemed to herald a relentless prosecution of the war. The army, Colonel W. H. Blake of the Ninth Indiana wrote Schuyler Colfax, has one central idea, to whip the rebels and dictate peace. It contained little abolitionist sentiment; but "there is a desire to destroy everything that in *aught* gives the rebels strength," "there is a universal desire among the soldiery to take the negro from the secesh master," and so "this army will sustain the emancipation proclamation and enforce it with the bayonet." [57]

But though the plain soldier, like Lincoln, thought of emancipation primarily as a war measure, in countless instances he also rejoiced in its enlargement of human freedom. As the Union troops in marching South studied the worst aspects of slavery, they quickly learned to hate it. When they saw the auction block, the whipping post, the iron gyve, when they glimpsed the field hand cringing under his master's gaze, when the fleeing slave bared his scarred back, or told a tale of young children wrenched from the mother's arms, they resolved that slavery must die.[58]

One result of the proclamation was to turn a potentially harmful convention of Northern governors at Altoona, Pennsylvania, into an innocuous farce. Its prime mover was Andrew G. Curtin of Pennsylvania, who early in September had written Andrew of Massachusetts that the time was ripe to give the war a definite aim, and that the loyal executives should take prompt, united, decisive action. Correspondence among various Northern governors followed. Tod of Ohio, Blair of Michigan, Berry of New Hampshire, Pierrepont of Connecticut, and others were drawn into the movement. It inevitably aroused some pernicious newspaper speculation that it was hostile to Lincoln, that it aimed at the overthrow of McClellan, that it was a maneuver by Andrew and Curtin to get themselves re-elected, and so on. Happily, these two governors had enough sense to go to Lincoln beforehand. He told them of his impending proclamation, and with characteristic considerateness asked if they wished him to defer

56 Sept. 30, 1862, Manton Marble Papers, LC.
57 Glasgow, Ky., Nov. 7, 1862, Colfax Papers, Ind. State Lib.
58 See T. F. Dornblaser, *Sabre Strokes of the Pennsylvania Dragoons*, 120–121, for a vigorous statement.

its issuance until they had requested him to act. They replied that he should by all means bring it out first, and they would follow it with a strong address of commendation.[59] This was done; the conference met on the Allegheny crest September 24, and agreed to a paper written by Andrew. All appended their names but Bradford of Maryland, who, aware how deeply his State was torn, remarked: "Gentlemen, I am with you heart and soul, but I am a poor man, and if I sign that address I may be a ruined one." Misrepresentation of the conference nevertheless persisted, and it had better never been held.

The fact was that some of these governors had been as deeply pained as Stanton and Chase by the reassignment of McClellan to command. John A. Andrew, for one, detested the general. Like many other leaders in this terrible crisis, he became overwrought at times. Once this summer he fell on his knees in his office to pray for emancipation, and made a visitor pray with him! He had written Count Gurowski on September 6: "Besides doing my proper work, I am sadly but firmly trying to help organize some movement, if possible to save the Prest. from the infamy of ruining his country." Curtin, Yates, and Austin Blair felt much the same. But now they knew that Lincoln, after all, had not fallen into reactionary hands or taken a wrong step.

[VII]

Two facts were now abundantly clear: Lincoln was running the war, the reins of power held tightly in his muscular grip; and he was determined to run it so that the North would keep the initiative on all fronts—military, economic, and moral. If McClellan were not a useful implement in maintaining offensive operations, he would discard McClellan. But the Union would relax no pressure and neglect no effort. And no man better grasped the essence of statesmanship, which is the achievement of what is practicable within the limits of what is desirable.

That Lincoln regarded the proclamation not merely as opening a sterner war, but as announcing a revolution, is clear from the message he shortly sent Congress. It *was* revolution, though he hoped to keep it a controlled revolution. When at this very time he made his before-quoted remark to T. J. Barnett about so shaping the tragic conflict that it should always have a peace in its belly, he made it plain that if the South did not yield during the hundred days before the preliminary proclamation gave way to the final document, it must face a mighty socioeconomic upheaval. "What I write," Barnett warned S. L. M. Bar-

59 The Austin Blair and Andrew Papers have full correspondence; see also the statement Curtin gave Rufus Rockwell Wilson in 1881, *Lincoln Herald*. W. B. Hesseltine in *Lincoln and the War Governors, passim*, presents evidence that the governors were anxious to maintain State authority as against Lincoln's growing use of Federal power.

low for the benefit of New York Democrats, "was indicated plainly enough by the President—but I know more of his spirit than his publications imply. The idea is this—From the expiration of the 'days of grace' the character of the war will be changed. It will be one of subjugation and extermination if the North can be coerced and coaxed into it. The South [i.e., the old Southern system] is to be destroyed and replaced by new propositions and ideas." [60]

To those who had eyes, the lineaments of Lincoln's greatness were emerging. His great decision, premature to some, tardy to others, had been taken with his acute instinct for the ripening moment. No journal expressed this fact better than the Springfield *Republican*: "The President's action is timely—neither too soon nor too late. It is thorough—neither defeating itself by halfway measures nor by passionate excess. It is just and magnanimous—doing no wrong to any loyal man, and offering no exasperation to the disloyal. It is practical and effective—attempting neither too little nor too much. And it will be sustained by the great mass of the loyal people, North and South; and thus, by the courage and prudence of the President, the greatest social and political revolution of the age will be triumphantly carried through in the midst of a civil war." [61]

But the most remarkable aspect of Lincoln's stroke was its impact on world opinion—a subject of momentous consequence, requiring careful examination.

60 Dated "Friday" (Sept. 25, 1862), Barlow Papers.
61 Sept. 24, 1862. Congress had approved of Lincoln's general plan for colonizing freedmen on the Chiriqui coast of Panama in New Granada (Colombia), and in April and June, 1862, had appropriated $600,000 for the settlement there of Negroes liberated under the Confiscation Act and in the District of Columbia. Secretary Usher of the Interior Department was ready to push the undertaking. But Lincoln, seeing that some "political hacks"—Senator S. C. Pomeroy of Kansas was one—hoped to enrich themselves from the contemplated contract, drew back. His hesitancy was shared by Seward, who had become doubtful about the title to the Chiriqui lands and the existence of good coal there. In October, Lincoln bade Usher to tell Pomeroy that the enterprise would be abandoned indefinitely.

10

Britain, France, and the War Issues

AMERICANS hardly watched more closely than Britons the fighting at Second Manassas and Antietam, nor did New York newspapers report it with much more accurate detail than London journals. For Europe as well as the Un States the war had critical meaning. Consequences of the greatest magnitude hung upon the deepening tension of European-American and especially Anglo-American relations in the late summer of 1862. It is hardly too much to say that the future of the world as we know it was at stake.

A conflict between Great Britain and America would have crushed all hope of the mutual understanding and growing collaboration which led up to the practical alliance of 1917–18, and the outright alliance which began in 1941. It would have made vastly more difficult if not impossible the coalition which defeated the Central Powers in the First World War, struck down Nazi tyranny in the Second World War, and established the unbreakable front of Western freedom against Communism. Anglo-French intervention in the American conflict would probably have confirmed the splitting and consequent weakening of the United States; might have given French power in Mexico a long lease, with the ruin of the Monroe Doctrine; and would perhaps have led to the Northern conquest of Canada. The forces of political liberalism in the modern world would have received a disastrous setback. No battle, not Gettysburg, not the Wilderness, was more important than the contest waged in the diplomatic arena and the forum of public opinion.

The popular conception of this contest is at some points erroneous, and at a few grossly fallacious. The framework of the received story is that the British aristocracy and "upper class" were bitterly hostile to the North; that by social pressure and the thunder of the London *Times* they controlled the Ministry, itself naturally unfriendly; that Lord John Russell, the Foreign Secretary, was ready to follow the eager Napoleon III in breaking the Union blockade and recognizing the Confederacy; that the heroic Lancashire cotton workers, starving but devoted to freedom, followed their champion John Bright in resisting intervention; and that Antietam and the emancipation proclamation came in the nick of time to prevent European interference and war. Thus stated, the story has all the fascination of melodrama—a melodrama that ends with the footlights blazing up, the orchestra playing "The Star-Spangled Banner," and liberal-minded Britons applauding the name of Abraham Lincoln as they prepare to pass the second Reform Bill.

This story has elements of truth, but equal elements of fiction. In reviewing it we must remember several corrective facts. It does injustice to the great intelligent middle class in Britain; it does some injustice to Earl Russell, and still more to the Prime Minister, Palmerston; it does injustice to other Ministers; it overstates the role of the Lancashire workers, and the immediate, though not ultimate, impact of emancipation; and it omits important elements. It attributes too much of British governmental policy to Machiavellianism. Palmerston and his Ministers were in fact actuated primarily by a desire to protect British interests in common-sense ways, keeping the realm out of trouble. While pursuing this policy they were acutely aware of the danger of some sudden embroilment in Europe, of the weaknesses of their navy, and of the flimsiness of their Canadian defenses. They were conscious, too, of the importance of respecting the right of blockade, for Britain had direly needed that right in Napoleonic times, and might direly need it again.

If the diplomatic scene had any key figure, it was Palmerston, experienced, wary, and doggedly devoted to those British interests which fared best in peace. He disclosed a fundamental attitude when he wrote October 16, 1861: "The love of quarrelling and fighting is inherent in man, and to prevent its indulgence is to impose restraints on natural liberty. A state may so shackle its own subjects, but it is an infringement on national independence to restrain other nations." [1] In brief, Great Britain did not like other nations to fight, but when they did, her true policy was not intervention but neutrality.

[I]

Americans were acutely sensitive to British opinion for various reasons. Great Britain was the one country which could heavily injure the United States. Old ties of kinship, two centuries of deference to British opinion, the universal influence of British literature, the economic and financial power of Britain, all counted strongly. "Why do Americans attack us and not France?" many Englishmen asked H. W. Beecher on his visit in 1863. "Because," he replied, "we in our deepest hearts care for England, and not much for France." [2]

[1] Max Beloff, "Great Britain and the American Civil War," *History*, N. S., XXXVI (Feb., 1952), 47.
[2] Brooklyn speech, Nov. 25, 1863, N. Y. *Tribune*, Nov. 26.

At the outset, when it was supposed the conflict might be short, British sympathy was primarily with the Federal government. "The English are really on our side," wrote Henry Adams from London, July 2, 1861, and his father the Minister said the same. But after Bull Run opinion became sharply divided.

The fact that after Bull Run most Tories and most of the aristocracy sympathized with the Confederate cause was patent. The London *Morning Star*, stanchly on the Union side, gibed at "that upper circle in which an aristocracy of blood acknowledges kinship with an aristocracy of color." [3] Charles Francis Adams wrote Seward that the chief desire of the aristocracy was to see the Confederacy victorious, and John Bright agreed. But it was by no means true that this attitude represented a deliberate calculation that a weaker United States would mean a stronger Great Britain. Rather, five principal reasons, all natural enough, might be assigned for the Tory predilection for the South.

One was a simple feeling of sympathy for the underdog. The Confederacy was so heavily outmatched, and her defeat after Donelson and New Orleans seemed so imminent, that the brilliant strokes of Lee and Stonewall Jackson aroused admiration. Another source lay in the belief, fostered by Thackeray's *The Virginians*, the fiction of John Esten Cooke, and much Southern oratory, that the South represented a Cavalier element, or at any rate, that Southerners were of good English stock, whereas the North was a motley conglomerate of British, Irish, Germans, Scandinavians, and whatnot. Much British journalism emphasized this view. Even William H. Russell, while giving accurate facts upon the "mean whites" in letters from the South, discovered gentlemen more easily there. And it was easy for English conservatives, perturbed by the growth of democratic and radical sentiment, to see that the collapse of American democracy would offer a good argument to check the movement. Lord Robert Cecil, later Lord Salisbury, who presently distinguished himself as an opponent of the Reform Bill, made the most of American troubles. Lord Derby had the same outlook. [4]

Another root of Tory unfriendliness to the North was the smoldering resentment over recent Yankee bluster and truculence. During the 1850's Lewis Cass, Douglas, and Ben Wade had continuously ranted against the British Government, even the reserved Jefferson Davis and cultivated Sumner had used harsh epithets in assailing British policy, and Seward had taken an occasional twist at the lion's tail. Britons remembered the hard American bargaining over the Maine boundary, the slogan "Fifty-four forty or fight," and the filibuster activities in Cuba and Central America. While Great Britain had her own record

3 May 12, 1862.
4 Herbert Paul, *Hist. Modern England*, II, 311. But Derby and other responsible Conservatives were consistently non-interventionist; W. D. Jones, "The British Conservatives and the Amer. Civil War," *Am. Hist. Rev.*, LVIII (April, 1953), 527–543.

of bullying, to Englishmen it did not seem so bad. So warm a friend of the North as John Stuart Mill wrote that the most operative cause of English feeling against the United States "is the general belief that Americans are hostile to England, and long to insult and humble her if they had but an opportunity; and the accumulated resentment left by a number of small diplomatic collisions, in which . . . through the reluctance of England to push matters to extremities, which do not vitally concern the national honor, bullying and blustering have been allowed to prevail." [5] Charles Francis Adams avowed to a close friend in 1861: "My feelings, as you know, have never been partial to the English. I suppose I owe the bias to those who have gone before me." [6] Why should he expect Earl Russell to be partial to the Americans?

The principal organ of upper-class anti-Northern opinion, the London *Times*, was the one British newspaper widely regarded throughout America. Its circulation of 60,000 did not compare with the *Telegraph*'s 200,000, but it had greater prestige than any other daily in the world. Lincoln, who knew that it represented old-time governing-class opinion, compared its power to that of the Mississippi.[7] Its manager at this time was Mowbray Morris, a Conservative whose West Indian birth gave him a sense of kinship with the South; its editor was J. T. Delane, who had visited the United States in 1856 without giving due attention to political and economic subjects. Before Sumter, Delane in a leader laid down the proposition that while the North was legally right on secession, it was impossible to keep so large and strong a portion of the nation as the Confederacy in the Union against its will, and that Lincoln was therefore wrong in condemning the land to the horrors of civil war in a hopeless undertaking.[8] The *Times* was not specially sensitive on slavery—it had published a review condemning *Uncle Tom's Cabin* as bad propaganda—and it had a high sense of British dignities and prerogatives.

In the early months of the war the *Times* showed editorial moderation, while its special American correspondent W. H. Russell was indefatigable, perceptive, and impartial. But after Russell returned home early in 1862 smarting under the castigation he had received for his accurate reports of Bull Run, of inefficiency in the volunteer army, and of the crudity of certain politicians, the United States, as we have said, paid a penalty for its ill treatment of this distinguished journalist.

Delane and Mowbray Morris chose as their new correspondent Charles Mackay, a popular versifier and former editor of the London *Illustrated News*

5 See his review of Cairnes's *Slave Power* in *Westminster Review*, (Oct., 1862).
6 To R. H. Dana, Jr., Aug. 28, 1861, MHS.
7 *Hist. of the Times*, II, 354-358, gives circulation; the *Telegraph* was a penny paper, the *Times* threepenny.
8 March 19, 1861.

who had lectured in the United States and written a shallow volume of impressions. They instructed him to mold his letters to the anti-Northern policy of the paper. Because he had presided at a secessionist lecture in London he met a frigid reception in Boston and New York, and found important Unionist sources of information closed. Fernando Wood, however, cultivated him and poured a special poison into his ear. From his residence on Staten Island, for he was less inclined than Russell to go into the field, Mackay sent home a series of prejudiced letters, making the most of military failures and evidences of popular discontent. His acrid reports, including one garbled by a proofreader to accuse both Northern and Southern soldiers of cowardice, gave so much offense that Bennett's *Herald* suggested tearing down his house. No single person did more during the war to create misunderstanding and animosity between Britain and America. At the end of the conflict Seward, a former friend, sent him a stinging letter: "I pray God to forgive you for the great crime you have committed." [9]

It should be added that the *Times* correspondent in the Confederacy meanwhile wrote well-informed, astute, and sympathetic articles.

Worse than Mackay's letters, however, were the malignant editorial articles of the *Times*. As the London *Daily News* put it,[10] the Thunderer dealt in "reckless misrepresentation, falsifying of facts, and tirades dipped in gall." The burden of the argument was that the North was spilling seas of blood and reducing large European populations to penury in a cruel effort to subjugate a section which asked only to be let alone. "Nine millions of people, inhabiting a territory of 900,000 square miles, and animated by one spirit of resistance, can never be subdued." [11] What of slavery? "Now, we are in Europe thoroughly convinced that the death of slavery must follow as certainly upon the success of the Confederates in the war as the dispersion of darkness occurs upon the rising of the sun." When the egregious John A. Roebuck, M. P., a Confederate supporter, called the Northern people "the scum and refuse of Europe," the *Times* applauded speaker and speech.[12] It assailed American taxation at a time when it

9 Mackay, (1814–1889), an irregularly educated Scot, was perhaps best known for his song "The Good Time Coming," which sold 400,000 copies. His *Life and Liberty in America* (2 vols., 1859) was not unfriendly, though he was much offended by politicians, Jefferson Brick journalists, and Irish agitators who continually insulted England. His autobiography, *Through the Long Day*, makes it clear that he wrote just what Delane and Mowbray Morris wanted. His garbled column on Oct. 14, 1862, declared that the recent heavy battles "proved anything but the courage of the combatants"; he had written "nothing but." Seward's letter, Nov. 3, 1865, replying to Mackay's note of sympathy after the attempt on the Secretary's life, is in *Through the Long Day*, II, 274. Marie Corelli was Mackay's illegitimate daughter. Cf. Cook, *Delane*, 165.
    10 Aug. 8, 1862.
    11 Feb. 7, 1862.
    12 Oct. 7, 1862.

was only half the British rate, spoke of "drafting day by day the youth of their country" when conscription was still unknown, and referred to Northerners as "these degenerate and insensate people." [13] An outrageous financial article suggested that slavery was a lesser evil than the new American tariff, which must alienate every commercial nation.[14] These articles and editorials, reprinted entire in many Northern journals with angry comment, were all too generally accepted as the voice of the dominant element in British affairs.

Yet it was noteworthy that the *Times* never advised British intervention, and repeatedly rejected the idea. After the fall of New Orleans, Delane remarked that the North had a right to anticipate early victory, and to expect the South to re-enter the Union "on the easy and honorable terms which the North would be glad to offer." When McClellan failed and Pope was defeated, he argued that the hope of a voluntary change of Northern policy offered cogent reason for standing aloof. The late autumn of 1862 found the *Times* anguished by the suffering of Lancashire. "Yet we are still willing to bear and forbear," it declared, "if by any means we can keep out of this unnatural quarrel, and avoid giving the dominant faction in America the power of saying that England, out of jealousy or revenge, broke up the Republic." From that stand the Thunderer did not budge.[15]

[II]

Americans erred when they assumed that the aristocratic classes, with the *Times, Morning Post,* and *Saturday Review* as mouthpieces, controlled the nation. When Charles Francis Adams early in the war wrote that "the great body of the people and very much the largest portion of the press do sympathize with us," he meant that most of the middle as well as lower class stood by the North. And John Stuart Mill had correctly written in 1840 that the British government "is progressively changing from the government of a few to the . . . regime of the middle class." Richard Cobden expressed the fact a little differently when he wrote in 1864: "The House of Commons represents the wealth of the country though not its numbers, and I have no doubt the members hear from all the great seats of our commercial ship-owning and manufacturing industries that the busy prosperous people there want peace."

13 See London *Daily News,* Aug. 8, 15, 1862, for an indictment of the *Times,* with quotations from reckless leaders.

14 This *Times* article, July 21, 1862, aroused great anger. No Southern journal had gone further in upholding slavery.

15 That Tory organ the London *Morning Post,* which specially appealed to fashionable society and the landed gentry, also repudiated interventionism with vigor; see its leaders, November 11, 14, 1862. In *Punch,* Sir John Tenniel's cartoons repeatedly wounded Northern feeling without doing anything to please the South, but it too was stubbornly opposed to intervention.

William Michael Rossetti, poet-brother of Dante Gabriel and Christina Rossetti, penning a retrospective analysis just after the war, took the same view as Adams. Distinguishing at least seven important schools of thought, he concluded that the most significant party believed the North to be in the right, but for a time doubted both its reformative zeal in dealing with slavery, and its ability to win. When the North dispelled these doubts, the party took its side with tremendous power.

Indeed, wrote Rossetti, many Britons cared about nothing in the struggle but its antislavery impact. At first the cautious utterances of Washington leaders suggested that the North hardly threatened slavery, but most middle-class Britons watched eagerly for every act, every speech, which proved the vitality of abolitionist sentiment. They thrilled to the manifestoes of Frémont and Hunter, the liberation of "contrabands" by Northern legions, and the enlistment of Negro auxiliaries. After the emancipation proclamation, they felt "a genuine veneration and even enthusiasm for President Lincoln." Thus they gradually cast off hesitancies which chilled their sympathy. "This party was diffused over the length and breadth of the land." It numbered some of the aristocracy, and a multitude of the laboring millions, but its chief strength lay in the hard-working, religious, philanthropic sections of the well-to-do middle class; the groups which gravitated toward radicalism in politics, dissent in church affairs, and good works in social practice. The people who thus slowly made up their minds that the North *would* end slavery, and *could* win, strengthened and at last made irresistible the party which stood for Lincoln and freedom.[16]

Herbert Spencer, looking back in old age on the wartime tides of British sentiment, felt sure that the main body of thoughtful middle-class opinion had been with the Union. This was Henry Ward Beecher's impression in 1863. Three influences, he said on his return from England, had swayed most of the upper classes against the North: commercial interest and rivalry, class pride and fear of contagious radicalism, and a feeling that the United States was growing too powerful. "But if England is to be judged by her middle class . . . she is with us." While the plutocracy was hostile, "the brains that represent progress in Great Britain are in our favor." It was true, Beecher remarked, that a majority of the friends of the North were still without the ballot, but he had learned in England the surprising fact that the voteless men, when united and determined, could control the men who voted. Bishop McIlvaine,

16 Emerson, whose chapter on the *Times* in *English Traits* had contributed to its American prestige, noted that "the privileges of nobility are passing to the middle class"; Ch. XI. Rossetti's long paper appeared in the *Atlantic*, XVII (Feb., 1866), 129–149. A Londoner born and bred, a civil servant, and a Pre-Raphaelite leader, he had access to varied social circles.

the Episcopal leader whom Washington sent to Britain to use his influence, reported to the same effect.[17]

Though hostile British voices often had waspish vehemence, the adherents of the North showed greater conviction and moral fervor. They felt more deeply; Cobden wrote in 1861 that he and Bright regarded the war almost with the sorrow of a personal affliction. To them the outcome would be the victory or defeat of a mighty world cause. William E. Forster, agent of the Quakers in the Irish famine and champion of universal education; Milner Gibson, who had denounced the Crimean War and in Parliament and Cabinet had upheld the tenets of the Manchester Liberals; Wilfrid Lawson, a young radical from northern England; James Stansfeld, intimate friend of Mazzini; Monckton Milnes, poet, politician, and friend of Henry Adams—all exhibited burning earnestness. The principal liberal editors put passion into their utterances. Hutton, editor of the *Spectator*, for example, declared that the Americans were "the only people who . . . are still consciously toiling on to a higher future."

Despite notable exceptions, the best intellectual leaders of the kingdom were on the Northern side. No pro-Southern pamphleteers showed the energy of John Stuart Mill, greatest of English political thinkers; Goldwin Smith, professor of modern history at Oxford; J. E. Cairnes, professor of political economy at Galway; Thomas Hughes, whose *Tom Brown's Schooldays* had earned him a wide popular influence; and the young journalist Edward Dicey, who in his book *Six Months in the Federal States* praised the volunteer army and expressed wonder over the newborn strength of the American people. An impressive array of magazines, church organs, and provincial newspapers fought for the North.[18]

It hurt Northern admirers of Carlyle to find him indifferent to the great issues of the conflict. He abhorred the war, and thought it irrational for white

17 Beecher in N. Y. *Tribune*, Nov. 26, 1863. He said: "Men that are struggling for a better future for themselves and their children, that class is on our side. . . . Our allies have been the common people of England." The county franchise was restricted to those with a holding of £50 rental. McIlvaine wrote Bishop Bedell, Jan. 10, 1862, Seward Papers, Rochester Univ.

18 Among magazines *Macmillan's*, the *Westminster Review*, a radical organ, the *Dial*, the *Observer*, the *Reader* (literary), the *Beehive* (trades union organ), and *Lloyd's Weekly News*, edited by Douglas Gerrold, with a circulation of 400,000 weeky, chiefly among workers. Among church organs the *Freeman* (Baptist), the *British Ensign* (Congregationalist), and the *Nonconformist* (for dissenters generally). Among provincial newspapers the Manchester *Examiner*, widely circulated in Lancashire factory areas, the Liverpool *Daily Post*, the Birmingham *Daily Post*, the Newcastle *Chronicle*, the Bucks *Chronicle*, the Leeds *Mercury*, the Bradford *Advertiser*, the Preston *Guardian*, the Carlisle *Examiner*, the Dundee *Advertiser*, the Edinburgh *Caledonian Mercury*, and the Belfast *Northern Daily Whig*. The immense influence of these provincial dailies has never been properly assessed by students of the period.

men to butcher each other over the position of the blacks. His little *jeu d'esprit*, "Ilias Americana in Nuce," or the American Iliad in a nutshell, betrayed his dislike of democracy and his blindness to the moral evils of slavery. Mill, his old friend, broke with him, and administered a delicate thrust by replying to Carlyle's "The Nigger Question" in an essay called "The Negro Question." But Trollope, Kingsley, George Meredith, and George Eliot were in varying degrees for the North, while the two Brownings, Clough, and Landor made their sympathy clear. These writers knew the mind and heart of the middle class. Pamphlets like Dicey's "Labour and Slavery" and W. E. Baxter's "The Social Condition of the Southern States" were addressed to the plain people.[19] Beecher thought that pro-Northern newspapers circulated a million copies daily, a conservative estimate. Antislavery clergymen certainly addressed millions every Sunday. Cairnes's book *The Slave Power* was initially presented in the form of popular lectures, which, like Baxter's speeches, struck a deep chord.[20] Dicey contrasted the Southern and Northern meetings in England:

At the former you had upon the platform peers, members of Parliament, merchant princes, and many of the . . . leading men of England, but in the body of the hall you have never had a free, crowded audience. The head has always been there but the body has been wanting. At the latter class, you have had few men of note as leaders. . . . But, in return, you have had audiences crowded to the very roof.

The power of working-class and middle-class opinion became a powerful restraint upon British elements which wished to interfere in America. So long as the North seemed flabby on slavery and its chances of success dubious, this opinion was uncrystallized. Its strength grew until, once the Lincoln Administration struck at slavery and evinced a grim determination to win, it became one of the impressive phenomena of the war. "Do not forget," Cobden wrote Beecher, "that we have in this case, for the first time in our history, seen the masses of the British people taking the side of a foreign government against its rebellious citizens. In every other instance, whether in the case of the Poles, Italians, Hungarians, Corsicans, Greeks, or South Americans, the popular sympathy of this country has always leaped to the side of the insurgents." [21]

Unfortunately for subsequent Anglo-American relations, most expressions

19 Both issued 1862; Baxter, a Scottish M. P., expatiated on the moral, social, and economic evils of slavery, with interesting quotations from a journal he had kept while traveling in the South.
20 Marcellus Hartley heard Bright deliver his masterly presentation of the Northern cause in the Birmingham town hall just before Christmas, 1862, and at once obtained permission to print and distribute 10,000 copies in Britain; later 5,000 more. See his article in the N. Y. *Times*, Jan. 22, 1898.
21 Beecher read this letter in public, Nov. 25, 1863; N. Y. *Tribune*, Nov. 26.

of friendly middle-class opinion went unnoticed in the United States. People quivered with anger over the taunts of the *Times* and *Morning Post,* and were stung by Tenniel's cartoons of Brother Jonathan in *Punch.* But they did not read the eloquent defense of Northern principles in the *Daily News* and *Morning Star,* or learn that the mayors of Manchester, Birmingham, and many other towns were with them, or see what a phalanx of veteran reformers upheld the Union cause. Northern resentment rose to the pitch which Sumner described to the Duchess of Argyll in April, 1863. He had talked with Lincoln. "When the rebellion is crushed," he told the President, "a more difficult piece of statesmanship still will be to keep from instant war with England." Half a million Irish were said already to be enrolled for the conflict. "And now the worst is to be told," wrote Sumner. "Those who have heretofore most cordially stood by England with admiration and love—the best educated, the best principled, and the wealthiest of the land—are now embittered beyond Irish and Democrat." Friends whose English sympathies were once intense, he continued, "talk to me and write to me as strongly against England as against the rebellion." Sumner liked to exaggerate bad news and stir up trouble, but this time his statements had some warrant.[22]

[III]

Because the Ministry was divided, Parliament was confused, and the sufferings of Lancashire were increasing, real danger existed in the fall of 1862 of some rash British spasm. The general election of 1859 had given the House only a few more Liberals than Conservatives. When Palmerston became Prime Minister he bestowed the foreign office on Lord John Russell, and the chancellorship of the exchequer on Gladstone, who was nominally a Conservative. Three dukes went into this Liberal Cabinet, in which Cobden, disliking its head, stubbornly refused a place.[23]

Palmerston, a political veteran and an imposing figure, was a fascinating mixture of qualities good and bad. He was nonchalant, jaunty, and iron-willed. Lord Clarendon termed him "an artful old dodger," while Queen Victoria linked him with Earl Russell as "those two dreadful old men." A writer in the *Daily News,* angered by his swaggering insolence, remarked: "He has made

22 Sumner to Duchess of Argyll, April 26, 1863, HL. Some British papers criticized Sumner severely, and he never forgot criticism. The half-million Irishmen pledged to war were actually ten or twenty thousand Fenians whose movement Mackay exposed in the London *Times.*

23 Palmerston, writes Herbert Paul, had a superficial Liberalism, but the Conservatives could not cooperate with the Radicals to overthrow his composite government. *History of Modern England,* II, 320, 321.

himself the political incarnation of the English bully." [24] But it could fairly be said that he had perfect public integrity, and always stood to his word; that however flippant, he was a hard worker; and that he felt not only a strong sense of the dignity of Britain, but an earnest concern for the nation's welfare. He had been called to aid Spencer Percival's cabinet in 1809, as Jefferson was just leaving the Presidency; now, at seventy-six, he was capable of driving to Harrow in a rain, opening a library there with a speech, driving back, and sitting in the House until 2 A.M.[25]

He was in some respects farsighted, consistent, and logical, with a gift for connecting current policies with long-term principles. He understood the force of the great nationalist currents which were creating nations in Italy and Germany, and keeping patriotism alive in Poland, Bohemia, Hungary, and the Balkans. Like Russell, he comprehended and valued the liberalism that found eloquent voice in Mazzini, Tocqueville, and Gottfried Kinkel. He wished to see the aspirations of suppressed peoples and the hopes of patriot dreamers realized, at least in part, with as little disturbance to the peace of Europe as possible, and he had enough belief in the old diplomacy to hold that this could be done while maintaining the uneasy balance of power. He knew when to be daring, and when to be cautious. He tended toward arrogance, using too much of the *fortiter in re* with too little of the *suaviter in modo;* he had the instincts, as Metternich once said of him, of an autocrat; he was full of prejudices, and Victoria correctly noted that he was vindictive.[26] But if his realism could be hard, cold, and tactless, it could also be sagacious—and in the end his realism benefited the United States.

That frail intellectual aristocrat Lord John Russell stood in sharp contrast with the downright, overbearing Palmerston. With an ardent, restless temperament, and some of the brilliance that made his philosopher grandson famous, he was doctrinaire in politics, holding extreme stands with opinionated tenacity.[27] He liked to meddle in international affairs, preaching sermons the while. Since entering Parliament in 1820 he had played the part of a true liberal, supporting Catholic emancipation, the Reform Bill, the repeal of the Corn Laws, and the aspirations of small peoples. In 1860 he had defied the reactionary Powers of Europe by penning the celebrated dispatch which became one of the cornerstones of Italian unity: "Her Majesty's Government turn their eyes . . . to

24 July 12, 1862. This writer declared that Palmerston had "corrupted by social bribery a powerful portion of the London press."
25 Paul, II, 316.
26 Queen Victoria's *Letters, Second Series,* II, *passim;* Bell, *Palmerston,* II, 273–354; Temperley and Penson, *Foundations of British Foreign Policy, 1792–1902,* 88–304.
27 Russell was approaching seventy; a brother of the Duke of Bedford, in 1861 he succeeded to a small Irish estate and became earl. Bertrand Russell sketches his grandfather, "warm and affectionate and kindly," in *Portraits From Memory.*

the gratifying prospect of a people building up the edifice of their liberties, and consolidating the work of their independence, amid the sympathies and good wishes of Europe." Victoria had good reason for characterizing him as selfish, vain, "and often reckless and imprudent." [28] He was abysmally ignorant of the United States. He wrote indiscreet papers. But twenty million Italians never forgot his generous part in committing Britain to their liberation; and Palmerston, to whose domination he had become submissive, could curb his recklessness.

It must be admitted that Russell had some valid ground for feeling irritation over Northern foreign policy. He knew from Lord Lyons the essence of Seward's mad proposal for provoking hostilities with Spain and France to bring the South back into the Union. Lyons detailed to him Seward's conversations of April and May, 1861, adumbrating this plan.

On May 10, for example, Seward suggested to Lyons that Britain and the United States sign a convention for suppressing the slave trade at which Spanish officials in Cuba winked, and guaranteeing the independence of Santo Domingo, on which Spanish troops had already landed. "For my own part," Lyons reported Seward as saying, "I would have no objection to make an anti-African Slave Trade demonstration against Spain; if she were rash enough to provoke it." [29] Lyons and Russell knew that the United States was not strong enough to fight the Confederacy, France, and Spain all at once, and they resented a proposal that Britain should enter into a virtual alliance with the North which would estrange her from France and radically align her against the South. Russell unquestionably read with distaste Seward's threatening statement to the *Times's* correspondent that no foreign power could receive the Confederate commissioners, even if they called informally to hand in a document, without risking a breach of relations with the American Government.

Russell may also have been ruffled by Northern uproar over the British proclamation of neutrality, an act which was not merely justifiable under international law but indispensable under the political circumstances. Bryant's *Evening Post* exploded as wrathfully over "Britain's Blunder" as Greeley's *Tribune*, while *Harper's Weekly* and the *Atlantic* pronounced the British grant of belligerent rights to the Confederacy inexcusable.[30] By the summer of 1862 Leslie's *Illustrated Newspaper* was making the wild assertion on which Sumner later

28 *Letters, Second Series*, II, 625.
29 Lyons, May 11, 1861, to Russell, FO/4 1137.
30 *Evening Post, Tribune*, May 29, 1861; *Harper's Weekly*, June 8; *Atlantic*, VIII (December, 1861), 761–769. If Lincoln's blockade was a reality, Britain had to enjoin a strict neutrality on her subjects. The very newspapers which berated England were themselves ready to treat the army, navy, and government of the Confederacy as those of a belligerent. The South stood in a very different position from the Carlist and Hungarian rebels to whom Britain had refused belligerent status.

based a huge bill for damages: "The Rebellion would have been dead today
. . . had not she [Britain] sided with the rebels and lent them moral encouragement and material aid." [31] These reproaches were as unreasonable as the
counter-complaints of the South, which assailed Great Britain for not at once
recognizing the independence of the Confederacy and breaking the blockade.
In point of fact, the North had only itself to blame for so promptly giving the
Confederacy the status of a belligerent. As Attorney-General Bates argued,[32] the
government would have acted shrewdly if it had simply proclaimed a closing
of the Southern ports instead of a formal blockade. The fact that Russell twice
saw the Confederate mission to London unofficially and without the slightest
commitment disturbed Northerners; the fact that he then refused to see the
members again angered Southerners. He was hewing to a neutral line.

Fortunately Russell did not know the worst about Seward's peculiar diplomacy. He did not know that on May 21 Seward had written a dispatch, No. 10,
which Adams' son and biographer justly characterizes as "so indecorous and
threatening as to be tantamount to a declaration of war." It declared that if
Britain gave shelter to Confederate privateers, the United States would once
more, as twice before, become her enemy. A global war would ensue, in which
Britain would have reason to lament her folly while the United States would
emerge comparatively unscathed. This paper, had it been delivered as first written, would have made a collision with Britain almost certain. Happily, Lincoln
took firm control, and not only expunged the offensive phrasing, but directed
Adams to regard the dispatch as a mere confidential instruction, to be communicated to nobody.[33] But Lord Russell, if he read the *Times*, did know that
Seward was indulging in the idea that a world-wide war would rescue the
United States, for the Secretary told the *Times* correspondent on July 4: "If
any European power provokes a war, we shall not shrink from it. A contest between Great Britain and the United States would wrap the world in fire, and
at the end it would not be the United States which would have to lament the
result of the conflict."

Nor, down to the late summer of 1862, could Lord Russell's displeasure have
been mollified by any sense of the moral superiority of the North. Seward's
early dispatches seemed almost to strike the slavery question out of the American contest. He expatiated on the Federal and State protection given to all the
existing interests of slavery, and instructed Adams not to discuss "opposing
moral principles." More than that, in a dispatch of July 5, 1862, to Adams, he

31   Aug. 9, 1862.
32   To Lieber, Aug. 23, 1861, Lieber Papers, HL. A majority of the Cabinet had wished
simply to shut the ports; but when Seward argued in favor of a blockade because the rules
governing it were clearly known, and it seemed less likely to create foreign difficulties,
Lincoln and the others agreed. Welles, *Lincoln and Seward*, 123.
33   For the text before and after Lincoln revised it, see Randall, *Lincoln*, II, 35–37.

VULCAN ARMING NEPTUNE.

(INFLUENCE OF THE *MERRIMAC-MONITOR* BATTLE.)

From Punch, or The London Charivari, April 19, 1862

treated armed rebels and emancipationists as equally guilty of trying to pre-cipitate a servile war, thus equating Jefferson Davis and Charles Sumner.[34]

As the North tightened the blockade and captured numerous blockade runners, Earl Russell deprecated the rigor, "beyond the usual practise of na-tions," with which the United States treated British subjects engaged in the traffic. He sent Washington a strong protest against this which arrived in the gloomy hour after Pope's defeat. Meanwhile, divergent national policies on two other matters, privateering and the slave trade, engendered temporary mis-understanding and friction.

As an outgrowth of the Crimean War, Great Britain and France had taken the lead in 1856 in a movement to abolish privateering and secure fuller respect for neutral commerce in time of war. The Declaration of Paris adopted that year by six powers obtained the assent of nearly all European and South American states. The United States, however, declined to give it the uncondi-tional adherence required. When Seward in 1861 moved hastily to accede, it was obvious that he did so in order to outlaw Confederate privateers. A civil con-flict having begun, Britain was unwilling to change the rules of war in a way favorable to either side. Russell declared that he would make no engagement which had any bearing, direct or indirect, on the contest; whereupon Adams testily remarked that he would rather a thousand times let the Declaration re-main unsigned forever than accept such a proviso.[35] The British government issued a decree June 1 that it would permit no privateer to bring prizes into its ports—which meant, practically, that the Confederacy could have no priva-teers. But the Foreign Office continued to believe that Seward had attempted a piece of sharp practice.

As for the African slave trade, as late as July, 1861, it was still to a consider-able extent promoted from New York. The Federal marshal there sent Seward in October affidavits of four crewmen of the American ship *Nightingale*, seized

34 For radical anger over this dispatch when it was finally published, see Pierce, *Sumner*, IV, 110, 111.

35 For several reasons the treatment of this and other episodes by Charles Francis Adams, Jr., in his life of his father (1900) must be taken with reserve. For dramatic effect, the biographer unduly heightens British hostility, and improperly presents his story as a personal contest between Adams on one side, Russell and Palmerston on the other. The Minister's diary in the Massachusetts Historical Society shows that he was treated with much more cordiality by high British circles than the biography suggests. The son also glosses over weaknesses of temperament and policy in Adams which the diary of Benjamin Moran dis-closes. Finally, the life greatly overestimates the capacity and achievements of Seward, with whom the Adamses had an old friendship, and underestimates Lincoln. (In 1873 Charles Francis Adams, Sr., delivered a singularly ill-informed memorial address on Seward to the New York legislature, portraying him as the real power in the Lincoln Administration. This was deeply resented by the surviving Cabinet members, Chase, Blair, and Gideon Welles; and Welles penned a small volume, *Lincoln and Seward* (1874), which completely crushed Adams's statements.) The Minister's achievements were great enough to need no exaggera-tion.

in the port as a slaver. The enormous profits of the Africa-Cuba run tempted men to run any risk. "Until a few months ago," wrote the marshal, "a very large proportion of the vessels engaged in the African trade have been fitted out at this port." This was no news to the British consul, who had employed detectives and paid bribes to ferret out information. He knew all about the operations of Abranches, Almeida & Co., and other New York agents for slavers. In view of the long record of American laxity in dealing with this atrocious commerce, British leaders had some excuse for doubt concerning Northern intentions.[36]

One diplomatic difficulty after another was conquered. The British decree of June 1 stopped all possibility of a quarrel over privateering. The American execution of Nathaniel Gordon, captain of a slaver, early in 1862, with the drafting of a new Anglo-American treaty for cooperative action in stamping out the trade, banished English doubts in that field. Not only was the *Trent* affair peaceably settled; when Mason and Slidell finally reached England, the London *Times* itself expressed a hope that nothing like an ovation would be given them. But the vital facts are two: first, that Secretary Seward, with his ideas about provoking a war with Spain and France, had not impressed the British government as wise, moderate, or farsighted, and second, that neither Seward's notes nor Lincoln's major acts down to Antietam had given the Northern cause an aura of high nobility. Lord Russell did not have to be excessively hostile to ask whether the conflict was worth while.

That question pressed on humane Britons high and low after the Seven Days and Second Manassas. The war was fast becoming the bloodiest and costliest of modern times. The slaughter, the devastation of rich countrysides, the fierce mutual hatreds, were appalling. Decent families on the Dee and Mersey went in rags and hunger because of the blockade; the danger that some sudden incident would spread the conflagration abroad could not be underrated. And to what end, so long as no high moral object threw a gleam of sunshine over the scene of horror? Countless religious people felt with the London *Record* that the bloodshed affronted common sense, Christianity, and humanity.[37]

Fortunate it was for the United States that it had so able, firm, and high-minded a representative in London as Charles Francis Adams. He had gotten his earliest education in Russia, France, and England, and indeed, some knowledge of the English character had been beaten into him at an Ealing boarding school. He had studied law under Daniel Webster, served in legislature and Congress, and become one of the Free Soil leaders. He had all the cultivation,

36 The Federal marshal, Robert Murray, wrote Seward on Oct. 12, 1861; Seward Papers. The British consul, E. M. Archibald, sent Lord Lyons several letters on the trade; see especially that of Feb. 1, 1861, FO 84/1137.
37 London *Record* (Anglican weekly), July 14, 18, 1862.

probity, public spirit, and immovable courage characteristic of his family, with all their power of pungent expression. His very faults were those the British leaders could most easily overlook, for in pride, reserve, tactlessness, and rigidity he was one with many of them. He was totally unable to reach public opinion in England; he attempted few public appearances, showed no faculty for dealing with the press, and made no firm friendships even among those who freely offered friendship. Complaining of the chill manners of some Englishmen, he admitted that Westerners addressed the same reproach to Yankees: "It is irksome to me who have the same cold manners to attempt to make acquaintances, so that I hardly know how I shall get on." With frequent opportunities to talk cordially with Bright and Cobden, Grote and Milman, Sir Henry Holland and Monckton Milnes, and to open other doors, he made little use of them. At least once Palmerston made a frank after-dinner effort to improve Anglo-American intercourse, suggesting that Seward showed too much *brusquerie* (and Adams admitted this "awkward *brusquerie*") toward Lord Lyons. More geniality in the Minister, and less suspiciousness, would have served America well. But if his championship of America had an iceberg frigidity, it had also an iceberg massiveness.

[IV]

Had Britain and France been linked in a close entente, the chances of joint intervention would have been greater. But the two nations had an ancient enmity, while most Englishmen regarded Napoleon III as a dangerous adventurer. As lately as 1858 the island had suffered a scare over the possibility of a Gallic invasion. In 1860 the government had sternly disapproved of Napoleon's annexation of Nice and Savoy, Lord John Russell warning Parliament that the success of this stroke would lead the warlike French into other acts of aggression. Since the French resented the British condemnation, this disagreement was slow to heal.[38] The troubled European scene, moreover, was constantly in the minds of British and French leaders, and limited their freedom to act together.

August Belmont, the well-informed American agent of the Rothschilds, wrote Seward from Paris in the fall of 1861 that Napoleon wished to recognize the Confederacy at once. He was so assured both in London and Paris. Thus Napoleon would stop the derangement of industry and trade caused by the war, made doubly disastrous by the total failure of French grain crops. But British cooperation was essential, and the British hung back. "The fact is," Belmont

38 Hansard, Third Series, CLXVII, 1257, 1258; Temperley and Penson, *Foundations of Br. Foreign Policy,* 286.

noted, "the feeling between the English and French people is at the moment anything but friendly, whatever efforts their governments may make." [39]

Nor did the French adventure in Mexico improve British confidence in Napoleon's policies. When the Mexican Congress in July, 1861, suspended payments on the foreign debt for two years, the culminating act in a long series of outrages against Europeans, the governments most aggrieved decided to deal drastically with the republic. President Benito Juárez, a full-blooded Indian, was an honest, large-minded attorney who had reached his post by ability and hard work. But the state was racked by civil war, insurrectionary armies ravaged wide countrysides, property and even life had become insecure, and the British legation in Mexico City itself was despoiled of a large sum of money. France, Britain, and Spain agreed, by a joint convention in the fall of 1861, to protect the persons and possessions of their subjects, and compel the fulfillment of Mexican obligations. They also agreed, Britain and Spain sincerely but France dishonestly, not to exercise in Mexico's internal affairs any influence prejudicial to the right of the Mexican nation to chose freely the form of its government.

After the bloodless occupation of Veracruz by the three nations, Britain and Spain soon withdrew. For one reason, the shrewd Juárez made reasonable concessions to satisfy them. For another, it became plain that Napoleon III intended to capture Mexico City, overthrow the republic, and create a Mexican Empire, with a Catholic monarch of his own choice as head. His motives were mixed: to heighten the prestige of his dynasty, obtain a fresh outlet for French manufactures, restore to France some of the New World glories won by La Salle and Cadillac, and establish a Latin civilization south of the Rio Grande to counterbalance the Anglo-Saxon culture north of it. The economist Michel Chevalier expatiated in the *Revue des Deux Mondes* on the role that France, the eldest daughter of the Church, was to play as leader on both sides of the Atlantic. The one consideration which reconciled Englishmen to Napoleon's theatrical stroke was stated by the London *Times:* "The best guaranty of peace is the direction of French enterprise or restlessness to places beyond the pale of the finely-balanced community of Europe." [40]

Almost from the beginning of the American conflict the French emperor was ready to recognize the Confederacy and break the blockade—if the British would act with him. We wish, he wrote his chief agent in Mexico in 1862, to

---

39 London, Oct. 21, 1861, Seward Papers, Rochester Univ. Belmont thought that the appointment of the two Orleans princes to McClellan's staff had irritated Napoleon III, who was very sensitive to Bourbon prestige.

40 May 27, 1862. The same view was stated by the *London Illustrated News,* favorable to the North, May 24, 1862: Mexican occupation "will afford an outlet to those feverish energies of the French people which find themselves 'cribbed, cabined, and confined' within the narrow limits of their native land."

see the United States prosperous and powerful, but we do not wish her to dominate Latin America. If we can establish a government in Mexico supported by French power, we and Spain can maintain control of our colonies in the Antilles, can extend a beneficial influence over the whole area from the Rio Grande to Cape Horn, and can open fresh markets and obtain indispensable raw materials. If the Confederacy gained its independence, as he anticipated, he knew that the antagonisms of the North and South would give him free rein. Mercier, the French Minister in Washington, visited Richmond to canvass with the Confederate leaders the possibility of French mediation, and reported that they were prepared to fight to the last for their independence. Unlike Palmerston and his Ministry, Napoleon III did not have to take constant thought of public opinion; and the French elements which suffered economic damage from the war were almost unanimous in their sympathy with the South, for they felt little of the passion for democratic freedom which pulsed in Lancashire.[41]

In short, it became clear in the winter of 1861–62 that Napoleon would intervene if Great Britain ever agreed; but it was also clear that France was too weak to expose herself to European animosities by acting alone.

Chief among the friends of the North in France were six men; Edouard Laboulaye of the Sorbonne; Count Agénor de Gasparin, leader of the Protestant Liberal group in French affairs and a prominent publicist; Henri Martin, the historian; Auguste Cochin, journalist and member of Parliament; Count Charles F. de T. Montalembert, the famous Catholic Liberal; and August Laugel, mining engineer and prolific author. The American Minister, Dayton, knew no French, and displayed little enterprise, but happily the consul Lincoln sent to Paris, John Bigelow, was a young man of rare accomplishments. He had been Bryant's associate in editing the *Evening Post,* had traveled widely, read French fluently, and combined enterprise and insight with gracious manners. With Laboulaye in particular, he formed an alliance of great benefit to the North. Some ten years earlier the French scholar, loitering on the left bank to examine the bookstalls, had found a volume in English by William Ellery Channing, paid a few sous for it, read some pages, and becoming fascinated, sat down in the Champs-Elysées to finish it. In high excitement, he sought the office of the editor of the *Journal des Débats.* "Today I have discovered a great man!" he announced. That influential newspaper shortly published three articles, one on Channing's writings, one on the movement of religious ideas in New England, and one on "The Present Condition and Probable Future of the Great Republic." In the fall of

---

41 Cf. L. M. Case, ed., *French Opinion on the U. S. and Mexico, 1860–1867, passim;* Detroyat, *Intervention Française au Mexique,* 167 ff.

1849 Laboulaye began lecturing at the Sorbonne on the American Constitution, and gradually made himself an authority on the United States.

Gasparin had brought out his treatise on the free-soil movement, *The Uprising of a Great People*, in 1861, dating his preface two weeks after Lincoln's inauguration. Laboulaye was eager to use his pen in the same cause. Soon after Bigelow arrived in Paris, he noticed two careful papers in the *Journal des Débats*, highly sympathetic to the North, by Laboulaye. The consul asked permission to call; Laboulaye declared that he was only too happy to serve a cause identified with liberty and justice; and from that moment his literary talents were always at Bigelow's disposal, without thought of any material reward. The *Débats* articles were apparently evoked by Gasparin's second book, *L'Amérique devant L'Europe*, which had then recently appeared. Bigelow reprinted them in pamphlet form, sending copies to members of the Institute, most of the Paris bar, the diplomatic corps, and the more prominent statesmen and journals of Europe.

Unquestionably, Bigelow demonstrated great shrewdness in managing the French press. It was well that he did so, for in France as in England the economic impact of the conflict was heavy. "Our war," wrote Bigelow, "has deranged the financial calculations of the governments and bankers of Europe to a greater degree than any of the wars or revolutions that have preceded it in Europe." The textile factories of France suffered at first even more than those of Lancashire, because supplies of raw cotton in storage were small. Some members of the government were open propagandists for recognition of Confederate independence. On May 14, 1862, the foreign minister, Thouvenel, frankly told Slidell that in his opinion if it had not been for the capture of Fort Donelson and of New Orleans, France would quickly have recognized the Confederacy; and if the fortunes of war ran against the North, she might yet take the decisive step.[42] Bigelow, often fearing the worst, knew that only a great decisive Union victory would end the danger. Instead, the dispatches painted a dismal scene. "The advance of the [McClellan] army," commented Bigelow, "does not seem to be much more rapid than the original colonization of the country."

Strenuously as Bigelow labored, however, he could not affect the course of the journals under government patronage and control. All of these semi-official sheets—the *Constitutionnel, Patrie, Pays*—were advocating recognition throughout the spring of 1862. They harped upon the rigors of the blockade. To Bigelow, the blockade was a mistake. He did not believe it would do much if anything to end the war, feared that it might force cotton-hungry nations to intervene, and believed that as a matter of world policy, all blockades ought in the long run to be abolished. Had his wishes been met, one of the greatest

42 Naval O. R., II, iii, 491; Clapp, *Bigelow, passim*; Bigelow, *Retrospections*, I, 371-587.

weapons of the United States in gaining its victory over the Confederacy, and
of the Allies in defeating Germany in 1918, would have been struck out of their
hands. His letters to Seward on this subject made no convert. Seward, indeed,
knew how to drive home to the French Government the fact that the blockade
was not the prime cause of the cotton famine; when Mercier suggested that it
be lifted, he made a counter-suggestion that the North put an embargo on wheat
to correspond with the Confederate embargo on cotton!

It was fortunate for the North, indeed, that wheat played so large a part in
the French situation. While Europe reaped a short grain crop in 1860–62, the
North had bumper yields. That fact, Bigelow wrote his old chief, Bryant, gave
America the whip hand in France. While one Southern State after another forbade cotton shipments to Europe in 1861, a free flow of Northern breadstuffs
left Northern ports for Liverpool and Bordeaux. But in France, as in England,
many idealistic men could not understand Northern hesitations to attack
slavery.[43]

At no time did the British Government respond to Napoleon's overtures.
Though the London *Daily News* declared that Palmerston was like the Emperor
in his arrogant irresponsibility, actually the Prime Minister was as wary as
Napoleon was reckless. The difference in their attitudes was dramatically illustrated in April, 1862.

One of the principal British interventionists, the shipowner William S.
Lindsay, M. P., crossed the Channel to confer with Slidell. On April 11 he saw
Napoleon, who told him that he was prepared to recognize the Confederacy
"if Great Britain set the example," but that he had twice proposed the step to
the British only to be tacitly rebuffed, and would make no further offer. Two
days later, however, if we may believe what Lindsay told the British ambassador in Paris, Napoleon did ask him to have private talks with Palmerston and
Russell, and to try to bring about Anglo-French recognition of Confederate
independence. As the British ambassador reported to Earl Russell, a "nasty intrigue" was being carried on, of which Thouvenel, the French foreign minister,
said he had no knowledge. On April 18 Napoleon saw Lindsay again. But then
came news of Shiloh and McClellan's impending peninsular campaign. We must

---

43 Thurlow Weed, who did really admirable work for the United States as an informal
agent in Britain and France, impressing everybody by his geniality, tact, and statesmanlike
vision, wrote Seward from Paris on Jan. 26, 1862; "There are two radical difficulties here.
The Tariff is a stumbling block. It gave the Emperor decided offense. But that is not more,
or perhaps not as serious, as the Slavery question. If ours was avowedly a War for Emancipation, this Government would sympathize with and aid us. My greatest difficulty with
the Count de Morny, Prince Napoleon (the Emperor's brother), and other distinguished
Frenchmen has been to explain our difficulty in this respect." Seward Papers, Rochester
Univ.

cling to strict neutrality, Thouvenel wrote Mercier in Washington on May 18, until we see how the struggle develops.

When London learned in June, 1862, that the French army marching from Veracruz to Mexico City had received a bloody check at Pueblo the previous month, liberal British circles were pleased. Napoleon's organ, the *Moniteur*, edited by Prosper Mérimée, had predicted that the French troops would be received with roses and cheers, but instead they were met with bomb and bayonet. Mexico began to look like a dubious gamble.[44]

[V]

At the same time that McClellan's and Pope's failures taught Americans that the war would be long, European opinion awoke to the same fact. This realization coincided with a sharp increase in the British and French sufferings from the shortage of cotton.

For months after Sumter the prevailing British belief was that the conflict could not drag far into 1862. In the complicated story of the cotton famine, it is certain that British textile interests did not at first realize how critical was their position. Imports of cotton in 1860 had been excessively high, so that stocks had grown oppressive, and overproduction had glutted the textile market. The stoppage of cotton shipments by the Confederate embargo and Northern blockade was therefore temporarily welcomed by some manufacturers as enabling them to work off their heavy inventory. But the autumn of 1862 brought a tightening pinch. Lancashire and Lyons were shocked when they heard of the wholesale Confederate burnings of cotton at New Orleans and along the Mississippi; they were alarmed when they saw the war would go into 1863, and perhaps 1864 or 1865. The movement for intervention gained a new background.[45]

From one point of view British economic distress has been exaggerated. In the kingdom as a whole the number of persons on relief did not rise materially during the war, for heavy as was the unemployment in the textile areas, other industries enjoyed a compensating boom. Arms makers, ironmasters, and metal workers generally received large war orders. Linen and woolen manufacture

44 Clapp, *Bigelow*, 170–172; see Bigelow, *Restrospections*, I, 514–520, for Slidell's report of his own official audience with Napoleon on July 16, 1862, in which the Emperor said that "the difficulty was to find the way to give effect to his sympathies." For a rough characterization of Lindsay, see Moran, II, 963 ff., 1040 ff. This story is well covered in J. M. Callahan's *Diplomatic History of the Confederacy*, 147–149. As Napoleon himself took a hand in editing the *Moniteur*, it was rather more than semi-official. The French Government published many of the Thouvenel-Mercier dispatches in a *Yellow Book* late in 1862.
45 See the Manchester cotton trade circular republished in N. Y. *Tribune*, June 12, 1862; it warned manufacturers to be prepared to see cotton supplies "hermetically sealed."

expanded to take the place of cotton goods. British shipyards and sea carriers profited from the steady increase in the use of iron for ocean vessels, the depredations of Confederate cruisers on American commerce, and the high insurance rates on Yankee vessels, so that by the close of the war Britain was securely reinstated in her old maritime supremacy. Gladstone, a truly great finance minister, devised prudent fiscal measures and impressed the government with the need for economy.[46]

Nevertheless, the hardship concentrated in a relatively small area—in Lancashire, Cheshire, Derbyshire, and part of Yorkshire—became heartrending. The whole number of British cotton mills in the summer of 1862 was 2,877, and the total of workers in the cotton trade was 540,000. July found 80,000 people totally unemployed, and 370,000 working only two, three, or four days a week. This meant that two million people in Lancashire, and a quarter million in Cheshire and Derbyshire, were plunged into want.[47] During the summer and autumn the pressure of poverty increased. By the end of the year fewer than 125,000 operatives were working full time, while nearly 250,000 were completely out of work. "Distress in the North" was a standing headline in most journals. Public meetings were held all over the kingdom, relief committees organized, and subscriptions circulated. In the stricken region workrooms were opened, public improvements undertaken—Preston employed men on the moor, the marsh, and the stoneyard—and soup and bread distributed. In Manchester, by November, more than one-tenth of the people were on relief.[48]

The patient heroism of the workers was admirable. As long as possible they subsisted on their savings. At no time did they give way to the slightest disorder. Karl Marx was busily writing in the British Museum, but they offered no forcible illustration of the class conflict. Many pawned their belongings until they slept on the floor and ate without table or chairs from a cracked bowl and pitcher, shivering before fireless grates;[49] still they made the best of their situation, picking oakum if no better work was offered, and flocking to voluntary schools opened to occupy their time. Some asked alms in the streets or in railway carriages. Groups went through the large towns, singing such songs as they knew for pennies, and made London squares resound with hymns. When workers read the newspapers they found nothing but dark predictions. "The prospect is gloomy in the extreme," warned the London *Daily News* late in August. "Competent authorities estimate that during the next six months there

46   Max Beloff, *History*, N. S., XXXVII (Feb. 1952), 45.
47   Figures given by Edmund Potter, in House of Commons, July 24, 1862, Hansard, Third Series, CLXVIII, 739; see also W. O. Henderson, *The Lancashire Cotton Famine, 1861–1865*, 52–118 *passim*.
48   *Illustrated London News*, Nov. 29, 1862.
49   See sketches of four tenement interiors, *idem*, p. 585.

will be only sufficient cotton to admit of the operatives having two days' work a week, and this is upon the supposition that not a single bale will remain in stack at the end of that period." [50] Yet their overwhelming sentiment was for the North and against intervention.

This was true even before the emancipation proclamation. It was not for nothing that they had read *Uncle Tom's Cabin*. "There are signs," said the London *Morning Star*, "of a renewed attempt to extract from the sufferings of the Lancashire operatives some support for the Confederacy. Outdoor meetings have been got up, ostensibly to petition for a relaxation of the poor-law code, but really . . . against the blockade." As it commented, such expectations were futile. "The operatives are well enough read in contemporary history to understand that the people of the Free States are subjecting themselves to great sacrifices for what they believe to be a righteous cause." [51]

One striking event after another underlined this statement. At Blackburn in July, for example, an open-air meeting was called to petition Parliament to offer mediation. A great throng assembled. The large cotton manufacturer who presided accused the North of fighting for aggrandizement and plunder. Another speaker put the motion: the time had come for the British Government to use its influence to end the war. At this a stalwart worker, secretary to the Weavers' Association, was on his feet with blazing words and a counter-motion: "That, in consequence of . . . the widespread destitution . . . this meeting is of opinion that it is the duty of the British Government to use every influence compatible with the maintenance of peace for the settlement of the American difficulty *by restoring the confidence of the Southern planters to the policy of President Lincoln, and the reorganization and preservation of the American Union*." Amid cheers the throng passed this counter-motion, voted resolutions condemning the anti-Northern agitation, and carried a motion of censure on a prominent anti-Northern member of Parliament. [52]

Yet however stanch the general body of workers, danger existed, once the McClellan-Pope failures advertised the certainty of a long war, that irritations would grow, and that a divided Cabinet and confused House might take rash action. The second wartime tariff seemed to many Britons and Frenchmen a blow in the face. [53] Merchants, shipowners, and manufacturers exhibited alarm and anger. Cobden was deeply offended. Americans, wrote the *Times*, were rejoicing "because they hope they have shut out half the world, in-

50 Aug. 25, 1862.
51 May 6, 1862.
52 Manchester *Examiner*, quoted in N. Y. *Tribune*, July 15, 1862.
53 The *Daily News*, and indeed all Manchester Liberal groups and organs, were likewise distressed. The law showed, said the *Daily News*, July 15, 1862, that American control had passed from the slave power to the industrial power.

sulated themselves from Europe, brought famine to several millions of British, French, and German firesides, and made the Atlantic ten times as wide to all practical purposes." [54] While the blockade was temporary, the high tariff might be permanent. Meanwhile, of course, the Confederacy was promising Europe a low-tariff policy.

On the American side, at this anxious moment, great indignation was aroused by the negligence of Britain in the case of the *Alabama*. The British Government in general tried honestly to enforce its long-standing neutrality legislation, which among other provisions forbade the construction and equipment in British harbors of ships for belligerents in any war in which Britain remained neutral. But here was an instance of gross and culpable carelessness.

Minister Adams knew that the Confederates were having a ship built by Messrs. Laird at Birkenhead for use as a cruiser. On June 23, 1862, he warned Lord Russell, sending his evidence. Russell referred the matter to British officials in Liverpool, a port full of Confederate sentiment; and here, though the legal adviser to the Commissioners of Customs declared that "the evidence was almost conclusive" for the guilty character of the vessel, nobody interfered. The commissioners merely promised that the officers at Liverpool would keep a strict watch on the vessel. At the suggestion of Lord Russell, Adams then had the American consul in Liverpool gather a mass of new evidence to submit to the collector of the port. This evidence, though conclusive to any reasonable man, the collector practically ignored. Adams thereupon retained a distinguished legal figure, R. P. Collier, Q. C., to whom he showed not only the old evidence but some fresh depositions. Collier's verdict was emphatic. "I am of opinion," he wrote, "that the collector of customs would be justified in detaining the vessel. Indeed, I should think it his duty to detain her. . . . It appears difficult to make out a stronger case of infringement of the Foreign Enlistment Act, which if not enforced on this occasion, is little better than a dead letter." But still the collector delayed! [55]

The outraged American Minister at this point sent Collier's opinion, with a mass of relevant papers, to Lord Russell. "I ought to have been satisfied . . . ," admitted Russell afterwards, "and to have given orders to detain the *Alabama* at Birkenhead." [56] Instead, he forwarded the documents to the senior law officer of the crown, Sir John Harding. To cap this fresh delay, fate played the British and American Governments a sad trick. Had the senior law officer been the Attorney-General, Russell could have been sure of prompt action. But as he was not a member of the Ministry, the Foreign

54 July 11, 1862.
55 *Diplomatic Correspondence*, 1862, pts. i and ii, *passim*.
56 *Recollections and Suggestions*, 235.

Secretary did not know that he was becoming insane. For five days the papers lay unread at his house—days during which the final touches were put on the *Alabama,* and a possible cause of war between Britain and America received no remedy. At last, on July 28th, the Attorney-General and Solicitor-General got hold of the evidence. They at once decided that the *Alabama* must be halted, and on the 29th so reported. But that very day the ship put to sea, without papers, under pretense of making a trial trip.

Once the *Alabama* was gone, Lord Russell saw what a fearful blunder he had made. He proposed in the Cabinet that orders be telegraphed to seize her in any British port which she touched. At least three other members of the Ministry, Sir George Cornewall Lewis, Milner Gibson, and the Duke of Argyll, deplored the escape of the cruiser, and Argyll approved of Lord Russell's proposal. But the plan came to nothing. The *Alabama,* with a crew largely British, proceeded to the Azores, where she took on arms and ammunition, and Captain Raphael Semmes assumed command. For the next two years she was the scourge of the ocean.[57]

When the *Alabama* began burning the prizes which she could not take into neutral ports, Northern anger was passionately expressed. The Chamber of Commerce of the State of New York, condemning British negligence, passed a resolution declaring "that all who willingly aided and abetted this crusade of fire against the commerce of the United States, must be considered as participators in a crime against humanity." [58]

[VI]

It was thus in a situation of growing tension that the tremendous question of British or Franco-British mediation (which, involving recognition of Confederate independence, carried a threat of imminent war) came to a head late in 1862. Lord Russell suggested to Palmerston on August 6 that the government might make some move in October, and it was arranged that

---

57 The Confederacy converted two highly effective commerce raiders of its own, the *Chickamauga* and *Tallahassee;* Coulter, *Confederate States,* 304.

58 Adams in a long letter to Russell, Nov. 20, 1862, and subsequent communications, laid claim to compensation for the depredations of the *Alabama,* and Russell on Dec. 19, 1862, energetically denied liability. These interchanges (*Diplomatic Correspondence, 1862* and *1863*), were first published in the American press Jan. 22, 1864, attracting wide attention. Northern newspapers consistently referred to Confederate privateers as "pirates." The *Florida,* built at Liverpool for the Confederate service, had taken to the high seas in March, 1862, at once sailing to the Bahamas for arms. Court proceedings were begun to condemn her, but the judicial authorities, in what the British later admitted was a miscarriage of justice, released her. Governmental neglect in this instance was less flagrant, but the destruction of American shipping by the *Florida* aroused only less indignation than that by the *Alabama.* See the British Blue Books, *Papers Relating to Proceedings of the Tribunal of Arbitration at Geneva,* 1872, *passim.*

the Cabinet should meet October 23 to discuss the subject. In September Russell explored the intentions of the French Government and found that Thouvenel, always warier than Napoleon, was unexpectedly cool, for he feared that serious consequences might follow a breach with Washington. Palmerston declared that Russia also must be consulted, and this meant another delay. Then news came of Lee's invasion of the North and of Union hopes that he might be crushed. On September 23 Palmerston told Russell that he was in favor of an offer of mediation only "if the Federals sustain a great defeat." Thus far the Palmerstonian realism was sound.

The Prime Minister, in fact, had consistently declared against any immediate effort at mediation as both useless and dangerous. In a lively debate in Parliament on July 18 he had opposed W. S. Lindsay's motion on the subject, declaring that full freedom must be left to the ministry, and the London *Times* had endorsed his stand.

Then early in October, the influential Finance Minister went off at half cock. Gladstone, speaking at Newcastle on the 7th, let complex emotions carry him away. "We may have our own opinions about slavery," he said; "we may be for or against the South; but there is no doubt that Jefferson Davis and other leaders . . . have made an army; they are making, it appears, a navy; and what is more than either, they have made a nation." This unwarranted statement, coming from a powerful member of the Ministry, gave many Britons an impression that the government was about to act. Undoubtedly Gladstone's motives were good. He believed firmly in the principle of what men later termed self-determination. Always an admirer of the American Constitution, he particularly liked its nice balance between national authority and State autonomy. He did not see how the North, even if its armies subjugated the South, could in any way compatible with free institutions control so great and disaffected a minority. As a humanitarian, he was anguished by the red slaughter, for a cousin, Colonel Neville, who spent three months with McClellan's army in the futile peninsular combats, had just sent him a vivid account of the heavy mortality and the sufferings of the wounded. But the effect of his outburst, since he had a strong personal following, was bad.[59]

59 Gladstone was a hater of slavery, a well-wisher of democracy, a man of liberal vision. But he feared that Northern liberty itself might be endangered by the steps needed to pin down a conquered people. As for slavery, he believed that it had thus far been sheltered by the Union flag, that Lincoln's Administration had emphasized their unwillingness to interfere with it, and that the abolitionists had been a small and futile body. If the South separated and world opinion was concentrated on that section, slavery would sooner die; while the North might have a purer, stronger political and social life if relieved of the problem of race relations. Neville's letters made Gladstone feel that Europe could not much longer stand a silent witness of such horrors as Malvern Hill and Second Manassas; and he

And Lord Russell chose this moment for circulating a memorandum to the Cabinet (October 13) arguing that the combined European powers consider proposing an armistice in America. He gave the proposal no explicitly anti-Union cast. He merely asked whether, in view of America's terrible position ("military forces equally balanced, and battles equally sanguinary and indecisive, political animosities aggravated instead of being softened, social organization not improved by a large and benevolent scheme of freedom for the human race, but embittered by exciting the passions of the slave to aid the destructive progress of the armies") Europe ought not to ask both parties, in friendly terms, to halt the fighting in order to weigh calmly the relative advantages of peace or continued bloodshed. But in effect he was proposing Northern acknowledgment of defeat under foreign pressure.

In this crisis the antimediation forces of Britain rapidly mobilized. The *Spectator, Daily News, Morning Star,* and other journals denounced Gladstone's speech.[60] On October 14 Sir George Cornewall Lewis, the war minister, delivered a speech that crushed Gladstone's hasty plea. Lewis, an earnest, high-minded man who had made thorough studies of the lot of the laboring poor in Britain and Ireland, joined a liberal temper to complete sincerity; he was one of the best-trusted members of the House. Cool exactness was his forte. He pointed out that the South had not established a *de facto* independence, was not a nation, and was hence not entitled on moral or legal grounds to recognition. And on the 17th Lewis circulated to the Cabinet an able counter-memorandum to that of Russell, masterly in its handling of international law and the political situation. He pointed out that any mediation proposal would be made not to dispassionate men, but to heated and violent partisans; that an armistice could not be equal in effect on North and South, but must give the Confederacy an advantage; that determination on both sides was rock-like, and the North would be heatedly against compromise; that Washington would be sure to show its resentment in a fashion that might lead to hostilities; and that even if the North acceded, Britain and Europe would be utterly helpless in offering advice on boundaries, the slavery question, and other intricate matters. Implicit in Lewis' argument was his conviction that Great Britain could not afford to wage a costly and dangerous North American war.[61]

Palmerston's caution at once returned. Sounding out Lord Derby, he

---

thought it would be an act of charity to open American eyes to Old World condemnation. C. Collyer, "Gladstone and the Amer. Civil War," *Proceedings Leeds Philosophical Society,* VI, pt. 8 (May, 1951), 583–594. All this does not alter the fact that Gladstone, as he admitted later, made a deplorable *gaffe* by his speech.

60 E.g., *Morning Star*, Oct. 9, 1862.
61 Printed copy, seven pages, War Office 33/12 (1862).

found the leader of the Opposition opposed to any action. On October 22 the Prime Minister wrote Russell that he was "much inclined to agree with Lewis, that we must continue merely to be lookers-on till the war shall have taken a more decided turn." [62] This proved decisive. No formal Cabinet meeting took place on October 23. Instead, a number of ministers, not including Palmerston, held a general discussion which showed that a majority supported Lewis as against Russell. As events proved, the British nation and government had now taken a fixed position against intervention—though one additional crisis of special nature was to occur. Palmerston in a Guildhall speech, November 10, declared the time had not arrived for friendly mediation in America by any European power; and the *Morning Post* and *Times* applauded this stand. Palmerston also expressed hope that India might in some degree supply the nation's cotton needs.[63]

The British emphasized their decision when at the end of October Napoleon III, who had replaced Thouvenel with the more complaisant Drouyn de Lhuys, suddenly let Slidell's promptings and his own adventurous temperament carry him away and proposed that France, England, Prussia, Austria, and Russia suggest an armistice. Palmerston summoned the Cabinet for November 7.[64] But it was hardly necessary for Cornewall Lewis to prepare a second memorandum which, as the Duke of Argyll put it, smashed up the remaining interventionists. This paper contained some good epigrams: "A single intervening power may possibly contrive to satisfy both the adverse parties; but five intervening powers have first to satisfy each other." "What would an eminent diplomatist from Vienna, or Berlin, or St. Petersburg know of the Chicago platform or the Crittenden compromise?" [65] The Cabinet not only rebuffed Napoleon but immediately made its decision public.

By this time the news of emancipation was known throughout Europe. In England particularly the response of the middle classes was tremendous. The spirit with which they greeted Lincoln's proclamation was expressed by the *Morning Star;* "It is indisputably the great fact of the war—the turning point in the history of the American commonwealth—an act only second in courage and probable results to the Declaration of Independence. . . . Is not this a gigantic stride in the paths of Christian and civilized progress?" The *Star* reminded its readers that Granville Clark's inscription in the Abbey hailed him as one who had saved Britain from "employing the arm of freedom to rivet the fetters of bondage." [66]

---

62 G. P. Gooch, ed., *Later Corr. of Lord John Russell,* II, 327, 328; Ephraim Adams, II, 55–57.
63 Nov. 11, 1862.
64 Temperley and Penson, 298.
65 "Confidential," War Office 33/12, twenty-five printed pages.
66 Oct. 6, 1862.

Among conservative groups, to be sure, the response to the proclamation was hostile. The *Times* sneered at the Lincoln Administration: "Exactly when its military and political powers are most broken, it threatens." Delane predicted that the inevitable separation would now be accompanied by horrible scenes of servile rebellion, and that Lincoln might quit office amid the massacre of white women and children, and the extermination of the black race.[67] But nearly all liberal journals and leaders shared the feeling of John Bright, who wrote Sumner that the Union was great only when it was a Union of Freedom, and that any retreat from the proclamation would be the most deplorable event in history. The *Spectator* qualified its approval only by saying that the proclamation should have been national and complete.

And when the prophecies of slave revolt proved empty, British opinion veered heavily toward endorsement of the Union position. The middle class was rising, and the breeze of favor soon became a gale. Crowded public meetings, beginning in December, were held in all the large commercial towns: Sheffield, Bristol, Glasgow, Liverpool, Leeds, Edinburgh, Birmingham, Manchester, York, and by the end of March, 1863, fifty other places. Bright made the Birmingham meeting memorable by one of his finest bursts of oratory.[68] The veteran abolitionist George Thompson spoke twenty-one times in one month. Fervently worded resolutions were sent to the American Minister assailing slavery, and praying the North to press on until not a bondsman was left on American soil. Letters upholding Lincoln multiplied in the press. The London *Times* declared that the gatherings were made up of nobodies, but Adams reported to Seward that they were composed of just the people who had stopped the slave trade and compelled emancipation in the colonies.

One London meeting, that in Exeter Hall on January 29, 1863, the largest the city had seen since the Corn Law agitation, resounded like a clap of thunder. Long before it began the main hall was jammed; a lower room rapidly filled up; and thousands more organized a meeting in the street. Emancipation and Reunion were proclaimed the watchwords of the evening.

---

67 Oct. 6, 21, 1862.
68 Bright invoked the names of Cavour, Mazzini, and Victor Hugo as symbols, with Lincoln, of the movement of world liberalism. He expressed his faith that the Western republic would never be riven asunder. "I have another and a far brighter vision before my gaze. It may be but a vision, but I will cherish it. I see one vast confederation stretching from the frozen North in unbroken line to the glowing South, and from the wild billows of the Atlantic westward to the calmer waters of the Pacific main—and I see one people, and one language, and one law, and one faith, and, over all that wide continent, the home of freedom, and a refuge for the oppressed of every race and of every clime." He continued making effective speeches. It is not strange that Lincoln a year later (Dec. 17, 1863), pardoned a rash young man from Birmingham, caught in a privateering expedition, "especially as a public mark of the esteem held by the United States of America for the high character and steady friendship of . . . John Bright."

The enthusiasm of the triple assemblage exceeded all expectations. Speakers were interrupted by dispatches reporting similar demonstrations under way in Bradford and Stroud; the recent Union victory at Murfreesboro was hailed with cheers as loud as if it had been a British triumph; and at the first mention of Lincoln's name the whole gathering rose and applauded wildly for several minutes.

"In the Indian summer of 1859," said the London *Illustrated News*, "the genius of Emancipation was incarnated in the persons of John Brown and his motley score of followers; in the autmn of 1862 her instrument is the President of the United States, wielding the military and financial resources of one of the richest and most powerful nations of the earth." Henceforth, added the editor, the conflict became a revolution.[69]

[VII]

A great war—even a civil war—is a calamity to the whole world, and an international peril. By its destruction of wealth, dislocation of commerce, and impairment of order and security, it injures everybody on the globe. Americans, by a reprehensible failure of statesmanship, had involved themselves in the bloodiest and costliest war since Napoleon's day. They could not expect other countries to treat it as a purely American affair. When it brought great British and French populations to penury, it became a legitimate concern of the governments in London and Paris.

The danger of Anglo-French involvement did not arise from Machiavellianism in high places. It arose, fundamentally, from the fact that when the supposedly short war of 1861 was converted into the patently long war of 1862, without any grand moral purpose to justify it, without any prospect that either side could rationally impose its will on the other, and with steadily increasing hardship to other lands, impatience inevitably seized foreign peoples and leaders. They were certain to respond to the same impulse that led President Wilson in January, 1917, to appeal to the Allies and Central Powers for a negotiated peace without victory. British policy alone had decisive importance, for Napoleon, who *was* Machiavellian, was too weak to be important. When a man of the intellectual and moral stature of Gladstone took an impulsive stand on the wrong side, people of foggier vision might well turn against both warring sections and call for an armistice. Lord John Russell's proposal to discuss mediation was not prompted by the tariff, or a desire to reduce American power, or sheer bad temper. It was prompted

69 Oct. 18, 1862. The song "John Brown's Body" had become well known in Britain.

mainly by perplexity over a terrible transatlantic disaster that seemed becoming an endless international nuisance.

The threat of intervention was averted, in the first instance, by the realism of British leadership. It was not ended by the stubborn stand of Lancashire workers; courageous as they were, they had no great political power. It was not ended by Cobden or Bright. It was not ended by the Emancipation Proclamation, for the decision was taken when that edict was new and was regarded dubiously in wide British circles. What ended it was Palmerston's circumspect common sense, George Cornewall Lewis' brilliant analysis of what interference would mean, the blunt opposition of Milner Gibson and the Duke of Argyll, and the Ministry's wholesome fear of middle-class opinion.

Later, and in the long run, the British decision against intervention was taken by massive middle-class and working-class opinion, swayed by two forces, one moral and one material. So long as the war lacked a high moral object, and so long as it seemed uncertain that the North had the stamina and skill to fight to victory, a great body of British opinion was gelatinous. The Emancipation Proclamation dispelled the first ground of British doubt. The news of Antietam and the immense Northern preparations for the campaign of 1863 ended the second doubt. British opinion ran parallel to large sections of Northern opinion, for many Northerners had little heart in the war until the government adopted emancipation, and many in the summer of 1862 feared that with his weak and bickering generals Lincoln could never win. After the beginning of 1863 so massive a body of British opinion was with the North that no leader could have brooked its might.

The South might at any time have vastly improved its chances of foreign support and recognition had it been able to take a single mighty step: to promise that on obtaining its independence it would gradually liberate the slaves. But that step was out of the question. In the eyes of many Southerners the Confederacy was fighting to maintain slavery. The time was to come, late in the war, when desperate Confederate commanders would recommend the enlistment of Negroes in the army, with freedom as a reward. But even then the suggestion aroused the bitterest antagonism, and in 1862–63 any step toward liberation lay outside the realm of political possibility. The Confederacy could offer Europe, for breaking the blockade, free trade, abundant cotton, and long-term friendship. It could not proffer the one reform that would have silenced many enemies and won countless friends.

Examined in detail, the diplomatic record of Britain, France, and the United States alike offers much to censure. Seldom has a foreign minister committed a costlier blunder than Lord Russell's mishandling of the *Alabama*. Not often has a prime minister lost his temper in a more regrettable way than

Palmerston did over Ben Butler's order that New Orleans women who insulted Northern troops should be treated as women of the town. "Pam" wrote Charles Francis Adams that he could not adequately express his disgust, for it was absolutely infamous "to hand over the female inhabitants of a conquered city to the unbridled license of an unrestrained soldiery." Butler's order, deplorable as it was, did not reach such depths as that! Adams was quick to ask Palmerston whether this was an official or unofficial communication; obviously, it was indefensible in either light. The greedy machinations of Napoleon III respecting Mexico, and his shifty, timid suggestions of interference in the war, were contemptible. But it must be acknowledged that Seward's desire to provoke a collision with Spain and his wishful talk of a world conflagration present him in a worse light than any in which Lord Russell appears. And while Adams' conduct was always officially correct, his stiff, icy pride, touching the borders of rudeness, stood in unhappy contrast with the genial courtesy always exhibited by Lord Lyons in Washington.

The great redeeming feature of the record is the decisive part played by considerations of decency, justice, and humanity as felt by the plain people on both sides of the ocean. The liberal sentiment of America decreed emancipation; the liberal sentiment of Britain responded. Lincoln realized the significance of these facts. On December 30, 1862, six thousand workingmen and others of Manchester sent him an address declaring that the erasure of the foul blot of slavery would make his name honored and revered by posterity. Greatly touched, Lincoln replied that he knew well the sufferings of the Lancashire workers. "Under these circumstances, I cannot but regard your decisive utterance upon the question as an instance of sublime Christian heroism which has not been surpassed in any age or in any country. It is, indeed, an energetic and inspiring assurance of the inherent power of truth and of the ultimate and universal triumph of justice, humanity, and freedom."

11

The War-Torn West

WE HAVE seen how the West, a region bright with Union hopes, suddenly darkened when on July 24 the advance troops of Braxton Bragg's Army of the Mississippi marched into the vital railway center of Chattanooga. In this area, too, Southern generalship outstripped the Northern. Bragg, whose brilliant management of his artillery at Buena Vista had never been forgotten by Jefferson Davis, was making an impressive new record. He had capably assisted Albert Sidney Johnston to organize his army at Corinth, had led a corps at Shiloh with energy and dexterity, and had helped reconcentrate the shattered forces after the retreat. Davis, making him a full general in charge of the Western Department, naturally turned to him when he lost faith in Beauregard after the evacuation of Corinth, and when the Creole general made the mistake of leaving his command at this anxious moment, without permission, to recruit his health.[1]

It was obvious that the Confederates, since Halleck so obligingly dissipated the grand Union army, had three main objects: first, to fortify Vicksburg so strongly as to make its capture almost impossible; second, to hold Chattanooga as a base of operations against Nashville or Louisville; and third, to use the forces of Sterling Price and Van Dorn to keep Grant occupied at Corinth. Bragg, who had graduated at West Point seventh in his class with Hooker, John Sedgwick, and Jubal A. Early, was a close student of war but not a masterly strategist. In fact, his rapid movement upon Chattanooga had been prompted by Kirby-Smith, stationed at Knoxville, who possessed a more incisive mind. He had many faults and limitations, for he was brusque, narrow, and quarrelsome; his troops detested him as a martinet; and he showed a fatal hesitancy at critical moments. But he possessed cleverness, a firm grasp of fundamental principles of army management, and abundant energy directed by a meticulous sense of duty. He successfully achieved all three of his immediate objects. Clearly, he was a fair match for his principal antagonist, Buell.

1 Seitz, *Bragg*, 123–167; Roman, *Beauregard*, I, 400–420; T. Harry Williams, *Beauregard*, 161. Beauregard by the latter part of June had reconstituted an army of 47,000 men to face Halleck's forces of 120,000. His record was excellent.

This Southwestern theater was a region of grandiose distances, where armies seemed at times swallowed up in the landscape, and long cavalry raids found special scope. While in the East rival generals maneuvered in the relatively narrow space defined by the Potomac, Shenandoah, and James, in the West the fighting seesawed over a broad empire from the Appalachians to Texas. Bragg was fortunate in the service of two brilliant cavalry leaders, John Hunt Morgan and Nathan Bedford Forrest, who made distance an ally.

Nothing better illustrated Halleck's folly in scattering small armies over a huge territory than the successful forays of these cavalry leaders. Morgan, a Mexican War veteran, a successful Kentucky businessman, and the organizer in 1857 of the Lexington Rifles, had fought at Shiloh. Grasping the opportunity to seize supplies and derange enemy communications, on July 4 he set out from Knoxville on a thousand-mile dash into his own bluegrass region of Kentucky. Though nominally heading a brigade, he never had more than 1,500 well-drilled men, and almost any loyal county in his path could have turned out an equal force. Yet he took hundreds of prisoners, terrorized half the State, captured valuable stores, and while Indiana and Ohio were hurrying forces to the rescue, got back safely to Knoxville.[2] Louisville had been so panic-stricken that its banks moved their money to safety and hundreds of citizens prepared to flee across the Ohio. Morgan's blow was the more stinging because the Confederates accompanied and followed it by similar strokes. Raiding parties cut the Nashville & Chattanooga and Nashville & Decatur railroads, crippling the communications of Buell's army. Squadrons of cavalry made sudden descents upon Florence in Alabama, Chickasaw in Mississippi, and Savanna in Tennessee, and temporarily blockaded the Tennessee River.

Immediately after Morgan's raid, Nathan Bedford Forrest, the unlettered son of a blacksmith, a man of native genius who had risen from farm laborer and slave trader to become a rich planter and an alderman of Memphis, delivered an even more humiliating thrust. He had begun the war by equipping a mounted battalion at his own cost. After extricating his command at Donelson and fighting at Shiloh he had now become a brigadier. On July 13 he and 1,400 hard-riding troopers caught a larger Union garrison at Murfreesboro, Tennessee, and with a loss of only 25 killed, captured 1,200 men, four guns, and a half million dollars worth of material. This surrender outraged Buell, then at Huntsville, Alabama. "Few more disgraceful examples of neglect of duty," he wrote, "can be found in the history of wars."[3] The Union troops in

2 B. W. Duke, History of Morgan's Cavalry, 114 ff.; Louisville corr., N. Y. Tribune, Aug. 7, 1862; Columbus, Ky., corr., N. Y. Tribune, Aug. 6, 1862. Morgan's report is in O. R., I, xvi, pt. 1, pp. 767–770.

3 General Order 32, July 21, 1862; O. R., I, xvi, pt. 1, pp. 810, 811, pt. 2, pp. 131–157; Wyeth, Forrest, 83–103.

northern Alabama, reduced to half rations whenever their railways were cut, shared his anger.

While these raids checked and embarrassed the Union forces, so did a sudden blaze of guerrilla warfare. The wide distances, the scattering of Union forces, and the absence of any heavy campaigning fostered it, for when open war ends, irregular fighting begins. Forrest and Morgan could not be called guerrilla leaders, nor M. Jeff Thompson, who in August did some smart fighting with Union forces near Helena, Arkansas. Eastern Tennessee, however, was infested with vicious guerrilla bands, the endemic guerrilla activity in Missouri became epidemic during the summer, and the same fever infected Union-occupied parts of Mississippi, Alabama, and western Tennessee.

The Missouri situation became particularly serious. Notorious rebel bushwhackers took courage from McClellan's failure, the Western standstill, and the factional bitterness between "claybanks" and "charcoals." They found unexpected aid in General John M. Schofield's policy of ordering the militia, which he commanded, into the field along with national forces, for this aroused the apprehension of Southern sympathizers that they would be drafted into the army, and thousands flocked to the guerrilla standards where hundreds had been expected. An indiscreet order by Stanton directing the military authorities to enforce the new Confiscation Act, though soon annulled by Lincoln, also fanned the embers.[4] Early in August some observers estimated that 10,000 Confederate guerrillas were abroad in Missouri, their temper so ferocious that in certain districts all able-bodied men took to camps in the woods and left only women and children to occupy the houses.[5] Once more, men could well question the wisdom of the order which late in 1861 had annulled Frémont's agreement with Price, under which hostilities were to be restricted to armies in the field, and guerrilla groups on both sides suppressed. Meanwhile, in East Tennessee one guerrilla outrage aroused special indignation in the North. Brave General Robert L. McCook, one of eight brothers who gained fame as "the fighting McCooks," seized while ill and carried in an ambulance, was slain in cold blood by rebel partisans.[6]

The disorders in Missouri were in part the natural result of the deep social and political antagonisms that divided the people, in part the fruit of the rash precipitancy with which Frank Blair and Nathaniel Lyon had opened the war there, and in part the consequence of the growing harshness with which Union

4 Schofield, *Forty-six Years*, 56, 57; R. S. Brownlee, *Gray Ghosts of the Confederacy*, 53–179.
5 So dilatory did Schofield seem to the radical faction in Missouri in repressing guerrilla warfare that a St. Louis meeting early in August appointed a committee to visit Lincoln and ask for a new commander, but it met a cool reception. *Ibid.*, 58 ff.
6 Nashville corr., dated Aug. 14 in N. Y. *Tribune*, Aug. 23, 1862.

commanders—Halleck, Schofield, Curtis—enforced military government. Martial law, first exercised by Frémont and formally authorized by Lincoln on November 1, 1861, was a necessity. The rigor of its application, however, was not. Halleck's arbitrary fines and assessments, his many death sentences, Curtis's wholesale arrests, the suppression of all freedom of speech and publication, the banishment of citizens and restrictions on trade, did more harm than good. They fomented bitterness, rebellion, and bloodshed.

Elsewhere the upflare was fiercely spasmodic. In Louisiana, Alabama, and western Tennessee, as Union detachments spread over a large area, helpless people fell into a mood of desperation. Many communities had been almost completely drained of able-bodied men; the overseers fled as troops approached; and large numbers of Negroes flocked into the Union camps, while those who remained were often insubordinate. Raiding parties of Union troops searched the countryside. Most planters had chafed under the cotton-burning activities of Confederate detachments, but they resented far more the rough seizures by Yankee forces, which took all the cotton in sight even to the widow's single bale, offered a pitiful compensation of ten or twelve cents a pound, and if that was refused, paid nothing. They also often seized livestock, grain, vegetables, and household possessions.[7] Inevitably, citizens past military age organized bands to attack the scattered Federal units, cut supply lines, and inspire Negroes with their old deference to white Southerners. When ably led, such groups not only heartened the Southerners, but crippled Union operations, playing almost the part of Marion and Light-Horse Harry Lee in the Revolution.[8]

We have said that all three of the main objects of the Confederates were achieved in the summer of 1862. Vicksburg, high on its bluffs from 100 to 200 feet above the Mississippi, was fortified front and rear. When Farragut's fleet ran past on June 28 the Confederate batteries possessed only 29 guns, with 10,000 troops in or near the city. More guns were mounted, the new well-armored ram *Arkansas* anchored under them in mid-July, and the capable engineer S. H. Lockett began about September 1 an elaborate system of redoubts, redans, lunettes, and field works.[9] Meanwhile, Grant in the wide new command which the departure of Halleck left him was immobilized, for Bragg posted 35,000 men at Grand Junction between Corinth and Memphis to menace his communications, and he dared not stir. At the end of August he had fewer than 50,000 men in the whole area from Cairo to Corinth, including Sherman's

7 E. L. Acee, Coahama County, Ala., to Gov. J. J. Pettus, July 29, 1862, Pettus Papers.
8 Edward Delong, June 26, 1862 to Earl Van Dorn, Palmer Coll. Western Reserve Hist. Soc.
9 For Lockett's account see *Battles and Leaders*, III, 482–492.

force at Memphis.[10] As for the final Southern objective, Bragg collected enough troops at Chattanooga to ensure the safety of that key point.

Indeed, Bragg had an army strong enough to attempt more. After he seized the invaluable railroad junction, his logical next step was the invasion of Kentucky. By mid-August a new drama was about to unfold in the West. It held terrifying possibilities to the North. If Bragg marched through Kentucky unchecked, the Union armies would have to take their stand on the Ohio; Nashville, isolated, would have to be evacuated; and the nation's battlelines in the West, as in the East before Antietam, would be pushed farther back than when the conflict began.

Thus began one of the most picturesque campaigns of the war. It had pictorial beauty in its theater, the Kentucky country of bluegrass, rhododendron, and laurel, of deep narrow rivers, limestone caves, and hazy peaks. Some of its leaders were impressive figures, like the blithe Kirby-Smith, a large-spirited man who delighted in books, war, and hunting, and the fearless, swaggering Forrest. The campaign was above all picturesque in its crisscross of movements, and its plunge on both sides from high aims to impotent endings.

[I]

Bragg of course took pains to mystify his opponent. Buell knew that he was planning an aggressive movement—but on just what line? He might drive into eastern Kentucky, he might strike at Nashville and central Kentucky, or he might attempt to move around Buell's northern flank and into his rear, severing his communications. What was certain was that, having gained the initiative by his concentration of forces and the cavalry raids, he meant to keep it. Both generals knew that they were playing for the highest stakes. If Bragg could defeat Buell he might regain most of the valleys of the Tennessee and Cumberland; but if he were so defeated that he lost Chattanooga, all of Kentucky and Tennessee would pass forever under Union sway, and the vital railroad which linked Richmond with Georgia would be severed. The stakes also included men and supplies, for if Bragg repossessed central Tennessee and lower Kentucky he might obtain thousands of recruits and valuable stores.

Like a pugilist whirling to meet an adversary, Buell shifted his forces to a new line running from Stevenson, Alabama, through Winchester, Tennessee, to Murfreesboro, facing east toward Bragg.[11] He had barely completed the

10 *Memoirs*, I, 395.
11 This new line gave middle Tennessee and southern Kentucky a better protection from Confederate invasion, but it abandoned the Memphis & Charleston Railroad in northern Alabama.

movement when on August 28 Bragg began to move northward. The Confederate War Department had advised the timing of Bragg's thrust: as Lee's rebel army invaded Maryland, Bragg's would strike at Louisville and Cincinnati. "The country is in peril," declared Greeley. "Viewed from the standpoint of the public estimate of 'the situation,' it is in extreme peril." [12]

In the West excitement ran high. Governor David Tod of Ohio reached Cincinnati on September 2 to find martial law in force, large numbers of men fortifying the hills on the Kentucky shore, and citizens enrolling themselves for home defense. That same day the Kentucky legislature met in emergency session in Louisville, where martial law also reigned. Governor James F. Robinson three days earlier had issued a proclamation calling the people to arms, and the legislature passed measures to strengthen the forces. Everywhere in Bragg's path towns were being evacuated by Union forces. Lew Wallace abandoned Paris to fall back on Covington and Cincinnati, and General H. G. Wright, under a supposed threat from Forrest's and Morgan's cavalry, was preparing to quit Lexington and Frankfort.

Bragg had decided against an attack on Nashville, for he had in view a bolder plan which if successful would leave that city an easy prey to subsequent movements. It was to thrust his army all the way from Chattanooga across Kentucky to Louisville, taking steps as he went to cut Buell's supply line, the Louisville & Nashville Railroad, and thus impede his intercepting movement. Relying upon Van Dorn and Price to hold Grant, he had expected other lieutenants to aid him in defeating Buell and overrunning Kentucky. E. Kirby-Smith, who held a coordinate command, would move his army from Knoxville, isolate the Union troops at Cumberland Gap, and take Lexington; General Humphrey Marshall would simultaneously descend from western Virginia into eastern Kentucky. "We confidently hope," Bragg wrote Van Dorn just before starting, "to meet you upon the Ohio." [13]

Did he have enough men for so dangerous a movement? The answer was doubtful. After the campaign Confederates were wont to say that they had been outnumbered two to one, and though the army statistics are foggier than usual, odds were clearly against them. Bragg's returns on August 27 gave him 27,816 officers and men fit for duty, while Kirby-Smith, who had headquarters at Knoxville to guard East Tennessee, wrote him that he would bring to Lexington about 12,000 effectives.[14] Against this total of about 40,000, Buell in

12 N. Y. *Tribune*, Sept. 4, 1862. Bragg as early as July 21 had telegraphed Davis that he meant to advance from Chattanooga (Seitz, 149); later on direct evidence of coordination with Lee's invasion appears. See Appendix II.

13 Cincinnati *Enquirer*, Sept. 2, 1862; Eggleston, *Confederate War*, II, 62.

14 Union officers as always overestimated Confederate numbers. Gen. A. M. McCook, putting a spy into Chattanooga, reported to Buell Aug. 19 that Bragg had 80,000 men! O. R..

June reported 57,706 in his scattered units present for duty. Bragg made a cardinal error in leaving 10,000 men in Middle Tennessee just to watch Nashville, for if incorporated in his army of invasion they would have heavily augmented his striking power. He had no choice but to attack.[15] After the defeats and retreats earlier in the year, the Western Confederacy demanded a victory, the army lost health and morale whenever it stood idle, and he desperately needed supplies and new recruiting grounds.

At first all went well for the Confederates. Kirby-Smith, at thirty-nine a marvel of energy, marched his 12,000 men through the mountains into the bluegrass region of Kentucky, struck a smaller force at Richmond, and totally routed it, taking some 4,000 prisoners, 10,000 small arms, 9 guns, and quantities of wagons and provisions. Union leaders after the battle could collect only 1,500 survivors. The result was the abandonment of nearly all central Kentucky to the invaders. "From the eastern borders of the State almost to the line of the Louisville & Nashville Railroad," wrote a correspondent, "the rebels have it now their own way." While Union troops in and about Lexington, with those along the Lexington & Covington, fell back to the Ohio, Kirby-Smith's ragged, partly shoeless, and till now indifferently armed forces occupied the town. Some Southern sympathizers flocked to his colors. "Kentucky is rising *en masse*," joyously proclaimed his chief of staff.[16]

In Cincinnati the versatile Lew Wallace had taken command and begun energetic preparations for battle. He felt certain that Kirby-Smith would march on the city. "Here is the material of war," he told an aide, "goods, groceries, salt, supplies, machinery, and so on—enough to restock the whole bogus Confederacy." Summoning citizens to work on entrenchments or shoulder guns, he brought out artisans, storekeepers, and professional men, with a large Negro contingent, to toil with desperate energy. A pontoon bridge built in a single day carried them across the Ohio to dig a semicircle of trenches, ten miles long. The works were garrisoned in part by Cincinnatians, and in larger part by a motley array of minutemen who poured in from half of Ohio—"the squirrel hunters." Young, middle-aged, and old, they had left the plow, anvil, and desk bearing all types of arms. While field pieces were wheeled into place, seven steamboats rudely fitted out as warships began patrolling the river.[17]

But though Southern reconnaissance units under General Henry Heath came

---

I, xvi, pt. 2, pp. 367, 368. The question of numbers is discussed in *Battles and Leaders*, III, 4–8; Ropes, *Civil War*, II, 393–405; Cist, *Army of the Cumberland*, 68, 69, without any absolutely dependable result. Eaton, *Story of the Confederacy*, 193, 194, gives Bragg 40,000 men, and Buell (ultimately) 58,000.

15 See Buell's defense of his campaign in O. R., I, xvi, pt. 1, pp. 21–65.

16 Louisville corr., N. Y. *Tribune*, Sept. 12, 1862; Parks, *Kirby Smith*, 220. Kirby-Smith had started so early that he took Lexington on Aug. 30.

17 T. B. Read, "The Siege of Cincinnati," *Atlantic*, XI (Feb. 1863), 229 ff. Read was a

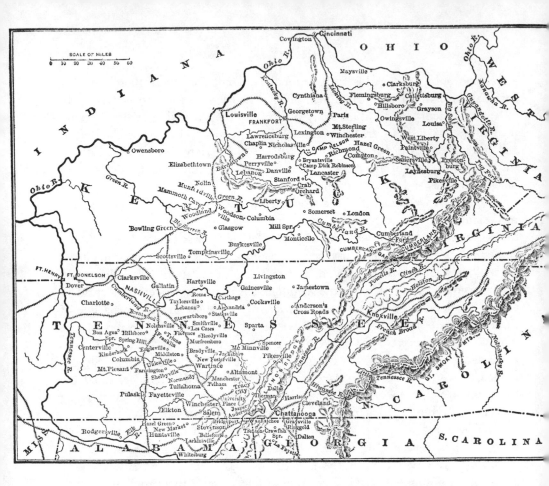

THE BRAGG-BUELL CAMPAIGNS

close enough to skirmish with Northern pickets, their main objective lay else-where. Wallace told Cincinnatians that they could boast to posterity of their impromptu fortifications: "The enemy came and looked at them and stole away in the night." The Confederate goal, however, was Louisville. By September 12 Buell, who had strengthened the forces at Nashville by three divisions under Thomas, realized the true direction of the Southern thrust, and called Thomas back. The two armies began a race for Louisville, using parallel roads—Bragg in front.

It was obviously Bragg's duty to intercept Buell's march, force a battle, and try to crush him. As Richard Taylor wrote later, Buell had so scattered his

---

staff associate of Wallace. The two men hold real if minor places in American literature. At first practically all work before Cincinnati was done gratuitously, but later laborers were hired. In St. Louis the fortifications which Frémont had built were hastily put in order for defense.

forces that the chance of besting him was good.[18] The crisis came just after mid-September, coinciding with that in Maryland. Bragg on September 16–17, in full drive for the Ohio, captured a strong Union fort at Munfordville, some sixty-five miles south of Louisville, taking 4,000 prisoners, 4,000 stand of arms and 10 cannon. His troops, greatly elated, expected to take a stand there, halt Buell's oncoming forces, and overthrow him. Their expectations rose high when Bragg placed his army in a strong position south of the Green River with the fort as part of his line. He was squarely across Buell's communications with Louisville, able to get ample supplies from middle Kentucky, and within easy reach of Marshall's and Kirby-Smith's reinforcements. All observers along Bragg's march were impressed by the destitute condition of many Confederate troops, and their poor physical condition. Neither in Lexington nor elsewhere had they found much. One weary barefoot soldier in Lexington was heard mournfully exclaiming: "Plenty of socks and drawers, but nary a shoe!"

On the 18th, writes Joseph Wheeler, the rebel cavalry leader, Bragg called him in and explained his plans for battle. "I never saw him more determined or more confident. The entire army was in the best of spirits. . . . It is true our back was to a river, but it was fordable at several places. . . ." [19] In fact, no better position could be wished from which to fight a battle.

And then, with one of the greatest opportunities of the war in his hands, Bragg fell a victim to his mortal weakness, lack of grit in a crisis. On the 20th Thomas united with Buell's army, while Kirby-Smith's independent force had not yet joined Bragg. Actually Kirby-Smith was waiting for Bragg's orders to march against Louisville. But Bragg would neither make that march nor fight Buell. He feared that the Union columns, which refused to attack his chosen line, were too strong to be met elsewhere. "With my effective force present reduced by sickness, exhaustion, and the recent affair before the intrenchments at Munfordville to half that of the enemy," he wrote later, "I could not prudently afford to attack him there in his selected position." He turned aside to Bardstown.[20] Bragg's statement cannot be reconciled with Buell's subsequent assertion that he was ready to give battle to Bragg at Munfordville if he remained there; that skirmishing took place, but the main body of Confederates withdrew that night; and that he drove Bragg's rear guard out of Munfordville next day, and pressed it "until he turned off the main road toward Bardstown." The fact was that neither general had stomach for a battle.

When he did so Buell pressed forward with determined speed, and easily

18 *Destruction and Reconstruction*, 101; cf. the exhaustive investigation of Buell's operations by a military commission, O. R., I, xvi, pt. 1, pp. 5–726.
19 *Battles and Leaders*, III, 10. Buell reached Bowling Green, Ky., more than a third of the distance from Nashville to Louisville, on Sept. 14.
20 Buell, *Battles and Leaders*, II, 42; cf. Bragg's report, O. R., I, xvi, pt. 1, pp. 1088 ff.

crossed the Green River, with a clear road ahead. On September 25th his advance guard was marching down the Louisville streets. All along the road his flank offered an inviting target for attack, but Bragg, Polk, and Hardee pleaded the exhaustion of their divisions as a reason for remaining inert. Once ensconced in Louisville, Buell displayed remarkable administrative power in reorganizing his troops, while he collected from Indiana and Ohio numerous fresh troops. The Western blow of the Confederacy had been parried at almost the same time that Lee's Eastern stroke was halted at Antietam.

It was now the turn of the Union forces to take the offensive. At the beginning of October, Buell's three corps moved southward from Louisville by forced marches over three roads to find and fight the enemy. By that time the Confederates had broken into numerous units scattered through seven or eight counties busily foraging and recruiting. They made few enlistments, for as Kirby-Smith wrote Bragg, although the hearts of many Kentuckians were with the South, their heads bade them cling to the bluegrass and their horses. And then, Bragg had won no great victory! The Union leaders expected that the approach of their army would force the Confederates to concentrate and retreat into Tennessee.

[II]

This Kentucky campaign, costly and inclusive, created deep dissatisfaction North and South. The North felt a sense of outrage when it heard that Buell had been compelled to leave northern Alabama and fall back across Tennessee, across Kentucky, in a frantic effort to save Louisville and Cincinnati. Andrew Johnson made an urgent demand for Buell's removal, which many Kentucky Unionists seconded; Governor Oliver P. Morton of Indiana led a still fiercer outcry in that State; Ohio throbbed with anger. Lincoln himself, to whom the borderland was especially dear, was perplexed and irritated. Buell, a cold, reserved, formal man, had never been popular with officers or men. "Now," wrote the Louisville corespondent of the New York *Tribune*, "the want of sympathy between him and his command has grown into utter hatred and contempt. . . ." Although an exaggeration, this expressed a widespread feeling.

As soon as Buell arrived in Louisville, Halleck had united all the troops of the region under his command so that three corps might be formed. General William Nelson, the former naval officer who had expedited Buell's march to Shiloh, had been working day and night to organize old troops, new regiments, and home guards to meet Bragg if he approached. He was a man of imperious temper, demoniac energy, and brutal manners. Nobody could come nearer doing the impossible in an emergency; nobody could earn the mortal enmity of more associates. His language to subordinate officers, soldiers, and citizens was often a mixture of forecastle profanity and Billingsgate obscenity, roared out in a way that earned him the name of "Old Bull Nelson." After his return from the defeat at Lexington he was said to have boasted that he cut down some Union men who fought badly. Indiana soldiers felt such hatred that many were thought determined to kill him in the first battle.[21] The day before Buell's army marched south against Bragg, an aggrieved Indiana officer, Jeff. C. Davis, had a hot altercation with Nelson in the Galt House and fatally shot him.[22]

At the same time, as a result of Western pressure, Washington ordered Buell to turn his command over to George H. Thomas. With characteristic modesty, Thomas, who knew how well Buell had met adverse circumstances, at once telegraphed Halleck requesting that Buell be reinstated. Capable division and brigade commanders also remonstrated, while some of Buell's old troops showed resentment. The outcome was his restoration, but his position remained precarious.

Northern anger at Buell, however, was nothing compared with Southern anger at Bragg. Why had he not required Kirby-Smith to unite with him? Why did he not fight Buell near Munfordville? If he did not mean to fight, why had he wasted precious days there instead of marching posthaste against ill-defended Louisville? He held all the aces, and then refused to play them.

It is true that certain excuses could be made for Bragg. His army was smaller than Buell's, and poorly armed; he had lost heavily by hard marches, sickness, and casualties; and he was fettered by the Confederate leaning toward independent commands, which gave Kirby-Smith an equal authority.[23] The result was that at the decisive moment the two Confederate armies were more than a hundred miles apart, neither was fully informed of the other's plans, and although Kirby-Smith was anxious to cooperate, he followed his own ideas about strategy. Nevertheless, a bolder general in Bragg's place would have occupied Louisville. Had he marched on the city just before or after the Munfordville fight, he could almost certainly have taken it. Buell on September 22 instructed Nelson that it would not be "advisable for you to attempt a defense of Louisville unless you are strongly intrenched." Once settled there, Bragg

21 Cincinnati *Enquirer*, Oct. 1, 1862.

22 *Papers*, Mil. Hist. Soc. of Mass., VII, 278–279. Davis's crime went unpunished, because of his good military record, the general feeling against Nelson, and the influence of Governor Morton, who had accompanied him to the Galt House; James B. Fry, *Military Miscellanies*. Chase (*Diary and Correspondence*, 98) commented on the contrast between Nelson's great talents and his "cruelty and passion and tyranny," especially when drunk.

23 Ropes remarks on "the folly, which both the Union and the Confederate Governments were so constantly committing, of having more than one commanding officer in one theatre of war." *Civil War*, II, 403.

could have refitted and rearmed his troops, left a small garrison, and marched out to meet Buell where he liked.[24]

While North and South thus hummed with indignant critics, Buell and Bragg commenced a short-lived game of hide and seek. The Confederate general still had it in his power, if he acted with decision and energy, to strike a heavy blow in a new direction. Since Nashville had been left with a weak garrison, he could turn thither, and by a rapid march seize the capital. This was precisely what Buell feared he would do. But Bragg's vacillation was matched by a dyspeptic pessimism. He decided against attempting a partial restoration of the Confederate lines held just after Donelson, for he was still much more interested in Kentucky than in regaining central Tennessee. Leaving his army at Bardstown under Leonides Polk, he wasted time in hurrying to Frankfort to assist in the futile inauguration of a provisional Confederate governor and to confer with Kirby-Smith. In the days that followed, Bragg and Buell, each with his forces scattered, each misconceiving the purposes of each other, fumbled nervously to bring on an encounter.[25]

When parts of the two armies stumbled on each other at Perryville, one of the most peculiar battles of the entire war in the West unexpectedly occurred. The date was October 8. A heavy drought had seared central Kentucky, with such severe hardship to men and beasts that the movement of troops was affected by desperate searches for water.[26] Bragg was on the field in person, though Leonidas Polk had selected the main position of the 16,000 rebels engaged. Buell, injured by a fall from his horse, was only a few miles distant, but conditions of terrain and atmosphere were such that the battle raged violently for hours without his knowledge. The most striking tactical feature of the combat was the assault of Cheatham's division upon the Union left, where two Northern generals fell and green troops gave way in panic. Savage fighting continued until dark, when the Southern troops held possession of the field. "At every point of battle," Joe Wheeler writes, "the Confederates had been victorious," [27] and Bragg later asserted that they had

24 "General Bragg is a good officer, a man of fair capacity," wrote Gen. Jones C. Withers this fall, adding that he was "self-willed, arrogant, and dictatorial"; Feb. 13, 1862, to C. C. Clay, Clay Papers, Duke. But his martinet qualities were of slight consequence compared with his hesitant defeatism. For a defense of him see K. P. Williams, IV, 108.

25 Bragg said he still hoped to give battle to Buell; O. R., I, xvi, pt. 2, p. 896; Polk, II, 147. But, when Buell's forces reached Bardstown they found Bragg gone.

26 Greeley, American Conflict, II, 217, 218. The examination of Buell by a court of inquiry, O. R., I, xvi, pt. 1, pp. 8–726, is a mine of information, and Lew Wallace, Autobiography, II, 641–653, furnishes a commentary.

27 Battles and Leaders, III, 17. One Union officer relates that as he reached the crest of a ridge, the whole sight and sound of the conflict burst upon him. "At one bound, my horse carried me from the stillness into the uproar of battle." Mil. Hist. Soc. of Mass., VII, 286. Perryville was heralded in the Northern press as a Union victory—"the rebels two to our one"; see N. Y. Herald, Times, Phila. Press, Oct. 15, 16, 1862.

driven their opponents back two miles. They had taken ten or fifteen cannon.

But if a Confederate victory, Perryville was also a Confederate blunder. It was folly on Bragg's part to let his army be drawn into battle before he had concentrated his troops with those of Kirby-Smith. Confronted now by immensely superior forces, he had no choice immediately after the fight but to retreat to Harrodsburg. There he did unite all the Confederate forces. But the preponderance of Union strength, the large number of sick and wounded, exceeding 4,500, and the difficulty of guarding supply lines, made the evacuation of all Kentucky imperative. So Bragg, Kirby-Smith, Polk, and Hardee decided, and on October 11 the army crossed Duck River southward.[28]

In their flight from Kentucky, screened by Wheeler's cavalry, the Confederates left behind hundreds of men too sick or badly wounded to move, and abandoned much of the spoils they had gathered. On his emergence into the Knoxville area Bragg was in as bad estate as when he had begun on his adventurous invasion; even worse. The general's defenders pointed out that he had ascertained Kentucky's real temper, obtained some clothing, and driven off large herds of beeves. What was more important, he had taken more than 5,000 prisoners with quantities of small arms and cannon. But in any large view his offensive had been a failure; he had not defeated Buell, had not inspired the Kentuckians to revolt, and had not captured any large city. The army was back in the Tullahoma-Chattanooga area where it had started, its cavalry resuming their old watch over the Union forces in Nashville.

On the Union side, the equally impotent conclusion of the campaign sealed Buell's fate. Neither people nor government could forgive his failure to defeat Bragg. The slaughter at Perryville sickened many, so that even the judicious General John M. Palmer lashed out at him in intemperate language.[29] Governor Morton could not contain himself. "Another three months like the last six," he wrote Lincoln October 7, "and we are lost—lost." Governors Yates, Tod, and Andrew Johnson also pressed for Buell's removal. Perspicacious soldiers in the field, like the future historian of the Sixth Ohio, believed that with his numerical superiority Buell early in October should have pinned Bragg down and wiped out his army.[30] Most Chicago, Indianapolis, and Cincinnati newspapers were sharply condemnatory.

A highly persuasive defense of Buell was published by a Confederate in a Lexington newspaper this fall. The author pointed out that when Bragg commenced his advance, Buell's forces were widely scattered. Gathering them together, he began his march, moving straight toward Louisville. Leaving Nash-

28 O. R., I, xvi, pt. 1, p. 1088, see *idem*, pp. 1088–1094, for Bragg's report.
29 Nashville, Nov. 8, Palmer Papers, Ill. State Hist. Lib.
30 Foulke, *Morton*, I, 196, 197; O. R., I, xvi, pt. 2, p. 634; Hannaford, *Story of a Regiment*, 374, 375.

ville to care for itself, avoiding any collision that would delay him, and yet braving the dangers inescapable if he were to accomplish his great purpose, he pressed on past Bragg and reached his goal. In Louisville he mobilized the large body of recruits there and started on the return march. Sending out three columns, he adopted the only plan that could promise success, probably hoping to fight at Bardstown, or to turn Bragg's flank and get in his rear. Morgan's troopers, said the author, knew well the difficulties of the route followed by Buell in his northward march, and how great was his feat.[31] But the West was in no mood to listen to such arguments. A court of inquiry, after hearing testimony by Generals Thomas, A. D. McCook, and T. L. Crittenden, presently declared that if Buell had concentrated his forces and attacked the rebel army before it crossed the Cumberland, he could have defeated it; and that if later, as Bragg was retreating, he had vigorously intercepted the Confederate columns from Perryville or Danville he could have crushed them before they got away.

Buell made matters worse by once more flatly disobeying orders in a matter close to Lincoln's heart: East Tennessee. After Perryville he followed the enemy to the upper waters of the Cumberland, but then halted and swung his columns toward Nashville. The Administration, directing him to press into East Tennessee, had not required him to follow the route which Bragg laid waste behind him. Halleck gave him two alternative roads, one eminently sagacious. He suggested that the Union army march directly across Tennessee to Chattanooga, for the road was nearly as short as that to Nashville, and led through a country whose autumn crops could subsist the troops. Had Buell taken this counsel while fine weather reigned, roads were firm, and Bragg was weak, he might not only have taken Chattanooga, but by repairing the railroad to Nashville could have laid a firm grasp on both cities. Halleck believed that it was possible to drive the rebels out of the whole area. "If we cannot do it now, we need never hope for it," he wrote.[32]

East Tennessee, harried by irregular warfare, had sent numerous regiments into the Union armies. Though Lincoln's attachment to it is sometimes dismissed as sentimental, most Northerners lamented that the loyal population had never been brought under Union protection. The President was distressed by Buell's rejection of Halleck's plan. He knew what strong political reasons existed for a vigorous campaign and the seizure of Chattanooga, for the elections were at hand, and the North needed positive victories. Buell, who should have realized that Lincoln could lose the war if he ignored politics and public opinion, apparently never gave the fact a thought. The conclusion of Lew Wallace, after careful study, that while Buell was a brave, industrious, and

31 "Morgan's Vidette" in Lexington *Observer and Reporter*, Nov. 22, 1862.
32 O. R., I, xvi, pt. 2, pp. 623, 626.

loyal general, capable in routine operations and brilliant in logistics, he was either too cautious or too rigidly methodical to meet a great crisis successfully, seems entirely justified.

On October 24, the Administration removed Buell, never to use him again, and put William S. Rosecrans in his place.[33] This West Point graduate and Mexican War veteran, still in his early forties, had a deserved reputation for hard application to military studies, and bore on his brow the laurels of his West Virginia campaign and his recent partial victory over Price at Iuka. He at once reorganized the Army of the Cumberland, as it was now called, with its base at Nashville. Bragg meanwhile revamped his Army of the Tennessee, and toiled hard to recruit its strength. But he too remained unforgiven; some Kentucky Confederates would gladly have burned him at the stake. President Davis, however, was unwilling to remove his old friend, and tried to soften the complaints of Kirby-Smith by writing him:

I have held long and free conversations with Gen. Bragg. . . . He has explained in a direct and frank manner the circumstances of his campaign and has evinced the most self-denying temper in relation to his future position. That another Genl. might excite more enthusiasm is probable, but as all have their defects I have not seen how to make a change with advantage to the public service. His administrative capacity has been felt by the Army of Misspi. his knowledge of the troops is intimate and a new man would not probably for a time with even greater ability be equally useful. Of the Generals, Cooper is at the head of the adjutant-general's Bureau, Lee is in command of the army in Va., Johnston still disabled by the wound received at Seven Pines, Beauregard was tried as Commander of the Army of the West and left it without leave when the troops were demoralized and the country he was sent to protect was threatened with conquest. Bragg succeeded to the command and organized the army and marched to your support with efficient troops.[34]

But it was not Kirby-Smith alone who had lost faith in Bragg; other generals, Breckinridge, Hardee, Cleburne, and Polk, were emphatically of the same mind.

[III]

In a real sense, the double invasion by Lee and Bragg represented the high tide of the Confederate cause. Never again would armies be as confident as those which almost simultaneously crossed the Maryland and Kentucky bound-

33 Buell, a man of character, showed an excellent spirit while kept waiting for orders, his record meanwhile the subject of investigation. Discharged from the volunteer service in the spring of 1864, he at once resigned his regular commission. See James B. Fry, Operations of the Army Under Buell, passim.
34 Kirby-Smith Papers, Southern Coll., Univ. of N. C.

aries; never again would they have so good a chance of victory. The fundamental causes of Confederate failure on both fronts were the same: lack of manpower, weakness in firepower, inadequacy of general equipment, and exhaustion after arduous marches and heavy fighting. The quartermaster and commissary departments of the Western forces, as J. L. M. Curry wrote President Davis this summer, had no system, no economic strength, and no efficiency whatever.[35] Lesser causes played a part: the divulgence of Lee's plan of campaign, the division of authority between Bragg and Kirby-Smith, Bragg's irresolution, and miscalculation as to popular support in both Maryland and Kentucky. But had Lee and Bragg possessed 10,000 more men apiece, well furnished with shoes, food, and firearms, possibly both would have won. The Confederacy failed in this supreme double effort partly because it was inferior in population and industrial resources, partly because the brains it put into mobilizing men and materials were inferior, and partly because States Rights sentiment crippled its efforts to get recruits and supplies.

These facts suggest that the Davis Administration would have been wiser to stand on the defensive in the West and summon all its available strength for the Eastern blow. It might have been able, without risking Chattanooga, to transfer 20,000 men from Alabama and Tennessee to the Virginia theater. Had it done this as soon as Halleck dispersed the great army at Corinth, these troops might have taken part in the Seven Days; had they arrived later, they might have shared Lee's invasion of Maryland. The practice of the South, like the North, was to let each department and section fend for itself; Davis and Seddon seldom tried a large-scale concentration of troops for a special campaign, and never until late in 1863 did they transfer a great body of men across the Alleghenies. A powerful reinforcement of Lee in the summer of 1862 might have produced incalculable consequences.[36]

Even as matters stood, the South was far from beaten. In the East fortune was soon to turn her wheel. In the West, Jefferson Davis placed his trust in new offensive operations. He told Kirby-Smith that he must stay in that area, and cooperate with Bragg. "To recover from the depression produced by the failure in Ky.," he wrote, "no move seems better than to advance into middle Tenn. If Buell comes he will be weaker than in Ky. and I hope will be beaten." [37] Davis hoped that if Bragg re-entered Tennessee he might obtain 30,000 new troops from Confederate sympathizers, soothe his almost mutinous officers, and reanimate the spirits of his drooping army.

35 Talladega, June 20, 1862, Davis Papers, Duke Univ.
36 Cf. Ropes, *Civil War*, II, 416–418; he believes Davis should have made the transfer.
37 Kirby-Smith Papers, *ut sup.*

[IV]

The great southwestern region, by the fall of 1862, was in a convulsed condition. An ill-defined line between Union and Confederate military control severed Tennessee, Alabama, Mississippi, and Arkansas into jagged, quivering halves, a broad zone in each State suffering from devastation, arbitrary martial law, and guerrilla warfare. Never before had large American populations lain in such terrible distress. To find any parallel men had to turn back to Thomas Sumter's horrifying account of the Carolinas late in the Revolution, when Whig and Tory bands turned the country into such a desert that the very buzzards went hungry.

Poverty, unemployment, disorganization, inflation, and shortage of necessities ruled from the Missouri and Ohio to the Gulf. In St. Louis early in 1862 a summons to wage earners filled Verandah Hall with ragged laborers and pinched seamstresses. After speakers expatiated on the prostration of industry, the meeting passed resolutions urging the national government to provide some remedy.[38] In Kentucky, Governor Magoffin's annual message to the legislature declared that trade was largely stopped, that wide regions had been desolated, that farm products lacked their old outlets, and that in much of the State property could not be sold for a third of its value. Universal gloom, said the governor, pervaded a once happy commonwealth, thousands of families had been broken up, and starvation stared many in the face. "You would shudder," one Union soldier wrote home from Kentucky, "to see how destitute some families are left." [39]

In the district around Corinth, Mississippi, General John M. Palmer was distressed by the abject poverty of small farmers. He had visited families with half a dozen children living in a roughly boarded log cabin almost empty of furniture. Their ignorance was pitiable. The women looked hungry and hopeless, the men sullen, the children frightened and wild. Yet they were being plunged into still deeper gulfs of want.[40] In Louisiana the tale was the same. When Union forces occupied Baton Rouge, many were so destitute that the authorities opened a center to which charitable people brought their surplus.[41] The French consul in New Orleans reported in the spring of 1862 that half the inhabitants of a city lately renowned for its opulence were on the verge of famine.[42]

38 St. Louis *Republican*, Feb. 6, 1862.
39 *National Intelligencer*, Feb. 22, 1862; S. F. Martin, Jan. 24, 1862, Palmer Coll., Western Reserve Hist. Coll.
40 May 6, 1862, to his wife, Palmer Papers, Ill. State Hist. Lib.
41 Gen. John McGrath, Baton Rouge *State-Times*, Dec. 3, 1915.
42 Gordon Wright, "Ec. Conditions in the Confederacy as Seen by the French Consuls," *Journal of So. Hist.* VII (May, 1941), 195 ff.

The guerrilla warfare which racked much of this great region afflicted the helpless civilian population even more than the troops. Many bushwhackers were just what the Memphis *Union Reveille* called them, "bands of heartless pirates," who preyed on Confederate and Union adherents alike.[43] In Kentucky, Tennessee, northern Mississippi, and northern Alabama the ghastly outrages inflicted on helpless people grew worse after the Bragg-Buell campaign. No man not bred in Central America, wrote a Confederate soldier from Arkansas, could form a conception of affairs in that state.[44] A press correspondent who journeyed to Holly Springs, Mississippi, in midwinter of 1862–63, found the roads as deserted and silent as the fields. Mile after mile he met nobody; on four plantations out of five he saw not a soul; sometimes gaping windows revealed a gutted shell, sometimes nothing remained but the tall chimneys whitened by the flames. Many men settled old scores, for family feuds had been frequent, by gun or torch. In a few Mississippi counties Unionists grew bold enough to raid Confederate stores, intimidate conscription officers, and seize and parole Southern soldiers; the authorities in retaliation then used bloodhounds to track them into the swamps, and shot or hanged them.[45]

One leader of Tennessee Unionist irregulars, Dave Beattie, was so ferocious that when Bragg caught sixteen of his men he promptly hanged them by the roadside. He was matched by the Confederate guerrilla Chamez Ferguson, who in the summer of 1862 boasted of dispatching thirty-two men, and when ordered by General Basil W. Duke never to murder prisoners, muttered that if he caught any hound who deserved killing he would slay him on the spot.[46] Late in the summer of 1862 bands in the mountainous tip of North Carolina, partly Unionists, partly draft evaders or deserters, captured the seat of Madison County and seized some stores. The colonel of the Sixty-fourth North Carolina retaliated with what Governor Zebulon B. Vance called shocking barbarity, shooting more than a dozen men and flogging women; and Vance protested hotly to Richmond.[47] Unionist Germans in western Texas meanwhile organized guerrilla groups which did severe fighting with rebels, whereupon the vengeful Confederates undertook to exterminate them. In one encounter only a dozen Union men out of eighty escaped shooting or hanging.[48]

Conditions in Missouri were the most appalling of all. The fanatic Indianian Jim Lane, recruiting a brigade of Kansas troops, led them into western Missouri

43 July 1, 1862.
44 Cyrus Franklin Nov. 30, 1863, Davis Papers, Duke Univ.
45 Letter Jan. 5, 1863, copied in Frankfort, Ky., *Commonwealth*, Jan. 29; J. K. Bettersworth, *Confd. Miss.*, 213–241.
46 Duke, *Reminiscences*, 123.
47 Vance, Feb. 28, 1863, to Secretary Seddon, Lieber Papers, HL.
48 Galveston *Union* article in N. Y. *Tribune*, Jan. 10, 1863.

to burn houses, shoot citizens, and loot shops. Charles R. Jennison with a body of Kansas cavalry was equally ruthless. When John M. Schofield took over the chief command, his militia retaliated against the outrages of Confederate irregulars by furious maraudings, hangings, and slayings. In the spring of 1862 a frightful guerrilla warfare burst into full flame. The murderous William C. Quantrill organized a band to combat Jennison and others, and was soon leading vicious raids into Kansas. In March, Halleck issued his General Order No. 2, declaring that any man who enlisted in an irregular band would, if captured, be hanged as a robber and murderer, thus going far beyond the order by Frémont which Lincoln had modified; and the natural result was that on both sides the fighters ceased to give quarter. The ferocity of the struggle increased so fast that by midsummer the richest and most populous counties were ablaze with warfare. On July 22, 1862, Schofield issued an order drafting every able-bodied man capable of bearing arms "for the purpose of exterminating the guerrillas that infest our state." [49] Great parts of Missouri and Arkansas by fall were verging on anarchy. Albert Pike exhorted the tribes of Indian Territory to defend themselves against Union attackers without rest, "for they are more merciless than wolves and more rapacious." In one Missouri county in six months rebel guerrillas killed nearly a hundred Unionists, while the militia in revenge dispatched thirty men, one eighty-six years old. [50]

Everywhere from the Great Smokies to the Nueces, groups of Confederate deserters, hiding in swamps and woods and preying on the countrysides, intensified the lawlessness of the region. Estimates of their number ran above 10,000 each for Arkansas and Mississippi, and companies of volunteer "rangers" took the field to hunt them down in what often became an implacable conflict.

One Union officer who distinguished himself by savagery was Ivan Turchin, a Russian who had come to the United States after serving in the Crimea, and had been made colonel of the Nineteenth Illinois. Insisting that war should be ruthless, he subsisted his men on the country so freely that Southerners called him the robber colonel. He gave notice that if his force was attacked after a town surrendered he would punish the community ruthlessly, and in Athens, Alabama, allegedly told his men: "I close my eyes for two hours." His troops looted stores and dwellings indiscriminately, destroyed civilian property in the most wanton manner, and insulted women. Buell ordered him court-martialed, and he was sentenced to dismissal. But the War Department made him a brigadier, his Chicago admirers presented him with a sword, and although

49 Jay Monaghan, *Civil War on the Western Border*, 251 ff.; Richard S. Brownlee, *Gray Ghosts of the Confederacy*, 53–109; O. R., I, xiii, *passim*, but esp. Schofield's report, 7–21.
50 Pike in O. R., I, xiii, 869–871; W. C. Reynolds to T. B. Garesche, June 23, 1862, Reynolds Papers, LC.

the South outlawed him and set a price on his head, many in the North regarded him as a hero.[51]

The Pope-Stanton general orders in Virginia for punishing civilians and levying on their property had a malign influence everywhere. From an early date, however, the most rigorous of the responsible Union leaders was W. T. Sherman, who became commander at Memphis July 21, 1862. Aware that most of the surrounding population was implacably hostile, and angered by Forrest's exploits, he jumped to a drastic conclusion. The government, he wrote Secretary Chase, should act on the principle that everybody in the South was an enemy of the North, and that all who could get arms would bear them either in proper regiments or guerrilla units.

From this generalization that the whole Southern population was in arms it was but a step to the conclusion that all should feel the wrath of the North. He assured his wife in the summer of 1862 that if the North could hold on, the war would soon take a turn toward the extermination not only of the rebel armies but of civilians. He quickly put his ideas in practice. Exasperated by the way in which Confederates fired on supply steamboats from the banks of the Mississippi, he ordered an Ohio colonel, September 24, 1862, to destroy every house in the town of Randolph, scene of such an attack, and this without inquiry into the guilt of the inhabitants. Three days later he ordered that for every instance of firing into a boat, ten families should be expelled from Memphis, and began placing rebel prisoners on boats exposed to attack. While we cannot convert the Southern people, he wrote Grant, we can make war so terrible that they will be ready to exhaust all peaceful remedies before taking up arms.[52] When further attacks on steamboats occurred, Sherman broke through all restraints. Insisting on condign penalties, he ordered his troops to lay waste all the houses, farm buildings, and fields in a strip for fifteen miles along the Arkansas bank of the Mississippi.

One exploit of Sherman's command, lying on the borderland between what was legitimate and what illegitimate in war, is related by General Benjamin H. Grierson in his unpublished autobiography. This brilliant cavalry commander in mid-November, 1862, overheard Sherman, then about to leave Memphis,

---

51 The New Orleans *Daily Picayune*, March 11, 1862, declared that 4,541 officers and men deserted from the Louisiana forces during the first year of the war and estimated Arkansas desertions at 10,029, Mississippi desertions at 11,604. See Edwin A. Leland, "Org. and Admin. of the La. Army During the Civil War," M. A. thesis, La. State Univ., 1938. For the story of Ivan (J. B.) Turchin, see *National Intelligencer*, July 22, 1862; MS Recs. of James Fenton, 19th Ill. Vols., Palmer Coll., Western Reserve; O. R., I, xvi, pt. 2, pp. 273–278.
52 O. R., I, xvii, pt. 2, pp. 259–262; John Bennett Walters, "Sherman and Total War," *Journal of So. Hist.*, XIV (Nov., 1948), 447 ff.

upbraiding his quartermaster for not supplying his transportation wants. The quartermaster protested that horses and mules were simply unobtainable. At this Grierson interposed. "There is no need for any trouble in the matter," he said, "for I can get you 2,000 mules and horses by tomorrow night, and more." Sherman turned toward him in amazement, exclaiming: "How? Where in the world can you get them?" "Take them from the rebels wherever they may be found," replied Grierson. Sherman smiled, and turning to the quartermaster, ejaculated: "We must have them. Do it, Grierson—do it!" "All right," the cavalryman responded, "I will do it by your order." During recent scouting expeditions he had kept his eyes open, and knew where the animals could be found. "I sent my men throughout the country," he relates, "and swept them in by tens, twenties, fifties, and hundreds. I stopped wagons and carriages and took the mules and horses from the traces, and scoured the plantations, and thus quickly obtained the animals from barns, corrals, and pastures." A hornet's nest soon raged about headquarters—but Sherman had his transportation.[53]

In Kentucky rebel forces at various times in 1862 burned hotels, railway stations, houses, and every other building that Union commands might use, while they consumed vast quantities of grain and fodder, and drove away all the horses and cattle worth having. Bragg early in the year, with great mortification, denounced acts of pillage, plunder, and destruction of Southern property by his own men; but when he retreated before Buell he felt constrained to lay waste a wide ribbon of country south of Green River, so that one inhabitant called it the Land of Sorrow. Stragglers became a great nuisance in both armies, living like locusts on the country. One of Greeley's correspondents wrote from Buell's army that hundreds of these loiterers occupied their time in stealing horses, wantonly shooting hogs and cattle, and insulting women.[54] The moment Union troops entered Louisiana they began to misbehave, and by the spring of 1863 were almost out of hand. Lieutenant John Merrilies of an Illinois artillery unit relates that as the troops advanced through the rich and beautiful country north of New Orleans a succession of blazing houses indicated the line of march.[55] When his company halted before some specially fine mansions he saw that every previous unit had taken a hand in destruction, smashing mahogany tables and damask-covered sofas, splintering china, breaking fine mirrors, and thrusting bayonets into oil paintings; but the soldiers of his own outfit completed the vandalism, till he was glad to seek quiet outdoors. The diarist of the Fifty-second Massachusetts, writing of the march through

53 MS "Lights and Shadows of Life," Ill. State Hist. Lib.
54 Lexington *Observer and Reporter*, Jan. 13, 1862, for typical devastation; "Junius," Frankfort, Ky., Oct. 12, 1862, in N. Y. *Tribune*, Oct. 17.
55 MS Diary, April–June, 1862, Chicago Hist. Soc.

the country about Opelousas, Louisiana, in April, 1863, was frank: "We have left an awful scene of desolation behind us." [56]

The climax was reached in Sherman's work of devastation in Mississippi in the spring and summer of 1863. Frank P. Blair, acting upon his instructions to lay waste the Yazoo Valley, destroyed half a million bushels of corn, immense stores of pork, and every grist mill in the area. While Grant repeatedly and peremptorily required the punishment of officers and soldiers caught in acts of violence or pillage, Sherman in general set such orders at defiance. In May his troops entered Jackson, Mississippi, primarily to destroy Confederate government property. This was effectively done and much sugar and tobacco was confiscated. "The town all day was a scene of the wildest confusion," writes Merrilies, "plundering going on universally among the stores, which the guards made very feeble efforts to prevent. . . . By night . . . private property was still being pillaged by the men." Later, in July, the sack of the capital was completed, the business section being burned and even churches and the State Library being looted.[57] One regiment alone, the Fourteenth New York, in the spring of 1863 seized 800 horses and 3,000 cattle in the neighborhood of Brashear City, Louisiana.[58]

To add to the distress of the white population, restlessness increasingly pervaded the slaves. Many remained loyal to their masters, so that Susan Dabney Smedes could later write that they were the greatest comfort of white women during the war, but many others became uncontrollable. Sometimes stragglers from the army persuaded slaves to quit work, and sometimes antislavery officers did so, but commonly they quit by their own impulse. While they usually fled to the nearest Union camp, in many parts of the South they formed gangs, hid in the brakes and woods, and raided plantations and farms to supplement the game and fish they caught. Often they stayed at home, but in a new status. Mrs. C. C. Clay of Alabama found that her Negroes would obey no orders: "They say they are free." If her husband left the place and the overseer tried to punish a hand, one slave told her, they would kill the overseer.[59] Her slaves would not even build fires or milk cows without grumbling and making threats.

A typical Mississippi planter of the better sort, John Huston Bills of the Holly Springs district, furnishes in his diaries a record of continuous anxiety over mounting evils. He suffered greatly from Union depredations in the late

56   J. F. Moors, *Hist. 52nd. Mass.*, 133, 134.
57   Merrilies, MS Diary, May 15, 16, 1863.
58   E. P. Pellet, *History of the 14th New York*, 45.
59   Mrs. Clay to her son, Sept. 5, 1863, Clay Papers, Duke University. "I have to work harder than I ever did," she writes, "but am patient, prayerful, and silent." On Sept. 19 she informed her son "I fear that if the cars run all the negroes that are capable will go. None work."

spring of 1862; his son-in-law was badly wounded at Shiloh; his debtors insisted on paying him in Confederate notes which, though they were "almost worthless" to him, he had to take under pressure of the law and public opinion; and he found that Confederate cavalrymen burned a hundred bales of his cotton in one swoop. The wanton, useless destruction of property by Northern soldiers, he wrote, would better suit an army of savages than of Christians. "The Negro girls cannot pick cotton in the field unless guarded by their husbands and brothers." But his principal concern was the growing insubordination of the slaves on his four fine plantations. On July 31, 1862, he wrote: "Gloom and despondency on the countenance of all property holders. We fear all the Negroes are demoralized and lost for further use." A few days later he made a trip: "Meet 40 to 50 Runaway Negroes Comeing in to join the Federals and be free." [60]

Now and then, moreover, the former slaves became violent. One planter near Selma watched them assist Northern troops in burning his dwelling and gin house. A friend to whom he told the story wrote: "The 'faithful slave' is about played out. They are the most treacherous, brutal, and ungrateful race on the earth." This, however, was a very unusual ebullition of feeling. Most masters knew quite accurately how much—or how little—reason their Negroes had for gratitude and attachment.[61]

Over all the conquered portions of the western Confederacy, meanwhile, brooded the spirit of exploitation and speculation. Despite Confederate efforts to carry out the law for the destruction of cotton and tobacco, large quantities of it escaped destruction. New Orleans, Memphis, Nashville, and other cities became centers of a feverish traffic in Southern staples, which drew into the region a cohort of buyers, some of them estimable men doing a legitimate business, but more of them a crew of adventurers and harpies. The significant fact is that the influx contributed to a social demoralization fast pervading the region. Grant denounced the cotton speculators whose love of gain surpassed their love of country, and he might have added that the greed for money made them contemptuous of all moral law. Corruption attended all their activities, and extravagance and vice followed in their footsteps. John M. Palmer wrote his wife in the autumn of 1862 that Nashville had become intolerable, for "the war has undermined and demoralized the whole foundation of society in Tennessee." Two years earlier the city had been prosperous, happy, and decent; now many families, with husbands and fathers away in the army, lived in utter poverty. The natural consequences of a choice between want and shame

60 MS Diary, Univ. of N. C. The Bills plantations were called Hickory Valley, Cornucopia, Bonnie Blue, and Home, and were evidently rich. Bills, while not enthusiastic about the Confederacy, supported it.
61 John F. Andrews to Mrs. C. C. Clay, July 10, 1863.

flaunted themselves everywhere, officers and soldiers spending all their pay on fallen women.[62]

Worst of all were the vindictive passions searing men's hearts. The human race, Lord Bryce wrote Charles W. Eliot just after the First World War, is subject to startling relapses. "That of our own time seems to me one of these; the saddest part of it being the virulence of hatred. . . ." In 1862 Parson Brownlow was touring the North, preaching grape for the rebel masses and hemp for their leaders; asserting that he would arm every bear, catamount, and crocodile, every devil in hell, to defeat the South, and would put down the rebellion if the task exterminated every man, woman, and child south of Mason and Dixon's Line. *Harper's Weekly* published unfounded atrocity stories of wounded men shot in ambulances, of poisoned wells, of decapitation and massacre. On the Southern side Howell Cobb, Robert Toombs, and other Georgia leaders preached unrelenting warfare, even to scorched earth, against an invader who came "with lust in his eye, poverty in his purse, and hell in his heart." No anger equals the anger of brother for brother, and none leaves a worse legacy of evil.[63]

Before the end of 1862 the upheaval of war had thus so racked and brutalized large areas from the Ohio to the Gulf that even if the conflict could then have been halted, the task of reconstruction and regeneration would have been staggering. Of numerous areas men might have said just what Charles D. Drake wrote later of Missouri: "Falsehood, treachery, and perjury pervaded the whole social fabric." The decent people of the republic were learning that sad as is the material destruction that accompanies war, the cultural, moral, and spiritual losses are far more fearful. And the struggle was not yet half finished!

62   Nov. 22, 1862, Palmer Papers, Ill. State Hist. Lib.
63   Fisher, *Bruce*, II, 274, 275; *Harper's Weekly*, June 14, 1862; Coulter, *Brownlow*, Ch. X.

The Voters and the Administration

WHEN McClellan fell back from Richmond to Harrison's Landing, the curtain had already risen on the nation's first wartime political campaign. In mid-June the Union men of Indiana, both Republicans and War Democrats, rallied by Oliver P. Morton, held a mass convention in Indianapolis; before the month ended the "regular" Democrats met there; and the next few weeks witnessed party conventions from the Kaw to the Kennebec. Everyone realized the gravity of the autumn elections. It was barely possible, though unlikely, that the Democrats would win control of the House. Certainly they might elect governors in New York and New Jersey who would hamper the Administration, and might choose legislatures elsewhere which would obstruct such earnest executives as Yates, Morton, and Curtin.

The Administration entered the political campaign under so many disadvantages that its supporters feared an ignominious defeat. It had staked its prestige on the Peninsular thrust and rapid opening of the Mississippi, and in both areas had failed. Prices and taxes were rising. Many farmers were caught between a glut of grain and high freight rates. Hatred of the draft was widespread. Arbitrary arrests and other invasions of fundamental civil liberties had created sharp resentment. Most disturbing of all in some States was the apprehension of an influx of liberated Negroes, which would take jobs away from white men, depress wages, and breed violence. The Democratic Party, naturally, was regarded as the strongest barrier against such a tide.

Seeing how desperate a fight they had to wage, Republican politicians took what hasty steps they could to strengthen themselves. They knew that they could make no direct use of Lincoln, who wisely chose to devote himself to the war, standing above the political melee. When Mark W. Delahay asked his advice on party strategy in Kansas, the President endorsed the letter: "Answered July 29 declining to suggest any course of action, preferring to rely upon intelligence and patriotism of friends." [1] The situation differed so widely from State to State that national leaders of the party left management

1 RTL Papers; this endorsement not in the *Works*.

and tactics in local hands. But they did try, wherever feasible, to effect a coalition of Republicans and War Democrats in a Union Party; they mobilized all their newspapers; and they assailed the Peace Democrats, who were talking of an armistice, a national convention, and the restoration of the old Union under the old Constitution.

This political campaign of 1862 was in various ways a confused battle. The North had no single date for polling: Connecticut, New Hampshire, and Rhode Island had held their elections in the spring, Pennsylvania, Ohio, and Indiana voted in October, and elsewhere the final decision waited until November. While Massachusetts, New York, and New Jersey would elect governors, the other principal States would choose only Congressmen and minor State officers. The most confusing fact, however, was the chaotic situation in the party system.

Parties, as everybody saw, were in a state of flux, with their ultimate character indeterminable. The War Democrats who invoked the name of Douglas and the Peace Democrats who shared the prejudices of Franklin Pierce heartily abominated each other. James Sheahan, the Douglasite editor of the Chicago *Morning Post*, assured Elihu Washburne in June that he was almost ready to join the Republican ranks, for he could never accept fellowship with Democrats of the appeasement school.[2] On the Republican side, everyone knew how bitterly the Wade-Chandler radicals detested the Seward-Blair conservatives. Many moderate Republicans hoped that a Union Party of national scope would soon emerge behind Lincoln—a party insisting on victory but disclaiming any desire for utter subjugation of the South and a complete social revolution there. Seward, Montgomery Blair, Bates, and conservative Senators like Preston King cherished some such dream. This new party might be brought into existence on a program embracing restoration of the Union, gradual compensated emancipation, and a mild reconstruction policy, but only if a large body of loyal Democrats lent their assistance.

Unfortunately for this dream, the campaign demonstrated that extremists in both parties were steadily gaining strength at the expense of moderates. As the strains of the war became more painful, tempers grew shorter. Throughout the summer and fall Lincoln's Administration was under a double fire, and if his Democratic opponents exhibited the more brutal manners, some Republican enemies were really more venomous and dangerous.

To be sure, the immediate tests applied to Administration policy by the opposed forces were entirely different. The radical Republicans had three principal demands: Would Lincoln dismiss McClellan? Would he confirm the emancipation of the slaves? And when he did this, would he arm them for

2 June 19, 1862, Washburne Papers, LC.

service in the Union armies? The "regular" Democrats hoped for the retention of McClellan, the deferment of emancipation, and the modification or non-enforcement of the confiscation laws. But the two camps agreed in their hostility to several Cabinet members, and particularly Stanton. The Secretary of War is distinguished only by cant, ignorance, and imbecility, said the New York *Express;* he has utterly lost the confidence of the people, grumbled the *World;* his attacks on slavery are merely a cover for his failures, asserted the Cincinnati *Commercial.*[3]

It is unquestionably true that, as F. L. Olmsted believed, confidence in Lincoln remained unshaken among the masses and slowly increased as people comprehended his firmness, patience, and sagacity. But from both sides, some leaders assailed him mercilessly. Sumner grumbled to intimates that he was honest but inexperienced, and had too much *vis inertiae.* Joseph Medill of the Chicago *Tribune* believed that Seward held him in a spell while "West Point pro-slavery generals, a rotten Cabinet, and a blind, cowardly Congress" were ruining the country. The Secretary "has been President *de facto* and has kept a sponge saturated with chloroform at Uncle Abe's nose all the while, except one or two brief spells." Henry Ward Beecher, temporarily editing the *Independent,* told its great body of churchgoing readers that neither Lincoln nor the Cabinet had furnished any kindling inspiration, for they had let Fear prove stronger than Faith. "Not a spark of genius has he [Lincoln]; not an element of leadership; not one particle of heroic enthusiasm." Senators Trumbull, Wade, and Chandler scolded as stridently. Thaddeus Stevens, denouncing McClellan on July 5 as a general who sympathized with slaveholders, extended his indictment to the President; Lincoln was the most honest of men, but altogether too amiable, and too much misled by malign Kentucky counselors.[4]

After every military defeat, it was natural for radical Republicans to call for more harshness, and for radical Democrats to protest that the nation's only salvation lay in conciliation. Voters tended to gravitate to one of two extremes.

3 All quoted in Chicago *Morning Post,* July 12, 1862. Its editor, Sheahan, early in the campaign remarked: "The few men who represent the extreme end of the Republican Party, men who were loudest in shouting for the election of Abraham Lincoln, are fast becoming his enemies. On the other hand, those who opposed his election from principle are fast becoming his friends." *Morning Post,* July 8, 1862.

4 Pierce, *Sumner,* IV, 83; Elmer Gertz, *Joe Medill's War,* 8; N. Y. *Independent,* July 17, 1862; *Cong. Globe,* 37th Cong., 2d Sess., 3125, July 5, 1862. Greeley was urging that the army accept at least a hundred thousand former slaves, giving them ax, spade, or rifle. "We do not fear that the right thing will not ultimately be done, but that it will be done too late." N. Y. *Tribune,* June 17, July 21, 1862.

[I]

By far the most important contest, that in New York, illustrated the move-ment toward violent attitudes. Governor E. D. Morgan had decided not to run for a third term. The Democratic strategist Dean Richmond, veteran of a hundred political battles, resolved to make the most of the war weariness. Re-fusing to listen to a proposal that the Democrats and Republicans unite on John A. Dix, he decided that the ideal candidate was Horatio Seymour, who though only fifty-two had been in public life for thirty years, and had made a creditable governor in 1853–54. This Utica attorney, immersed in his profes-sion and conscious that his sensitive, subtle character hardly fitted him to be an opposition leader in a bitter civil war, was reluctant, but the boss refused to take no.

And Richmond, coldbloodedly intent on party victory, brought Seymour forward in the most effective way possible. A group of old-line Whigs opposed to emancipation and other radical policies held a Constitutional Union conven-tion in Troy early in September. Here Richmond saw to it that a well-controlled body of delegates effected Seymour's nomination; and the very next day a Democratic convention in Albany ratified this choice.[5] Party heads could thus assure voters that the Democrats, renouncing partisanship, had accepted the nominee of the Constitutional Unionists, who included Millard Fillmore. The regular Democratic organization was actually in complete control—an organiza-tion which Richmond and Seymour would soon dominate more powerfully than any pair since Marcy and Van Buren.[6]

The platform on which Seymour stood gave comfort to all enemies of the Administration and most sympathizers with the South, for it re-emphasized the Crittenden Resolution, and while pledging a hearty effort to suppress the rebel-lion, declared that the Democrats would endeavor to "restore the Union as it was, and maintain the Constitution as it is." One plank denounced arbitrary ar-rests. Seymour, who was present, assailed emancipation as "a proposal for the butchery of women and children, for scenes of lust and rapine, and of arson and murder, which would invoke the interference of civilized Europe." [7]

While personally the man who used this intemperate rhetoric was an ap-pealing figure, politically he was both puzzling and offensive. Even the aboli-tionist Gerrit Smith admitted that he was a gentleman of wide reading, winning manners, and pure life. Essentially a moderate, before the war he had opposed nativism and prohibition, and had denounced Northern and Southern firebrands

5 N. Y. *Herald, Tribune,* Sept. 10, 1862.
6 Stewart Mitchell, *Seymour,* 245; Blaine, *Twenty Years,* I, 437 ff.
7 Mitchell, 245; Alexander, *Pol. Hist. N. Y.,* III, 18, 19.

with equal fervor. He was hard-working, conscientious, and talented. But he was fiercely hostile to the more advanced Administration measures: to attacks on slavery, the confiscation laws, the draft, and all restrictions upon civil rights. When nominated, he expected to meet defeat, but hoped to demonstrate the existence of a strong party which would oppose the forcible subversion of the white South and a reign of intolerance in the North. "I enjoy abuse at this time," he wrote his sister, "for I mean to indulge in it." [8] Certainly his acceptance speech was abusive of the Administration. His unique combination of cultivated manners and acrid partisanship, of candor and casuistry, was always to make his course hard to understand.[9]

So strong a nomination demanded an effective counterstroke. Of the two men most discussed for the Republican leadership, James S. Wadsworth and John A. Dix, both had originally been Democrats; but Wadsworth, heir to the greatest landed estate in western New York, had always been sternly antislavery, had helped organize the Free Soil Party, and had become a fullfledged Republican by 1856, while Dix had remained a Democrat, so recognized when Buchanan gave him a Cabinet post and Lincoln appointed him major-general. Wadsworth was fifty-five, Dix sixty-four. While Wadsworth had never occupied a political position and had never even practiced law, Dix had held high offices. Patriotic men might well hesitate between two leaders so able and earnest. But radical Republicans naturally favored Wadsworth, while conservatives preferred Dix. The Greeley-Bryant-Preston King half of the party was aligned against the Seward-Weed-James Gordon Bennett half.[10]

All the currents of the hour set in favor of the radical Republicans, for many believed that no successful fight could be made against Seymour if the party took Seymour's conservative stand. While Wadsworth wrote letters protesting that the military situation required him to keep his command of the Washington defenses and that he hoped he would not be nominated, actually he was receptive if he could get an aggressively radical platform. Thurlow Weed, seeing which way the Republican cat was going to jump, had a long talk with Chase, and tried to ingratiate himself with that leader; it was clear that he had concluded that Wadsworth would be nominated and elected, and did not wish to be left shivering in the cold. A few days later he sent word to Chase that he was

8 Sept. 18, 1862; Mitchell, 146, 147.
9 A State Rights conviction almost as impassioned as Calhoun's was one key to the man. In a speech nearly a year earlier, Oct. 26, 1861, Seymour had inveighed against Republican leaders "animated by a vindictive piety or a malignant philanthropy," and had declared against emancipation in stringent terms: "If it be true that slavery must be abolished to save this Union, then the people of the South should be allowed to withdraw themselves from the Government which cannot give them the protection guaranteed by its terms." N. Y. *Times*, Oct. 29, 1852; *Public Record of Horatio Seymour*, 32 ff.
10 Pearson, *Wadsworth*, 150–152; Martin Lichterman, MS Life of John A. Dix.

ready to make Wadsworth's nomination unanimous if it were "not to be considered a triumph over him"; that is, if he could have his share of loaves and fishes afterward. Wadsworth, however, could afford to refuse any pledges, for his selection was inevitable. On September 22 he dined with Chase, and when told of Weed's overtures, declined to budge an inch.[11]

The Republican convention, meeting two days later in Syracuse, was a complete triumph for the radical wing. In the atmosphere produced by Lincoln's proclamation, any other outcome would have been a repudiation of his policy. Raymond of the *Times*, chosen to preside, told the delegates that he favored Dix because his chats with politicians had convinced him that Wadsworth could never be elected,[12] and the War Democrats attending the convention shared this view. On the first ballot, however, Wadsworth received the nomination, and the convention tailored a platform to suit him, hailing emancipation and urging a relentless prosecution of the war. Bryant's son-in-law Parke Godwin was head of the resolutions committee, and Bryant and Greeley were exultant. Both had often said that slavery was the deadly foe of the nation, and Wadsworth typified the determination to crush it.

The campaign was inevitably tinged by bitterness. Seymour in his convention speech had thrown down a gage which the Republicans were quick to catch up. Greeley indulged in an orgy of villification, and even the mild Henry J. Raymond declared that a vote for Seymour was a vote to destroy the Union. According to the *Tribune*, Seymour was hand in glove with men openly hostile to the war. Actually, copperheadism at this time was weak except in New York City, and the great mass of voters demanded an earnest continuance of the struggle; but some excited upstate editors were almost as vitriolic as Greeley.

Seymour, after his first harsh speech, conducted his battle on a high plane. Fully aware of his responsibilities, he emphasized his loyalty to the Union, spoke of Lincoln respectfully (protesting, indeed, against abuse of him), and founded his appeal primarily on the failure of Republicans to save the country. The victorious Democrats, he promised, would give Lincoln fuller support than radicals like Chase and Wadsworth. Democratic victory, moreover, would bring the Administration back to the right track—the crushing of the rebellion, as distinguished from the overthrow of the Southern social system—and thus reduce the danger of foreign interference.[13] But some of Seymour's supporters were

11 Chase, *Diary* (Amer. Hist. Assoc. *Report*, 1902, II), 83, 90; cf. Van Densen, *Weed*, 295 ff.
12 Brown, *Raymond*, 237; N. Y. *Tribune*, Sept. 25, 1861.
13 Of Seymour's patriotism no doubt whatever exists. But it was also politically expedient for him to follow a dignified and moderate course, for thus he could best win War Democrats and conservative Republicans to his side. August Belmont, for example, a War Democrat, would have voted against Seymour had he hesitated. While in Europe in 1861–62, Belmont had tried to make himself useful to the country, and in all his talks with

wildly intemperate, declaring that Northern boys were being killed merely to satisfy antislavery fanatics. Bennett in the *Herald*, for example, predicted that if Wadsworth were elected, he would inaugurate a reign of terror worse than anything since the French Revolution—for his acts while commander in Washington proved it. On the Republican side, Weed and Seward remained chilly, and a letter Seward finally sent in behalf of Wadsworth disgusted Charles Sumner by its feebleness. We need a bugle note, he snorted, and Seward gives us a riddle!

So disruptive did the campaign become that some frightened men tried to get both Seymour and Wadsworth to retire in favor of a new coalition of moderates under Dix. Bennett's *Herald*, which had opposed Wadsworth, on October 13 vainly urged Seymour to use a great meeting that night in Cooper Union to surrender his place to Dix.[14] General Wadsworth did not appear in the State until October 30, when he arrived in the metropolis to address a mass meeting. Conservative Republicans were shivering in anticipation, for they knew, as Weed said later, that he would make an emancipationist speech which might throw away the State.[15] All efforts to persuade him to confine his remarks to Lincoln and the Union met a peremptory rejection. Whether his uncompromising deliverance lost votes it is impossible to say, but it was certain that Seymour's final speech, unflinching in its insistence on restoration of the Union, won him a host of friends. The Democratic majority, as we shall see, was to prove decisive.

[II]

In Massachusetts the extremists triumphed in a different fashion. A Republican victory was certain, and in that party Sumner and John A. Andrew, two thorough-going radicals, carried everything before them.

Nearly everybody had a high regard for Andrew's gifts. This aggressive, generous, choleric little man, the Miles Standish of the Bay State, had proved far-sighted, fearless, and unwearied. To be sure, his judgment was erratic, for he was emotional and impulsive; he was tactless, and his fierce bluntness made many enemies. He liked to write fiery letters about the sins of Ben Butler and other opponents, and declaim them aloud to everybody within earshot. His fits of

European statesmen had defended the Lincoln Administration. He thought that the people both South and North were "in the hands of reckless politicians, and are dragged willing victims, to ruin and desolation." But as a Union Democrat he wished to see Lincoln upheld, and scolded S. L. M. Barlow vigorously for carrying his opposition too far. See Belmont to Barlow, various letters, Aug., 1862, Barlow Papers.

14 Dix helped spike the movement by declaring that he could not leave his Maryland desk; N. Y. *Herald*, Oct. 20–25.

15 To S. H. Gay, Nov. 7, 1862, Gay Papers.

impatience, his violent language, his exaggerated loves and hates, however, were easy to forgive, for he put a manly honesty into all his acts. Working day and night, seeing far ahead, and planning astutely, he made Massachusetts a pillar of strength for the Union. In spite of his one occasional weakness, a Websterian taste for drink, he was unquestionably the ablest of the war governors. To Sumner much stronger objection could be made. His vanity, fanaticism, lack of humor, savage use of invective, and belief in his own infallibility had raised up a host of antagonists. But Massachusetts in general was proud of him—proud of his eloquence, learning, dignity, and elevation.[16]

When the Republican convention met in Worcester on September 9, a stubborn group of conservatives—R. H. Dana, Jr., Leverett Saltonstall, Joel Parker of the Harvard Law School, and others—were ready for battle. They were mainly old-time Whigs, resentful of the ascendency of former Free Soilers. They knew that nothing could prevent Andrew's renomination, or Sumner's re-election once the Republicans won the legislature, but they did hope to prevent any formal endorsement of emancipation and Sumner. Dana proposed that the platform should consist merely of a brief resolution supporting the government in the prosecution of the war.[17] The devoted antislavery men, with the Puritanical young George Frisbie Hoar a prominent figure, quickly overrode this move. With a roar of ayes, they carried resolutions calling for the destruction of slavery and re-election of Sumner, and then renominated Andrew.[18]

Chagrined and angry, a group of conservatives, chiefly former Whigs, left the hall prepared to create a new party—the People's Party, supporting Lincoln, the war, and the Constitution alone. But seldom has a schismatic movement been so quickly crushed. Dana, Saltonstall, and others, with the approval of the Springfield *Republican*, prepared a manifesto which, after assailing Sumner's incessant outcry for emancipation, declared: "We want no impotent proclamations now." The next morning Massachusetts men, opening their newspapers at the breakfast table, saw the headlines over the Emancipation Proclamation! We hope, wrote one journalist, that Parker had finished his coffee and muffins before he read this impotent paper! [19]

Andrew rejoiced that the enemy was delivered into his power. "*Go in for the war*," he exhorted his friends. "Hurry up the recruitments. Have grand *war*

16 H. G. Pearson, *John A. Andrew*, II, Ch. IX, offers a good portrait; see the *Nation*, XXXIII (July 28, 1881), 77–78, for another.
17 Dana's letter to C. F. Adams, Sr., Nov. 25, 1861, crisply states: "We cannot justify war on the domestic institutions of the Southern States as an end and object." Adams, *Dana*, II, 260. Joel Parker of Massachusetts and the Joel Parker elected governor of New Jersey this year had no relationship except their devotion to Democratic conservatism.
18 Pearson, *Andrew*, II, 54; Pierce, *Sumner*, IV, 100, 101.
19 W. S. Robinson (Springfield *Republican* corr.), *Warrington Pen Portraits*, 286.

meetings all over the State." He thought they could destroy the dissenting movement in ten days. The new party, composed of Democrats, Bell-Everett Whigs, and conservative Republicans, did take shape at a convention in Faneuil Hall on October 7, but it was pitifully weak. Brigadier-General Charles Devens, reluctantly accepting the nomination for governor, refused to leave his Virginia command to take part in the campaign, and when Charles Francis Adams was chosen to stand for the Senate, his son John Quincy instantly withdrew his name.[20] The natural result was that the Democrats, who on October 8 endorsed Devens, took charge of the opposition, and after that happened, the parties battled with increased ferocity. John Chipman Gray, an anxious young Bostonian, compared America with France in 1793.[21] So alarming did the enhanced fanaticism of the hour seem to conservative men!

But Andrew and the whole slate of Administration Congressmen were certain of triumph by wide margins.

[III]

Since Pennsylvania, Ohio, Indiana, and Illinois elected no governor, their campaigns lacked the drama of the battles in New York and Massachusetts. All presented the familiar spectacle of radical Republicans berating the Administration from the rear while Democrats and ultraconservative Republicans abused it from the front. The most distinctive feature of the struggle, however, was the part played by public apprehension of a large Negro immigration. All four states bordered upon slave territory, and their people realized that a rush of freedmen across the Potomac and Ohio could create appalling problems. The Philadelphia *Inquirer*, a Republican paper, pointed out two days before Lincoln's proclamation that while New England and upper New York would receive few liberated slaves, States further south might get many. Their voices should therefore be potential; "and they *have* spoken, every one of them"—for Ten Eyck of New Jersey, Cowan of Pennsylvania, Sherman of Ohio, Wright of Indiana, and Browning of Illinois had uttered warm remonstrances.[22]

Ohio had long felt distinct tremors on the subject. When the legislature met at the beginning of 1862 petitions had been submitted against any further immigration of colored people, while one even demanded the removal of those already in the State. The House laid this inhuman plea on the table by the close

20 Devens, a Worcester man, had been severely wounded at Fair Oaks; see memoir by J. C. Ropes, *Mass. Hist. Soc. Proceedings*, Series II, Vol. VII (Nov., 1891), 104–117.
21 *Gray-Ropes War Letters*, 6–14, Oct. 15–20, 1862. Gray, of a wealthy family, was commissioned lieutenant this fall. The Springfield *Republican* after the Democratic endorsement of Devens turned back to Andrew and Sumner.
22 Phila. *Inquirer*, Sept. 20, 1862.

vote of 53 to 51. Memorials for debarring Negroes continued to pour in from all parts of the State, to increase in number, and to receive wide press publicity.[23] S. S. Cox played heavily on the fear that Ohio would become the chief asylum for the slaves of Virginia and Kentucky.[24] A lively apprehension that Negro competition would take the bread from the mouths of poor laborers inspired midsummer race riots in Cincinnati and Toledo, where colored men were employed on boats and along the waterfront. Though the Cleveland *Leader* ascribed these outbreaks to the machinations of Democratic agitators among the ignorant Irish,[25] their source was plainly economic.

Indiana also took the Negro question with intense seriousness. The State in 1860 had about 11,000 colored people, and many thought that number quite enough. When the Emancipation Proclamation appeared, the New Albany *Sentinel* and other papers predicted that a deluge of lazy, helpless, and thriftless freedmen would roll across poor Hoosierdom. In Illinois, too, where the latest census had reported a colored population of 7,628, the subject had become painful as soon as the capture of Donelson and Nashville brought a host of refugee slaves into Cairo.[26] David Davis warned the President in mid-October that if they infiltrated into central Illinois, they would do the party grave injury in the election, and Governor Yates telegraphed Lincoln to the same effect. Since 1853 Illinois had on its statute books a law which imposed a heavy fine on every Negro, slave or free, who entered the State, and though many regarded it as unconstitutional, in certain localities it had been enforced. Now, shortly before election day, the Secretary of State prohibited any further entry.[27]

Everywhere, as the campaign rolled forward, the "regular" Democrats accepted the issue drawn by the Emancipation Proclamation, and made the most of it. But to *loyal* War Democrats the proclamation offered a more painful issue, for it posed two plain alternatives. The Administration intended to use every weapon to achieve victory, and it meant to reconstruct some Southern States, if not all, without slavery; should the party acquiesce, or should it demand that what Lincoln had done must be undone? For us, T. J. Barnett warned S. L. M. Barlow, "The issue is, shall we sustain the President, or is a revolution necessary?"[28] Either the country would witness a rigorous effort to carry out Lin-

23 See Cleveland *Leader*, Jan. 16, 1862, for petitions, with editorials April 18 and May 2 on public sentiment; John R. McLean's *Enquirer* verged toward copperheadism.
24 David Lindsey, *Cox*, 62–65.
25 Editorial, July 19, 1862.
26 See, for example, Chicago *Morning Post*, Aug. 30, 1862.
27 Davis to Lincoln, Oct. 14, 1862, RTL Papers; Cole, *Era of the Civil War*, 225, 226. The statements by Davis and Yates measured their fear of a disastrous change in Illinois. Lyman Trumbull warned Lincoln that Democrats there were led by men who, if they gained control, would paralyze the war effort of the State, and perhaps even turn it against the Union. Sept. 7, 1862, RTL Papers.
28 Sept. 25, 1862, Barlow Papers.

coln's policy, or it would see a general overthrow of his authority. Could the Democratic party risk demoralizing the army, inciting generals to mutiny, and creating political chaos throughout the North? War Democrats said no; and the effect of the proclamation was thus to deepen the schism between them and the Democrats who demanded reunion under the old Constitution, leaving slavery untouched.

[IV]

It was inevitable that the party battle should involve the issue of disloyalty. Democratic speakers made the air resound with their championship of civil liberties. "I am glad to see that you follow up the subject of illegal arrests," Horatio Seymour wrote Manton Marble of the *World*. "It must be made the issue." [29] No aspect of the campaign was more interesting than the widespread protest against suspension of the writ of habeas corpus, arbitrary arrests, and interferences with the press. On this issue of civil rights the Administration had laid itself open to an attack based upon principles which every true American revered.

Lincoln's primary anxiety, unescapably, was for the nation's safety. As he later wrote, a limb must often be amputated to save a life, but a life must never be given to save a limb. "I felt that measures, however unconstitutional, might become lawful by becoming indispensable to the preservation of the constitution, through the preservation of the nation." As a broad guiding rule this was unexceptionable. It implied Holmes's later test of clear and present danger.

The difficulty was that the unsystematic Administration, struggling with a thousand problems at once, devised no workable system to implement the rule. The whole problem was clumsily handled. Attorney-General Bates, approaching seventy, inclined to boggle over details, and erratic of judgment, was unequal to the task. Lincoln assigned the field to Seward, who seemed a good choice, but who had quite enough to do in supervising foreign affairs, and was sometimes too irresponsibly casual for the preservation of exact justice. It could be said for the Administration that it executed nobody, established no police state, and rather than institute a reign of terror, let many petty traitors escape its net. But it could also be said that it never created a machinery adequate to protect all innocent men from injustice, that to the end of the war it too often preferred the swift judgment of military tribunals to civil procedures, and that it indulged in too many arbitrary arrests and imprisonments.

Lincoln had solid grounds for authorizing General Scott in April, 1861, to suspend the habeas corpus along the vital communication lines between Phila-

29 Nov. 11, 1862, Manton Marble Papers.

delphia and Washington, a power which Scott deputed to his subordinate commanders.[30] The crisis was desperate; the Constitution provided for suspension if in cases of invasion or rebellion the public safety required it.[31] But the military arrests in Maryland, where heads of the Baltimore police, certain secessionist members of the legislature, and others were clapped into prison, troubled many observers. Futile descents were made by officious Dogberries, sometimes a mere captain, and the grounds alleged for detention were often flimsy. General Banks, in seizing the police officers, merely asserted that they entertained "some purpose not known to the government" which was believed inimical to safety!

During the latter half of 1861 arbitrary arrests had become more numerous, and produced so much resentment that as soon as Congress met in December Lyman Trumbull introduced a resolution calling on Seward to report the number of persons being held, and to state under what law they had been jailed.[32] Various Senators expostulated with Trumbull. If Lincoln and Seward had not seized the dangerous men undermining the government in the North, said Dixon of Connecticut, they would have been guilty of moral treason themselves. Henry Wilson recalled what dire perils had beset the government just after Bull Run, with the army defeated, the ninety-day men leaving, and treason stalking the very Capitol.[33] But Trumbull stood by his guns: "Sir," he said, referring to vital civil liberties, "it is in just such times as these that the greatest danger arises."

While arbitrary arrests continued to excite dissension in the North, the question of the President's right to suspend the habeas corpus reached the courts. John Merryman, who had been drilling some secessionist volunteers near Cockeysville, Maryland, and preaching rebel doctrines, had been arrested May 25, 1861, by General George Cadwalader, and thrown into Fort McHenry. He petitioned Chief Justice Taney, sitting as Federal Circuit Judge, for a writ ordering the general to bring him into court for a hearing. Taney issued the writ, and Cadwalader at once refused to obey it. Thereupon Taney sent a marshal to serve the commander with a citation for contempt of court. The officer, who expected this, ordered men with bayonets to prevent entrance to the fort. The helpless Taney could only prepare a written statement denying the constitutional right of the President to suspend the writ, file it in the Circuit Court, and send a copy to Lincoln, calling upon him to perform his constitutional duty by see-

30 For Lincoln's rule, see *Works*, VII, 281, 282; for the suspension, O. R., II, i, 567, 568. On Oct. 14, 1861, Seward notified Scott that the military line for suppressing the rebellion having been extended as far as Bangor, Maine, "you and any officer acting under your authority are hereby authorized to suspend the writ of habeas corpus in any place between that place and the city of Washington"; Seward Papers, Rochester Univ.

31 Cf. speech by Andrew Johnson, *Cong. Globe*, 37th Cong., 1st Sess., 289, 290. During the Revolution Pennsylvania authorities had suspended the writ.

32 *Cong. Globe*, 37th Cong., 2d Sess., 90 ff.

33 *Ibid.*, 97, 98.

ing that the civil process of the nation was enforced; whereupon Lincoln obtained the Attorney-General's opinion that his suspension order had been quite correct.[34]

By no means all objectionable seizures were made without legal formalities. In the second half of 1861 numerous citizens were arrested on sworn charges which were often of the most trifling character. This was notably true in Kentucky. During the spring of 1862, 34 citizens were indicted in Bourbon County, and after the invasion by Bragg and Kirby-Smith later that year, 205 persons were indicted in Fayette County.[35] Some arrests, however, were amply justified. A great pother, for example, was made over the detention of former Governor Charles S. Morehead, and his release from Fort Warren early in 1862 aroused wide rejoicing in Kentucky; but he was thoroughly disloyal, and soon appeared in England as an agent of the Confederacy—a "blatant traitor," said Senator Henry Wilson.[36]

While the total of arrests throughout the country continued to grow, not one case came into court for a real hearing. This neglect to bring a single person to trial out of the many seized diffused an unhappy impression of governmental inefficiency and fairness. The *National Intelligencer* and *Evening Post* agreed that the Administration's methods savored of the old *lettres de cachet*,[37] and this judgment was heightened by Seward's insouciant remark to W. H. Russell that whenever he wished to arrest any suspect, he had only to touch a little bell on his desk. Horace Greeley, deeply troubled, took steps to lay an eloquent protest before the Secretary. Of course fomenters of sedition must be locked up, he wrote, but Seward should understand that the essential question was whether men should act according to law, or according to Jack Cade's rule, "My mouth shall be Parliament." In Maryland the government, obstructed as it

34 Randall, *Const. Probs. Under Lincoln*, 152-163; O. R., II, i, 574 ff.; White, *Trumbull*, 194-196. The British consul in Baltimore, Frederick Bernard, was in the courtroom when Taney declared the validity of the habeas corpus. He congratulated the aged jurist. "He made a very feeling reply," Bernard wrote Lord John Russell, "that he had been brought up to study, and revere, the English common law, and that, pained as he was to be so obliged at such a moment, he would not shrink from asserting its glorious principles, which were likewise those of the Constitution of the United States." May 30, 1861, FO 5/784. During the Napoleonic Wars the British Government had gone to great lengths to preserve the validity of the writ of habeas corpus. Merryman was shortly released to the civil authorities, and indicted for treason, but the case—like practically all others of the sort—never came to trial. For Bates's opinion sustaining Lincoln see O. R., II, ii, 34.

35 J. T. Dorris, "President Lincoln's Treatment of Kentuckians," *Filson Club History Quarterly*, XXVIII (Jan., 1954), 3-20. Henry Clay's son John was arrested but released on bail, as were many others. A large business of oath-taking, bond-filing, and paroling sprang up in Kentucky, the amount of bond required ranging from $500 to $20,000. Five volumes of records in the Federal Circuit Court file in Louisville measure the extent of this business.

36 *Cong. Globe*, 37th Cong., 3rd Sess., 35.

37 *Nat. Intelligencer*, Feb. 12, 1862; Greeley, Oct. 3, 1861, to Samuel Wilkeson, Seward Papers, Rochester.

was by bad Federal judges, might have to move in a highhanded way. But in New York and Connecticut it had no occasion to use any law except such as was bound in sheep; "and when you grab such men as Col. Wall of New Jersey," wrote Greeley, "you tear the whole fabric of society."

Public irritation was increased by well-founded reports that prisoners were being treated inhumanely. Much disturbed, some influential New Yorkers went to Henry W. Bellows, head of the Sanitary Commission, asking that he investigate, and on October 5, 1861, he requested permission to visit some of the New York jails.[38] He found several scores of civilians confined in Fort Lafayette in New York bay. In one small casemate twenty-three prisoners, two-thirds of them in irons, were crammed together without beds, bedding, or the commonest necessaries; in other casements, fourteen feet by twenty-four, they were almost equally crowded. According to a remonstrance which some of the prisoners sent Lincoln, the misery of inmates approached that of slaves on the middle passage. Two battery rooms, dark and close, held sixty-nine men. Though many of the prisoners had become ill, they had no fresh water except for drinking, and little of that, while their food consisted of coarse soldiers' rations badly cooked.[39] Yet they included such distinguished men as Severn Teackle Wallis, a leader of the Maryland bar, reformer, and philanthropist, and Charles J. Faulkner, who after representing a Virginia district in Congress for eight years had been Minister to France.

Conditions at Forts Monroe and McHenry were similar.[40] But the most dismal of all prisons was one in Washington within an easy walk of Congress and the White House.

This was the Old Capitol, a decaying jail hastily refurbished for captured Confederates, refugee Negroes, blockade runners, and state prisoners. The verminous rooms stank of open drains, sweaty inmates, and the eternal fare of salt pork, beans, and rice. A military guard clattered its arms on the cobblestones outside while patrols thumped up and down the wooden hallways. The dark, ill-ventilated cells, kept full to bursting, became breeding places for all kinds of maladies. During 1862 a midsummer influx of captured Confederates raised the population to 600. The one redeeming feature of this ramshackle barn was its convivial jollity, for most prisoners were herded into five large second-story rooms partitioned out of the great chambers which had been occupied by Congress just after the burning of the Capitol in 1815. Here, by pooling their resources, the inmates could while away the hours with poker, dominoes, tobacco, whisky, and talk.

38 Nat. Intelligencer, Oct. 5, 1861.
39 Memorial of State prisoners in Port Lafayette to Lincoln, Oct. 8, 1861, Seward Papers, Rochester.
40 Dix to Seward, Sept. 18, Oct. 21, Seward Papers.

[V]

By 1862 the lengthening roll of prisoners, the irritation of the public and Congress, and the demands of military leaders, made it imperative for Attorney-General Bates to take some action. General Buell laid the problem squarely before him. Bates in reply tried to draw a line between judicial arrests on one side, and political or military arrests on the other, saying the judicial cases must go to the civil courts, but the others were subject to the "somewhat broad, and yet undefined, discretion of the President, as political chief of the nation" and commander in chief. The Attorney-General wisely decided that the Department of Justice had no powers in connection with prisoners held on political or military grounds, for it could deal only with offenses against clear Federal statutes.

Bates was also wise in making it clear that he was anxious to avoid indictments for treason, so strictly defined in the Constitution, except when the offense was flagrant and clear.[41] He knew how many difficulties the First Amendment threw in the way of prosecutions. Early in 1862 he instructed the Federal attorney in Missouri, J. O. Broadhead, that a few examples should be made, if only to prove that the Union was vigorously alert; but no cases should be pushed to trial except those in which conviction was certain. Not only was treason a crime hard to prove, but conviction often accomplished nothing except to create a political martyr. Federal officers had to beware of men who made charges and demanded trials out of personal malice or love of publicity, and should remember also how much harm a series of acquittals would do the government. It would be far more politic, Bates thought, to try to punish internal enemies for vulgar misdemeanors or felonies than to proceed against them for treason, which had an aura of dignity.[42]

Two conspicuous instances of arbitrary confinement were military, but they had a political coloration. Though a certain murkiness attaches to the case of Major Justus McKinstry, he was unquestionably handled tyrannically. As acting

41 "Overheated zeal," he wrote, would produce a reaction; Randall, *Const. Probs.*, 87. Incidentally, the Attorney-General had but a tiny office force. In fact, when the war began, he had only an assistant, a clerk, and a messenger. This force was enlarged in August, 1861, to eight persons, the salaries of the nine totaling $20,500. Yet his duties, even at the outset, were considerable. An Act of Aug. 2, 1861, gave the Attorney-General supervision over Federal district attorneys and marshals, authorized him to employ counsel to assist them in their work, and required them to report to him. A. G. Langeluttig, *The Dept. of Justice*, 6–8.

42 Bates to Broadhead, April 10, 15, 16, etc., Dept. of Justice Records, Letters Sent, Nat. Archives. In the spring of 1862 Pierce Butler of Philadelphia brought suit against Simon Cameron for trespass, assault and battery, and false imprisonment, Cameron having supplied the troops who arrested Butler. A similar suit was brought against Gideon Welles. Lincoln instructed the Justice Department to defend such suits. Attorney-General Bates took appropriate action, and Congress passed protective legislation. See Bates to U. S. Dist. Attorney G. A. Coffey, May 5, 1862, Justice Dept., Letters Sent, Nat. Archives.

quartermaster in St. Louis with Harney, remaining on as quartermaster of the Western Department under Frémont, this Regular Army officer incurred the hostility of the Safety Committee which had broken Harney. He was arrested November 13, 1861, and confined in the arsenal. No basis for the arrest was stated, and seven months later he was still ignorant of the grounds. General S. R. Curtis, who gave the order, received it from somebody else. From whom? Horace Greeley, who became interested, made inquiries which showed that the President, Secretary of War, and Adjutant-General knew nothing about it. Reports were meanwhile circulated that McKinstry had handled contracts corruptly. But the Judge-Advocate in St. Louis found no facts to support such charges, the board of claims sitting in the city discovered nothing to impeach his integrity, and when the Van Wyck committee repeated the charges, he published a detailed refutation. He was seemingly a passable officer, but the affair had blasted his military career, and early in 1863 Lincoln confirmed his dismissal.[43]

Still worse was the arbitrary eight months' imprisonment of Brigadier-General Charles P. Stone, which in time became a *cause célèbre*. This graduate of West Point, veteran of the Mexican War, and friend of McClellan was held responsible by Congressional radicals for the Ball's Bluff disaster, and sharply questioned by the Committee on the Conduct of the War. Stanton then ordered his arrest, and on February 10, 1862, he was confined at Fort Lafayette, on charges vaguely reported as misconduct in the battle, correspondence with the enemy, treachery in letting the Confederates build a fort under his guns, and an intention of sacrificing his whole command. He was guiltier than people supposed, declared the New York *Tribune:* "The knell of traitors within already tolls." [44] Pleading in vain for trial, he lingered in prison more than six months. Lincoln had written: "Whether he be guilty or innocent, circumstances required, as appeared to me, such proceedings to be had against him for the public safety." McClellan, who might have insisted on an early trial, played an equivocal part. When on August 16 Stone was curtly released it was without acquittal, and—though he did serve later with Banks in Louisiana and with the Army of the Potomac—he was never restored to important command.[45] He

---

43 N. Y. *Tribune,* Jan. 18, 1862; see the documented pamphlet, "Vindication of General McKinstry." As provost-marshal in St. Louis, McKinstry had tried to restrain sedition by numerous arrests high and low. But Frémont had handled such arrests with judgment. He brought with him to St. Louis a Cincinnati attorney of distinction, Richard M. Corwine, whom he appointed judge-advocate; and Corwine (succeeded later by Gustav Koerner) sat on cases, took depositions, and recommended releases or courts-martial. Koerner, *Memoirs,* II, 170–173.

44 Editorial, Feb. 12, 1862.

45 Flower, *Stanton,* 136; T. Harry Williams, "Investigation, 1862," *American Heritage,* VI (Dec. 1954), 16–21; *Committee on Conduct of War, Report,* II, 252–510. Stone, though

thought that Stanton lied about the affair, and that McClellan treated him very shabbily. Certainly the episode must be regarded as one of the grossest breaches of civil liberty in our history. During his prison days Stone sent a friend a letter that might have come out of Russia.[46] "For one hundred and thirty days," he wrote, "I have been hoping what you have hoped—a trial and acquittal; but up to this time have not advanced so far as to receive a word of charges."

Lincoln was well aware early in 1862 that he must find some fairer solution of this problem, and the advent of Stanton to office offered an opportunity for turning a new page. An executive order of February 14, 1862, therefore decreed that all political prisoners in military custody should, after due inquiry, be released on parole, with an amnesty for past offenses; that all extraordinary arrests should be made in the future under the direction of the military authorities alone; and that spies, secret agents, and others whom the Secretary of War regarded as dangerous to the public safety, should be held in custody under his control. Much was to be said for thus handing the subject over to the War Department. After all, arrests usually had to be made, wherever military rule prevailed, by armed force, and the line between civil and military offenses was often thin. Yet some men who knew Secretary Stanton must have shuddered, for of all members of the Cabinet, he had the least judicial mind and most arbitrary temper.

Free as yet from the kind of odium that had gathered about Seward, Stanton began with a fairly clean slate. He adopted a sensible course for sifting the great mixed body of prisoners on hand, appointing John A. Dix and Edwards Pierrepont of New York commissioners to examine each case separately and render a verdict. These men held personal interviews, allowed friends of the accused to appear, and invited written statements, all with dispatch—in one day at Fort Lafayette they handled ten cases. Visiting one jail after another, they completed their work before May, 1862, releasing most of the prisoners. Meanwhile, with all eyes fastened on the advances of McClellan and Grant, and hope of victory running high, extraordinary arrests almost ceased. Public opinion warmly approved of the clearance of prisoners and the relaxation of tension.[47]

However, the liberalization of government policy during the first half of

---

not a knave, was a good deal of a fool. His second wife was a Louisiana woman, and he showed sympathy with slavery. Commanding on the Maryland shore in the early days of the war, he issued an order which his officers took as calling for active enforcement of the Fugitive Slave Act. When John A. Andrew censured an officer of the Twentieth Massachusetts for following the order, Stone wrote an insulting letter on the "usurpations" of the governor. Pearson, *Andrew*, I, 312–316.

46 To S. L. M. Barlow, June 26, 1862, Barlow Papers.

47 Exec. Order No. 1 Relating to War Prisoners, O. R., II, ii, 221–223; Pierrepont was a noted attorney of New York.

1862 proved only a prelude to new rigors in the second half. Military failure East and West bred pessimism and distrust, so that disloyalty grew bolder, while the Administration became less inclined to take risks. Moreover, the first limping draft act in July provoked evasion and resistance, to meet which the War Department had to exercise extraordinary powers. Hence on August 8, 1862, the War Department laid down a whole series of stringent rules. Draft eligibles were forbidden to quit the country or make uncontrolled journeys at home. Any man who left his community to evade enrollment might be instantly arrested and sentenced to nine months (the usual draft period) in the army. The habeas corpus was suspended for all persons guilty of "disloyal practices," which now specially meant the discouragement of enlistments. Many detentions, some of them highly controversial, followed.

Happily, within a short time Stanton introduced a certain regularity into his procedures. He had Major L. C. Turner, judge-advocate for the Washington district, take charge of political arrests, and decreed that none should be made except on Turner's warrant, or (within military districts) that of commanders, or of governors of States. Responsibility was thus concentrated in a small number of men. Turner might cite any arrested civilian for trial by a military commission, but this was not mandatory, and most prisoners were released without appearing before any tribunal. Late in September, 1862, Stanton by War Department order provided for the appointment of provost-marshals in the several States, responsible to a provost-marshal general; and to this last office he temporarily assigned Simeon Draper of New York, an intimate friend of Seward and Weed, and a genial, broad-minded merchant of shrewd judgment. The men named as state provost-marshals were in general civilians, and were well chosen.[48]

But the habeas corpus remained suspended with respect to persons held for disloyal practices, and during the summer and fall many men suffered. Two Iowa editors, Dennis A. Mahony of the Dubuque *Herald* and Dana Sheward of the Fairfield *Constitution and Union*, were arrested, carried to Washington, and thrown into the Old Capitol prison. At the same time a number of prominent Illinoisans were seized, including William J. Allen, who had been elected to Congress from Logan's district, and three judges, Andrew D. Duff, C. H. Constable, and John H. Mulkey. In Ohio the arrest of Dr. Edwin B. Olds of Lancaster aroused great indignation; in New Jersey, that of an able attorney and writer, James W. Wall. The country had applauded the apprehension of draft "skedaddlers" as they tried to escape into Canada, but the jailing of prominent Democrats for their denunciation of Lincoln's policies was a different matter. It was significant that Manton Marble, whose *World* had at first

48 Weed, *Memoir*, II, 483. Stanton allowed the travel restrictions to die.

treated the extraordinary arrests as largely an unfortunate necessity, now joined other editors in angrily indicting *lettres de cachet* and bastilles. The *World* was a real power, for it had a circulation of 40,000, and a brilliant editorial staff.

Moreover, Stanton's characteristic arrogance had made itself felt. A case in point was offered by two brokers in substitutes whom he had the New York police summarily arrest in the summer of 1862. They had advertised in the press that they would obtain substitutes for draft eligibles. Stanton decided that this was an interference with enlistments, and after keeping the men several days in a city jail, sent them to Fort Lafayette. He did not allow the story of the arrests to be published until one day after the report that he had decided that such brokerage was improper. Thus the public got the impression that a warning had preceded the offense; but when Judge-Advocate Turner visited Fort Lafayette he was horrified to learn that the prisoners had not been warned, and were being held on *ex post facto* proceedings. And though Stanton laid down rules, he allowed vast confusion to envelop the subject. Overzealousness by officers who made arrests was followed by carelessness in getting charges tried and endless buck-passing. Thus in the Mahony case the buck was passed from Marshal Hoxie to the provost marshal, then to the military governor of Washington, then to Assistant Secretary Watson, then to Judge-Advocate Turner, then to Halleck, and then to Stanton—and nothing was done until after the election! Mahony had powerful friends to follow the buck, but what of those who were friendless? [49]

Horatio Seymour and other Democratic leaders hence met a large response from independent voters when they made the arrests a major issue of the fall campaign. Some of the imprisoned men profited from their political martyrdom. Mahony was nominated for Congress; Allen was renominated and reelected; a citizen who had been arrested in Galena was chosen mayor. Lincoln made matters worse by an ill-timed proclamation on September 24 announcing that the habeas corpus could not be invoked on behalf of persons who discouraged enlistments, resisted the draft, or engaged in "any disloyal practice." He was simply trying to clarify Administration policy, but as he gave no argument justifying his course or explaining his intentions, his statement seemed

49 Mahony wrote a crisp, vivid book, *Prisoner of State*. He and Sheward appealed to Stanton and Lincoln by letter, in vain; then Charles Mason, former chief justice of Iowa, took up their case. Assistant Secretary of War Watson actually told Mason: "Let them prove themselves innocent and they will be discharged!" In his diary Mason gives a fascinating account of the way in which Turner, Halleck, Stanton, and others all evaded his efforts to gain a hearing for the editors. He became convinced that partisan politics was behind their detention during the campaign. MS Diary, Columbia University. But Allen, unlike many others, would seem to have deserved his arrest. A Tennesseean by birth, he had openly proposed to Logan that Illinois be divided so that the southern half could join the Confederacy, and he advised young men to go south to fight; Cole, *Era of the Civil War*, 302. In the House he played a role considerably more clownish than sinister.

to many to offer a threat of overriding all opposition by punitive arrests. Senator Bayard and other Democrats declared that any man who protested against the draft, or expressed gloomy views about the war, or quarreled with any Administration activity, might be accused, thrown into jail, denied trial, and kept in some fort, arsenal, or other place of confinement until the close of the war.[50]

In the midst of the battle an Indiana grand jury issued a report (August 4) which estimated that the Knights of the Golden Circle had 15,000 disloyal members in that State, and handed down 60 indictments for treason, conspiracy against the government, and other crimes. Democrats were quick to declare that this document reflected a keener interest in the fall elections than in the safety of the nation, and its estimate was certainly a wild exaggeration. The Knights flourished especially in areas of Southern blood. Founded long before the Civil War to promote filibustering and expansion in the circle around the Caribbean, their secret order had been readily converted in 1861 to underground support of the Confederacy. Just how numerous, active, and dangerous it was nobody will ever know, for its activities were clandestine.[51] It was true that some Knights were trying to embarrass enlistments and encourage desertion. But it was also true that Governor Morton was a partisan who foresaw that a Democratic legislature would resist efforts to make the war (in his words) "instant and terrible," [52] and would try to keep it moderate. Probably the indictments did the Administration ticket more harm than good.

It was clear, as election day approached, that the civil-rights issue was strengthening the Democrats by stiffening their lines and converting uneasy citizens. Even the Springfield *Republican* asserted that the methods which the Administration employed did not befit a free government.[53]

[VI]

The October elections revealed a powerful wave of discontent—but not an overwhelming current. In Pennsylvania, Ohio, and Indiana the Democrats

50 *Cong. Globe*, 37th Cong., 3rd Sess., 72.
51 The founder, G. W. L. Bickley of Cincinnati, set energetically to work in 1861 in transforming the order. After planting lodges in Kentucky and Tennessee, he encouraged agents who established others in Southern Indiana and Illinois. Prentice of the Louisville *Journal* in 1861 charged that the Knights were the very brain and soul of secession in Kentucky. Governor Morton in Indiana used Colonel Henry B. Carrington in an excited, harsh, and vindictive warfare against their machinations which all too often presumed that nearly every Democrat was a potential traitor. See George Fort Milton, *Lincoln and the Fifth Column*, Ch. IV; Stampp, *Indiana Politics*, 151, 152.
52 Foulke, *Morton*, I, 118.
53 Editorials, Sept. 27, Nov. 1, 1862. The *Republican* thought Lincoln's proclamation of Sept. 26 badly timed, badly phrased, and unfortunate in omitting qualifications and restraints.

polled a majority of the popular vote and took a majority of the House seats. Their margins, however, were moderate. In Pennsylvania the vote stood 219,140 to 215,616; in Ohio, 184,332 to 178,755; and even in Indiana only 128,160 to 118, 517. In Pennsylvania, the two major parties split the Congressional places almost evenly, but in Ohio the Democrats won fourteen seats and the Republicans only five, while in Indiana the Democrats took seven of the eleven seats. Vallandigham lost his place only because a Republican county had been added to his district. Although these three States definitely aligned themselves against the Administration, Republicans could find a good deal in the results to comfort them. In Pennsylvania, for example, part of the slender Democratic margin was provided by the sheer efficiency of the party organization, far surpassing that of the Republicans. In Ohio the small Democratic margin could be traced, at least in part, to the absence of many Union men in the army, and to the fact that, as the Cincinnati *Commercial* put it, "the prejudice of race has been inflamed, and used by the Democratic party with an energy and ingenuity perfectly infernal." [54]

All eyes now turned to New York, New Jersey, and Illinois—and particularly to the first. The real stake in the New York contest, it seemed to many, was national power. Behind the mask of Wadsworth, conservatives of both parties saw the sinister figure of Chase, archenemy of Seward and of moderate policies; already staggered by the Republican defeat in Ohio, the Secretary must not be allowed to triumph in the Empire State. Not only Seward, but Montgomery Blair and Bates, were believed to be at heart against Wadsworth, and it is certain that Thurlow Weed was lukewarm if not disloyal in the Republican cause. Bennett's *Herald*, professedly for Lincoln and the Union, exerted all its influence to help elect Seymour. On the Democratic side, efficient city machines for once worked in unison. The Mozart Hall Democracy and Tammany Democracy had made a bargain which ensured Fernando Wood, his brother Benjamin Wood of the *Daily News*, James Brooks of the *Express*, and Anson Herrick of the *Atlas* seats in Congress; these three newspapers gave stanch support to each other, while the halls united with the Albany Regency in forming a solid front behind Horatio Seymour. McClellan could hardly contain his hatred for Wadsworth. "I have so thorough a contempt for the man and regard him as such a vile traitorous miscreant that I do not wish the great State of New York disgraced by having such a thing at its head." [55]

54 *Tribune Almanac*, 1863, *passim*; *Annual Cyc.* 1862, *passim*. Of the Pennsylvania seats, according to the *Tribune Almanac*, 54, the Democrats took eleven, the People's Union Party (Republicans) ten, the War Democrats one, independent Union ticket one, and Independent Republican one. In Pennsylvania a Republican legislature had done some gerrymandering. See S. L. Davis, *Pennsylvania Politics, 1860–65*, 176 ff.

55 *N. Y. Tribune*, June 16, 1863, describes the bargain of the halls; McClellan Oct. 17, 1862, to Barlow, Barlow Papers.

The November elections gave the New York Democrats a decisive victory. Seymour had a majority of nearly 11,000, and the Democrats won 17 Congressional seats, the Administration only 14. Roscoe Conkling, Lincoln's brilliant young supporter in the House, lost his place. Though weariness, Republican disunity, and resentment over arbitrary arrests all counted in the result, here the major explanation lay simply in the military reverses. Bryant had written Lincoln just before the election that Seymour's election, "a public calamity," might be averted if the armies would only win a timely battle, but that continued military inactivity would lose New York and other States.[56] And John Cochrane later wrote Lincoln that the adverse vote expressed not hostility to him, but disappointment in the dragging war.[57]

If Bryant thought New York a disaster, he might well have called New Jersey a debacle. Joel Parker, a tall, dignified, well-educated Douglas Democrat, ran away with the governorship by a vote of 61,307 to 46,710, while Democrats took four of the five House seats, and gained full control of the legislature. In Illinois a similar dissatisfaction prevailed. "If we are beaten in this State two weeks hence," Horace White telegraphed Lincoln late in October, "it will be because McClellan and Buell won't fight." On election day the Democrats carried Illinois 136,662 to 120,116, taking nine of the fourteen House seats. The President's friend Leonard Swett was defeated in a district which had been Republican in the last two elections. Lyman Trumbull, anticipating a dark future, wrote Zach Chandler that the results might prove revolutionary. "Should not be surprised if the Democrats in the end became the war party. This is their true policy. I fear a humiliating compromise. . . ."[58] Unquestionably the reverse in his own prairie home cut Lincoln to the heart.

In peripheral States, where emancipation had been the chief issue, the outcome was somewhat equivocal. Kansas elected a Republican Congressman. Final Missouri returns gave Congressional seats to two Democrats, as against seven men who labeled themselves Republican, emancipationist, or independent Unionist—one of them Frank P. Blair; a result hailed as a notable victory for the Administration. Emancipation had won, said one editor, because the people had seen slavery and freedom in competition, and taken note of the superior prosperity of the free States.[59] The fact was, however, that an ordinance the previous June had disfranchised many Missourians, that the polls were guarded by troops who barred anyone who had not taken an oath of allegiance to the

56 Samuel J. Tilden wrote the peroration for one of Seymour's speeches, promising the South if it but re-entered the Union absolute local self-government and fresh guarantees of equal rights; Letters and Memorials, I, 167.
57 N. Y. Times, Nov. 5, 1862; Cochrane, Nov. 5, 1862, RTL Papers.
58 White, Oct. 22, 1862, RTL Papers; Trumbull, Nov. 9, 1862, Chandler Papers.
59 Providence Journal, Nov. 17, 1862. Andrew carried Massachusetts 70,000 to 50,000; Pearson, Andrew, II, 60.

Union and the provisional State government, and that numerous citizens were absent in the Confederate army. Delaware chose a Democratic Representative; Maryland and Kentucky held no elections.

Altogether, the oft-repeated statement that the Border States stood by Lincoln while almost the whole North outside New England went against him is inaccurate. After all, Michigan, Iowa, and California took their stand beside the Yankee Northeast, while a change of 2,000 votes in Pennsylvania and 3,000 in Ohio would have altered the whole outcome there. Considering the unfavorable circumstances, the Administration did fairly well in the North. As for the borderland, its voice was muffled by force. In Missouri even loyal Democrats felt an element of intimidation; that State was not, indeed, to know a full, free, and fair election until 1876. In Delaware also the use of troops to guard the polls aroused lasting resentment, for more than a thousand soldiers were brought into the State.[60]

That the election was a serious Administration reverse nobody ever doubted. It filled Democratic leaders with exultation, and encouraged disloyalists. It was a vote of want of confidence, and under a parliamentary system, the government headed by Lincoln might have been compelled to resign. Though under existing conditions, with the South gone, it was almost impossible for the Republicans to lose the House, their strength was sadly shaken. The best computation available, based on the vote for Speaker in the next Congress, gives 77 out-and-out anti-Administration members against 101 Administration men.[61] Had they taken fifteen additional seats, the Democrats would have gained control. As it was, the Administration on clear-cut party measures could carry the day. But measures were seldom clear-cut, and as we have said, the party situation was chaotic. Lincoln had as many foes in the Senate on the Republican side as on the Democratic, while in the House many members, from Thad Stevens down, were ready to show their independence. Time was to prove that, like Presidents before and since, he would have to rely on bipartisan support to carry some of his most cherished measures.

Lincoln's explanation of this reverse, set forth in a letter to Carl Schurz, was inadequate. He believed three main causes were responsible. The Democratic voters had been left in a majority by the departure of Administration supporters for the war; their leaders had taken advantage of this by making frenzied efforts to reinstate themselves in power, and part of the Republican press, by villifying the Administration, had given them the weapons. He added a fact of greater weight: "Certainly the ill success of the war had much to do with this." Secretary Chase expressed his feelings acridly: "But after all can

60 Lucien Carr, *Missouri*, 354–356; H. Clay Reed, *Delaware*, I, 163 ff.
61 Greeley, *American Conflict*, II, 254; *National Almanac*, 1864, pp. 78, 79.

we complain that the people are not satisfied with an unfruitful debt and a mismanaged war?" [62]

Unquestionably many elements, including high prices, high taxes, talk of corruption, the suspension of the habeas corpus, the arrests, the draft, and fear of Negro competition in the labor market, had played a part in the grand result. If the Emancipation Proclamation gained votes for the Administration in New England, northern Ohio, and Michigan, it lost votes in other areas. But looming above all other considerations was the failure of the government to bring a close of the horrible struggle within sight. "The people," said the Cincinnati *Gazette*, "are depressed by the interminable nature of this war, as so far conducted, and by the rapid exhaustion of the national resources without progress." [63] That was the gist of the matter.

62   To Hiram Barney, Oct. 15, 1862, Chase Coll., Pa. Hist. Soc.
63   Editorial, "The Moral of the Election," Oct. 17, 1862. The RTL Papers are full of letters to Lincoln on the subject. He wrote Schurz on Nov. 10, 1862, and Schurz replied that the people had some reason to administer their "severe reproof."
    Administration interferences with freedom of the press also played a part in the election. But these became graver at a later date in the war, and full treatment is reserved to a subsequent chapter. Thomas F. Carroll offers a sound introduction in "Freedom of Speech During the Civil War," *Virginia Law Review*, IX (May, 1923), pp. 516-551.

13

Lincoln Dismisses McClellan and Faces Congress

IN THE weeks preceding and following the election, Lincoln was far less concerned with politics than with the progress of the war. Antietam was too indecisive to satisfy him, for McClellan had merely parried Lee's blow, striking none in return. In the West, Perryville and its sequels were equally disappointing. When Buell's sluggishness seemed to match McClellan's, young Nicolay dryly commented: "It is rather a good thing to be a major-general; one can take things so leisurely." To the President, as to Cabinet and Congress, one question was paramount: Would the Army of the Potomac try to crush Lee before the first wintry storms?

One of the many evidences of Lincoln's anxiety for action lies in the irritable telegraphic exchanges between Halleck and McClellan. The President's long strides carried him several times a day to the War Department, where he not only conferred with Stanton and Halleck but shaped many of their dispatches. Stanton hated McClellan, for he could never forgive the general's bitter reproaches after the Seven Days; Halleck was taciturnly antagonistic; Lincoln was grimly patient.[1] Why, Halleck demanded by wire, did McClellan not pursue the enemy instead of tarrying to bury the dead? How many had been slain and wounded on each side? What was the exact position of the two armies? When would he move? Lincoln's own sense of frustration breathed in these messages.

The President put the same queries to Allan Pinkerton when that confidential agent of McClellan brought his Scots accent into the White House on September 22. Knowing that Pinkerton would report everything to his chief, Lincoln took pains to mention the priceless value of the two recent victories. But—why had McClellan been so slow in reaching South Mountain? Why had

---

1 Stanton freely expressed regret that Burnside had not taken the army after Pope's failure; Butterworth, Sept. 23, 1862, to Barlow, Barlow Papers. For Halleck's antipathy see Comte de Paris, II, 540; for the Halleck-McClellan exchanges, O. R., I, xix, pt. 2, 339 ff.

he not renewed the battle the day after Antietam? Why had he allowed the
rebels to recross the Potomac? Pinkerton expatiated upon the superior strength
of the enemy (crediting Lee with 140,000 men at Antietam!), the exhaustion
of the Union troops after the battle, and the facilities which the low stage of
the Potomac gave for Lee's retreat. The agent thought he had made an impression upon Lincoln. "For myself, you know," he wrote McClellan, "I am rather
prejudiced against him—but I must confess that he impressed me more at this
interview with his honesty toward you and his desire to do you justice than he
has ever done before." [2]

The dreary story of McClellan's delays and excuses, which had so long
exasperated the radicals in Washington, was being resumed. Some of his soldiers
read his pleas of fatigue and discouragement in the ranks with incredulity. "To
us of the Thirteenth Massachusetts," wrote one, "it seemed just possible that
the enemy might be equally tired and a good deal more discomfited." Many
officers felt the same. Robert Gould Shaw records their disappointment when
Lee withdrew. "When we heard that he had gone, the day after the battle, we
said it would ruin McClellan." The general had not properly exploited his victory, Meade informed his wife: "I think myself he errs on the side of prudence
and caution. . . ." As we have noted, Lee, falling back to the area of Winchester and Bunker Hill where the rich Shenandoah Valley afforded full
supplies, indulged his veterans in a much-needed rest while he labored strenuously to refill his ranks; and Richmond aided him so effectively that by October
he had about 70,000 fighting men. McClellan meanwhile satisfied himself with
reoccupying Harpers Ferry as a bridgehead on the south side of the Potomac,
and putting Sumner with two corps in possession of it and the fortified heights
above. His own strength was not far from twice Lee's, but he did not think it
safe to go beyond Harpers Ferry, lest he provoke the overwhelming enemy
host! [3]

The chagrin of Administration leaders when they found that no effort was
being made to press Lee was explosive. Barnett of the Interior Department
talked at length on September 23 with Lincoln and Caleb Smith. "I am convinced," he wrote Barlow, "that the government, if they dared, would supersede Mac." [4] Why did they not dare? Because they feared the resentment of
the army; because, too, they did not know whom to put in his place. "Oh, put
anybody!" said Ben Wade, but Lincoln replied: "Wade, *anybody* will do for
you, but I must have *somebody*."

    2 Pinkerton, Sept. 22, 1862, to McClellan; Pinkerton Papers.
    3 C. E. Davis, Jr., *Three Years in the Army*, 142; Nicolay, *Lincoln's Secretary*, 149;
Shaw to his wife, Jan. 10, 1863, Shaw Papers; Meade, *Meade*, 319. On Oct. 20, 1862, McClellan reported an aggregate of 159,860 present, with 144,433 effectives; Lee at the same time
had 79,595 present for duty, with 68,033 effectives.
    4 Sept. 23, 1862, Barlow Papers.

The visit to the front was significant. In his uneasiness, Lincoln felt that he must carry his demands directly to McClellan. Cabinet members demurred, Stanton in particular declaring that McClellan would use the visit as an excuse for thereafter writing the President direct instead of going through channels. Lincoln however insisted, and taking a special train to Harpers Ferry on October 1, met the general at Sumner's headquarters. He reviewed Sumner's corps, riding along its ranks as unit after unit dipped colors, presented arms, and cheered. Everyone thought him thin and careworn; a future President, Hayes, noted that, mounted on a white horse with his trousers hitched nearly to the top of his boots, Lincoln was heedless of the ludicrous figure he cut.[5] One corps commander, Hooker, was not there, having been invalided to Washington. But Lincoln talked with other generals, viewed the two battlefields, looked at the John Brown engine house, and in particular conferred with McClellan.

The public impression that he wanted to hurry little Mac was correct. In fact, he told the general emphatically that he must now act with spirit, or he was lost. The President wished him to cross the Potomac east of the Blue Ridge, thus keeping his army between Lee and Washington, while McClellan wished to cross west and attack Lee in the Shenandoah. On his return, Lincoln issued an order, through Halleck, which any other officer would have regarded as peremptory (October 6):

The President directs that you cross the Potomac and give battle to the enemy or drive him south. Your army must move now while the roads are good. If you cross the river between the enemy and Washington, and cover the latter by your line of operations, you can be reinforced with 30,000 men. If you move up the valley of the Shenandoah, not more than 12,000 or 15,000 can be sent you. The President advises the interior line between Washington and the enemy, but he does not order it. He is very desirous that your army move as soon as possible.

Lincoln was peremptory because he had come back totally unable to understand why an immediate forward movement was not undertaken. The troops seemed rested and well equipped, and the officers eager for movement. Several of McClellan's generals had written strong complaints to Cabinet members. Hooker, holding a series of conferences in his Washington sickroom with Secretary Chase, assured him that it was not true that the troops or officers idolized the little Napoleon, that McClellan really had no dash or boldness, and that he was unfit to lead a great army.[6] Garfield, waiting for a new command, agreed. Pinkerton, learning all this at the War Department, hastened to warn

5 Fitz-John Porter hailed Lincoln's arrival in a note to Manton Marble: "The President is here. His visits have been always followed by injury. So look out—another proclamation or war order." Sept. 30, 1862, Manton Marble Papers, LC.
6 "Hooker is looking for promotion to be General-in-Chief," wrote Fitz-John Porter, "and will turn a somersault to get it. . . . Watch him. . . . He is ambitious and unscrupulous." Lincoln's order above is in O. R., I, xix, pt. 1, p. 72.

McClellan that he faced a clear alternative: If he attacked and won a reasonable success, he would be advanced to the highest command, but if he stood still, he would be dismissed.

For two main reasons McClellan elected to stand still. He must wait until the Potomac rose to be sure Lee would not recross it; and he must finish drilling new recruits, reorganizing his forces, and procuring sufficient blankets, shoes, uniforms, and camp equipment. A wrangling interchange between McClellan and Halleck continued through most of October and grew steadily more acrimonious. The War Department insisted that it had furnished adequate supplies, and certainly Meigs made every effort to do so. But Meade was telling his wife that hundreds of his men were shoeless, and nothing would satisfy McClellan. "The men cannot march without shoes," he wrote, at precisely the same time that Lee was confiding to Jefferson Davis what pain it gave him to watch 8,000 barefoot veterans "limping over the rocky roads." During October 95,000 pairs of footgear were sent to McClellan.[7]

As McClellan waited, Jeb Stuart made a daring raid into Pennsylvania with 1,800 hard-riding troopers at his back. At dawn on October 10 he drove through Mercersburg, occupied Chambersburg that night, and swept south again into Virginia, bringing out some prisoners, 1,200 fresh mounts, and valuable information. Three Union cavalry leaders, Averill, Pleasanton, and Stoneman, had ridden furiously to intercept him, and gotten nothing but hard knocks for their pains. Why did you not catch Stuart in your toils? demanded the War Department of McClellan. His explanation that the government had provided a wretched remount service angered Meigs, who hotly replied that he was furnishing 1,500 horses a week, meeting strict national specifications, but that McClellan's troops did not know how to take care of them.[8]

At this point Lincoln resumed the process which Nicolay termed poking sharp sticks under Little Mac's ribs. On October 13 he sat down to remind the general of a previous rebuke for overcautiousness. Was he not overcautious when he assumed that he could not do what the enemy was constantly doing? McClellan had telegraphed Halleck that he could not subsist his army at Winchester until the railroad from Harpers Ferry to that town was repaired. But Lee was now subsisting his army at Winchester without rail communications, wagoning stores a distance twice as great as that from Harpers Ferry, and with half the wagons that the Union army possessed. Time was essential to the

7 Pinkerton to McClellan, Oct. 6, 1862, Pinkerton Papers; O. R., I, xix, pt. 2, 422–424, 465, 466.
8 Thomason, *Stuart*, 291–319. The Confederate remount service is treated in Charles W. Ramsdell, "General Robert E. Lee's Horse Supply, 1863–1865," *Am. Hist. Review*, XXXV (July, 1930), 758–777. McClellan's army of 122,000 at this time required 34,000 draft horses, 6,850 artillery horses, and 5,000 cavalry horses, or about 46,000 in all; Report of General Rufus Ingalls, O. R., I, xix, pt. 1, 94–97.

Union, Lincoln declared. Why not attack Lee's communication lines, so badly exposed, forthwith?

Change positions with the enemy, and think you not he would break your communication with Richmond within the next twenty-four hours? You dread his going into Pennsylvania. But if he does so in full force, he gives up his communications to you absolutely, and you have nothing to do but follow, and ruin him; if he does so with less than full force, fall upon, and beat what is left behind all the easier.

Exclusive of the water line, you are now nearer Richmond than the enemy is by the route that you *can*, and he *must* take. Why can you not reach there before him, unless you admit that he is more than your equal on a march? His route is the arc of a circle, while yours is the chord. The roads are as good on yours as on his.[9]

The President recalled how he had suggested that McClellan move down east of the Blue Ridge, thus at once menacing Lee's communications with Richmond. If Lee should then advance into Pennsylvania, McClellan could follow him closely; if he should retire toward Richmond, McClellan could try to reach that city first, meanwhile giving battle on any good opportunity:

If he makes a stand at Winchester, moving neither North nor South, I would fight him there, on the idea that if we cannot beat him when he bears the wastage of coming to us, we never can when we bear the wastage of going to him. This proposition is a simple truth, and too important to be lost sight of for a moment. In coming to us, he tenders us an advantage which we should not waive. We should not so operate as merely to drive him away. As we must beat him somewhere, or fail finally, we can do it, if at all, easier near to us than far away. If we cannot beat the enemy where he now is, we never can, he again being within the entrenchments of Richmond. . . .

This letter is in no sense an order.

But McClellan continued to delay, putting Lincoln off with a vague reply. He would give the President's views the fullest consideration, and would advance "the moment my men are shod and my cavalry are sufficiently renovated."[10] Lincoln, beset by Bryant, Raymond, and a hundred other editors to give the country some progress, returned to the charge. On October 21, through Halleck, he repeated his order of the 6th, stating that while he did not expect impossibilities, he was very anxious that the continued good weather should not be wasted by inactivity. "Telegraph when you will move, and on what lines you propose to march." An epidemic had broken out among the

9 *Works*, V, 460–462.
10 Oct. 17, 1862; O. R., I, xix, pt. 1, 16. From Harpers Ferry to Washington was five hours by train. McClellan could have left the Ferry any day at noon, conferred with Lincoln, Stanton, Halleck, and Meigs for two hours, and gotten back soon after midnight. But his relations with all were such that he did not want a conference, nor would one have been fruitful.

army horses, giving them sore mouths and backs, and McClellan on the 24th made this an excuse for immobility. Lincoln returned one of the sharpest messages of his career. "I have just read your dispatch about sore tongues and fatigued horses," he telegraphed. "Will you pardon me for asking what the horses of your army have done since the battle of Antietam that fatigues anything?"

At last McClellan, on October 26, began throwing his army across the Potomac at Harpers Ferry and Berlin, an operation which took him six days. He followed this by a rapid march to the New Baltimore–Warrenton area. At the outset he was east of the Blue Ridge, Lee on the west; he had the inside line to Richmond; but his deliberate movements enabled Lee, leaving Jackson's force in the Shenandoah, to cross the Blue Ridge at leisure and place himself at Culpeper between McClellan and the Confederate capital. Lincoln had told John Hay that if McClellan sacrificed the advantage of inside lines, he would relieve the general. Would he now act? [11]

[I]

McClellan's last movement was strategically sound. By his forward swing to Warrenton he had put himself in position to strike between Lee at Culpeper and Stonewall Jackson west of the Blue Ridge, thus either fighting each army separately, or forcing them to concentrate as far south as Gordonsville. He should have told Lincoln of this plan. But he failed completely to keep Halleck, Stanton, or the President advised of his intentions, telling them only of his fears and demands. He sent long telegrams October 25–30 on measures to guard the Potomac against an attack on Maryland during his advance, but he did not inform Washington just what this advance contemplated.

And if Lee and Jackson concentrated at Gordonsville, what then? Would McClellan fight, or would he find more excuses for delay? On November 5–6 water froze and snow fell; winter was beginning.[12] McClellan's subsequent report of operations throws doubt on his determination to give battle. Once he faced Lee at Gordonsville, he writes, the army would be "in position either to adopt the Fredericksburg line of advance upon Richmond, or to be removed to the Peninsula if, as I apprehended, it were found impossible to supply it by the Orange & Alexandria Railroad beyond Culpeper."[13] The Peninsula again! How long would removal to the James take? And if Maryland was in danger

11 Lincoln, *Works*, V, 460–462.
12 N. M. Curtis, *From Bull Run to Chancellorsville*, 215. On the 7th Virginia had one of the heaviest snowfalls in years; Richmond *Examiner*, Nov. 8.
13 O. R., I, xix, pt. 1, 84–87. McClellan worried lest Bragg's faraway troops suddenly join Lee!

while McClellan lay at Warrenton, what about Washington after he moved down to the Peninsula? The President feared a resumption of the old postponements.

And Lincoln, who wished to keep politics out of military operations, was doubtless also uneasy about McClellan's political attitudes. The President had just dismissed Major John J. Key, brother of one of McClellan's staff, for saying that the "game" was to prolong the war until both sides were worn out, when the Union might be saved with slavery intact. He knew that, as Schurz tells us, such silly treasonable talk was rife among the staff, and hoped that an example might cut it short.[14] Everyone knew of McClellan's tenderness toward Southern institutions. In his order to the army publishing the Emancipation Proclamation, he had not only avoided any word of approbation, but had forbidden political discussion with a pregnant hint: "The remedy for political errors, if any are committed, is to be found only in the action of the people at the polls." [15] This, a few weeks before the November elections, was sure to be given a partisan interpretation. It was said that he even prepared a public protest, which his officers induced him to suppress. The President had no anxiety about the general's possible insubordination, and when John Hay spoke of the matter responded sadly: "McClellan is doing nothing to make himself either respected or feared." Nor was Lincoln in the least inclined to follow Madison and Polk in letting party considerations affect his own decisions. He wrote at this very time that "in considering military merit, the world has abundant evidence that I discard politics"—as the names of McClellan, Buell, and Halleck proved. But he had to give consideration to the fact that McClellan had around him men who wanted a compromise peace.[16]

Lincoln at this moment commands our deepest sympathy. Winter was coming with no prospect that the long record of Eastern defeat and stalemate would be broken; Congress, partly angry, partly sullen, was about to meet; though the elections showed that popular impatience was rising, still more men and more money would have to be demanded from the country. He was bitterly assailed by men who wanted sterner war, and men who wanted peace. The governors, as the Altoona Conference had shown, were restive. The Cabinet was filled with dissension to a degree which interfered with public business, and though Lincoln did not know it, early in October Chase and Stanton were talking together in harsh terms about the President's shortcomings, and trying to enlist Gideon Welles.

Lincoln was still reluctant to remove McClellan, for he thought the man

14 *Works*, VIII, 47–49; Schurz, *Rems.*, II, 382.
15 O. R., I, xix, pt. 2, 395, 396.
16 Nicolay and Hay, VI, 180; Lincoln, *Works*, V, 486.

might deserve another chance, and he told friends that he was not certain anybody else could effectively maneuver a great army. Sumner was too old, McDowell had lost the troops' respect, Buell wavered at critical moments, and Grant and Sherman were too inexperienced, or at least too little known in the East. There remained Hooker and Burnside, neither surely known to be qualified, and the former at sword's point with McClellan. From Halleck, meanwhile, Lincoln got no useful advice. At a Cabinet meeting on November 4, Stanton sneeringly remarked that Halleck did not consider himself responsible for army movements or deficiencies east of the Alleghenies, for McClellan did not report to him but to the President direct. Lincoln cut in sharply to say that Halleck would and should be considered responsible; he had told Halleck that he would remove McClellan at any time he required it, and would bear the public brunt of the decision.[17] Clearly, nobody had an exact idea of just what Halleck's functions were. As the discussion continued, Lincoln said, with full Cabinet concurrence, that Halleck was quite unfitted for field command, and shirked the position he held; in Welles's words, he was a moral coward.

Had Lincoln decided to keep McClellan, he would have had to face the condemnation of almost all the really determined Union leaders.[18] The President of course acted on his own reasoning. He knew that McClellan could organize a splendid army, hold its devotion, and save it from calamity; that he could protect Washington and the North. But the Union could never be restored in that way. What he needed was a general who would hit hard, boldly, and often. He had been all too patient.

On November 5, 1862, Lincoln relieved McClellan and appointed Ambrose E. Burnside in his stead. With McClellan went Fitz-John Porter. O. B. Willcot was assigned Burnside's corps, while Hooker took Porter's. The order carried by General C. P. Buckingham reached McClellan in his tent at night on the 7th, taking him by surprise. Reading it with a silent smile, quite alone, he exclaimed: "Alas for my poor country!" Some of his officers advised him to refuse to obey. He might, he wrote later, have led his troops against Washington to take possession of the government—an idea that should never even have occurred to him. But on November 10, in a painfully impressive scene, he parted from his great army of 120,000 men.[19]

---

17 Welles, *Diary*, I, 179 ff. At this meeting Lincoln reviewed his relations with McClellan, and belatedly read his long patient letter to McClellan dated Oct. 13. Halleck's moral cowardice is shown by the fact that although he was anxious to get rid of McClellan, he said nothing to Lincoln; see his letter to C. P. Buckingham, Dec. 22, 1862, Ill. State Hist. Lib.
18 Including Montgomery M. Meigs, whose letters refuting McClellan's charges of inadequate supply were withering invectives; O. R., I, xix, pt. 2, pp. 422 ff., 465.
19 Stanton asked Gen. Buckingham to carry the orders (1) because he might specially persuade Burnside to take the command—and Burnside indeed accepted only when told that Hooker would get it if he refused; and (2) because Stanton, doubting McClellan's loyalty,

[II]

If Lincoln's removal of the general was questionable, as many army officers believed at the time and many military analysts have written since, it was a decision rendered unavoidable by McClellan's faults. The Young Napoleon could waste weeks before Yorktown, fail before Richmond, drag his feet in bringing aid to Pope, fail once more in not attacking on the morrow of Antietam —and still be forgiven; but his whole course since Antietam seemed to presage continued failure. That battle had been fought September 17. But McClellan, despite Lincoln's orders, despite Halleck's reiterated demands, did not move his army forward until six and a half weeks later—forty days which saw precious autumn ebbing away. Had he taken but four weeks and explained his course thoroughly to his superiors, he might have kept his command, for he had good reasons to justify a limited wait. Many of the regiments he had taken from Pope were wasted by fighting and desertion to two or three companies apiece; Pope's loss of stores caused a grievous shortage of equipment, and many of Pope's troops were demoralized. Antietam had inflicted new losses of men and material and left some units exhausted. Many incoming regiments, too, were green and ill disciplined.[20]

But McClellan was stubbornly reticent. Instead of explaining his situation, he wrote ill-tempered letters about wagons, tents, and horses. To the end he gave Lincoln and the War Department no clear indication that he meant to fight before winter halted operations. The breakdown of confidence between him and the leaders of Congress and Cabinet was perhaps not adequate reason for dismissal—though McClellan's total indifference to popular opinion in a war of the people was inexcusable. But the breakdown of effective communication between his headquarters on one side, and the White House and War Department on the other, a breakdown for which he was primarily responsible, was a very broad ground for his ouster. His successor's first important step was to send Lincoln a detailed plan of campaign.[21]

McClellan returned to New Jersey, out of the war for good, a victim not of

---

feared that the general would refuse to give up the army. This was the same unworthy suspicion that some men had held of Frémont in 1861, and just as unfounded. Buckingham in Chicago *Tribune*, Sept. 4, 1875; Comte de Paris, II, 555, 556. If we may believe Montgomery C. Meigs's notes on Lincoln and Stanton in his papers, the President had been willing to put Burnside in command just before the Seven Days; if we may believe Orville H. Browning (*Diary*, I, 589, 590) he had been willing to do so when Lee invaded Maryland.

20 See G. W. Bicknell, *Hist. of the Fifth Maine*, 142 ff., on army needs.

21 O. R., I, xix, pt. 2, 552–554. Some critics of McClellan accused him of delaying action until after the election to further Democratic chances; critics of Lincoln accused him of delaying the removal lest he hurt Republican fortunes. Lincoln at least was far too high-minded to put party above national welfare.

incapacity or inexperience but of his character and temperament. Impatient of authority, querulous under criticism, religiously certain of divine guidance, deeply egotistical, he lacked the central quality of a great commander as defined by a famous modern soldier. "Most vital of all," writes General Archibald Wavell,[22] "he must have the fighting spirit, the will to win"; he must be "the man who plays his best when things are going badly, who has the power to come back at you when apparently beaten, and who refuses to acknowledge defeat." Napoleon remarked: "If the art of war consisted merely in not taking risks, glory would be at the mercy of very mediocre talent." McClellan excelled at not taking risks; a perfectionist, he was reluctant to move until the last linchpin and map case was ready, while he always feared that just over the hill the enemy had unseen reserves. This spirit would save the army and lose the nation.

Much was lost when McClellan departed. (1) The changeover of command entailed friction and fumbling. The staff work of the Army of the Potomac had reached immense volume, and all but one or two top staff members left with the general.[23] Subordinate staff officers, a numerous body, had to establish working relations with Burnside's entourage. (2) McClellan, unrivaled in organizing ability, had been brigading depleted veteran regiments with units recently raised and taking other steps to improve army arrangements; this work was now broken off. (3) Above all, the confidence and energy of many troops were impaired when the popular McClellan gave place to a little-known general who at Antietam had not done conspicuously well. Numerous regimental histories describe the grief which the troops manifested when McClellan rode through the camps on November 10 to take leave.[24] The ranks sent up wild cheers and cries of farewell; some men heaped sweeping denunciation on the government; the color bearers of Meagher's brigade cast their flags in the dust for the general to ride over. The army he so splendidly organized, declared Meagher, "has been grossly outraged." Edward S. Bragg wrote his wife: "Little Mac has gone, and my heart and hopes have gone with him." Meade commented on the general gloom, and Francis A. Walker, though far from uncritical of the general, wrote: "When the chief had passed out of sight, the romance of war was over for the Second Corps." [25]

22 "The Qualities of a General," N. Y. *Times*, March 16, 1941; see also Wavell's book, *Generals and Generalship* (1941).
23 Comte de Paris, II, 557 ff.
24 E. g., C. B. Fairchild, *Hist. of the 27th N. Y. Vols.*, 111.
25 Meagher, Nov. 10, 1862, Barlow Papers; Bragg, Nov. 16, 1862, Bragg Papers; Meade, *Meade*, I, 325; Monroe, *Walker*, 57. C. F. Walcott, *Twenty-first Massachusetts*, 217-219, states his opinion that the general sentiment of the army would have sustained McClellan if he had refused to recognize the order of removal "until after the probably impending battle had been fought." McClellan made Meagher's troops pick up the flags.

Press comment was what might have been anticipated, with the Republican newspapers approbatory, and the Democratic journals critical. Greeley, rejoicing over McClellan's severance from what courtesy called active service, genially added that all his friends were traitors. Raymond's *Times* expressed relief and hope, saying that the general's calamitous inactivity had given strength to the rebels and encouragement to foreign enemies.[26] But the Democratic press sharpened its knives for the Administration. The *World*, accusing Lincoln of removing McClellan for party reasons and under Cabinet pressure, placed squarely on his shoulders "the terrible responsibility" of displacing a tried soldier "from the command of a great army actually in the field and moving in the face of an enemy."

Southern comment on the removal was naturally restricted and acrid. In the past he had been treated favorably, partly through genuine admiration for his organizing talent, partly perhaps because Southern victories seemed sweeter if he were credited with genius, and partly because of his strict adherence to rules of civilized warfare. Now he was treated more caustically. The Richmond *Whig*, for example, savagely dissected his record. "The Yankees might have taken Richmond after the battle of Seven Pines, when our forces were in confusion," it said, had he seized his opportunities. "After the battle of Hanover Court-House he might have done the same thing. After the battle of Antietam the same." And the *Whig* concluded by saying he was the victim of his own pretensions. "How fortunate for us that he was chosen chief of the Yankee army!" Such comment must be taken with as much reserve as the now-familiar story that Lee later declared McClellan by all odds the best of the Union generals; a story from dubious second-hand sources reported long after the event. Lee had shown his real opinion of McClellan by dividing his forces before South Mountain, and staying in his positions after Antietam.[27]

The removal was a misfortune, but under the circumstances an unavoidable misfortune. McClellan had left the patient President no choice but to act as he did. The selection of Burnside as McClellan's successor, another misfortune,

26 Both the *Times* and *Tribune*, Nov. 10 ff., carried reports from field correspondents ridiculing the tales of excitement and dismay in the army. Two *Times* writers declared they heard only expressions of rejoicing from the soldiers, and a *Tribune* man quoted some officers as saying that McClellan's removal had saved the army from going to pieces. Certainly some soldiers took the removal philosophically. D. W. Judd, in *The Story of the Thirty-third N. Y.* (p. 217), for example, states that the whole Ninth Corps had begun to question McClellan's capacity when he failed to attack after Antietam. B. W. Crowninshield, *First Mass. Cavalry*, 38, 39, indicts him for his failure. One of his staff, Van Vliet, informed S. L. M. Barlow just before his removal that he might have been commander-in-chief if he had advanced in mid-October, adding: "We *should* have marched, perhaps, though it is not for me to decide." This is a significant admission. Oct. 22, 1862, Barlow Papers.
27 Richmond *Whig*, April 21, 1863; R. E. Lee, Jr., *Lee*, 415, 416; K. P. Williams, *Lincoln Finds a General*, II, 478, 479. Hassler offers an able defense in *McClellan*, 296-330.

seemed a logical act, for Lincoln could only take the most promising subordinate. The fact that Burnside had twice declined the command, and that he now wept, declaring himself unfit for the place, was a bad omen. In the Crimean War, when Raglan died amid general relief, General James Simpson had been named commander after he opposed his own appointment and bore testimony to his own incapacity; and after three months of failure he resigned. But—what better man was in view than this graduate of West Point, a veteran of Scott's march to Mexico City, inventor of a superior carbine, the victor of Roanoke Island and New Bern, and a corps commander known to have favored renewal of the battle the day after Antietam? He was a truly chivalric leader, as his recent order sternly forbidding indiscriminate plundering and the unauthorized seizure of private property had demonstrated.[28]

Happy were the Confederates who faced no problem of supreme command, but rested content with Lee, Stonewall, Longstreet, the two Hills, and Jeb Stuart. During this beautiful autumn of dry sunny weather half of Lee's sick recovered, and most of his stragglers, protected, fed, and often equipped by friendly Virginians, rejoined his ranks. "In the shelter of the dense woods about Culpeper," wrote the London *Times* correspondent from Confederate headquarters November 14, "in wonderful spirits, with physique ineffably improved since the bloody days of Sharpsburg, are clustered the tatterdemalion regiments of the South. It is a strange thing to look at these men, so ragged, slovenly, sleeveless, without a superfluous ounce of flesh upon their bones, with wild matted hair, in mendicants' rags, and to think when the battle flag goes to the front, how they can and do fight." Lee had told this correspondent, "There is only one attitude in which I should never be ashamed of seeing my men, and that is when they are fighting." With this heroic force, led by two of the greatest commanders of history, the much-tried Army of the Potomac was now required to grapple.

But hardly had Lincoln dealt with the exigent problem of army command before he had to turn the equally heavy responsibilities presented by the assembling of Congress. He had in fact to meet one of the most formidable crises in the governmental history of the nation, a crisis thick with difficulties.

---

28 At New Bern, on March 15, 1862, Burnside had faced a well-built Confederate breastwork and several redoubts protected on one side by the Neuse River and on the other by an impassable swamp. These works were defended by about 5,000 men, 3 field batteries, and 13 heavy guns; but Burnside moved his troops within short range, formed them in battle order, charged, and carried the entrenchments with a loss of only about 600 killed and wounded. He was to remember this victory when he faced entrenchments at Fredericksburg. For his General Order No. 8 against the Stanton-Pope scheme of looting see Poore, *Burnside*, 156, 157.

[III]

Difficulties of Congress—and his own official family. "The Cabinet are far from being a unit. Part of them really hate each other. Blair hates Chase and speaks openly on the street—and so it is with others. [Caleb B.] Smith says Lincoln don't treat a Cabinet as other Presidents—that he decides the most important questions without consulting his cabinet." So David Davis wrote late in November after four days of talk with Lincoln and his associates.[29]

His statements were true, and the transfer of the army to a new leader naturally stimulated a demand for changes in the Cabinet. Most of the radical editors, long hostile to Seward in particular, wished to see shifts made all along the line in the interests of greater unity and a more aggressive policy. If the armies were to hit hard and fast, so should the government. The Cleveland *Plain Dealer*, and Cincinnati *Commercial*, reiterating their familiar demands for more energy and less queasiness in attacking slavery, spoke for scores of other papers in asking for a drastic reorganization.[30]

The general utterances of the radical politicians indicated an apprehension that Lincoln would vacillate or even retreat, and must have a sterner set of advisers. Even Raymond's *Times* declared that any Administration "less timid than that which has now possession of power" would have ousted McClellan long before—as if timidity were dominant.[31] Nothing could be more certain than that when Congress met its extremists would bring pressure for the removal of several men. Fessenden, whom many wished to see in Seward's office, wrote the Boston capitalist John Murray Forbes that the prime need of the hour was to get the New Yorker out of the Cabinet. This would be difficult, for he would never willingly retire, and the President was so blind to the importance of a change that they would just let the ship of state drift. "For myself," protested Fessenden, "I can only say that there is no political calamity I should look upon with so much dread as being asked to share the responsibility of guiding it." What this meant was that he was aching to step into Seward's shoes.[32]

In the jangling Cabinet, Chase was the mainspring of opposition to the President. He not only talked with Stanton about Lincoln's faults, but discussed them with various Senators and Representatives. A story crept around Washington that just after the elections Lincoln had expressed grave doubts about pursuing the policy of emancipation; whereupon Chase had faced him defi-

29 To Leonard Swett, Nov. 26, David Davis Papers, Ill. State Hist. Lib.
30 Nov. 17, 1862.
31 Nov. 10, 1862.
32 J. M. Forbes, *Letters and Recs.*, I, 336-338.

antly, threatened to join forces with the radical leaders of Congress, and declared that sooner than carry on the war without destroying slavery they would stop it by cutting off all appropriations.[33] This was a fable, but Lincoln did tell Frank P. Blair about this time that Chase "runs the machine against me," and years afterward Montgomery Blair expressed the opinion that Chase was the one man whom Lincoln actually hated—that is, disliked, for Lincoln was incapable of hate. Chase's egotism made him sublimely condescending toward the President, whom he pronounced kindly, sensible, and honest, but "greatly wanting in will and decision, in comprehensiveness, in self-reliance, and clear, well-defined purpose." [34]

The mistrust of Lincoln, strongest in New England and some Yankee communities of the mid-West, was rooted in ignorance. Lincoln led, and Seward, so far as his innate selfishness permitted, gave him loyal support. If Lincoln's leadership was cautious, it was firm and increasingly masterful. Where the President really lay open to censure was in failing to consult his Cabinet adequately as a body, as Wilson later consulted his in the First World War, and to improve its unity and harmony. While Presidents have obeyed no rule in their use of the Cabinet, public interests suffer if it is rent by dissension, and Lincoln had read enough history to know of the experience of John Adams and Andrew Jackson with unruly heads of departments.

But the Chief Executive, watching Burnside move his army from Warrenton to Falmouth on the Rappahannock, and putting the final touches on his annual message, appeared unperturbed. His calm, sagacious outlook on affairs was reflected in a conversation with T. J. Barnet at the close of November. Barnet, calling informally at the White House, read the President a letter from the Democratic leader S. L. M. Barlow without divulging the name. Later he described to Barlow its reception.

The President gave me to understand that he should abate no jot of his emancipation policy; but that by imperceptible (comparatively) degrees, perhaps, military law might be made to relent. He says that he highly appreciates the loyal sensibilities of the Opposition—and he scouts the idea of impugning their motives—but he remarks that issues are swept away so fast by over-topping

33 This story was given in a cock-and-bull version in the N. Y. *Herald*, Nov. 10, 1862. T. J. Barnet reported it to S. L. M. Barlow on Nov. 18 in less sensational form: "Chase has got the inside track against the predisposition of the President to regard the late elections from a desirable standpoint, by threatening him with a conspiracy among the Radical members of Congress to stop the supplies, and end the war in that way, making him have the responsibility. This has been the course pursued by Mr. Chase—and for the moment, at all events, he has overslaughed the opinions of the President, of Seward, and Smith." Barlow Papers.

34 F. P. Blair, Jr., to father, n.d. but just after McClellan's dismissal, quotes Lincoln; Blair-Lee Papers. Welles, who like Seward deeply distrusted Chase, records Chase's estimate of Lincoln in his *Diary*, I, 413.

facts that no party will have time to mature until after the war. He thinks the foundations of slavery have been cracked by the war, by the Rebels; and that the masonry of the machine is in their hands—that they have held its fate and can't complain. He believes that there will be no intervention and derides the notion that servile insurrection is stimulated by his proclamation. He feels that Emancipation will occur, if at all, as hitherto it has progressed, etc.

Lincoln, according to Barnet, thought that he could make it clear to the nation that he usurped no power by the Proclamation. Barnet went on:

What most troubles him is to provide for the blacks—he thinks still that many of them will colonize, and that the South will be compelled to resort to the Apprentice System.[35]

[IV]

As Congress assembled at the beginning of December, the two questions which most troubled members were whether Lincoln would carry the Emancipation Proclamation into effect January 1, and whether he would retain the existing Cabinet. They troubled the whole North. All doubt on the first issue, however, was quickly dispelled. Lincoln told responsible newspapermen that the proclamation stood and he would recommend legislation to carry it into effect. He had promised that he would once more urge Congress to adopt the policy of gradual compensated abolition, and this promise he had to keep. But as he assured Congress, neither the war nor proceedings under the proclamation would be stayed because of this recommendation.

Much of his annual message, published in the newspapers on December 2, was devoted to an enlarged version of his old Border State plan. He recommended that Congress should offer the several legislatures a constitutional amendment, to consist of three articles: first, providing compensation in Federal bonds for every State which should abolish slavery before 1900; second, guaranteeing freedom to all slaves who had gained it by the chances of war, but compensating loyal owners; and third, authorizing Congress to make some provision for colonizing freedmen abroad. In arguing for this plan, Lincoln—who felt that it offered the only means of recreating a fraternal Union—reached a new height of eloquence, and illustrated as never before his largeness of view.[36]

He looked forward not to the next year, but the next generation; he dealt not with slavery alone, but with the far graver problem of race adjustment. The Northern people, he argued, should unite behind a broad and permanent

35 Barnet, Nov. 30, 1862, "confidential," Barlow Papers. I have broken the letter into two paragraphs.
36 Nevins, "Lincoln's Plan for Reunion," *Abraham Lincoln Assn. Papers*, 1930, pp. 51–92.

policy. "By mutual concession we should harmonize and act together. This would be compromise; but it would be compromise among the friends, and not with the enemies of the Union." One editor spoke of the quaint simplicity, the rough-diamond quality, of Lincoln's style; and although it now seems incredible, it is actually true that the predilection of many Americans of that era for stump-speech rhetoric blunted their appreciation of Lincoln's lucidity, force, and grace.[37] He begged the people of the North to remember that they were as much responsible for the original introduction of slavery as the Southern people. He urged them not to give way to selfish fears that the freedmen would displace white workers. "If they stay in their old places, they jostle no white laborers; if they leave their old places, they leave them open to white laborers." He pleaded with them to abandon any mean prejudice against colored settlement in their communities. Equally distributed over the land, the Negroes would be but one colored to seven whites. "Could the one, in any way, greatly disturb the seven?" And in closing, he spoke with lofty eloquence of the necessity for rising to the height of the crisis:

Fellow-citizens, *we* cannot escape history. We of this Congress and this Administration will be remembered in spite of ourselves. No personal significance, or insignificance, can spare one or another of us. The fiery trial through which we pass will light us down, in honor or dishonor, to the latest generation. . . . In giving freedom to the *slave* we *assure* freedom to the *free*—honorable alike in what we give and in what we preserve. We shall nobly save, or meanly lose, the last, best hope of earth.

Lincoln really hoped that his plan, when adopted by five Border States and perhaps two Southern States (for seven slave States would have to join the North in ratifying the amendment before it became (effective) might halt the fighting.[38] The South could obtain peace, partial payment for its bondsmen, and a transitional period in which it could still keep vestiges of the former labor system; would this not be better than continued bloodshed and a probability of abrupt emancipation without a cent of recompense? Lincoln spoke of ratification of the amendment as a consummation which "would end the struggle now, and save the Union forever." He spoke hopefully also of colonization abroad, and of the emptiness of Northern fears of a wide Negro dispersion. "Their old masters will gladly give them wages at least until new laborers can be procured; and the freedmen, in turn, will gladly give their labor for the wages, till new homes can be found for them, in congenial climes, and with people of their own blood and race."

37 *Works*, V, 518–537.
38 Lincoln's emancipation proclamation of Sept. 23 had applied to the States and districts at war against the Union; his amendment, though not limited in application, would seem to be aimed primarily at the North, the border region, and the three States fast approaching reconstruction, Louisiana, Tennessee, and Arkansas.

This trust in reason was rather naïve; the Southerners after their many victories could not now be diverted from their struggle for independence, and colonization was always an impracticable will-of-the-wisp. In the North it was certain that radicals and extreme conservatives alike would reject Lincoln's plan. After he had read the draft of his message to the Cabinet, rather for their information than their criticism, Chase had warned him of this fact. The subtle Ohioan, while paying tribute to the noble sentiments and admirable language of the message, suggested that it would be wise to omit the plea for a constitutional amendment. No probability existed that a two-thirds vote could be mustered in Congress to support one, or that it could obtain approval by the States. Would it not weaken rather than strengthen the Administration thus to march forward to certain defeat? [39] The conservative Orville H. Browning termed Lincoln's scheme a hallucination; the radical Charles Sumner character-ized it as mere "surplusage" in his message, to be ignored. Ben Wade and Horatio Seymour, for divergent reasons, were both scornful and both certain of its futility.

The newspaper press was similarly almost a unit in rejection. To free the slaves by instalments, observed the *Evening Post*, was like cutting off a dog's tail by inches to get him used to the pain. The New York *Herald* did its best to tear the plan to pieces. "We have always admired the President as a joker, but we never imagined that he could so aptly blend exquisite humor and practical common sense in an official document. He knows that the agitation about slavery hinders the war, and he is right in deciding to postpone this agi-tation. In fact, a truce on the negro question until 1900 is a military neces-sity. . . ." This was the *Herald*'s usual heavy irony. Greeley's *Tribune*, while praising Lincoln's sincerity, condemned his ideas on colonization—"Our coun-try has no laborers to export"—and declared that slavery should be ended at once, not gradually. The Cincinnati *Commercial* had a conviction that the fanatics in both parties would reject his plan, and disliked the colonization feature—there would be time later to decide what was best for the colored folk.[40] *Harper's Weekly* similarly scoffed at the colonization scheme. Thus far, it commented, persons with dark skins had shown the same predilection for staying in their own country as persons with white skins, this being patriotism in the whites but stupidity in the blacks.

In general, however, comment was moderate, and much Republican disap-proval was veiled under silence. Even Greeley avoided any detailed discussion. Give us six months' fair trial of rigorous emancipation, he exclaimed, the Union forces pressing southward with freedom pinned to their bayonets, and if that

39 Nov. 24, 1862; RTL Papers.
40 See files of the journals named Dec. 2–6. Some papers, like the *Herald,* voiced somewhat varying opinions in successive editorials. The Phila. *Press* (Dec. 2) and Cincinnati *Commer-cial* (Dec. 4) gave Lincoln a sustained personal eulogy.

does not bring the traitors to their marrow bones, we shall be glad to talk of a compromise peace. In the same spirit other papers avoided criticism of the President by ignoring gradual compensated emancipation, and emphasizing Lincoln's assertions that slavery must be given a death sentence. A number of journals, echoing much popular comment, expressed regret that Lincoln had said so little about the progress of the war and the means of expediting it.[41]

[V]

The temper of Congress had been worsened by recent events. The Republican Jacobins, as John Hay called them, interpreted the military defeats and the election as requiring much more drastic and pugnacious action. Democrats and Border Republicans, on the other hand, interpreted them as requiring a return to strict interpretations of the Constitution and the single war-object of restoring the Union. More fighting, more confiscations of rebel property, more liberation of slaves, and full use of colored fighters—these were the demands vociferated by extreme Republicans. An instant stoppage of arbitrary arrests, a repudiation of emancipation as unconstitutional, or inexpedient, and a halt in the headlong progress toward despotism—these were the ultimatums of extreme Democrats.[42]

One powerful figure, in a speech long remembered, struck not only at the Congressional minority but at the Administration. When Thad Stevens rose to assail the contention of Representative A. B. Olin of New York that the rebellious States were still inside the Union, and that their loyal people were entitled to its full protection, he took issue with Lincoln as well. Stevens at least subconsciously cherished a resentful belief that he and not Cameron should have sat for Pennsylvania in the Cabinet. He never saw Lincoln when he could help it, and never spoke cordially of him. While close to Chase, whom he had known for full twenty years and with whom he worked closely in meeting the financial needs of the nation, he felt contempt for Seward, and dislike for Montgomery Blair. It would have been well had Stevens devoted himself exclusively to financial affairs; but this iron-willed man held deep con-

41 The message astonished Orville Browning by "its singular reticence in regard to the war"; *Diary*, I, 591, Dec. 1, 1862. On foreign affairs the President diplomatically made little comment. Touching on finances, he declared that on the whole the best mode of raising money for the war was by establishing a system of banks of issue, whose notes should be uniform in appearance and based on the deposit of United States bonds in the Treasury; but he left details to Chase.

42 Cf. Donnal V. Smith, *Chase and Civil War Politics*, 60 ff. Cox and Vallandigham in the House, and Bayard in the Senate, brought forward resolutions against the arbitrary arrests; G. H. Yeaman of Kentucky and John Crisfield of Maryland among others assailed the Emancipation Proclamation as unconstitutional. *Cong. Globe*, 37th Cong., 1st Sess., pt. 1, *passim*.

victions about the war, in which force must be used to the utmost, and about the peace, in which the North must show no softness, no spirit of compromise, no magnanimity. In brooding over what he regarded as Lincoln's delays and excessive generosity, Stevens sometimes exhibited a frenzy of anger.

So it was as 1862 closed. For the past fifteen years, asserted Stevens, he had always been a step ahead of the Republican Party, and always the party had caught up. Once more, he predicted, they would have to overtake him before this infamous and bloody revolt was ended. They would find that they could not execute the Constitution in the seceded States, and must forget that document in levying war. "They will come to the conclusion that the adoption of the measures I advocated at the outset of the war, the arming of the negroes, the slaves of the rebels, is the only way left on earth in which these rebels can be exterminated. They will find that they must treat these States now outside of the Union as conquered provinces and settle them with new men, and drive the present rebels as exiles from this country; for I tell you they have the pluck and endurance for which I gave them credit a year and a half ago in a speech which I made, but which was not relished on this side of the House, nor by the people in the free States. They have such determination, energy, and endurance, that nothing but actual extermination or exile or starvation will ever induce them to surrender to this Government." [43]

Stevens knew well that this talk of conquered provinces was so much shrapnel aimed directly at the White House. He had to be taken much more seriously than Martin F. Conway of Kansas, who on December 15 introduced resolutions calling for the conquest of the South, the extirpation of slavery, and the reorganization of the executive, the alternative to be a cessation of the war.[44] By a vote of 132 to 1, the House tabled these resolutions. But everyone knew that Sumner, Chandler, Wade, Henry Winter Davis and others took the same view (barring extermination) as Thad Stevens. Washington correspondents reported secret meetings of radical intriguers—Senators, Representatives, generals, and some Cabinet members—to plan a new leadership and a drastic new tendency in the war. An ominous sense of coming changes, of dramatic political events impending, filled the air of Washington.[45]

The Democrats meanwhile were eagerly discussing the best means of using their recent election victories. Daily, Bayard, Cox, Vallandigham, and others gathered to exult over the popular discontent and lay plans for fomenting it. The best of them, like Cox and Powell, regarded themselves as patriotic defenders of constitutional liberty; the worst, like Bayard and Vallandigham,

43 *Cong. Globe,* 37th Cong., 3rd Sess., pt. 1, pp. 242, 243; Jan. 8, 1863.
44 *Ibid.,* 91, 92.
45 For example, N. Y. *Herald,* Dec. 8–15, 1862.

were sympathizers with the South and with slavery. Bayard stood for peace at almost any price, frankly avowing that he would rather let the Confederacy go than continue a war ending in Southern subjugation and the establishment of a centralized despotism.[46]

A passing flurry of peace talk gave the closing weeks of 1862 a bizarre touch. It was started by a Marylander named Chase Barney, who came home from a sojourn in Richmond with what he pretended were Southern proffers of terms for returning to the Union. The mischievous Fernando Wood shortly made a New York speech outlining these supposed terms. They included, he said, the restoration of the old Constitution unchanged, adoption of the Crittenden Compromise, assumption of the Confederate debt, and ejection of the French from Mexico, to be followed by the annexation of that country to make nine slave States.[47] Having made this preposterous statement, Wood maneuvered to bring about an exchange of views with Lincoln. Through Mayor George Opdyke he sent the President an impudent letter stating that he had learned from an unnamed source that the South would send members to the next Congress provided they be given full amnesty; and he begged Lincoln to let him conduct negotiations with the Confederate leaders.

The President brushed Wood aside with a reply marked "confidential." If the South would cease all resistance and submit to the national authority, he stated, the war would stop, and he would be willing within a reasonable time to grant a general amnesty. But he did not think it proper to communicate this to the Confederates, who already knew it, and could at any time approach him directly.[48] Meanwhile, other men took part in the talk about peace: among them Horace Greeley, who wrote Lincoln December 12 that he was confident the rebels were sick of war, and an eccentric humbug named J. Wesley Greene, who stung the President into penning a short memorandum exposing his real character. But before Lincoln dismissed Greene's shallow deception, Greeley had published in the *Tribune* an editorial speculating hopefully on the peace feelers. Actually, of course, the South had no idea whatever of surrender, for while suffering terribly from the strain of the conflict, it rejoiced in the fact that Lee's army, checked but not defeated, still held Union forces at bay in the East, while Confederate armies still firmly gripped Vicksburg and Chattanooga in the West.

And suddenly, in the midst of this talk, occurred a series of events which elated the South, depressed the North, and brought the demand for Cabinet reorganization to a head.

46 "Occasional" in Phila. *Press*, Dec. 10, *et seq.*; *Cong. Globe, ut supra*, 67, 68; Dec. 11, 1862.
47 Barney to Lincoln, Nov. 23, RTL Papers; Wood's speech in N. Y. *Tribune*, Dec. 1.
48 *Works*, V, 517, 518; N. Y. *Tribune*, Dec. 11, 1862.

14

Fredericksburg and Government Crisis

IT WOULD be difficult to overstate the anxiety with which all patriotic Northerners during November awaited the movements of Burnside. Despite recent snows and rains, the authorities in mid-November still expected nearly a month of good weather for campaigning. Newspaper accounts emphasized the imposing strength of the army McClellan had just left, corps on corps advancing like mere regiments. It was unquestionably well clothed, well fed, well armed, and in excellent spirits. Lying about Warrenton, it was only some twenty miles from Lee's main force at Culpeper, the Rappahannock between them. As McClellan returned North to meet a warm demonstration in Trenton and hear "Prince" John Van Buren suggest him for the Presidency to a New York meeting, all eyes were turned on his successor. He bore the scrutiny well. Modest, dignified, of imposing presence, Burnside impressed Lincoln by his evident strength of character. In North Carolina and at Antietam he had shown high gallantry under fire; his management of troops combined firm discipline with a kindly, parental attitude; and he had a remarkable power of attaching people to himself. The vital question of his intellectual endowment, however, was unanswered.

McClellan had intended to advance against Lee by striking southward between Culpeper and the village northwest of it called Washington, but Burnside decided to swing east and establish a new base at Fredericksburg.[1] That McClellan's plan was much the better there can be no doubt. Without much fighting, he would doubtless have compelled Lee's retreat to Gordonsville, and might then by a march south of the Rappahannock have seized Fredericksburg, whence he would have a choice of two routes toward Richmond: the water path to Harrison's Landing on the James, or a land path along the railroad through Hanover. Burnside's plan was more difficult, because instead of leaping the Rappahannock at its easy headwaters, he would have to make a considerable march downstream to a point where crossing might be hard. The

---

1 McClellan's *Report* (1864), 435, 436. Hassler, *McClellan*, 309, points out that Lee had fervently hoped that McClellan would advance up the Shenandoah Valley.

initial question was whether he could effect the transit at Fredericksburg by surprise. He would have to get his pontoon bridges, which had been in the vicinity of Harpers Ferry, sent down the Potomac and waggoned by Aquia Creek to Falmouth, opposite that town. If his army and the bridges arrived simultaneously by stealth, a surprise attack would be possible; if they failed to arrive together or the movement was detected, the Confederates would make Fredericksburg bristle with cannon and bayonet.

Halleck, conferring with Burnside on November 11, expressed a preference for McClellan's plan. The new leader, however, insisted on his own, and three days later, Halleck telegraphed Lincoln's authorization for the move: "he thinks that it will succeed if you move rapidly; otherwise not." Secrecy was important. Yet the Philadelphia *Press* on November 19 was blurting out its endorsement of the thrust against Richmond by way of Fredericksburg. As delays ensued, Northern editors grew pessimistic. Bennett's *Herald* on November 28 accused the radical press in Philadelphia and New York of disclosing the plan of campaign to the enemy, and then depressing the North by gloomy pictures of Burnside's prospects. On November 26–27 Lincoln visited the general on Aquia Creek, and soon after he returned to the capital Burnside followed for hurried news conferences. Why? The New York *Times* told its readers that he had gone to Washington to ascertain why his pontoon bridges were coming up so tardily.

Actually, Burnside, Lincoln, Stanton, and Halleck had discussed the whole miltary situation, which Lincoln termed "somewhat risky." The pontoons were but part of the picture. Lincoln had proposed that the crossing of the Rappahannock be accompanied by some diversionary action, the fleet assisting. When Burnside and Halleck rejected the idea, he gave the general full freedom in executing his movement.[2]

The story of the delayed pontoons, one of the worst pieces of blundering in the whole war, exhibited gross incapacity in Halleck and some of his subordinates. McClellan's chief engineer had ordered the bridges sent down the Potomac to Washington, and Halleck on November 12, from Burnside's Warrenton headquarters, had directed that they be forwarded to Aquia Creek. It was natural for Burnside, setting out on a march which made direct communication with Washington impossible for several days, to rely on Halleck to push the transfer through. As a matter of fact, Meigs, Haupt, and Halleck had all visited Burnside's headquarters,[3] and it would seem that one or all of the three could have arranged for rapid transport of the pontoons to the

---

2 Comte de Paris, II, 560, 561; Swinton, 234–240; Ropes, II, 448–450; K. P. Williams, II, 502–505; Shelby Foote, 766, 767.
3 Daniel Reed Larned, Nov. 13, 1862; Larned Papers, LC.

Fredericksburg area. But Halleck allowed indistinct orders, carelessness about details, and general confusion to entangle the operation and fatally impede the transfer.

Burnside and his army marched at top speed, covering forty miles from Warrenton to the Rappahannock opposite Fredericksburg in two and a half days, so that advance units reached Falmouth November 17. But the pontoons, after appalling delays, did not get to Aquia Creek until the 18th, and were not on the Falmouth shore until the 25th. Too late! [4]

The *Tribune* correspondent who suggested that this footless blundering might cost several thousand lives did not overestimate the penalty. Lee, to be sure, was not quick to grasp the new threat. He at first, on November 15, suspected the direction of Burnside's movement and started some small reinforcements toward Fredericksburg; he then hesitated, mistrusting even reports sent him by Stuart's cavalry; and not until November 18–19 did he move four of Longstreet's divisions toward the town. But he did not need to be quick. By the 25th, when the pontoons were ready, Longstreet's fifth division had arrived; by the 26th Stonewall Jackson, the two Hills, and Lee's main body were rapidly coming up. [5]

And once more the Virginia river gods turned against the Union army. The day that Sumner's troops marched into Falmouth, November 17, rain fell lightly, and on the 19th a heavy downpour began. While roads turned to sloughs, the Rappahannock swelled into a deep barrier in front of the massing Union forces. Burnside's communications with Washington were poor, for the landing piers at Aquia Creek were wretched, and the railroad for the dozen miles thence to Falmouth, using Haupt's new bridge over Potomac Creek, was inadequate; his long wagon trains of provisions crept at snail's pace across the countryside. The troops suffered from shortages. They suffered still more from seeing Longstreet's grim legions, while they fretted on the northern shore, settle into formidable positions opposite. Lincoln's emphasis on speed had been correct, for instead of taking the Confederates by surprise, the slow Union movement had simply enabled them to gain the shelter of a difficult river.

Rain and cold might at any time give way to freezing weather. In fact,

---

4 Kenneth P. Williams gives the best account of Halleck's tangled blundering, and convicts him of trying to cover it up afterward; II, 502–505. For a good description of pontoon bridgebuilding, see J. P. Bloodgood, *Personal Rems.,* 121, 122.

5 Freeman, *Lee,* II, 429–438, praises the Confederate leader for marvelous prescience; Williams, II, 509–514, by stricter analysis of evidence, shows his uncertainty and hesitation. But for the delayed pontoons, he would have had to face Burnside's superior army after it gained a strategically favorable position, holding Fredericksburg securely. Yet Lee's intelligence service was incomparably superior to Burnside's, as it had been to McClellan's; Freeman, II, 439, 440. Ropes gives a somewhat different view of Lee's strategy; II, 451–455.

Nicolay in Washington wrote his wife on December 7 that real winter had begun. "It snowed day before yesterday, and last night froze up tight and fast. I pity the poor soldiers who had to do guard and picket duty last night." [6] The roads would get worse, so that even if Burnside effected a crossing and drove Lee back, he could not follow far. Two sensible alternatives presented themselves; he could go into winter quarters where he lay, or transfer his army to the James. If he took the first course, however, Northern opinion would rage at his inaction, while if he took the second, he would merely adopt McClellan's plan while the public chafed under new delays. He had 145,500 officers and men, of whom nearly 120,000 with 312 pieces of artillery could be mustered for combat, while Lee had only 92,000 officers and men, of whom but 72,500 were ready for battle. Burnside knew that his superior strength might compensate for a disadvantageous position if he handled his troops well. The Administration and country had expected him to move forward, find Lee, and attack him. He therefore resolved to stake everything on a frontal attack, and on the night of December 10–11 laid two-thirds of his pontoon bridge.

Northern expectations were indeed maintained at a curiously high pitch. The field correspondent of the New York *Times* reported on December 3 that Burnside had come back from his visit to Washington well satisfied with his conferences. He "will now be let alone—allowed to follow out his own plans, in his own time and way, free from bureaucratic dictation at Washington, and confident that he will have from the government all the assistance he asks for." Editorially, Raymond was so fearful that the rebels would make use of delaying tactics that he urged Burnside on December 6 to attack at once.[7] The general was under heavy pressure to justify his appointment by an energetic offensive.[8]

[I]

The response came; on December 12, the press flamed with dramatic news. Columns of jubilant writing described how Burnside had crossed the Rappahannock under fire, seized the town, and begun preparations for assaulting the enemy on the heights beyond. Rejoicings over this initial success were fervent and universal.

It was a bright, gay, picture-book action, this river crossing. From the Confederate side the scene was one of the most magnificent of the war. As noon

6 Nicolay Papers, LC.
7 Dec. 3, 1862, and dates following.
8 The Wash. corr. of the N. Y. *Times,* reported that Lincoln had said, "The war is now virtually at an end." We may be sure he did not, but Seward did utter such a prophecy.

approached on the clear, sunny morning of the 11th, Burnside ordered all of the hundred or more guns within range of Fredericksburg to fire fifty rounds into it. Some women and children were still in the town. To Southern watchers on Marye's Heights the streets were half veiled in a dry haze, out of which rose only the steeples. Above and within this canopy incessantly bloomed the fire-hearted clouds of bursting shells. Soon high over the mist rose three or four columns of thick black smoke, lifting vertically in the still air hundreds of feet before they shredded apart. Beyond the town the river glistened dimly, and beyond that the Union bank for two miles was studded with batteries which incessantly jetted flame and smoke. Still farther back, their dark blue uniforms and glistening rifles set vividly against the brown landscape, lay the massed formations of more than a hundred thousand infantry, with endless orderly parks of white-topped wagons and ambulances, awaiting the hour of clear transit across the stream. High above the troops, a thousand feet or more, hung two large balloons. The scene, as a Confederate officer wrote, conveyed a memorable impression of the disciplined power of a great army, and of the vast resources of the nation which had sent it into the field.[9]

Completion of the bridge that day was a nightmare. Two-thirds of the pontoon structure had been laid in the previous hours of darkness, and the engineers, aided by Michigan and Massachusetts infantry, undertook to finish it under a hot fire of Mississippi sharpshooters. Ever and anon the builders would be driven back, and come rushing over the lip of the bank dragging their wounded and dying with them; then they would re-form, dash down again, push out another boat under a new hail of bullets, and lay a few more planks—frequently just in time to catch the bleeding bodies of the men who bore them. At last the fire grew so furious that the builders could no longer reach the bridge end; halfway across, timber and men would go down in a heap together or topple into the water.[10] Infantry had to be rowed across to dislodge the sharpshooters. Franklin on the 11th and 12th got two corps over the Rappahannock farther down and aligned them for battle where the ridges along the river ended and the country opened out. But Sumner's two corps did not cross till the 12th.

Meanwhile the Confederates finished their concentration. Jackson's outlying divisions under Early and D. H. Hill reached the scene of action on the morning of the 13th. Once more fate had denied Burnside an opportunity. Had he pushed his troops over in time to attack on the afternoon of the 12th,

9 Alexander, *Military Memoirs*, 290–292. It was perhaps with such pageantry in mind that Lee next day made his famous remark to Longstreet: "It is well that war is terrible, or we would grow too fond of it."

10 C. H. Weygant, *Hist. 124th N. Y.*, 62, 63, covers the bridgebuilding.

or (as Franklin urged) at daybreak next day, he might have taken advantage of the small remnant of Confederate dispersion. As it was, he faced an iron front; when the sun lifted on the 13th, the Confederates were ready for him.

At this point Burnside, realizing that his preparations had miscarried, lost his nerve. Had he massed all available forces on his left, in the open area downstream, he might have crumpled up the Confederate right flank, where Jackson had just arrived to take command and Hood had erected only weak defensive works. Instead, he decided on a bifurcated attack, Sumner to assault the Confederate left at Marye's Heights while downstream Franklin, with six divisions on a line more than three miles long, was to deal a blow at Jackson's intrenched troops. By thus rejecting a single powerful thrust at the weakest point of the Confederates in favor of two isolated advances, he threw away his last chance of achieving a success.[11] The movement against Marye's Heights was folly, for here the Confederate line, occupying the low ridge back of the town, embodied Telegraph Road, sunk three to five feet below the surrounding terrain, and affording a broad trench with parapet, invisible from the front.

In a short winter's day the Union army suffered the cruelest defeat in its history. At noon, under the bright cold sun, Sumner's troops began to swarm out from the smoldering town, where Union forces had been sheltering from the continuous Southern fire—and indulging in considerable looting.[12] They deployed in dense lines at the edge of the fields below the heights.

Instantly the carnage began. As the troops advanced into the great slaughter pen in front, they met so terrific a storm of shell, grape, and canister that even the bravest quailed. To one Pennsylvanian the air seemed so full of missiles that even a finger could not be pointed up at the Confederate lines without being hit; a New York soldier declared, "We might as well have tried to take Hell." [13] The infantry knew that they were in a death trap, even the simplest

11   Alexander, 294, 295. Burnside's reason for separating the two attacks, as stated in orders to Franklin, were "with a view of avoiding the possibility of a collision of our own forces, which might occur in a general movement during the fog." O. R., I, xxi, p. 71.

12   D. H. Larned of Burnside's staff wrote a friend Dec. 16: "While [we were] waiting for the means to cross the river, the enemy have fortified their position to make it impregnable. From this side of the river we can count 20 crests and hills, each mounting from two to five guns, and all can be brought to bear on any given spot. Each line of earthworks is covered by a second or third, which can be held independently of the first and second, and from the guns that opened on our infantry on Saturday from the high hills and woods in the distance there are batteries which we have not seen. These guns are so placed that they rake every street in the city running at right angles with the river, and their sharpshooters are concealed in every bush and behind every stone wall and rock, so that it was certain death for anyone to show himself beyond our pickets." Larned Papers.

13   T. H. Parker, Hist. of the 51st Pa. Vols., 270; G. H. Washburne, Hist. of the 108th N. Y. Vols., 26, 27.

realizing that assault was hopeless; but with steady step and even ranks they advanced as indomitably as if Columbia cheered them on. When their resolute march brought them within range of Cobb's and Kershaw's troops in the sunken road, a fierce hail of musket balls struck them down in companies. Within minutes the ground was carpeted with the dead and dying. As at every step men fell, some with clean bullet wounds, some with legs or arms torn off, some with brains oozing out, the ranks broke. They rolled back "like chaff before the wind," writes one Confederate, and as they retreated, the artillery fire swept through their ranks anew.[14]

The first attack had hardly ended before fresh troops began filing out of Fredericksburg to the assault. This time the tide swept nearer Cobb's defenders in the sunken road, but again the ranks were blown back like chaff. As a third assault ended and a fourth began, over ground so filled with bodies as to impede the marchers, Lee became alarmed lest such stubborn bravery might yet pierce his defenses. "General," he told Longstreet, "they are massing very heavily, and will break your line, I am afraid."[15] A fifth charge came and recoiled; a sixth fell back across a field heaped with bodies. But the Union forces did not retreat entirely. Regiment after regiment flung itself on the ground, until in some areas eight or ten lines of battle were thus extended, the troops frenziedly loading and firing until the hundred rounds they had brought were spent. At dark Sturgis reported by telegraph to Burnside's headquarters: "Our men only eighty paces from the crest and holding on like hell."[16]

Then night closed on the field. Under bright stars in freezing cold the sound of gunfire ceased, and from the windrows of wounded came a dolorous symphony of pain and despair: screams, groans, cries for help, for stretchers, for water. Rescue was impossible, for Union regiments held picket lines on the field, no truce was considered, and any movement drew a dozen balls. As the gray morning of the 14th broke, writes Longstreet, "the spectacle we saw upon the battlefield was one of the most distressing I ever witnessed." On the Confederate right, where Franklin by a determined attack might have won a success ("he would in all probability have given us trouble," concedes Long-

---

14 James Longstreet, *Battles and Leaders*, III, 79.
15 *Ibid.*, 81.
16 Larned, Dec. 16, 1862; Larned Papers. William McCarter, in his MS volume on life in the army, NYPL, says that the troops who returned that night to the town saw a scene of wild demoralization. Every house still standing was rapidly filled with wounded men; the principal streets were blocked by disabled horses, dismounted guns, and debris; and the sidewalks and alleys were choked with troops so full of excitement and anger that officers gave up trying to control them. Other survivors declare that the men execrated Burnside. "No epithet could be severe enough to express their sense of his folly and stupidity," says Augustus Buell, *The Cannoneer*, 60 (a dubious source, but here accurate).

street) he accomplished nothing. Because of unintelligible orders, he brought only about half his men into battle,[17] and Jubal Early's reserves, from superior positions, threw them back. In this area, too, the scene of butchery appalled even hardened Confederate officers.

In one day Burnside's splendid army had lost approximately 12,650 killed, wounded, and missing, and was as far from Richmond as ever. Why the general persisted in his futile assaults on Marye's Heights after the first two or three waves failed is incomprehensible. Midway in the action Hooker remarked: "There has been enough blood shed to satisfy any reasonable man, and it is time to quit." [18] William Swinton, who was with Burnside's staff, thought that a mood of desperation seized the unhappy general as he watched line after line recoil. Certainly such a mood must have dictated his preposterous notion of renewing the assault with the Ninth Corps, himself at its head, the next morning. When Sumner and others vehemently expostulated he gave it up, and with tears running down his cheeks ordered the evacuation of Fredericksburg. General William F. Smith, calling at headquarters December 14, found him alone in his tent, pacing up and down in anguish. "Oh, those men! Oh, those men!" he exclaimed, pointing across the river to the field of dead and dying. "Those men over there! I am thinking of them all the time!" [19]

He might well feel that central responsibility for the disaster rested on his head. At last men knew how much intellect he had. Too late in the war for either, an improvised general had fought an improvised battle.

[II]

The storm of sorrow and wrath which at once swept the North fell more heavily on Lincoln, Stanton, and Halleck than on Burnside, whose reluctance to command was well known. Privately if not publicly, people castigated Lincoln worst of all, for they did not know that he had warned Burnside that he would fail unless he moved promptly, and that he had given the general complete freedom. He had in fact sent Burnside no message, much less orders,

17 As Greeley says (*Amer. Conflict*, II, 346), a Blücher would have found in such orders as Franklin received a warrant for throwing his whole force against Hill; but the orders were certainly badly worded. See F. W. Palfrey, *The Antietam and Fredericksburg*, 174-180.
18 *Battles and Leaders*, III, 82. Larned writes of the afternoon of the battle, "Hooker expressed his mind very freely at headquarters—ungentlemanly and impatient"; undated memorandum, Larned Papers.
19 Burnside's anguish was sincere, but he was not the man to feel it long. At the end of the week he went to Washington to see Lincoln. The Sunday after this lament he was eating a splendid dinner at the table of the Assistant Secretary of War, John Tucker, with game, oyster patties, *mouton en papillote*, fruit, and wine, and sitting late to enjoy the brilliant talk of Robert J. Walker. Larned Papers.

since their meeting in late November. But many naturally held him responsible for what Joseph Medill called the Central Imbecility.[20] George Bancroft was extremely severe. "How can we reach the President with advice?" he demanded of a friend. "He is ignorant, self-willed, and is surrounded by men some of whom are as ignorant as himself." The Democratic press of course seized the occasion for lamenting anew the President's removal of McClellan, and correctly observed that he would not have committed Burnside's blunder. At the other political extreme Zach Chandler was writing his wife: "The fact is that the country is done for unless something is done at once. . . . The President is a weak man, too weak for the occasion and those fool or traitor generals are wasting time and yet more precious blood in indecisive battles and delays." [21]

Such defeatism seized many observers that even firm patriots were heard to talk of a war for boundaries. When the head of the Chicago *Tribune* did so we may be sure that frailer spirits succumbed. Medill assured his old friend Elihu Washburne that as the rebels could not be defeated by the existing machinery, and they must fight for a division of territory, the Northwest should see to the conquest of the whole Mississippi Valley and the Southwest before a partition took place. "An armistice is bound to come during the year '63." Before it came, they must take Vicksburg and Port Hudson, clear the Mississippi, and make sure that Missouri, Arkansas, Texas, Louisiana, and the Territories would stay in the Union. Once Grant had conquered the whole Mississippi River, they could offer an armistice, at the end of which the Confederacy might be established with only seven States. After that, the Northern republic could wait on events—a reconciliation or a reconquest; and meanwhile, added the highminded Medill, "we might grab Canada to indemnify us for loss of territory." [22]

This type of defeatism, joining surrender with sectional selfishness, was the worst possible. Of course most men remained resolute in holding that the war must be fought through to victory. But the demand for a reorganization of the Administration now swelled up more loudly and widely than ever. The New York *World* beseeched Lincoln to call the best men to his aid in a final effort for the salvation of the republic, and get rid of Stanton, Chase, and Halleck at

20 Lincoln's recent experience had made him wary of interfering with generals. Herman Haupt relates that he brought the first news of Fredericksburg to Lincoln before midnight of the day it was fought. They went together to see Halleck. Haupt heard the President direct Halleck to telegraph orders to Burnside to withdraw to the north bank; but when Halleck expostulated, Lincoln dropped the demand. *Century Magazine*, March, 1882, XXIII, 796, 797.
21 Bancroft to Lieber, Oct. 29, 1862, Lieber Papers, HL; Norton to G. W. Curtis, Nov. 12, *Letters*, I, 258; N. Y. *Herald*, Dec. 16; *World*, Dec. 17; Chicago *Times*, Dec. 17; Cincinnati *Enquirer*, Dec. 17–22, etc.
22 Medill, Jan. 14, 1863, Washburne Papers, LC.

once. Raymond of the *Times*, without suggesting names, wanted new personnel. American opinion had gone beyond the point reached in 1814, when it
compelled Secretary of War Armstrong after the capture of Washington to
resign. Ever since Congress met there had been talk of resignations; now many
people wanted not a scapegoat, but a sweeping change.[23]

Lincoln had reeled in anguish under the news. What he first learned of the
defeat from Burnside himself was fragmentary and misleading. He had no
complete account of the extent of the disaster until the war correspondent
Henry Villard supplied its details on the evening of the 14th. Next day brought
confirmation, and the President told a friend: "If there is a worse place than
Hell, I am in it." [24]

On Tuesday, December 16, immediately after the Senate's adjournment in
early afternoon, Republican members met in secret caucus. When the doors
were shut Anthony of Rhode Island asked someone to state the purpose of the
gathering. Thereupon Lyman Trumbull, rising, set the stage by asking what
the Senate could do to rescue the nation; and Wilkinson of Minnesota, taking
the cue, launched into an invective against Seward, who had ruined the country
by his halfhearted, compromising views. Other Senators followed in a vehement
clamor against the Secretary. All were convinced that he was the nation's evil
genius. He had obstructed a vigorous prosecution of the war, constantly advocated a patched-up peace, and overruled the demands of the earnest members
of the Administration. Lincoln was criticized on various grounds, but the general view was that he was blameworthy for yielding too much to Seward's
influence.[25]

It soon became clear that behind Wade and other critics loomed the figure of
Salmon P. Chase, who had spread his poison into every channel he could reach.
Fessenden, who spoke at length, held close relations with Chase and in indicting
Seward made it plain that his information originated with him and Stanton.

23 Seaton of the *National Intelligencer* had written Seward on Dec. 12 asking if the
Secretary had really resigned his office; Seward Papers. For the quoted opinions see N. Y.
World, Dec. 17, 18, 1862; *Times*, Dec. 19. *Harper's Weekly* declared that the loyal North
was rapidly becoming filled with sickness, disgust, and despair. The people had shown
unexampled patience. "They have borne, silently and grimly, imbecility, treachery, failure,
privation, loss of friends and means, almost every suffering which can afflict a brave people.
But they cannot be expected to suffer that such massacres as this at Fredericksburg shall be
repeated. Matters are rapidly ripening for a military dictatorship." Dec. 27, 1862.

24 H. Wadsworth reported this to S. L. M. Barlow, Dec. 18, Barlow Papers. Wilkeson
also reported it, adding that Lincoln was "awfully shaken"; Dec. 19, Gay Papers.

25 Several members, like Chandler, had worked themselves into frenzy, for Zach's letters
suggest a psychopathic state. He thought that McClellan and Franklin had approached
treason. As for Seward, he was a traitor. "I believe sincerely," Zach wrote his wife Feb. 10,
1863, "that he is today plotting for the dismemberment of the government. I believe he
would prefer to see England or France intervene rather than see the Rebellion crushed by
force of arms." Chandler Papers.

Indeed, he used a phrase about Seward's "back-stairs influence" which came straight from Chase's lips.[26] Grimes, whose closest Washington friends were Chase and Fessenden and who had declared that the nation was going to destruction as fast as imbecility and corruption could carry it, spoke in the same vein; so did Collamer of Vermont. Everyone seemed agreed that in so terrible a crisis, the Senate could not rest upon its strict constitutional duties, and must intervene in executive affairs. But how? Ben Wade proposed that the Senators go in a body to Lincoln to demand Seward's removal. Grimes, knowing that this would offend the President and country, made a counter-suggestion that Anthony be instructed to present a resolution in the Senate expressing want of confidence in Seward.

For a few minutes it seemed that the Senate and President were about to be brought into direct collision. But Preston King of New York and others protested against Grimes's proposal, and several members agreed with Orville H. Browning that the best course would be to send a deputation to call on the President, learn the true state of affairs, and give him a frank statement of their opinions. The caucus broke up to sleep on the matter. When they met next day, feeling against the Administration had hardened. Several Senators even wished to propose a resolution calling on the President to resign. Trumbull, like Browning the first day, warmly defended Lincoln, extolling his high character, asserting that he wished to fight the war with all his might, and declaring that only a bad Cabinet and worse generals had thwarted his purpose. The conservative Harris of New York proposed a resolution for general reconstruction of the Cabinet. But to this John Sherman objected that it sounded as if the whole body were to go: "No one wishes Mr. Chase to leave the Treasury, which he has managed so ably." And, added Sherman, merely changing the Cabinet would not help, for the root-trouble was with Lincoln, who lacked proper dignity, orderliness, and firmness.

Finally the caucus decided to pass a resolution calling for "a change in and partial reconstruction of the Cabinet," and to send a deputation to call on the President. Of thirty-two Senators present, thirty-one voted for the resolution. The deputation included seven radicals, Wade, Trumbull, Howard, Fessenden, Sumner, Grimes, and Pomeroy, and two moderates, Collamer and Harris; Collamer by an astute stroke was named chairman. Its work done, the caucus

26 Chase had written Chandler on Sept. 20, 1862, that he knew nothing of affairs outside his own department. "There is no Cabinet except in name. The heads of departments come together now and then—nominally twice a week; but no reports are made; no regular discussions held; no ascertained conclusions reached. Sometimes weeks pass by and no full meeting is held." Chandler Papers. Chase had also written Rosecrans lamenting that his influence with the President and War Department in military affairs was weak. "Had it been greater some serious disasters would have been avoided. . . ." Rosecrans Papers, UCLA Library.

broke up in high spirits. The majority believed that they had sealed the political death warrant of Seward, and made certain of radical domination of the Cabinet.[27]

Some dissenters, however, were convinced they had gone too far. Preston King of New York, an old friend of Seward, took immediate steps to warn the Administration. Rushing from the caucus to Seward's house, he told the Secretary what was taking place on Capitol Hill. At once Seward declared that he would not allow the President to be put in a false position by his unpopularity, wrote out a curt resignation along with that of his son the Assistant-Secretary, and dispatched both to the White House. King followed on the messenger's heels.

Lincoln, astounded at his dinner hour by the sudden resignations, turned to the portly New York Senator to demand an explanation. When King told him about the caucus action, his perplexity increased. Later that evening the dismayed President went to Seward's house to get him to withdraw his resignation, but all arguments were in vain—Seward would not budge. If he remained obdurate, the radicals would have won a sweeping victory at one blow—and Lincoln roused himself to prevent that disaster.

He was not helped in this by some confused counsel from the elder Blair, who came to the White House that same evening—for he had doubtless heard what the Republicans were doing—and next day wrote Lincoln an emphatic letter.[28] Perhaps Lincoln told him that Seward had resigned; more probably he did not. But Father Blair, as Lincoln called him, at any rate knew that a strong movement to reconstruct the Cabinet was afoot, and offered his own ideas. He urged the President to recall McClellan, get rid of Stanton, and put Preston King into the War Department. This of course would make Seward stronger than ever. The reinstatement of McClellan, thought Blair, would rally the army, which was a great political as well as military machine, behind the Administration, while the choice of King would replace the unpopular Stanton by a man of admirable judgment, business talent, and nerve, who was also politically strong in the Empire State. It need hardly be said that this scheme for putting the ultraconservatives in control was politically preposterous.

Lincoln of course knew that the proposal was in part motivated by family

27   This whole account is based on the diaries or reminiscences of Welles, Chase, Bates, Fessenden, Browning, W. E. and F. H. Seward, and others, contradictory in detail, but in essentials generally agreeing. The MS Diary of Fanny Seward, in a long retrospective passage of unclear date, relates that during the crisis no Senator called on Seward. "Father and Fred went to dine at Baron Gerolt [the Prussian Minister], and there C. Sumner had been invited, accepted, and recalled his acceptance at the eleventh hour." T. Harry Williams, *Lincoln and the Radicals,* offers a thorough study of the political background.
28   Blair to Lincoln, Dec. 18, 1862, RTL Papers.

hatred of both Chase and Stanton. The Blairs had detested Stanton ever since the Buchanan Administration. But the Blairs also honestly thought that Preston King would make a much better head of the War Department than Stanton, an untenable opinion. "Pardon my zeal—it is love for the cause and you—no selfish promptings," concluded old Blair. Lincoln ignored his proposals.[29]

Collamer, after drawing up a statement of the sentiments of the caucus and getting members of his committee to approve it, asked for an appointment with Lincoln on the evening of Thursday the 18th. To this the President, deeply hurt and despondent, assented. He knew what injurious reports were flying around the city—reports summarized by Samuel Wilkeson of the *Tribune* in a private letter to his managing editor:

Fessenden has refused to go into the State Department unless the whole Cabinet rookery is cleaned out. He has said if that were done he would consider if he could serve the country by taking the place.

Lincoln said yesterday that if there were any worse Hell than he had been in for two days, he would like to know it. He is awfully shaken.

The feeling is everywhere of exultation at the prospect of getting rid of the *whole Cabinet*. There is no exception to this in Congress or anywhere else.

There is little doubt left that Burnside made his awful blunder on his own responsibility.

Just one fortnight ago Seward sent off the thousandth reiteration of his dispatch that the Rebellion was just going to be crushed. A foreign minister remarked today that Congress should long since have passed a law forbidding Seward to prophesy, for horrible disasters always followed his efforts in that line.[30]

One rumor announced that a delegation of the solid businessmen of New York was coming to Washington to demand from Lincoln a change of men and measures. The distressed Executive, talking to his old friend Orville H. Browning, asked what the caucus Senators really wanted. Browning replied that he hardly knew, but that they were exceedingly hostile to the Administration, and that the resolution adopted was the gentlest action acceptable to the majority: "We had to do that or worse." Lincoln dejectedly remarked that he believed the Senators wished to get rid of him, and was half disposed to let them. The country, he mournfully declared, stood on the brink of ruin: "It appears to me the Almighty is against us, and I can hardly see a ray of hope." Browning, who loathed the radicals, advised him to stand fast, for the main force of the onslaught was directed against Seward, and this statement simply

29 Smith, *Blair*, II, 194 ff., 228 ff.; Flower, *Stanton*, 255; Blair-Lee Papers.
30 Collamer's note, Dec. 18, is in RTL Papers; Wilkeson's letter, "Friday night" (Dec. 19), is in the Gay Papers. Wilkeson raged against the telegraph censorship, which forbade his sending direct news of the Cabinet crisis to the *Tribune*. Its only effect in the case of Seward's resignation, he wrote, was to enable the men Seward told of the affair to buy stocks for a fall in New York; "'Tis said this was done."

added to Lincoln's sad perplexity. "I wonder," he said in effect, "why sane men can believe such an absurd lie as the charge of Seward's malign influence over me."

Everybody in Washington was now remaking the Cabinet. Father Blair was buttonholing men, urging them to call on Lincoln to oust Stanton and Halleck, and place Preston King and McClellan at the head of military affairs. Browning thought that Collamer would make a good head of the State Department, Banks of the War Office, and Thomas Ewing of the Treasury. Reverdy Johnson wanted Dix for the War Department. Ewing suggested the pompous cotton-Whig, Robert C. Winthrop, as Secretary of State. Meanwhile in the White House, Lincoln, aghast at the thought that the radicals under Chase might seize the helm, pondered means of keeping his quarrelsome family intact.[31]

[III]

On Saturday evening the President received the caucus committee with his usual urbanity. Collamer read the prepared statement, which demanded that Lincoln give the country a Cabinet composed exclusively of men determined upon vigorous prosecution of the war, and entrust military operations only to generals in hearty accord with the objects for which the war was being fought. Wade, Grimes, Howard, and Fessenden spoke, repeating the old charges against Seward. When Fessenden referred to the imperfect support the Administration had given to McClellan, Lincoln produced and read letters showing that he and Stanton had sustained that general to their utmost ability. Sumner then brought up Seward's recently published diplomatic correspondence, saying that he had subjected himself to ridicule at home and abroad, and had written some letters that were most objectionable. To this Lincoln replied simply that he had no memory of these offensive dispatches. As chairman of the Foreign Relations Committee, Sumner had a special right to criticize Seward's correspondence.[32]

In making its demands on Lincoln, the committee offered an amazing new interpretation of the Constitution. As phrased by Collamer, whose study of

31 Browning, *Diary*, 599–602; the press was also busy suggesting changes. For a good general summation of public attitudes toward the President see Herbert Mitgang, *Lincoln as They Saw Him*.

32 Sumner and others particularly objected to Seward's Dispatch No. 287 to Adams, July 5, 1862, reading: "It seems as if the extreme advocates of African Slavery and its most vehement opponents were acting in concert together to precipitate a servile war—the former by making the most desperate attempts to overthrow the Federal Union, the latter by demanding an edict of universal emancipation. . . ." But he had made other offensive statements. See the long letter signed Truth and Courage (perhaps Sumner?) in N. Y. *Tribune*, April 15, 1863.

history should have taught him better, it ran: "The theory of our government and the early and uniform construction thereof, is, that the President should be aided by a cabinet council, agreeing with him in political theory and general policy, and that all important public measures and appointments should be the result of their combined wisdom and deliberation." This was a thrust at the coalition character of Lincoln's Cabinet. As if Washington, balancing Jefferson against Hamilton, had not possessed a similar Cabinet! The committee asked for changes that would bring about unity at once, but it wanted unity on its own lines, and actually proposed that the President should make appointments only *after* submitting names to the Senate and getting its approval. No wonder that ex-Governor Dennison of Ohio wrote:

Is it not a dangerous innovation for Senators to interfere in Cabinet matters in caucus form? Will it not be a precedent that may in future completely subordinate the Executive to the Legislative branch of the govt., and thus virtually destroy the whole theory of our political system? Will not the next step be for Congress to vote its want of confidence in the President and so embarrass as to compel him to resign? Was not some such purpose in the Senatorial caucus?[33]

The committee obviously wanted a Cabinet congenial to Chase.[34] Throughout the three hours' discussion, indeed, the figure of Chase was always in the background. It was plain that he had been conferring with radical Senators, was the source of half the criticism of Seward and Stanton, and hoped to dominate the new Cabinet. Lincoln, as he allowed the Senators to do most of the talking, was studying them coldly, and at the end he ushered them out with the noncommittal statement that he would think the subject over. If they had expected him to yield, they were much disappointed.

Actually, he had determined to recede not an inch. His first step was to call the Cabinet together, with Seward of course absent. After asking them to keep his statements secret, he told them all he knew of the Republican caucus, of Seward's resignation, and of the committee's call on him. He described the Senators' attitude fairly, saying that they were "earnest and sad, not malicious nor passionate, not denouncing anyone, but all of them attributing to Mr. Seward a lukewarmness in the conduct of the war, and seeming to consider him the real cause of our failures." [35] They thought that whenever the President had any good purpose, Seward contrived to suck it out of him. Lincoln explained that he had defended his Cabinet loyally, and was most emphatic in repelling the idea of a general upset. He could not go on without his old friends,

33 Dec. 22, 1862, to Blair, Sr., Blair-Lee Papers. Dennison was conservative.
34 The committee knew that Seward had resigned; Fessenden says he heard rumors Wednesday evening, confirmed Thursday morning.
35 Bates, *Diary.* Lincoln plainly feared precipitate new resignations, discrediting the Administration and weakening morale.

and declared that this unjustifiable movement should never be allowed to break up the Cabinet.

Thus far the President had worn the air of a man who held a losing hand, but suddenly he placed an ace card on the table. He proposed that the Cabinet meet with him and the committee that night; thus he would have the support of his associates in facing Wade, Sumner, Fessenden, and the rest, and would put Chase in a spot where he would have to show whether he stood with the President or with the radicals. Though neither Chase nor Bates liked the idea, Welles and Blair spoke so heartily in favor of it that finally everyone acquiesced. Both were anxious to see Chase forced to show his true colors; for every perceptive person in Washington now believed the Ohioan was at the bottom of the whole movement.[36] Lincoln's intentions were becoming plain. He did not think that a Senatorial junta should be permitted, at the height of a terrible civil war, to dictate Cabinet membership and Administration policies to the President; and he did not think that anyone in his Cabinet should be allowed to play the traitor.[37] He did not object to one unimportant change in his official family, the long-contemplated resignation of the colorless Caleb B. Smith of Indiana, who had been given the Interior Department as a reward for helping deliver his State delegation in the Chicago convention. Smith left December 31 to accept a judicial post, and was at once replaced by John P. Usher. But Lincoln was resolved to permit no drastic alteration.

That night, from seven-thirty till almost midnight, the White House witnessed one of the most momentous meetings in the nation's history. Lincoln managed it with superb adroitness. He did not make the mistake of having the Cabinet with him when the committee arrived. Instead, the committee (without Wade) and Cabinet (without Seward) gathered in the same anteroom. The committee trooped into Lincoln's office first, and he asked their permission to admit the Cabinet for a free discussion; when they came in, fourteen in all were seated. The President opened the proceedings in a carefully matured speech. After reading the committee resolutions and recapitulating the previous night's conference, he launched into a defense of his Cabinet relations. He did not pretend, of course, that the Cabinet had decided all policies, for everyone knew that *he* made the critical decisions; he mentioned instances, including the appointment of Halleck, the restoration of McClellan before Antietam, and the new Banks expedition to Louisiana, when under emergency pressures he

36 Tom Ewing, who was an active Washington lawyer and heard all the gossip, so told Orville Browning; Browning, *Diary*, I, 602.

37 See Welles, I, 193, for Smith's attacks on Seward. He had made up his mind to leave because of failing health and interest. David Davis hit the nail on the head when he wrote Swett: "Smith has no faith and no hope and wants to retire on the District Judgeship. Smith repels me very much. There can be neither heart nor sincerity about him, and he cannot be a man of any conviction." Nov. 26, 1862; David Davis Papers.

had acted without Cabinet consultation or even the knowledge of several members. But all the members had acquiesced once a policy was determined.

"Did they not?" he demanded, turning to the Cabinet. Calling upon them to say whether there had been any lack of reasonable consideration or unity, he looked pointedly at Chase. Indeed, all eyes fell on Chase. The Secretary was horribly embarrassed, for he was trapped in an equivocal position; he had to make good his accusations to the radicals, or his loyalty to his chief. Blurting out that he would not have come had he known he would be arraigned before such a body, he looked about for a way of escape. According to Gideon Welles, he endorsed Lincoln's statement, but regretted the lack of a thorough discussion of every important measure in open Cabinet. According to Fessenden, he said that questions of importance had usually been weighed by the Cabinet, though not as completely as might have been desired, and that acquiescence had indeed been the rule, no member opposing a measure once it was adopted. By either account, he made a weaseling statement.[38]

Fessenden, one of the astutest lawyers of Maine, was irritated to the point of tart speech by Chase's dodging. He assured the Cabinet that the Senators had no idea of offering dictation to the President, only friendly advice. Then, turning to Chase, he answered the charge of arraignment by saying that it was the President who had unexpectedly brought the two bodies together. He went on to express his own views with deep feeling. Lincoln, he thought, had settled too many questions without Cabinet advice—he should have had all important questions discussed, though he was not bound to follow the majority —and had leaned too much on Seward. He spoke approvingly of an instance in J. Q. Adams' Administration in which the Cabinet, led by Clay, had overruled the President. Collamer expressed the same opinions, stressing the value of combined wisdom.[39]

The most radical members, Sumner, Grimes, and Trumbull, were emphatic in condemning Seward. "I have no confidence whatever in him," said Grimes. Sumner, agreeing that he should be ousted, once more brought up his alleged misconduct of foreign affairs, reading aloud his letter about emancipation and servile revolt, which shocked even stout Gideon Welles. "For one in his place," reflected Welles, "he is often wanting in careful discrimination, true wisdom, sound judgment, and discreet statesmanship." Trumbull, who had been angered by Seward's arbitrary arrests, was equally unrelenting in his condemnation. These three agreed that the main issue was no abstract question of Administration unity; it was Seward.

38 Fessenden, *Fessenden*, I, 244 (Fessenden wrote a long record of the whole affair, apparently soon after it occurred); Bates, *Diary*.
39 Welles notes the tartness for which Fessenden was famous; I, 196–198.

Bates and Montgomery Blair with rambling prolixity came to the defense of Lincoln, insisting that no President need consult his Cabinet unless he pleases; and Chase did Seward the justice of recalling that he had offered suggestions which strengthened the emancipation proclamation. But Lincoln, making several speeches and lightening the occasion by deft anecdotes, was his own best advocate. Near the end he brought the Senators up to the point of responsible action by asking them bluntly whether they still wished Seward to leave the Cabinet, and whether this step would please their constituents. Grimes, Trumbull, Sumner, and Pomeroy answered yes. But Fessenden, Collamer, and Howard declined to commit themselves, while Harris said that Seward's influence in New York was so great that his departure would hurt the party. Fessenden, still in irritable mood, declared that while he could not answer for his constituents, he believed that many who had formerly been zealous friends of Seward had lost their confidence in him. As for himself, he did not wish to discuss the subject until he learned whether the President meant to follow the wishes of the Republican Senators; if so, he would try to ascertain these wishes.

As the meeting broke up, Trumbull came to the President with angry mien: "Lincoln, somebody has lied like hell!" Lincoln coolly replied, "Not tonight." Fessenden among others remained to press Lincoln on the acceptance of Seward's resignation, and to repeat his offer to canvass the Republican Senators. Lincoln good-naturedly parried every attack, and to Fessenden's query about polling the Senators replied: "I think not." He made it plain that he desired to avoid any Cabinet changes whatever, for he feared that if Seward left, Chase and Stanton would also withdraw in "a general smashup." [40]

The unhappiest man that evening was Chase. Fessenden was angry at him for his double-dealing; Stanton commented that he was ashamed of the way Chase had lied about the manner of doing business in the Cabinet—*he* would not have done it, for the Senatorial charges were true; Caleb Smith said later that he had been strongly inclined to contradict Chase on the spot. Doubtless Chase passed a sleepless night. Conscious that his duplicity had been discovered, that the President was indignant, and that if the radicals forced Seward out the conservatives would demand his own head, he saw that he must write his resignation. Yet no more than Seward did he wish to leave; no more than Seward did he think he could safely be spared; and much more than Seward, he thought he would make a good Presidential replacement in 1864.

Gideon Welles also had passed a sleepless night, for it seemed to him a

---

40 Helen Nicolay had the "lied like hell" story from Robert Todd Lincoln; *Abraham Lincoln Quarterly*, V (March, 1949), 287. Nicolay and Hay, VI, 267, write simply that Trumbull turned back after leaving the room to tell Lincoln vehemently that Chase "had held a very different tone the last time he had spoken with him."

national calamity to let a Senatorial cabal dictate to the President the make-up of his Administration. Fessenden, too, fearful that Stanton and Chase would go, was racked with anxiety. Calling on Stanton, Fessenden to his relief found that pugnacious man determined to stay. "Seward shall not drive *me* out," he blazed. Posting over to the Treasury, however, Fessenden was startled to learn that Chase had already decided to resign. If he stayed, he explained, he would be accused of having maneuvered to get Seward out (hardly a false accusation!), while conservative attacks would make his Treasury burden, already crushing, quite intolerable. In vain did Fessenden expostulate; Chase insisted he would leave.[41]

Welles, meanwhile, went at an early hour to the White House. His white beard tremulous with agitation, his stern eyes blazing, he bade Lincoln stand firm, for it was his duty to maintain the rights and independence of the Executive. He remarked that while Seward obviously had grave faults, his self-exalting ways and invasions of the sphere of his associates, from which Welles had suffered much, did not call for Senatorial interference. Lincoln fully agreed, observing that if he yielded, the whole government must "cave in." At the President's request, Welles then hurried to see Seward and repeat Lincoln's words. He found the Secretary much excited, deeply wounded and chagrined, and voluble on the subject of his own sagacity and invaluable services to the nation—for his vanity never failed. That he—*he* in his own eyes practically the architect of the Republican Party, the founder of its success, and the sheet-anchor of the Administration—should be thus assailed by men who had once professed the greatest deference, was an outrage without parallel.

And this New Yorker whose whole career had been founded on shifts and compromises had the effrontery to criticize Lincoln for not taking an adamant stand. The President, said he, should have rejected his resignation without hesitation, and defied the Senate majority by refusing to talk with its committee. Delighted by Welles's attitude, Seward told him he might inform the President that the resignation could quickly be withdrawn. As if Lincoln did not know this! Welles, elated, hurried back to the White House.[42]

Here occurred the culminating scene of the crisis. When Welles entered the President's office Chase and Stanton were there, the President out. Welles spoke to them of his strong opposition to Seward's resignation, and thought them evasively acquiescent. The President entered, his eye on Welles. "Have you seen the man?" he demanded. "I have, and he assents to our views," replied Welles. Thereupon the President turned to Chase and said that he had sent for

---

41 Fessenden, *Fessenden*, I, 249, 250.
42 Welles, I, 200, 201. Seward's own diary is silent, but his son writes that he had begun to pack for his return to Auburn; *Seward in Washington*, 146–148.

him because he was deeply troubled by the situation—an obvious hint. The Secretary, expressing pain over the previous night's conference, replied that he had prepared his resignation.

"Where is it?" demanded Lincoln, his eyes lighting up. Chase hesitantly took it from his pocket. "Let me have it," ejaculated the President, stretching out his long arm. The Secretary wished to say something, but Lincoln ripped open the seal and hastily scanned the letter. "This," he said with a triumphant laugh, "cuts the Gordian knot." An expression of deep satisfaction overspread his face. "I can dispose of this subject now without difficulty," he went on, turning in his chair. "I see my way clear." Stanton interposed with a pompous offer of his own resignation, which Lincoln waved aside. "The trouble is ended," he said, and dismissed all three.[43]

[VI]

The crisis was indeed over. Lincoln, holding both resignations, could let the radicals understand that if Seward went Chase must go too. In his delight he fell back upon frontier imagery. "Now I can ride," he told Senator Harris. "I have got a pumpkin in each end of my bag." He told another man: "Now I have the biggest half of the hog. I shall accept neither resignation." Later he remarked to John Hay that he was sure he had managed the affair correctly. "If I had yielded to that storm and dismissed Seward the thing would all have slumped over one way, and we should have been left with a scanty handful of supporters." The radicals were actually too few and weak to govern the country, and when Lincoln formally announced December 22 that he had requested both Seward and Chase to withdraw their resignations, public comment admonished them of the fact.[44]

The storm not only cleared the air, but taught a needed lesson to all concerned, not excluding the President.

Chase, so abruptly exposed, had most to learn. His standing with his old friends sank; Fessenden accused him of betraying them, and Wade, Chandler, and Sumner saw that their movements would no longer find a secret ally inside the Cabinet.[45] When Collamer reported to the Senatorial caucus on the com-

43 Welles describes the scene in detail, I, 200 ff., and says that Chase left "moody and taciturn."

44 Nicolay and Hay, VI, 271; Dennett, ed., *Hay Diary*, 111. William H. Schouler, head of the Massachusetts Military Administration, wrote Seward that all Boston was cheering. When it heard the Secretary was out, the city was plunged in gloom; one man had offered to bet that within sixty days the nation would have a military dictator; and if it had appeared that Sumner was responsible for the breaking of the Cabinet, the Legislature would probably have refused to re-elect him to the Senate. Winfield Scott sent Seward his fervent congratulations. Seward Papers.

45 "You have no right to abandon your friends in this way," said Fessenden when he

mittee meeting with Lincoln and the Cabinet, Orville H. Browning asked how Chase, after telling Senators about Seward's backstairs work, could have made his statement on Cabinet unity. Collamer answered: "He lied." After this lesson, Chase restrained his tongue, and somewhat modified his attitude toward the President. Lincoln's secretaries tell us that it had varied between active hostility and benevolent contempt, and it had certainly lacked due respect; but now he had a new insight into both Lincoln's masterful qualities and his magnanimity—for the President repeatedly thanked him for remaining in the Administration. He continued to criticize and to intrigue, but less offensively.

Seward, too, learned a sharp lesson. Egotistical, erratic, meddlesome, he had long helped diffuse a totally false impression that he managed the Administration. By devious methods, unsleeping vigilance, use of his great experience, and skillful exploitation of Lincoln's friendliness, he had indeed done more to affect public policy than his colleagues; and boasting of his activities to friends, he flaunted them in the face of foes. To Chase, Smith, Welles, and Stanton he had behaved with exasperating insolence. Now he suddenly learned that half his own party not only bitterly hated him but thirsted for his blood. He saw that his ideas, methods, and loose use of words had raised a storm from which only Lincoln's consummate skill had saved him. He was henceforth content to confine himself to State Department business.

The President was triumphant. His expedient of bringing the Cabinet and Senate committee together was a perfect illustration of his grasp and shrewdness, combining frankness, honesty, dexterity, and insight into human nature. He alone emerged from the crisis with enhanced prestige. Yet he also had a lesson to learn, and knew it.

Lincoln's conception of his functions as wartime administrator and organizer was defective. He had no taste for administration, not the slightest experience in it, and little aptitude; he did not organize even his own office very well. Had he been more imaginative about governmental machinery, he might have enlarged his Cabinet for war purposes, for somebody of Cabinet rank was needed to deal with arms, munitions, supplies, and transport, leaving Stanton and Welles to direct the recruitment and general management of the army and navy. With no chief of staff yet dreamed of, the vagueness of Halleck's role was painful. And Halleck was undependable. Lincoln, long conscious of this, fairly lost patience with him after Fredericksburg, as a stern letter of rebuke on New Year's Day showed. Halleck had known that Burnside's strategy was wrong, yet let him go ahead; he had helped pave the way to defeat by his blundering with pontoons; and when later Burnside wished to recross the

learned of Chase's resignation; and he speaks pungently in his memorandum about Chase's change of tone on Seward and Cabinet unity; Fessenden, *Fessenden*, I, 250 ff.

Rappahannock and his best generals disapproved, Halleck failed to visit the spot, find out the true state of affairs, and deliver a decided judgment. As Lincoln wrote, all Halleck's "military skill" was useless unless he used it firmly. Yet Lincoln did not dismiss Halleck.[46]

It was wonderful how well Lincoln managed matters on which he thought deeply; it was also wonderful how completely he refused to think about some matters at all. Administration was one of them. The lack of liaison between McClellan and Halleck had remained painful till the day McClellan left; McClellan and Stanton, hating each other, had hardly been on terms of communication; and a painful failure of rapport between Halleck and Stanton had developed. To say that the public interest suffered is an understatement. It was defective administration which permitted the decision to send Banks's expedition to Louisiana without consulting Welles in advance, though Welles had to make the naval preparations. Welles wrote December 14, when he had not yet heard of the defeat at Fredericksburg: "It has struck me as strange that Banks was not sent up James River with a gunboat force. Such a movement would have caused a diversion on the part of the Rebels and have thrown them into some confusion, by compelling them to draw off from their strong position at Fredericksburg."[47] It was indeed strange, and much of the informal public agreed with the Secretary.

That Lincoln did not use his Cabinet efficiently is clear. While he was right in holding that he alone should make the great decisions, and that its consultative value was limited, he could have used it more largely for mutual exchange of information. He went to the War Office daily, and saw Seward frequently, for Seward was a "comfort" to him; the others he neglected. Chase, though a leader of one of the two great wings of the party, fell into the role of mere financial specialist, and resented the fact. Stanton complained that in important military matters the President took counsel of none but army officers, though he ought to be consulted, or at least be kept informed. Yet Stanton himself in Cabinet meetings imparted little information, and had a way of drawing Lincoln into a corner and talking with him in a low voice. Seward meanwhile aroused ill feeling by sending his son Frederick, the Assistant Secretary, to some Cabinet meetings, which provoked Stanton to declare that he would discuss no important business while an outsider was present, a feeling shared by others.

Fessenden, Sumner, Lyman Trumbull, and Grimes were highminded, patriotic men, sincerely anxious to promote the national welfare. The movement

---

46 Welles wondered that Lincoln gave such weight to the judgment of "the dull, stolid, inefficient, and incompetent" general; *Diary*, I, 320.

47 *Ibid.*, I, 192.

which they helped to lead had four capital objects: (1) to insist on a vigorous prosecution of the war; (2) to drive home the principle that no important military enterprises should be entrusted to lukewarm generals; (3) to ask the President to get rid of any Cabinet members who were not "cordial, resolute, unwavering supporters" of a determined war—meaning Seward; and (4) to induce Lincoln to give his Cabinet more, and take more from it. On the first two objects all were agreed; the third was improper; but the fourth was sound, and needed pressing home.

Lincoln learned from the crisis that, unsystematic, often abstracted, so intent on great aims that he thought little of minutiae, he had neglected details which, each trifling, amounted in the aggregate to something important. He realized that his principal associates were entitled, as Chase put it, to full systematic accounts of the progress of the struggle, the purposes entertained, and the means to be used. Full of natural good will to everyone, he had forgotten that some might resent his apparent favoritism toward Seward. At the next Cabinet meeting, December 23, the proposed creation of West Virginia received exhaustive discussion; and at the two following sessions the President, inviting careful discussion of his draft of the final Emancipation Proclamation, heard criticism from Chase, Welles, Blair, and Seward, and adopted some of their changes, including apparently a felicitous closing sentence by Chase invoking the considerate judgment of mankind and the gracious favor of Almighty God.

This proclamation enabled Lincoln to end a year full of frustration and failure with a document breathing hope and inspiration. On New Year's Day Seward and his son took the sheet to the White House for signature. Lincoln, dipping his pen, held it suspended as he observed: "I never, in my life, felt more certain that I was doing right than I do in signing this paper. But I have been receiving calls and shaking hands since nine o'clock this morning, till my arm is stiff and numb. Now, this signature will be closely examined, and if they find my hand trembled, they will say 'he had some compunctions.' But anyway, it is going to be done." With firm hand, he signed the declaration that all slaves throughout the areas in rebellion were then and forever free.[48]

[VII]

With the crisis behind him, the President could deal firmly with the military situation in Virginia. He was willing to give Burnside another opportunity to show what he could do. That commander behaved in sportsmanlike fashion. When he learned that rumor placed responsibility for his march against Fred-

48 Seward, *Seward in Washington*, 151; Lincoln, *Works*, VI, 23–31.

ericksburg on Lincoln, he sent Halleck a letter (December 17) assuming complete blame: "The fact that I decided to move from Warrenton on this line, rather against the opinion of the President, Secretary of War, and yourself, and that you left the movement in my hands, without giving me orders, makes me responsible." [49] The army, however, was dejected and demoralized. Late in December, Burnside decided to march up the Rappahannock to the fords above Fredericksburg and make a sudden movement across the river there. His chief subordinates sharply disapproved, and two brigadiers, John Cochrane and John Newton, hurried to tell the President that any such stroke might be ruinous. Lincoln therefore curtly directed Burnside not to move the army without letting him know.

While officers continued to express opposition, Burnside determined to proceed with his plan. After talking with Lincoln, he notified him of his resolve, enclosing his resignation if the President rejected the plan. Dry weather had hardened the roads; he commanded nearly 200,000 men, of whom 120,000 stood before Lee's forces; and he thirsted to retrieve his fortunes. Lincoln was deeply perplexed. On New Year's Day he wrote Halleck, bidding him for once to do his plain duty: to go over the ground with Burnside, confer with his officers, ascertain their temper, and decide whether the movement was good or bad. Halleck cast his vote in favor of the movement, saying it would not do to keep the large army inactive, and Lincoln assented—though still with doubts, for he enjoined Burnside: "Be cautious, and do not understand that the government, or country, is driving you." [50]

Then General January interfered. As the troops began to move, a terrific rainstorm turned the countryside into a quagmire in which the army bogged down. Artillery, pontoon trains, and supply wagons stuck fast, pushed on a few feet when men with spades dug them out, and stuck fast again. Infantry sank to their knees. It was obviously impossible to keep on. As Burnside the second day admitted failure, his army dragged its wet, miserable way back to its old camps.

But it did not return to a continuance of Burnside's command. That general, angered by the resistance of his best officers to his ideas, and by an ill-tempered interview Joseph Hooker had given a newspaperman, had attempted a drastic housecleaning. He prepared orders dated January 23, 1863, dismissing Generals Hooker, Newton, Cochrane, and W. T. H. Brooks, and relieving Generals W. B. Franklin, W. F. Smith, Samuel D. Sturgis, and two others from duty. At the same time he telegraphed Lincoln for an appointment, and seeing him early on the 25th, declared that if the President did not endorse

49 Lincoln was pleased; Sandburg, *Lincoln*, 1-vol. ed., 356.
50 O. R., I, xxi, 998.

the dismissals, he would resign.[51] Just what Lincoln said to him we do not know. But the President summoned Stanton and Halleck at ten that morning, and announced that he had made up his mind to relieve Burnside and place Hooker in command. He knew that the army, which was so outraged by Burnside's incompetence that it treated him in public with icy silence, would receive the news with gratification.

The mud march, the new change of commanders, and a shower of reports showing that the Army of the Potomac was ill sheltered and ill fed, did nothing to relieve the gloom in the North. Soldiers fed on salt pork and hardtack were actually dying of scurvy. Frigid tent-hospitals were so poorly provided with nurses and orderlies that some patients froze to death for want of fires and blankets. Meanwhile soldiers savage after months of defeat sent letters home that lowered public morale. "I am sick and tired of disaster," declared one, "and the fools that bring disaster upon us." Charles Dudley Warner believed that many soldiers in the army had become "McClellanized," and by tens of thousands wrote home to express a conviction that "we can never whip the South." This was unfair to a devoted army, which had good reason to excoriate Pope and Burnside, but which never lost its dogged courage. Yet the Northern discouragement for the moment plumbed great depths. People said later that this was the Valley Forge winter of the war.[52]

One measure of the discontent and bad discipline East and West was the high desertion rate. More than 200,000 men deserted during the conflict; 25,000 from New York units alone, 24,000 from Pennsylvania. The monthly desertion rate during 1863 averaged 4,650 and was especially great after Fredericksburg and the mud march. It would have gone hard with the Union armies had not the Confederate desertions been equally heavy. The percentage of desertions, strangely enough, was much higher among the regulars than the volunteers.

But it was in the Northwest that the situation seemed most alarming. Here, too, the people heard sorry news from troops in the field. The health of Western soldiers was so bad that some regiments had more men sick than well; the commissary arrangements were no better than in the East; and medical work was so mishandled that invalids died on hospital steamers for sheer lack of nourishment. Many of the people were as downhearted as the volunteers. They wrote letters, as an Illinois captain put it, "which would discourage the most loyal of men." The Northwest gave the President some of his chief worries. It had hitherto achieved the most; if it now faltered, all would be lost. Sumner wrote Francis Lieber in January: "The President tells me he now fears

51 *Works*, VI, 77, 78; O. R., I, xxi, 1008, 1009. Burnside's march began January 20; it broke down on the 22d; he saw Lincoln, as here stated, early on the 25th.
52 Warner to J. R. Hawley, Jan. 18, 1863, Hawley Papers, LC; Catton, *This Hallowed Ground*, 206: N. Y. *Tribune*, Feb. 11, 1863, etc.; Dorsheimer to F. P. Blair, Sr., Dec. 3, 1862.

'the fire in the rear'—meaning the Democracy—especially the Northwest—
more than our military chances." [53]

What was the real situation in this vast area of hill, prairie, and river valley?
What were the forces and events which made Lincoln so uneasy in thinking
of it?

53 Ephraim A. Wilson, *Memoirs*, 151; Pierce, *Sumner*, IV, 144. On desertion see O. R.,
III, v, 109, 757 ff.; Ella Lonn, *Desertion During the Civil War, passim.*

15

The Darkest Hours of the Northwest

FOR SEVERAL reasons the difficulties and defeats of 1862 had an especially malign effect in the Old Northwest, and particularly in Indiana and Illinois. All the States bordering on the Ohio, but most notably the two named, had many citizens of slave-State extraction. Their southern counties were full of folk drawn from Virginia, Kentucky, and Tennessee. Many, of course, were as strong free-soilers as Moncure D. Conway, Benjamin Harrison, and John M. Palmer, three men of Virginia blood who made their mark in Ohio, Indiana, and Illinois respectively, but many had proslavery sympathies. These sympathizers felt but faint approval of the war, which they blamed equally on Southern fire-eaters and Northern abolitionists. When they perceived that it would be long and burdensome, they became restive.

At Xenia, Ohio, in the summer of 1861, Moncure D. Conway, trying to arouse the people, had emerged from his hall to hear an excited Democrat exclaim, "Every word was as false as hell!" In Dayton, Conway argued that the President could abolish slavery by martial law. Vallandigham rejoined in his Dayton newspaper: "It seems to us that about three months in Fort McHenry, in a straight uniform, with frequent introductions to the accommodating institution called the town pump . . . would have a tendency to improve the gentleman mentally." [1] After military reverses, such dissidents were sure to revolt.

In Ohio, Indiana, and Illinois the Democratic Party had a historic ascendancy. Of twenty-three governors from admission to 1860, Ohio counted fifteen Democrats. In Indiana all the governors but two were Democratic from admission until 1861, while every governor of Illinois was a Democrat until W. H. Bissell took office in 1857. The party simply regained its old position in Indiana and Illinois when it swept the elections of 1862. Ohio remained Republican. But the Hoosiers put Democrats in the lesser State offices by more than 9,000 majority; and Lincoln's own State gave the Democratic candidate for Congressman-at-large 53 per cent of the vote, placed the legislature firmly

[1] Conway, *Autobiography*, I, 338, 339.

in Democratic hands, and strengthened the influence of such sharp critics of the Administration as William A. Richardson. Well it was for Lincoln that Governors Oliver P. Morton and Richard Yates held four-year terms, and that in Ohio the Union Party chose in David Tod an executive of the stanchest temper.

Another element in the rising discontent was the war losses. In all three States the Democrats, in true Jacksonian spirit, had done their full share in sending volunteers to fight. In Illinois, for example, the adjutant-general's report for 1862 showed that of about 270,000 men liable for duty, the State had sent nearly one-half, or 135,000, into service. Democratic counties like Massac, Union, and Williamson had actually led the way, and an exceptionally high proportion of those liable to duty had volunteered. Early in the war the legislature in Indianapolis created a voluntary militia organization called the Indiana Legion. As it was most active where border raids were feared, southern Indiana bore the chief burden of State defense, and thousands of men passed through it into the Union armies.[2] A natural consequence of exuberant volunteering from Democratic areas was heavy casualty lists in these counties. The four relatively indecisive battles of Iuka, Corinth, Perryville, and Murfreesboro late in 1862 cost the Northwest at least 3,000 slain and 12,000 wounded, totals which outran the cost of Antietam or Fredericksburg in the East.

The Democratic population meanwhile suspected that what had begun as a national war to save the Union had become a Republican war to destroy slavery, create a strong centralized government, and hold the South in permanent subjection. The partial draft after McClellan's failure angered much of the public; in Indiana, for example, men forcibly resisted it in various places.[3] Arbitrary arrests and other infractions of civil liberties simultaneously aroused widespread resentment. Early in 1863 General Burnside took command of the Department of the Ohio. He no sooner reached Cincinnati than he kicked over a hornet's nest by his General Order No. 38, proclaiming that he would not tolerate "the habit of declaring sympathy for the enemy" or allow any form of "expressed or implied" treason. This doctrine of implied treason, new to Anglo-Saxon law, evoked angry protests from the Democrats. A little later Burnside, if Governor Morton had not interfered, would have declared martial law in Indiana.[4]

Most of all were conservative Democrats offended by the emancipation proclamation. Many thousands of people who had sprung from slaveholding

2 *Report*, Illinois Adjutant-General, 1862; Stampp, *Indiana Politics*, 80. Frank L. Klement's *Copperheads in the Middle West* appeared too late for use in this volume.
3 Stampp, *op. cit.*, 155, 156.
4 O. R., I, xxiii, pt. 2, 147, 237; pt. 1, 398, 728.

areas, and who had relatives and friends in them, knew what bitter hardship any abrupt military emancipation would cause. They sympathized with the Southern feeling that the problem of race relations was too delicate to be surrendered to rough surgery. A New Englander who had never been near a slave State could afford to be callous, but not an Illinoisan who had scrutinized the relations of Negro and white in Kentucky. And as we have seen, countless people of Ohio, Indiana, and Illinois deeply feared an influx of freedmen. This fear was held without respect to party, though it was naturally keenest south of a line drawn from Quincy east through Springfield and Indianapolis to Columbus.

The Illinois constitution had long penalized the introduction of free Negroes. In 1862 the voters strengthened this constitutional barrier by a new provision authorizing the legislature to pass laws for discouraging, and if possible totally preventing, any such immigration. The winter session of 1863 had hardly begun when a member introduced a bill punishing any Negro attempting to enter by fine, imprisonment, and thirty-nine lashes. Harsh items blossomed in the Democratic press:

The Contrabands at Cairo.—There are now nearly 1500 "contrabands" at Cairo, 500 having been sent up from Columbus last week. They are a dirty, ragged, and filthy lot of human beings, most of them being the refuse of Southern plantations which the owners were very probably glad to get rid of. Only a small portion of the whole number are able or willing to work. The smallpox is among them, and there is an average of ten deaths a day.[5]

As still another cause of discontent, an apprehension was spreading that the war was being used to enrich Eastern industrial, mercantile, and banking groups, and injure Mississippi Valley farmers. Hundreds of articles, editorials, and speeches expressed this feeling. Just after Fredericksburg, $100 in gold would purchase $135 in greenbacks. A banker with $7,500 in gold could buy enough greenbacks to purchase $10,000 in United States gold bonds, paying 6 per cent and redeemable in five to twenty years. The interest, $600 in gold, would buy almost enough greenbacks every year for another $1,000 bond. Then in 1868 or later all the bonds would be redeemed in gold. While the poor bled, many said, the wealthy would grow richer.

The wartime tariffs, meanwhile, seemed as hurtful to agriculture as they were helpful to industry. They raised consumer prices while limiting foreign ability to buy foodstuffs. Daniel Voorhees of Indiana in 1862 made protection the target of bitter attacks in the House, and that summer the Democratic

5 Chicago *Morning Post*, Jan. 25, 28, 1863. The *Post* declared that about two-thirds of the Republicans of Illinois had voted for the new constitutional provision for excluding Negroes.

State Committee published an appeal against it in the Indianapolis *Sentinel* which was later reprinted as a campaign document.[6] In Illinois one of Douglas' Chicago friends, Samuel S. Hayes, made a number of speeches in the winter of 1862–63 denouncing the tariffs, and when the legislature met he argued that the North could best cajole the South back into the Union on a free-trade basis. As Democratic leaders pointed out, Eastern manufacturers got the great majority of war contracts. The trunk-line railroads, mainly owned by Eastern capitalists, were garnering a rich harvest from war traffic and the closing of the Mississippi. Agrarian groups complained of extortionate freight and elevator rates.

All the while, of course, the Northwest shared the ardent longing of the whole nation for victory. To Westerners victory meant above everything else the clearing of the Mississippi. The East-West railways had not yet taken the place in men's imaginations so long held by the central river system. The Northwest never forgot Douglas' asseveration that the men of Illinois would follow the Mississippi inch by inch with the bayonet to the Gulf. When defeat followed defeat in the East, some Westerners began to fear that Washington might fight for boundaries and let the cotton States go. If that happened, many said with Joseph Medill, the Northwest would secede, continue the war until it conquered the Valley and the Southwest, and erect its own republic.

[I]

In the West, in the winter of 1862–63, the armies were held in a deadlock which encouraged the widening discontent. The Union lines had pushed down to the long southern boundary of Tennessee, at some points slightly below it, as at Corinth, and at others above it, as northwest of Chattanooga; there they seemed almost immobile. Grant commanded in West Tennessee, with movable headquarters. His forces were much scattered, but the armies might be regarded as comprising a left wing at Corinth under Rosecrans, a center to the northwest of that town under Edward O. C. Ord, and a right wing based on Memphis under Sherman. Grant could readily manage all of them, except part of Sherman's, by telegraph, and did so with more expertness than good luck in the early autumn battles of Iuka and Corinth.

Grant's own account of Iuka is fair and lucid. This pretty village, a resort with mineral springs twenty miles east of Corinth on the Memphis & Charleston Railroad, and only seven miles from the Tennessee River, fell without resistance to Sterling Price in mid-September, 1862. "I was apprehensive," writes Grant, "lest the object of the rebels might be to get troops into Tennessee

6 *Cong. Globe*, 37th Cong., 2d Sess., 1150; Stampp, *op. cit.*, 139, 140.

to reinforce Bragg." The apprehension was well founded. Before Bragg began his northward march, he had informed Price and Van Dorn that he left the enemy in West Tennessee to them. Later, supposing that Rosecrans, then at Tuscumbia, was moving north to join Buell in pursuit, he had directed Price to follow; and Price with about 12,000 men had seen his chance to take the exposed post at Iuka, where large Union stores had been collected. Of course Grant, who kept well informed of Confederate movements by cavalry reconnaissances, saw that it was important to crush him. Rosecrans did not have enough men at Corinth to attack the enemy singlehanded. But Grant

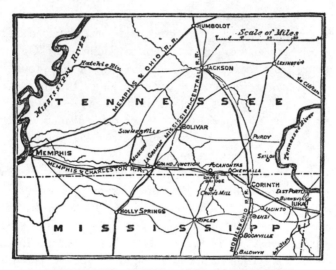

MEMPHIS, IUKA AND CORINTH

believed that if he sent Rosecrans with 9,000 troops and Ord with 8,000 to fall simultaneously on Price, one from the west and the other from the northwest, their combined strength would carry the day. Unfortunately, faulty maneuvering by Rosecrans, and the tardy arrival of Ord on the battlefield, ruined the effort, so that Price escaped without crippling damage, and joined Van Dorn. This result gave Grant, who had been almost certain of annihilating his foe, the greatest chagrin. "I was disappointed," he writes in his memoirs, "but I had so high an opinion of General Rosecrans that I found no fault at the time." Word of the abortive fight (September 19) reached Northern hearths on the heels of news of Bragg's victory at Munfordville (September 17) and of Antietam.'

7 For Iuka see *Battles and Leaders*, II, 701–736; O. R., I, iv, 175–565; Grant, *Memoirs*, I, 404–413.

As Bragg drove on north in Kentucky and joined Kirby-Smith at Frank-fort, Van Dorn and Price prepared to make a determined onslaught on Rose-crans at Corinth—for the Union general returned to that town on the 26th. Grant and Rosecrans knew that it was vital to hold Corinth, with its im-mense stores. If they were defeated there, Bolivar and Jackson to the north might also fall, West Tennessee to the gates of Memphis would again come under Confederate sway, and the victorious Van Dorn–Price army would establish communication with Bragg's troops through Middle Tennessee.

On October 2 Van Dorn's army camped ten miles from Corinth, and early next morning the battle began. On the first day the Confederates seemed to carry everything before them. By fierce charges they hurled the Union forces from a key hill, capturing two guns, and forced them back to the out-skirts. Van Dorn sent an exultant telegram to Richmond: "Our troops have driven the enemy from their positions. We are within three-fourths of a mile of Corinth. The enemy are huddled together about the town. So far all is glorious." All night Rosecrans stayed on the field, while Negroes threw up a fresh fort.[8] At first on the 4th the Confederate drive again seemed irresistible; but as the Union artillery asserted its superiority, the Southerners fell back. They knew that Northern reinforcements were at hand, and in fact, as the bat-tle ended McPherson unloaded a body of fresh troops from the cars.

Once more Rosecrans failed to show promptness. Had he moved with dis-patch in pursuit of Van Dorn the moment the Confederates began retreating, he might have annihilated their army. Grant had given him specific orders to follow without delay. But he did not begin his march till the morning of October 5th, took the wrong road, and let his troops be hampered by a wagon train. "Two or three hours of pursuit on the day of the battle," writes Grant disgustedly, "without anything except what the men carried on their persons, would have been worth more than any pursuit commenced the next day could have possibly been." Rosecrans' excuse was that his troops needed rest, while the thicketed country made progress difficult by day and impossible by night. Badly mauled, Van Dorn got clean away. After a brief futile chase, Rose-crans returned to Corinth to find the press full of his praises. In the aura of his imperfect victory he was ordered to Cincinnati, where he found that the government had given him Buell's place in command of the old Army of the Ohio.[9]

The Northwest was distressed to learn how sadly this force (now re-named the Army of the Cumberland) was weakened and demoralized. In nine months it had accomplished little beyond a hazardous retention of Ken-

---

8 Rosecrans himself describes Corinth in *Battle and Leaders*, II, 737–756. See also his testimony in *Report, Committee on Conduct of War*, Second Series, III, 1–109.

9 Lossing, *Civil War*, II, 538; John Fitch, *Annals of the Army of the Cumberland*, 367 ff.; Van Horne, *Army of the Cumberland*, Chs. XVI, XVII.

tucky and Nashville. Its effective numbers had fallen from about 100,000 to 65,000; the absentees, including about 10,000 in hospitals, were estimated at 33,000. The cavalry were far less efficient than Forrest's and Morgan's hard-riding commands. Recent events, in the words of its provost-judge, had left "its spirit broken, its confidence destroyed, its discipline relaxed." Many citizens believed this the fault not of Buell, a Democrat, but of neglect by the War Department; and the way in which Oliver P. Morton and other Republicans had accomplished Buell's dismissal angered Western Democrats just as McClellan's ejection angered their Eastern brethren.

Rosecrans, an excitable, temperamental man who possessed keen intelligence but only spasmodic energy, knew that he was expected to strike a blow. When he took command he found that Bragg had concentrated the rebel forces at Murfreesboro, where they covered northeastern Alabama, Georgia, and the vital rail line through Chattanooga to Richmond. Only thirty miles or so southeast of Nashville, Bragg menaced that city while himself feeling quite safe as he entertained Jefferson Davis at the handsome house he made his headquarters. Balls and parties enlivened Murfreesboro, for few expected a winter campaign. The Confederates, their ranks augmented by a rigid conscription, in fact felt so confident that they sent a large body of cavalry into western Tennessee to harass Grant, and another into Kentucky to try to cut the railroad north of Nashville.

But having amply supplied his forces, Rosecrans the day after Christmas pushed them southward in three columns under George H. Thomas, Alexander M. McCook, and T. L. Crittenden. Driving back outlying units, they reached the main Confederate position on Stones River before Murfreesboro on the 30th. Here, as 1863 ended and the new year began, they fought one of the stubbornest battles of the war. In chill, rainy weather, over rough and partially wooded terrain, some 75,000 effectives, in fairly equal numbers,[10] grappled in grim charges and hand-to-hand fighting. Though Rosecrans had expected to hold the offensive, Bragg by prompter movement on the 31st seized it from him. For a time that first day, as two divisions on the Union right buckled, Northern defeat seemed almost certain.

Fortunately, the Union officers had learned much about fighting since Shiloh;[11] fortunately also, Thomas and Sheridan held their positions against heroic Southern attacks. Soldiers called a particularly bloody segment of the

10 Livermore, p. 97, states that Rosecrans had 41,400, and Bragg about 35,000; but Cist, *Army of the Cumberland*, credits Bragg with 46,600 effectives, Rosecrans with 43,400.
11 "Our generals are now learning how to fight and save their men," wrote Lieut.-Col. James I. Davidson of the Seventy-third Illinois. "We fight a great deal lying flat on our breasts making breastworks of rocks, fallen trees, stumps, or anything we can get, and never allow the enemy to come upon us in full overwhelming force and take advantage of us. We place the batteries whenever practicable on high land or the edge of timber where our infantry can be concealed." Davidson Papers, Ala. State Archives.

field "Hell's Half Acre." One Northern colonel thought it wonderful anybody survived. "The shells, grape, balls, railroad iron and such like fired
from the enemy's cannon was a constant storm. Their columns came on with
yells as fierce as devils. . . ." William B. Hazen's brigade of 1,300 Ohio, Indiana, Illinois, and Kentucky volunteers beat back every wave, though one-
third its men went down. At the end Sheridan greeted Rosecrans elatedly:
"Here we are, all that are left of us." He might well say this, for his command
alone had lost seventy-two officers. The struggle closed when at noon on
January 3 Bragg, in council with his generals, decided to retreat behind Duck
River. Both armies had been terribly mangled, each reporting more than
9,000 men killed or wounded, while the combined death roll alone came to
about 3,000.[12] If Bragg had lost the field, Rosecrans had lost the larger number of prisoners, twenty-eight pieces of artillery, and much of his wagon-
train.

In effect, Murfreesboro or Stones River was a drawn battle. Fierce dissensions broke out among the Confederate officers. Breckinridge, Hardee,
Cleburne, and Polk agreed that Bragg had mismanaged his army and should
be removed from its command, while he was so violently assailed by the press
and general public that he appealed to President Davis for vindication or dismissal. On the Union side, Rosecrans' army was immobilized for the next six
months, for the brilliant Confederate cavalry leaders constantly threatened
its long single-track communication line with Louisville. Among the Northern
officers special criticism fell upon the right wing commander, McCook. On
both sides, the devotion of the common soldiers defied praise. Bragg spoke of
their "glorious work," and Rosecrans paid them a more emphatic tribute: "the
sturdy rank and file showed invincible fighting courage and stamina, worthy
of a great and free nation, requiring only good officers, discipline, and instructions to make them equal, if not superior, to any troops in ancient or
modern times." This devotion accounted for the heavy losses.

Altogether, in the indecisive battles of autumn and early winter, the Western armies of the Union suffered fully 25,000 casualties. Disease took larger
toll in the Western forces than the Eastern. Thinking of so many fresh graves,
of the cripples in the streets, and of the coffins stacked in railway stations,
countless Northwesterners asked, "To what end?"

Everyone who knew the West realized that political as well as military reasons made early capture of Vicksburg and clearance of the Mississippi desirable.
Yates and Morton knew it; editors like Medill and James Sheehan knew it; the

12 Livermore, 97, gives the Union losses as 1,677 killed, 7,543 wounded, and 3,686 missing,
a total of 12,906; the Confederate losses as killed, 1,294, wounded, 7,945, and missing, about
2,500, a total of 11,739. But Confederate officers estimated the number of their missing as
not over 1,000; Polk, *Polk*, II, 197. Full dispatches and reports are given in O. R., I, xx.

popular Democratic politician John McClernand knew it. The President had a clear grasp of the fact. Orville H. Browning, Senator until the end of January, 1863, was on terms of warm intimacy with the Lincolns. One day when he called, Lincoln picked up a map and pointed to the counties on each side of the river from Memphis downward, showing that Negroes averaged three-fourths or four-fifths of the population. Rapping the line of the Mississippi, he said: "I tell you, I am determined to open it, and if necessary will take all these Negroes to open it and keep it open." [13] His mind was receptive to men who had a plan, as Morton and McClernand did.

Morton's plan, unfortunately, was poor. He wrote Stanton just after the fall elections that the fate of the Northwest trembled in the balance, and that an immediate advance was imperative. Most Democratic leaders, he declared, believed that rebellion would triumph and the South gain its independence. The Democrats, asking what Ohio, Indiana, Illinois, and Iowa should then do, were replying that they should form a Northwestern Confederacy to save the Mississippi; and their arguments had wide appeal, for even ignorant men saw the value of the channel. "I give it here as my deliberate judgment," Morton told Stanton, "that should the misfortune of arms, or other causes, compel us to [grant] the independence of the Rebel States, Ohio, Indiana, and Illinois can be prevented, if at all, from a new act of secession and annexation to these States only by a bloody and desolating Civil War." But his program? He proposed that 100,000 men be immediately sent by sea to conquer and hold Louisiana, Texas, Arkansas, and the whole west bank of the Mississippi. This, he thought, could be done in ninety days. Thus even if the cotton States made good their new republic, the free navigation of the Mississippi could be secured. As a plan for putting 100,000 troops out of the war, this was superb.[14]

McClernand, the stout Jacksonian who had left Congress to become a brigadier, and since March, 1862, a major-general, perceived the military requirements of the hour much more accurately. He had been in Washington during the late summer drumming up support for an ambitious scheme. The 10,000-mile river system with its immense commerce was locked up, as he had written Lincoln, by a comparatively small garrison at Vicksburg. He would enlist a new force of his own—a special appeal to Democrats was implied. Then he would strike at that key city with not less than 60,000 men and a fleet of river gunboats. In this he would use what then seemed a shrewd plan of attack. That is, he would send transports laden with troops

13 The Brownings stayed in Washington till midsummer of 1863 and were much missed when they left; *Diary*, I, 512–568.
14 Morton's letter, Oct. 27, 1862, is in the Stanton Papers, LC.

down the Mississippi to the mouth of the Yazoo just above Vicksburg; have them ascend that river to the first eligible landing on the side toward Vicksburg; and thus throw his powerful force within about a dozen miles of the city. After capturing Vicksburg, the army should seize Jackson forty-five miles to the east, and march on to Meridian, from which railroad junction it could menace either Montgomery or Mobile.[15]

But the story of autumn and winter operations against Vicksburg was one destined to keep the Northwest in painful suspense.

Grant had been having a difficult time the whole summer and fall of 1862. As commander of the Army of the Mississippi, he had suffered from the haziness of his authority. Halleck had been uncommunicative. "Practically I became a department commander," Grant writes, "because no one was assigned to that position over me and I made my reports direct to the general-in-chief"; but he felt uncertain of his authority and tenure. The mediocre performance of Rosecrans and Ord distressed him. He was constantly worried by guerrilla warfare, and by the activities of cotton traders, which demoralized his troops. The public criticism he had received after Shiloh, the humiliations visited upon him by Halleck, exaggerated stories of his drinking, and the hawklike surveillance by Rawlins to see that these stories gained no substance, created a certain self-distrust. Since his dreary garrison duty at Humboldt Bay in 1853 Grant had been through harsh experiences, but none more galling than the anxieties of this dark national period.

While he, too, had a plan for taking Vicksburg, he did not offer it until in late October the government put him in command of the new Department of the Tennessee with clear powers. He had been waiting, he explained to Halleck, for guidance. "You have never suggested to me any plan of operations in this Department," he wrote October 26. Grant's troops were badly scattered on overextended lines.[16] He proposed concentrating them, and moving them down the Mississippi Central Railroad toward Jackson, Mississippi; an advance which he thought feasible because once his column reached Grenada it could be supplied from Memphis by way of the railroad connecting those two cities. When his army reached points east of Vicksburg, Grant believed it would force the evacuation of that place.

15 McClernand's important letter was written to Lincoln from Washington on Sept. 28, 1862; McClernand Papers, Ill. State Hist. Lib. We may repeat that as a veteran of the Black Hawk War, lawyer, Congressman, and opponent of the Kansas-Nebraska bill, he knew Lincoln well; and he talked with him in the White House.

16 The Army of the Tennessee under Grant supplanted the Army of the District of Western Tennessee and the Army of the Mississippi; Phisterer, 53, 54. Of Grant's forces in October, 4,800 were in Kentucky and Illinois, 7,000 in Memphis, 19,200 from Mound City south, and 17,500 at Corinth; reinforcements soon came in. Memoirs, I, 420, 421. Grant humbly assured Halleck that he was ready to do whatever that general might direct with all his might and without complaint; Oct. 26, 1862, Grant-Halleck Papers, Ill. State Hist. Lib.

Of the three plans advanced, the Administration chose McClernand's, which was soundest. Though his vanity, grasping ambition, and want of tact made him an unpleasant figure, the idea that his project represented either political intrigue or military insubordination, as some critics have stated, is absurd. On the contrary, it was a thoughtful effort to meet the political exigencies of the period by prompt action to clear the Mississippi under a Democratic leader who had wide influence with his Northwestern party.[17] It was strategically superior to Grant's plan because a river advance would be far safer from interruption by raids than an advance down a railroad. Moreover, McClernand's proposal for raising fresh forces for the expedition was sound, for he had already been prominent in recruiting men. The country needed more Jacksonian Democrats thinking as constructively as he did.[18]

At the end of October, McClernand, after long interviews with Lincoln, Stanton, and others, was back in Springfield. He had obtained confidential orders from Stanton to range through Indiana, Illinois, and Iowa, organize troops he found there or could freshly collect, and forward them immediately to Cairo, Memphis, or some other spot. This was "to the end that, when a sufficient force, not required by the operations of General Grant's command, shall be raised, an expedition may be organized under General McClernand's command against Vicksburg. . . ." He immediately established close relations with Morton, Yates, and Kirkwood. "I feel deep interest in the success of the expedition," Lincoln endorsed on the order, "and desire it to be pushed forward with all possible dispatch, consistently with the other parts of the military service." The newspapers laid hold of the news, which afforded good Western ammunition for the Administration just before election, and the popular response seemed enthusiastic.[19]

By November 10, McClernand had sent twenty regiments of Indiana, Illinois, and Iowa troops, with two batteries, to Columbus, Kentucky, and Memphis. He urged Stanton to continue supporting him, writing that the popular delight in the Mississippi expedition would curdle into anger and disillusionment if any neglect ruined it. Among the officers eager to join him was Frank P. Blair, Jr., who also had been raising troops.[20]

Grant watched all this with unhappy gaze. The newspaper praise and

17 John Fiske in *The Mississippi Valley in the Civil War*, 202, calls it political intrigue, and F. V. Greene in *The Mississippi*, 60, "a violation of all military discipline"; both statements ignore the Lincoln-Stanton endorsement and Northwestern unrest.

18 For McClernand's services see Cole, *ut sup.*, 262, and Force, *From Fort Henry to Corinth*, 21, 28, 38 ff.

19 Stanton's orders were dated Oct. 20–21; McClernand Papers. For newspaper publicity see John M. Thayer, St. Louis, Oct. 24, 1862, to McClernand, *ibid.*, and files of the Chicago *Morning Post*, *Illinois State Register*, and Indianapolis *Daily State Sentinel*.

20 McClernand to Stanton, Springfield, Nov. 10, McClernand Papers; Blair to McClernand, Nov. 12, *ibid.*

popular congratulations showered on McClernand worried him. He thought two commanders in the same field one too many, and was quick to express concern over McClernand's inexperience, the possibility that he would get his raw troops into trouble, and the chances of imperfect cooperation. He therefore on November 6 asked Halleck whether he was to lie inert while this expedition was fitted out from Memphis, or whether he could push as far ahead as possible. Halleck well realized that Grant outranked McClernand, and always favored professional soldiers. He knew that Stanton had authorized McClernand to move only when he had a sufficient force not required by Grant's operations, and that Lincoln wished to expedite him only in a way consistent with other parts of the service. He therefore assured Grant: "You have command of all troops sent to your Department, and have permission to fight the enemy where you please." [21]

At this point everything began to go wrong for Grant. The general, according to his plan, concentrated his forces at La Grange, Tennessee, marched south on November 20 along the line of the Mississippi Central, and had Sherman move from Memphis (November 24) to join him on that railroad. On December 5 they camped side by side at Oxford and College Hill in northern Mississippi. The Confederates under Pemberton retreated before them to Grenada, about 140 miles by road from Vicksburg. All looked roseate until the perils of dependence on a long line of railway appeared. Grant had established his main depot at Holly Springs, to which he had to bring supplies by 180 miles of track from Columbus, Kentucky, a precarious lifeline. If he pushed on south to capture Grenada he would reach the direct lateral line from Memphis, but it was in bad condition. Moreover, at Grenada he would still be 140 miles by road from Vicksburg, while the railway in advance had been torn up, the highways were poor, and Pemberton was sure to gather strength to meet the advance. Grant realized that he had made a false start.[22]

On December 8, therefore, he decided to divide his forces for *two* movements against Vicksburg. He ordered Sherman to return to Memphis with one division, collect enough troops thereabout to give him more than 20,000 men, and move down the river with Admiral Porter's gunboats in a strong amphibious expedition. Grant would meanwhile hold his army ready to advance against Vicksburg from the central Mississippi rear, immobilizing Pemberton. If the Confederate army opposed one force, the other could snatch the

---

21　Nov. 12, 1862, Grant-Halleck Papers. Grant states his objections in *Memoirs*, I, 426. Full military papers are given in O. R., I, xvii, pts. 1 and 2, *passim*.

22　Greene, 63, 64; Liddell Hart, *Sherman*, 160, 161. Much light is thrown on Grant's serious supply problem by the papers of Col. (later Gen.) Lewis B. Parsons, who had charge of river transport; Ill. State Hist. Lib. For his Mississippi Central expedition he wanted more locomotives, for that line had only eighteen in working order; Grant, Nov. 12, 1862, to Halleck, Grant-Halleck Papers.

prize. But two blows immediately befell Grant. The Sherman-Porter amphibious advance would be using what was essentially McClernand's plan. It is not strange that when Sherman reported his orders, Halleck warned him the President might insist on keeping the original projector in charge. After all, McClernand had a better claim than Sherman, his junior in years, rank, and influence. And Lincoln did just this. On December 20 Sherman steamed down the river with 20,500 troops, to be reinforced at Helena by 9,500 more; but meanwhile, on December 18 Halleck telegraphed Grant that, by the President's direction, McClernand was to lead the river expedition.

And then suddenly, just after mid-December, the Confederates completely smashed Grant's supply line and main base by two brilliant cavalry strokes. Forrest, with 2,500 horsemen based on Columbia, Tennessee, destroyed numerous stretches of track along sixty miles of Grant's supply railroad. And simultaneously Earl Van Dorn with 3,500 cavalry, striking from Grenada, fell upon Grant's supply base at Holly Springs, captured 1,500 of the Union troops guarding it, and burned $1,500,000 worth of supplies. Grant was outraged by the feebleness of the commander, who had 2,000 effective men able to shelter behind brick walls and cotton bales, and who had been given ample warning. "The surrender at Holly Springs was the most disgraceful affair that has occurred in this Dept.," he wrote.[23]

Yet Grant himself was censurable for not making sure that so vital a point had a heavy defense force under competent officers. His position was now sad indeed, for with his principal depot gone and his communications broken he was compelled to retreat. To stand still long was to starve, while to go forward, depending on the country for food, was too dangerous—though he seriously contemplated doing just this. For a time he sustained himself by collecting supplies from the district about Oxford. He sent out scores of wagon trains, heavily guarded, for twenty-five miles on every side. They stripped the country bare of livestock, grain, and forage, and when the inhabitants begged for enough to live on, Grant sternly bade them move further south. Then, putting his men on three-quarter rations, he turned back behind the Tallahatchie, and retreated to his starting point near La Grange. On January 10, 1863, he himself was in Memphis. He made the more haste to reach that city because he had been stung by the telegram giving Lincoln's order that McClernand, not Sherman, should lead the river expedition against Vicksburg.[24]

23 Grant, Jan. 14, 1863, to "Dear Cousin," Grant Letters, Colo. State Hist. Soc.
24 Grant, *Memoirs*, I, 422–436, gives a vigorous account of his movements. See Liddell Hart, 162, for his desire to get to Memphis to cut out McClernand. McPherson wrote Grant on Dec. 20 of the Vicksburg expedition: "I would, if in your place, proceed to Memphis and take command of it myself. It is the great feature of the campaign, and its execution

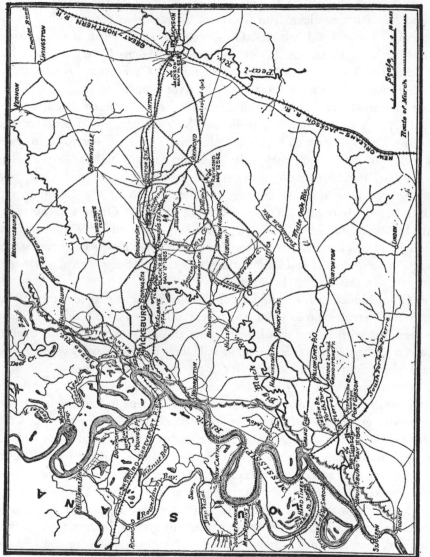

THE VICKSBURG CAMPAIGN

Grant had not covered himself with glory. He had marched from Grand Junction nearly a hundred miles to Oxford, and then marched back again. His two months of effort had merely lost valuable supplies and demonstrated that his route was badly chosen. If he and his staff had learned a good deal about handling a large body of troops, it was an expensive education. Meanwhile, Sherman continued to execute the plan of a rapid amphibious descent of the Mississippi, followed by a drive up the Yazoo just behind Vicksburg—in effect, McClernand's plan. For Lincoln's order that McClernand should take command had been received by Grant just as Forrest cut all communications, so that it was relayed neither to Sherman in Memphis nor to McClernand in Springfield. Sherman put all speed into the assignment Grant had given him because both men were anxious to forestall McClernand, and because he hoped to take the defenders of Vicksburg by surprise, perhaps capturing the city by a single blow.

In other respects this was not Grant's happiest hour. On December 17 his headquarters in Holly Springs published General Orders No. 11: "The Jews, as a class violating every regulation of trade established by the Treasury Department and also department orders, are hereby expelled from the department within twenty-four hours from the receipt of this order." Post commanders were to eject "all this class of people" and to arrest anyone who returned. Plenty of chicanery, thievery, and illegal dealing in connection with cotton shipments could be found in the department, but more Gentiles than Jews were concerned in it. Indignant Jewish delegations at once visited Washington to protest. One was headed by Rabbi Isaac M. Wise of Cincinnati. They had no trouble seeing Lincoln, who promptly revoked the order. The President, whose antagonism to Know-Nothingism was well known, told Rabbi Wise that he would never permit any citizen to be in any manner wronged on account of his place of birth or his religion.[25]

[III]

But Sherman fared as badly as Grant, for once more the Union leaders reckoned without Confederate enterprise. The Southerners had spies in Memphis to report the start of his expedition on December 20, and yet more spies

---

rightfully belongs to you." Liddell Hart thinks that Grant might well have remained in Pemberton's front to keep him from reinforcing Vicksburg. James Harrison Wilson in *Under the Old Flag*, I, 120–127, relates that he had seen much in Washington during October of McClernand, who offered him a place on his staff. McClernand thought poorly of Grant, but Wilson warned him that Halleck would assuredly favor Grant for chief command of the Vicksburg expedition.

25 For Grant's order see O. R., I, xvii, pt. 2, p. 424; for Halleck's statement on it, *idem*, p. 530; for Wise's report, *The Israelite*, Jan. 8, 1863. Bertram W. Korn's full analysis in *American Jewry and the Civil War*, 121–155, should be read.

to record its hourly progress. As this army descended the river, Forrest was capturing small posts behind Grant, while Van Dorn, leaving the Holly Springs base in ashes, was mopping up Union detachments in that area. Grant was estopped from furnishing Sherman any cooperation and his letter of December 23 announcing that he had been compelled to fall back did not reach Sherman until long after its intelligence was of any value. The result was disaster. When Sherman the day after Christmas landed three divisions on the bank of the Yazoo, Pemberton had 13,800 men facing them in entrenched positions on hills. The Union attacks during the next three days met a bloody repulse. Nearly 1,800 Union soldiers were lost in an action which one participant, Frank P. Blair, Jr., acridly described:

The Grand Mississippi Expedition has been a failure. Everybody in the West supposed it would contain at least 100,000 men, [but] it numbered 30,000. Grant, it seems, preferred to operate in two lines, one interior and the other by the river. His communications were cut off and he with 45,000 men compelled to fall back on Memphis. The enemy then concentrated against us at Vicksburg. Sherman instead of concentrating his force at some one point of the fortifications of Vicksburg scattered them along the whole line from Haines Bluff on the Yazoo to the city of Vicksburg.[26]

Meanwhile, the defenses of Vicksburg were being feverishly augmented. "The work here goes bravely on," reported the Vicksburg correspondent of the Yazoo *Banner*. "General Pemberton's energy and skill have accomplished wonders. He is a great worker. What he lacks in genius he makes up in industry. He has not established any headquarters yet. One day he is with the army of the north, the next at Jackson, the next at Vicksburg. . . . The whole place is being fortified. Forts, breastworks, and batteries outside the city, riflepits and intrenchments in the streets. The line of defense is twenty-odd miles in length. . . . The iron-clad is not feared." [27]

While Sherman was being repulsed, McClernand, who had at last discovered that he was entitled to command before Vicksburg, was hastening down the Mississippi. He reached the mouth of the Yazoo on January 2, 1863, to find the defeated Sherman glad to subside into the position of a corps commander.[28] As nobody knew how long it would be until Grant arrived—cer-

26 Blair-Lee Papers; casualty lists reached the Northwest along with those of Murfreesboro.
27 Dec. 17, 1862.
28 McClernand suspected that Lincoln's order putting him in command had been deliberately withheld. Certainly Grant was not to blame—he had tried to relay it promptly; but why had Halleck not sent a copy direct to Springfield? "Either accident or intention has conspired to thwart the authority of yourself and the Secretary of War and to betray me," McClernand wrote Lincoln from Memphis on Dec. 29, "but with your support I shall not despair of overcoming both." He complained he had to push down to his command at Vicksburg, running a gauntlet of guerrilla bands, in a common river steamer. His letter is in Rufus Rockwell Wilson, "President Lincoln and Emancipation," Lincoln *Herald*, LI (June, 1949), 43, 46.

tainly not within a fortnight—Sherman proposed that while awaiting him the army and gunboats should move against the so-called Post fifty miles up the Arkansas River, where a garrison of about 5,000 under T. J. Churchill presented a threat to Mississippi operations. McClernand, who had already thought of this, agreed. On January 11, 1863, gunboats silenced the fort's artillery, Union troops pushed to within a hundred yards of the intrenchments, and the white flag went up. With just over a thousand casualties, McClernand and Porter took 4,800 prisoners, killed or wounded 110 more, and captured 17 guns.

At this point Grant dealt with McClernand in an arbitrary spirit. His feeling against that officer suggests a jealous determination never to let him get the credit for capturing Vicksburg. Thus far, the "political general" had done better than Grant himself. But on the very day Arkansas Post was taken, Grant sent a letter of stern disapproval, ordering him back to the Mississippi unless he was acting under superior authority. He simultaneously telegraphed Halleck that "McClernand has gone on a wild goose chase to the Post of Arkansas," a most unjust statement. Halleck was glad to seize on this telegram as a basis for action. Without waiting to learn the facts he replied: "You are hereby authorized to relieve General McClernand from command of the expedition against Vicksburg, giving it to the next in rank or taking it yourself." When on the 13th Grant heard from McClernand of the capture of the fort he directed him to return to Milliken's Bend, clearly intending to reduce him to subordination as corps commander. But as soon as Grant learned that Sherman had advised the operation, he praised it as a wise step! [29] The best that can be said for the victor of Donelson is that he was acting on incomplete knowledge, and that at a time when both the situation and orders from Washington demanded an immediate strengthening of the Mississippi River column, he had been genuinely alarmed by a dispatch from McClernand implying that the general might go on from the Post to a rash foray through Arkansas.

Throughout the war it was all too often evident that when a professional soldier blundered his West Point associates helped gloss over the slip, and whenever a West Pointer scored a success his friends made the most of it; but any error on the part of an officer from civil life was unpardonable. Had McClernand marched a large army to Oxford and back again he would have been accused of something worse than a wild-goose chase; had he lost Holly Springs with 2,000 men and large stores he would have been assailed as mercilessly as Frémont after the loss of Lexington. The statement of reasons

29 Sherman deals with Arkansas Post in Ch. XII of his *Memoirs*, emphasizing McClernand's vanity as he boasted of his star "ever in the ascendant." It is unfortunate that McClernand left no personal record. Nearly all judgments of him have been based on *ex parte* evidence, without examination of his papers or his son's MS biography in the Illinois State Historical Library.

for attacking Arkansas Post which he now sent to Grant's adjutant-general was an honest and reasonable document. He pointed out that the necessity for reducing the Post was obvious—he had urged General W. A. Gorman at Helena, on his way down the river, to seize or invest it; that after Sherman's repulse at Chickasaw Bayou, the movement against Vicksburg could obviously not be renewed for some time; that Grant's retirement had left Price's army at Grenada free to reinforce Vicksburg; and that if he had not made this attack his forces would have rusted in idleness. He added two sentences which must have stung Halleck like a whiplash: "Vicksburg cannot be reduced by a front attack, unsupported by cooperation from the rear of the place, except by a very large land and naval force, and after great delay. *The golden moment for the reduction of Vicksburg was allowed to pass unimproved.*" [30] It was Halleck who, after his slow march on Corinth, had neglected that moment.

McClernand, with all his faults, understood the situation in mid-January more clearly than his superior. Grant scolded him because Grant entertained three glaring misapprehensions. He believed that N. P. Banks would lead his army up from the south into the Vicksburg area any day; that with this augmentation a fresh attack on Vicksburg could succeed; and that Arkansas Post was of little consequence. The truth was that Banks did not even reach Port Hudson until late in May, and then was disastrously repulsed; that even his 15,000 additional men would not have enabled the Union forces to make a successful attack on Pemberton from the Yazoo; and that Arkansas Post was too troublesome a threat on the Union flank to be tolerated. The Confederates, as Sherman assured Grant, believed they had made it impregnable. "Could we have followed up," added Sherman, "the capture of Little Rock would have been easy; but even as it is. . . . I assure you when next at Vicksburg I will feel much less uneasiness about our communications." [31]

McClernand no sooner got Grant's order to return to Milliken's Bend than, on January 14, he assured Grant that he would obey it immediately. He left Arkansas Post, however, with a feeling of pique. Why had he not been allowed to move against Vicksburg by the Yazoo route in early December with all the troops available? Why had Grant waited two months, let his communications be cut, and allowed his base to be destroyed? Why had Sherman, hurrying to forestall him, stumbled so clumsily into defeat? When

30 O. R., I, xvii, pt. 1, p. 709; my italics.
31 Napoleon, Ark., Jan. 17, 1863, to Grant; O. R., I, xvii, pt. 2, pp. 570, 571. Some of Grant's biographers have accused McClernand of being ready to commit his army to a hare-brained attempt to seize Little Rock; but the record plainly shows (1) that Sherman believed this possible if the Arkansas River remained high, and (2) that McClernand was closely watching the stage of water, fully aware that he must not let transports get stranded upstream. See McClernand to Sherman, Jan. 14, 1863, O. R., I, xvii, pt. 2, pp. 563, 564.

at last he, McClernand, had been permitted to appear on the scene he had gained a victory only to be loaded with reproaches. A core of truth lay in the foolish letter he sent Lincoln from Arkansas Post on January 16:

> I believe my success here is gall and wormwood to the clique of West Pointers who have been persecuting me for months. How can you expect success when men controlling the military destinies of the country are more chagrined at the success of your volunteer officers than the very enemy beaten by the latter in battle? Something must be done to take the hand of oppression off citizen soldiers whose zeal for their country has prompted them to take up arms, or all will be lost.[32]

McClernand still hoped that Grant, keeping his headquarters in Memphis to exercise over-all control, would give him a free hand in taking Vicksburg. This dream quickly vanished. On January 13, 1863, Grant had informed General J. B. McPherson in La Grange, Tennessee: "It is my present intention to command the expedition down the river in person." [33] For the good of the country, this was a wise decision. There is truth in Sherman's observation that McClernand excelled in short-range views of any situation, but was poor in long-range judgment; that he, Sherman, excelled in long-range plans, but went astray in short-range thinking; and that Grant was good in both. But February and March were to pass before any real progress was made, just as in the East an even longer period was to expire before the Army of the Potomac initiated any movement.

Western officers, it is true, were beginning to see the lines of future success. "Russ" Jones, a cotton-trader friend of Elihu Washburne, rode on the steamer *Magnolia* on January 27–28 with Grant, Rawlins, and other staff officers between Memphis and the mouth of the Yazoo. Writing Washburne, he made it plain that he had listened to the talk of officers lounging on deck. One fact was especially interesting:

> Grant has about 36,000 men down below. Will get 6,000 men from Helena and has about 16,000 at Memphis ready to come down making in round numbers about 60,000 and as many gunboats as can be used at one time. He has ammunition enough here for present use and enough on the way to give each man 700 rounds, with artillery ammunition in proportion. I was under the impression that Sherman failed for lack of men, but he tells Grant that he had as many men as he could use, that the result would have been the same if he had had 700,000 men. *As I understand it, the only hope of getting Vicksburg is in being able to get below it and in behind. If that can be done we are all right, if not it is doubtful.* On the 2nd water had entered the Butler Canal and that may

---

32 O. R., I, xvii, pt. 2, pp. 566, 567.
33 *Ibid.*, p. 557. Grant in a report to the War Department on Jan. 20, 1863, stated this intention—unless the government interfered, which of course it did not.

prove available. I told Grant I hoped he would not let the outside pressure influence him to be in too great a hurry.[34]

Yet as winter passed into early spring, doubts about the capacity of Grant persisted. Lincoln felt them; he told a New York *Tribune* man on March 20 that he was not sanguine about capturing Vicksburg. Radical leaders felt them: Grimes of Iowa went to the White House to demand the removal of Grant as an incompetent utterly callous about human life, and when Lincoln refused, flounced out of the office in a rage. Cadwallader C. Washburn, who as a commander of Wisconsin troops had full opportunities for observation, was completely skeptical. "Grant has no plans for taking Vicksburg," he wrote his brother Elihu on March 28, "and he is frittering away time and strength to no purpose. The truth must be told even if it hurts. You cannot make a silk purse out of a sow's ear." This to Grant's chief political sponsor! Like some others, "Cad" believed Rawlins infinitely Grant's superior.[35]

[IV]

While the winter thus passed in discouragement, the tide of Northwestern discontent rose. Every setback gave it strength. A number of editors and politicians trod the narrow zone between legitimate criticism of the government and treasonable obstruction of the war effort. The Chicago *Times*, which the city board of trade late in 1862 denounced for almost daily articles calculated to give aid and comfort to traitors, was one. Cyrus H. McCormick had financed its purchase by W. F. Storey, who after the emancipation proclamation bitterly attacked the Administration. Samuel Medary's Columbus *Crisis*, edited by a professional agitator who supported Vallandigham, was so objectionable to Unionists that angry soldiers wrecked its press in the spring of 1863. Such other organs of the Peace Democrats as the Cincinnati *Enquirer*, which declared the idea of a Union established by force ridiculous, the Detroit *Free Press*, and the Indianapolis *Sentinel*, were abetted by smaller newspapers like the Peoria *Demokrat*, which the government excluded from the mails, the Terre Haute *Journal and Herald*, which was mobbed, and the Ashland (Ohio) *Union*, which termed Lincoln a bloodstained tyrant.

34 Jan. 28, 1863, Washburne Papers, LC; italics mine. By the Butler Canal, Jones meant the canal that had been started by General Thomas Williams the previous summer, under directions from Farragut, across the peninsula opposite Vicksburg, in an effort to bypass and isolate that city.

35 A. D. Richardson, March 20, 1863, to Gay, Gay Papers; W. M. Thayer, *Grant*, 208, 209; Washburn, Helena, Ark., to Elihu Washburne, Washburne Papers, LC. The Chicago *Morning Post* strongly took McClernand's side. The troops had been greatly disheartened, wrote its army correspondent, by the repulse of Sherman's attack, "which was insane in conception, and inspired, it is affirmed, by jealousy"; but the victory at Arkansas Post had restored confidence. Letter from the front Jan. 10 in issue of Jan. 29, 1863.

The precise strength of disloyalty was for three reasons difficult to measure: a clear definition was impossible; its worst manifestations were kept secret; and its vigor fluctuated from place to place and day to day. Who was disloyal? Any patent conspirator for Confederate success, like Dr. William Bowles of French Lick Springs, Indiana, who organized the Knights of the Golden Circle along the border, was certainly a traitor. So was any Northerner who strove actively for peace at the price of disunion, or on the basis of a new nation to include the South and exclude New England. Any man who corresponded with Confederate leaders, tried to block recruiting, committed acts of sabotage, or disseminated false reports designed to cripple the government, could be termed disloyal. But a twilight penumbra surrounds such words. Seward himself had stood for peace at the price of temporary disunion; multitudes of good citizens asserted that they would support recruiting and heavy taxation to save the Union, but not to enforce emancipation. The Newark *Evening Journal* declared: "It will be seen that Mr. Lincoln has called for another half million of men. All who wish to be butchered will please step forward. All others will please stay at home and defy Old Abe. . . ." [36] Were such words treasonable?

The epithet "traitor" was assuredly used with reckless looseness. The wealthy Illinois landholder Isaac Funk, losing his temper this winter in the State Senate, burst into a violent philippic. "These villains and traitors and secessionists in this senate," he vociferated, "are killing my neighbors' boys, now fighting in the field." The galleries rang with applause as he went on: "Mr. Speaker, these traitors on this floor should be provided with hempen collars." He glared at some of his colleagues. "Hell itself could not spew out a more traitorous crew than some of the men who disgrace this legislature." Radical members of the assembly agreed that the legislature contained downright traitors. Morton of Indiana, certain that traitors abounded in the Northwest, described their conspiracy as Machiavellian:

The Democratic scheme may be briefly stated thus: End the war by any means whatever at the earliest possible moment. This, of course, lets the Rebel States go, and acknowledges the Southern Confederacy. They will then propose to the Rebels a reunion and a reconstruction upon the condition of leaving out the New England States; this they believe the Rebel States will accept, and so do I. It would withdraw twelve votes from the Senate, and leave the Slave States in a permanent majority. . . . Govr Seymour and the leading Democratic politicians of New York and Pennsylvania are in the scheme. . . . [37]

Yet a great deal of so-called treason was no worse than the utterances of the eminent S. F. B. Morse, who urged men to stop fighting as long as emancipation

36 Quoted in Robert S. Harper, *Lincoln and the Press*, 126.
37 E. M. Haines of the Illinois legislature described the situation on Jan. 10, 1863, to Elihu Washburne; Washburne Papers, LC. Morton's letter is in Stanton Papers, Feb., 1863.

was made an object of the war. The veteran Jacksonian Amos Kendall wrote him that if he would not fight the enemy unless the President first recalled his proclamation, the chances were that he would soon have neither constitution nor ballot box to fight for.[38] And who would apply the epithet of traitor to Nathaniel Hawthorne? He assured a close friend in the fall of 1861 that he did not wish to see the Union restored as it was. "Amputation seems to me much the better plan; and all we ought to fight for is the liberty of selecting the point where our diseased members shall be left off. I would fight to the death for the Northern Slave States, and let the rest go." The next spring found him of the same mind: "It would be too great an absurdity to spend all our Northern strength for the next generation in holding on to people who insist on being let loose." And even after Gettysburg, Hawthorne clung to his belief: "The best thing possible, so far as I can see, is to effect the separation of the Union, giving us the west bank of the Mississippi, and a boundary line affording us as much Southern soil as we can hope to digest in another century." [39] But no more than Morse would Hawthorne have performed an act of overt hostility to his country.

In Indiana and Illinois many people thought that a midwinter crisis offered imminent peril to the nation. Governor Yates was impressed by letters making accusations of disloyalty in various localities. Washburne and Trumbull in Washington received word from town after town that the "secesh" were more dangerous than ever before. Early in the new year disturbing news reached Springfield. The 109th Infantry at Holly Springs became insubordinate, some men deserting while others declared they would never fight for emancipation; and though the colonel remained true, numerous officers and privates had to be arrested, and Grant disbanded the regiment. It had been raised in Union County, where most people were of Southern ancestry, and where the Knights of the Golden Circle, with their mummery of oaths and passwords, had fostered hostility to antislavery measures. News of the mutiny threw the "copperheads" of the section into a fever of excitement. Democrats who had at first winced under this epithet began wearing heads of Liberty punched from big copper cents or polished cross-sections of a butternut, and holding angry meetings. Yates wrote Secretary Chase in alarm that he was sitting on a powder keg, and the Administration should recall John M. Palmer, with at least four regiments, to Illinois ready for instant hostilities.[40]

38 Kendall, March 28, 1864, Morse Papers, LC.
39 See Hawthorne's correspondence with Horatio Bridge, *Century Magazine*, N. S., XIII (Jan., 1888), 489, 490. He wrote President Chamberlain of Bowdoin May 26, 1861: "I rejoice that the old Union is smashed. We never were one people and never really had a country since the Constitution was adopted." N. Y. *Times*, Jan. 25, 1883.
40 See the Yates, Trumbull, and Washburne Papers, Dec.–April, 1862–63, for numerous letters from citizens on "treasonable" activities. Yates's letter to Chase, Feb. 2, 1863, is in the Stanton Papers, LC. The term "copperhead" was used at least as early as July 30, 1862,

In Indiana, Morton was equally frightened. He knew well that his autocratic regime had aroused deep resentment. The vast majority of Indiana folk were entirely loyal, but his vehement radicalism and acquiescence in arrests had aroused the detestation of Democrats. So had his enforcement of the draft of 6,000 men when, as it was later shown, Indiana had really met the full quota under Lincoln's calls.

When the new Democratic legislatures gathered in the snows of Springfield and Indianapolis, they presented programs which indicated that copperhead leaders of the two States were working in unison. The extremists brought forward resolutions denouncing emancipation, the tariff, and the arming of Negroes. They proposed that a national convention of State commissioners be held in Louisville in the spring to arrange terms of peace, Congress meanwhile agreeing to an early armistice. They also undertook to reorganize the administration of the militia, the plan being to establish new boards and transfer to them all the governors' powers over home troops, camps, and arms.

It is clear that the danger was by no means so great as the excited governors supposed. Organization of revolt was impossible. Local malcontents could not communicate with each other, could not drill without inviting the attentions of home guards and the military, and could find no real leaders. Under these circumstances sedition was like the ghost in Hamlet; it was here, it was there, it was nowhere.

When the Indiana houses met on January 8, 1863, rhetorical Democrats, attacking the usurpers ruling Hoosierdom, asserted they would not give another man or dollar to the war. At this the Republican members of the Senate refused to go into an election of United States Senators unless the Democrats would first pledge themselves to vote for appropriation bills, and for resolutions urging a vigorous prosecution of the war. Their bolt aroused such sharp condemnation in some Republican as well as all Democratic quarters that they reconsidered, and returned to their seats long enough to let their opponents send Thomas A. Hendricks and David Turpie to Washington. Then the Democrats brought forward a reapportionment bill, and a measure which placed primary control of the militia in the hands of a new board of Democratic State officers. At this Morton blew up with a loud bang. "I knew that, if passed," he wrote later, "it would involve the State in civil war in twenty-four hours." [41]

---

when it was employed to stigmatize Democrats of the Indiana State Democratic Convention; see Cincinnati *Gazette* of that date. For the "copperheads" see Paul S. Smith, *Amer. Hist. Rev.*, XXXII (July, 1927), 799, 800; Wood Gray, *The Hidden Civil War*, 140, 141; James F. Flower to Lucius Fairchild, March 26, 1863, Fairchild Papers, Wis. State Hist. Lib. For the early history of the Knights of the Golden Circle see Nevins, *Emergence of Lincoln*, II, 306, 328.

41 Foulke, *Morton*, I, 198–251; Stampp, *op. cit.*, 166 ff.; see Chicago *Morning Post*, Jan. 14, 1863, for Republican censure of the Senate bolt. We shall recur to Morton's feat in keeping spies within the Knights of the Golden Circle.

Actually it might never have passed. It went through the house, but the senate might have stopped it, and if he vetoed it both chambers would have to give it a majority once more. But he took no chances. "I knew there was but one way to prevent the passage of that bill, and that was to break up the legislature. The Republican members determined to withdraw from the House."

This extralegal step was in reality not so much a coup to frustrate a treasonable conspiracy as a party maneuver to make political capital, keep control of militia patronage, and block reapportionment. The struggle was selfish enough on both sides. For a time it seemed that the angry Democratic rump would itself take extralegal action. It proceeded with the forms of a legislative body, threatened to pass the military bill without a quorum, and debated resolutions denouncing the carnage and demanding a war for the restoration of the Union alone. But in the end the legislature died, not to meet again until early in 1865. As it failed to pass any appropriations, Morton had to resort to unconstitutional measures. By strenuous effort, he obtained loans for $135,000 from county officials and private sources, and $250,000 from a special fund held by the War Department. Placing these funds in an extralegal bureau of finance which he created, he carried Indiana through the two crowning years of the war with an energy for which he deserves enduring fame.

Thus the conflict between parties in Indiana temporarily destroyed constitutional government, and made Morton as much a dictator as Charles I. He long edified Union meetings with the tale of how his vigilance had saved a commonwealth on the brink of revolution. Democratic leaders for their part boasted how, if the legislature had been let alone, they would have taken weapons from the arsenal to arm 90,000 men and make sure that the radicals did the people justice. These were revolutionary times, in which dangerous precedents are set.[42]

Governor Yates had to intervene in Illinois with equal directness. At Springfield the Democrats held such control of the legislature that they could maintain a quorum. After electing William A. Richardson to Douglas' old Senate seat, they took up a measure to revamp militia controls, a habeas corpus bill aimed to stop extralegal arrests, and an inquiry into the public and private conduct of Yates. Finally their conduct became so exasperating that Yates decreed the first prorogation of the legislature in the history of the State. The House continued its sessions for a fortnight, but its position was so clearly illegal that the troublemakers gave up in defeat. Not one of their important bills passed.

Indeed, a reaction soon set in throughout the Northwest. Militantly loyal mass meetings were held in all the large cities to answer the anti-war gatherings.

42 Indiana affairs can be most closely followed in the Indianapolis *Daily Journal* and Cincinnati *Commercial*, Jan.–Feb., 1863.

At a tremendous gathering in Indianapolis on February 26, for example, Andrew Johnson read the original manuscript of a letter by Andrew Jackson assailing Calhoun's nullification movement. The sight of the rigid handwriting of Old Hickory moved veteran Jacksonians to tears.[43] Citizens of Chicago organized a boycott of the Chicago *Times*, which some smaller communities supported. "Things look better to me," a Chicago friend wrote Elihu Washburne on February 20, 1863, and a Galena neighbor was equally reassuring: "Everything looks much better than it did thirty days ago . . . these scoundrels are again hunting their holes and keeping quiet." [44] Albert D. Richardson, a shrewd correspondent of the New York *Tribune,* reported early in April, after a week of travel in the Northwest, that the tone of the people had never been better, and that the men of the Valley would sacrifice more for the country than the East. King Sedition would do no more for the Confederacy than King Cotton:

As Prentice has it, the Rebels went in for cotton, and got worsted. Their greatest delusion now is concerning the North-West. Their leading politicians and editors actually seem to believe that, while the great manufacturing and commercial interests of New-England, New-York, Pennsylvania, are fostered and fattened by the war, the farmers of the North-West are in a state of pecuniary ruin, if not of starvation. They would be astonished to see the evidence of prosperity everywhere visible in the great agricultural districts. Chicago, today, is the most flourishing city on the continent, and the vast grain-producing region tributary to it, the most flourishing section.[45]

Spirited war rallies were held in many smaller cities throughout the Northwest. More and more Western regiments in the field held meetings, passed resolutions, and sent them home with indignant letters. As spring approached and the Union girded itself for mighty new efforts, patriotic sentiment mounted.

[V]

This ebb in the opposition to the war revealed the essential weaknesses of Northern disloyalty. It suffered from the fact that while loyal support of the war effort was ever better organized and ever more united, dissent remained amorphous. Malcontents could gather in a single community or a State legislature, but found it impossible to adopt coherent plans on a regional basis. Sedition suffered also from the fact that many of its adherents, like Irish laborers in New York and the rural folk of southern Ohio, Indiana, and Illinois, were poor, ignorant, and illiterate. It suffered from the violent acts and language of hot-

43 "The largest and most enthusiastic meeting ever held in Indiana," ran the N. Y. *Tribune* report; March 3.
44 J. R. Jones, Chicago, and C. L. Stephenson, Galena; Washburne Papers.
45 N. Y. *Tribune,* April 10, 1863. Anthony Trollope's book of wartime travels presents a vivid impression of exuberant growth and prosperity in the Northwest.

heads, for the threats to assassinate Morton in Indiana repelled decent men. It was hampered by inability to gain complete control of any single State government. In the East the legislatures were Republican; in Iowa, Illinois, and Indiana the governors were a citadel of strength for the Union. Despite inflation, prosperity sucked the life out of much of the discontent. But above all, disloyalty was crippled by weak leadership.

The strongest Democrats whom the election of 1862 swept into office were fundamentally loyal. Horatio Seymour as governor of New York knew how searching would be the gaze turned upon him. One of his first acts was to offer Major John T. Sprague of the United States Army the post of adjutant-general as evidence that he desired a man able to work harmoniously with the War Department.[46] He took another judicious step in conferring with Chief Justice John D. Caton of Illinois. Caton, while emphatic that the West would never consent to Southern independence, agreed with him that prostration of the South would upset the proper balance of Union; and Seymour prompted the judge to publish a letter declaring that the North must fight not to crush the South, but to crush the rebellion. The President, thought Caton, might liberate himself from the wild men about him, whereupon the moderates of the South would respond. He and Seymour called themselves conservative Unionists.[47]

Seymour had discounted Lincoln's quasi promise of what he would do if the governor wheeled the Democratic party into line. "Tell him for me," Lincoln bade Weed, "that if he will render this service to his country, I shall cheerfully make way for him as my successor." [48] Weed had delivered this message to Seymour, only to be disappointed by the tone of his inaugural address. The fact was that impassable differences of principle lay between the governor and President—differences centering mainly in the issue of State rights and the future position of the South. Seymour hotly opposed centralization in government, and a "bloody, barbarous, revolutionary" emancipation policy that would disorganize a whole section. But his devotion to national unity and his anxiety to overthrow the Confederacy were indubitable. "For the preservation of this Union I am ready to make every sacrifice," he wrote Lincoln on April 14, 1863. In this he stood with two abler Democrats, Samuel J. Tilden and Abram S. Hewitt.

"Damn those New York men!" said one Cabinet member. "They bleed well, fight well, grumble like hell, and *submit like patriots*."

The strongest opposition editors, too, were entirely with the Union. The idea of its possible overthrow horrified nobody more than James Sheahan in

46 Mitchell, *Seymour*, 333, 157.
47 Caton, *Miscellanies*, 17–31; see Hesseltine, *Lincoln and the War Governors*, 282–284, for Seymour's emphasis on the importance of maintaining a balance among the sections.
48 Weed, *Memoirs*, 428.

Chicago and Manton Marble in New York. Marble was responsible for some bad policies, but when the *Tribune* characterized the *World* as a secessionist journal, he sent Greeley an indignant protest. The epithet was false, he declared. "You know it to be so. The *World* is not in any possible sense a 'secessionist' newspaper. You know that it is not. You know too that whatever means it may advocate or oppose for the suppression of the rebellion and the overthrow and utter discomfiture of the secessionists, its desire for that speedy consummation is as ardent and patriotic as that of any living being." He might have added that it was firmer for the national cause than were a good many nominal patriots who thought only of their wealth.[49]

No editor made louder protestations of patriotism than Medill of the Chicago *Tribune*, but none did more harm by his defeatism than this Republican. His newspaper columns reflected the statements he made in letters to friends: that the armies could not be filled even by drafts, that an armistice was bound to come during 1863, and that the proper goal was to fight for a boundary, confining the Confederacy to the seven coastal slave States. They reflected his belief that the Administration was a "central imbecility," in which Lincoln was but half awake.[50] Douglas' old lieutenant James Sheahan of the Chicago *Morning Post* compared well with Medill. Such Illinois critics as Sheahan, Caton, William A. Richardson, and Storey were often indiscreet, and consistently offensive to Northern radicals. But they had every right to differ from Lincoln and Congress on emancipation, on financial measures, on arbitrary arrests, and on Southern reconstruction. Their dissent was a token of democratic vitality. Lincoln was quite right in saying that those who were not for saving the Union were against it. But it could be saved with varying degrees of departure from the past, and the country needed men who would put brakes on the now sweeping revolution.

Vallandigham, the most theatrical fomenter of sedition, lacked the weight to command any large following. This handsome Ohioan, forty-one when the war began, a graduate of Jefferson College when that Pennsylvania institution had a Southern clientele, had been a friend in Congress of many Southerners and a devotee of State rights. He was essentially a dogmatist, who in any era of

49 Francis Lieber called them the rich fogies. "I was at Senator Fish's last evening," wrote Henry W. Bellows, Feb. 11, 1863, to Frederick Law Olmsted; "met half a dozen men, Aspinwall, Dodge, Beekman, Roosevelt, and so on. The talk *not* good and wholesome! I had to pitch in very extensively, and *put on my jacket*, as you do. I feel full of fight with these rich and lazy do-nothings who use their comfortable castles to make desperate raids with their tongues into the public confidence. Talk—idle, conceited, ignorant talk—is our most fatal enemy." Olmsted Papers, LC. For striking glimpses of the feeble-hearted, selfish, defeatist old-family millionaires of New York see the third volume of the diary of George Templeton Strong. T. J. Barnett, May 13, 1863, reports the Cabinet member's remark; Barlow Papers.

50 To Elihu Washburne, Jan. 16, 1862, Washburne Papers.

religious struggle would have been a Torquemada. Though intelligent, and in his humorless way attractive enough to become speaker of the Ohio house in his mid-twenties, he was unhappy unless he was immolating himself and others for a cause. At Jefferson College he had quarreled with the president on a constitutional question and refused to accept his diploma. Setting his face against the war from the outset, he refused to vote a man or penny toward its continuance. With noncoercion his original shibboleth, after the Emancipation Proclamation he made tolerance of slavery a new watchword.

Vallandigham would rather have seen the nation lost by strict interpretation of constitutional powers than saved by broad construction. The idea of a violent revolt against Washington was always a sweet morsel under his tongue; so was the idea of martyrdom—of course properly publicized. Early in 1863 he told Congress that rather than abet the war, "I had rather my right arm were plucked from its socket, and cast into eternal burnings." As Lincoln wrote, the whole tenor of his speeches had been to arouse men against the conflict, and justified the inference that he was obstructing the war effort. But this perverse mixture of exhibitionist, fanatic, rabble-rouser, and traitor, highly adept at rallying Ohio malcontents, never gained a substantial following outside his own State, and approached so close to the line of the ridiculous that a single adroit push by Lincoln was presently to send him tumbling across it.

The fact that, thus lacking any strong leader, sedition subsided in the late winter and early spring of 1863, justified a greater moderation in dealing with political offenders. The conscience of liberals, as we have seen, had long been sensitive. William Cullen Bryant, commenting on Seymour's inaugural, wrote that his arguments against arbitrary arrests and martial law had so much force and truth that they must appeal to a majority of all parties. The conviction of Samuel Bowles, Bryant, and George William Curtis was that while harsh measures had been a necessity when the war first began, the abatement of the crisis made leniency desirable. Without stern action, declared Bryant, we would have lost Maryland, Missouri, and Kentucky; now it was no longer needed.

Thanks to the growth of an improved organization for administering the war,[51] a workable system for policing troublemakers emerged by the spring of 1863. Control under Stanton had been concentrated in the offices of Joseph Holt as Judge-Advocate General, and James P. Fry as Provost-Marshal General. Both offices had been specially created by Congress. Lincoln personally had selected Holt, confident that this Kentucky Democrat, whom he appointed September 3, 1862, would deal justly with political prisoners. He brought to his duties courage, energy—and ruthlessness. While it was the intention of Congress that civilians suspected of disloyal acts should be arraigned before

---

51 See *National Almanac*, 1863, 1864, sections on War Department, for its steady growth; L. D. Ingersoll, *Hist. of the War Dept.*, 344-352.

civil courts, Lincoln believed that trial by military commissions was often preferable. Holt adopted a policy which enabled the military authorities to arrest, imprison, and try many supposed political offenders who were never properly subject to courts-martial.

As for Fry, an Illinois graduate of West Point, he was recommended for his post by Grant. Taking over his duties on March 17, 1863, he showed the traits of an efficient martinet. Much the greater part of his work concerned recruiting, conscription, and desertions, but he was expected also to deal with general enemies of the government. He did this by the appointment of provost-marshals for each Congressional district, who in turn named deputy provost-marshals for the counties. The machinery thus created soon became one of the most potent arms of the government, systematic, thorough, by no means free from corruption, and widely hated. By the time the war ended Fry was as hotly controversial a figure as Holt, which is saying a great deal.[52] But the treatment of political offenders had unquestionably been given system, and officers worked by rule, not whim.

Some of the worst injustices, meanwhile, had been partially rectified. Just before Congress met in December, 1862, the Administration directed the liberation of all persons confined on charges of discouraging enlistments or impeding the draft. At once a sweeping release began. Prisoners who had sighed in as many as four different "bastilles" heard the locks grate to release them. As we have seen, Marshal George V. Kane of Baltimore and nine fellow townsmen long in jail breathed free air again. Stanton had previously empowered Judge-Advocate Turner of the Washington district and others to release prisoners, after inquiry, pretty much at discretion. Colonel Lafayette C. Baker, appointed a special provost-marshal, had become head of an alert body of War Department spies, and enjoying use of the Department's secret fund, he came perhaps as near a Fouché as the United States could produce. His jurisdiction touched political offenders as well as deserters, bounty jumpers, shady speculators, and saboteurs, and his zeal outran his sense of propriety.[53] But if the government still had to observe the rule of safety first, the period of its worst offenses against civil liberties was now over.

[VI]

"Mammoth War Demonstration. Immense Meeting at the Cooper Institute. Unity and Victory the Battle Cry." These were the headlines which the New

52 The Univ. of Chicago has a doctoral dissertation by Mary B. Allen on Holt. Fry was highly praised by Nicolay and Hay; for a more critical estimate see Milton, *Lincoln and the Fifth Column*, 250, 251.
53 Baker's cloak-and-dagger thriller, *Hist. of the U. S. Secret Service*, must be used with reserve.

York *Herald* on March 7, 1863, placed over its account of a demonstration headed by War Democrats; the largest and most fervent gathering in the metropolis, it declared, since the Union Square mass meetings of 1861. William Cullen Bryant had presided. Similar meetings of War Democrats, as we have seen, took place in the Northwest.

Even more significant of the nation's purpose was the fact that the Congress which adjourned March 4, 1863, had carried through the first clearly national conscription law. The work primarily of Henry Wilson in the Senate and Thaddeus Stevens in the House, it made every able-bodied male citizen between twenty and forty-five liable to military service. An elaborate machinery for its enforcement was provided, and the War Department left no doubt that it would be employed with rigor. Lincoln had urged the legislation, writing that the country could no longer waste time in trying to revamp a volunteer system that was patently inadequate. The terms of the new draft act, as we shall see, were highly unfair; its application was to encounter heavy difficulties, and its history to reveal gross inefficiency and scandal. It in fact disgraced a nation which might easily have profited from Europe's long experience with conscription. But the determination which dictated it and the defiance of disloyal and half-hearted groups which inspired its passage were thoroughly creditable.

Five Union forces, as spring drew on, stood poised against five points in the long Confederate line; the armies of Hooker on the Rappahannock, Rosecrans in southern Tennessee, Grant before Vicksburg, and Banks near Port Hudson, with the squadron of Flag Officer S. F. DuPont before Charleston. The North waited prayerfully, hopefully, resolutely to see what they would accomplish.

In each previous spring of the war men had confidently hoped that the conflict would end by New Year's. Millions had believed this in 1861; millions again in 1862. Now Northerners were too disillusioned to indulge in prophecy. Here and there a voice was lifted in encouragement to the people, as when the New York *Tribune* in March asserted its faith that the next Fourth would be celebrated throughout a restored and peaceful Union, but such statements had a hollow ring. When men thought of the future, too, they now realized that peace would merely raise the curtain on a complex array of harassing new problems. Every day brought nearer the time when Johnny would come marching home. It also brought nearer the time when men must grapple with financial disorder, a new economic world, the reconstruction of conquered States, the care of the freedmen, and a dozen other situations so tremendous and so baffling that prewar America began to look like some far-off peaceful Arcadia.

16

Roads to Vicksburg

IT WAS clear to men in Washington that even amid reverses, Lincoln revealed a steady augmentation of self-confidence and decision. The Emancipation Proclamation had enhanced his prestige. He had fully established his personal and Presidential authority. As he had defeated Seward at the outset, so now he had defeated the Congressional radicals by compelling them to revise their Confiscation Act, and drop their intended reorganization of the Cabinet. He knew how far to trust Stanton, whose brutal temper seldom impaired a sound judgment and an unshakable devotion to the cause. He knew how to use Chase, whose Presidential ambitions, as he said, were like a horsefly on an ox, keeping him up to his work. A Lincoln legend was gaining currency: the legend, as John W. Forney put it, of a great, peculiar, mysterious man who with quaint sagacity did his work in his own honest way without regard to temporizers or hotheads.[1]

Though now emphatically commander-in-chief, his attitude toward the army had a certain ambivalence. He was ready to make and unmake commanders with decision. He had brusquely displaced, or approved the displacement, of generals who proved incompetent or put themselves in impossible situations: McDowell, Frémont, McClellan, Buell, Burnside. As in civil affairs he told Sumner and others, "My policy is to have no policy," so in military affairs he was ready to experiment pragmatically. To some extent the appointments of Halleck and Pope had been the result of radical machinations directed less toward the elevation of these men than the destruction of McClellan; but to a greater extent they sprang from Lincoln's despair over McClellan's delays and willingness to use trial, error, and retrial. He had been swift to discard Pope. Unfortunately, his field of choice was always limited. He knew when he turned to Hooker that the general had a bad record of drinking, gambling, and emotional instability; but who else was so available? Welles wagged his gray beard

---

1   Welles, *Diary*, I, 212, 219, 227, etc.; Forney's statement to a Gettysburg crowd in the fall of 1863 is in Hay, *Diary and Letters*, Dennett ed., 121.

dubiously and Montgomery Blair spoke of John Barleycorn, but they suggested no alternative.[2]

As a practical man, Lincoln knew that although West Point could teach engineering and old-style tactics based on Jomini, with a little strategy, it could do no more to guarantee character than Oxford or Harvard. While it prided itself on fostering standards befitting "an officer and a gentleman," its graduates in the slack atmosphere of the regular army all too often developed what were euphemistically termed habits. And certainly West Point singularly failed to armor its officers and gentleman against the sin of selfish jealousy. In political life personal jealousy is a much larger element in conduct than is usually supposed: the mutual jealousy of a Jackson and a Clay, a Blaine and a Conkling. In military affairs it may be far more dangerous, for it plays with human lives. On January 21, 1863, Lincoln approved the verdict of the court-martial which, under General David Hunter, had tried Fitz-John Porter on accusations growing out of Second Manassas.[3] Pronounced guilty of all the charges preferred, Porter was immediately dismissed from the service. The finding was dubious. After a long interval, a board of review was to report in Porter's favor (1879), and the President was to cancel his disqualification from holding office under the United States (1882). The verdict nevertheless underlined the fact that after the appointment of Pope, McClellan and his army partisans had failed of the zealous cooperation that was their duty, had chilled the spirit of their troops, and had contributed to the loss of a great battle and thousands of lives.

It is probably just to say that Porter deserved removal, but that dismissal in disgrace was too severe a penalty, and it was imposed for the wrong reasons. He had a strong defense for his conduct at Second Manassas. But that his spirit was viciously bad is proved by his many letters, some prudently left unsigned, in the papers of Manton Marble of the *World*. "Bah!" he burst out at one point. "You have fools at the head of our country, and our people are no better." On August 5 he predicted Pope's imminent failure, and the overthrow of Halleck if that general did not succeed in ousting Stanton—with a possible revolution. He was venomously suspicious of Lincoln, whom he accused of trying to cause McClellan's defeat to prolong the war, and violently hostile to all who wished to fight "an abolition war." He was better out of the army.

Lincoln had no patience with the harsher disciplinary ideas of professional soldiers. He knew that a great citizen army gathered from an undisciplined

2 Welles, *Diary*, I, 229, 230. Welles learned that Hooker "indulges in the free use of whisky, gets excited, and is fond of play." Everyone knew that he talked too much and too indiscreetly.

3 Besides Hunter, the judges were Generals Hitchcock, Rufus King, Garfield, Prentiss, Ricketts, Casey, Buford, and Morris. Lincoln acted on an able review by Judge Advocate-General Holt. For army ideas cf. David Donald, *Lincoln Reconsidered*, Ch. 5.

democracy could not be treated like the professional army of an Old World kingdom. If hard-jawed generals insisted on regular "butcher's days" for sleeping sentinels, men absent without leave, and other delinquents, the people would rebel. His repeated interference with military executions reassured the Northern public.[4] Lincoln believed also that the military mind often adhered to strategic preconceptions at the expense of common sense. He so concluded when Rosecrans insisted that the proper time to attack Bragg would be not while Grant was approaching Vicksburg, but after he had taken the city; and he told Rosecrans this in no uncertain terms.[5] While McClellan initially conceived of his campaign in terms of sieges of Yorktown and Richmond, Lincoln kept trying to make him comprehend that the real object was the destruction of Lee's army in open battle.

Yet Lincoln at the same time showed high respect for army organization and the leadership of professional soldiers. Halleck had a profound regard for both, and great as was the President's irritation over Halleck's limpness and total incapacity for any active command, he was influenced by his adviser's attitude. Halleck constantly exerted himself against what he called political generals. He helped frustrate the many radical friends of Frémont who pressed Lincoln to give him another army; he helped frustrate radical friends of Sigel, like Bryant; he stood in the way of Lew Wallace, who had once expressed contempt for him all too freely. He was undoubtedly pleased when another political figure, Ben Butler, was relieved on November 9, 1862, from command of the Department of the Gulf, closing next month his efficient but controversial administration in New Orleans. For Lincoln to keep Halleck as nominal head of the armies and confer with him steadily was to give partial assent to his strong professionalism, particularly as Stanton supported it.[6]

Lincoln showed his deference to professional soldiers when he acquiesced in Grant's assumption of the chief command of the Vicksburg expedition on February 2, 1863. Sometime in December, Blair in the Cabinet had alluded to the fact that McClernand was being crowded aside, saying that a combination existed to prevent his getting the command. Records Welles: "The President started from his chair when the remark was made and said it should not be so." Stanton reassured him. But now it *was* so. Grant, three weeks after McClernand's

4 For one of many examples see Lincoln's order May 21, 1863, stopping the execution of T. M. Campbell; *Works*, VI, 225.

5 Lincoln to Rosecrans, Aug. 10, 1863; *idem*, VI, 377, 378.

6 A strong New York committee, supported by Greeley, Bryant, and Daniel S. Dickinson, urged Lincoln on May 30, 1863, to give Frémont command of 10,000 colored troops; and Senator Sumner endorsed the project. Lincoln assented to the idea in principle, but practical obstacles were insuperable; *idem*, VI, 239, 242-244. For Lew Wallace, see *Autobiography*, II, 579, 580. The MS Diary of Fanny Seward, who liked Butler, reflects his ambitions.

capture of Arkansas Post, had taken full control. All McClernand's protests were in vain. The President assented because Grant outranked McClernand, had far better professional equipment, and possessed Halleck's firm support. He wrote McClernand that he must accept the situation, for he was doing better for himself and the country than he could if he provoked a controversy—and Lincoln already had enough Army squabbles on his hands.[7]

The Union, as spring in 1863 stole up from the South, possessed a new and untested commander in Virginia, Hooker. It possessed three commanders in the Mississippi Valley whom people regarded as still on trial: Grant, Rosecrans, and N. P. Banks. The first two had inconclusive records, and Banks no record at all. The general situation was not bright. During the fall the Army of the Potomac had been forced back into Maryland, and the Army of the Cumberland back to the Ohio; Grant's march down the Mississippi Central had been broken up with loss and confusion. Lincoln, in daily consultation with Stanton and Halleck, could find little encouragement in recent minor gains in ground.[8]

[I]

Banks was a clever, interesting, showy politician without much depth or purpose. But he was a favorite of Seward's, and a man of influence in the Bay State, where he had honestly earned his prominence. The son of a cotton mill superintendent, he was almost as much self-educated as Lincoln, for he had been taken out of school to become "the bobbin boy of Waltham." He trained himself in languages, public speaking, acting, and law. At thirty-seven, after service in the legislature, he was chosen president of the able State constitutional convention of 1853. Three years later, in 1856, a nominal Know-Nothing but actual Republican, he was elected speaker of the national House after a historic struggle; and in that office he displayed tact, fairness, and decision. Nobody did more that year to bring forward Frémont, with whom he formed a fast friendship. Elected governor of Massachusetts, he made a shrewd and progressive record, paying special attention to education. When Sumter fell he volunteered, and Lincoln lifted him from his new presidency of the Illinois Central to become a major-general. But he lacked high capacity, and his service in the Shenandoah suggested that he had little aptitude for war.[9]

The inception of the Banks expedition had been peculiarly maladroit. Ref-

7   Welles, *Diary*, I, 217; Lincoln, *Works*, VI, 70, 71.
8   Uncertainty in Washington as to Grant's capacities was reflected in Browning, *Diary*, I, 591, and Welles, *Diary*, I, 387. Welles states that as late as the fall of 1862 neither Stanton nor Halleck cared much for Grant. Cf. Cadwallader, *Campaigning With Grant*, 60–62.
9   For caustic estimates of Banks see Moncure D. Conway, *Autobiography*, I, 235; Welles, *Diary*, II, 18, 26.

ugees from Texas had assured Stanton that their State might easily be won back
to the Union, while a Northern force could also cut off the large flow of
European supplies overland from Matamoras. With Stanton's consent, they
applied to Governors Curtin, Morgan, and Andrew for troops. With characteristic enthusiasm, Andrew assented on the understanding that the expedition
would invade Texas, that Frémont would be put in command, and that the
volunteers should be given facilities to settle there as a staunch Union community. Other Northerners shared his hopes. But the plan went completely
awry. In the first place, the Administration sent the troops not to Texas, but
to Louisiana, largely because it felt it had to displace Butler from New Orleans.
(A small force that did go to Galveston was soon compelled to surrender.)
In the second place, Stanton gave the command not to Frémont, but to Banks,
and in the third, all idea of permanent settlement in the area soon went glimmer-
ing. Banks quickly found his energies fully occupied in fighting.

As Ben Butler's successor, he was expected to hold the conquered parts of
Louisiana, seize the lower Red River as highway to an early conquest of Texas,
and move up the Mississippi to help Grant take Vicksburg. It was a large assignment; too large for an army of about 30,000, half of which had to be used
for garrison work. Banks reached New Orleans in mid-December, 1862. A third
of his force immediately ascended to Baton Rouge, which Brigadier-General
Cuvier Grover recaptured with little fighting.[10] This brought the Union troops
within eighteen or twenty miles of Port Hudson, a natural stronghold which
the Confederates had diligently fortified. Using abundant slave labor, they had
mounted twenty heavy siege guns along the bluff eighty feet above the river,
and built strong defenses on both the water and land sides of the town. The
garrison numbering about 15,000 men, Grover's 10,000 could not assault the
place. Yet to reach the Red River and then approach Vicksburg, Banks had
somehow to get through. Both Port Hudson and Vicksburg drew most of their
supplies from the Red River Valley.

His first plan, which he tried to carry into effect late in January, 1863, was to
move a force up west of the Mississippi, through a country full of rivers,
bayous, and swamps, past Port Hudson to the Red. This force was stopped by
an accumulation of debris blocking a vital bayou. Meanwhile, the Confederate
capture of two Union warships which had run past Vicksburg and entered the
Red River alarmed Farragut, who decided he should take his fleet past Port
Hudson at once.[11] It was important to Grant's movements that Northern ves-

10 Fred H. Harrington, *Fighting Politician: Major-General N. P. Banks*, 119.
11 One of the captured ships was the new ironclad *Indianola*, armed with nine- and
eleven-inch Dahlgrens; the Confederates briefly hoped to use her to command this section
of the Mississippi, but in a panic over an attack by an old ship disguised as a Union ram
shortly blew her up. *Lossing*, II, 590.

sels command the 200-mile stretch of the Mississippi between Vicksburg and Port Hudson, and blockade the Red.

Farragut asked Banks to make a diversionary demonstration against Port Hudson while he steamed past the guns. He gathered his fleet of four frigates, five gunboats, and six mortar boats at a convenient island while Banks mustered 12,000 men for a simulated attack. But although the admiral managed the movement with skill and dash, he met only partial success. His squadron began moving before ten at night (March 13) under a plan that the big ships would do the fighting while the smaller ones added power. The Confederates, however, touched off bonfires which made the river light as day; the force of the current slowed the vessels; the enemy fire proved extremely hot and effective; and the troops gave no help. Receiving word that Banks was five miles away, Farragut growled: "He had as well be in New Orleans or Baton Rouge for all the good he is doing us." In the end the flagship *Hartford* and gunboat *Albatross* got by, but the others were forced back, and the frigate *Mississippi*, set on fire, blew up with sixty-five men missing.

Much pained, Farragut used the word "disaster" in his report to the Navy Department. Nevertheless, he had accomplished the greater part of his purpose. The two ships he had taken up could not patrol the 200 miles to Vicksburg, but they could blockade the Red and cut off its supplies. Their utility justified the risk he had taken. "The Mississippi is again cut off," Pemberton lamented to Richmond on March 19, adding that "neither subsistence nor ordnance can come or go." The next day he sent word to General Richard Taylor on the west bank: "Port Hudson depends almost entirely for supplies upon the other side of the river." One of Taylor's commissary officers, rejoicing on March 17 that four supply steamers had just arrived from the Red, wrote that the prospect for more was gloomy. "Five others are below with full cargoes designed for Port Hudson, but it is reported that the Federal gunboats are blockading the river." [12]

Banks would have done well to keep his army near Port Hudson, where the garrison was soon threatened by hunger. His best usefulness lay in aiding Grant's movement to clear the Mississippi. But he found the temptation of the wide Louisiana hinterland irresistible. April 20 found him marching into Opelousas, where he announced plans for a corps of Negro troops which would ultimately reach eighteen regiments. Early next month he reached Alexandria on the Red River only a few hours after Admiral Porter's gunboats had seized the place. This town is almost in the center of Louisiana, and Banks's operations had brought under control a region of fertile plantations, cattle ranches, and great forests, interlaced by waterways and swamps. His troops were delighted by

12 Mahan, *Farragut*, 200–225.

what they had accomplished. They had defeated enemy columns, taken mountains of cotton bales and a mass of booty, and captured twenty guns. Thousands of slaves had fled to their army camps. But all this contributed little to the main Union object.

In a sharp reprimand, Halleck pointed out to Banks that his real duty was to maintain a heavy pressure on the Mississippi. It was all too true that, as Halleck declared, the enemy rejoiced in Banks's relaxation of grip. Kirby-Smith termed it one of the most desirable events of the war. Not until May 14 did Banks, yielding to the War Department, begin to swing his army back to invest Port Hudson. He had just heard from Grant, by a letter dated May 10, that the Northern forces in the Vicksburg area had crossed to the east bank of the river below that city. On May 23–24 Banks's troops encircled Port Hudson as if for a siege. They were commanded by generals of ability, Grover, C. C. Augur, T. W. Sherman, and Godfrey Weitzel; and Farragut was at hand to shell the Confederate works.[13]

Then, on May 27, Banks committed a terrible blunder. Before his army was fully assembled, before his officers had finished reconnoitring the position, he made a furious but ill-coordinated assault. Two regiments of colored troops, the First and Second Louisiana, fought in this first important test with a valor matching that of the white soldiers. The defenders, with every advantage of entrenchments and artillery, held the Union forces at bay along the whole line. When the day closed Banks had lost nearly 300 dead and 1,550 wounded, while Confederates casualties fell short of 300. Under the hot June sun, Banks then began a close siege; the garrison suffering more and more from shortages of food, medicine, and general supplies.

[II]

More than 300 miles northeast of Vicksburg as the crow flies, Rosecrans in his hard-won occupation of Murfreesboro faced a question mark. If Bragg had retreated to Chattanooga, the Union army could have turned in that direction without anxiety. But Bragg had marched instead to Tullahoma, almost due south of Murfreesboro. Here he could move by rail or road to protect Chattanooga; he could equally send troops to the Vicksburg area. Nor was Rosecrans, at late as April 1, 1863, free from apprehension that reinforcements from both

13 Harrington, *Banks*, 119 ff. James K. Hosmer in *The Color Guard* describes the plantations, ranches, and bayous, the fighting, and the plundering. He saw mansions sacked with ruthless destruction of furniture and mirrors. This was war. "Great barbarities, however, I fear have been committed. They say ear-rings have been torn from the ears of women, and brooches from their bosoms, while they sat with children in their arms."

Vicksburg and Virginia might swiftly be sent to Bragg, who would then advance against the areas which Rosecrans was protecting; against Nashville, against Kentucky.

On the Confederate side Joseph E. Johnston, recovering from his wound at Seven Pines, had been assigned late in November, 1862, to chief command in the West, with the armies of Kirby-Smith, Pemberton, and Bragg under his supervision. He arrived at Chattanooga, his headquarters, on December 4, to learn that Pemberton was falling back before Grant's march down the Mississippi Central, and that Richmond had peremptorily ordered Lieutenant-General T. H. Holmes and his army near Little Rock to reinforce him. He also learned that Jefferson Davis, fearful that Holmes might not arrive in time, requested him to detach sufficient troops from Bragg's command to succor Pemberton. Johnston replied that the Little Rock forces could get to the Vicksburg area much more quickly than any of Bragg's, and that it would be unwise to weaken the army in Middle Tennessee. He contented himself with telegraphing Bragg to send a large cavalry force to raid in Grant's rear and cut his communications. The alert Bragg had already acted, and we have seen how effectively cavalry tore up the railroad behind Grant and destroyed his Holly Springs base.[14]

The Confederate government had in fact been highly alarmed in December for the safety of Vicksburg. Jefferson Davis hastened westward to examine the situation in Mississippi and Tennessee. "Private information from many sources," wrote R. G. H. Kean, third in rank in the War Department, on December 13, "represents the tone and temper of the people of the Mississippi Valley as very unsound. *They are submitting.*" [15] At Murfreesboro and Chattanooga the uneasy Davis, overruling Johnston, ordered 9,000 of Bragg's infantry and artillery transferred to Pemberton's command; a force that at the moment was useless to Pemberton, but would have been invaluable to Bragg at Murfreesboro. In mid-January Governor Pettus of Mississippi convoked the legislature to mobilize the whole military force of the State behind Pemberton. Although the retreat of Grant and repulse of Sherman gave Southerners momentary relief, they remained anxious in the extreme. Johnston, visiting Vicksburg with Davis on January 20, was disheartened by errors of fortification.[16]

Johnston had grounds for personal despondency in the vague and precarious nature of his command, in his uncertain health, in the dissensions between Bragg and his chief officers, and in the weak information services of the widely scattered Western forces. He was nominally in command of three Confederate

14 Johnston, *Narrative*, 147–150.
15 Edward Younger, ed., *Inside the Confederate Government*, 33.
16 Johnston, *Narrative*, 152.

armies. But how real could his command be? One army was on the Tennessee; another, hundreds of miles away, was on the Mississippi; still another, Kirby-Smith's, soon operated behind the river in Louisiana. Each had its special object and problems; each faced an adversary with a special goal. How could one general direct all three? When Johnston explained this to Davis, the President replied that since Richmond was so distant, it seemed necessary to have an officer in the West possessing authority to transfer troops in an emergency from one command to another. Johnston rejoined that such transfers were impracticable, for each army was weaker than its foe, and the forces were too far separated to help each other effectively. This exchange did not soften the mutual dislike long felt by the two men, and thereafter the testy Johnston made his lack of confidence in the President and Secretary Seddon plainly felt.[17]

Meanwhile, grave dissensions in Bragg's camp after Murfreesboro threatened not only his summary overthrow, but an impairment of public morale throughout that part of the South. A quarrel had long smoldered between him and Breckinridge. When Bragg retreated from Kentucky his volunteers from that State, realizing they were going into a long exile, grumbled that they were being marched south to protect the Mississippi and Alabama planters; Breckinridge expressed sympathy with them; and the two generals became deadly enemies. Soon afterward a Kentucky soldier was tried for a small offense, and Bragg ordered him shot. He was quoted as saying that Kentucky blood was too feverish for the health of the army, and that he intended to stop the corn-crackers' grumbling if he had to execute every man. Breckinridge, angrily declaring that Kentuckians would never be treated like slaves, asserted that the shooting would be military murder. Company after company of Kentucky troops, swept by angry excitement, rushed from their tents to stack arms. With difficulty the mutiny was composed—and the man was shot. Then, after Murfreesboro, some Kentucky soldiers charged that Bragg had ordered them to make an attack which he knew would end in useless slaughter.[18]

In fact, Kentuckians and Tennesseeans demanded Bragg's retirement as hotly as Ohioans and Indianians had demanded Buell's. He was a martinet whom men would have hated even without his failures. A Louisianan who traveled through the region in January found the people violently denouncing him. Intelligent citizens averred that he had never intended to hold Kentucky, and that from

17 *Ibid.*, 154, 155. Kean wrote April 12, 1863, of Johnston: "He treats the Department as an enemy with whom he holds no communication which he can avoid and against which he only complains and finds fault."
18 This is the account given in the Frankfort, Ky., *Commonwealth*, Feb. 11, 1863, in a long editorial purporting to be authentic; and in the Nashville *Union* quoted in the Chicago *Morning Post*, Feb. 23, 1863.

the time when, standing between Buell and Louisville, he failed to crush the first and take the second, they had lost all faith in him. Most of his own officers called his campaign indefensible.[19]

Bragg quarreled with Leonidas Polk, who condemned his mismanagement of the forces at Perryville. He quarreled with Buckner, who refused to answer his questions upon the extent to which he had sustained Polk in what Bragg called "acknowledged disobedience." One reason why he kept silence, Buckner explained, was that he did not wish to "aggravate the feeling which public rumor imputes as existing between you and your subordinate commanders." Bragg also quarreled with Hardee. When he sent a belated report of his Kentucky campaign to Davis late in May, he explained its tardiness on the ground that he had waited to gather evidence refuting the charges against him by Hardee and Polk; charges which, if unanswered, "would subject me to the severest criticism and injustice." All these officers, while disliking Bragg's frigid manner, morose temper, and harsh acts, were actuated primarily by a belief that he had proved utterly incompetent; that, as General Basil W. Duke later put it, his vacillation and timidity had thrown away one of the greatest Southern opportunities to win the war. They made it clear to Richmond that they wished him removed.[20] When Bragg himself queried Generals Breckinridge, Cleburne, and Hardee upon their attitude, they told him bluntly that they believed a change in the command of the army was imperative.

Davis, who never forgot his Mexican War debt to Bragg, went so far as to send Johnston in late January to make an investigation at Bragg's headquarters. But his faith in his old favorite remained unshaken, and when Johnston advised against removal—on the ground that the troops retained a strong fighting spirit —he kept Bragg in command. The general's army, however, was soon much weakened. On May 10 Johnston sent two of his brigades west to reinforce the Confederates struggling to save Vicksburg, and a fortnight later ordered Breckinridge's division to follow.[21]

The Union army in Middle Tennessee meanwhile fared better, but remained quite inert. Rosecrans was as popular with his officers and men as Bragg was unpopular. He was an excellent organizer and disciplinarian, and a tremendous worker. As he needed little sleep, he sometimes toiled at his desk from ten in the morning until one or two that night—to the anguish of his aides. He had a keen instinct for system, and when he took over the army from Buell immediately reorganized its staff work. He established courier lines connecting head-

19 J. G. Leach, Waterproof, La., Feb. 2, 1863, to R. M. McKee; McKee Papers, Ala. State Archives.
20 Polk, *Polk*, II, 198 ff.; Buckner, April 26, 1863, to Bragg, Palmer Coll., Western Reserve Hist. Soc.; Duke, *Reminiscences*, 308.
21 Johnston, *Narrative*, 161, 162.

quarters with all the camps, collected military maps from every source, called in Unionists from the surrounding area to give information, and kept a large body of clerks hard at work on papers. Slovenliness angered him, for he regarded war as an exact science. Any officer who brought in an incomplete report was sternly rebuked: "How did you know this? How did your informant know? Why didn't you get all the particulars? What are you an officer for? War means killing!" No officer was allowed to take a furlough or resign unless his health broke. He was swift to get rid of incompetents. "I care not for individuals," he would say. "Everything for the service, nothing for individuals."

Yet he spent much time among troops, riding out for reviews or inspection. Examining equipment with searching care, he would sharply rebuke a private for not getting a defective bayonet, canteen, or knapsack replaced. "Go to your captain and demand what you need," he would order. "Go to him every day for it. Bore him for it!" He liked young men, full of vigor and snap. "Young men without experience are better than experienced old men, for they will learn." And he did his best to lick young officers into shape. "Your knowledge of geography is bad," he would say raspingly. "You make a poor statement. You don't observe closely." One of his fixed ideas was that cavalry must be energetically employed as the eyes of the army, and he lost no time in forming a strong mounted force under General David S. Stanley. Using the cavalry, he strove to improve his maps, which were one of his passions.[22]

Yet the lively, temperamental Rosecrans was one of the many officers who displayed high capacity in routine tasks, but who in the hour of adversity became prey to irresolution and frustration. Grant's distrust grew after Iuka and Corinth. When Charles A. Dana found opportunity to study "Old Rosey" closely in the field he noted a curious mixture of weakness and strength. "He has invention, fertility, and knowledge," Dana reported to the War Department "but he has no strength of will and no concentration of purpose." This accurate judgment harmonized with the conclusions of the correspondent Cadwallader. Intensely ambitious, and fond of command, the general was feeble at just those times when decision was most needed. At critical junctures he became erratic in judgment and deficient in administrative grasp. One fault was his inability to depute work; he insisted on personal supervision of every department, so that subordinates could not act until he gave the word. Another fault was "his passion for universal applause," and his reluctance to hurt the feelings of high officers by censuring their blunders.[23]

22 W. D. Bickham (Cincinnati *Commercial* correspondent), *Rosecrans' Campaign, passim;* N. Y. *Tribune*, Jan. 8, 1863; *Diary and Letters of Rutherford B. Hayes*, II, 27 ff. For Grant's critical views see his *Memoirs*, Ch. 40.

23 Dana to Stanton, Chattanooga, ct. 14, 17, 1863, Dana Papers, LC, offer a thorough estimate; Cadwallader's MS Diary, Ill. State Hist. Lib., "Four Years with General Grant,

This winter and spring found him managing his army well, but also keeping it inert. With Vicksburg the central goal in the West, his refusal to contribute anything toward its capture gravely offended Grant and Sherman in the field, and Lincoln and Stanton in Washington.

Struggling to seize his prize, Grant sent repeated petitions for help. At first his desire was simply that Rosecrans should occupy Bragg sufficiently to prevent him from sending aid to Pemberton. He wrote repeatedly to Halleck urging that the army be moved energetically in one of two directions: to threaten Bragg at Tullahoma, or lay Chattanooga open to capture. Halleck, approving the proposal, repeatedly ordered Rosecrans to advance. But the general took a stubborn stand on the old military maxim which forbade commanders to fight two decisive battles at the same time. As Grant later dryly remarked, it would be bad to be defeated in two decisive battles fought the same day, but it would not be bad to win both! [24]

His inaction puzzled and offended the President. When Lincoln learned that part of Bragg's force had gone west, he felt keen anxiety lest Grant be overwhelmed by a concentration of enemy strength. As he wrote Rosecrans later, he thought this "the exactly proper time for you to attack Bragg with what force he had left." At one point he told Halleck that he should give explicit orders to this effect, and Halleck replied that he had already done so in substance. "Soon after," Lincoln recalled in reviewing the record with the general, "dispatches from Grant abated my anxiety for him, and in proportion abated my anxiety about any movement of yours. When afterwards, however, I saw a dispatch of yours arguing that the right time for you to attack Bragg was not before but would be after the fall of Vicksburg, it impressed me very strangely. . . . It seemed no other than the proposition that you could better fight Bragg *when* Johnston should be at liberty to return and assist him, than you could *before* he could so return to his assistance." [25]

The important fact was that as Grant before Vicksburg received no aid from Banks, so he got none from Rosecrans. That general could say much for his position. He not only gave the detachment of aid anxious thought, but on June 8 queried all his principal officers for their opinion. Without exception,

---

1862–66," contains passages on Rosecrans omitted from the printed version. Dana's criticism of the general was sharp: "His mind scatters, there is no system in his use of his busy days and restless nights, no courage against individuals in his composition. . . ." Cadwallader also summed him up harshly: "a military demagogue of the most pronounced type." But Rosecrans had important virtues; he was hard-working and conscientious, he looked after his troops' welfare, and he was more dynamic than Buell. Rosecrans Papers, UCLA.

24 Grant, *Memoirs*, Ch. 40. See Bruce Catton's admirable study, *Grant Moves South*, 304 ff.

25 Aug. 10, 1863, *Works*, VI, 377, 378.

all of them—Sheridan, Thomas, T. L. Crittenden, and others—advised against it, most of them in strong terms. "If Grant fails before Vicksburg," wrote John M. Palmer, "it would be unfortunate if this army is then found entangled in the interior of Tennessee." However, Rosecrans might well regret later that he had not taken a bolder course.

[III]

It was a mighty force which Grant commanded when at the end of January, 1863, he arrived at Young's Point before Vicksburg to take direct charge of the movement against the fortress; and mightily did he employ it. Jefferson Davis had said at Jackson on his Western tour that retention of the Mississippi was a question of life and death for the Confederacy. If Vicksburg and Port Hudson fell, all the men and supplies in the rich areas of Arkansas, Texas, western Louisiana, and the Yazoo district of Mississippi would be lost to the South. Hope ran high in Confederate circles that the Union troops, repulsed in their first effort at a breakthrough, could be baffled. Some Northern officers of the army were daunted by the obstacles, but with the dogged determination that always marked him, Grant was ready to take every risk to win.[26]

With determination, with faith in his Western fighters—and with the courage of desperation, for Grant knew that he was still on trial, and that a long delay or new retreat might send him home broken. His enemies and detractors were urging that he be removed, and some newspapers were insisting on it. Before long Lorenzo Thomas was sent from Washington on a double mission; one errand to examine conditions in the contraband camps along the river and encourage military use of the Negroes, the other to investigate military affairs with an eye to a possible reshuffle of high officers. On his heels would come Charles A. Dana, also with a double charge; ostensibly to straighten out delays in the paymaster service, actually to ascertain the true capacity of Grant and others. The commander knew that he had to do something, and do it soon. But it was part of his character to drive forward against all impediments, and he took heart from the mighty panoply under his orders. He had a hundred thousand volunteers, reported the press; and though this nearly doubled his real num-

---

26 Jesse Grant, paying a visit to his son's department early in 1863, paused at Covington on his return to write Elihu Washburne. Ulysses, he commented, had a big contract on his hands; he had a good many generals with him in whom he placed confidence; but "I have been thinking it might be good policy to send one of the able generals from Washington now out of command to advise with him. I mean Franklin or Burnside. Franklin was his classmate at West Point, and I know he has a high opinion of his skill and abilities." Jesse added that this idea was original with himself. Grant would not have thanked him for it!

bers, it was true that he possessed a massive superiority—if he could bring it to bear on the enemy.

Grant in fact had a quadruple ordeal to face, with enemy forces not the principal threat to his future. He had to meet all the obstacles of an impracticable country, the river, the bayous, the mud, the high water, and a sickly climate. He had to face resentment amounting almost to enmity in McClernand, now reduced to corps commander. Not least, he had to face weakness in himself, and a possible stumble of which his ill-wishers would take instant advantage. Finally, of course, he had to defeat Pemberton, possibly reinforced by Johnston. Never did he have to cope with greater dangers than this spring, and never did he act with more heroic resolution or greater skill.

After a talk with Sherman, McClernand, and Porter at Napoleon on January 17, Grant concluded that time and a large force would be required to take Vicksburg. The four men agreed that McClernand and his 13th corps should at once drop down the river to Young's Point on the Louisiana shore, nine miles above Vicksburg. The city lay near the top of a great loop of the stream; at Young's Point was the opening of the canal planned months before to cut across the bottom of the loop and thus bypass Vicksburg. McClernand landed his men on January 22, and they and Sherman's 15th corps began toiling in the watery clay, tortured by incessant rains, rising water, uncertain commissary arrangements, and malaria. Only a few days passed before churning paddle-wheels and resonant whistles heralded the arrival of Grant with more troops. Additional armored gunboats came in to augment Porter's fleet. The smoke of a hundred vessels at a time floated over the town on its high bluffs; batteries were planted on the west bank to cut off Confederate vessels from Port Hudson; the camps grew ever larger. Plainly, a supreme effort was under way.[27]

But the canal, badly placed and not greatly improved by a slight re-siting under Grant's orders, proved an abortive undertaking. The commander no sooner saw it than he lost all faith in it, for an eddy at its head thrust the current away from it. Father Mississippi was a giant who moved as he pleased. Grant kept on with the effort because the soldiers were better busy than idle, and because Washington pressed him. Gustavus V. Fox wrote Porter early in February that the canal should be opened farther upstream, and that the whole army should be set to work on this new line. "I dislike to see you all sit down for a long siege at Vicksburg. The country cannot stand it at home or abroad. The President is of my opinion that you had better cut through farther back and do it at once." [28] Grant, despite private pessimism, had the troops toil on.

27   Vicksburg observers Jan. 25 reported 93 transports and 14 gunboats; N. Y. *Tribune*, Feb. 16, 1863.
28   Feb. 6, 1863; Fox Corr., NYHS.

They toiled in a world of broken levees, rising water, dark skies, wet tents, viscid clay, and rain, rain, rain. Every day it seemed more likely that the swelling river would flood the camps, and with spade and dredge the troops threw up an embankment to protect them. Finally on March 8 came catastrophe. The river broke through the protecting dam at the head of the canal in an eight-foot rush which buried channel and implements, and forced men to run for their lives.

Already Grant had shrewdly turned to other efforts to flank Vicksburg, for though some men talked of a frontal attack, he knew it would end in appalling losses and defeat. An amphibious expedition of 7 gunboats and 18 transports bearing 5,000 troops was making an attempt to get to high ground northeast of the city by way of a chain of waters—Yazoo Pass, the Coldwater River, the Tallahatchie, and finally the Yazoo. But they were completely blocked in mid-March by Confederate obstructions and batteries at Fort Pemberton on the upper Yazoo, and on March 23 Grant ordered them to come back. Meanwhile, another attempt to flank Vicksburg on the east by getting into the Yazoo through Steele's Bayou and other waters met difficulties of navigation; the bayous and streams which Porter's boats had to thread were narrow, full of snags, and half blocked by overhanging trees. After heavy toil, the troops and vessels were glad to turn about. And on the west side of the Mississippi, a plan for moving troops and gunboats past the city through Lake Providence, a couple of bayous, some intervening streams, and the Tensas River—a long, tedious, untrustworthy route—also broke down, though not until Grant had invested heavy labor in digging channels and cutting stumps.[29]

The last week of March found the Union army seemingly defeated by the tough river country. It had explored every possible flanking line in the soggy bottoms. To many it seemed that Grant would have to give up, return north to Memphis, and try once more a march down the precarious Mississippi Central. The possibility that he would be removed was very real. As Francis Vinton Greene writes, his real qualities were as yet unknown; for a year he had apparently done little, and for three months his army had been seemingly lost in the swamps, with no news but of fruitless expeditions, fever, smallpox, and sinking morale; and many thought he was just another in the dreary line of failures that included McClellan, Frémont, Burnside, and Buell.[30] But at this crisis of his career Grant had no intention of turning back; he meant to go forward. He would march down the west side of the river, get the gunboats and empty transports to run the Vicksburg batteries, and establish a

29 Adequate accounts in Greene, *The Mississippi*, Ch. IV; *Battles and Leaders*, II, 441 ff.
30 See C. C. Washburn, March 24, 28, 1863; Washburne Papers, LC. "Cad" suggested using most of Grant's troops to reinforce Rosecrans and defeat Bragg.

base at Grand Gulf below. On March 29, two days after Sherman returned from his abortive Steele's Bayou expedition, Grant ordered McClernand to move down the river toward the villages of Richmond and New Carthage, with some point below the Warrenton defenses his objective. He simultaneously wrote Porter explaining this movement, and proposing that the gunboats run the Vicksburg gantlet to engage the enemy at Grand Gulf and protect a landing in that area.

How did the idea for this bold stroke originate? Grant tells us in his memoirs that all winter he had contemplated a movement by land to a point below Vicksburg, waiting only for the improbable success of some one of the expedients used to achieve a different base. Keeping the plan secret even from his staff, he believed that he had first mentioned it to Porter, whose cooperation he could request but not command.[31] Porter's story is slightly different. Grant, he states, had from the first the idea of turning Vicksburg, but *how* to do it he did not know. He knew he was dependent on transports for troop carriage and provisions, and feared that the shore batteries would quickly disable these frail vessels. But when the Yazoo enterprises failed, he made up his mind. "I will go below Vicksburg," he said, "and cross over if I can depend on you for a sufficient naval force. I will prepare some transports by packing them well with cotton bales, and we'll start as soon as you are ready." Porter replied that he would be ready by sunset next day.

Other men in time made claim for the origination of the bold concept. James Harrison Wilson, serving on Grant's staff, was one. He relates that just before he departed on a fruitless Yazoo expedition he talked with Rawlins. Arguing that such operations were dubious, and that a direct assault from the Vicksburg wharf would be suicidal, he declared there was only one alternative. It was to run the batteries with the ironclads, gunboats, transports, and barges and march the troops to such a point below as might be selected as the base of operations against the interior of the State and the defenses of the city.[32] And Farragut also made a claim. Late March found him and the *Hartford* patrolling the river between Port Hudson and Vicksburg. On the 20th, lying only a few miles below Vicksburg, he communicated with Grant, asking him and Porter to send down two rams and an ironclad from above. On the 26th he and Grant met on the flagship for a talk. The ship log merely states: "Major-General Grant came on board." But when Farragut dined later in the war at George Bancroft's house in New York he told of their conversation. "I made Grant's acquaintance off Grand Gulf on the Mississippi," he recalled, "and told him *that* was the direction for threatening Vicksburg.

31 *Memoirs*, I, 460, 461; Grant gives no dates.
32 *Under the Old Flag*, I, 156–158.

He reflected, studied the map carefully, and instantly changed the whole plan of campaign. He had caught my idea." [33]

All this is an oversimplification. Grant already knew the concept well; he has grasped it, others had grasped it. What Farragut doubtless did was to encourage him in the idea and assure him that a dash of the requisite naval forces past Vicksburg was quite practicable, for several ships had recently dashed past. All this the general and the admiral unquestionably discussed on the *Hartford*.[34] As Grant says in his memoirs, his campaign was developed by circumstances. He could not flank Vicksburg east or west by bayou and lake; he could not deliver a frontal assault from the river. If he took his army back to try marching down the Mississippi Central again, public anger would force his removal. Elihu Washburne had been so disturbed by one all-is-lost letter from his brother Cadwallader, saying that Grant was surrounded by a drunken staff, and predicting that when the weather turned hot, the men would die by regiments, that he sent it to Chase. That Secretary had so little faith in Grant that he favored using most of his army to reinforce Rosecrans in a push against Chattanooga. In dismay, he took the letter—this was about April 10—to the White House, and read it to Lincoln, who seemed much impressed.[35] Fortunately, the President remained patient, for he liked Grant's fighting temper. But if the general had not moved forward decisively on the one road open to him, his head—and he well knew this—might soon have rolled beside Buell's; and McClernand was second in rank.

[IV]

Actually the plan for an amphibian movement adopted by Grant, Porter, and Farragut had two components, one so spectacular that it has eclipsed the other and equally important feature. The army was to link together a line of bayous, roads, and bridges west of the Mississippi extending from Milliken's Bend and the Young's Point area to New Carthage about thirty miles below Vicksburg. This meant much canal digging, road repairing, and bridgebuilding. Advance detachments pushed slowly forward on this route, skirmishing as they went. The wagon trains on some stretches struggled through beds of bottomless black mud, and at other points took to clumsy barges. Sometimes the troops followed the levees; elsewhere they used the highway. "What we

33 A. Laugel, "A Frenchman's Diary in our Civil War Time," *Nation*, July 24, 1862.
34 Farragut to Porter, Naval O. R., XX, 12; Grant to Farragut, *ibid.*, 14. Cf. C. L. Lewis, *Farragut*, 189; Mahan, *Farragut*, 226, 227.
35 Grant, *Memoirs*, I, 574, 575. C. C. Washburn declared that he feared some catastrophe; that Grant was desperate, and might undertake a ruinous frontal assault. Chase would gladly have seen Grant ousted and blamed Lincoln for delay; to Elihu Washburne, April 11, 1863, Washburne Papers.

planters . . . had been anticipating," ruefully wrote a Southern lady of the district, "came to pass. Grant perceived that he could very easily march down the Richmond road, where we drove our carriages at nearly all seasons of the year except during an overflow of the river." [36] On April 6 advance troops occupied New Carthage; by the 14th McClernand's remaining divisions took the road; and the 20th found the whole corps assembled at the first goal.

Meanwhile, the river navy had done its part. On the night of April 16, Porter's veteran flagship the *Benton* led his flotilla of eight gunboats and three cotton-protected transports (of course without troops) past the waiting batteries of Vicksburg. As they approached the dark heights, bonfires of tar barrels, pine, and blazing buildings lighted up the levee, city, and forts as if the sun shone. Confederate guns spat shells and solid shot as fast as the men could serve them, and Porter's warships answered with all their broadsides. The transport *Henry Clay*, catching fire, belched flame like a volcano, her men leaping into the water to save themselves. Another transport was hulled and disabled by two direct hits. Shells bursting against the boats threw blazing cotton bales into the stream until the water was strewn with fragments of burning material, a thousand floating lamps. The fleet needed an hour and a half to pass the four miles of guns, and by the time it reached the last battery a dozen vessels seemed afire. The panorama of smoke and flame struck Porter like a picture of the infernal regions. Yet when the ships anchored off New Carthage he found that only one (with a few coal barges) had been lost, and but a single man killed.[37] He writes:

When daylight broke . . . I was besieged by the commanding officers of the gunboats, who came to tell me of their mishaps; but when I intimated that I intended to leave at Carthage any vessel that could not stand the hammering they would be subject to at Grand Gulf, everybody suddenly discovered that no damage had been done their vessels, which, if anything, were better prepared for action than when they started out. Generals McClernand and Osterhaus came on board the *Benton*. . . . Osterhaus was beaming all over:

"Now," said he, "does dampt fellers, dey'll catch it; give dem gunboat soup." [38]

Grant reached New Carthage by land on April 17, assured himself that the naval movement was completely successful, and returned to Milliken's Bend to hasten forward the remainder of the army. Because of high water about New Carthage, that town proved unsuited to the concentration of a

36 Sarah W. Dorsey, *Recs. of Henry W. Allen*, 158; Greene, *The Mississippi*, 110.
37 Porter, *Incidents and Anecdotes*, 178. Each ship was under fire about a half hour when off Vicksburg, and perhaps ten minutes at Warrenton. The unwieldy steam ram *Queen of the West* had passed the Vicksburg batteries at the beginning of February in a spectacular run described in the N. Y. *Tribune* of Feb. 12.
38 N. Y. *Tribune*, May 26, 1863.

large army. McClernand, however, by reconnaissance discovered two points farther downstream, Perkins's Plantation and Hard Times, where bodies of men could be camped, and Grant ordered the army moved there at once. On the 29th most of it was at Hard Times, nearly opposite Grand Gulf, and seventy miles from the Bend. It was ready for ferriage to the east bank of the river, and Porter's squadron struck hard at the Grand Gulf fortifications, with Grant midstream in a tugboat watching. The attack miscarried. Porter's vessels, throwing some 2,500 projectiles, many from nine-inch and eleven-inch guns, failed to silence the Southern batteries, and killed only three defenders, while two of his ships were badly damaged. It was clearly out of the question to throw the army across at Grand Gulf.

Undaunted, Grant simply decided to drop downstream to the vulnerable neighborhood of Port Gibson. McClernand took the van. Confederates who had expected an assault on their fortifications were left bewildered. "When McClernand gave Grand Gulf the go-by," wrote one correspondent, "and pushed his corps swiftly up the hillsides ten miles to the south, they were confounded. They had for once been fairly outwitted and out-generalled. They met us with a force wholly inadequate, and were routed before their reinforcements could save them." As Union troops marched into Port Gibson on May 2, the Confederates at Grand Gulf realized that they had been cut off in the rear. They blew up the magazines, dismounted the guns, and abandoned the place without substantial resistance. The river navy at once took possession.

Grant's main army, 41,000 strong, was now firmly ensconced on the east bank of the Mississippi, some twenty-five miles as the crow flies from the Vicksburg lines. His rapid movements, disconcerting the enemy, had at last turned the Confederate flank. On the other bank of the river, protecting his communications, he had about 10,000 men. The whole North—even men doubtful, like Lincoln, of the wisdom of going below Vicksburg—took heart at the spectacle of energetic action. His aggregate force of some 51,000, which was soon reinforced, faced Confederate armies which if united would have nearly equal strength, but which were divided. Could he maneuver to defeat them, and take a city so heavily fortified that Sherman called it a veritable Gibraltar?

For, giving up his initial thought of uniting with Banks against Port Hudson first and Vicksburg second, he had resolved to strike directly at the greater fortress. He received at Grand Gulf a letter from Banks saying that he could not be at Port Hudson in less than ten days, and then with only 15,000 men. "The time was worth more than the reinforcements," wrote Grant later; "I therefore determined to push into the interior of the enemy's country." [39] In this decision we see Grant at his best; his instinct for rapidity of action was marvelous. On May 3 he sent directions to Sherman for bringing the 15th corps to reinforce him. "It's unnecessary for me to remind you of the overwhelming importance of celerity in your movements," he wrote. And after speaking of the engagement at Port Gibson in which they had driven the Confederates back with large losses, he continued: "The enemy is badly beaten, greatly demoralized, and exhausted of ammunition. The road to Vicksburg is open; all we want now are men, ammunition, and hard bread. . . ." [40]

Charles A. Dana had been with Grant since April 6, when he arrived at the Milliken's Bend headquarters by way of Memphis. Some of Grant's staff, regarding him as a spy from Washington, had proposed giving him a cold shoulder, but Rawlins wisely overruled them, treating him with the utmost cordiality. Grant and he took to each other at once. He found the general elated by the opening of the road down the west shore to New Carthage, and confident that a combination of siege operations and starvation would shortly reduce Vicksburg. In the ensuing weeks Dana performed two memorable services. He encouraged Grant in the course chosen, and he sent Stanton a series of letters giving complete information on plans, shrewd estimates of all the officers, and hopeful views of the future. He made it plain to Washington that while Grant's staff was a queer mixture of good and bad, the general deserved the utmost confidence. Influenced by Grant's and Rawlins' dislike of McClernand, he praised Sherman and McPherson highly as corps commanders at the expense of the former Congressman. If anything happened to Grant, it would be McClernand who would automatically succeed; and Dana made it quite clear that while McClernand might be a passable corps commander, he could never direct a great army. [41]

39　It was a decision which, according to Dana, he had hesitated to take when on April 10 he received a letter from Halleck ordering him to Port Hudson. "It is now determined," wrote Dana on the 12th, "that after the occupation of Grand Gulf, instead of operating up the Big Black toward Jackson and the bridge in rear of Vicksburg, the main force shall proceed against Port Hudson. Dispatches will at once be sent to cooperate. There is still some uncertainty respecting the time of the movement." On April 24 Dana added: "It is now settled . . . that McClernand will not go farther than to Grand Gulf, but will remain there to command the post, while General Grant himself will go on to Port Hudson, taking McPherson and thirty thousand troops with him. Enemy still, however, have no idea of the movement, but look constantly for an assault on Haines' or Vicksburg." Grant however reached Grand Gulf on May 3, he heard there on May 10 that Banks did not expect to get to Port Hudson until the 25th at earliest, and he hence took his final decision; Greene, *The Mississippi*, 223, 224.

40　May 3, 1863; Grundlach Collection, Amer. Art. Assn. Catalogue, May 3, 1927.

41　Dana to Stanton, April 27, 1863; Stanton Papers.

[V]

When during the autumn of 1862 Richmond belatedly realized the gravity of the situation in the West, and sent Johnston to Chattanooga with military power over the area between the Alleghenies and the Mississippi, it acted without proper forethought. Johnston, wary, deliberate, and temperamentally pessimistic, was not the proper man for a position demanding lionhearted courage and dynamic action; the authority given him was not the proper authority. We have seen how quickly he pointed out to Jefferson Davis that with three armies separated by vast distances under his nominal control, he was in an impossible predicament. "I must either take the immediate direction of one of the armies, thus suspending its proper commander, or be idle except on rare occasions when it might be expedient to transfer troops from one department to another." In the first contingency he would deprive an officer of the command he had earned; in the second he would be an inactive and distant spectator. He earnestly begged to be appointed to a less equivocal position.

The request was denied. Johnston was inspecting fortifications at Mobile on February 12, 1863, when he learned that the War Department ordered him to take direct charge of the Army of Middle Tennessee, Bragg having been ordered to Richmond for conferences. Because Bragg's wife was believed lying at the point of death, Johnston withheld the orders from him, but he did assume command of the army at Tullahoma. While here he learned that Farragut with the *Hartford* and *Albatross* had passed Port Hudson into the stretch of river just below Vicksburg. This fact, he realized, greatly reduced the value of both Port Hudson and Vicksburg, for the South no longer held control of the stream between them. A few days later he fell seriously ill, and Bragg reverted to active control of his forces.[42] While he was still weak, Grant threw his troops across the river south of Vicksburg and seized Port Gibson and Grand Gulf. A crisis had arisen. Richmond at once, on May 9, ordered Johnston to try to meet it:

Proceed at once to Mississippi and take chief command of the forces there, giving to those in the field, so far as practicable, the encouragement and benefit of your personal direction. Arrange to take for temporary service with you, or to be forwarded without delay, three thousand good troops who will be substituted in General Bragg's army by a large number of prisoners returned from the Arkansas Post capture.[43]

Johnston set out for Mississippi on the first train from Tullahoma. We can well imagine the anxiety he felt as his train made its bumpy, uncertain

42 Johnston's *Narrative*, 163–174.
43 *Idem*, 172, 173.

crawl through lower Tennessee, upper Alabama, and on to Jackson, which he reached the evening of May 13. From that point he sent a despairing message to Secretary Seddon that the enemy was already between him and Pemberton, cutting off communication: *"I am too late."* He meant that Pemberton and Seddon had been too late, but in fact all three stood indicted by events.[44]

Pemberton, with the rank of lieutenant-general, had been in command of his department since October 13, 1862. A man now forty-eight, of Philadelphia Quaker stock, West Point education, and long military experience, for he had served in the Seminole hostilities, the Mexican War, and the Mormon expedition, he was a captain when the Civil War began, with a brevet as major for gallantry at Molino el Rey. Married to a Virginia girl, and holding strong State Rights views, he took the Southern side although every consideration of personal interest counseled him to remain with the Union. His rise since had been rapid. As major-general early in 1862, he had seen that Sumter was worthless for the defense of Charleston, and had built Fort Wagner and Battery B instead. When he took command at Vicksburg he had shown skill and energy in erecting forts and batteries. Time, however, disclosed two crippling weaknesses. Primarily an engineer, and vigorously capable in defensive operations, he was confused and uncertain in mobile field activities. His public relations were always bad. Though utterly loyal to the South, his Northern birth and education inspired distrust and even wild charges of treason; and his chill, stern demeanor, severity of speech, and disciplinary strictness augmented his unpopularity.[45]

Because Pemberton had long thought it impossible for Grant to approach Vicksburg from the south, he had taken inadequate precautions there. The batteries at Grand Gulf, though in a strong position, were small; a force of only 6,000 men held that place and Port Gibson; a small picket force lay at New Carthage, and a camp of instruction, a battery, and a cavalry company at Lake Bruin—that was all. On April 17, after Porter's flotilla sped past the Vicksburg batteries, he awoke to his peril; he notified Johnston in Tullahoma that Grant could now transfer his army to the east bank. Later he blamed

---

44 *Idem,* 506.
45 Pemberton, *Pemberton,* 1–48. "Pemberton seems confused and uncertain about everything," wrote Pickens June 12, 1862; Pickens Papers, Duke Univ. A New Orleans refugee in Pike County, Miss., reported to the governor on March 3, 1863, that recent events combined with Pemberton's antecedents had created a growing distrust of the general. "A Lovell's incompetency lost New Orleans—a Pemberton's treachery may bring worse evils." Pettus Papers, Miss. State Archives. On the other hand, the perceptive Thomas C. Reynolds wrote a friend from Camden, Ark., April 13, 1863: "Here, as at Charleston, the evidences of his capacity have overcome, in great measure, the prejudices engendered, on first acquaintance, by his martinet foppery"; Reynolds Letterbooks, LC.

Johnston for not acting to meet the fast-deteriorating situation. *"Then,"* he wrote a friend, "(if such an order was ever proper), was the time to have directed me to unite *all* my forces, if Grant should land, to beat him. Had he then said, 'it is my order, that if Grant lands on this side of the river, you will, if necessary, abandon Port Hudson and Vicksburg and its dependencies to beat him,' I could not have been in doubt as to his intentions." [46] Yet he knew that Johnston favored a concentration of the forces of Pemberton, T. H. Holmes, and Frank Gardner, commanding at Port Hudson, in the field. [47]

It was Pemberton's fate to suffer from the radically conflicting views of his two superiors, Johnston and Davis, and from his own indecision. President Davis believed it vital to hold Vicksburg even at the risk of losing a powerful army, and instructed Pemberton to defend the city at all costs. Johnston, knowing that Union warships ranged the river north and south of the city, believed it of secondary value compared with Pemberton's force of 32,000 well-armed men; the main object to him was to preserve this army intact, unite it with other troops, and seek an opportunity to strike Grant a decisive blow. Davis, as the situation of Vicksburg grew desperate, might have asked Lee to send several divisions—or at least one, Pickett's—west to help relieve the place; but Lee believed that this would be tantamount to a sacrifice of Virginia, and he and Davis hoped for a new invasion of the North, while considerations of time and geography stood in the way. The Confederate President did make strenuous efforts, by telegraph, to summon assistance from every quarter; from Charleston, from Arkansas, from the militia and home guards of Alabama. All these efforts failed. His insistence on the supreme importance of the stronghold, however, harmonized with Pemberton's natural taste for a defense of fortifications, so that the general determined to hold it. [48]

The hour of decision for Pemberton was May 14. Johnston the previous day, ill and exhausted, had sent from Jackson a message which he hoped would effect an immediate concentration of the Confederate forces. He had just come, he had incomplete and uncertain information on Grant's movements, he possessed only 6,000 infantry of his own, and he was prey to the defeatism exhibited in his telegram "too late"; but he broke through his palsy with his first peremptory orders. "I have lately arrived," he wrote, "and

46 To Sarah W. Dorsey; Dorsey, *Allen,* 182, 183.
47 Johnston did write Pemberton from Tullahoma on May 2: "If Grant crosses, unite all your troops to beat him. Success will give back what was abandoned to win it." This was equivocal. He did not order Pemberton to abandon Vicksburg and Port Hudson for field operations, yet he could later say (indeed, his partisans did say) that this was what he meant. Certainly Pemberton could have accepted it as an order. *Idem,* 194.
48 Figures on Confederate strength are in O. R., I, xxiv, pt. 1, p. 273. Davis's telegrams asking reinforcements are in Pemberton, *Pemberton,* 51–56.

learn that Major-General Sherman is between us, with four divisions, at Clinton. It is important to reestablish communications, that you may be reinforced. If practicable, come up in his rear at once; to beat such a detachment would be of immense value. The troops here could cooperate. All the troops you can quickly assemble should be brought. Time is all-important." [49]

Had Pemberton acted on this order, a junction of the small force in Jackson with Pemberton's army could possibly have been effected, and the joint command might have preserved mobility; but the chances were against this. In any event, Pemberton took a different course. He called a council of war and argued against Johnston's orders. A majority of the council voted for accepting them; a minority wished to try to cut the communications of the advancing Federal forces. Though Pemberton was adverse to this, he accepted the plan. He thus determined upon a measure of which he and a majority of his council disapproved, and which violated the orders of his superior. In so doing, Pemberton was actuated by a conviction that he must not abandon his base at Vicksburg, as he explained to Johnston in a note of May 17. His movement to cut the Federal supply line failed after involving him in some circuitous marching, and a stinging little defeat at Baker's Creek. The next certain news that Johnston obtained was that Pemberton, after a futile effort to hold a bridge over the Big Black River behind Vicksburg, had retreated to that city. [50]

One important factor in Confederate weakness and fumbling was the difficulty in filling the ranks of the army, and in supplying the men with shoes, uniforms, and blankets. The conscription law worked so badly that officers grew wrathful over its poor enforcement. Longstreet wished a provost-marshal placed in every town in the Confederacy, with deputies authorized to round up all stragglers; he wished evaders punished, and men who furnished substitutes held liable if the substitute deserted. Robert W. Barnwell was shocked by the reluctance to serve and the innumerable evasions in Georgia and South Carolina. [51] In Mississippi the situation was as bad as anywhere, and in Louisiana it was worse than in most States. "Desertions are numerous and frequent and the demoralization of the militia complete," one brigadier told Governor Pettus early in 1863. As Union forces marched through Louisiana many able-bodied men, concluding that the struggle was hopeless, refused to fight. In Arkansas, General Holmes reported the same situation to President Davis. Numerous State officers having taken the oath of allegiance to the

49 Johnston's *Narrative*, 523.
50 *Idem*, 181–188; Pemberton, *Pemberton; Battles and Leaders*, III, 478, 479.
51 Aug. 17, 1863, to Senator Wigfall; Wigfall Papers, Univ. of Texas. Barnwell, Nov. 2, 1862, *ibid*.

Union, the whole machinery of Confederate law was paralyzed. Bands of deserters openly resisted conscription, even murdering suspected informers. Holmes put his finger on the principal grievance of those Southerners everywhere who grumbled over the rich man's war and poor man's fight:

The greatest cause of complaint is the feature of the conscript law exempting the owner of 20 negroes, and the state law that requires a white man to remain on every plantation where there are negroes. This has effectually aroused the non-slaveholders, and as there is really in many places very great suffering among the poor, the disposition of disloyal persons to raise bands for marauding purposes is almost unopposed.[52]

Grant believed that Pemberton's troops were better armed than his own. But many of them, like many of Holmes's, Kirby-Smith's, and Johnston's troops, were in rags, with rough rawhide shoes or none. As the winter had set in, Major-General Hindman at Fort Smith had predicted that unless the nakedness of his troops was cured, half of them would die ere spring. Food shortages in the Arkansas-Mississippi region were growing, for although Grant's troops found the country south of Vicksburg full of grain and livestock, in other areas the wholesale removal of Negroes southward, and the ravages of armies and guerrillas, had stripped the country bare. The British officer Lieutenant-Colonel Fremantle of the Coldstream Guards, who reached Natchez from Matamoras this spring and pressed on to Jackson and Virginia, found Mississippi and Alabama in an extremity of anguish. He saw boys of fifteen and sixteen badly wounded, and sometimes vain over a missing limb. He visited farmhouses where the women had scarcely any clothes, nothing but the coarsest side meat and cornbread to eat, and sweet-potato coffee to drink; they were in miserable uncertainty as to the fate of their relatives and their own future. When he ate with Johnston and his staff the only cooking utensils were a battered coffee pot and frying pan, and they shared a one-pronged fork among them. He found the railroad to Meridian almost unusable; the cars had proceeded but five miles when the engine left the track.[53]

52 Gen. J. J. George, Grenada, Miss., Jan. 12, 1863, Pettus Papers; Holmes, Little Rock, Jan. 21, 1863. Desertion in the South, like the North, early became a tremendous problem. The New Orleans *Daily Picayune*, March 11, 1862, estimated that 8,024 officers and men deserted from the Louisiana forces during the first year of war; it put Arkansas desertions at some 10,000 men, and Mississippi desertions at 11,604. See Davis, *Rise and Fall*, II, 218, for the revolt en masse of the garrison at Fort Jackson. Late in 1863 Gen. W. H. Allen reported to the Confederate government of Louisiana that 8,000 deserters were skulking in his vicinity in that State. Edwin A. Leland in "Org. and Admin. of the La. Army During the Civil War," M. A. thesis, La. State Univ., 1938, concludes that the nonslaveholding farmers of the State, averse to authority under any circumstances, resisted conscription with desperate tenacity.
53 Fremantle, *Three Months in the Confederacy, passim.*

But the genuine rebel, as Fremantle observed, with his bare feet, ragged garb, and thin rations, would fight grimly on.

Difficulties of transport also beset Johnny Reb, and even on the defensive he had to envy the better Union fortune. Command of the Western waters was as important as that of the Atlantic and Gulf, for sea power wrought its triumphs there as elsewhere. Northern domination of the Ohio, Tennessee, and Mississippi was an extension of the Atlantic and Gulf blockade, shutting off supplies from the Confederacy. Amphibious fighting, supply boats, hospital boats, dispatch boats, all at Northern disposal, were totally out of Southern reach. Johnston repeatedly complained of the difficulties of movement. "The whole of the [Mississippi] valley is said to be impassable for large wagon trains," he declared early in March. Reinforcements between May 20 and June 4 brought his own force up from 6,000 to about 24,000 infantry and artillery. This small army, not one-third, he thought, that of the enemy, lacked ammunition, batteries, but above all transport, so that it could not be moved with any hope of success. The country had been so stripped of horses and mules that draught animals did not arrive from distant points until too late. Food could be found, but for want of wagons and horses could not be brought in. Had he wished to attempt the relief of Port Hudson, want of transport would have blocked him. The same deficiency put Vicksburg in its terrible predicament, for stores could not be collected to endure a long siege. The railroads, lacking proper fuel, rolling stock, and personnel, and crippled by bridge burning, were breaking down.[54]

In despair, Johnston on May 18 sent Pemberton a final appeal. If he were invested in Vicksburg, he must ultimately surrender. "Under such circumstances, instead of losing both troops and place, we must, if possible, save the troops. If it is not too late, evacuate Vicksburg and its dependencies, and march to the northeast." But Pemberton, who thought the march impracticable, made no effort to carry out the order—if such it could be called. With sixty days' rations, he decided to hold Vicksburg to the end in the hope that Richmond would relieve it. "I still conceive it to be the most important point in the Confederacy," he wrote.

[VI]

Grant, aware when he reached Grand Gulf that he must strike hard and fast, carried out in the next eighteen days a campaign as brilliant as any

54 See Johnston to Wigfall, March 4, 1863, Wigfall Papers; Johnston's final report to Adjutant-General S. Cooper, Nov. 1, 1863, on the campaign. The letters of President W. Goodman of the Mississippi Central R.R. and Supt. J. L. Fleming of the Mobile & Ohio to Gov. Pettus in the Alabama State Archives throw light on the endless railroad difficulties.

of Marlborough's or Napoleon's. If his numbers and equipment were not overwhelmingly greater than those of Pemberton, his confidence, mobility, and generalship were incomparably superior. His troops, tough men from the Western prairie who made hard-bitten, tenacious fighters, were in fine fettle. He pushed his army northeastward along the line of the Big Black between Vicksburg and Jackson, so as to separate Pemberton and Johnston; McClernand's corps at first leading the way, Sherman's following close behind, and McPherson's striking forward on the right flank to threaten the capital and cut the railway between the two cities. Sharp fighting occurred at Raymond and other points on the march. On May 14, after another action, Grant occupied Jackson, which the army systematically reduced to a shell; on the 16th he fought a heavy battle at Champion's Hill, completely routing Pemberton's forces; and on the 17th he flung Pemberton's disheartened troops back across the Big Black. The Southern general, his command so mauled and scattered that only about 21,000 effectives were left, retreated hastily toward Vicksburg.

This succession of victories, after the months of defeat and immobility, filled the North with delight. "Within the last three days," trumpeted "Xenophon" in the New York *Tribune*, "God has crowned our arms with two decisive victories; not simply repulses leaving our columns bleeding and crippled; not simply steady advances in the face of an enemy beaten, but still at bay and defiant; not victories on a small scale over a puny antagonist, and securing small results, but victories in the largest sense of the word, with all their laurels and trophies, rout, pursuit, disorganization of the enemy, capture of prisoners, ensigns, and cannon; victories on the grandest scale, over a vast and desperate enemy in the heart of his own territory and defending his great stronghold." [55] Lincoln and Stanton were now hopeful of the early liberation of the Mississippi. The country had at last the military hero for which it had longed, and Grant's name was on every lip.

Reporters wrote with enthusiasm of a rapidity of advance entirely novel in the war. The enemy had been taken by surprise, defeated, followed up before he had time to rally, and defeated again and again by a strategy that put two Union divisions at every point where Confederates posted one. Under the May sun the blue columns rolled swiftly through a singularly variegated country of hills, ravines, clumps of timber, and high open plateaus, the lines of bayonets flashing under the waving flags; skirmishers in advance, artillery close at hand, ammunition always ample. Impedimenta was reduced

55 Behind Vicksburg, May 20, in *Tribune* of June 1; the two battles referred to were Champion's Hill, much the bloodiest of the campaign, and Big Black River Bridge. In eighteen days Grant marched 200 miles, captured 88 cannon, took 4,500 prisoners, and inflicted heavy losses, while his own casualty list was only 3,500; Greene, *The Mississippi*, 170, 171.

to the lowest point; the men lived on the country. "I am afraid Grant will have to be reproved for want of style," Elihu Washburne, who had been West, wrote Lincoln. "On this whole march for five days he has had neither a horse, nor an orderly nor servant, a blanket, or overcoat, or clean shirt, or even a sword; that being carried by his boy 13 years old. His entire baggage consists of a toothbrush." Soldiers feasted on hams, cornmeal, dried apples and peaches, honey, butter, molasses, and preserves; they shot the cattle and roasted the fowls. From all quarters slaves flocked into the camps, some on foot, some in carts drawn by their masters' horses and bearing their masters' goods, and some driving pigs and sheep.[56]

Grant's victories rendered Haines's Bluff on the Yazoo untenable, and Union forces were eager to reach that river and re-establish direct communications with the North. "My first anxiety," writes Grant, "was to secure a base of supplies on the Yazoo River above Vicksburg." He and Sherman impatiently joined the advance, and amid whistling bullets climbed to the very point on Walnut Hills from which the Confederates had repulsed the Union troops in December. At the brow Sherman turned to Grant. "Up to this moment," he said, "I doubted your plan of campaign. Now I am absolutely certain of its success." The army was delighted by the reopening of direct transit with Memphis and Cairo. They had missed their bread and coffee, and as Grant came back to the main line, after watching pioneers building a road from the Yazoo, they greeted him with a chorus of "Hardtack! Hardtack!"

Southern soldiers and harsh terrain were not the only obstacles with which Grant contended; all spring he had been fighting a battle with his old enemy, drink. In this as in his military planning Rawlins was his sleepless aide. Gossip about the commander's old weakness was incessant. His onetime West Point associate, Brigadier-General Charles S. Hamilton, wrote a Wisconsin friend in February: "I will now say what I have never breathed. *Grant is a drunkard.* . . . When he came to Memphis he left his wife at La Grange and for several days after getting here was beastly drunk, utterly incapable of doing anything. Quinby and I took him in charge, watching him day and night and keeping liquor away from him and we telegraphed to his wife and brought her on to take care of him." As relations between Hamilton and Grant were strained, this statement might be rejected, but other evidence bears it out.[57]

56 Correspondence N. Y. *Herald, Times, Tribune,* and Chicago *Tribune* May 25–June 10; Washburne, Hay Papers, Ill. State Hist. Lib.; Fremantle, *Three Months,* Ch. 5. Details of men on the march slaughtered enough beeves and poultry each night to supply the army. "The chivalry through this region," wrote the Chicago *Tribune* correspondent, "are perfectly confounded and horrorstricken."
57 Hamilton, Feb. 11, 1863, to James R. Doolittle; Doolittle Papers, Wis. State Hist. Lib. Hamilton thought Grant an able commander, but Sherman still abler. See also "Unpublished War Letters of Grant and Halleck," *North American Review,* March, 1886.

The correspondent Cadwallader describes a spree on which Grant embarked while on the steamboat *Diligence* in the first week of June. "He made several trips to the barroom of the boat in a short time, and became stupid in speech and staggering in gait." Cadwallader locked him in his stateroom, threw his whisky out of the window, and fanned him to sleep. But later Grant obtained a new supply, and while intoxicated ordered the boat to proceed to Chickasaw Bayou. "If we had started then," writes Cadwallader, "we would have arrived at the Bayou about the middle of the afternoon, when the landing would have been alive with officers, men, and trains from all parts of the army. To be seen in his present condition would lead to utter disgrace and ruin." Measures were taken to delay the boat, which did not reach the Bayou until sundown. But Grant had been drinking again, and on leaving the gangplank put spurs to his unruly horse, which carried him through the dusk at breakneck speed over a tortuous road and dangerous bridges. The correspondent followed, hid him for a time, and about midnight got him back to camp in an ambulance. He had slept off his liquor, and climbing out, started to his tent as steadily as he had ever walked. Cadwallader concludes:

My surprise nearly amounted to stupefaction. I turned to Rawlins and said I was afraid that he would think I was the man who had been drunk.
But he replied in suppressed tones through his clinched teeth, "No, no. I know him. I know him. I want you to tell me the exact facts—and all of them, without any concealment. I have a right to know them, and I will know them." The whole appearance of the man indicated a fierceness that could have torn me into a thousand pieces had he considered me to blame.[58]

Even this circumstantial account might be discounted did not the Rawlins papers contain a letter to Grant, dated at one in the morning on June 6, which gives it color. "The great solicitude I feel for the safety of this army," wrote Rawlins, "leads me to mention, what I had hoped never again to do, the subject of your drinking." He had heard that one Dr. Mcmillan had induced Grant, at Sherman's headquarters, to take a glass of wine; and that day he found a box of wine in front of Grant's tent, and had learned that he forbade its removal. Then "tonight . . . I find you where the wine bottle has just been emptied, in company with those who drink and urge you to do likewise; and the lack of your usual promptness and decision, and clearness in expressing yourself in writing, conduces to confirm my suspicion." Rawlins went on:

You have the full control over your appetite, and can let drinking alone. Had you not pledged me the sincerity of your honor early last March, that you would drink no more during the war and kept that pledge during your

---

58 MS Diary, Ill. State Hist. Lib.; not in the printed selections.

recent campaign, you would not today have stood first in the world's history as a successful military leader. Your only salvation depends upon strict adherence to that pledge. You cannot succeed in any other way. . . .

As I have before stated, I may be wrong in my suspicions, but if one sees that which leads him to suppose a sentinel is falling asleep on his post, it is his duty to arouse him; and if one sees that which leads him to fear the General commanding a great army is being seduced to that step which if he fails to sound the proper note of warning, the friends, wives, and children of those brave men whose lives he permits to remain thus in peril, will accuse him while he lives, and stand strict witnesses of wrath against him in the day when all shall be tried.[59]

We hear of no more faltering. Possibly some of the harshness with which Grant treated McClernand, and the alacrity with which he soon found an excuse for sending him back to Springfield, derived from his knowledge that if he were ever discovered drunk, McClernand (to the dismay of the army) might succeed. But the important fact was that Grant almost completely overcame his one frailty.

[VII]

On May 18 the first worn division of Pemberton's army, under General M. L. Smith, filed into the fortifications on the northeastern outskirts of Vicksburg, throwing out skirmishers behind as it did so. Within a half hour the line of skirmishers was under rifle and artillery fire—so closely did the blue press on the heels of the gray. By nightfall half of Grant's army was within sight of the works about the city. Next day, after the two armies had spent the morning disposing their men, Grant delivered a preliminary attack which was thrown back with serious losses. At various points the Union troops planted their flags on the parapets, but could maintain no foothold. They had hoped to find the Southerners demoralized after their retreat, but as Pemberton telegraphed Jefferson Davis that day, sending his message out by courier, the Confederates had quickly recovered their morale.[60] Though Grant planned another early assault, it seemed clear the struggle would be prolonged and grim. One of the famous sieges of history was about to begin.

But while the flag made such stirring progress in the West, a darker story was being written in the East.

59 Dated "Before Vicksburg"; Rawlins' father had been ruined by drink. Captain John M. Shaw of the 25th Wisconsin, a Galena friend of Rawlins, made this letter public after the war, with an endorsement by Rawlins attesting its genuineness. Cadwallader's story may deal with a different incident, or may be a distorted and exaggerated remembrance of this one. Cf. Catton, *Grant Moves South*, 463–465.
60 O. R., I, xxiv, pt. 1, p. 274; pt. 3, p. 842; Pemberton, *Pemberton*, 180–184.

17

Hooker at Chancellorsville, and After

THE CENTRAL fact of the war situation by the spring of 1863 was that the South could win a great battle and emerge permanently weakened, while the North could lose again and again with an Antaeus-like growth in strength.

Though a Confederate soldier could with difficulty be replaced from a white population which conquest had now reduced to five or six millions, Union losses were easily restored from the natural increase of twenty-odd millions, and the stream of European immigration. A wrecked Confederate cannon imposed a fresh strain on the only two sources of heavy ordnance, the Tredegar works and the Selma foundry, but a wrecked Union cannon could be made good by a score of firms. Secretary Mallory of the Confederate Navy wrote President Davis in the summer of 1862 that iron shortages were "severely felt throughout the Confederacy," and the evacuation of much of Tennessee and North Alabama increased the pinch. But from Trenton to Pittsburgh, meanwhile, furnaces roared and rolling mills rumbled to meet every order. Want of textile machinery made Southern clothing scarce even while Confederate squads burned cotton, yet the North remained well clad. The strain on Southern railroads was becoming insupportable; the president of the Mississippi Central, for example, reported this spring that unless he got supplies from abroad, his dilapidated line must soon be abandoned.[1] Confederate resourcefulness and devotion were accomplishing wonders in the manufacture of powder, muskets, medicines, shoes, and harness. But the blows of attrition and the coils of the blockade nevertheless made the South a land of want, makeshift, and dread.

---

1   The South rolled no railroad iron during the war; C. W. Ramsdell, "The Confederate Govt. and the Railroads," *Amer. Hist. Review*, XXII, July, 1917, 794 ff.; Black, *Railroads of the Confederacy*, 22 ff., 85 ff. Goodman sent his complaint to Secretary of War Seddon, Jan. 23, 1863; O. R., IV, ii, pp. 381, 382. In a message to Congress, Nov. 18, 1861, Davis emphasized the importance of closing some bad gaps in the Confederate railroad system, but the sorely needed link between Danville, Va., and Greensboro, N. C., was not finished until late in May, 1864, and that from Augusta, Ga., to Columbia, S. C., was never built. Southern gauges ran from four feet, eight and one-half inches to five feet, six inches, and two different gauges were laid during the war. Black offers the best railroad map.

The North as the besieging power, prospering and growing, felt only two heavy pressures for victory in battle: it would sustain morale at home and bolster prestige abroad. But these pressures *were* heavy. Every such blow as Fredericksburg encouraged the copperheads and inclined Napoleon III to lend a readier ear to the wily John Slidell. Down to May Grant's success in the West was still dubious, and in the grim Eastern slugging match, the press, politicians, and plain citizens demanded a victory as overdue.

It is clear that Du Pont's attack on Charleston in April, 1863, was undertaken for reasons quite as much political as military. The government, to be sure, wished to release the blockading fleet off the city, partly to help hunt down Confederate cruisers on the high seas, partly for operations in the Gulf. But it was actuated mainly by other motives. The seizure of the cradle of the Confederacy, the proud capital of nullifiers and secessionists, would humiliate every follower of Calhoun and exalt every Northern heart. It would prove to Europe that the new American navy was a power to be dreaded. Since Roanoke Island, Port Royal, New Orleans, and Memphis, the armored ship seemed to many invincible.

Secretary Welles and Gustavus V. Fox were encouraged in aiming their blow against Charleston by the rapidity with which the navy was being strengthened. The first monitors under the extensive new building plan had been delivered late in 1862, and had proved their fair-weather seaworthiness in coastal voyages. The navy also received the *New Ironsides*, a casemated warship of more than 5,000 tons, whose 16 Dahlgren guns and 2 Parrott rifles on pivots were able to deliver a broadside of 1,100 pounds. Her four-inch iron plates covered the heaviest oak framing ever put on a ship, and extended four feet below the waterline. With this ironclad, and eight monitors each mounting an eight-inch and a fifteen-inch gun, Fox expected to deal the Carolinians a stunning blow. Du Pont was less sanguine. He had taken pains to make two tests of the single-turreted monitor *Montauk* against Fort McAllister in Georgia, and his report to Welles on January 28 was decidedly chilling, for he listed three grave objections. To begin with, while ironclads might be impenetrable, they were not sufficiently destructive against forts, their slowness of fire affording the garrison time, as some said, to smoke a cigar between shots. In the second place, success against strong coastal forts would always be uncertain without the help of troops. Finally, it was difficult if not impossible to remove sunken obstructions in shallow water under fire.[2]

2 Naval O. R., I, xiii, 503 ff.; Dudley W. Knox, *Hist. U. S. Navy*, 264, 265; *Battles and Leaders*, I, 671–691. The *Naval Register* for 1863 listed 530 vessels, of which nearly 140 had been constructed since Sumter as warships, and nearly 50 were ironclads. Immediately after the *Merrimac-Monitor* battle the Navy Department ordered 20 monitors built.

The Navy Department heads did not realize how energetically Beauregard had ringed Charleston with formidable guns and impediments. He had strengthened the walls and batteries of Forts Moultrie, Wagner, and Johnson, made Sumter more dangerous than ever before, and filled the channels with mines, pilings, and ropes to tangle propellers. The harbor batteries could concentrate a heavier volume of fire on an assailant, it was said, than the defenses of any other port in the world. Moreover, the area possessed ample troops. According to James Chestnut, Jr., who made an inspection trip through the State only a fortnight before Du Pont's assault, South Carolina had 21,300 effective soldiers, and the forces between Savannah and Charleston were capable of holding five times David Hunter's 10,000 men at Port Royal. The proud Carolinians could be trusted to fight to the last ounce of powder. Wade Hampton, home on furlough, assured Beauregard how happy he would be to give everything to the defense, and Judge A. S. Magrath declared complete destruction of the city preferable to its surrender.[3] Some Northerners had doubts of the issue. Lincoln let Fox know early in April that he believed the fleet would be repulsed, and made the same statement to Sumner.[4]

Reluctantly, Du Pont began his assault early on the afternoon of April 7. Four monitors moved in against the forts; he followed on the *New Ironsides;* then came four more monitors. Immediately the fleet found itself in trouble. Shallow water and strong tidal currents made steering difficult. Once the flagship had to drop anchor to avoid grounding; a little later it collided with two monitors and had to drop anchor again. John Rodgers of the *Weehawken*, leading the line, decided that he could not breach the channel obstructions, and turned aside, followed by other monitors. Thereupon Fort Sumter opened fire at point-blank range (700 yards), and Moultrie and Wagner quickly followed. For an hour and forty minutes ships and forts exchanged a tremendous fire in which the batteries had much the best of it. Then, discouraged by his steering difficulties, Du Pont signaled the fleet to withdraw. Though he intended to resume the attack next morning, a gloomy evening council of the captains dissuaded him. The ships had fired only 139 shots against some 2,200 from the batteries; the *Keokuk*, hit 90 times, was so badly hurt that she sank next day, and others were extensively damaged.

"I attempted to take the bull by the horns, but he was too much for us," wrote Du Pont on April 8. "These monitors are miserable failures where forts are concerned." Not only Welles but Lincoln was disappointed. Fearful

3 James Chestnut, Jr., March 22, and Magrath, June 14, 1863, to Davis in Jefferson Davis Papers, Duke Univ.; Hampton, Columbia, Feb. 26, 1863, to Beauregard in Beauregard-York Papers, CU.
4 Sumner to Lady Argyll, April 13, 1863, Sumner Papers, HL.

of public opinion, the Navy Department tried to throw a shroud of partial secrecy about the event, and to cast the blame on Du Pont, whom it accused of failing to push the attack with the imagination and pluck which Farragut had shown at New Orleans. Critics declared he had made no use, for example, of his wooden gunboats, keeping them out of range. The real blame, however, lay with the ships, not the admiral. The monitors could neither sustain the fire they met, which jammed the turret gear of some and closed the port stoppers of others, nor return it with effect. Moreover, their poor design made them purblind—the officers could not keep a clear outlook. Members of Congress were soon violently denouncing the whole investment in monitors.

The public thus had to digest still another defeat. It was discouraging, for plainly the fleet could never take Charleston, and it was the harder to accept because European naval experts found proof in the battle that the claims made for the monitors after the Hampton Roads affair were quite unfounded. American naval designers obviously had much to learn.[5]

But all Eastern eyes now turned to Virginia and Hooker's impending campaign.

[I]

When news of Hooker's appointment to head the Army of the Potomac had flashed to the country at the end of January, 1863, Northerners plucked up hope. Observers had been impressed by the dashing courage he had shown at Williamsburg, Fair Oaks, Malvern Hill, and Antietam. Taking the Fifth Corps when Fitz-John Porter was removed, he had handled it well. It was known that Lincoln liked him. The President, meeting him after Bull Run, had been impressed by his confident analysis of that battle; he had been pleased later on by Hooker's ardent desire to open the Potomac; and he rewarded the general's stubborn courage at Williamsburg by making his commission as major-general date from that action. Halleck, who possessed first-hand knowledge of Hooker's raffish life in old California days, was hostile to the appointment, and his dislike infected Stanton. Both had been irritated by the general's flagrant maneuvers to get the command when McClellan was removed, and by his indiscreet talk. But Secretary Chase and the radicals of

5 See London *Times*, Jan. 7, 1864, with long quotations from the N. Y. *Times*; Henry Winter Davis in *Cong. Globe*, 38th Cong., 2d Sess., App., 34–40; H. W. Wilson, *Ironclads in Action*, I, 86–97. Du Pont's report in Naval O. R., I, xiv, 5–8, declared that the outer defenses of Charleston should first have been taken by land forces. H. A. Du Pont, *Du Pont*, 213–270, spiritedly defends the admiral.

the Committee on the Conduct of the War favored this impetuous son of Massachusetts.[6]

Hooker took charge of an army which had clearly lost moral tone and unity in the three months since McClellan left. Two of its corps historians declare bluntly that it had been controlled by West Pointers who often made patriotism subservient to military ambition, and that other officers had placed political aims above country. Carl Schurz was alarmed by its mood of surly discouragement. "I have spent several days here," he wrote Lincoln from Stafford Court House the day before Hooker's appointment, "and feel compelled to say to you, that I have seen and heard a great many things which deeply distressed me." Several of the generals, he continued, had systematically undermined the spirits of the men and their confidence in Burnside. The mud march had worn out many regiments, they were badly fed and badly housed in rain-damaged tents and huts, and many had not been paid in six months. "I have heard generals, subordinate officers, and men say that they expect to be whipped anyhow, that 'all these fatigues and hardships are for nothing' and that they might as well go home." [7]

That the new commander had done his share in fomenting army discontent Lincoln well knew from Henry J. Raymond and Burnside. Hooker was moreover accused of chronic bad temper, immoral conduct, and weakness for drink, while his vindictiveness toward opponents was as notorious as his devotion to those who did him a service. Critical, cynical, and outspoken, he left enemies wherever he walked. A nervous man, working with rapid intensity and going at every task with a dash, he was always blowing off steam, as tactless as he was talkative. The worst trait in his volatile nature, however, was not his sharpness of tongue, but his tendency toward intrigue. His recent remark to William Swinton of the *Times* that Lincoln and his Administration were "played out" was harmless compared with his underhand activities first against McClellan and later Burnside.[8] Lincoln, aware of

6 For Lincoln's attitude see N. Y. *Herald*, Jan. 27, 1863, and W. F. G. Shanks, "Fighting Joe Hooker," in *Harper's Mag.*, XXXI (Oct., 1865), 640–642. For the attitude of radical leaders see *Report, Committee on Conduct of War*, 1865, I, 175; Warden, *Chase*, 488; Hebert, *Fighting Joe Hooker*, Chs. XI, XII. Chase was suspected of planning a tacit compact to promote Hooker's military fortunes in return for Hooker's support for the Presidency. Stanton and Halleck strongly favored Meade for control of the army.

7 A. C. Hamlin, *The Battle of Chancellorsville*, 33, 34, and J. H. Stine, *Army of the Potomac*, 310, are frank on the bad spirit of the officers. Hebert, *Hooker*, 174, quotes H. E. Tremain of Hooker's staff as saying that some regular officers were reluctant to end the war because they would lose their high rank in the volunteer service.

8 Hebert, *Hooker*, Chs. XI, XII. Gen. Charles P. Mattocks and others in the volume published by Massachusetts when the Commonwealth erected a statue in 1903 do justice to Hooker's heroism, tactical insight, and brilliant charm. But of his vindictiveness Judge W. M. Dickson of Ohio gives a harsh instance in *Century Mag.*, N. S., XIII (April, 1886), 961, 962.

his faults yet appreciative of his fighting temper, now wrote him a letter that was kind yet sharply admonitory.

"I think," declared the President, "that during Gen. Burnside's command of the Army, you have taken counsel of your ambition, and thwarted him as much as you could, in which you did a great wrong to the country, and to a most meritorious and honorable brother officer. I have heard, in such a way as to believe it, of your recently saying that both the Army and the Government needed a Dictator. Of course it was not *for* this, but in spite of it, that I have given you the command. Only those generals who gain successes, can set up dictators. What I now ask of you is military success, and I will risk the dictatorship. The government will support you to the utmost of its ability, which is neither more nor less than it has done and will do for all commanders. I much fear that the spirit which you have aided to infuse into the Army, of criticizing their Commander, and with-holding confidence from him, will now turn upon you. I shall assist you as far as I can. Neither you, nor Napoleon, were he alive again, could get any good out of an army, while such a spirit prevails in it."

Lincoln also understood Hooker's impetuosity. "And now, beware of rashness," he concluded. "Beware of rashness, but with energy and sleepless vigilance, go forward, and give us victories." To Raymond the President remarked that it was true Hooker talked badly, "but the trouble is, he is stronger with the country today than any other man." In a people's war, Lincoln had to give due weight to the fact that Hooker was more popular with press and Congress than Meade. He apparently handed the letter to the general at a White House interview of which little is known; only that Hooker felt rebuked, and that, apprehensive of Halleck's hostility, he arranged to communicate directly with the President.[9]

For two months Hooker devoted himself to reorganization and the restoration of Army morale. The rolls showed that absentees from their regiments had reached the shocking total of 81,964 soldiers and subalterns, and 2,922 officers, the great majority without valid excuse. Desertions had risen to 200 a day, some families sending their sons bundles of civilian clothing to aid their escape! With restless energy, Hooker improved training, discipline, and general confidence. He increased the quantity and raised the quality of the food, seeing that the men had an abundance of beef, bread—

9 *Works*, VI, 78, 79; H. W. Raymond, "Extracts From the Journal of Henry J. Raymond," *Scribner's Monthly*, XIX (1879–1880), p. 705. Much criticism of Hooker was irresponsible. Charles Francis Adams, Jr., for example, caustically writes (*Autobiography*, 160–163), that he was "little better than a drunken West Point military adventurer," showy but without character, and that he brought to his side two other totally unprincipled men, Sickles and Butterfield. This was the testy prejudice characteristic of aging Adamses.

fresh bread twice a week—soup, potatoes, and onions. He enforced rules of camp sanitation which reduced mortality to the level of a city of similar population. Although he punished deserters severely, he granted many furloughs to those who had earned them. Small festivities and the visits of officers' wives were allowed. Early in April, Lincoln, Mrs. Lincoln, Attorney-General Bates, and others visited the camp and took part in an imposing review of some 12,000 men. From the hills beyond Fredericksburg the Confederates, using glasses, could see the broad plain black with moving masses of infantry and horses.[10]

Abandoning Burnside's organization of the army in four grand divisions, which had worked badly, Hooker regrouped the troops in corps: the First Corps under John F. Reynolds, the Second under Darius N. Couch, the Third under Daniel E. Sickles, the Fifth under George G. Meade, the Sixth under John Sedgwick, the Eleventh under Franz Sigel, and the Twelfth under Henry W. Slocum, youngest of the number. Burnside and the Ninth Corps were remanded to Fort Monroe. General George Stoneman's body of 10,000 cavalry was concentrated into one corps, which was better than leaving it distributed by regiments throughout the army; and the artillery was henceforth to be considered still another corps in the general organization of forces, though Hooker neglected to regroup it and reofficer it properly. As Sigel was discontented with his place, he was relieved, and O. O. Howard, a West Pointer of thirty-two with the unique distinction of never drinking or swearing, was put in his stead; a change which displeased the Germans constituting nearly two-fifths of the unit, who thought that Howard had crowded their old chief aside. All the corps commanders except Sickles were worthy officers, and two, Reynolds and Meade, were men of high distinction.

Hooker's chief of staff was Daniel Butterfield, a graduate of Union College who had become an express-company executive in New York City, and had there distinguished himself in militia activities. The Twelfth New York under his colonelcy had been the first regiment to enter Virginia. Quick, industrious, and judicious, he had become major-general and head of the Fifth Corps before Fredericksburg. During the previous spring he had prepared a careful manual on camp and outpost duty for infantry, which appeared from Harper's early in 1863, quickly selling more than 10,000 copies. McClellan

10 E. K. Gould, *Major-General Hiram G. Berry*, 241-243, gives a lively account of a wedding in camp attended by ten bridesmaids and ten groomsmen, followed by banqueting, drinking, and a ball at Sickles' headquarters. He also describes a St. Patrick's Day hurdle race witnessed by all the ladies in camp, with drinking, gambling, and such reckless fence jumping that two horses and one man were killed. Such scenes gave Hooker's camp a bad name, but they no means justify C. F. Adams's statement that his headquarters were "a combination of barroom and brothel." Actually, his headquarters were under constant, close, and critical scrutiny by many men, and he worked like a slave day and night.

urged the War Department to distribute it wholesale and Sherman bought a large order. Butterfield also originated the shoulder patch as a corps insignia. Under McClellan he had unsuccessfully urged the marking of troops, artillery, ambulances, and baggage wagons with corps and division badges, and the flying of special headquarters flags. On the Peninsula, Philip Kearny had given his division troops a red patch with good effect. Now, with Hooker's support, Butterfield distributed to each corps its distinctive badge, two inches square, to be worn on cap or shoulder. This fostered *esprit de corps* in a literal sense, and served as a means of quickly indentifying wounded men, culprits, and stragglers.[11]

Altogether, by the latter part of April, Hooker's firm hand had brought into existence a new army of 125,000, happy, united, and vigorous. The troops were paid at last. Their rebuilt huts and repaired tents kept them comfortable; fresh vegetables banished scurvy; the new sanitary regulations cut the sickness rate from 10 per cent to 5; the rule that not more than one field officer or two staff officers could be absent from a regiment at once, and not more than two privates in a hundred could take a furlough simultaneously, kept the ranks filled. Picket lines had been made so tight that Confederate spying was almost impossible. The general kept the troops healthfully busy with drill and maneuvers.[12] Northern newspapers this month were full of Grant's spectacular advance, Banks's showy marches, and the sweeping Republican victories in Connecticut and Rhode Island. The Eastern troops must keep pace with the Western; Lincoln was eager for an early offensive, for the terms of at least 23,000 men would soon expire, and Lee must not be allowed to capture the initiative.

Hooker was eager too, promising that he would put every reserve unit into the next battle, for he was determined either to gain a complete victory or suffer overwhelming defeat. He had created a special agency to collect information on the foe, and felt utterly confident of success. "So are all who know anything of the situation here," wrote a friend from headquarters to Manton Marble. "We have a moral certainty of all that it is necessary to know in regard to the enemy, every regiment and brigade, division, etc., all their latest arrivals and departures, etc., all collated, compared from many sources, and fully confirmed. The secret service of Gen. Hooker is far superior to anything that has ever been here before." Whereas McClellan and Burn-

---

11 Julia L. Butterfield, *Butterfield*, 116–118, 119 ff.

12 Alden, *Harper's Hist. of the Great Rebellion*, 484; Survivors' Assn., *Corn Exchange Regt.*, 165, 166; Bates, *Diary*, 287 ff. Hooker's General Order No. 52 reduced to formal system the best sanitary practice in the army. Tents were to be pitched on fresh ground with drainage ditches eighteen inches deep; refuse and garbage were to be burned or buried daily; latrines were to be dug eight feet deep and covered with a half-foot of earth every night; personal cleanliness was to be enforced. Adams, *Doctors in Blue*, 198.

side had possessed the murkiest half-facts about Confederate affairs, Hooker could see the situation clearly: "nothing transpires in the enemy's camp which he is not speedily informed of." [13]

The Virginia spring this year was chill and wet, retarding operations. On April 23, after another soaking rain, the roads were such red quagmires that wags declared movement possible in only one direction—downward. Then, after a final storm on the 24th, the army on its muddy hills above the Rappahannock began to dry out. Sunday the 26th found the camps full of movement. At daybreak on Monday three corps, those of Meade, Howard, and Slocum, struck their tents and marched westward, aiming at fords twenty-five to thirty miles upstream. They found pontoon boats in readiness, and early Tuesday evening Howard's troops began crossing the river at Kelley's Ford, above the junction with the Rapidan. Lee's guards reached upstream only as far as the Rapidan, along which he had strung out some small detachments. He did not suppose that the Union forces would march higher over difficult roads into a country where they must depend on transported stores, or would cross the two rivers, both likely to flood under sudden rains, in order to attack his left flank. But this was just what Hooker with 45,000 men was attempting.

Hooker possessed nearly twice as many men as Lee had in his entrenched lines behind the Rappahannock, some 115,000 effectives against Lee's 61,800. His bureau of military information apprised him that Lee held only three days' rations at one time, so that if his lines were cut he must retreat. Hooker had therefore originally meant to send Stoneman's 10,000 cavalry up the Rappahannock and across it to describe a wide circle in Lee's rear, cutting off his supplies, compelling his retirement, and then harassing his columns. "Let your watchword be Fight! and let all your orders be Fight!" he instructed Stoneman. But when storms swelled the Rappahannock and delayed the march, he fixed on a larger enterprise. "I concluded," he said later, "to change my plan and strike for the whole rebel army, instead of forcing it back upon its line of retreat. . . ." His basic concept for his movement was masterly.[14]

In a sentence, the plan was to catch Lee between two powerful Union forces, each nearly equaling his whole army. He would send three corps far upstream to cross beyond the hostile lines, and with cavalry assistance turn

13 Frederick Law Olmsted to Mark Skinner, April 24, 1863, Olmsted Papers; J. E. Hammond to S. L. M. Barlow on Hooker's new military information bureau, April 22, Barlow Papers.

14 See Hooker's testimony in *Report, Committee on Conduct of War*, Second Series, I, 120 ff.; Hebert, *Hooker*, 180, 191; Bigelow, *Chancellorsville*, Chs. 1–3; N. Y. *Times, Herald, Tribune*, April 24–30. A useful table of official returns of the Army of Northern Virginia is in Alden, *Harper's History*, 383.

Lee's flank. Meanwhile the four other corps would make threatening movements at Fredericksburg and the fords nearer that town. Sedgwick was ordered to march his own corps and those of Reynolds and Sickles a short distance downstream, cross there, and open a demonstration against Lee's right wing. The hope was that Lee, fancying the operations near Fredericksburg the true threat, would concentrate his troops to resist them. Then, in Hooker's words, the three corps which had crossed the upper Rappahannock and Rapidan would sweep down the riverbank, "knock away the enemy's force holding the United States and Banks's Fords by attacking them in their rear," open these fords, and join the men of Couch's corps in a grand assault. If Lee tried to bring up reinforcements from his right, Sedgwick's blue host, fully 55,000 men, would be upon him instantly, and his whole army would be ground like wheat between two millstones.

At first all went magnificently. Meade's, Howard's, and Slocum's troops made a swiftly efficient march up the Rappahannock. Wednesday, April 29, saw the fields beyond Kelley's Ford covered with their dense moving masses. In two columns they pushed on to the Rapidan fords, taking the Confederates so unawares that they captured a small bridgebuilding party. That same day Sedgwick's troops broke across the Rappahannock four miles below Fredericksburg, and deployed in fighting order.

News that the army was across the river electrified the North. "Lee," exulted Greeley's *Tribune*, "has beyond question been deceived, flanked, and probably forced from his position—in other words, out-generaled." [15] Meade's forces continued eastward along the south bank of the Rapidan and past its junction with the Rappahannock, to the neighboring United States Ford, eleven miles from Fredericksburg. As the two Confederate divisions guarding the ford retreated, Couch's troops on the north bank greeted Meade's column with a cheer and began laying pontoon bridges. They were soon across, with Sickles's corps ready to follow. Altogether, four corps, with a fifth at hand, were now massed on Lee's left, with Sedgwick's powerful force on his right. Meade and Couch might have pushed on toward Fredericksburg had not Hooker, at 2:15 on the afternoon of April 30, warned them not to go beyond the crossroads and brick mansion called Chancellorsville. Here, about a fifty-acre clearing where a plank road and macadam turnpike intersected, he ordered them to concentrate.

[II]

The principal reason why Lee had only 62,000 men was that Longstreet's corps had been detached early in the year for service south of the James.

15 Editorial, May 2, 1863.

Union forces under John J. Peck, advancing from the Norfolk area under gunboat protection, had seized Suffolk, an important railway junction on the line to Petersburg, and Longstreet with 24,000 men whom Lee could ill spare had been charged with holding him back. He readily accepted the task because he thought he would not be needed on the Rappahannock. In fact, he had informed D. H. Hill that he really believed Burnside's mud march would be the last against the Army of Northern Virginia, that they could hold their line with a reduced force, and that the war would be over in five or six months at most. "Our Army seems somewhat spoilt," he crowed. "The troops seem to think they can whip the Yankees with the greatest ease whenever they may choose to come, and wherever they come. I have more confidence myself than I ever had before, and I believe that I have always had more than any other man in the Confederacy." At the very crisis of Hooker's advance he kept his aplomb, and before he heard the final result wrote Hill again that he was certain "we had abundance of time to operate whenever we chose." Abundance of time! Yet it was essential to maintain Longstreet where he was, his department (which soon included Richmond and North Carolina) requiring its 44,000 effective troops, for Northern forces were as strong.[16]

The other main reasons for Lee's numerical weakness lay in the bad operation of the conscription laws, widespread evasions and desertions, and crippling shortages of transport, food, and clothing. The heavy toll of the Seven Days, Second Manassas, and Antietam, with the steady drain from disease and exhaustion, could not be made good. The draft act passed in the spring of 1862, applying to male whites between seventeen and thirty-five, was amended that fall to raise the age limit ten years higher. But the exemptions from the outset included a wide range of men: civil officials, railroad and river workers, miners, laborers in cotton, woolen, and metals establishments, ministers, college and academy teachers, and hospital personnel. Moreover, they were soon enlarged. Any master or overseer controlling twenty or more slaves was exempted, and any stockman with 500 head of sheep or cattle or 250 horses and mules.[17] Skulking, cheating, and malingering stained the splendid record of Southern heroism as badly as the Northern. Fraudulent exemption papers were as well known in the Confederacy as in the Union, diseases were as often feigned, and bombproof positions in the government were as anxiously sought. Conscripts could hire substitutes among men not subject to the draft, and a brisk brokerage business in supplying them arose. And as absence without leave more than decimated every Northern camp, so it played havoc with the Southern army. Some deserters were Union sympathizers conscripted against their will, some were men whose wives wrote that they were

16 Longstreet, Jan. 29, May 6, 1863, to Hill, D. H. Hill Papers; Freeman, *Lee*, II, 499 ff.
17 Coulter, *Confederate States*, 314-330.

barefoot and ragged and their children crying for proper food, and some, of course, were plain slackers.[18]

Confederate authorities had estimated that the conscription laws of 1862 would add 105,000 men to the armies, raising their totals to about 500,000; only those between 35 and 40 years of age being called out immediately. The problem of supply was so difficult that a larger number could not well be kept in the field. Uniforms, footgear, meat, grain, and above all transportation were painfully limited. Lee was especially troubled by shortages of horses and forage, while supply trains moved on the railways with increasing uncertainty.[19] Along the railway lines an immense congestion was becoming evident, and a city or army might be threatened by famine while the countryside bulged with food, and supplies piled up at a bottleneck fifty miles away. The shortage of labor for military work was approaching a crisis which would compel Davis to consider gathering tens of thousands of slaves by purchase or confiscation.

But however few and ill-supplied Lee's veterans might be, their heroism never wavered; and the smaller the army, the firmer the bonds which knit it togther. Seeing his men brave heat, thirst, ravines, thickets, and murderous artillery fire to attack at Malvern Hill, Lee had exclaimed: "No fighting on earth could surpass it." Yet again and again the Southern troops equaled that display of combined endurance and valor. They would advance unhesitatingly to certain death, as Hood's men did in the cornfield at Antietam. Their very hardships, patiently shared, gave them a sense of fast comradeship. Building "merrimacks," or improvised lean-tos, for night shelter; cooking dough by twisting it around a ramrod and holding it over the fire; eating calamus, green corn, bullfrogs, and anything else remotely edible; charging with the rebel yell—through it all they took pride in the sense that they were making history. Some youths suffered from homesickness, and then became so attached to comrades, the camp mess, and the company file that when on leave they longed to get back, a strange conflict between homesickness and campsickness raging in their breasts. The drafted men fought as bravely as anyone, though a certain stigma did attach to the name "conscript." Vigorous boys found delight in a leisurely march, twenty miles a day,

18 Conscription is fully treated in Coulter, *Confederate States*, Ch. XV; Moore, *Conscription and Conflict in the Confederacy*, 114-161; Wiley, *Life of Johnny Reb*, 123-150; and Wesley, *The Collapse of the Confederacy*, 74-104, as in numerous military biographies.

19 Freeman, *Lee*, II, 491-495, describes Confederate shortages, the cruel severity of the winter of 1862-63, the onset of scurvy, and the danger that lack of wagons, horses, and feed would paralyze artillery as well as needed supplies. Appendix I of Freeman, *Lee's Lieutenants*, I, 677 ff., offers an analysis of the weakness of Virginia railroads. They began the war with 136 good and 44 defective locomotives, and 2,220 passenger and freight cars. But sidings and turnouts were inadequate, the 432 wooden bridges could easily be destroyed, and even when lines served the same city managers often refused to connect their tracks.

through the Virginia landscape, ending with camp in the woods where fire after fire sprang up in the darkness, gleaming redly on stacked arms and dark forms moving about the blaze.[20]

The individualism of the Confederate soldier excelled that of the Eastern troops in the Union army. The men marched loosely, and though they might go into battle in good order, the first shots from enemy rifles scattered the ranks and set every man to fighting for himself. He might stand up, kneel, or lie down, he took shelter as he liked, and he spoke freely to his comrades: "How many cartridges you got?"; "Looky here, Butler, mind how you shoot, that ball didn't miss my head two inches"; "Cap'n, don't you think we'd better move up a little, just along that knoll?"[21] Sometimes a quick-eyed private in the line would see an opportunity that must be seized without delay. He would spring up, shouting "Charge, boys, charge!" and with a volley of shots and yells, the long, loose-jointed line would coil rapidly forward, while its slain and wounded dropped here and there. Many a Southern lad had a touch of poetry in his nature. One North Carolinian who became a Northern prisoner thus hymned the Confederate battleflag:

The colors drop, are seized again—again drop, and are again lifted, no man in reach daring to pass them by on the ground—colors, not bright and whole and clean as when they came first from the white embroidering fingers, but as clutched in the storm of battle with grimy, bloody hands, and torn into shreds by shot and shell. Oh, how it thrilled the heart of a soldier, when he had been long away from the army, to catch sight again of his red battle-flag, upheld on its white staff of pine, its tatters snapping in the wind!—that red rag, crossed with blue, with white stars sprinkling the cross within, tied to a slim, barked pine sapling with leather thongs cut from a soldier's shoe! This rough red rag my soul loved with a lover's love. How often in long prison days have I sat and dreamed over it, imagining friends come to release us, and my first meeting with its fairness! How I clasped it in my arms, and kissed it, and cried over it![22]

How could such soldiers, magnificently led, be defeated?

[III]

"I have Lee's army in one hand and Richmond in the other," Hooker exultantly told his aides as he rode up to Chancellorsville. But did he? He had to reckon with Lee.

That general, recently ill and under medical attention at Guiney's Station,

---

20   Joseph Clay Stiles Papers, HL; Henry Kyd Douglas, *I Rode With Stonewall, passim.*
21   MS Recs. of Henry Greenwood Benson, Univ. of N. Carolina.
22   *Ibid., ut sup.*

and just returned to duty, was asleep when one of Jackson's staff captains awoke him with news that the enemy was crossing. "Well," he remarked genially, "I thought I heard firing, and was beginning to think it was time some of you young fellows were coming to tell me what it was all about. Tell your good general I am sure he knows what to do. I will meet him at the front very soon." He at once joined Stonewall in studying reports of Union movements in the fogbound territory as couriers came in. His first telegram to Richmond gave warning of a general advance, and asked that troops not needed south of the James be moved up. His second telegram the same day, April 29, was more urgent. Hooker was crossing downstream in large force while upstream at Kelley's Ford the 14,000 infantry of Howard's corps, with cavalry and artillery, had swarmed over. He wanted all available troops sent by rail or road as rapidly as possible.[23]

As Hooker's main forces concentrated by various lines at Chancellorsville crossroads, Lee saw that their primary object was to crush the Confederate left. The wide area covering the western approaches to the crossroads, filled with scrubby trees and brush, was called the Wilderness. Its unworkable clay soil, boggy in spring and brick-hard in summer, was useless for crops, and in places nearly as impassable as an Amazonian jungle. Union troops had swarmed into this tangled terrain by three roads, pushing through it to a point beyond, where a ridge and open field gave advantageous scope for maneuver; then Hooker had called them back to a really detestable position on low flat ground amid the trees and thickets. Lee saw that he must swing his northward-facing army around toward the west to confront them. This he did, leaving Early on the river at Fredericksburg. As the Confederate lines stiffened, their scouts and advanced parties felt out the whole line of the Northern forces. They made strong feints, drove in pickets, and used sharpshooters to kill officers and artillery horses. From their reports Lee gathered that the four corps which assembled at Chancellorsville, after their swift advance, had unaccountably paused, as if their leader had yielded to timidity. Hooker had obviously forgotten his injunction to Stoneman and the cavalry: "Celerity, audacity, and resolution are everything in battle."

Even so, to the Southern commanders the situation must have seemed desperate; for they were outnumbered two to one, taken in flank, and forced hurriedly to reshift their lines. Far into the night of May 1, Lee and Jackson debated their slender possibilities. What could be done? Lee had ascertained by a reconnaissance that the Union left was too powerful in numbers and too well protected by Mineral Springs Run to attack, and he now received

23 Greeley, *Amer. Conflict,* II, 354; cf. Freeman and McWhiney, *Lee's Dispatches to Jefferson Davis,* 84–86.

reports that the center was almost impregnable. There remained Hooker's right. As the generals talked, Jeb Stuart rode up with fateful news. Fitzhugh Lee with his cavalry had found the enemy there badly exposed, its lines resting on no stream or hill, and its entrenchments facing in only one direction, south. Lee might throw part of his army around it by rapid stealthy marches, and take it in flank or rear.[24]

The decision was swiftly taken, and just as swiftly Lee confided the movement to Jackson, whom he could trust to march without pause and fight with demoniac energy. "General Stuart will cover your movement with his cavalry," he promised. Jackson, glowing with pleasure, rose and saluted: "My troops will move at four o'clock." But just how would he move? That question was resolved before dawn. A chaplain whose family owned land in the district, and who therefore knew something of the roads, said that he had heard of a route across Hooker's front to his right, and the proprietor of an iron furnace deep in the woods furnished the clinching information: a twelve-mile woods road, fit even for artillery and largely concealed from Union view, led around to the desired point.

Before eight o'clock of a cloudless day, May 2, the head of Jackson's column took up its march along the Wilderness byway or "furnace road" thus pointed out, and a little later men standing by the highway saw Stonewall and his staff pass on horseback. He and Lee had parted with a few pregnant sentences. Asked how many men he proposed to take, Jackson replied, "My whole corps." This meant fifteen brigades, or 28,000 infantry, and would leave Lee dangerously weakened. In fact, he would have fewer than 20,000 effectives. But a dire crisis justified dire risks, and after a moment's reflection Lee calmly rejoined, "Well, go on." This was the last meeting of the two great captains.[25]

Jackson's flanking march was efficiently but not hurriedly executed. He took no provisions, admonishing his men that they must either capture the Union supplies or starve. He ordered that all stragglers who failed to rejoin their commands and fight must be shot. Every effort was made to avoid detection, a cloud of cavalry scattering out to the right, with a line of skirmishers behind them, to drive back any Union scouts. In passing over ascents the troops crouched half-bent, trailing their arms, behind bushes. At the outset some Northern artillery on a distant hill shelled them, and once or twice sharpshooters fired into the column. They saw Lowe's balloon in the sky, and felt sure it had espied them.[26] Noon came, and they marched

24 Thomason, *Jeb Stuart*, 375-377, offers a vivid record.
25 Henderson's account is excellent, *Jackson*, II, 432; Freeman's in *Lee's Lieutenants*, II, 540-551, still better.
26 See army corr. in N. Y. *Tribune* May 8, quoting prisoners.

steadily forward. Early afternoon found them deep in the tanglewild between
the Culpeper plank road and the Rappahannock. They must attack and win
before dark. Jackson was now separated from Lee by many miles of brake,
ravine, and forest, and if he were repulsed, he might lose the war, for Hooker
could then drive his powerful center between the two Confederate leaders
and destroy them both.

It was past two when Stonewall halted his men along and south of the
plank road until, with Fitzhugh Lee as guide, he could reconnoiter the Federal
position. Slipping to the top of a cleared hill, the two officers saw below them
the Union entrenchments facing south, with an abattis in front, arms stacked
in the rear, and two cannon on the turnpike running east to Chancellorsville.
The soldiers were congregated in small groups, cooking, eating, sleeping, or
playing cards, with one knot butchering cattle. Jackson, who must have
worried throughout the march lest he find the foe strongly fortified on
the west and sternly alert, felt inexpressible relief. "I watched him closely
when he gazed on Howard's troops," writes Fitzhugh Lee. "His expression
was one of intense interest, his eyes burnt with a brilliant glow, and his face
was slightly flushed, radiant at the success of his flank movement." His lips
moved in prayer. Seeing at once that Fitzhugh Lee was right in recommending an attack along the turnpike, he ordered three divisions to form in line
of battle. At that moment Hooker and nearly all other high Union officers
were persuaded that Lee was retreating toward Richmond. Hooker at 4:10
P.M., in fact, ordered Sedgwick to capture Fredericksburg and vigorously
pursue the Confederates: "We know that the enemy is fleeing, trying to save
his trains." [27]

In the disposition of his troops Jackson took the greatest pains. He saw
that every brigadier and colonel had his instructions, posted staff officers to
maintain liaison among the divisions, and made sure that his guns were ready
for action. At six o'clock his preparations were completed. "Are you ready,
General Rodes?" asked Jackson. "Yes, sir," replied Rodes. "You can go
forward, then," quietly instructed Jackson. The bugles rang out, their last
notes drowned by the rebel yell. Confederacy artillery bellowed, and the
musketry of the advancing line rattled.

The Union cannon planted on the road were instantly taken. The two
outer regiments on the Northern flank, German troops under Leopold von
Gilsa, were thrown into a helpless huddle before they fired three rounds.
Regiments behind them, attacked on three sides, were routed and driven
back in sheeplike confusion. The whole right brigade of Howard's corps was
quickly churned to pieces, and when another brigade faced about it was

27 O. R., I, xxv, pt. 2, p. 363.

shattered by Jackson's canister and the overwhelming rush of the Confederate mass. Union officers died in scores trying to form their lines, their men strewed the field, and General Devens was carried back wounded. For a time it seemed that the whole Eleventh Corps would be captured before any of it could rally on the open ground about Hooker's headquarters at the Chancellor house, and if one of Rodes's brigades had not lost touch and halted, this might have happened.[28]

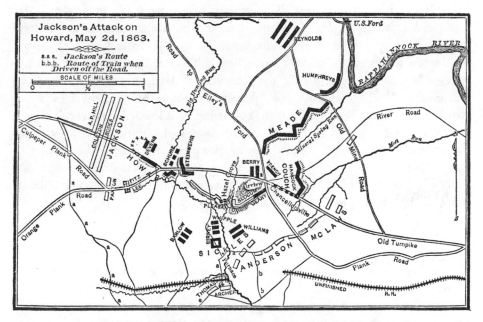

JACKSON'S ATTACK ON HOWARD

Within an hour, or before seven, the Confederates had completely defeated the 10,000 men of Howard's corps, and had scattered their remnants through the woods west of Chancellorsville, or sent them flying past that crossroads. Then the rebel advance slowed down. As twilight drew on, Confederate units became inextricably mixed in the broken fields and woodland, the men unable to find their leaders. Still Jackson, galloping along the lines on horseback, his hair streaming, his face alight with enthusiasm, urged his troops forward. The growing darkness, the thickening numbers of the enemy,

28 Howard's defensive story, *Autobiography,* I, 347-377, is less honest than might have been expected of "the Christian General."

the exhaustion of his men after sixteen hours of marching and fighting—some died of sheer fatigue—he disregarded. Before the action ended they must, if possible, seize the White House road half a mile ahead, the only road by which Hooker could retreat to the United States Ford. A full, brilliant moon shone down from the clear sky, and by its light the struggling Southerners fired, reloaded, and fired again, while Union and Confederate shells burst together in the thick, scrubby woods.

Meanwhile Lee had been attacking on his front. When he heard the boom of artillery and clatter of musketry in the distance, he passed word along the line: "Jackson at work; press them heavily everywhere." [29] Press them Mc-Laws did, attacking along the plank road and pike, and keeping the Second and Fifth corps so busy that Hooker sent in hot haste for Sickles and Pleasanton to hurry to his aid. For a bad half hour, half-ringed by the up-roar of battle, hearing the yells and drumfire of Jackson's men draw nearer, and seeing Howard's fugitives sweep past the house, Hooker must have felt that all was lost. But the broken remnants of Howard's Eleventh Corps finally formed a line. Other units hastened to their support, artillery raced up and opened with fifty guns on the Southerners, and as the troops of Rodes and Colston groped blindly in the gloom and Wilderness tangle, the rebel advance stopped. The firing died away, and officers of some Confederate units ordered their men to lie down on their arms.

[IV]

Hooker, after an able beginning, had made a cardinal error. He had gotten his army across the Rappahannock, had united the bulk of his troops there, and had pushed through the Wilderness and out into the open country beyond. He had compelled Lee to swing around to meet him. Had he then instantly used his superior force to crush Lee's main body, he would have been in a position to take in the rear the Confederates who under Early and Barksdale were holding the fortified ridge behind Fredericksburg. He had about 78,000 men as against Lee's 47,000, and by swift action might have carried everything before him. Who can explain why at the critical moment he lost his nerve, drew back from the open manueverable country, made his army fortify itself along the tangled Wilderness, and handed the initiative to Lee? While he entrenched, he left his right wing in the air, its flank un-protected. This particular blunder was not so much his own as Howard's, for when Hooker, aware that the flank was exposed, sent an extra brigade

29 London *Times,* June 16, 1863; corr. from Lee's headquarters dated May 6.

and battery to reinforce it, Howard rejected them as unnecessary. But the major error was all his own.

It arose from his irreparable delay at the critical moment. When he had concentrated four corps about Chancellorsville before 6 P.M. on April 30, with a fifth at hand, Lee's main force was still at Fredericksburg, for he had feared that Sedgwick would initiate the main attack there. Had Hooker pushed forward only four miles that evening, he could have seized favorable ground, gained perfect command of Banks's Ford, thus bringing Sedgwick's force much closer, and compelled Lee to fight under signal disadvantages. But as he failed to press on, the Confederates next morning gathered formidable forces in front of him and threw up entrenchments. When on May 1 he finally did move he got a hot reception from the enemy. He also found that his rear forces were impeded by the heavy thickets through which they had to move, the brush breaking up his regiments, sending aides wandering about aimlessly, and preventing concert of action as effectively as a heavy fog. Dismayed and confused, he ordered the army to draw back. Warren, Couch, and other officers protested bitterly, for they knew that only on open ground could large infantry forces and artillery be used freely. They knew, too, that Hooker's whole talent lay in the offensive, that the troops would be disheartened by a retrograde movement, and that while the absence of his cavalry—for Stoneman had started on his expedition—was not of prime importance while he advanced, he would miss its scouting and screening activities as soon as he fell back to the defensive.[30]

But Hooker had insisted on his stand. He had notified his army that he was giving up the initiative by an order at 4:30 P.M. on May 1: "The major-general commanding trusts that a suspension in the attack today will embolden the enemy to attack him." [31]

The main Union line on Saturday morning, May 2, the day of Jackson's flanking march, ran from the Rappahannock southwestward along Mineral Springs Run to the Chancellorsville crossroads, thence turning westward to form an obtuse triangle. It was a well-connected, well-fortified line, strong everywhere except on the right extremity. In a single night Howard's troops could have felled trees for an abattis, built breastworks, and placed artillery in redoubts which could sweep the ground west as well as south, but they remained inert. Hooker, inspecting the line at dawn, saw the defenseless nature of Howard's position. When he returned to his headquarters he learned

30 Doubleday, *Chancellorsville and Gettysburg,* 9–16; Bigelow, *Chancellorsville, passim;* Walker, *Second Army Corps,* 202–234; De Trobriand, *Four Years,* 435–470; Howard, *Autobiography,* I, Ch. XXII.
31 O. R., I, xxv, pt. 2, pp. 360, 361.

that enemy forces had been seen moving northeastward across his front, and realized that this might presage a flank attack. At 9:30 A.M. he therefore sent Howard and his neighbor Sickles identical warnings to examine the ground for favorable positions in the event of such a blow, and to keep strong reserves in hand.[32] He was explicit and emphatic. "The right of your line does not appear strong enough. No artificial defenses worth naming have been thrown up, and there appears to be a scarcity of troops at that point, and not, in the general's opinion, as favorably posted as might be. . . . Please advance your pickets. . . ." This while Jackson's column was stealthily moving on!

Though Howard later denied receiving this order, it is clear that Carl Schurz at his headquarters both read it to him, and put it in his hands. A few minutes later Howard received another and shorter order of the same purport.[33] Tired, sleepy, and convinced that Lee was retreating, he may have listened inattentively. He certainly paid no heed to Schurz's energetic monitions, based on information of his own, that the Confederates might at that moment be coming to fall upon his flank. "General," Schurz argued, "do you not think it certain that the enemy, attacking from the west, will crush Gilsa's two regiments, which are to protect our right and rear, at the first onset? Is there the slightest possibility for him to resist?" Howard merely mumbled, "Well, he will have to fight." In desperate mood,[34] Schurz took two regiments from his line facing south, and placed them facing west. Here, as we have seen, they were shortly caught in one of the great "skedaddles" of the war; a flight so headlong that some of the participants, streaking toward Fredericksburg with cries of "*Alles ist verloren*," ran through the Union battle line and picket line on the east into the Confederate ranks.

Even after the collapse of the Eleventh Corps, a body on which Hooker had never counted heavily, the contest remained undecided. Sunday morning, May 3, found Hooker in a better position than the previous evening. His main forces were intact, and he still outnumbered his foe eight to five. The divided Southern army could apparently reunite only by the heaviest fighting, for two divisions of Sickles' corps held a position between Lee and Jackson. Had they been maintained on their high ground here at Hazel Grove, a junction of the separated Southern forces would in fact have been impossible. But Hooker threw this last golden chance away by ordering the troops to fall back at dawn of May 3 to specified positions; and the moment they left, one of A. P. Hill's brigades seized the elevation. Jeb Stuart, grasping its

32   O. R., I, xxv, pt. 2, pp. 360, 361; *Battles and Leaders*, III, 196.
33   Text in Bigelow, *Chancellorsville*, 276, 277.
34   Schurz, *Reminiscences*, II, 416.

vital importance, crowned it with artillery, and began a brisk bombardment of Chancellorsville and other Northern positions below. He was able to enfilade the Union lines from the position which Hooker had thus presented him, and his murderous fire contributed largely to the result of the battle. The Union forces were pushed back into the Wilderness north of Chancellorsville and the house was set on fire.[35]

At its height the carnage and horror of this second day's battle surpassed the first. The fighting was "mad and desperate," writes one participant.[36] Behind the Northern breastworks which Stuart's fire raked, the dead were piled in every attitude of agony; along the roads were heaps of slain, mutilated horses, cannon overturned, and men still contending fiercely. When the woods caught fire many of the wounded, shrieking with fear, tried to clear away the brush and leaves from their position, and some were burned alive. Hooker, leaning against a column of Chancellorsville House when a cannonball struck it, was incapacitated for several hours, unable to give commands. Not for this reason, but because he was obsessed with the idea that he must keep a strong reserve ready for emergency, he never brought anything like his full force into the battle. Some 37,000 men, near at hand, eager to fight, and able if properly handled to sweep back Stuart's tired 26,000, were never used.

All the while Lincoln was tormented by fear that Hooker was not using all his forces. Butterfield telegraphed him early on May 3 that a battle was in progress. Lincoln telegraphed back: "Where is Gen. Hooker? Where is Sedgwick? Where is Stoneman?" To this Butterfield replied later in the day that Hooker was at Chancellorsville, Sedgwick was three or four miles from Fredericksburg on the road to Chancellorsville, and headquarters did not know where Stoneman was. Immediately on receiving this message Lincoln wrote an anxious reply: "I assume that Howard, Meade, and Slocum were in the main fight with Hooker. Was Sickles in it? Was Couch in it? Was Reynolds in it? Where is Reynolds? Is Sedgwick fighting Lee's rear? Or fighting the intrenchments around Fredericksburg?" He had in mind the order he had given Hooker when he reviewed the troops: "In your next fight, put in all your men." [37]

Although Meade and Reynolds wished to fling their fresh corps against

---

35 Doubleday, *Chancellorsville*, 45, 46; Dodge, *Chancellorsville*, 182 ff.
36 De Trobriand, *Four Years*, 457.
37 O. R., I, xxv, pt. 2, p. 377, with Hooker's own telegram to Lincoln, p. 379; Lincoln, *Works*, VI, 196, 197; N. M. Curtis, *The Sixteenth New York*, 254. When it was too late to help, Stoneman's cavalry raid did reach the outskirts of Richmond. A. L. Holliday wrote from that city May 8: ". . . had the Yankees chosen, I am confident that last Sunday night they might have dashed into Richmond and remained long enough to burn the Tredegar Works and the depots and then have gotten away with trifling loss." Cabell Papers, Univ. of Va. Library.

the Confederates, Hooker refused to let them do so. Later, when he was prostrated with pain, the line in front sent an urgent request for reinforcements, and he directed General Meade, who was with him, to take what action he thought best. It was an opportunity which Meade should have seized, for he could have turned the tide and driven the Southerners back. But because he did not wish to act without a clear order by Hooker or the next in command, Couch, and because of the late stage of the battle, he declined the responsibility. Reynolds also waited for orders. Meanwhile, an attempt by Sedgwick, who had crossed the Rappahannock three or four miles below Fredericksburg, to crash through Lee's rear and unite with the main Union army at Chancellorsville, achieved only a limited success. He overran Fredericksburg, took Marye's Heights behind the town, and then, after an unfortunate delay, moved forward only to meet a check. When darkness ended the fighting, the Confederates still held their lines between him and Hooker, they had the night to strengthen their position, and they were in less peril than Sedgwick himself—for Hooker made it plain to a messenger that he could not aid the general.[38]

Next day, May 4, while Hooker's army lay inert, Lee, after elaborate preparations, attacked Sedgwick on three sides. He forced the Union troops back toward the river, so that when night came on with a heavy fog, Sedgwick was glad to recross the Rappahannock. He had lost almost 5,000 men and accomplished nothing.

That night Hooker called a council of his corps commanders, stated the situation, and invited them to decide whether to remain on the field or fall back behind the river. Howard wished to remain for the poor reason that he hoped his corps could retrieve its reputation. Meade also wished to stay for the equivocal reason that he thought a crossing unsafe. Reynolds, exhausted, had gone to sleep saying he would vote as Meade decided. Sickles and Couch were for retreat. Hooker had in fact already decided to fall back. The force thus returned to its original ground, leaving its killed and wounded on the field, and abandoning 14 guns, 20,000 stand of arms, and other spoils to the Confederates. The total Union casualties, 12,197 killed or wounded and 5,000 missing, materially exceeded the Confederate losses of 10,266 killed and wounded, and 2,753 missing.[39] But such figures are far from stating the full truth. The Union army had again suffered a bitter blow to its morale, and the North was once more sunk in discouragement; the Confederate dead or disabled were irreplaceable.

38 E. S. Welch, Sedgwick, passim; G. T. Stevens, Sixth Corps, 200 ff.
39 These are Doubleday's figures. Freeman, Lee's Lieutenants, II, 644, puts the Union casualties at 16,804; the Confederate at 13,156.

[V]

One gap torn in the Southern command, indeed, made the Confederacy reel. We have seen that on the night of his attack Jackson, as his battle lines paused in the Wilderness, had insisted on pressing his advance to the vital Union road ahead. Meeting one brigadier, he gave peremptory orders, "Push right ahead, Lane; right ahead." General A. P. Hill came up and got the same directions: "Press them; cut them off from the United States Ford, Hill; press them." He hoped that the Confederates could extricate themselves from their disorder, reform their lines, and sweep onward. He could guess, though he did not know, that in front of him Union regiments were frenziedly using bayonets and canteens to scoop up earth, and with bare hands piling it in improvised breastworks.[40]

While he was thus heroically occupied in the front lines, with late twilight deepening the gloom among the trees, an officer expostulated with him. "You should not expose yourself so much," he pleaded. Jackson cut him short. "The danger is all over—the enemy is routed," he said. But the officer was right. Skirmishers on both sides were firing wildly; the lines of battle were stiffening. As Jackson and some companions turned their horses toward the Eighteenth North Carolina, an officer, alarmed by the strange horsemen coming from the direction of the Union forces, gave the order to fire. The volley brought down men and steeds. Jackson received three bullets—one through the right hand, two mangling the left arm and cutting the artery. As his horse Sorrel bolted, he was struck by a low branch in the face. An aide caught the steed and helped him to the ground. To A. P. Hill, who arrived on the scene after himself being fired on by Confederates, he said that he was badly hurt. So intertwined were the advance forces of the two armies that even while Hill spoke to him, two Union skirmishers emerged from the thickets a few feet away. Under heavy Union shelling, he was taken toward the rear. As he went, a brigade leader, Pender, told him that he feared his men must retreat. Jackson roused himself. Writes an eyewitness:

At this moment the scene was a fearful one. The air seemed to be alive with the shriek of shells and the whistling of bullets; horses riderless and mad with fright dashed in every direction; hundreds left the ranks and hurried to the rear, and the groans of the wounded and dying mingled with the wild shouts of others to be led again to the assault. Almost fainting as he was from loss of blood, desperately wounded, and in the midst of this awful uproar, Jackson's heart was unshaken. The words of Pender seemed to rouse him to life. Pushing aside those who supported him, he raised himself to his full height,

40 Freeman, *Lee's Lieutenants*, II, Ch. XXXIII; Henderson, II, 450; De Trobriand, *Four Years*, 449 ff.

and answered feebly, but distinctly enough to be heard above the din, "You must hold your ground, General Pender; you must hold out to the last, sir." [41]

Before dawn, Jackson's surgeon, Dr. Hunter McGuire, amputated his arm. The general recovered to learn that Hill had been wounded and that the Confederate lines were in great disorder; then he sank into exhausted sleep. Stuart ably took his place. The battle came to an end short of that complete victory which Stonewall might have won had he lived to carry his troops forward to the road which commanded the United States Ford.

The general, transferred to Guiney's Station, fell ill of pneumonia, sank, and on May 10 died. His last delirious words were characteristic. From the beginning of the war three ideas had burned in his brain: battle, the welfare of his soldiers, the hope of ultimate peace. "Order A. P. Hill to prepare for action! Pass the infantry to the front!" he ejaculated. Then, "Tell Major Hawks to advance the commissary train." And after an interval, very distinctly: "Let us cross over the river, and rest under the shade of the trees." [42] The words rang across the South:

> Yet even in battle-dreams, he sends supplies
> To those he loved so well.
> His army stands in battle-line arrayed;
> His couriers fly: all's done: now God decide!
> And not till then he saw the Other Side
> Or would accept the shade. [43]

The Southern wounded, in their base hospitals about Richmond, heard the tolling bells and knew what they meant. "Such gloom therefor as fell upon all the people!" wrote one. [44] Not since the death of Washington had the South so mourned a son. People had come to look on him as a man made invulnerable by his mission—to believe that the Providence in which he so firmly trusted would armor him against mischance. Their gratitude for his services, admiration for his character, and faith in his genius were given warmth by a deep affection for his personal traits. He was one of the two men whom the South could not spare.

Both armies were exhausted. With the Rappahannock between them, both were glad to settle into their former lines and rest. To be sure, unused Federal troops could have been thrown into battle again at once—had they possessed any confidence in Hooker. But most of the Union army had been badly mauled;

41   Quoted in Henderson, II, 452; cf. Burke Davis, *Jeb Stuart*, 293, 294, quoting W. F. Randolph of Jackson's staff. Lenoir Chambers, *Jackson*, II, 411–423, gives all the facts.
42   Henderson, II, 471; Freeman, *Lee's Lieutenants*, II, 670–682; Hunter McGuire, *Jackson*, 227–229.
43   Sidney Lanier's poem, written in 1865.
44   H. G. Benson, MS Recs., Univ. of N. C.

the men were torn by briers, stung all over by mosquitoes and flies, chilled by sleeping on the wet ground at night, dirty, tired, and discouraged. The Confederates had marched and fought until they could hardly stand; their units were badly disorganized; the damage done their railroads by Federal cavalry had put them on short rations. In Richmond, moreover, many men in the government hoped that a pause might lead to peace negotiations on the part of the North. All winter and spring the South had taken false hope from the outcries of the copperheads. Ever since Fredericksburg multitudes had shared Longstreet's belief that peace might be only a few months away. The great new victory seemed to open the way for a surge of Northern sentiment which would compel the Lincoln Administration to put an end to the bloodshed and suffering; and a cessation of fighting might give that sentiment opportunity to register itself.

This was of course a miscalculation. As the North reviewed the battle, feeling was divided between confusion over its course, for even the higher officers did not understand its complications, and disgust with the blundering leadership. "Once more the gallant army of the Potomac," exclaimed the *World*, "controlled by an imbecile department and led by an incompetent general, has been marched to fruitless slaughter." [45] Soldiers wrote home that they were unable to understand why, when Hooker had victory in his hands, he so stupidly let that golden prize turn into apples of Sodom. Bragg of the Wisconsin Iron Brigade told his wife that the whole experience seemed a wild, baffling nightmare. "I heard guns, shells passed over me, bullets whizzed by me, but whether discharged by friend or foe I know not. We were in a dense wilderness and backed out in an immense storm. I am alive—can eat—ride horseback—swear and smoke—that's about all the humanity there is left in me." [46] As fuller information filtered in, men were able to assess Hooker's follies: the folly of sending away his cavalry, which could have scouted Jackson's march; the folly of stopping his triumphant advance, retiring into the Wilderness, and tossing the initiative to Lee; the folly of employing his best arm, the artillery, so feebly; the folly of leaving nearly 40,000 troops unused in the battle; the final folly of giving up the vital ground of Hazel's Grove. They could see that his staff work had been poor, his boasted intelligence bad, his communications weak. Of what avail the immense Northern strength if put in such hands?

Yet no true patriot thought of giving up, and the Union began girding itself for still more titanic efforts. Some expressions of its fighting temper were unfortunate. The day real fighting began at Chancellorsville, May 1, Clement L. Vallandigham addressed a Democratic meeting at Mount Vernon, Ohio. Among

45 May 8, 1863.
46 May 10, 1863; Bragg Papers, Univ. of Wis.

the audience were two captains in plain garb taking notes. Nearly a month earlier Burnside, now head of the Department of the Ohio, had issued General Order No. 38, declaring that assertions of sympathy with the enemy, or any other manifestations of treason, real or implied, would not be permitted. Learning that Vallandigham had said that the "wicked and cruel war" was an attempt to erect a Republican despotism on the ruins of slavery, the general decided that he had breached the order. He sent soldiers who broke into Vallandigham's house in Dayton, arrested the ex-Congressman, and amid a riotous demonstration by would-be rescuers, haled him to Cincinnati, where he refused to plead before a court-martial.[47]

Sober men at once saw that large constitutional questions were bound up in the case. It was debatable whether Burnside had any right to arrest the man. It was still more questionable whether Vallandigham's speech justified his detention, for S. S. Cox, appearing in his defense, maintained that he had merely appealed to the public forum and the ballot box. The civil courts were open. Southern Ohio, now that the threat of the previous fall to Cincinnati had rolled far away, was no longer properly under martial law. Vallandigham should have been cited to a judge and grand jury. Instead, in a two-day trial the court-martial found him guilty of attempting to cripple the government, and sentenced him to close confinement until the war ended. Being a shrewd politician, Vallandigham used the pedestal to which he had been elevated to make a ringing appeal to the Democrats of Ohio to rally to his side in defending the Constitution, the laws, the Union, and liberty.

It was indispensable that Lincoln should act, for he was commander-in-chief and Burnside merely his lieutenant, and he was also guardian of civil liberties and constitutional right. With his fine sense of justice and of the spirit of Anglo-American law, he was taken aback by the arrest. Yet he could not feel sure that Burnside did not have real provocation, and he feared the effect on the army and public sentiment of a flat annulment of what the general had done. "All the Cabinet," the President telegraphed Burnside,[48] "regretted the necessity of arresting . . . Vallandigham, some perhaps doubting there was a real necessity for it; but being done, all were for seeing you through with it." This was the voice of expediency, which ill suited Lincoln. How deeply the President was troubled was made manifest by his action in altering Vallandigham's sentence of imprisonment to one of transfer within the Confederate lines. Thus made a figure of mockery, "Val" was taken under military escort to rebel outposts, and was soon being greeted, none too enthusiastically, by Southern leaders.

47 J. L. Vallandigham, *Life of C. L. Vallandigham*, 277 ff.; N. Y. *Times, Tribune*, May 6–7, 1863.
48 May 29, 1863; Nicolay and Hay, *Lincoln*, VII, 329–339.

Lincoln's sensitiveness was further illustrated by the pains he took in composing a long justificatory document. Addressed to Erastus Corning and other protestants against military arrests, it was in the main a labored and unhappy document. Here and there, however, it was illumined by touches of the simple eloquence that was seldom far from his pen. He met the objection to Vallandigham's arrest on two grounds: that the man was damaging the army, on which the existence of the nation now depended, and that since the government was compelled to shoot deserters, it had an unquestionable right to deal severely with wily agitators whose words induced guileless soldiers to desert.[49] The first argument raised a question of fact; the second the dubious claim that men might be punished for the *tendency* of their words. It was true, however, that Lincoln's duty was to think first and foremost of the nation's safety, now desperately imperiled, and that he could well wonder, as he remarked, whether posterity would not censure him for arresting too few men rather than too many. The land in which Vallandigham now began wandering had far less liberty of speech and action than the North. Infringements on the right of free speech were not carried to such an unjustifiable extreme during the Civil War as later during and after the First World War, when the Espionage and Sedition Acts of 1917–18 lent authority to deplorable interferences.

But for the reasons why the nation took in its stride not only such episodes as this, but grave reverses in the field, we must turn to the progress it had made in organizing its energies.

49 June 12, 1863; *Works*, VI, 260–269. I shall later resume this subject. The best modern thought endorses Justice Jackson's statement of 1950 (in 339 U.S., 442, 443): "While the Governments, State and Federal, have expansive powers to curtail action, and some small powers to curtail speech or writing, I think neither has any power, on any pretext, directly or indirectly to attempt foreclosure of any line of thought." Cf. David Fellman, *The Limits of Freedom*, 87–123.

18

Business of War

"THE GOVERNMENT," wrote Seward as the news of Chancellorsville sank in, "is performing its painful duty with no abatement of energy, and no diminution of confidence."[1] Lincoln, visiting the Army of the Potomac once more, declaring that he would gladly take a hundred thousand colored troops into the service, trying to allay the chronic disorder in Missouri by appointing John M. Schofield to command, and studying the problem of reconstruction in Louisiana, was certainly doing his best, as he assured the Presbyterian General Assembly, to keep the ship of state afloat. Chase, toiling to organize the national banking system which Congress had authorized early in the year, and helping Jay Cooke sell the 5-20 bonds, was indefatigable. Stanton never paused in his labors. Had military leaders done as well as the Administration, the country would have been in happy estate.

Several commanders were particularly vexatious. Burnside followed his arrest of Vallandigham by a still more unjustifiable order June 1 forbidding circulation of the New York *World* in his department (Ohio, Indiana, Illinois), and suppressing the Chicago *Times*. A meeting of representatives of fifteen New York dailies and weeklies, with Greeley as chairman, delivered a spirited protest. Interferences with freedom of the press are particularly obnoxious, and Lincoln asked Stanton to revoke or suspend the *Times* order. Hooker, meanwhile, was demonstrating his lack of character in two ways, by garbling the news of his defeat, and encouraging friends to shift the blame to Howard and Sedgwick.

Making no report on the battle, Hooker issued instead a mendacious general order dated May 6, 1863. The army had added to its glory, he wrote; it had executed long marches, crossed rivers, surprised the enemy in his trenches, inflicted heavier blows than those received, taken 5,000 prisoners, and put *hors de combat* 18,000 troops. Only the subordinate generals, he made it plain, had failed! What was worse, Hooker and his intimates spread reports through the army and press that Halleck, ignorant and prejudiced, had hampered him on every hand and fatally botched his plans. He even intimated that he had been

---

1 May 19, 1863; *Seward at Washington*, III, 166.

given only two hours to attend to the battle, the other twenty-two being absorbed by the Washington authorities.[2] Another center of discontent was Carl Schurz, eager to see Howard displaced and Sigel restored to his corps command. Hooker, quite ready to have Howard made a partial scapegoat, encouraged the tactless Schurz to use all his influence with Lincoln, and promised that if Sigel came back he would strengthen his force and help him use it.[3]

Not unnaturally, the press demanded a general shake-up of officers. Chase, who continued to stand behind Hooker, was as usual slightly two-faced. Visiting Washington, Howard talked with Chase as "my friend and favorite"; yet Chase had written Hooker a few days earlier urging that Sigel be put in place of Howard.[4] Radical members of the Committee on the Conduct of the War of course rallied to Hooker as their old favorite, and in due time issued a report which whitewashed him and stained the scutcheons of other officers. Halleck wanted to oust the commander. For the time being, however, the patient Lincoln made no changes. He determined not to remove the young "Christian general" without another trial, telling critics: "Give him time, and he will bring things straight." [5] He also decided to give Hooker a longer tenure, though he remarked with unwonted acidity: "If he had been killed by the shot that stunned him, we should have been successful." Couch with equal acidity declared that the trouble with Hooker at the critical moment was not that he had too much liquor, as some men falsely asserted; it was that he did not have liquor enough.

2   *Works*, 234–254. Many soldiers believed such stories; see David Craft, *Hist. 141st Pa. Vols.*, iii; J. D. Bloodgood, *Personal Rems.*, Chs. VII, VIII. The fact was that between crossing the Rappahannock and retreating behind it Halleck had no communication with Hooker; neither did Stanton; and Lincoln merely telegraphed for information on the struggle and the use of troops. Halleck to Lieber, Oct. 13, 1863, Lieber Papers, HL. For Hooker's letter of Feb. 28, 1864, placing on Sedgwick the onus of the failure to win victory, see *Century Mag.*, N. S., XIII (April, 1888).

3   Schurz was horrified by press criticism of the German troops and particularly his own division for their confusion and panic. He wrote in his official report of May 12 that "we have been overwhelmed by the army and the press with abuse and insult beyond measure. We have borne as much as human nature can endure." It was not his division that was driven back, but Devens'. The angry general wrote Howard so bitter a letter that, said Howard, "I thought I should never survive it, but I have." See Schurz's letters in Sigel Papers, N. Y. Hist. Soc.; *Rems.*, II, 432–433; Gen. George N. Gordon, *A War Diary of Events*, 149.

Some German troops did fall into panic at Chancellorsville, just as Yankee troops ran elsewhere. Ella Lonn's *Foreigners in the Confederacy* and *Foreigners in the Union Army and Navy*, taken together, explode the myth that a polyglot Union army fought a completely Anglo-Saxon Confederate army. She proves on the one hand that tens of thousands of foreign-born helped fill the Southern ranks. On the other, she shows that nearly four-fifths of the Northern soldiers were native-born. These books, like those of Bell I. Wiley, make it clear that Yank and Reb were surprisingly alike. The Northerner was more literate, more intellectual, more political-minded, and more practical; the Southerner had more humor, more imagination, a warmer emotionalism, and a deeper concern for his cause.

4   Carpenter, MS Life of Howard; Schuckers, *Chase*, 467.

5   Howard, "Personal Recs. of Lincoln," *Century Mag.*, N. S., LXXV (April, 1908), 873–877

But Hooker's days as head of the army were numbered. The most dangerous of all generals is the general who loses his nerve in a supreme crisis. A. K. McClure said of "Fighting Joe": "He could play the best game of poker I ever saw until it came to the point when he should go a thousand better, and then he would flunk." And Lee was about to bet ten thousand!

The North quickly rallied from the news of Chancellorsville, for it saw that its main strength was untouched. The strain of war, felt with such increasing rigor in the South that May opened with an ominous bread riot of white-faced, emaciated people in Richmond,[6] was accepted by the North with elasticity. From early June people were hopeful of the capture of Vicksburg—"within a day or two," predicted the *Tribune*'s Wall Street column of June 8. News that the Negro outfit at Port Hudson, the Second Louisiana Native Guards, had lost 600 out of 900 men in its impetuous charge, dispelled some of the doubts about colored troops. "The repulse of Hooker and the disappointment attending it," Charles Eliot Norton assured Olmsted, "have strengthened and improved the public spirit. Our defeats are doing more to make us a nation, and to free the land from slavery, than our victories." [7]

[I]

By the standards of the time, the war administration in the middle of 1863 had become an enormous machine. The executive departments were no longer grossly understaffed, and their labors were increasingly complicated and proficient.

Visitors at the War Department, for example, which now hummed like a hive in several buildings, found Stanton working three chief assistants to death—quite literally in at least one instance: Peter H. Watson, who had taken over most of the duties once performed by Thomas A. Scott, John Tucker, who handled the large contracts and the shipping, and C. P. Wolcott, who supervised State relations and most other correspondence. Stanton and Watson had been law partners, and when Stanton was offered the Secretaryship at $8,000 he had told his associate: "Why, I cannot afford to give up a practice worth three or four times as much." Watson sternly reminded him of his patriotic duty. Later Stanton summoned Watson to Washington, and when he arrived, handed him his appointment as Assistant Secretary at $3,000. "Why, I cannot afford—" began Watson; and Stanton instantly turned the tables on him.[8] Elsewhere in the department nearly two score executives

---

6 For McClure, *Hebert*, 225; for the riot, Strode, *Davis*, 381-383.
7 May 20, 1863, Olmsted Papers, LC.
8 L. D. Ingersoll, *Hist. War Dept.*, 345, 346. Tom Scott left the War Dept. in June, 1862, and C. A. Dana became Asst. Secretary in December, 1863; Dana, *Recs.*, 156 ff. Wolcott sank under overwork.

pushed and tugged at the careening car of Mars; and two of them, Montgomery C. Meigs as Quartermaster-General and William A. Hammond as Surgeon-General, displayed superlative imagination and address.

The Navy Department similarly had not only Welles as head and Fox as Assistant Secretary, but a score of bureau chiefs and their aides supervising ever-crescent activities—equipment and recruiting, yards and docks, construction and repair, provisions and clothing, medicine and surgery. The Treasury Department, with George Harrington as Chase's able Assistant Secretary, again mustered a score of important functionaries, of whom Joseph J. Lewis as commissioner of internal revenue and John J. Cisco in charge of New York affairs were the chief. All the departments groaned under a load of paper work that old-time bureaucrats found stupendous. The mere enumeration of the excise taxes to be collected filled seventeen pages of fine print;[9] the list of Army rolls, returns, and reports to be sent continuously to the War Department made filing clerks and auditors shudder. And the undertakings of every department seemed to ramify endlessly.

An illustration of this fact is furnished by the government railroad and telegraph service. Railway transportation was indispensable to haulage of supplies and most active field operations alike. After the emergency activities of Scott and Carnegie in 1861, Congress early the next year authorized the President to take possession of all roads and telegraph lines in the nation, and if necessary operate them for the government's benefit. In February, 1862, Stanton appointed Daniel C. McCallum as military director and superintendent of railroads, with full power to seize and use all equipment necessary. This Scottish-born engineer, bridgebuilder, and poet, beginning with the seven-mile line from Washington to Alexandria, steadily expanded his corps of construction workers. Most of his activities in the first two years lay in Virginia, where he built and rebuilt roads, raised and re-raised bridges, as the battle lines swayed back and forth. He was indispensable in McClellan's Peninsular and Antietam campaigns, and in Pope's, Burnside's, and Hooker's operations. Near the close of 1863, his Eastern railroad corps being fully organized and trained, he went West to take up his headquarters at Nashville. Before the war ended he administered more than 2,000 miles of railway, bossed 11,000 construction workers at a time, built about 650 miles of lines, and spent nearly $40,000,000.[10]

"Not only were the men continually exposed to great danger from the regular forces of the enemy, guerrillas, scouting parties, etc.," wrote McCallum later, "but owing to the circumstances under which military railroads must

9   See text in *Natl. Almanac*, 1864, pp. 90–107.

10   McCallum's Report on Mil. Railroads of the US, 39th Cong. 1st Sess., House Exec. Doc. No. 1; Ingersoll, *War Dept.*, 353–360; Weber, *Northern Railroads in the Civil War*, 134–168.

be constructed and operated, what are considered the ordinary risks upon civil railroads are vastly increased on military lines. . . . It was by no means unusual for men to be out with their trains from five to ten days, without sleep, except what could be snatched upon their engines and cars while the same were standing to be loaded or unloaded, with but scanty food or perhaps no food at all for days together. . . ." The expertness of McCallum's men excited admiration. One story related that as the enemy was about to blow up an important tunnel, a Confederate exclaimed that it was no use; the Union army carried long duplicates of all tunnels! The total length of McCallum's wartime bridges was put at twenty-six miles.

Principles upon which McCallum and his friend and subordinate Herman Haupt could efficiently work were laid down by a War Department directive in the fall of 1862. Officers were ordered on pain of discharge to refrain from interference with the civilian superintendents of the roads, and to furnish them sufficient men to load and unload cars promptly.[11] McCallum worked in particularly close liaison with quartermasters. Over the lines going south went troops, arms, ammunition, forage, clothing, food; over the same lines coming north passed the wounded, sick, refugees, prisoners, freedmen, and captured war material. He had altogether 419 engines and 6,330 cars under his control. Both he and Haupt showed admirable leadership, and both faced up to military commanders with unflinching nerve. When the drunken Sturgis at the crisis of Second Bull Run held up four trains which were carrying wounded and were needed to bring back reinforcements—an act that kept 10,000 men out of the battle—Haupt threatened him with arrest. As Burnside began his inept command of the Army of the Potomac, Haupt told him bluntly what an idiot he was to think the Orange & Alexandria could be counted on to supply his troops.[12] Then Haupt went on to make the line almost accomplish the impossible.

Rates for government work on the privately owned lines were a matter of complex difficulty. The War Department by a circular of July 12, 1861, fixed a general tariff of two cents a mile per man for troops, and normal first-class rates for equipment, munitions, and supplies. But the government encountered so many instances of exorbitant charges that it called a convention of representatives of the principal railroads in Washington in February, 1862; and this body drew up an elaborate schedule which Quartermaster-General Meigs shortly approved.[13] It continued the general rate of two cents a mile for carrying troops, each man being allowed eighty pounds of baggage.

11 Weber, Northern Railroads, 158.
12 Haupt, Rems., 74, 76, 79, 158, 159.
13 Meigs, Circular, May 1, 1862, QMG Letterbook No. 60, pp. 33-35, NA.

The general charge for supplies, munitions, and other freight was to be 10 per cent below the printed tariffs of the various companies. The department for its part gave the lines assurance that it would not deliberately encourage harsh competition for the purpose of bringing down rates.[14] Meigs also made every effort to divide freight equitably among the available roads, materials carried West, for example, being apportioned among the Erie, the New York Central, and the Pennsylvania lines. It appears that the government did its best to treat the railways generously. For example, Meigs early in 1863 recommended that the Louisville & Nashville be allowed prewar freight rates, exceeding those fixed by the convention, to compensate it for its repair of damages inflicted by military action.[15] The government instructed its agents always to negotiate with the proper company officers, and to allow them to direct all transport operations free from meddling interference.

The provision of sufficient cars, locomotives, and appurtenances was another thorny problem. Congress empowered the President to take possession of needed equipment, but did not specifically authorize purchase. McCallum therefore at first obtained cars and engines on loan, it being understood that he would get an impartial valuation made, pay a per diem allowance for ordinary use with an extra sum for any unusual depreciation, and make full compensation for any property not returned. The railroads proved reluctant to lend their stock, however, and once more the government bowed to their wishes, buying material in the regular markets and contracting for manufactures.[16] In the summer of 1862 McCallum placed his first contract for 20 locomotives and 250 cars, and April, 1864, found manufacturers delivering the government one locomotive a day. Outright purchases of rolling stock were meanwhile made from the Illinois Central and other roads.

"There was but one way," he later wrote,[17] "to secure the locomotives and deal fairly with the manufacturers. They were required to discontinue work in their then existing contracts, and use the materials in and upon engines to be built at once for the Government, for which they were to be paid such additional costs for material as they could satisfactorily show had arisen. . . . I was met by them in a spirit of hearty cooperation."

The railway administration made steady contributions to the unification of

14 Meigs to Trowbridge, March 4, 1862, QMG Letterbook No. 58, p. 325; NA.
15 Meigs to Stanton, March 19, 1863, QMG Letters to War Dept., Book No. 7, pp. 32, 33; NA. The railroads did not always show equal scruple in return. Rebates, pooling arrangements, the short-and-long-haul abuse, and other practices later indicted by the Grangers, were already common, as government officers found; so were overcharges. On this subject more will be said later.
16 McCallum to A. P. Robinson, March 21, to G. O. D. Lilly, March 29, 1862, Press Copybook Office of Supt. of Govt. Rrs., Series A; NA.
17 McCallum to Meigs, Aug. 26, 1862, *ibid.*

the rail system of the North. It forged links between separated lines, as in connecting the North Missouri with the St. Louis & Iron Mountain, and the Allegheny Valley with the Pittsburgh, Fort Wayne, & Chicago, in 1862. It built extensions to the roads converging in Pittsburgh so that they all reached the arsenal there.[18] It altered the gauges of some lines—for example, the 5-foot gauge of the Norfolk & Petersburg—to make them conform to the standard English gauge of 4 feet 8½ inches. It improved terminals, and gave efficiency to their freight handling. This mobilization of the railroads was one phase of Union operations which deeply interested a group of German observers, including Count Zeppelin, who visited the country, and they later applied its lessons in the wars of 1866 and 1870.[19]

[II]

The first task of the government, as it girded itself in 1863 for greater efforts, was to fill up the armies; the second was to improve their arms, equipment, and sustenance. Under the bludgeon of disaster, the unsystematic nation was learning system, the formless society was taking form, the adolescent economy was gaining maturity. Progress, however, was sometimes timid and blundering—and nowhere more so than in the management of recruiting.

If any fact was clear to the North early in 1863, it was that volunteering was inadequate and that the nation needed more system instantly to fill its ranks. Battle and disease had struck heavily in the previous year. The 88,000 militia who had enlisted under Lincoln's August call for nine-months' men would begin going home in May; and few now believed that victory could be won before the terms of the three-years' regiments of 1861 expired. These 300 regiments of veterans could ill be spared. Meanwhile, discharges for disability, an inevitable sequel of worthless physical examinations at the time of enlistment, continued numerous. The Sanitary Commission had reported to Lincoln, on the basis of a survey, that probably a quarter of the men accepted during 1861 were unfit for service; and it and C. S. Tripler, medical director of the Army of the Potomac, agreed that some examining doctors had been bribed to fill up regiments.[20] The horrifying total of desertions presented a problem so baffling that when Provost-Marshal General Simeon Draper made

18 Watson to J. Rollins, April 22. 1862, War Office Military Book 49b.
19 Cf. Edwin A. Pratt, *Rise of Rail Power*, 23, 24, on McCallum.
20 Halleck informed Banks June 27, 1863, that he could not send him more troops; the discharge of nine-months' and two-years' men "has so reduced our forces that we can hardly defend Washington and Baltimore." Early in August he wrote Gov. Austin Blair of Michigan that those discharged and to be discharged amounted to something over 70,000. Halleck Papers, HL.

an estimate late in 1862 that 100,000 men were absent without permission, he believed that not more than a third could be caught. Meanwhile, said Henry Wilson, "volunteers we cannot obtain." [21]

One reason why seven million white Southerners had been able to hold more than twenty million Northerners at bay, as Greeley's *Tribune* said, was that the South had a better recruitment system. It resorted to a general draft nearly a year before the North. When men were accepted, the South distributed them among the old regiments, keeping each as nearly as possible up to full strength; the North, on the contrary, kept raising new regiments and letting the old ones dwindle to weakness. "Our many memorable successes," wrote Davis, "are with justice ascribed in large measure to the reorganization and reinforcement of our armies under the operation of conscription." [22] Some of the Northern defeats could be ascribed to the failure to intermingle veterans and raw recruits. In theory, everybody applauded Napoleon's plan of dividing regiments into battalions, one of which, the depot battalion, stayed at home in a garrison town, training and forwarding troops. McClellan's dictum that 50,000 recruits in old regiments would be better than 100,000 in new ones was well remembered. But the government kept on letting the States raise new outfits.

Congress at last, by the law which Lincoln approved March 3, 1863, decreed a general conscription of male citizens between 20 and 45, for three years' service. It permitted few exemptions: none but the mentally or physically unfit, high government officers, and the only sons of dependent parents. Conscripts were to receive the same advances and Federal bounties as volunteers. Henry Wilson declared that it would be used to restore the strength of shattered units: "The nation needs not new regiments and more officers; it needs new bayonets in the war-wasted ranks of the veteran regiments." This seemed a momentous step. The measure passed the House 115 to 49, received wide editorial praise, and was hailed by commanders in the field. Rosecrans predicted that two months of the draft would increase the power of his army by half; Sherman wrote Grant that if the men were really used to fill the old regiments, a work which would require 600,000 men in all, the step would be more important than the capture of Vicksburg and Richmond together. Under the new law the Provost-Marshal General's office became a separate bureau in the War Department. Colonel James B. Fry correctly anticipated that

---

21 *Cong. Globe*, 37th Cong. 3rd Sess., 976 (Feb. 16, 1863). Of the nearly 200,000 men who deserted from the Northern armies during the war, not quite 76,000 were arrested and sent back; Lerwill, *Personnel Replacement System*, 76. Lincoln on March 10, 1863, proclaimed an amnesty to all absentees who reported for duty on or before April 1, 1863.

22 N. Y. *Tribune*, Feb. 6, 1863; *Messages and Papers of the Confederacy*, I, 294.

about 3,000,000 men would be enrolled, but he was all too optimistic in his calculation that some 425,000 would flow into the fighting forces.[23]

No measure of the war was a more stunning disappointment than this Draft Act of 1863. If the spirit had merits, the text was hopelessly blundering. To begin with, Congress, influenced by old militia practices, foreign examples, and bad arguments, provided that any drafted man might furnish a substitute or by payment of $300 obtain total exemption. It seemed to some members that citizens holding important civilian positions or with special family responsibilities should have the right to hire an alternate. It also seemed to them that with $300 for extra bounty, the government could hire as good men as most draftees. But Congress really opened a Pandora's box.[24] In the second place, Congress wrote into the law a provision that whenever a regiment fell below half the legal maximum, its companies were to be consolidated and its surplus officers discharged. Commanders in the field protested that this would deprive them of an indispensable array of the most experienced officers. They were able to resist execution of the foolish clause and minimize its effects, but it did harm nonetheless. And in the third place, the law was so loosely written that the government could easily forget about filling up depleted regiments. Just after Chancellorsville the War Department began permitting governors to enlist quite new units—forty regiments in all.

Amid sharp criticism, and in many places angry hostility, Fry's bureau organized a costly machinery, calculated the quotas of States and districts, and enrolled citizens. By July 1 it was actually drafting men in some areas. Grave difficulties instantly arose. The size of quotas was fixed according to the proportion of the population of a given district previously furnished to the armed services. Several States had already sent more than their share to the front, and were hence exempted. The computation of quotas proved an intricate matter. Figures of prior enlistments were often disputed; Fry's mode of reckoning, which made one enlistment for three years equal to four enlistments for nine months, was disputed; New England States which had long sent males West and kept females at home disputed the justice of balancing a million people in Massachusetts against a million in Illinois: and each State was ready to dispute about the number of its sons who had enlisted elsewhere. In New York, Governor Seymour expressed suspicion that Fry's office had assessed excessive quotas upon the Democratic districts of Man-

23 Sherman to Grant, June 2, 1863, O. R., I, xxiv, pt. 3, pp. 372, 373. Sherman wrote that the Western regiments did not average 300 men. Lerwill, *Personnel Replacement*, 93, 94, gives Fry's predictions.

24 Lieber to Halleck, March 16, 1863, Halleck Papers, HL; Morton to Stanton, March 6, Stanton Papers, LC. The money-commutation privilege was restricted in 1864 to conscientious objectors; Shannon, *Admin. and Org.*, II, 87. O. R., III, i, pp. 19–1198 covers recruiting and the draft fully, with illuminating letters by Fry.

hattan and Brooklyn to make sure that the Republicans would carry them in the next election, and he demanded an inquiry. Altogether, a running battle soon raged between governors and the War Department, with plenty of popular and official obstruction of the draft. The fierce local and State antagonism and the ebullitions of open violence we shall treat later.

It was soon plain that the draft would require a costly system of enforcement. It was also clear that it would breed swarms of cheats and cormorants, and that its directors would have to guard against the most ingenious evasions and frauds. Bounty jumpers, substitute brokers, and corrupt doctors appeared in noisome swarms. Their activities in all the large cities became one of the chief scandals of the war. Agents tried to palm off cripples, old men, escaped lunatics, and dipsomaniacs as substitutes. Emigrant-runners and sailor-kidnapers turned to the new source of revenue. In some districts a majority of the men drafted refused to come before the boards until compelled to do so. Substitutes by thousands pocketed their payments and bounties, deserted, and sold themselves over again. Fry, giving up hope of nearly a half-million new men, declared before the end of the year that the law was not really designed to raise and maintain an army, and that no sophistry could disguise its failure.[25]

A failure it was; yet not entirely so. The Draft Act did something, as its authors had expected, to stimulate volunteering. A young man reaching twenty was obviously wiser to offer his services, escape the stigma of conscription, get special State and local benefits, and join the regiment he liked, than be taken by the neck for service. For the War Department, as we have seen, authorized governors to recruit quite new regiments. This defeated the hope that the thin veteran units would be substantially strengthened. Altogether, they received only 21,331 men in the first ten months of 1863, with the result that one army corps which fought at Chickamauga this fall reported that its 33 regiments had an average strength of only 325 men.[26] Some regiments were kept alive only by the zealous exertions of their officers in canvassing farms, villages, and towns in occupied parts of the Borderland and South for recruits. In the end the drafts of 1863–64 gave all the armies a direct accretion of fewer than 170,000 men, and continued to offer a lesson in how *not* to manage recruiting.[27] But 170,000 men were worth a great deal, and the value of the Draft Act in its spur to volunteering, its proof of the

25 Fry to H. S. Lane, Dec. 20, 1863, O. R., III, iii, 1175–1177; Lerwill, *Personnel System*, 94, 95; "Examinations and Exemptions," N. Y. *Tribune*, Sept. 28, 1863; "The Recruiting Business in our City," N. Y. *Tribune*, Feb. 16, 1864; Gov. Austin Blair's message, Detroit *Free Press*, Jan. 20, 1864; Whitelaw Reid, *Ohio in the Civil War*, I, 204 ff.
26 Lerwill, *Replacement System*, 99.
27 O. R., III, iv, 927, 928; v, 486, 487. Of this number about 46,000 were conscripts and 118,000 substitutes. Nearly 87,000 men paid commutation money.

determination of the government, and its illustration of the possibilities of nation-wide organization, was by no means slight.

The national forces that had a total strength of 556,000 officers and enlisted men when 1862 ended had grown to a nominal 918,121 a year later. So many veterans had re-enlisted that the armies had gained in skill and toughness. Two Britons, Lieutenant-Colonel T. L. Galloway of the engineers and Captain H. J. Alderson of the artillery, who made an inspection tour early in 1864, pronounced the soldiers well behaved, brave, intelligent, and possessed of remarkable initiative.[28] The discipline of the artillery was good, of the infantry poor, and of the cavalry wretched; the visitors concluded that its defects arose from the scarcity of good officers and noncoms, but American individualism was probably a larger factor. Certainly the desertion rate alone proved bad discipline. But that the great volunteer armies were growing stronger, and that they showed splendid fighting qualities when led with even halfway talent, nobody could deny.

[III]

One prime source of increased army strength was the steady improvement in arms, equipment, commissary, and medical care. By Chancellorsville the infantry had enough good Springfield and Enfield rifled muskets (though not always well distributed), with an ever-larger sprinkling of Spencer repeating rifles. An equally great advance in firepower lay in the artillery, which in the East, as D. H. Hill on the Confederate side wrote, was "always the most effective arm." [29]

The artillery did a great deal, in the war of movement during the first three years, to overcome the general Confederate advantage of defensive positions. Throughout the century and the world, the defense was gaining in strength. Competent authority has estimated that in the Napoleonic Wars 20,000 fighting troops to the mile, including reserves—the number Wellington had at Waterloo—were normal to a defensive position. In the first three years of the Civil War 12,000 to the mile were regarded as standard, and later 5,000 were found sufficient, Lee holding the long Richmond-Petersburg line with even fewer.[30] If the Union superiority in artillery and general firepower could not atone for bad leadership, on such a field as Antietam it could make up for disadvantages of position.

We have noted the care which McClellan took before his Peninsular

28 *Report Upon the Mil. Affairs of the U. S. A.*, Br. War Office, 1864. The tour was made Feb.–June, 1864, and the report was expert.
29 D. H. Hill, *Battles and Leaders*, II, 355.
30 Liddell Hart, *Manchester Guardian Weekly*, June 25, 1959.

campaign to provide a powerful artillery arm under William F. Barry. He wished every division to have four batteries, consisting of at least four and if possible six light fieldpieces. He especially liked the 12-pounder smooth-bore Napoleon, a handy bronze muzzle-loader with an extreme range of 1,300 yards for solid shot and half as much for canister. He also insisted on an artillery reserve of a hundred guns, and a siege train of at least half that many— actually he took nearly a hundred to Yorktown. Altogether, when his forces set out in March, 1862, they had 92 batteries of 520 guns, with 12,500 men and 11,000 horses. In the broken, forested Virginia terrain, where canister and shrapnel were much more effective than long-range shells, McClellan correctly thought two-thirds of his guns should be Napoleons, but it was not until Antietam that he was able to approach the desired proportions. He could well pay tribute to the feat of the ordnance bureau in providing within seven months, by manufacture, purchase, or supply from arsenals, the splendid panoply he had for use.[31]

After the Peninsular campaign Barry's place was taken by H. J. Hunt, who had managed a hundred guns at Malvern Hill with memorable skill, and who remained the capable chief of artillery till the end of the war. Both men were West Pointers, Mexican War veterans, and members of the board which in 1856 had adopted a new set of artillery tactics. Hooker neglected his artillery, and paid a heavy price for it. At Murfreesboro, Rosecrans had 39 batteries, and put 27 of them into the contest under his able chief of ordnance, Horace Porter, who was later to become one of Grant's best aides. In the West Grant and Sherman made effective use of artillery. Just before the siege of Vicksburg the returns showed that Grant had 224 fieldpieces and 88 heavy guns, and was then ordering more from the North. Sherman always believed that ordnance was more important to raw troops than to veterans, but he employed it well.[32]

After the first two years Northern artillery supply never posed an acute problem. The ordnance bureau bought more than 2,000 cannon during 1862, and issued about 8,000 pieces altogether during the conflict; and the supplies of shot and shell were adequate. The weird early variety of calibers and patterns, which had compelled the government to carry 600 different kinds of ammunition, was rapidly reduced to manageable size.

But in artillery design the bureau showed the same conservatism as in its

31 *Own Story*, 115–118. State troops brought with them a conglomeration of cannon, causing ammunition difficulties. American facilities for making wrought-iron and cast-iron guns were at first much superior to those for making bronze pieces. Washington fortifications had to take large coastal cannon for lack of light artillery; O. R., I, xix, pt. 2, pp. 391–393. Just after Antietam, McClellan's army had 126 Napoleons and 64 light Parrotts as against 128 larger guns; *ibid.*, 407.
32 *Memoirs*, II, 396.

approach to small arms. Although it would have been easier to experiment with the breech-loading principle in designing ordnance than it was in buying the first sorely needed Springfields and Enfields, for the emergency was less desperate, the head, J. W. Ripley, set his face against innovation. He rebuffed a manufacturer who offered to make breech-loading cannon for him with the curt declaration that however perfect such a piece might be, it would not suit the service, for a muzzle-loader of equal weight must necessarily be stronger, cheaper, simpler, and less liable to derangement. He also declined to support experiments with steel fieldpieces in place of bronze. No single prototype of small-caliber artillery was ever adopted, though among larger cannon the 15-inch Rodman gun, made in Pittsburgh by the Fort Pitt Foundry, found special favor.[33]

The British officers who reported on Northern military affairs in the first months of 1864 found that the Army of the Potomac had an ample supply of artillery, both smoothbore and rifled. Two-thirds of its light artillery was smoothbore for the simple fact that in fighting over rough country small shot was the best ammunition; most artillerymen going into battle liked to carry one-third canister, one-third shrapnel, and one-third solid balls. Four different field guns were in common use: the Napoleon, the 10-pounder Parrotts, a 3-inch ordnance gun, and a 20-pounder as a gun of position.[34] The officers also saw the large Parrotts made at Cold Spring on the Hudson, great cast-iron guns strengthened at the breech by wrought-iron hoops. They thought the operation very rough, and reported a number of instances in which the guns had bulged their hoops, burst at the breach, or blown off their muzzles.

As for small arms, the North did better and better. By Chancellorsville the early deficiencies had been so well cured that, as we have seen, the government was refusing to make new foreign contracts and letting the old ones run out; though it still bought some first-class Enfields on a non-contract basis. Marcellus Hartley, who had been sent abroad to purchase for the government, had returned in the spring of 1862 after doing a memorable piece of work in buying good arms, breaking up a combination of British maunfacturers, and frustrating the activities of Confederate agents. He received Stanton's warm praise, and it was not considered necessary to send him back again.[35] During 1862 the ordnance bureau bought 734,500 rifles and

33 To H. F. Mann, May 28, 1862, Misc. Letterbook No. 55, p. 285; to McClellan, July 7, 1862, *ibid.*, 447; Watson to Normal Ward, April 22, 1863, War Office Mil. Book No. 52c, p. 242.
34 Report, Br. War Office, 1864; cf. O. R., III, iii, 108.
35 For Hartley's remarkable work see L. W. Hartley, *Marcellus Hartley*, 33-49; Alden Hatch, *Remington Arms*, 100-102; O. R., III, i, ii, iii, *passim*, cover munitions thoroughly.

muskets, 48,000 carbines, and 120,000 pistols. The spring campaigns of 1863 found it with 381,000 rifled muskets in storage, expecting the delivery of 80,000 Enfields under contract, and obtaining new Springfields from the national armory at the rate of 30,000 a month.

In short, good arms were so abundant that Grant's statement that the Confederates before Vicksburg carried better weapons than his own troops excites amazement. This may have been true of some units, but not of the armies as a whole. The government could now afford to be contemptuous of the vast quantity of inferior foreign muskets that had seeped into the country. It warned the States against them, bought 18,000 bad Prussian guns at $4 for free distribution to militia for drill, and before the summer ended, allowed merchants to send the rusting foreign hardware back to the place of original shipment.[36] Meanwhile, it encouraged the domestic manufacturers who strove to make the Union self-sufficient.[37]

Little by little, first in the cavalry and later the infantry, breechloaders were reaching select bodies of troops. Ripley remained the Great Obstructor. Fussily swathed in red tape, he was skeptical of their merits, irritated by the number of types placed before him, and disturbed by prices which averaged $28–$30.[38] In the early period of the war he had been quite right in concentrating on a full supply of good muzzle-loaders. Many Army officers, for that matter, shared his opinion that men firing breechloaders tended to waste ammunition, and that careful training would be needed. But by energetic and farsighted action in 1862, when shortages eased, he could have made sure that a large part of the troops at Gettysburg and Chattanooga had the efficient new weapon. Prussian officers ever since 1861 had been confidently asserting the superiority of the needle gun type of breechloader, declaring that it fired three times faster than the Minié muzzle-loader. The Swedish army had turned to breechloaders. The two British observers found officers of the Army of the Potomac in 1864 generally agreed that a number of the more intelligent men in each regiment, at least, should carry breechloaders.

Repeating rifles were particularly valued, and the troops fortunate enough to get seven-shot Spencers were positively enchanted by them. George D. Ramsay, who succeeded Ripley in September, 1863, and was far more progres-

---

36 Ripley to Casey, Aug. 25, 1862, Ord. Misc. Letterbook No. 56, p. 50; Watson to J. B. Hupey, Aug. 18, 1862, *ibid.*, Letterbook No. 50; Watson to Naylor, May 11, 1863, *ibid.*, No. 52c; Hardie to Joseph Foulke's Sons, Sept. 7, 1863, *ibid.*, No. 53a.
37 See G. D. Ramsay's endorsement, Nov. 2, 1863, Ord. Letters to War Dept., Book No. 14, pp. 375, 376, praising Abram S Hewitt's production of fine gun metal.
38 Ripley wrote Lincoln May 5, 1862, that he did not think it wise to increase the number of breechloader types on the market; Ord. Misc. Letterbook No. 55, p. 183. Later he wrote Stanton to the same effect; Jan. 9, 1863, Ord. Letters to War Dept., Book No. 14.

sive, was anxious to enlarge their use. Beyond doubt, he declared in the spring of 1864, "repeating rifles are the greatest favorite with the army, and could they be supplied in quantities to meet all the requisites, I am satisfied that no other arm would be used." Of the three types of repeaters available in limited numbers in 1863, he thought the Spencer alone really cheap, durable, and efficient.[39] When he wrote, only 9,502 Spencer rifles and 9,500 carbines were in service, and the demand for more was tremendous. "It seemed as if no soldier who had seen them could be satisfied with any other." Along with their other merits, they used a copper cartridge which could not be injured by water and obviated all need for caps.

Ramsay advised a policy which the bureau should have adopted much earlier: "These facts are significant and should teach us to offer every encouragement to the manufacturers of the repeating arm using the copper cartridge." The visiting Britons were much impressed by what they heard from General A. H. Terry of the performance of the Spencers at Olustee, Florida. Here, on February 20, 1864, a Connecticut regiment maintained a rapid continuous fire which kept the enemy completely "subdued" and their own losses trifling.

During 1863–64 owners of Spencers were writing home enthusiastically of the powers of that arm. It was "a most formidable piece," declared a Massachusetts lad; "equal to a small battery in itself," stated a Pennsylvania volunteer.[40] The only difficulty was that of supply. The Burnside Rifle Company, for example, was so tardy in its contract for making 30,500 Spencer-model repeaters that it did not get them in until the very end of the war. Too little and too late was the general story. When firing stopped probably a hundred thousand breechloaders were in the hands of Union troops; had twice that many repeaters been ready in the middle of 1863 the war might have been cut short by a year.[41]

Imagination sometimes seemed conspicuously lacking in the Northern war effort. The soldiers even in 1862 were asking for a portable regimental oven to bake fresh bread, which private firms could then supply but which the government never troubled to furnish in quantity. A British general, Hugh M. Rose, in a celebrated thousand-mile fighting march in burning heat during the Indian Mutiny, had demonstrated the value of khaki uniforms, and Britain shortly used them in her Abyssinian campaign (1868); but though

39 He pronounced Colt's and Henry's too expensive, Colt's dangerous to the user, and Henry's too delicate for service; see his endorsement on applications of Burnside Rifle Co. and Sharps Co. for new contracts. Ord. Letters to War Dept., Book No. 14, p. 46. But Rosecrans thought the five-shot Colt rifle first-rate and demanded 5,000 for his cavalry arm; Bickham, *Rosecrans*, 25. Cf. Holt-Owen Report, 37th Cong., 2d Sess., Sen. Exec. Doc. No. 72.
40 Survivors Assn., *Hist. 121st Pa. Vols.*, 45; J. L. Bowen, *Hist. 37th Mass.*, 354, 355.
41 Cf. *War for the Union*, I, 361–363.

its six-pound woolen uniform was much too hot in summer, the North never experimented with a cool, dust-repellent cloth. The Prussian army had developed an excellent nine-ounce cooking tin in two fitted parts, large enough that one man might cook meat and vegetables for several while another boiled coffee; but Americans stuck to kettle and pan. It was to the Army's credit, however, that it did widely adopt the small shelter tent, which if made of waterproof cloth had more uses than a blanket; or rather, this was to the credit of the great supply bureau under whose sheltering wings it fought the war.

[IV]

That the quartermaster bureau under Montgomery C. Meigs accomplished a herculean task with remarkable efficiency, honesty, and expedition no reasonable person could deny. It performed so great a work indeed that Meigs should be given a place near that of Seward and Stanton, Chase and Gideon Welles. He brought to his office a high reputation as supervisor of the principal prewar undertakings, both architectural and engineering, for the improvement of the capital. A man of dogged industry, marked reserve, and utter devotion to the nation, he sometimes seemed a mere machine for toil. Yet his papers actually reveal a kinetic spirit and a warmly emotional nature, sensitive to blame and responsive to praise. The terse diary which he kept discloses his intense pride in his son John, who graduated from West Point in 1863 with honors, and his still intenser grief when the next year this promising lieutenant of engineers, "a noble boy, gallant, generous, gifted, who had already made himself a name in the land," was slain by guerrillas near Sheridan's Virginia headquarters. One younger son, fortunately, survived.

The diary also reflects a singular streak of martial ardor in this quiet executive. Viewing the capture of Missionary Ridge, he was thrilled beyond words by the wonderful sight, and could only write: "I am rejoiced—I took part in it—a wonderful day." In the spring of 1864 he thirsted to join Grant at his Virginia headquarters, but Stanton wisely decided that for the time being he could not be spared from his Washington post.[42]

Unescapably, Meigs was often violently criticized, for every step he took involved friction. "He is a most arbitrary man," declared Senator John P. Hale. His acrimonious correspondence with McClellan's chief quartermaster, Rufus Ingalls, upon the supply services just after Antietam, gave him particular pain. But he triumphantly outrode every storm, even McClellan

---

42 Meigs Papers, LC; brevetted major-general July 5, 1864, Meigs commanded Grant's supply base at Belle Plain later that year, and refitted Sherman's army at Savannah early in 1865. Russell F. Weigley, *M. C. Meigs*, analyzes his work as administrator.

acknowledging his efficiency. Spending about one and a half billion dollars, or nearly half the direct cost of the war, and directing it into channels that largely remade the American economy, he was an ideal administrator.

The extent of his well-organized activities was impressive. The quarter-master bureau had to supply the army with horses, mules, wagons, carts, harness, fuel, and forage, while even after the government had a cavalry bureau Meigs purchased cavalry mounts. He had to build barracks, quarters, storehouses, and hospitals. His bureau gave the troops their uniforms, over-coats, underwear, blankets, shoes, and mess gear. It delivered them their ambulances. It provided stoves and office furniture. It erected portable saw-mills. It paid the costs of army spies and interpreters, met the expense of courts-martial, and furnished many of the coffins for officers who died on duty. It shoed mules and hired veterinaries. To do all this required tremendous depots of supplies in appropriate cities—veritable department stores. A large staff of procurement officers and inspectors had to be maintained to buy everything from steamboats to pins; every regiment had its own quarter-master; and the commander of every company was accountable to the bureau for national property. It swam in a flood of paper work.[43]

As the first confusions of the war were conquered, the government gradually formalized its control over quartermaster contracts. By Federal law, bureau officers had to advertise for sealed bids, basing their advertisements on approved requisitions. While minor contracts might be let on the spot, all large orders had to be submitted to Meigs himself. Contractors were required to make an explicit statement of quantities, qualities, and terms of delivery, guaranteed by posted bonds. Though some regimental quarter-masters were dishonest, the central activities of Meigs' bureau were never touched by scandal; his code of integrity was perfect.

As he was constantly under severe pressure from State politicians and regional business interests, Meigs saw that it would be wise to scatter his orders as widely as possible. He insisted that wagon contracts, for example, be distributed among different areas and as many capable firms as seemed practicable, for this would spread employment and assure at least minimal deliveries. But time soon proved that many small new firms were inexpert or un-reliable, and in the end he was compelled to trim his sails to the wind of an increasingly concentrated economy. It was the big horse dealer, the big tent-maker, the big ambulance supplier, who increasingly got the orders, for in the emergent industrial America the big establishments usually showed more

---

43 For the organization of the bureau see O. R., III, iii, 894-897; for the Meigs-Ingalls corr. see O. R., I, xix, pt. 2, pp. 168-587. Ch. XXV, Laws of the 37th Cong., approved Feb. 9, 1863, outlines Meigs' main duties. His annual report for 1863-64 (O. R., III, iv, 874-902) is especially illuminating. He has been scandalously neglected by Civil War historians; Rhodes barely mentions him thrice, and Channing, Schouler, and McMaster not even once.

efficiency. We find him instructing an agent in clothing procurement to reject bids which appeared certain to plunge the contractor into loss, or force him to put his workers on a sweatshop basis, or require the cribbaging of materials. If several of the most respectable houses divided the order, "I am convinced that in the end the service, the soldier, and the government will be benefited." [44]

As the war went on stricter rules became necessary. Inflation and the ebb and flow of fortune on the battlefield caused violent fluctuations in the price of materials. The government therefore forbade long-term contracts, for if prices rose contractors failed with disastrous results, while if they dropped the bidders made fortunes. Congress asked for monthly estimates of needs, monthly advertisements, and monthly reports of contracts. Meigs always insisted, however, that a heavy burden of red tape would injure the war effort. For example, he attacked a Congressional proposal that every contract should carry affidavits sworn before a magistrate, pointing out that many purchases had to be made in the field amid all the confusion of advance or retreat, when nobody had time for affidavits, and that some army quarter-masters signed so many contracts that they would have to hire a magistrate as full-time office clerk. He was hostile also to an excessive centralization of supply operations in Washington, arguing that responsible buyers and inspectors scattered all over the map should be allowed due discretion.[45]

Army consumption rapidly grew staggering. To outfit a single regiment with clothing even at the low prices of 1861 required $20,000, so that the 500 new regiments authorized that July meant an initial expenditure of ten millions; and an active soldier would wear out a good uniform in three months of camp, or a few rough marches. Shoes needed constant replacement. Meigs assumed that after Burnside's army marched from Harpers Ferry to Falmouth, it needed a complete new supply of shoes. And what a wild conglomerate of other demands had to be met! The records of a high quartermaster officer in the Army of the Potomac have been kept. They show him receipting within a short period for 39 barrels of coal, $7\frac{1}{2}$ tons of oats, 23 boxes of bandages, 31 of soap, 4 of lanterns, 80 beef cattle and 450 sheep, 180 mules, a miscellany of ropes, nails, rags, forges, lumber, and wagons, rolls of canvas, shipments of stoves, parcels of wire, "sundries," and sacks—how the army needed sacks! He had to sign for everything, and keep accurate records of distribution.

At first the shortages had been appalling. Meigs had written just after Bull Run: "The nation is in extremity. Troops, thousands, wait for clothes to

44 To D. M. Vinton, Sept. 9, 1861, QMG Letterbook No. 18, p. 407.
45 To E. D. Morgan, Aug. 7, 1861, QMG Letterbook No. 56, p. 167. The States helped with supplies, but had to be reimbursed. For the liberal affidavit provisions actually enacted, see Acts of the 37th Cong., Ch. XXII, approved Feb. 7, 1863.

Office of Assistant Commissary General of Subsistence. No. 4 State-st., New-York, May 13, 1863.

PROPOSALS WILL BE RECEIVED BY the undersigned until 4 o'clock p. m., on WEDNESDAY, the 20th instant, for supplying for the use of the United States Army SUBSISTENCE STORES, to be delivered in New-York or Brooklyn, as follows, viz: For delivery on the 3d of June:

1,000 barrels first quality new MESS PORK, or PRIME MESS PORK, to be full salted, 200 ℔ meat, in full-hooped oak barrels, with two iron hoops; meat to be free from rust or stain.

1,000 barrels of first quality NEW EXTRA MESS BEEF. The meat to be packed in full-hooped oak barrels, with two iron hoops.

Five barrels to be examined as a sample before accepting the bids, and to be retained until all shall be delivered.

25,000 pounds first quality THOROUGHLY SMOKED NEW BACON SIDES.

12,500 pounds first quality THOROUGHLY SMOKED NEW BACON SHOULDERS.

62,500 pounds of first quality *thoroughly cured* SMOKED HAMS. Proposers will state whether their Hams are pickle-cured or dry-salted; also their average weight.

The bacon and hams to be delivered in bulk for inspection and packing, at such points in the cities of New-York or Brooklyn as may be designated.

750,000 pounds first quality PILOT BREAD, to be made of good sound Extra Ohio or other equally good flour; crackers to be thoroughly baked and perfectly dried before being packed, and in size, thickness, openness, &c., to conform to standard samples which can be examined at this office; to be packed in boxes of 50 pounds bread to each box; boxes to be made of fully seasoned wood, of such kinds as will impart no taste or odor to the bread; bottom and top of single pieces, or if two pieces, tongued and grooved together. Boxes to be strapped with light straps of suitable wood. The Flour and Bread will also be examined by the Inspector, who will reject all that in the quality of the flour or in any other respect is inferior to the standard Samples. Bidders to state the location of their bakeries

50 barrels first quality kiln-dried CORN MEAL. The barrels to have two iron hoops and to be full head-lined.

500 bushels of first quality NEW WHITE BEANS, well seasoned and dry—to be packed in good, bright, well coopered flour barrels, to be full head-lined with green hickory.

50,000 pounds of prime RICE, in clean, good, stout oak barrels, like samples to be seen at this office.

7,500 pounds first quality white flint corn HOMINY, in well-coopered, head-lined flour barrels

12,500 pounds prime RIO COFFEE, to be packed in barrels, like samples to be seen at this office.

50,000 pounds prime RIO COFFEE, to be roasted, ground, and packed in barrels, like samples to be seen at this office.

Parties offering to furnish Coffee, either green or to be roasted, are required to send in full-ch p-samples in the green state of all the coffee they propose to furnish.

12,500 pounds carefully selected TEA, in half chests, ¼ Green, ¼ Souchong, ¼ Oolong; boxes to be well strapped and in perfect order. Cargo and Chop-marks to accompany the usual samples. Bidders are requested to offer not more than two samples of each kind of Tea.

45,000 pounds of good hard SOAP. Bidders to give the location of their manufactories.

POTATOES—Such quantity as may be required during the month of June; 60 pounds to the bushel, in good, ordinary, well-coopered barrels.

All the stores will be carefully inspected before their delivery, and compared with the retained samples. Returns of weights signed by a professional Public Weigher must be furnished whenever required.

Payment, as heretofore, to be made in such funds as may be furnished by the United States.

Contractors are expected to hold their goods, without expense to the United States, until required for shipment.

Proposers whose bids are not accepted, are requested to send for their samples on MONDAY, 25th instant.

Blanks for Proposals will be furnished at this office, which must be inclosed in an envelope addressed to the undersigned, and indorsed "Proposals for Subsistence Stores."

A. B. EATON, Colonel and A. C. G. S.

ADVERTISEMENT FOR PORK AND OTHER SUPPLIES

From The New York *Tribune* for May 18, 1863

take the field. Regiments have been ordered here [Washington] without clothes. Men go on guard in drawers." At the onset of winter he had to place large orders for blankets in England.[46]

But by the middle of 1862 surpluses were developing in many items, depots were becoming well stocked, the placing of foreign orders had been stopped, and even domestic contracts were being restricted. Meigs wrote in April, 1862: "The hurry is over. There can be little occasion now for purchases of clothing, tents, etc., under such urgency as would justify purchase without advertisement." In August he estimated that the supplies on hand would furnish 600,000 new recruits with clothing and general equipment.[47] Most of the shortages thereafter were traceable to distributive difficulties. Footgear, for example, had long been one of his worries, and like Kipling's warrior he must have been haunted by a vision of boots, boots, boots. When Second Manassas was fought, however, the armies had enough shoes; the Washington depot alone held 116,000 pairs, and issued an average of 25,000 weekly. Offers of foreign shipments were rejected. Carts, stationery, and blacksmith's outfits were all abundant.

The worst difficulties were connected with transportation, from steamboats to wagon trains and ambulances. Horses and mules were required in seemingly endless numbers. Even in September, 1861, the Army of the Potomac needed 20,000 cavalry horses and 20,000 artillery and transport animals, and this was but the beginning. Small contracts were at first made for lots of 200 to 1,000 at an average price per horse of $120. In the summer and fall of 1862 a weekly average of 1,500 horses were supplied to the Army of the Potomac, and McClellan still grumbled that he did not get enough. Because the government had political reasons for favoring the border States, rather high rates were allowed for Kentucky stock, this decision being taken, Meigs explained later to his aides, "after the parties representing Kentucky interests had seen the President, the Secretary of War, and other members of the Cabinet."[48]

The bills grew so high that Meigs earnestly exhorted officers to take better care of their animals. That outrageous cruelties and abuses were common there can be no doubt. Cavalry horses were sometimes ridden by heavy and unskillful men for twenty-four or thirty-six hours without rest, while artillery and wagon horses suffered just as badly. Battle losses were also high; at Murfreesboro alone men estimated that more than 1,500 horses of all branches

46 Meigs to Vinton, July 24, 1861, QMG Letterbook No. 16 (Clothing and Equipage), 185, 186; to Cameron, Oct. 14, 1861, QMG Letters to War Dept., Book No. 5, p. 487.
47 To Allen, April 12, 1862, QMG Letterbook No. 19, p. 393; to Vinton, Aug. 12, 1863, *ibid.*, 693.
48 Meigs to Swords, Dec. 7, 1861, QMG Letterbook No. 57, p. 383.

were killed. The national supply in 1863 ran so low that one agent who was sent out with a fund of $100,000 to replenish the Army stock reported that he would get nowhere against other buyers unless he could go above the allowed price of $110.[49] By July, Meigs was willing to pay $150 for a good cavalry or artillery horse delivered in Washington, and the next year the price went to $170. It is not strange that he burst out in a violent admonition to Rosecrans:

Compel your cavalry officers to see that their horses are properly groomed. Put them in some place where they can get forage near the railroad or send them to your rear for grass and ear corn. When in good order start them, 1,000 at a time, for the rebel communications, with orders never to move off a walk unless they see an enemy before or between them; to travel only so far in a day as not to fatigue their horses; never to camp in the place in which sunset finds them; and to rest in a good pasture during the heat of the day. [Also], to keep some of their eyes open night and day, and never to pass a bridge without burning it, a horse without stealing or shooting it, a guerrilla without capturing him, or a negro without explaining the President's proclamation.

Operate on their communications. Strike every detached post. Rely more upon infantry than upon cavalry, which in the whole war has not decided the fate of a single battle rising above a skirmish, which taxes the Treasury and exhausts the resources of the country, and of which we now have afoot a larger nominal strength than any nation on earth. We have over 125 regiments of cavalry, and they have killed ten times as many horses for us as for the enemy.[50]

Meigs felt severely the burden of feeding all the animals in camps, depots, and on the march. While both the Union and Confederate armies made use of meadows and pastures, the Union forces relied much the more heavily upon delivered hay, corn, and oats. Moreover, the Northern troops carried a far greater bulk of impedimenta than the Southern. Like Sherman in the West and Butterfield in the East, Meigs believed that the armies might usually cut in half the amount of freight they dragged over the countrysides. According to his estimates, 40,000 men ought to get their necessities into 500 wagons, instead of the 1,200 for which they asked. He thought that McClellan had carried egregiously large trains down to the outskirts of Richmond. "After all its losses," he grumbled to Halleck in the summer of 1862, "the Army of the Potomac had in camp on the James River nearly 2,800 wagons, which was at the rate of 28 wagons to a thousand men."[51] Every wagon meant four or six draft animals.

49   C. E. Fuller to Meigs, May 13, 1863, QMG Letterbook No. 68, pp. 504, 505.
50   Meigs to F. W. Kellogg, July 23, 1863, and to Rosecrans July 1, 1863; Letterbooks Nos. 69 and 70. Lincoln in the fall of 1863 forbade the export of horses. During the first nine months of 1864 cavalry horses were purchased at the rate of 500 a day, which was the rate of destruction; O. R., III, iii, 289.
51   Meigs to Halleck, Aug. 18, 1862, QMG Letterbook No. 62, pp. 79, 80.

In the following spring the Army of the Cumberland had about 3,000 wagons, most of them with six-mule teams, or enough, if formed in one line, to extend thirty miles; it had about 600 ambulances; and its horses and mules numbered about 50,000. At one time it had on hand 24,000 bales of hay and 200,000 bushels of grain, the hay costing at the base about 25 dollars a ton, and the corn 25 cents a bushel.[52] As armies grew, so did the trains. Grant in the spring of 1864 had about 4,000 wagons in Virginia; and in the middle of that year the forces East and West were using 300,000 horses and mules. Meigs continually urged Halleck in Washington and the generals in the field to make more summer use of grass, green fodder, and wheat or oats in the sheaf. He implored them to get rid of bulky Sibley tents, officers' camp beds, and all like luxuries. He wished a clearance made of many of the sutlers, who sold illicit liquor, traded slyly with the enemy, and above all choked the roads with their wagons; it was hard enough to get necessities to the troops without giving space to their candies, pies, soft drinks, and gewgaws. In all this he had the support of Herman Haupt, who was disgusted with the way in which baggage trains impeded army movements.[53]

The West fared better than the East in transportation because of its river arteries. We have already noted the efficient work of Lewis B. Parsons. Commissioned captain in the quartermaster service, and ordered to St. Louis, he took charge in the last days of 1861 of all water carriage in the department. Soon rising to the rank of colonel, he continued in control until late in 1864. All the important expeditionary forces were transported under his direction. Grant's army was taken to Pittsburgh Landing before Shiloh by a great fleet of 153 river transports; Sherman's army of 40,000 was lifted from Memphis to its point of attack above Vicksburg in eight days. "Since the commencement of the war," wrote the chief quartermaster officer at Louisville on August 14, 1864, "no western army has ever been thwarted for the want of transportation or the lack of supplies." An ordinary steamboat of 500 tons capacity could carry enough stores in one trip to subsist 40,000 men and 18,000 horses nearly two days. The quartermaster-general's bureau found an ample supply of boats of low tonnage which could be brought up to the bank almost anywhere to disembark troops, animals, wagons, cannon, and general supplies.

One of the sorest initial shortages, that of ambulances, also began to be filled in the latter part of 1862. By October a total of 3,500 had been bought by Meigs. Hundreds of them were of the two-wheel model, cheaper by $27

52 *Annals of the Army of the Cumberland*, by an Officer, 274–288.
53 Meigs to Clarey, Aug. 27, 1862, QMG Letterbook No. 62, p. 201; Haupt, *Rems.* In the summer of 1863 Stanton actually nursed the crazy idea that he might mount cavalry on large-size mules; to Meigs, Aug. 17, 1863, War Office Military Book No. 52b.

than the $170 four-wheel type, but productive of agony, grating bones, and loss of blood in their heavy jolting over uneven ground. After 1862, happily, the government bought no more. But still this was one of the areas in which the record was bad. Near the end of 1862 a trial was made of litters, fitted on the backs of mules, for carrying wounded. Poor Yankee lads!—maimed, hauled to the rear on balky, uncertain mules, and then perhaps turned over to a quack surgeon for unnecessary amputations. The wretched quality of many of the four-wheel ambulances excited frequent complaint. Their axles broke, their bolts slipped out, their bodies splintered, and their covers admitted the rain. Meigs, denying that the surgeon-general's office could have done better than he, laid the blame for shortcomings on the pressure of war emergencies.[54]

But in 1863 even ambulances were at long last fairly adequate in numbers and equipment.

[V]

The commissary bureau, too, was mastering most of its difficulties. The poor, ill-balanced, ill-prepared diet given the troops in the first months, nearly as serious a cause of sickness as camp filth, was less the fault of Joseph P. Taylor, the commissary-general, than of custom, haste, ignorance of nutrition, and bad distribution. The old army ration of salt pork or beef, hard bread or flour, coffee, and dried beans or peas, was so obviously inadequate that Congress in the summer of 1861 took steps to have potatoes and fresh meat, whenever possible, added to the menu. Vinegar and molasses were also put on the ration list. Initially the quality of food was often inferior: the "sowbelly" was fat and stringy, the beef tough, the hardtack so weevily that soldiers called it "worm castles." And despite official prescription, vegetables were so hard to get at some seasons and so difficult to transport great distances that for long intervals the men seldom had a taste of fresh food. But, with the press raising frequent complaints and the best officers and medical service cooperating, the commissary did increasingly well. Many members of Congress regarded Taylor as one of the most capable administrators in Washington. Surgeon-General Hammond thought that the troops had the best basic army diet in the world, and foreign observers were impressed, especially when they saw dried apples, pickles, and canned or pressed vegetables served to the messes. Sutlers and local peddlers helped to vary the fare.[55]

Voluntary initiative was especially valuable in meeting emergency short-

54 To Henry I. Bowditch, Oct. 20, 1862, QMG Letterbook No. 63, p. 400.
55 Adams, *Doctors in Blue*, 206 ff.; Wiley, *Billy Yank*, Ch. IX; Maxwell, *Lincoln's Fifth Wheel*, 34–36.

ages and supplying fresh food. The Sanitary and Christian Commissions were both active. On March 4, 1863, telegrams throughout the Northwest announced: "Rush forward anti-scorbutics for General Grant's army." The results were astounding. Newspapers scattered the appeal broadcast; committees sprang up in hundreds of localities; from every Northwestern State vegetables, jellies, and dried fruits poured into Chicago, down the Illinois Central, and down the Mississippi. Soon a traffic link of a thousand barrels a week connected Chicago with the Vicksburg area.[56] The previous summer soldiers with McClellan on the James had testified that they were well fed. Wrote one: "I must say that a very great change is being and has been brought about in the diet. Vegetables are now furnished by each commissary."[57] Some observers, like Frederick Law Olmsted with Grant in the summer of 1863, and the British officers in Virginia in 1864, believed that the rations could hardly be improved except by a diminution in quantity, for in camp especially, soldiers tended to overeat. Much always depended, of course, on the ability of the regimental commissaries.

National expenditures for army rations, culminating in an appropriation of $140,000,000 for the fiscal year 1863–64, were always adequate. The occasional shortages and hardships, amounting sometimes to brief semi-starvation, were an inescapable accompaniment of the fighting. But the improvement was fairly steady, and was attributable to four principal factors. One was the rising efficiency of Taylor's commissary bureau, strengthened by Congress in 1863. One was the heightened understanding of dietary principle: army surgeons knew from the beginning that the Russian defeat in the Crimea had been largely attributable to a wretched diet, and that vegetables were essential; they gradually learned that onions and apples were better than potatoes, and that berries and salads, even of weeds, were valuable. A third factor was the increasing reliance of troops upon foraging: they lived off the country when they could, and so got more milk, fresh meat, and garden produce. Finally, the army profited from the growth of the canning and meat-packing industries during the war. Experiments with desiccated potatoes and with a combined baked-wheat ration and sausage ration invented by E. N. Horsford of Harvard were failures, but tinned vegetables became more and more widely esteemed. Canneries of sea food, peas, and sweet corn had flourished along the Atlantic Coast before the war, the first recorded Western cannery had been established in Cincinnati in 1860, and a year later the Van Camp Company began its activities in Indianapolis.

56 Andreas, *Hist. of Chicago*, I, 319, 320, gives an account of this episode. The Cincinnati *Commercial*, July 1, 1862, describes the work of the Sanitary Commission of that city in improving Army fare.
57 Seth Paine, July 31, 1862, to E. Wilkeson, Gay Papers, Columbia Univ.

The business of Gail Borden, who opened his first large condensed-milk plant at Wassaic, New York, in 1861, was given immediate impetus by the war. His manufactory was issuing cans of sweetened condensed milk when Sumter was bombarded, and the troops and government made eager customers. In pork packing Philip Armour, who began business in Milwaukee in 1859, and Nelson Morris, who reached Chicago the same year, profited and expanded with the aid of war orders. Taylor's commissary bureau became an enterprise of a magnitude scarcely conceivable in prewar years; and its activities stimulated undertakings that were to seem tremendous before it went out of existence.[58]

United States Sanitary Commission. — The Treasurer acknowledges the receipt of the following contributions since Feb. 16:

Sunday-School Class in High-st. Church, Portland, Me, by. B. Thurston (additional)	$1 10
M. J. L., N. Y.	3 00
John Taylor Johnston. (additional)	100 00
Citizens of Washington Territory, by W. W. Miller, Treasurer	4,520 77
Lieut. F. B. Crosby, U. S. A.	15 00
Citizens of Spanish Ranch, Plumas Co., California, by Thos. J. McCormick, Marysville	107 00
Premium on Gold from do	71 33
Chas. B. Hart, N. Y.. (additional)	25 00
Sawyer, Wallace & Co., by John T. Agnew	500 00
Woodland Soldier's Aid Society, Woodland, Yolo Co. Cal., by Mrs. C. W. Lewis, President, Mrs. F. S. Freeman, Treas., Mrs. G. D. Fiske, Sec.	1,222 60
Seven Gold and Silver Bars from Storey Co., Nevada Territory	19,866 37
Premium on do	10,554 67
One Silver Bar from Ladies' Social Benevolent Society, Gold Hill, Storey Co., Nevada Territory	860 16
Premium on do	468 73
Edmund H. Miller, New-York (additional)	250 00
Citizens of Oregon, by the Hon. A. Holbrook	377 84
Citizens of Walla Walla, Washington Territory, by the Hon. A. Holbrook	427 00
The Hon. Wm. H. Seward, being funds placed in his hands for the benefit of the Army by American residents of Santiago de Chili	8,688 84
George G. Briggs, Santa Barbara County, California, by Fowler & Wells	100 00
Thomas C. Smith	50 00
Anonymous, proceeds of a bet	25 00
N. R. Vail, St. John's, N. F., by J. M. Requa	150 00
Lathrop, Ludington & Co	250 00
Proceeds of Concert by Young Men's Association, West Troy, by S. H. Rogers, Secretary	152 50
Citizens of California, by James Otis, Treasurer, San Francisco	15,000 00
Premium on gold from do	8,006 50

GEO. T. STRONG, Treasurer, No. 68 Wall-st. New-York, March 18, 1863.

COLLECTING FUNDS FOR THE SANITARY COMMISSION

From The New York *Tribune* for March 19, 1863

The chariot of Mars was gaining momentum. On every side, by the date of Chancellorsville, observers could see evidence that improvised war was giving away to large-scale organized war, and that a new republic was emerging. The wagon trains of the armies were modeled on those of the Western plains, with practically the same vehicles, but were gigantic in comparison.

58 Much general material on activities of the commissary and quartermaster bureaus is scattered through O. R., III, iii and iv, Meigs's annual reports being specially valuable.

The four chief depots of quartermaster supplies, in New York, Philadelphia, Cincinnati, and St. Louis, closely resembled general stores, but were so much larger that even A. T. Stewart would have found them marvelous. The military telegraph system under Colonel Anson Stager and Major Thomas T. Eckert was growing toward the total of 6,500 miles which it would reach before the end of 1864.[59] One undertaking in social welfare, the rescue of the Negro refugees who had flocked to Washington, with the provision of housing, schools, police, and water, and the finding of employment, was unprecedented in government annals.

Northerners everywhere were learning entirely new lessons of resourcefulness, initiative, and organization. Herman Haupt's bridge over the Potomac Creek chasm was one of the marvels of 1862. In Napoleon's time trestle bridges of more than one story had been regarded as impossible, but this four-story structure lifted a railroad eighty feet above the stream bed. Built in nine working days in May, almost entirely of materials growing about the site, the 400-foot structure looked fragile—"corn stalks and beanpoles," said Lincoln—but it daily carried ten to twenty heavy trains in each direction and withstood severe storms. Yet other engineering feats were as remarkable, and some works, such as the model planning and construction done at Forts Richmond and Lafayette, defending New York harbor, were to be far more durable.[60] The nation's topographical engineers were giving a new vigor to mapmaking; in 1862–63 they made 8,841 military maps. Medicine was being regenerated by the war. As S. Weir Mitchell later recalled, the conflict found it with little professional status, self-confidence, or national regard; but the building and staffing of great base hospitals "left it with a pride justified by conduct which blazoned its scutcheon with endless sacrifice and great intellectual achievements." [61]

Most important of all were the lessons learned in organization. Frederick Law Olmsted pointed out that the meaning of the word was hardly known in prewar America. But young James A. Garfield, Rutherford B. Hayes, and Benjamin Harrison as brigade commanders necessarily learned organization. And how many others! Francis A. Walker was but twenty-two when, twice wounded at Chancellorsville, he became assistant adjutant-general in Couch's Second Corps of the Army of the Potomac. He had to collect and interpret every day the innumerable facts on the fighting strength of the corps; to digest the thousands of complaints, requests, and bits of information which welled up from 20,000 men; to conduct all correspondence and help frame

59 W. R. Plum, *The Military Telegraph During the Civil War*, tells an impressive story.
60 Haupt, *Rems.*, 45–50; Chanal, *The American Army*; Gilbert Thompson, "The Engineer Battalion in the Civil War," Occasional Paper 44, U. S. Army Engineer School.
61 Introduction, *In Wartime*.

all orders; to ride camp and battlefield alertly; and advise his commander. This training fitted Walker for directing two national censuses and building the Massachusetts Institute of Technology into the world's greatest engineering institution.

The inevitable outcome of the war was foreshadowed by the fact that while in defeat the North grew stronger, in victory the South became weaker. In the larger view, however, it was the steady growth not only of a more powerful Northern society, but a new type of society, which was significant. The old Pilgrim chronicler Nathaniel Morton, relating how the founders of Plymouth had taken leave of Europe, committed themselves to a fateful experiment, and by hard labor triumphed over their first trials, concluded that from their late estate they were forever parted: "If they looked behind them, there was a mighty ocean which they had passed, and was now as a main bar or gulph to separate them." When Americans in 1863 looked back a short three years, they saw that they were separated from their former world by a stormy ocean, and that an impassable chasm shut them off from their earlier history. To discern just how wide that main bar or gulph was, we must turn to the changes in private industry.

19

Shape of Revolution: Anvil, Loom, and Piston

UNSTEADILY, sometimes obscurely, but inexorably, forces of internal change by 1863 were transforming American life. The South stood face to face with a socioeconomic revolution from which not even victory could extricate it. In the North the multiform changes, the most powerful of them economic, were still more significant. Parallel with the waste and sorrows of war ran a stimulation of individual initiative, a challenge to large-scale planning, and an encouragement of cooperative effort, which in combination with new agencies for developing national resources amounted to a great release of creative energy. The principal Northern cities by the end of 1862 seemed electric with fresh ambitions, ideas, and methods. It was as if the shock of arms, with its tremendous affirmatives, had invigorated a people too long fettered by hesitancies. As a mighty human upheaval, the industrial resurgence outstripped the military effort.

Even in its worst months of defeat and discouragement, the period from the Seven Days through Chancellorsville, the country was steadied by a sense of economic well-being. Cheap and abundant food, ready employment at fair wages, heavy business profits in many lines, and a steady continuance of western settlement, sustained Northern courage. "Our people bear the burdens of the war without inconvenience," declared a circular of Samuel Hallett & Company in the summer of 1862, "because they have an abundance of everything that supports war—men, money, food, clothing, and munitions of all kinds. All these can be had in the greatest profusion upon such terms as the government offers. A similar strength, stability, and confidence displays itself in all the operations of society. Prices of property of all kinds are well maintained. There is no check to the progress of all useful enterprises that bid fair to be remunerative." [1]

[1] The writer of "Why the Country is Prosperous," an editorial in the Chicago *Tribune*, Oct. 31, 1861, found the explanation in increased exports, diminished imports of luxuries, and gold receipts from the Far West.

From the economic prostration just before and after Sumter, the North had made a sharp recovery in the first battle autumn. One of its sources lay in the abundant harvests gathered to meet an unprecedented world demand. Another root sprang from the war contracts which expanded so rapidly after Bull Run, and a third from the practical exclusion of many foreign commodities from the home market by the Morrill Tariffs, shipping difficulties, and incipient inflation with its resulting exchange difficulties. Not the least important source was the imagination displayed by industrial leaders in adapting themselves to changed demands. Finally, the use of new machinery and technological devices in field, factory, and foundry had its effects. This recovery had been continued into 1862 as a firmly rooted prosperity, which by 1863 was bearing gaudy flowers of wealth, speculation, and luxurious spending.

Nathaniel Hawthorne, studying the country, marveled at the rapidity with which it took on a military veneer. The demand just after Bull Run for a new army of half a million was translated into the sudden appearance of soldiers everywhere, parading on New England greens, clattering along Philadelphia streets, crowding prairie railway stations; privates buttoning their French-gray overcoats against the autumn chill, officers fingering their swords and gilt buttons. War contracts were translated into another language. They meant the hammering of countless carpenters on new buildings, the scream of saws hewing out gunstocks, the roar of forges making wagon tires. Bank presidents sat up late studying applications for credit. Newspaper editors, "free," said Grant, "to the point of open treason," toiled to distribute their swelling circulation by newsboys and post offices. Storekeepers wrung the hand of the departing clerk and asked the deacon if his bright daughter would like the place. In Washington, in State capitals, in city halls, administrators saw that the kind of regulation Andrew Jackson had established when he forbade the employment of women would have to be jettisoned. The manpower shortage meant higher wages, employment of young and old, and an eager search for labor-saving devices.

The United States, an underdeveloped nation in 1860, needed more capital, more entrepreneurial brains, more organization, more technology; in short, more of what a later generation called economic dynamism.[2] By mid-1863 the dynamism was a rushing flood.

2 The principles of capital formation and growth were not at this time understood anywhere. For these principles see the volume by the National Bureau Committee for Economic Research and various university scholars, *Capital Formation and Economic Growth* (Princeton Univ. Press, 1956), and Simon Kuznets, W. E. Moore, and J. J. Spengler, *Economic Growth: Brazil, Japan* (Duke Univ. Press, 1956).

[I]

The changes of these years were the more dramatic for being set against the brief paralysis which accompanied and followed secession. The failure of banks whose notes were based on Southern bonds, the collapse of firms to which Southern interests owed large debts, the embarrassment of businesses trading in Southern cotton, sugar, and naval stores, the suspension of commission houses acting for Southern shippers, all added heavy blows to the initial shock and uncertainty. The breakdown of Illinois banks, for example, which had based their note issues on Southern State bonds, was calamitous. In all Illinois only the fourteen or fifteen banks which had been wise enough to prefer Northern State securities survived. As for merchants, hundreds staggered and fell. Greeley's *Tribune* bitterly remarked that although some individuals had made money from the South, New York City and other centers had in general lost, for repudiation in the bad years 1827, 1837, 1841, 1854, 1857, and 1861 had wiped out all profits. Just how large the total debts of Southerners to the North were nobody knows, but $150,-000,000 would be a median estimate. This suspension of debt payments must not be discussed in moralistic terms, for Southerners found themselves without money to pay, but it created indignation as well as pain in the North.[3]

All businessmen, as the South seceded, turned nervous eyes to that great pillar of the Northern economy, the cotton business. Cotton textiles excelled any other branch of American manufacture in value of product, employment of capital, and importance to internal and foreign trade. With some reason, Southerners had believed that cotton was king in several Northern states as well as Britain and France. Nearly half of the nation's spindles were in Massachusetts and Rhode Island. New England employed about 200,000 operatives, or half as many as the mother country. Fortunately for the Yankee millowners, they had laid in a full annual supply of cotton during 1860, for they knew that the crop was heavy and that prospects for the future

3 For the breakdown of the Illinois banks, see *Annual Statement*, Chi. Bd. of Trade, 1861; Cole, *Era of Civil War*, Ch. XVI. One authority, J. C. Schwab, places the total of Southern obligations as low as $40,000,000; *Hist. Confederacy*, 111, 112. R. G. Dun & Company, after a close examination of their books, estimated it at about $300,000,000; they reported (N. Y. *Times*, Jan. 2, 1862) that the total owed to New York businessmen was $159,800,000; to Philadelphia businessmen, $24,600,000; and in Baltimore, $19,000,000. The Southern journalist E. A. Pollard puts the debt at not less than $200,000,000; *Jefferson Davis*, 183. Philip S. Foner, *New York Business and Slavery*, 218, sets the amount at $150,000,000. On May 21, 1861, the Confederate Provisional Congress made suspension legal by prohibiting debt payments to Northerners; those owing money were authorized to pay the amount due to the Confederate Treasury, which would give them a certificate payable after the war in specie or its equivalent.

suggested a diminished yield as well as political uncertainty. Even so, the out-break of war instantly disrupted the cotton-textile trade, for it cost the North the large Southern market, and faced the businessman with fears both spectral and substantial.

Between Sumter and Bull Run, most large mills completed their orders and shut down either completely or in part. The venerable Merrimack Company in Lowell, Massachusetts, made what that city long remembered as a stupendous blunder, for believing that the war would end soon and suddenly, the managers closed its mills, dismissed its hands, and began to sell stocks of raw cotton which soon became almost priceless. Some other mills followed this unlucky example. After Bull Run the industry relapsed further into the depression, for cotton spinners perceived that the war might last long, business might get worse, and the market could not absorb their textiles if they hastily manufactured all their reserve cotton. The Pepperell Company on the Saco, for example, in August discharged all but 200 or 300 of the 1,400 hands in its three mills. For the first year of war American mills averaged about half-time. Meanwhile, machinery makers found orders for textile equipment dwindling to a trickle.

In the closing weeks of 1861 observers doubted whether half the cotton mills were operating on any considerable scale. The export trade for the year had fallen by a quarter, and many discouraged hands had enlisted or found other employment. Suffering among the mill workers would have been seri-ous but for enlistments and the fact that many women simply scattered to rural homes. Only a few favorable circumstances had saved the cotton-textile busi-ness from being beaten prostrate. For one, prices of goods had slowly risen, so that even on reduced sales many maufacturers could show a profit. The mills closed the year with 75,000 bales still on hand, a stock augmented by meager shipments slipping through from the South, or returned from Europe by speculative holders anxious to take advantage of the high market; and this stock gave manufacturers hope they could hold on until McClellan overthrew the Confederacy. Even so, the outlook was gloomy, for raw cotton cost so much that many mills could not afford to buy new supplies and process them.[4]

Meanwhile, the Northern trade in many other commodities experienced an agonizing wrench. New York had special reason for feeling the national up-heaval. The loss of credits to the South, of shipping business, of brokerage

4 *Annual Reports*, Boston Bd. of Trade, 1861 and 1862, cover textile manufactures in New England. The Commissioner of Agriculture stated the cotton crop of 1860 at 5,192,746 bales, of which 3,812,345 bales were exported in that year, leaving 1,384,599 bales for domestic consumption; Annual Report, 1862, p. 561. In England, writes John Watts, "mills began to run short time or to close in the month of October [1861], but no noise was made about it"; toward the end of the year in England, speculation in cotton became unusually active. *Lancashire and the Cotton Famine*, 113.

and banking fees, and of a large retail trade through Southern ports, hit the city hard. It had stood supreme in the sugar trade, and now Louisiana shipments and Southern orders went by the board. It had been the chief market for naval stores, and dealers groaned when the last parcels of crude turpentine were sold in October. Shoe manufacturers and jobbers, catering almost entirely to the South, were left with a dead weight of stock on their hands. Until late summer, the sale of all kinds of iron and ironware was so completely checked that furnaces in the Hudson Valley, which had specialized in expensive grades of charcoal iron, had to be blown out.[5]

Philadelphia, with an advantage over most centers in the variety of her manufacturing, fared better. The census had shown that the city had 1,523 clothing factories, 525 textile factories, and 649 iron and steel works, producing about $60,000,000 worth of goods a year. But in addition, Philadelphia had a remarkable range of establishments making wagons, farm implements, paper, leather, glass, wooden wares, pottery, soap, and chemicals, a situation which facilitated its adaptation to new conditions. When cotton supplies ran low, some factories quickly put in woolen machinery, and when luxury goods fell their producers turned to army supplies. "Business has, of course, been greatly disturbed and deranged," remarked the Board of Trade in its review of 1861, "and heavy losses have ensued to many parties"; but, it added, industry had shown such resourcefulness that the great majority of employers and workingmen were fully and usefully occupied.[6]

The trade of Baltimore, however, was nearly paralyzed well into the summer of 1861, and recovered but slowly. Providence, which had specialized in cotton textiles, found that instead of receiving 160,000 bales as in 1860, it obtained little over one-third of that amount during 1861.[7] Most iron furnaces on the Susquehanna and Schuylkill shut down. Pittsburgh suffered from the interruption to the iron trade. All the cities along the border—Wheeling, Cincinnati, Louisville, St. Louis—were for a time badly hurt, for they expected more fighting than they actually saw, and were rent by factional divisions.

Cincinnati in particular had a well-justified fear from the beginning that its trade would be largely shattered. When war became imminent most of the people of Yankee and German origin called for an interdict on all traffic with the Confederacy. Pork packers, manufacturers, and merchants protested angrily that they would be ruined, but majority sentiment prevailed. While competitors in Louisville, St. Louis, and other places continued sending mixed shipments south, for the government imposed no blockade until May, the

5 See *Fourth Annual Report*, Chamber of Commerce, State of N. Y. (1861).
6 See *29th Annual Report*, Phila. Bd. of Trade (1861).
7 Theodore Collier, "Providence in Civil War Days," *R. I. Hist. Soc. Colls.*, XXVII, Nos. 3 and 4 (October, 1934), 102.

patriotic Cincinnatians paid a heavy price. In the fiscal year 1860–61 the city had butchered nearly twice as many hogs as Chicago, but now its Southern trade collapsed, and when 1861 closed it held the only oppressive stocks of pork in the West. Its expanding manufacture of furniture, designed largely for the Southwest, almost went to pieces; in the five months beginning with April it shipped only 27,000 pieces as against 78,000 in the same months of 1860. Iron manufacturers had to suspend wholly or in part. Altogether, Cincinnati underwent severe hardships.[8]

The trade of Chicago with the South had been lucrative. Merchants shipped cereals, flour, hay, and meats—for the city excelled in packing beef as Cincinnati did pork—by the Illinois Central and Alton railroads to St. Louis and thence by packets down the Mississippi and up every large tributary. A return river-rail traffic in cotton and sugar was just becoming appreciable, and nourished a dream of Northwestern cotton mills. The link between the Illinois Central and Mississippi Central was so far advanced that men had hoped to run through trains between Chicago and New Orleans early in 1861. Lately, moreover, buyers from Richmond, Charleston, and other points in the South Atlantic area had appeared in Chicago markets. The sudden curtailment of business by the political upheaval in the winter of 1860–61 dismayed everyone. "The South was never so bare of provisions and breadstuffs as at the present moment," remarked the annual trade review as 1860 ended. Until midsummer the depression persisted.[9] St. Louis meanwhile, as we have seen, suffered a paralysis as severe as Baltimore's.

But for most interests the war quickly healed the first wounds it created. Shuttered stores, smokeless factory chimneys, and ragged clumps of unemployed faded like a bad dream. Throughout the summer of 1861 men commented on the plethora of money which made call loans easily obtainable at 4 to 6 per cent. Though in the panic of 1857 notes signed by the best names had sold as high as 5 per cent a month, during the troubled early weeks of the war good paper was sought at legal interest rates. "One was a financial and the other a political panic," remarked the New York *Tribune*.[10] R. G. Dun & Co. reported more Northern failures in 1861 than in 1857, but for diminished totals; 4257 mercantile failures in 1857 for $265,800,000, as against

8 The Cincinnati Chamber of Commerce published annual reviews Sept. 1–Aug. 31, which are supplemented by annual reports of the Ohio State Commissioner of Statistics.

9 For Chicago's hardships see *Annual Statements*, Chi. Bd. of Trade, 1861–63; Chicago *Tribune*, 12th, 13th, and 14th annual reviews of trade and commerce, 1860–62; A. T. Andreas, *Hist. of Chicago*, II, 616 ff.; and Bessie L. Pierce, *A Hist. of Chicago, 1848–73*, pp. 127–129. The war shattered the dream of through Chicago-New Orleans rail traffic; direct trains did not run until the end of 1873.

10 N. Y. *Tribune*, June 29, 1861; as early as May 29 a *Tribune* editorial had predicted great war prosperity.

5935 failures in 1861 for $178,600,000. Jobbing houses had been the greatest losers.[11] And before the autumn began, a great change was under way. As early as July the Allegheny arsenal at Pittsburgh was employing 400 hands. In October the Cleveland *Leader* remarked that business was better than before the war, for machinists, manufacturers, shipbuilders, railroads, and clothing merchants were all filling war orders.[12]

[II]

Recovery came first in an unprecedented sale of grain, meats, and other farm staples to Great Britain and Continental Europe. During three years, 1860–62, British crops were a failure, and in one of these years the whole European crop was wretched.

Chicago, already the nation's chief rail center, boasted at the end of 1861 that it had carried on a richer commerce in cereals than ever before. "Our city may well be proud of her position." It forwarded much more than twice the flour shipped in the year Lincoln was elected, it was drawing ahead of Cincinnati in pork packing, and its receipts of lumber fell little short of the previous year's mark. Cold statistics tell little, but one may be cited: against shipments of just over thirty-one million bushels of grain and flour in 1860, Chicago in 1862 sent out more than fifty-six millions.[13] The city was a center of trade not only in cured meats, but in livestock on the hoof. In the summer of 1862 the New York *Tribune* noted that every channel to the Atlantic coast was teeming with agricultural products—"Illinois alone sends now to the great market at New York an average of 2000 head of cattle weekly." [14] Transportation facilities in the fall of 1861 were overtaxed, with every lake vessel fully employed and car shortages on all the railroads.

Other centers made the same report. The trade of St. Louis, which reflected army as well as civilian demands, curved upward during the fall. That city had shipped 443,000 barrels of flour in 1861; the figure rose to 484,000 in 1861, to 647,500 in 1862, and to 689,000 in 1863. Foodstuffs went down the Mississippi and up the Tennessee, Cumberland, and Arkansas rivers in the wake of the armies. Cincinnati also took courage from the avidity of the European market. Lard and meat exports to Britain broke all records in

11 N. Y. *Times*, Jan. 1, 1862.
12 Baldwin, *Pittsburgh*, 318; Cleveland *Leader*, Oct. 19, 1861.
13 Chicago had forwarded 698,000 barrels of flour in 1860; in 1861 it forwarded 1,604,000 barrels; and in 1862 it sent 1,828,000. *Annual Statement*, Chi. Bd. of Trade, 1865, p. 24; C. B. Kuhlmann, *Devt. of the Flour-Milling Industry in the U. S.*, 94 ff. For the decade before the war the United States had averaged wheat exports of about twenty millions a year, but in 1862 it sent overseas three times that much. *Statistical Abstract*.
14 July 29, 1862.

1861, for British consumers took the equivalent, from all America, of two million hogs. "Nothing like this ever happened before," wrote Cincinnati's trade annalist. "It shows . . . that there is now secured a market for our pork in Great Britain and on the Continent of such magnitude that . . . the amount consumed heretofore in the Southern States sinks into comparative insignificance." In Philadelphia the Pennsylvania Railroad erected large grain elevators for the export trade.[15]

The sizable military markets which appeared in the fall of 1861 rapidly widened to immensity. Providence noted the brisk new demand in September. Several firms held contracts for army cloth, a tool company had a contract for 25,000 rifles, Corliss and Nightingale were making breech-loading cannon, and other establishments were turning out bayonets and the Burnside rifle: "plenty of work, good prices, and general contentment." [16] By the end of August the New England shoe trade was busy on its first army contracts. Cincinnati clothing makers received batches of army orders early in the fall, and by September, 1862, had contracted for more than six million uniforms. The shoemakers found that they had cut back their facilities too sharply when Southern demand fell, for as the armies began engrossing the Eastern supply, a Midwestern shortage appeared which the revived factories could not meet. Pittsburgh, meanwhile, was busy making river steamboats, army wagons, and a variety of arms. New York found the consumption of sugar rising, for soldiers consumed more.[17]

Another stimulant to industry, the tariff, first became strongly felt in the summer of 1862. The original Morrill tariff, passed just before Sumter, had been moderate in temper, its most important changes being the enhanced duties on iron and wool. Its authors had asserted that they meant simply to restore rates to those of the Walker tariff of 1846. But the second Morrill tariff (July 14, 1862) went well beyond the avowed purpose of Thaddeus Stevens and Justin S. Morrill, the compensation of domestic producers for the sharp internal revenue taxes just laid. Western Democrats in Congress protested that the high duties, made still higher by the fact that they had to be paid in gold, laid an unjust burden on Western agriculture for the benefit of Eastern industry. "Let this process go on a few years, and the wealth of the West will be transferred to the pockets of New England monopolists and capitalists." And Francis Lieber wrote his friend Sumner declaring that such enactments fed the very real hatred which other sections felt for New

15 Annual Reviews, Cincinnati Ch. of Commerce, 1861, 1862; St. Louis Union Merchants Exchange, Annual Report, 1865; 29th Annual Report, Phila. Bd. of Trade, 12.
16 Theodore Collier, "Providence in Civil War Days," R. I. Hist. Soc. Colls., XXVII, Nos. 3 and 4 (July, 1934), 82.
17 5th Annual Report, Ch. Commerce, State of N. Y., 1862, p. 104.

England. The tariff actually shut out many articles so completely that it failed of its revenue-raising goal, and forced the growth of certain lines of industry as in a hothouse.[18]

In particular, it and a thousand war requirements revived the iron industry with galvanic effect, and with special benefit to Pennsylvania. Several other States, as prices soared, hastily refurbished old furnaces, rolling mills, and forges, and opened new ones. New York turned to disused shafts in the Adirondacks, and the Cooper-Hewitt works at Trenton increased their demands on New Jersey ores. But Pennsylvania drew ahead of all rivals—another step in that process of national disequilibrium which Horatio Seymour had deplored in his inaugural speech.[19]

During 1862 two extensive rolling mills were opened at Allentown and Bethlehem, with an annual capacity of 40,000 tons, another began operation at Sharon, and two steel works were established in Pittsburgh. The war never completely stopped railroad construction, while it accelerated the demand for rolled iron, merchant bars, forgings, and plates. The Phoenixville Iron Works soon made a specialty of the widely used three-inch rifled guns; the Fort Pitt Works at Pittsburgh, enlarged in 1862, turned out castings so huge that they were a wonder of the time. Meanwhile the heavy burden on existing railways created an urgent requirement for rails, cars, and locomotives which Pennsylvania did more than any other State to fill. Before the conflict ended the State doubled its output of iron rails, and its shops made most of the 3,000 freight cars and 50 locomotives put into service by the Pennsylvania Railroad alone.

By 1863 Philadelphians were rejoicing over a clear national primacy. Eastern Pennsylvania had turned out 381,000 tons of anthracite iron the previous year, and expected to make 580,000 tons in the current twelvemonth. "It is certain that the production of iron, which has been immensely stimulated during the last two years, has more than ever been concentrated in Eastern Pennsylvania, establishing our supremacy. . . ." The pig-iron production of the whole nation in 1860 had been roughly 920,000 tons. That of the North alone dropped in 1861 to 730,500 tons; reached 788,000 tons in 1862; and in 1863 broke the old records with a total of 947,600 tons.[20]

18 Taussig, *Tariff Hist.*, 162–170; S. S. Cox's speech in House, Jan. 22, 1863; Lieber, Jan. 14, 20, 1863, to Sumner, Lieber Papers, HL. New England for the good of the nation should "relax her protective acerbity," declared Lieber; but Pennsylvania was an equally greedy champion of protection, while Ohio sheep-growers benefited from the wool duties.

19 Nevins, *Hewitt*, 206 ff. Bernard Levin, "Penna. and the Civil War," *Pa. History*, X (January, 1943), 1–10.

20 Insofar as the United States had an infant Ruhr, it was in the Schuylkill and Lehigh Valleys. In 1862 the Lehigh Valley produced 178,000 tons of iron; the Schuylkill furnaces 80,000 tons. The Juniata and Cambria furnaces made 63,500 tons, the former specializing in

But the most interesting stimulant of industrial expansion in 1861–63 was the resourcefulness and ingenuity of Northerners, an asset worth an army. Of a thousand possible illustrations of quick adaptation to new circumstances that furnished by the Waltham Watch Company will suffice. Thrown on its beam ends in 1861, like other luxury craft, the corporation first reefed sail. Then, the managers, noting that the tariff, high exchange, and insurance rates had shut out foreign watches, while international complications made people favor a home product, began studying the market. They saw that soldiers, clerks, and workmen wanted cheap watches within the $12–$18 price range; and sales and profits climbed until in 1863 they were a third higher than in the last prewar year.[21]

[III]

Some industries were so altered and dilated by the war that men were tempted to call them new industries. The transformation was sometimes manifest in the rapid utilization of newly invented machines for quantity production or the replacement of lost manpower; sometimes in the adaptation of facilities which furnished one type of goods to the making of a substitute staple; and sometimes in the swift development of a quite novel resource. The use of the new shoe machinery offers a classic instance of the first kind of resiliency; the expansion of woolen manufactures to take the place of cotton goods an example of the second; and the rise of the petroleum industry an illustration of the third.

No chapter of our economic history has more drama than the wartime transformation of the boot and shoe industry. This was one of the largest industries of the nation, employing in 1860 some 123,000 persons in 12,500 establishments, and producing goods valued at $91,900,000—a sum not prodigiously below the $115,600,000 total for cotton textiles. But when the war began it was still mainly in the stage of domestic production, most so-called factories being mere assembly rooms for products fabricated at home. In New England, the consolidation of small shops into big factories had become pronounced in the 1850's, and had been accelerated by the panic of 1857,

charcoal and coke for fuel. Though steel production was trifling by subsequent standards, more was being made in the United States than most people realized. It was needed for files, saws, cutlery, and edged tools in general; and the N. Y. *Tribune* of Feb. 18, 1861, stated that twenty-one establishments were making at least 13,800 tons a year, some of it better than the Sheffield make. The N. Y. *Times* attacked the first Morrill tariff on steel as prohibitory, but the *Tribune* declared that it was time the British monopoly was ended. Files of the *Iron Age* contain much on iron manufacture, tariffs, the brisk wartime search for new iron deposits, and the shipments of Lake Superior ore, which dropped badly in 1861, recovered to the prewar level in 1862, and broke records (203,797 tons) in 1863.
21 C. W. Moore, *Timing a Century*, 42 ff.

for the factory system checked waste, speeded production, and insured a higher standard of work. The largest single establishment, that of the Batcheller family at Brookfield, Massachusetts, in 1860 produced goods valued at $750,000, and it and four other factories under the same proprietorship made more than a million pairs of boots and shoes. But uppers were as yet generally hand-bound to soles in homes, and often the whole shoe was made there.

Lyman R. Blake, who in 1858 patented a machine to sew the uppers to soles, and Gordon McKay, who promoted it, made it possible to abolish the principal bottleneck in shoe manufacturing; but their invention needed the war and the shortage of manpower to accomplish its rapid adoption. Blake's device consisted of a hollow arm tapering to a small rounded end with a hooked needle, and an accompanying mechanism for making a loop of thread, which the needle caught and drew through the sole. The early months of war found him, still only twenty-five, traveling about New England with McKay to introduce his machine, improve it, and instruct workers in its use. He began, he related later, by sewing shoes for the Massachusetts Light Artillery. "Next I sewed the shoes for one or two regiments, and afterwards many thousands of pairs of army shoes. This army work was very heavy, and was undertaken with a view to test the machines, that they might be rendered nearly perfect before they were sold to the public." In 1862 he patented an improved machine. That same year McKay organized a company with a capital of $250,000 to distribute it, and then leased it to manufacturers for a down payment of $500 and a royalty of 5¢ for each pair of shoes stitched.[22]

The new machine came in steadily. Seth Bryant, a Massachusetts manufacturer, helped break a path for it when he took samples of machine-sewed shoes to Washington to show Stanton. The War Department gave him a contract on condition that he would guarantee the sewing, to which he agreed with the stipulation, in return, that as he would stamp his name on every

22 The North could have made shoes for its armies by the old methods, for more shoes were produced just before the war, selling both North and South, than at any time during the conflict. But shoe workers enlisted heavily, and women could not fully close the labor gap; machine-sewn shoes were stronger and more flexible than handmade shoes; and the machines kept prices down. These factors rather than army exigencies brought in the new era. Blake had been unable to finance his invention himself, and in 1859 had sold his rights for $50,000 to men who, when they ran into difficulties, induced Gordon McKay to take an interest. Blake then joined McKay on a wage basis supplemented by a limited royalty payment. During a period of three years he experimented with improved models, and produced 150,000 pairs of shoes for the army, of which 30,000 were rejected. Army contracts stipulated oak leather, which was staple in the Pennsylvania area, whereas hemlock leather was common in the Massachusetts market, and this handicapped New England manufacturers. See B. E. Hazard, *Organization of the Boot and Shoe Industry in Massachusetts Before 1875*, 112 ff.; C. H. McDermott, *History of the Shoe and Leather Industries of the U. S.*, I, 58 ff.; and D. N. Johnson, *Sketches of Lynn or the Changes of Fifty Years*, passim.

pair, Stanton should compel all other makers to do the same. While this contract for 300,000 pairs gave Bryant little profit, it did afford the new machine an effective advertisement. At the end of 1863 about two hundred machines were in use, and had already stitched two and a half millions of shoes. Steam power could of course be applied to quantity manufacture. A typical newspaper article in the Lynn *Reporter*, describing the growth of factories at the expense of domestic output, related that little handicraft shops were being vacated all over town, while "operatives are pouring in as fast as room can be made for them; buildings for shoe factories are going up in every direction; the hum of machinery is heard on every hand." McKay's ingenious idea of leasing rather than selling the machines saved small factory owners from burdensome capital charges and thus encouraged the change. As the skill of the Yankee handworker was now less important, factories appeared in cities of the Middle West, where the cattle industry furnished a plentiful supply of leather.[23]

An equally remarkable transformation occurred in the woolen industry, the swift rise of which was partly a compensation for the crippling of cotton textiles, and partly a response to voracious military needs. Here was one of the most impressive economic shifts of the time. When fighting began, the army had clothing stocks for only 13,000 men. The inability of mills to meet the sudden demand for uniforms, leaving a gap that foreign importations and the use of wretched cloth did not fill, resulted in a frenzied effort to increase facilities and output, which the war spurred on without pause. Early autumn in 1861 found the wool market swept bare; the new clip had been taken voraciously, and California shipments were sold before arrival. Within six weeks prices rose by a full third. Demand for woolens continued to outstrip supply, and as the war continued many millowners reaped large fortunes. In 1862 the mills took nearly half again as much raw wool as the previous year, and in 1863 double the 1861 total. Philadelphia, Providence, Lawrence, and Lowell, in that order the largest makers of woolens, could hardly find enough hands.

"The woolen machinery of the country is now fully employed," re-

23 At the beginning of 1862 the Boston board assured Montgomery C. Meigs that as the State probably had more machinery in motion than any other, "and as our people adapt themselves to circumstances with wonderful facility, we think it entirely safe to remark that in a year's time our shoe towns could provide for an army of half a million, of as good materials and workmanship, and at a lower price, than elsewhere." *Eighth Annual Report* (for 1861). A typical conversion story was that of T. H. Nowell of Portsmouth, N. H. Early in the war he gave home workers their materials, each handmaking the whole shoe and averaging three pairs daily. Then he introduced machinery and filled a large room with employees. Each team of five men thereafter finished thirty-six pairs daily, and as wartime wages rose, this gain of 133 per cent in labor output was important. Portsmouth *Journal*, Aug. 27, 1864.

ported the Boston board of trade for 1863. New mills had sprung up like Jonah's gourd, while old ones were renovated into something (literally) rich and strange. The Pacific Mills at Lawrence, for example, a combined woolen, cotton, and textile-printing establishment, wrote under Abbott Lawrence a striking page indeed of business enterprise. When Sumter roused the nation it threw away the red ink used since the panic of 1857, increased its profits under the new tariffs, and was soon a dazzling success. The Riverdale Mill in Providence, managed by a sagacious Scot, Robert Blaikie, became equally noted. The Assabet Mill at Maynard, Massachusetts, grew rapidly into the largest woolen (as distinguished from worsted) establishment in the nation. With high prices as stimulants, such factories ran day and night and maintained an urgent pressure on machinery makers. Down to the war the industry had lagged far behind the English mills in mechanical equipment, but now their facilities became equal to any in the world.

The sudden new demand for raw wool was felt over half the globe. In every pastoral country sheep growers responded to it; Australia, Canada, South Africa, Argentina, New England, the Far West, and the Scottish border all saw flocks whitening their green pastures so that Yankee looms might be kept whirring. The sunshine of high prices brought out a May-fly dance of speculators. Half the foreign wool taken for American mills came from Buenos Aires and Montevideo, with Britain and Europe the next largest sources. Everyone made money from the staple: Ohio farmers, Victoria station-owners, jobbers, shippers—but above all, manufacturers. Stockholders in the Pacific Mills, after investing $2,500,000, drew out wartime dividends aggregating nearly $3,000,000. The James Steam Mills Corporation of New-buryport in twelve months beginning May 1, 1862, earned $240,000 on a capital of $250,000, paying dividends of 80 per cent while increasing its reserves. A student of company reports finds evidence that dividends rose from an average of 9 per cent during the eight years before the war to 25.2 per cent in 1865.[24]

Contrary to a widely accepted legend, the ready-made clothing business was well established in America before the war. The first systematic manu-facture, with coarse materials and rough workmanship, had begun in the 1830's. Garments ready-made in large quantities were sold to seamen, miners,

---

24 In this quick growth of the woolen industry statistics take on a certain aura of romance. The wool clip of the twenty-three loyal States in 1860 was 47,901,000 pounds; by 1864 the increase of sheep and improvement of breeds had lifted it to 97,385,500 pounds—it had more than doubled. *Ann. Cyc.*, 1865, p. 4. W. C. Ford, *Wool and Manufactures of Wool*, 317, gives the imports of raw wool as 31,000,000 pounds in 1861, just over 43,000,000 in 1862, some 73,200,000 in 1863, and 90,200,000 in 1864. See also A. H. Cole, *The American Wool Manufacture*, I, 268 ff.; and "Report Upon Wool" in *Reports* of U. S. Commissioners, Paris Exposition of 1867. Cole, I, 380, gives figures on wartime profits.

farm hands, and above all, owners of slaves. The invention of the sewing machine accelerated the business, while by the later 1850's woolen mills were manufacturing materials on a large scale. Use of sewing machines, and, just as the war opened, power cloth-cutters, assisted in the supersedure of many small shops by large wholesale establishments. This change is forcibly indicated by the fact that during the fifties the capital invested in the business nearly doubled, yet the number of establishments fell by 11 per cent. Trousers, cloaks, and vests were more readily made on a factory basis than coats, which required some skill in craftsmanship.

The disappearence of the Southern slave market confronted the ready-made trade with a crisis which war orders helped to erase. A single manufacturer received an order for $1,250,000 worth of uniforms. At first uniforms were made largely on the old "inside" system of manufacture; that is, workers went to a wholesaler for materials already cut and marked for putting together, and on completing them returned the garments for payment. As demands for Army clothing became exigent, however, factories were erected for the making of complete uniforms and nothing else. The government furnished measurements better adapted to males of various sizes than those previously used in the trade. The subdivision of labor increased, standards of workmanship became better established, and efficient new factory methods were introduced. The second Morrill Tariff, placing a duty of 24 per cent *ad valorem* on ready-made garments, almost completely excluded foreign competition. By 1863 Boston, New York, Rochester, Philadelphia, and Cincinnati were thriving centers of the business.[25]

In the swift development of a novel resource, the oil business meanwhile astonished not only America but the world. "Colonel" Edwin L. Drake had rubbed his Aladdin's lamp at Titusville, in the forested Allegheny hills, only fourteen months before Lincoln's election. The rush to northwestern Pennsylvania had taken on dramatic proportions before Sumter. In dash, color, and the exuberant production of wealth the oil boom rivaled the California and Australia gold rushes.

In certain essential respects this was not so new a business as it looked.

25 See the *Report* on clothing and woven fabrics by the U. S. Commissioners, Paris Exposition of 1867; U. S. Dept. of Commerce, *The Men's Factory-Made Clothing Industry* (1916), p. 9 ff. The wagon industry enjoyed an expansion not unlike that of the woolen industry. Carriage making in New York, like other luxury trades, was hard hit in 1861. But harbingers of revival appeared when the Union Defence Committee in June, 1861, ordered 50 ambulances, and that month and the next the Quartermaster's Department took 906 baggage wagons and 380 ambulances. In November, 1861, the New York *Coach-Makers' Magazine* was able to report: "The number of wagons, ambulances, and gun-carriages manufactured in this city and other places, for the army, is immense." By December, 1861, some 2,500 men were employed in making army wagons in Cincinnati; *Scientific American*, Jan. 2, 1862.

The extraction of lubricants and illuminants from coal had become a lucrative industry in various Eastern states during the prewar decade. Processes of distillation, well-designed lamps, and methods of barreling and selling "coal oil" (which was precisely that) had become well accepted. Petroleum was able to build on this foundation. However, the novelty of oil pumped in huge quantities from the earth, the quick returns made in "black gold," and the wide ramifications of oil-refining astonished observers. Amid bulletins of battle, the North read of fortunes made by the click of a drill, of frantic, noisy, populous towns like Oil City rising magically from the mud, and of the narrow gorge of Oil Creek studded for fifteen miles with derricks. The business soon developed the widest extensions. It gave half a dozen railroads a new source of freight for which they competed savagely, it required the swift building of tanks, terminals, docks, and warehouses; it replaced teamsters by pipelines; and it impelled a resourceful Englishman to establish a line of direct oil-carrying steamers to Liverpool. Lake and river shipping profited.

Though some cautious souls feared that the Pennsylvania fields would soon run dry, by the end of 1863 the economic importance of the flow was unmistakable; with an estimated production of ten million barrels that year, it was feeding refineries from Portland to Baltimore and from New York to Toledo. The market was insatiable, for petroleum furnished much the cheapest illuminant yet known. It made candles a luxury. Though the price of kerosene rose from 28 cents a gallon in 1860 to 41 cents in 1864, even the latter charge was only a third of the old-time cost of coal oil. Lard-oil, camphene, and other "burning fluids" were able to keep the merest vestige of customers. The fleets of whalers seeking sperm oil would have vanished from the seas, even had Confederate cruisers not assisted in scattering them. To fill the gap left when turpentine shipments ceased, petroleum derivatives were used with partial success for paints and varnishes. By the time Fredericksburg was fought, Pittsburgh had perhaps sixty refineries, the "oil regions" forty, and Erie, Pennsylvania, twenty. Speculation led to the rise of disreputable stock-peddling concerns and the formation of an excessive number of both producing and refining companies, many of which soon withered under excessive competition and high Federal taxation. A mining-camp atmosphere, with plentiful violence, enveloped the oil fields. But shrewd or lucky men made large profits, and before the last shots of the war were fired it was estimated that $450,000,000 had been invested in the "regions" alone.[26]

26 A meeting of crude-oil dealers held in New York on June 10, 1862, to combat some hostile Brooklyn restrictions, heard interesting facts from its chairman, A. C. Ferris. He declared that the bulk of the export trade centered in New York; that more than a million dollars had been invested in and around the city in it; and that the business grew mar-

This new industry brought a rising flow of much-needed gold into the country. New York in 1863 exported nearly half a million barrels, and other ports lifted the total to more than 800,000. In fact, oil shouldered its way up beside grain as an earner of foreign gold. "During the latter part of the year 1863," commented the Philadelphia board of trade, "petroleum exports constituted the leading article relied upon by the commercial cities for the creation of exchange in Europe." While Liverpool, London, Havre, Antwerp, Bremen, and Amsterdam were the largest importers, literally every important land on the globe, from China to Peru, wanted its quota of oil.[27]

[IV]

A number of other industries, new or renovated, added to the tale of business enterprise. Ironmasters, shipbuilders, textile makers, and arms manufacturers almost universally took the view that it was *their* war and they should monopolize the task of supply. If the government would only confine its orders to home interests, and compensate for heavy taxes by high duties, they would meet all its needs. A roar of protest went up from New England woolen men when word got about in the fall of 1861 that Quartermaster-General Meigs was about to buy five, or ten, or according to some, sixty million dollars worth of foreign cloth. The Boston board of trade telegraphed that this was entirely unnecessary and injurious to government and people, for home manufacturers could meet any demand. Meigs replied with asperity. Many soldiers were half naked; the governors were daily complaining that enlistments must stop unless abundant clothing was instantly sent to the camps; a hundred thousand uniforms were desperately needed at once; and having tried vainly to buy them at home, he felt justified in spending $800,000 —for that was all—abroad. Yet he had to agree that if home supply sufficed, he would hold the imported cloth for reserve supplies only.[28]

Advances in technological skill were illustrated by the arms factories, farm-implement shops, locomotive works, printing establishments (especially newspapers), machine shops, food canneries, and a hundred other businesses.

velously although the government taxed petroleum half its value. "The oil belt," he explained, "reached from Canada to the Gulf. . . . Another oil belt extended from Texas through Kansas to the Mississippi River. . . . Also upon the Pacific Coast there was a belt beginning about San Diego and so on by Los Angeles to Upper California." One man at the meeting held interests in 187 oil wells in Pennsylvania. N. Y. *Tribune*, June 11. Arnold Daum's MS history of "The Revolution in Illuminants," treats the coal oil industry and the superimposed oil industry in its early years; S. J. M. Eaton, *A Hist. of the Oil Regions of Venango County, Pa.*, 211, 271 ff., offers graphic material on early production.

27　*Annual Cyc.*, 1865, p. 700; Giddens, *Birth of the Oil Industry, passim.* The annual reports of the Phila. Bd. of Trade cover the petroleum industry.

28　Boston Bd. of Trade, *Eighth Annual Report*, 40 ff.

In the second year of the war 490 patents were granted for improved agricultural devices. Better reapers, mowers, threshers, grain drills, gangplows, and cultivators were needed to save manpower and bring in the large wartime harvests. Every curious foreigner visited the large meat-packing plants, and August Laugel was equally impressed by the Chicago elevators. He wrote:

> Imagine an immense building without windows, very high, and divided on the inside into several storys; the ground floor is cut in two by a long gallery, where two trains and their engines can come in. . . . The Chicago River flows on one side of the elevator, a canal on the other connected with the river, so that boats can lie alongside the building as easily as trains can go inside. When a car loaded with grain has gone inside, a door on the side is opened, and the corn pours out into a deep trench. . . . An iron axle turns at the top of the enormous building, put in motion by a 130-horsepower steam engine. This shaft supports a drum at intervals, on which runs a belt to which buckets are fastened. These come down and are filled with corn . . . and raise it to the upper story; a few turns of the wheel bring the corn to the roof, and there it is emptied into a square wooden box of great size. The river of nourishment flows, flows incessantly. . . .
>
> Thirteen elevating wheels raise each one 4,000 bushels an hour, so that 52,000 bushels can be stored in that space of time. The whole building can be filled in half a day.[29]

The engineer John Fritz gives us an illustration of the way in which war contracts, tariff protection, and general industrial activity facilitated the installation of superior equipment in iron mills. In 1861–62 he erected a stone building on the Lehigh River for the Bethlehem Iron Company and began installing furnaces and machinery. By the fall of 1862 the mill, with all its features, was completed. In every respect it met new standards. "The roll housings were of new design and were dressed out inside with hammer, chisel, and file; the fittings inside were fitted up in the same manner. The furnace plates, being corrugated, were strong and handsome . . . ; the train was of the largest diameter used in any rail mill in the country." Machine shop, foundry, blacksmith shop, and pattern shop were all of improved design. For some years the Bethlehem Works were a Mecca for iron men. We may

---

29 *The U. S. During the War*, 127, 128. As much as four and a third million bushels of grain were stored in Chicago in 1861 at one time; *American Agriculturist*, October, 1861, p. 292. The importance of the grain elevator in the growth of traffic centers has been overlooked. An English correspondent wrote his editor just after the war: "That the grain elevator has made the cities of Buffalo and Chicago is not saying too much; and Mr. Joseph Dart made the elevator. . . . Today Buffalo has 27 of these buildings, storing together 5,830,000 bushels, handling daily 2,808,800 bushels. . . . In fact, a vessel alongside may either receive or discharge in six hours a cargo of 150,000 bushels of wheat or corn by means of the elevator. What the elevator means may be understood from the trade of both last year (1865). Buffalo did 40,937,000 bushels, and Chicago came up behind with 40,836,000 bushels." *English Mechanic*, Vol. III, No. 66 (June 29, 1866), 275.

take with reserve Fritz's boast that they were the best ironworks in the world, for after the war American experts found British, French, and German iron and steel plants vastly superior; but they did mark an advance.[30]

Perhaps no changes were more remarkable than those in the shops which equipped the navy and mercantile marine. Depredations of Confederate cruisers, high insurance rates, and the shift from wooden to iron vessels made the war period disastrous for American ocean shipping. Its collapse was but the culmination of a process already well advanced by the time of Sumter. But the fleet employed in the coastal, lake, and river trade maintained its growth, reaching 2,600,000 tons in 1862. When the Navy Department added its special contracts, establishments making marine engines found themselves choked with orders.[31]

A deafening rumble arose by 1863 from a score of machine shops in the New York area: the Neptune, the Morgan, the Novelty, the Continental, the Allaire, the Delamater, the McLeod, and others. They were turning out engines both vertical and horizontal, boilers, furnaces, plates, anchors, and miscellaneous fittings. The Fulton Iron Works, for example, were using seven hundred men to supply engines for eight government vessels, boilers for two more, twenty-four heavy buoys, and equipment for some privately owned vessels. The Novelty Iron Works with twelve hundred men were rebuilding the *Roanoke* with more than a thousand tons of armor and three revolving turrets for fifteen-inch guns, and making a beam engine for a Pacific Mail steamship and machinery for three side-wheel steamers. As various ship-yards were building warships for Italy, Russia, and China, the machine shops furnished engines for them too. Although the decline of the merchant marine made the ultimate outlook gloomy, as long as the war crisis lasted the machine shops did well, and their precision, ingenuity, and scope grew as in no previous period.[32]

[V]

This industrial advance was accomplished by a far-reaching transformation of commerce. As soon as the Mississippi was closed, it became evident that the shift of trade from north-south to east-west channels, begun years before, would be accelerated. When some 1,600 steamboats ceased moving up and down the Ohio-Mississippi system with freight and gave way to war

30 The Bethlehem Works added a second furnace of novel design before they began rolling rails in September, 1863; Fritz, *Autobiography*, 141.
31 J. G. B. Hutchins, *The American Maritime Industries and Public Policy, 1789-1914*, 304-306. The appearance of low-cost iron-hulled steamships, British built and owned, to carry immigrants, had been especially disastrous to American packets.
32 Able articles appear in the N. Y. *Tribune*, Jan. 31, 1861, Feb. 7, May 1, 1863, etc.

flotillas, a huge tonnage of grain, meats, hay, and merchandise that had floated down to the Gulf had to turn toward the Atlantic by rail, lake, and canal.

Though no adequate statistics of steamboat trade exist, a table of steamboat arrivals at Cincinnati, chief commercial center of the Ohio Valley, is eloquent of the change. In the five years ending 1860 the average annual arrivals of steamboats from New Orleans had been 157, and from St. Louis 265; in the five years ending 1865 the arrivals from New Orleans fell to 41, and from St. Louis to 99. And most of what traffic still followed the river during the war served martial and not peaceful purposes.

The transports black with troops, the rams and "tinclads" with protrusive cannon, the sluggish flat-bottomed hospital boats and supply boats, kept the stretch south from Cairo busy; but Midwestern freight to and from the seaboard and Europe depended more and more on rails. For a decade three separate branches of water commerce had been declining. The movement of Western crops and manufactures to the South and Europe by way of New Orleans had declined; transfers between the Ohio Valley and the seaboard by canals had declined; and the movement between the Ohio River and the upper Mississippi and Missouri had declined. The war accentuated this threefold drop. While nobody can cite dependable figures, Cincinnati, Louisville, and St. Louis all now witnessed the final passing of the scepter from river packet to railway train.

The principal railroads paid off their floating debts, resumed dividends suspended in the recent panic, extended their lines, and in some instances accumulated surpluses. "At no former period," declared Greeley's *Tribune* late in the war, "has the whole Northern railroad system been so prosperous." [33] This prosperity encouraged the consolidation of small lines into trunk systems, and the building of new railroads for districts poorly served.

The Pennsylvania system, under the presidency of the brilliant engineer J. Edgar Thomson, achieved a highly successful series of consolidations. During the secession winter, replacing a short-term lease of the Harrisburg-Lancaster railroad by a 999-year lease, it obtained absolute control of a through line from Philadelphia to Pittsburgh. Before Donelson was fought it took another 999-year lease on the uncompleted Philadelphia & Erie, which would connect the main line with the Great Lakes and the oil district. Work was briskly pressed to finish this 289-mile road. For its connection with the Middle West the Pennsylvania used the Pittsburgh, Fort Wayne & Chicago, itself a merger of several lines, and by interlocking directorates and ownership of stock, the Pennsylvania managers obtained perfect control of this 465-mile road through Ohio and Indiana to Chicago, with branches to Cleveland

[33] Jan. 27, 1864.

and Toledo. During the war Thomson also effected a close alliance with several short roads from Pittsburgh southwestward to the Ohio, thus gaining connections with Cincinnati and St. Louis. Altogether, by 1863 his powerful combination of lines was able to collect in St. Louis and Chicago the Midwestern crops, in Cleveland the Lake Superior ores, and in Erie the Michigan lumber, while it would soon tap the oil fields.[34]

The closing of the lower Mississippi to grain traffic, and the plans for a Pacific railroad, encouraged other roads to wrap their iron tentacles around more territory between Lake Michigan and the Missouri. The Rock Island line was one. The Chicago, Burlington & Quincy, which grew from a small feeder of the Michigan Central into a powerful network—as John Murray Forbes wrote, "located, planned, and built by the right set of men"—was another.[35] When Congress passed the Pacific Railroad bill in 1862 the stock of the Rock Island rose twenty points in a few weeks. The Chicago & Northwestern, however, was first in the race to reach Omaha.

The most ambitious railway built during the war was the Atlantic & Great Western, an arresting example of the nation's power to expand while fighting a tremendous conflict. It had originated in the fertile brain of Marvin Kent of Ohio, an entrepreneur who had managed such diverse enterprises as a woolen factory, a flour mill, and glass works. About 1850 he decided that a line of six-foot gauge connecting the Erie Railroad with the embryo Ohio & Mississippi might greatly benefit the Middle West. Obtaining an Ohio charter in 1851, he cast about for means of building across Pennsylvania. To go to the legislature directly was beyond his means, that body, as Horace Greeley wrote, "being then one of the rottenest and the surrounding lobby the most rapacious and shameless on earth." But, learning that the Pittsburgh & Erie possessed charter powers which would furnish the required facilities, Kent induced several other capitalists to join him in buying that road for $400,000. Another half-defunct line, the Erie & New York City, he purchased as a basis for building into New York. Then, all his legal preparations complete, he began collecting subscriptions. Desperate efforts, however, availed to furnish only a million, and this being obviously insufficient, he sent an agent to Europe to procure additional capital.

---

34 H. W. Schotter, *Growth and Devt. of the Pa. R. R. Co.*, 52–60; *Amer. R. R. Manual*, 1873, pp. 227, 228. Late in 1860 the Pennsylvania had taken a car full of Philadelphians on a three weeks' visit to all the chief Midwestern cities; *Annual Report*, Phila. Bd. of Trade, 1860.

35 Van Oss, *Amer. Rrds as Investments*, *passim*, contains a wealth of accurate material on mid-century growth. See also A. T. Andreas, *Hist. of Chicago*, II, 133 ff.; Bessie L. Pierce, *Chicago, 1848–1871*, pp. 147, 148; and Cole, *Era of Civil War*, 359, 360. The career of Forbes, who turned from the China trade to use Yankee capital in promoting the Michigan Central and C. B. & Q., sums up much of the best enterprise of the period; *Letters and Recs.*, I, 163.

The tangled financial history of the road involved the well-known Anglo-American capitalist James McHenry and much British money, while the construction history involved the remarkable Sir Samuel Morton Peto, who had played a leading role in railway building in Australia, Canada, Denmark, and France. But the important facts are that construction began, that the war did not interrupt it until the seizure of the *Trent*, and that after this cloud blew over, it was energetically resumed in 1862. The English engineer prosecuted the work so tenaciously that a year later, despite labor scarcity and rising costs, he had trains running from Salamanca, New York, to Akron, Ohio, with branch lines into the oil regions; in all, about 200 miles of track. In the month of Gettysburg the managers leased the Mahoning Valley line, a coal and iron road, and at once laid an extra rail, giving them a broad-gauge track into Cleveland. At the same time, rails were being laid from Akron to Dayton, whence an existing line, when widened, would carry trains to Cincinnati—the Salamanca-Cincinnati stretch covering 438 miles. Machine shops and a hotel were erected at Meadville, Pennsylvania.[36]

Even during peace the construction of this line within two years would have been a notable feat. Amid the din of war, in districts which the oil-rush and iron-boom had helped to drain of hands, it was a spectacular exploit. By this enterprise, remarked Greeley's *Tribune*, Cincinnati and St. Louis gained closer communication with New York, "while Columbus, Dayton, Indianapolis, and nearly the whole of Indiana and Illinois have secured a new and in many respects superior outlet to the seaboard. The value of the Erie Railroad to its stockholders and to our city is nearly doubled by it."[37] Had as much planning, integrity, and respect for the public interest gone into subsequent management as into the building, the nation would have reaped large gains; a statement applicable to the Erie as well.

Richer, greater, and ever more firmly rooted became the east-west trade as the war went on. New Orleans had been taking from the Northwest about ten million bushels of grain and flour annually; Chicago in 1860 had shipped twice that much. Now that New Orleans was stricken from the list of exporters, while crops and foreign demand swelled, Chicago moved far to the front. During the war years it shipped an annual average of forty-five million bushels of corn, wheat, and flour.[38] This increase represented the expansion of agriculture and the railroads far more than a mere transfer from the Mississippi, but the transfer counted. The growth of east-west trade was assisted by the fact that transportation rates, instead of rising with the general

36 N. Y. *Tribune*, Jan. 19, 1864. See my *Rockefeller*, I, 177, 180 ff., and Mabee, *Railroads and the Oil Trade, passim,* for the importance of this railroad to the oil regions.
37 Jan. 19, 1864.
38 E. D. Fite, *Social and Ind. Conds.,* 47 ff.

inflation, actually fell during the war. The competition of the truck-line rail-roads with each other and with the Great Lakes-Erie Canal route kept them in check. The narrow and shallow canal greatly needed enlargement.[39] Nevertheless, it transported a great deal more wartime tonnage than the New York Central and Erie Railroads combined. The lake boats fixed their freight rates first, and for the greater part of the year the railroads had to adjust their charges accordingly.

As early as January, 1861, the superintendent of the Michigan Central was able to assert that "this secession movement is making the North rich"; that his line was carrying great quantities of fresh pork which would not other-wise have come to it; and that "the products of Kentucky, Tennessee, and so on are all coming this way on account of Southern troubles." The London *Economist* commented on the spectacle of Southwestern cotton and pork moving up the Mississippi instead of down. Ohio's commissioner of statistics reported at the close of 1863 that the revolution in channels of business was unquestionably permanent. "Producers, merchants, and carriers have all found that the markets of New York, Baltimore, and Boston are more stable and reliable than the Southwestern ports have been or can be. The great stream of western produce is running steadily and strongly to the North Atlantic cities—thence a large part of it is shipped to Europe." [40]

Agricultural products were by no means the only great component of the flow, for a rich body of copper, iron ore, and lumber also came by the Soo canal from the upper lakes, or by rail from Milwaukee and Chicago. Iron-ore shipments through the Soo rose from 45,000 tons in 1861 to 113,000 tons in 1862, and to 161,500 in 1863. Particularly remarkable were the figures for lumber. Ax and saw, long busy in the white pine and hardwood forests of Michigan, were now at work in Wisconsin, where the Chippewa River valley contained the most impressive stand of white pine in the world. Although much of this lumber went down the upper Mississippi for wide distribution over the Middle West to build towns, villages, and farmhouses, shipments eastward through the Soo rose from 384,000,000 feet in 1861 to 1,411,000,000 in 1863.[41] During the war, in fact, lumber was rebuilding America. Midway

---

39 Circular of Samuel Hallett & Co., June 9, 1862. This firm reported that even with the small canal boats, freight produce could be transported down the lakes and canal for $60 a ton. In winter, when cold closed the lakes and canal, railroads sharply advanced their rates. Moreover, carriers between the Missouri River and the lakes tended to overcharge. The Chicago Canal Convention of 1863 expressed irritation over high east-west freight charges.

40 N. Y. *Tribune*, Jan. 16, 1861; London *Economist*, Feb. 2, 1861; Ohio Bur. Statistics, *Seventh Annual Report* (for 1863), p. 21.

41 George G. Tunell, *Report on Lake Commerce* (Bur. Statistics, Treasury Dept., 1898), 24.

in the conflict the Chicago *Tribune* remarked that on every street and avenue new buildings were going up—immense stone, brick, and wooden business blocks, and new residences; and the next year, 1864, Chicago building surpassed all previous records, every street being choked by bricks, mortar, and lumber. While in New York building declined, in Brooklyn it reached remarkable levels. In Philadelphia the new factories erected rose from 9 in 1861 to 37 the next year, and 57 in 1863, while the new dwellings built in the same period rose from 1,535 to 2,462.[42]

Altogether, before the war was halfway through it was clear that the future of American transportation would belong to the east-west channels, and that on the economic landscape no giants could for years to come rival the trunk-line railroads; the Pennsylvania, New York Central, Baltimore & Ohio, and Erie, the longer lines west of Chicago, and the new Union Pacific. It was also clear that the railroad system would at last soon become standardized. Among the eight or more different gauges that of four feet eight and a half inches, the Stephenson gauge of England, was emerging as dominant. It already prevailed in the northeastern part of the country. When in 1862 the Pacific Railroad gauge had to be fixed, everyone realized that it would determine the future width of all roads. Of the eleven railroad presidents asked to suggest a gauge, seven recommended the Stephenson standard; and though Lincoln, as we have noted, favored five feet, this was under a misapprehension, and he promptly adopted the majority view. Other roads soon conformed.[43]

[VI]

The exuberant growth of Northern population, agriculture, and industry registered its force in the rise of a new security and finance capitalism, in the multiplication of corporations, and in the emergence of business captains of large vision and practical grasp. New York became unmistakably the nation's financial center. Investment and management demanded companies able to carry on transactions of unprecedented magnitude. Business leaders, and especially the younger leaders, brought a new imagination to affairs. The expansion of western and world trade alone would have begun to revolutionize the thinking of industrial chieftains; instead of dealing with a restricted region,

42 *Thirty-third Annual Report*, Phila. Bd. of Trade, p. 81; Fite, 213 ff. Receipts of lumber in Chicago doubled during the war, rising from 249,000,000 feet in 1861 to 501,000,000 in 1864–65.
43 Fite, 56, 57. The before-mentioned revolutionary occurrence of Jan. 11, 1863, when the first train of cars passed from New York into Ohio, was made possible by the fact that the new Atlantic & Great Western had the same six-foot gauge as the Erie.

they had to concern themselves with half a continent and lands overseas.

The chief money market, New York, was far from efficient prior to the change wrought by the national bank act of 1863. It has been well called an organization without a head, a witless monster, for no central bank exercised leadership in financial affairs. The reserve funds of the land flowed into a number of banks, not one; they were invested for the behoof and profit of separate banks, not of the banking system as a whole; and instead of being used according to rational plan by wise heads of a central reserve bank, they went in great part to the call loan market. When the cash reserves of New York banks fell by more than half in ten months, reaching a low point of $29,350,000 on December 7, 1861, the suspension of specie payments became inescapable. The nation's total bank circulation on New Year's Day, 1862, just after this event, was only $132,000,000, inadequate for the needs of government and industry alike. The Treasury called for an issue of legal tender notes, and by March 3, 1863, Congress had authorized the printing of $450,000,000 in greenbacks.[44]

These issues, augmented by fractional paper currency and large issue of short-term interest-bearing notes, made money abundant. The rapid expansion of local bank circulation during the first two years of the war added to the inflation, and helped furnish capital for new enterprises. By the second anniversary of Lincoln's inauguration, New York banks had deposits of $174,000,000, very nearly $40,000,000 in specie, and outstanding loans, with call money at 6 or 7 per cent, of $171,000,000; the total loans of New York, Boston, and Philadelphia banks came to $297,000,000.[45] The creation of money and credit on an enormous scale by the war had much to do with the nation's economic dynamism.

It also had much to do with less pleasant accompaniments of the conflict. "The current of speculation in the stock market sweeps on with undiminished volume," said the *Tribune*'s financial editorial for May 16, 1863; and gambling swept into every business area.

Speculation accompanied the secession movement. Sam Ward and others used inside knowledge to play the stock market. It accompanied every step of the war. When McClellan landed his army on the Peninsula, stocks rose; his first reverses brought them down; they went up again on news of the fall of Williamsburg and New Orleans, combined with a report of high earnings by the Hudson River Railroad; and they sank once more with the defeats on the Chickahominy. The speculative excitement was accelerated by in-

44 Margaret G. Myers, *The N. Y. Money Market*, I, Ch. X; John Crosby Brown, *A Hundred Years of Merchant Banking*, Chs. VII, XII, presents the Civil War atmosphere.
45 N. Y. *Tribune*, March 6, 1863, commercial column.

flation. A fluctuating currency, a constant rise in values, a sellers' market for most goods, a sense of virile national growth, all made business hum with speculators as a clover field hums with bees. Their activities sometimes reached frenzy:

The excitement in stock circles today we have never seen equalled in our very long experience of the street [wrote the *Tribune*'s financial editor January 8, 1862]. The amount of transactions . . . is, we think, larger than ever before known in the history of stock speculations, and the intense desire to buy almost any kind of securities amounted almost to insanity. No better illustration of the excitement in the Board can be found than that the same stock on the same call was often selling at one and two per cent higher at one end of the room than at the other. The oldest members of the Board cannot remember such a day of rampant speculation. The greatest rise, and one which has no precedent in the history of the Board, was in Toledo & Wabash stock, which sold yesterday at 40, and today at 60.

Commodity speculation was equally violent. Many shrewd capitalists saw early in 1862, for example, that wool was bound to soar. Thus, as the New York Chamber of Commerce noted, arose an army of speculators of every nation under the sun in New York, and as the prices advanced, the army grew. A Cincinnati annalist the following year noted that participants in the drygoods trade had made almost incredible profits. Many dealers speculated, and all who had stocks on hand became rich by the advance, several firms showing net profits of more than $100,000. Petroleum was a paradise for speculators. The receipts from a single Pennsylvania well opened in March, 1862, eventually reached $1,700,000. Andrew Carnegie drew such tropical dividends from the Colombia Oil Company, organized in 1861, that the subsequent erection of his steel mill became much easier.[46] The iron trade had its share of eager gamesters, who complained bitterly in 1863 that the furnaces were so far behind their orders for pig iron and the contracts for more were so numerous that no stocks for speculation existed. A production half again as great would sell instantly without giving the speculator a chance at a gain.[47]

While speculation in cotton became almost a national disease, grain speculation was a widespread occupation. Many a businessman in the army would have echoed Major-General C. C. Washburn's letter to his brother Elihu in 1863: "If I could now be at home, I would rake down largely!"[48] As it was, this lumberman and lawyer, acting from the Sixteenth Corps head-

---

46 *Fifth Annual Report of the Chamber* (for 1862), pp. 156–161. *Annual Statement*, Cincinnati Bd. of Trade, year ending Aug. 31, 1863, pp. 25, 26. Giddens, *Birth of the Oil Industry*, 42, 43.
47 *Sixth Annual Report*, Ch. of Commerce N. Y. (for 1863), pp. 105–107.
48 July 12, 1863, Washburne Papers, LC.

quarters, sold logs and lumber on a broad scale at high prices. Even as a soldier, he raked down quite a bit.

The leap in transportation securities was especially sweet to speculators. From early in the conflict freights exceeded carrying capacity, and net earnings for many lines surpassed the most roseate calculations. Between the beginning of January, 1862, and the same date in 1863, New York Central stock rose from 87 to 130, Illinois Central from 57 to 125, and Pacific Mail Steamship from 111 to 236. Railway securities were specially vulnerable to "movements" managed by bulls and bears. Rock Island Railroad shares in the winter of 1863–64 rose swiftly from 106 to 147, and then slid down to 115, this particular maneuver giving manipulators a reputed profit of a million. The period witnessed the first heavy combats between Vanderbilt and the New York Central on one side, and Drew, Gould, Fisk, and the Erie on the other, the "street" supplying ammunition. Years before, Jacob Little, autocrat of speculators, had familiarized men familiar with dashing operations in which fortunes were made and lost in a day; now a new set of gamblers carried out raids which excited the indignation of law-abiding citizens.[49]

Particularly outrageous were the activities of gamblers in gold. When the New York Stock Exchange, conservatively managed, forbade its members to sell government bonds at a discount or speculate in gold a plain need dictated the formation of the Gold Exchange; but that need was abused. In late winter of 1862–63 "the Jeff Davis gold gamblers," as Greeley called them, forced prices to high levels. As twenty-year 6 per cent United States bonds were selling at 85 or better, and greenbacks were convertible at par into such bonds, the premium on gold ought to have been limited; yet at one time it was forced up to 73—that is, $173 in greenbacks was needed to buy $100 in gold. Union men insisted that the speculation was pushed by interests sympathetic with the Confederacy and hostile to Chase's efforts to maintain the national credit. Excitement rose to a peak on March 6, with transactions aggregating perhaps three millions; the gamblers sold desperately, "in the vain hope of repelling the rising tide of loyal faith in the nation's future"; and the press rejoiced that a drop of seventeen points ruined most of them.

"We do confidently believe," trumpeted the *Tribune*, "that the secesh gold gamblers have received their quietus"; but the worst was still ahead.[50]

Secretary Chase had a limited power to check gold speculations, but no

49   Table in *Hunt's Merchants' Magazine*, XLIX (Sept. 1883), 221; N. Y. *Tribune*, financial column, Feb. 13, 1864. Daniel Drew, chosen a director of the Erie in 1857, used his position for stock manipulation shamelessly. In the famous Harlem Railroad corner planned by Vanderbilt and others in 1864 he was badly worsted.

50   N. Y. *Tribune*, March 5, 6, 7, covers this flurry; gold sank from 173 to 148, then back to 158, then down again (March 20) to 153.

legal mechanism existed to discourage raids in the railroad stock market, corners of supplies, or the sale of worthless oil shares to servant girls. Instead, some government operations underwrote the business of making fortunes at public expense. Whisky speculation was promoted by three successive increases in the Federal excise, not one of which, as the law was administered, applied to existing whisky stocks. As the tax rose from twenty cents to two dollars a gallon, the profits from this Federal wand-waving amounted to perhaps a hundred millions. This gift to one group, without a parallel in the tax history of any modern nation,[51] would have made buyers of government securities in anticipation of Hamilton's funding law livid with envy. Many rates in the second wartime tariff, obtained by lobbying and logrolling, were written to enrich special localities, groups, or even individuals at the cost of the general public. The duty on spelter, for example, was inserted by Elihu Washburne for the benefit of zinc manufacturers at Galena, Illinois, and Bethlehem, Pennsylvania, and largely for one man, Joseph Wharton.[52]

A striking example of skill in gaining special privileges was offered by the Onondaga Salt Company. It had silently lobbied through the Albany legislature a law giving it a monopoly of the great salt deposits near Syracuse. Three successive tariff rises brought the duty to forty cents a bushel, after which almost no foreign salt entered. The company at once more than doubled the price of its salt, while it watered its stock to conceal the egregious size of its dividends. Within five years, on a capital of $160,000, it distributed profits of $5,858,000! One member of the company had been speaker in Albany, and another sat on the ways and means committee in Washington.

In the fall of 1861 the *Herald* carried an editorial on the Shoddy Aristocracy of profiteers. Though they had filched the nation's money without giving value in return, it remarked, so had similar gentry in all the great military nations from France to Russia. They wanted to ape the knickerbocker, the cotton, and the codfish aristocracies, and were not much more vulgar; but their reign, predicted the *Herald*, would be brief. Instead, it proved long. Even the New York Chamber of Commerce admitted at the close of the conflict that the city had sold the government great numbers of pasteboard and shingle-stiffened shoes, and recalled the manufacturer who apologized for a boot whose sole dropped off after a half-hour march by saying that it was designed for cavalry use. The war on one side produced countless magnificent examples of heroism and self-sacrifice; on the other, it made dishonesty common. Fat contracts, speculative gains, the sight everywhere of

51 So stated Revenue Commissioner David A. Wells, 39th Cong., 1st Sess., House. Exec. Doc. 62.
52 See Joseph Wharton's letter, July 1, 1862, to Washburne, Washburne Papers, LC.

men making easy fortunes, were demoralizing. People despised Jim Fisk; but what about the respectable Dean Richmond, who with his picked directors controlled the lucrative Buffalo & State Line Railroad, and sold insiders at par a large issue of 7 per cent bonds which at once shot to 117? [53]

When the merchant Abiel A. Low just after the war reviewed the recent changes in business life, he fastened upon two as pre-eminently significant: the rise of establishments which made and shipped goods on a great scale to every important European market, and the multiplication of large corporations. But Low should have included two other major developments. One was the rise, after the national bank act approved February 25, 1863, of a sturdy new banking system centered in New York. The clearance house totals in the metropolis in the year beginning October 1, 1860, had been $5,916 millions; in the year beginning October 1, 1864, they were more than $26,000 millions.[54] The other was the appearance on the American scene of a bold new type of business captain.

It was in these war years that the firm of Plankinton, Armour & Co. was formed in Chicago (1863). Philip D. Armour, just over thirty, was ready for enterprising coups which before Appomattox netted him some two millions. The Havemeyer family began to assert their paramount position in the sugar business, its young members—one of them destined to be mayor of New York—succeeding the founder when he died at the beginning of the war. Wartime operations gave new vigor to the enterprises of Frederick Weyerhaeuser in lumbering, of Collis P. Huntington, far out in Sacramento, in general merchandising, and of Clement Studebaker in the wagon business. All Americans are familiar with the impetus which these years lent to three future titans, Rockefeller, Carnegie, and Morgan. Marshall Field, a young man from Massachusetts who had reached Chicago in 1856 and four years later had borrowed his way into a promising drygoods firm, gained such profits from the overwhelming wartime demand for goods of all kinds that he was able to join Levi Leiter in taking control of Potter Palmer's great merchandise business. A thousand lesser men, like Philo Remington of the famous gun works, achieved note as planners and organizers. The whole national map, in retrospect, appears studded with young entrepreneurs whose imaginations were stirred by the new era opening before them. Each had a marshal's baton in his knapsack, and several were future Napoleons.

One of the most significant facts of the era was the sudden complete release of organizing energy in the nation. Many of the new business captains

53 See James Parton's pamphlet exposé of the nefarious stock-manipulating activities of Wm. B. Ogden in connection with the Chicago & North Western, *Manual for the Instruction of Rings, Railroad and Political* (1866).
54 *Annual Report*, Ch. Commerce N. Y., 1866–67, Pt. 1, p. 7.

who took charge of this release had learned lessons of command and organization as majors and colonels; others had learned as head of new firms furnishing the nation essential wartime supplies. They were intent on making fortunes, and sometimes did so unscrupulously. But the important fact was that they were planners and organizers, and knew that they enjoyed such opportunities for planning and organizing as no business groups on the planet had ever before seen. They could create a new economic world as the Revolutionary generation had created a new political world. Tremendous natural resources, new fountains of credit, steady technological advances, a high wall against world competition, and the sense of confidence born of the tremendous war effort—these combined to put the future into their hands. They would swiftly remake America.

20

Shape of Revolution: Chattels No More

"WHERE ARE ye marching, soldiers, with banner, gun, and sword?" As Union forces pulled themselves together for fresh efforts after Chancellorsville and the first Vicksburg repulse, a larger answer could be given the query. They were marching to the liberation of a race, and the advance guard of the race marched with them. T. J. Barnett, Lincoln's Indiana friend, had important news for the lawyer-politician Sam Barlow just after Chancellorsville. "At present," he wrote, "the President is busy arranging his program for a negro army as a Southern reserve; he is perfectly assured, from facts which he gets from cavalry raids, that the whole available force of Rebeldom is in front; that the negroes understand that they are free; that the interior of rebeldom is now helpless in view of our threatening lines everywhere—and hence he is in fine spirits for a summer and fall negro campaign." [1]

Within a fortnight after this letter three resounding events took place. On May 22 the War Department established a bureau for colored troops with Assistant Adjutant-General C. W. Foster as head. On the 27th the Negro troops of the First and Third Louisiana Native Guard sharply and conspicuously engaged the enemy at Port Hudson. Under a capable colonel, the 1,080 men struggled over broken ground and through a tangle of felled trees to make repeated attacks on a strongly entrenched force. One out of five fell, but they never flinched. White officers, including Generals Banks and Daniel Ullman, declared that they had behaved magnificently.[2] And the next day the Fifty-fourth Massachusetts, the first colored regiment organized by a Northern State, paraded through Boston and was reviewed on the Common by Governor Andrew and Senator Henry Wilson. The scene as it left for the front, its band playing "John Brown's Body," was unexampled; no other regiment had shown greater discipline and dignity, none had collected such vast crowds, and none had been cheered so fervently. A second Negro regiment, the Fifty-fifth, was ready to follow.

1 May 15, 1863, Barlow Papers.
2 Banks to Halleck, O. R., I, xxvi, pt. 1, p. 45; Cornish, *The Sable Arm*, 142, 143. A later chapter in this work will deal with the general position of the freed slaves.

A notable story of State effort the Fifty-fourth represented; a story of which the Commonwealth could be proud when the dusky soldiers marched to death at Fort Wagner this summer, and when years later St. Gaudens reared on the Common, in their honor, the nation's finest battle monument, adorned by one of Lowell's most eloquent stanzas. The country had expected Massachusetts to lead in this field, and under Andrew it did. His service lay not in originating a Negro command—that had been done before; it lay in giving the well-chosen troops the most careful officering and training, and the fullest support of the State. He had entrusted the recruiting of the Negroes to his rich merchant friend George L. Stearns, Sumner's intimate and the whilom protector of John Brown, and Stearns had put unwearying exertions into drawing the men from many States. For colonel, Andrew turned to Robert Gould Shaw, of a distinguished Boston and Staten Island family, an officer who had given exemplary field service to the North from the outset; for lieutenant-colonel he selected Norwood P. Hallowell, scion of a Philadelphia family noted for philanthropy and antislavery zeal.

"This," Andrew wrote Shaw's father, "I cannot but regard as perhaps the most important corps to be organized during the whole war." [3] He wished to lend it all the prestige possible. The junior officers represented other prominent families. The readiness with which young Shaw and Hallowell left their comrades of the Second Massachusetts and Twentieth Maine respectively, and the scorn with which they faced Confederate threats of execution for all officers leading Negro recruits, were as honorable as the statement Shaw's mother made when she heard he had been offered the command. "I shall be nearly as proud to hear that he has accepted," she said, "as I would be to hear that he had been shot."

The national record down to these events of May was much less stirring. Congress in two acts of the summer of 1862 had expressly authorized the employment of colored men for labor or for military service, at the discretion of the President. But months elapsed before Lincoln thought the time ripe for putting arms into black hands. Opposition along the border, particularly in Kentucky, the hope of getting much of the South to accept compensated emancipation, and the desirability of letting events educate Northern Democrats, all reinforced his natural dislike of precipitate steps. He accepted Negro service in principle, but was concerned over the timing of the step.

Of three widely separated attempts, in fact, to marshal colored commands, all had been hesitant and irregular, and two were in the end disappointing. When General David Hunter took command over the sea islands at Port Royal in the spring of 1862, he began recruiting Negroes for a proposed regiment.

3   Jan. 30, 1863, Andrew Papers, MHS.

He actually dragooned many of them. But he got no pay for his recruits, was denied authority to muster them in, and was kept on the defensive by Stanton, hostile Congressman, and Edward L. Pierce, the Treasury agent in charge of a grandiose cotton-growing project in the islands. He finally disbanded all his men but one company, which did irregular garrison duty on St. Simon's Island. Meanwhile, in Kansas the irrepressible Jim Lane, not only without authority but against Stanton's express warning, also recruited colored men for projected regiments. His First Kansas Colored Volunteers drilled, scouted, and did a little fighting with Confederate bushwhackers in Missouri, but was not accepted by the government until early in 1863. The troops impressed newspapermen by their energy, discipline, and neatness, but accomplished little of military value.[4]

Greater material results flowed from the efforts of Ben Butler, who at first had low expectations of the Negroes as fighters, but found apt materials at hand. Governor T. O. Moore of Louisiana had enlisted a body of some 1,400 free Negroes in the militia during 1861. When the Union took New Orleans, they gladly forsook the Southern cause, and Butler shortly called on them to enroll in the volunteer service of the United States. Asking only for free colored men, he assured Halleck that he was keeping clear of the vexatious question of arming the slaves—though Southerners would have called many of them just that. The darkest of his recruits, he wrote Stanton, "will be about the complexion of the late Mr. Webster." Although the War Department gave him no specific approval for his action, in rapid succession he took into his forces the First, Second, and Third Native Guards. The free Negroes of New Orleans were a superior group, and they supplied him with some able company officers. It was two of these regiments that fought so manfully at Port Hudson, and one captain who died heroically close under the Confederate ramparts was given a funeral in New Orleans that rivaled Albert Sidney Johnston's. These fighters proved the martial spirit of their race.[5]

But a large-scale enlistment of colored troops waited on decisions in Washington.

4 Hunter's intentions were good but his methods outrageous; see Pierce's report, O. R., III, ii, 50–60; Cornish, *Sable Arm*, Ch. II. Lane, now a brigadier, built his activities on the long-standing free-soil and abolitionist tradition in Kansas; see the early pages of W. H. Stephenson, *Pol. Career of Gen. James H. Lane;* Cornish, 69 ff.

5 D. E. Everett, "Ben Butler and the Native Guards," *Journal So. Hist.,* XXIV (19-58), 202–217; for Stanton's clandestine support see Flower, *Stanton,* 186.

[I]

The earliest clear evidence that the Administration was dropping its opposition to military use of the Negro appeared in Stanton's orders of August 25, 1862, to General Rufus Saxton, military governor at Beaufort, authorizing him to arm and equip not more than 5,000 colored men as part of the volunteer forces of the nation. For the first time the government, and not a general acting independently, would be responsible. Saxton found his task difficult. Many officers showed a prejudice against the blacks; he divided his authority with Hunter's successor, J. M. Brannan; and many colored men had gone into the navy or the quartermaster service. But he finally mustered enough men for a weak regiment, the First South Carolina, and early in November sent a company on a profitable raiding expedition along the coast of Georgia and upper Florida. It fought with bravery and coolness. Later that month Colonel Thomas Wentworth Higginson arrived to take command, a happy choice. This militant antislavery clergyman of Massachusetts, widely known in the East for his essays and lectures, his book on Kansas, and his share in the attempted liberation of Anthony Burns, made a superb drillmaster and leader. What was equally important, his pen soon gave the fighting spirit of his troops a record eagerly read throughout the North.[6]

But even after the orders to Saxton the Administration necessarily carried water on both shoulders. Stanton, who held advanced views on emancipation and the arming of blacks, appealed to radical sentiment by his bold step; Lincoln by his silence appealed to the conservatives and Border State men. As long as he hoped that the South might make some response to the offer in his preliminary emancipation proclamation, the President could do nothing to close the door.[7]

Meanwhile, pressure for affirmative measures increased. Negro enlistment seemed a great cause, to which old-time free-soil leaders, most churchmen, and many editors rallied with fervor. To some it served a military necessity, to still more an idealistic purpose. Once Lincoln issued his final emancipation

6 Higginson's glowing report on the Edisto expedition of his colored troops, N. Y. *Tribune*, Jan. 20, 1863, is a good illustration of his graphic writing.

7 In any list of first places for Negro soldiers, Hunter's troops would be the first under fire, Lane's the first to lose men in combat, Butler's the first to become members of regiments accepted by the nation and to fight in a heavy action, and Shaw's the first to immortalize themselves and their leader. But Hunter deserves great credit for his pioneer efforts, by virtue of which the First South Carolina, though officially the fifth Negro regiment, should really be accounted the earliest—for it was a reorganization of the force he had recruited. Cf. Benjamin Quarles, *The Negro in the Civil War*, 108 ff.; Cornish, *The Sable Arm*, 92, 93.

proclamation, the movement became overwhelming. As Chase and Stanton pointed out to the President, the best way to render that paper something more than a bull against the comet was to make full use of freedmen in waging war. Thaddeus Stevens fulminated in the House, Trumbull in the Senate, and radical governors outside. Wendell Phillips toured Northern cities delivering his oration on Toussaint l'Ouverture, the central thesis of which was that Toussaint had taken a people demoralized by two centuries of slavery and "forged a thunderbolt." Greeley in the *Tribune* asserted that the Union could arm 50,000 black soldiers in the Carolinas alone. John Murray Forbes spoke for conservative businessmen anxious to shorten the conflict. And Frederick Douglass pleaded with passion for his race: "Give them a chance. I don't say that they will fight better than other men. All I say is, Give them a chance!"

The inevitable opposition of most Borderland leaders and copperhead Democrats was not easily overcome. All informed men realized that any really important body of colored troops would have to come from the South, and from the recent slaves. The Fifty-fourth Massachusetts was not prophetic of a coming army, for the North lacked an adequate Negro population. Superintendent J. C. G. Kennedy of the Census estimated the total free colored men of arms-bearing age in the free States at about 45,000. The free Negro males between 18 and 45 in Vermont numbered 140; in Wisconsin 292; and even in Illinois only 1,622. New York and Pennsylvania could possibly raise three regiments apiece, but no other State but Ohio could enlist even one of full numbers within its own borders.[8] And the arming of recent slaves seemed to some a reckless step. Even after emancipation many Northerners doubted whether large numbers of Southern freedmen could or should be used for anything but military labor. Might Negro regiments not touch off bloody slave revolts? Might they not rekindle Southern anger and prolong the war? Troops of Southern antecedents, as from southern Indiana and Illinois, or of marked color prejudice, found the idea that Negro recruits would suddenly become their equals repugnant.

William Tecumseh Sherman was so deeply opposed to the use of black troops to fight white men, and even to the placing of Negro garrisons in Southern cities, that his critics accused him of an almost criminal dislike of the race. Frank P. Blair, Jr., took a similar attitude. The colored people, in his opinion, should be colonized abroad. When General H. R. Milroy took command of troops in Western Virginia he found some of them habitually beating and abusing Negro teamsters and laborers. Peremptorily ordering them to stop, he explained to Schuyler Colfax: "I have labored hard and had much

8 Kennedy's report to the Interior Dept. is in O. R., III, iii, 43–45; Feb. 11, 1863.

trouble in abolitionizing my Virginia regiments. . . . Ignorance and prejudice are the great barriers in the way." General Thomas G. Stevenson, assigned to the sea islands, said publicly early in 1863 that he would rather have the Union forces defeated than win with Negro troops; whereupon General Hunter clapped him under arrest. White Middle Westerners who saw officers employing some handsome young Negro as orderly, mounting him on a fine horse, and taking him on dashes through the camp, were resentful.[9]

Friends of the Negro had therefore to contend not merely for his right to fight, but for his right to be trusted by other men. General Hunter, replying to the sharp interrogatories of Congress, was the first high officer to enter a wholehearted defense of the fighting power of the blacks. They are sober, docile, attentive, and enthusiastic, he wrote; "eager above all things to take the field and be led into action"; and in the unanimous opinion of their officers certain to prove invaluable auxiliaries.[10] Ben Butler was soon converted to their side. He later testified of his first three regiments of infantry that better soldiers never shouldered a musket; that not only were they brave, intelligent, and obedient, but they had learned to handle arms and march more readily than Harvard or Yale men could have mastered these arts, for they were already drilled and were highly imitative. This was the opinion of John C. Palfrey, son of the Massachusetts Congressman and historian. They drill well, he wrote his father from Ship Island in the summer of 1863; for working, marching, and roughing it they are splendid; and with good officers they make good soldiers. In short, he wished a Negro command. Higginson diffused through the North a particularly discriminating but sympathetic verdict on Negro capabilities.[11]

It was the pressure to fill Union ranks after the failure of volunteering, however, which most effectively broke down the opposition. Representative John M. Broomall of Pennsylvania drove home the point crisply: "I have never found the most *shaky* constituent of mine who, when he was drafted, refused to let the blackest Negro in the district go as a substitute for him." And Charles G. Halpine helped to effect a broad change in public sentiment when he addressed to his fellow-Irishmen the song "Sambo's Right to be Kilt." This happy effusion of his invented character, Private Miles O'Reilly, asserted that some might think it a shame to let the Negro fight, but as for himself

9 Liddell Hart, *Sherman*, 352, 353; Milroy's General Order No. 28 and his letter are in the Colfax Papers, Ind. State Hist. Lib.; for Stevenson see N. Y. *Tribune*, Feb. 27, 1863; for Middle Western attitudes, see Chicago *Morning Post*, July 22, 1863. Robert K. Murray in "Sherman, The Negro, and Slavery," *Negro History Bulletin*, XXII (1959), 125–130, concludes that Sherman was a lifelong believer in Negro inferiority and white supremacy.
10 *Amer. Conflict*, I, 516; cf. O. R., I, xiv, 3–469.
11 Palfrey, Aug. 16, 1863, Palfrey Papers, Houghton Lib.; Higginson summed up his conclusions in the *Century Mag.*, N. S., XXXII (1897), 194 ff. See *Butler's Book*, 494, 495.

> Don't think I'm tippin' you chaff,
> The right to be killed we'll divide wid him,
> And give him the largest half! [12]

Lincoln's change of front after the final Emancipation Proclamation, which declared that former slaves would be received into the armed forces, was complete. He unquestionably approved Stanton's order of January 26, 1863, authorizing Andrew to proceed with his regiments. When Higginson's First South Carolina took a gallant part in the reoccupation of Jacksonville, Florida, he warmly congratulated Hunter, noting the significance of the fierce Confederate counterattack. "It is important to the enemy that such a force shall *not* take shape, and grow, and thrive, in the South; and in precisely the same proportion, it is important to us that it *shall*." [13] He and Stanton agreed late in March to send Adjutant-General Lorenzo Thomas to the Mississippi Valley with plenary authority to enlist and officer Negro regiments. Thomas would start in at Cairo and move down the river to Grant's headquarters and beyond, creating Negro commands at such places as Helena, Columbus, Milliken's Bend, Corinth, Memphis, and Nashville. He was a narrow, plodding, dour-tempered man, whom Stanton was glad to get out of the War Department for a while, but he threw himself into this labor with enthusiasm—Washington supporting him to the best of its ability.

"I would like to raise on this river twenty regiments at least before I go back," Thomas presently told the troops at Lake Providence, Louisiana. Grant gladly collaborated with him. The record of the Western forces had not been good. Complaints had reached Stanton, as Halleck wrote the general, that many officers not only discouraged the Negroes from seeking Union protection, but by ill treatment forced them to return to their masters.[14] Quite without prejudice himself, Grant assured Halleck that he welcomed the new policy, and he saw that his subordinates supported it. At least three of his corps commanders, he reported on April 19, were zealously helping to recruit and arm the Negroes. "They at least are so much of soldiers as to feel themselves under obligation to carry out a policy (which they would not inaugurate) in the same good faith . . . as if it was one of their own choosing." And the Western troops had a new object lesson in the quality of colored soldiers at the end

---

12 R. B. Roosevelt, *Coll. Works of Charles G. Halpine.* The son of a talented Church of England minister in Ireland, for a time editor of the Dublin *Evening Mail*, Halpine remained a Protestant, but attached himself to the Young Ireland Party. His patriotic lyrics did much service to the colored folk as well as to the Union.
13 April 1, 1863; *Works*, VI, 158. Negroes of the Second South Carolina under James Montgomery fought alongside Higginson's men.
14 March 31, 1863, Lieber Papers, HL; Halleck added that he expected Grant to use his personal and official influence to remove prejudice.

of May. One of the naval officers in the Vicksburg area penned a spirited account of their heroism:

A boat came rushing down from Milliken's Bend (about 15 miles above here on the Mississippi) and said that about 5,000 rebels had attacked our troops there. The Union troops at the Bend consisted of about two negro regiments and part of a white regiment. The *Choctaw* and a Light Draft were immediately sent up there, and shortly after, the Flag Ship went up. The *Choctaw* arrived just in time—the negroes fought bravely (their white officers running away), but they were outnumbered, and were beginning to give up, when the *Choctaw* opened on the rebs with her big guns, and drove them away.

We went ashore and took a look at things. There were about 100 dead bodies on the field, about equally divided, half secesh and half negroes. The blacks fought like bloodhounds, and with equal numbers would have won the day. . . .

Grant later that summer expressed to Halleck his high opinion of colored volunteers. They stood the hot climate better than whites, they preserved discipline with less oversight, and "all that have been tried have fought bravely." [15]

Lincoln meanwhile gave orders to Banks paralleling those to Lorenzo Thomas; he and Stanton sent General Daniel Ullman to enlist freedmen in Baton Rouge, where a multitude of hungry, ignorant, and almost naked Negroes, 7,000 in two days, were pouring into the Union lines; and he wrote a singularly hopeful letter to Andrew Johnson, now military governor of Tennessee. Its tone bears out what T. J. Barnett had reported of his elation in planning a grand Negro campaign. The black population offered the Union its greatest untouched resource for victory, he told Johnson. "The mere sight of 50,000 armed and drilled black soldiers upon the banks of the Mississippi would end the rebellion at once." Why did he believe this? He did not say, but the plain implication is that he thought a formidable Negro army would arouse such fears of a general slave insurrection that Southern soldiers would break for home to protect their wives and children.

[II]

If Lincoln did believe this, he miscalculated; Southernors were not so much frightened by the early Negro regiments as angered. In Kentucky the Frankfort *Commonwealth*, a Union paper of copperhead tinge, had expressed the attitude of most slaveholders toward Negro enlistments: "The

15 Grant's letter of April 19, 1863, to Halleck, is in the Eldredge Papers, HL; his letter of July 24 on the fine quality of the Negro troops is in the Grant-Halleck Papers, Ill. State Hist. Lib. For the description of Milliken's Bend see C. F. Guild, June 1, 1863, to G. V. Fox, Fox Corr., N. Y. Hist. Soc.

vile injustice and barbarity of the proposition overshadow its unconstitutionality." The official Confederate position was one of extreme harshness modified by a prudent fear of Northern retaliation. Jefferson Davis had lost no time after the emancipation proclamation in telling the Confederate Congress that unless it otherwise directed, he would order all Union officers captured at the head of colored troops to be delivered to the States to be dealt with under their laws for punishing those who excited servile insurrection. This implied a death penalty. Congress showed more restraint. By joint resolution it declared that such officers should be put to death or "otherwise punished" at the discretion of a military court. Mere privates were to be sent back to their States of origin.

Certain Southern leaders at first showed a reckless temper. When General H. W. Mercer captured a uniformed Negro soldier in South Carolina in the fall of 1862 he wrote Beauregard suggesting a "terrible punishment," and Beauregard referred the matter to Secretary Seddon. He in turn laid it before Davis with the Christian endorsement: "With his concurrence my decision is that the negro be executed as an example. J. A. S., Sec'y War." Late the next summer some Negro troops were captured on James Island. Beauregard was for summary and ignominious penalties: "Let the execution be with the garrote." Davis, when consulted by Governor Bonham, advised against execution. It is certain, however, that four Negroes taken in uniform on St. Catherine's Island *were* put to death.

As it was in the Mississippi Valley that most Negro recruiting was done, there the Confederates faced the most acute problem in dealing with colored soldiers. They knew that they were on precarious ground. The Tennessee legislature in the first autumn of the war had empowered Governor Harris to enlist free Negroes for military service, Moore of Louisiana had paraded 1,400 Negro militia, and various Southern officers had used slave labor for fortifications. Nevertheless, so cultivated a gentleman as E. Kirby-Smith, West Point 1845, issued brutal orders. When Richard Taylor's troops first captured Negroes in arms, Kirby-Smith rebuked him for not killing them on the field. Refusal to give quarter would offer the simplest (he did not need to add the cruelest) way out of a painful dilemma, for if the South executed Negro soldiers by formal order, the North would assuredly execute as many Southern soldiers with the same formality. Secret murder was the only safe method. Secretary Seddon was guilty of the same cowardly type of brutality. Recommending to Kirby-Smith that Negro soldiers be treated kindly and returned to their masters, he advised that their white officers be dealt with "red-handed" on the field or immediately afterward.

It was in the West, too, that executions and denials of quarter were most frequently reported: the murder of twenty Negro teamsters in Union service near Murfreesboro, the public hanging of three Negroes at Holly Springs, and so on. How much truth the atrocity stories contain it is impossible to say; Grant flatly contradicted one. At various times Southern troops humanely returned disarmed Negroes to their masters. On the other hand, the Confederates unquestionably killed some black prisoners summarily, and they may even have followed Seddon's counsel by slaying some white officers. The tale of Fort Pillow we shall tell later. After the Milliken's Bend engagement General Richard Taylor remarked in his official report that many Negroes had been killed, but "unfortunately, some fifty, with two of their white officers, were captured"; he meant it was unfortunate that they had not been dispatched on the spot. One encounter in Arkansas, according to a Confederate participant, left the battlefield a sickening sight, for defying all restraints, the Southerners fell on the surviving colored soldiers and butchered them in great heaps.[16]

The Northern use of colored troops directly affected the vexatious question of the exchange of prisoners. In fact, it was the basic obstacle which first interrupted the exchange, and kept tens of thousands in the misery and starvation of prison camps.

When Secretary Stanton learned that three colored soldiers captured in South Carolina had been confined at hard labor, he ordered the same treatment given three South Carolinians. Other incidents of the same sort soon occurred. Agreements for exchanging prisoners presently covered the South Carolina area, but no colored troops were returned. At this a storm broke in the North. John Murray Forbes called for putting a proper number of Southerners in irons; Frederick Douglass declared he could no longer urge Negroes to enlist. Lincoln was prompt to take action. In a General Order of July 30, 1863, he asserted that the law of nations permitted no distinction of color in the treatment of prisoners of war, and that the United States would give equal protection to all of its soldiers. He directed that for every Union soldier murdered a rebel soldier should be executed, and that for every man enslaved by the enemy a Confederate soldier should be put at hard labor on the public works. Since the Confederacy took the stand that it would not return Negro prisoners on the same basis as white men, exchanges stopped.

16 For Confederate legislation on captured Negroes, see *Journal Confed. Congress*, III, 386, 387; for the Davis-Seddon approval of the execution of four Negro soldiers, see O. R., II, iv, 945, 946, 954, the final order being dated Nov. 30, 1862; for the Davis-Seddon exchange of views with Governor Bonham, see Seddon's letter of Sept. 1, 1863, Pickens-Bonham Papers, LC; for Kirby-Smith's rebuke of Taylor for not murdering Negroes, see O. R., II, vi, 21, 22, June 13, 1863; for Seddon's advice on red-handed action, see O. R., I, xxii, 964, 965; for Beauregard's invocation of the garrote, see *Amer. Conflict*, II, 523; and for the Arkansas engagement of tragic aftermath, see Cornish, *Sable Arm*, 177.

As an assertion of moral principle, the Northern attitude was admirable. But unquestionably the War Department was actuated by practical as well as moral principles, for it wished to deprive the South of as much manpower as possible.

A calamitous deadlock resulted; calamitous at least to a host of poor fellows North and South who gave up their lives in Camp Douglas, Andersonville, and other lethal detention holes.[17] Each side was too stubborn to yield. Northern generals, including Grant, were as determined as Lincoln and Stanton; Lee was as determined as Davis. To Southern leaders the Negroes were property—the property of white Southerners; to Northern leaders they were freemen and equal soldiers. The fact that the Union had far more prisoners than the Confederacy, which desperately needed more men, accentuated Washington's unwillingnesss to reopen the exchange, and the impasse was destined to last out the war. Naturally Negroes who believed that they would be murdered, or kept in hopeless durance, fought all the more frenziedly.

It meanwhile became clear that the systematic arming of freedmen involved a thrust against not only slavery but caste lines. To this fact Greeley attributed much of the opposition in Congress, the press, and conservative Northern circles. Charles B. Sedgwick of New York, supporting a Negro-enlistment bill in Congress, avowed that it had a class character—it was aimed at the detestable Southern aristocracy. That caste, he said, was the foe of labor, free public education, commercial prosperity, and true democracy; it was proud, intolerant, and insolent, and it must be brought low.[18] Many Southerners were quick to perceive that a new era was opening for the colored race —and for themselves.

Thus Julian Alcorn, a North Carolinian, described to his wife a visit he paid to the camp of General N. B. Buford near Mound City, Mississippi, where he and the general reviewed the Negro troops—"truly a fine looking and well drilled body of men." In the neighborhood were a so-called contraband area where several thousand Negroes were fed at government expense and a freedmen's district where Negro farmers were tilling twenty-acre plots carved from abandoned plantations. White teachers conducted two schools with ninety pupils. At church on Sunday a Methodist minister presided over an Episcopal service, the Negro soldiers and their white officers filling the pews on one side, while Negro and white citizens, men and women, mingled at will on the other.

17 By the end of 1863 the Union held some 26,000 prisoners, the Confederacy some 13,000; Cornish, *Sable Arm,* 171. Greeley gives a contemporary view of the problem; *Amer. Conflict,* II, 525; Rhodes emphasizes the North's material reasons for wishing to hold its prisoners, V, 498. We shall later consider prison camps and exchanges more fully.
18 *Cong. Globe,* 37th Cong., 3d Sess., 629, Jan. 30, 1863. "The cornerstone of this aristocracy is slavery," said Sedgwick.

"My observations at headquarters," wrote Alcorn, "induced melancholy reflections. The poor miserable southerners that cringed at the feet of power presented a contrast with the saucy well dressed negroes with faces bright, head erect, and scornful look at the 'poor secesh trash' that graciously yielded the walk to their sable superiors in position." He added that the South used to scoff at the idea of Negro garrisons in her cities. "But here is an important post, near the heart of the southern confederacy, that is garrisoned by negroes, and I believe our people think the place very securely held." [19] At such places one phase of Reconstruction was beginning. The best of the Northern recruiting officers knew that their long-term object was to make not merely good soldiers but good citizens.

[III]

General Thomas' mission, concluded in May, was successful. Though the Negro troops were subjected to unfair discrimination, getting only $10 a month and one ration while white volunteers received $13, full rations, and free uniforms, they came forward with alacrity. Thomas earnestly exhorted the white troops to welcome all refugee blacks, to feed and clothe them, and to give the able-bodied men arms. He had power to dismiss anybody guilty of maltreating Negroes. He also had authority to give commissions to white soldiers, irrespective of rank, who showed enthusiasm for using colored volunteers. Creating a line of regiments down the valley, he laid a foundation for steady continuance of the work. It was after his return in May that the War Department opened its new bureau, and systematized the enlistment of freedmen by General Order No. 43.[20] That fall recruiting stations were established in Maryland, Missouri, and Tennessee, loyal slaveholders who manumitted their hands and offered them for enlistment receiving $300 each. By December, more than 50,000 men had been organized and were in actual service, while the total was swelling daily. Thomas could later boast that he had initiated the organization of about two-fifths of all the colored regiments in the war.

Northern believers in the Negro read with pride of the number who became good officers, about a hundred gaining commissions. The white officers were carefully selected, particularly after General Silas Casey, author of a famous manual of infantry tactics, became head in Washington of the busiest of the several examining boards. He and others set high standards. Governor Austin Blair of Michigan was much irritated when, trying to officer the First Michigan Colored Regiment, he found the board examining his initial nominee

19 J. Alcorn, Mound City, March 22, 1864; Alcorn Papers, Univ. of N. C.
20 Most accessible in *Ann. Cyc.*, 1863, p. 27.

in trigonometry and conic sections; subjects which, he sarcastically wrote Zach Chandler, even Lincoln did not know. There was no lack of applicants for places, and two out of five of them were rejected. Most Northerners were delighted by stories of the rapturous enthusiasm of the Negroes. A private who marched through Beaufort, for example, declared that he had looked neither right nor left: "Eb'ry step was worth a half-a-dollar." As the recruiting progressed, all observers could reach the wise conclusion which Grant stated this summer:

The people of the North need not quarrel over the institution of slavery. What Vice-President Stephens acknowledges the corner stone of the Confederacy is already knocked out. Slavery is already dead and cannot be resurrected. It would take a standing army to maintain slavery in the South if we were to make peace today guaranteeing to the South all their former constitutional privileges.
I never was an abolitionist, nor even what could be called Anti-Slavery, but I try to judge fairly and honestly and it became patent to my mind early in the rebellion that the North and South could never live at peace with each other except as one nation, and that without slavery. As anxious as I am to see peace reestablished I would not therefore be willing to see any settlement until this question is forever settled.[21]

The situation of the colored troops remained in some respects unpleasant. They were usually regarded as inferiors. The discrimination in pay, despite Stanton's protests, endured until the close of the war. Many officers were disposed to use Negro units only as labor outfits, a tendency against which William Cullen Bryant conducted a crusade in the Evening Post. Other slights were numerous; and Northern States were soon sending recruiting agents south to enlist colored men and thus make up their quotas, a discreditable type of exploitation.

Segregation was the general rule, though the summer of 1863 saw one mixed force of Negroes, Indians, and whites winning the battle of Elk Creek on the Southwestern frontier. It could not be considered a hardship, for the colored man preferred association with his own people. But it was noteworthy that no effort was made to break it down. When Robert Gould Shaw's father questioned him on the subject, he replied that any intermingling would have to be preceded by a long process of education. White orderlies, he had noted, made no objection to living in the same tent with black orderlies; but if white volunteers were asked to receive Negroes in their regiments, they would object fiercely.[22] The navy, with a specially creditable record of

21 To Elihu Washburne, Vicksburg, Aug. 20, 1863, Grant-Washburne Papers, Ill. State Hist. Lib.
22 Shaw's letter is in the R. G. S Papers, privately held; courtesy of Mrs. Pierre Jay.

colored recruiting, showed that more could have been done than was attempted. At the beginning of the war Secretary Welles had directed officers to accept the services of everyone, black or white, who promised to be useful. An order in the spring of 1863 instructed the flag officers of blockading squadrons that as the sickly season was about to begin, and contrabands were acclimated, Negroes should be enlisted without constraint.[23] Both free Northern Negroes and Southern freedmen thus served at sea alongside white sailors, though at generally lower pay; and Stringham at Hatteras and Du Pont at Port Royal praised the work of the colored gun crews. In the West, Commodore Porter enlisted hundreds of Negroes on his river gunboats. But the army kept the colored soldier with his own folk—where, to be sure, he was most content.

The year 1863 was definitely a year of apprenticeship for the colored soldier, in which he proved himself. General Saxton, when given a long list of questions about the Negro's qualities, ordered his secretary to draw a line through them, and write: "They are intensely human." This nearly covered the ground, and by 1864 the army was ready to accept them as invaluable fighting reinforcements.

All the more discreditable was the conduct of Northerners who, like Horatio Seymour, continued to oppose any military use of colored men. The full story of Seymour's obstructiveness is full of drama. New York was one of the two Northern States which could send a really strong contingent of its own free Negroes to the front. As fighting ended at Chancellorsville a meeting was held in the metropolis to take measures for enlisting large numbers of colored volunteers, and a deputation immediately afterward waited on Lincoln, who told them that the national government could not support the undertaking until it was assured of the governor's cooperation. Memorials were thereupon laid before Seymour, who ignored them. A pertinacious citizen of Albany, asking that a well-known colonel be empowered to raise one colored regiment, finally got a curt reply: "I do not deem it advisable to give such authorization, and I have therefore declined to do it." Prominent citizens of New York rallied to the battle. Peter Cooper, Bryant, Henry J. Raymond, William E. Dodge, and others formed an association, and applied themselves anew to Lincoln and Stanton. The newly formed Union League Club joined the fray. Still Governor Seymour, making fresh excuses, was a lion in the path. If he could help it, New York would never arm a Negro.[24]

23 See approbatory editorial, Wash. *National Republican*, May 13, 1862. Representative Sedgwick, reviewing naval use of Negroes (*Cong. Globe*, 37th Cong., 3d Sess., 630), stated that the navy at the beginning of 1863 had about 5,000 colored seamen.
24 Bellows, *Union League Club*, 83–87; Mitchell, *Seymour*, 300; Flower, *Stanton*, 241; Strong, *Diary*, III, see index for numerous favorable references to Negro troops; Alexander,

In the end the angry citizens persuaded the War Department to take the units they organized into the army under national, not State, authority. The Twentieth New York, departing for the front, was given an ovation which in heartfelt enthusiasm equaled that tendered the Seventh New York in the first days of war. Two more colored regiments followed. But Seymour had hopelessly delayed the effort of the Empire State, which should have outstripped that of Massachusetts.

The Massachusetts story came to its stirring climax in midsummer of 1863, when an amphibious force under General Quincy Adams Gillmore and Admiral John A. Dahlgren undertook to renew the assault on Sumter and Charleston in which Du Pont had failed that spring. The first point of attack was Fort Wagner on Morris Island, commanding the central channel into Charleston Harbor. If this were taken, Union guns could batter Sumter to pieces, and perhaps throw shells into Charleston, the spires of which were plainly visible. A force under General G. C. Strong landed on the island, took possession of three-fourths of it, and pushed their lines up to within musket range of the fort. It was a formidable position, fully garrisoned by Confederate veterans under that Congressional fire-eater of the fifties, Lawrence Keitt, and sure to be tenaciously held—for if it was lost, Charleston might be lost. The approach was by a narrow road of sand with the sea on one side and a creek and marshes on the other; a deep ditch had been dug in front of the fort; and strong bastions at the corners mounted howitzers. Strong's preliminary assault on July 11 was thrown back with loss.

Just a week later Gillmore's artillery and Dahlgren's monitors opened a heavy fire on Wagner, while a storming party of three brigades formed on the island. From noon until dusk the roar of Parrotts, mortars, and light artillery continued. The Confederates made little reply, their flag still waving over their works, and actually they lost only four men killed and fourteen wounded. As night fell the first assault column moved toward the fort— the Fifty-fourth Massachusetts in the van. When Strong offered the regiment this post of honor, Robert Gould Shaw might have declined, for his Negro troops had been marching for two days through sand and marsh, in pitiless heat, and were worn out; but he accepted with exultation. The knightly young officer knew that the eyes of the country were upon his men. He gave the order of quick-march, to become double-quick. The troops had almost reached the ditch when a sheet of musket fire flared from the parapet, and as they pressed on hand grenades and the howitzers caught them. An

Pol. Hist. N. Y., III, 77–80. But the story of Seymour's intransigence is best covered in the New York press, and in Henry O'Rielly's pamphlet "First Organization of Colored Troops in the State of New York."

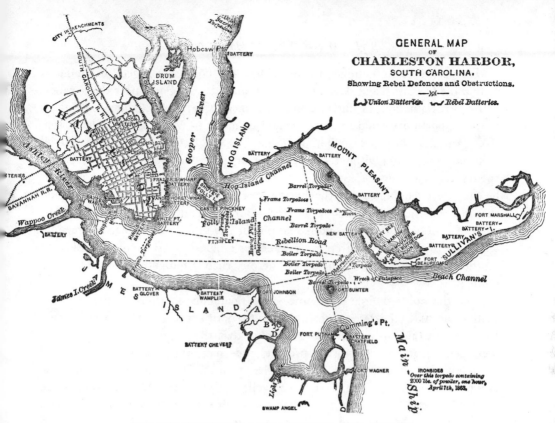

GENERAL MAP
OF
CHARLESTON HARBOR,
SOUTH CAROLINA.
Showing Rebel Defences and Obstructions.
—)o(—
Union Batteries. Rebel Batteries.

CHARLESTON AND FORT WAGNER

intrepid group gained the interior of the fort, planted the colors there, and then had to fall back. Shaw fell dead among scores of his followers. Nearly half of the black troops were slain, wounded, or missing, and more than half of the officers.

The death of Shaw sent a wave of sorrow over the nation as heartfelt as that which had followed the loss of Elmer Ellsworth. Vindictive Southerners buried him under his Negroes. The immediate request of his father that the Union forces forgo all effort to recover the body, leaving him with the men he led, added a fitting touch to the battle; they mingled their dust in a common glory. Colonel Charles Russell Lowell, who later this year married Shaw's sister Josephine, and who himself was to perish in battle, sent her the most fitting words of comfort: "The manliness and patriotism and high courage of such a soldier never die with him; they live in his comrades." In reality, Shaw, who had died calling "Forward, my boys!" was to live in the memory of a State, a nation, and a race; all colored Americans stood on higher ground after Fort Wagner.

Heroism was not confined to the soldier; the colored refugees, the millions of humble freedmen and slaves, exhibited it abundantly. Soon after the Emancipation Proclamation an illiterate black woman of Franklin County, Virginia, found opportunity amid the war turmoil to move to Malden, near Charleston, West Virginia, her three children trudging most of the way. They had lived in a one-room cabin without wooden floor or glass windows; the littlest, a boy aged seven, had never slept in a bed, and had sometimes been so hungry that he ate the corn boiled for the livestock. He had heard his mother praying that she and her brood might be free—and in Malden they *were* free. His name was Booker T. Washington, and one of the first uses he made of freedom was to apply himself to a copy of Webster's blue-backed spelling book. His mother was neither less nor more heroic than thousands of other black women.

But the colored fighters, whose large final contributions to the war we shall treat with the later campaigns, were path-breakers in a special sense. Lincoln had said in his December message that the dogmas of the quiet past were inadequate to the stormy present, and that men must think anew and act anew. Late this summer, writing that peace seemed nearer, he paid the Negro soldier the tribute he had so well earned: "And then there will be some black men who can remember that, with silent tongue and clenched teeth, and steady eye, and well-poised bayonet, they have helped mankind on to this great consummation; while, I fear, there will be some white ones, unable to forget that, with malignant heart and deceitful speech, they have strove to hinder it." The neglected slave, clothed in the national uniform, and realizing that he was battling for his own freedom and dignity, was lifted to the height of the great national purpose, and showed that he too had in him the stuff for epic deeds.

[IV]

No change in the fortunes of war could now long halt the multiform revolution of the time: the emergence of the North to industrial strength, the replacement of improvisation by plan and organization, the shattering of the slave system. Reflections on the subject must have haunted the pillow of a Confederate senator who lay dying this summer in his Alabama farmhouse. Nobody had done more than William L. Yancey to blow the glowing coals of sectional alienation into the flame of war. Without him the Confederacy might never have been born. He had written the Alabama Platform of 1848 demanding positive national protection of slavery in all the Territories; he had led in splitting the Democratic Party asunder as a prelude to dividing the nation; he had penned the Alabama ordinance of secession. Although on his deathbed he clung passionately to the principles he had long upheld, he knew that all his hopes were dust and ashes. His mission to England had been a failure. He comprehended before he died on July 27, 1863, that the tread of Union armies already shook Alabama, and that the old slaveholding civilization was doomed.

But fresh Union defeats East and West could still have the gravest consequences, and with nerves on edge Northerners waited in June for the latest news from Mississippi and Virginia. Grant delivered his second assault against Vicksburg on the 22nd, and his 35,000 men were again flung back with serious loss. Plainly, he must begin a regular siege. In Virginia as June opened, Lee's elated veterans still held the Rappahannock at Fredericksburg, and their commander was bending his eye northward. Striving to ascertain his plans, Hooker sent Pleasonton's cavalry corps on a reconnaissance; and on the 8th these forces struck Jeb Stuart's command at Brandy Station in the heaviest cavalry battle of the war. The Southerners kept the battlefield and inflicted the greater loss, but Hooker learned that Lee was moving some of his men toward the Shenandoah, the natural avenue for invasion of the North.

The Confederate Government had just confronted the most fateful dilemma of the war. Should Lee's troops be used to strike once more at the heart of the North, or should they stand on the defensive while strong detachments were sent west by rail to assist Johnston and Pemberton? Secretary Seddon understood the strategic importance of the West better than any other man in the Richmond administration. As early as April 6 he had suggested to Lee that two or three of Pickett's brigades, with perhaps one other, would give an encouraging reinforcement to the Army of the West, and he later repeated the proposal.[25] But Lee, determined to invade the North, was against any such step. On May 26 one of the most important cabinet meetings of Confederate history discussed the question. John H. Reagan of Texas pleaded earnestly for sending immediate assistance to Pemberton, but the majority overbore him. We are already greatly outnumbered by the enemy in the East, declared Lee, and Jefferson Davis took his side. The troops would be held for a great Eastern Thrust.

Of this debate the North knew nothing, but with rising anxiety it saw storm signals mount in the sky. "Lee's Force Nearly Doubled," ran headlines in the New York *Tribune* of June 13, 1863. "East Virginia and All North and South Carolina Drained. The Rebels Preparing a General Movement."

---

25 After Hooker's defeat, Beauregard suggested that Longstreet's corps should be dispatched with all possible speed on the two railroad lines available to Chattanooga, and used to defeat Rosecrans. Thomas Jordan, Notes, extra-illustrated *Battles and Leaders*, HL.

Bibliography and Appendices

Bibliography and Appendices

BIBLIOGRAPHY

MANUSCRIPT SOURCES

In this list *LC* signifies Library of Congress; *NYPL*, New York Public Library; *MHS*, Massachusetts Historical Society; *IHS*, Illinois State Historical Society; *UNC*, University of North Carolina Library; *CU*, Columbia University Library; and *HL*, Huntington Library. The author specially thanks Mrs. Pierre Jay for access to the diary of Josephine Shaw and the papers of Robert Gould Shaw; Mrs. Laura Stryker for partial use of the Frederick Law Olmsted Papers in the Library of Congress; and S. L. M. Barlow for entry to the valuable archive of his distinguished grandfather of the same name. He thanks also Bruce Catton, E. B. Long, Freeman Cleaves, and many others whom he cannot name for transcripts of valuable documents.

MANUSCRIPT COLLECTIONS

Charles Francis Adams Papers and Diary, MHS; William Allen Papers, LC; John A. Andrew Papers, MHS, Mass. State Archives; Gen. Christopher C. Augur Collection, IHS.

S. L. M. Barlow Papers, HL; Samuel G. Barnes Diaries, LC; Edward Bates Papers, LC, Missouri Historical Society; John A. Bayard Papers, LC; Henry W. Bellows Papers, MHS; H. G. Benson MSS Recollections, UNC; John Huston Bills MS Diary, UNC; Jeremiah S. Black Papers, LC; Austin Blair Papers, (Burton Collection), Detroit Public Library; Blair Family Papers, LC, Mo. Hist. Soc.; Blair-Lee Papers, Princeton Univ.; Francis A. Boyle Diary, UNC; Edward S. Bragg Papers, Wisconsin State Hist. Soc.; Brock Collection, HL; Orville A. Browning Papers, IHS; Bryant-Godwin Collection, NYPL; Buchanan Papers, Dickinson College, Pennsylvania Hist. Soc.; Buchanan-Lane Papers, LC.

Sylvanus Cadwallader Papers, IHS; Cadwallader-Washburn Papers, Wis. State Hist. Soc.; Simon Cameron Papers, LC; John D. Caton Papers, LC; Zachariah Chandler Papers, LC; Salmon D. Chase Papers, Pa. Hist. Soc., LC, Ohio State Hist. Soc.—see preface to *Inside Lincoln's Cabinet: the Civil War Diaries of Salmon P. Chase*, edited by David Donald; Civil War Collection, Mo. Hist. Soc.; C. C. Clay Papers, Duke Univ.; Cornelius Cole Papers, Univ. of California (Los Angeles); John Coleman Papers, Mo. Hist. Soc.; F. P. Corbin Papers, NYPL, Duke Univ.; W. W. Corcoran Papers, LC; Samuel S. Cox Papers, LC, New York Hist. Soc., NYPL, Ohio State Hist. Soc.; S. W. Crawford Papers, LC, IHS; John J. Crittenden Papers, LC, Duke Univ.; William A. Croffut Papers, including E. A. Hitchcock material, LC; J. L. M. Curry Papers, LC; S. R. Curtis Papers, IHS; Caleb Cushing Papers, LC.

John A. Dahlgren Papers, including Ulric Dahlgren Diary, LC; Charles A. Dana Papers, LC; David Davis Papers, IHS; Jefferson Davis Papers, Confederate Museum, Richmond, Duke Univ., LC, HL, NYPL. See introduction on sources in Dunbar Rowland, *Jefferson Davis, Constitutionalist, His Letters, Papers and Speeches*, I, iii–xi; J. D. B. De Bow Papers (include three MS volumes on the Confederate Treasury), Duke Univ.; John A. Dix Papers, N.Y. State Hist. Library, and family possession; Stephen A. Douglas Papers, Univ. of Chicago; Dubose Papers, Alabama State Archives.

Eldredge Collection, HL; William G. Eliot Papers, Mo. Hist. Soc.; William H. English Papers, Indiana State Hist. Soc.; John Ericsson Papers, LC; Edward Everett Papers, MHS; Thomas Ewing Papers, LC.

Lucius Fairchild Papers, Wis. State Hist. Soc.; William Pitt Fessenden Papers, Palmer Collection, Western Reserve; William B. Franklin Papers, LC; John C. Frémont Papers, Univ. of California (Berkeley), LC, CU.

Hamilton R. Gamble Papers, Mo. Hist. Soc.; S. H. Gay Papers, CU; Joshua Giddings Papers, Ohio State Hist. Soc.; Gillespie Papers, Chicago Hist. Soc.; William A. Graham Papers, UNC; U.S. Grant Papers, LC, IHS, HL, MHS, NYPL; Grant-Lee Papers, IHS; Grant-Washburn Papers, IHS; Horace Greeley Papers, LC, NYPL, HL. Greeley Papers are scattered everywhere; see notes on sources in the lives by William A. Linn, Glyndon C. Van Deusen, William Harlan Hale, and R. R. Fahrney's *Horace Greeley and the Tribune in the Civil War;* Gen. Benjamin H. Grierson Papers, IHS.

Henry Wager Halleck Papers, IHS, LC, HL; William J. Hardee Correspondence, LC; George Harrington Papers, HL; John Hay Papers, IHS, LC; Heintzelman MS Diary, LC; William H. Herndon–Jesse Weik Papers, IHS; D. H. Hill Papers, Virginia State Library; Ethan Allen Hitchcock Papers, Mo. Hist. Soc.; Ethan Allen Hitchcock Diary in W. A. Croffut Papers, LC; Rev. Mr. Moses Hoge Diary, Mission to London, 1863, Univ. of Va. Library; Joseph Holt Papers, LC; Howard Papers, Bowdoin College.

Andrew Johnson Papers, LC; C. J. Johnson Papers, Louisiana State Univ.

Robert Garlick Hill Kean, MS Diary, Univ. of Va. Library, admirably edited by Edward Younger (1957), but the author had used the MS; Laurence M. Keitt Papers, Duke Univ.; Horatio King Papers, LC; Gustav Koerner Papers, IHS.

Robert E. Lee Papers, LC, Duke Univ., Confederate Museum—see notes on MS sources in Douglas S. Freeman, *R. E. Lee, A Biography,* IV, 543–8; Gen. Stephen D. Lee Papers, UNC; John Letcher Papers, Va. State Archives; Francis Lieber Papers, HL, CU; Abraham Lincoln Papers, LC, HL, MHS, Chic. Hist. Soc., NYPL, IHS, including Abraham Lincoln Assn. Photostats of Lincoln documents—see the foreword by Roy P. Basler to the *Works of Abraham Lincoln,* 9 volumes; Robert Todd Lincoln Papers, IC; Martin Lichterman, MS life of John A. Dix, private possession.

George Brinton McClellan Papers, LC, NYPL; Gen. John A. McClernand Papers with MS biography by his son, IHS; Hugh McCulloch Papers, LC; Edward McPherson Papers, a valuable collection made by a member of the 36th and 37th Congresses, who became clerk of the House in 1863, LC; Gabriel Edward Manigault, MS autobiography, UNC; Manton Marble Papers, LC; Charles Mason MS Diary, CU; Montgomery Meigs Papers, LC; William M. Meigs Papers, LC; John Merrilies MS Diary, Chic. Hist. Soc.; William Porcher Miles Papers, South Caroliniana Library, UNC; W. O. Moore Papers, La. State Univ.; E. D. Morgan Papers, N.Y. State Library; S. F. B. Morse Papers, LC.

John G. Nicolay Papers, LC; John G. Nicolay and John Hay, MS, proofs, and notes used in writing *Abraham Lincoln: A History,* IHS.

Richard J. Oglesby, letters and papers, IHS; Frederick Law Olmsted Papers, LC; J. A. Orr, Papers and Scrapbooks, UNC.

Palmer Collection (Civil War Papers), Western Reserve; Gen. John M. Palmer Papers, IHS; Lewis B. Parsons Papers, IHS, Mo. Hist. Soc.; Marsens Patrick MS Diary, LC; J. J. Pettus Correspondence, Alabama State Archives; Andrew Pickens Papers, Duke Univ.; Pickens-Bonham Papers, LC; Allan Pinkerton Papers, IHS.

Charles H. Ray Papers, HL; Whitelaw Reid Papers, LC; Thomas C. Reynolds Papers, Mo. Hist. Soc.; W. C. Reynolds Papers, LC; David F. Ritchie MS Diary, private possession; Edmund Ruffin MS Diary, LC.

Carl Schurz Papers, LC, NYPL, Wis. State Hist. Soc.; see prefatory note to Joseph Shafer, *Intimate Letters of Carl Schurz 1841-69;* James A. Seddon Papers, Duke Univ.; William H. Seward Papers and Fanny Seward Diary, Univ. of Rochester, N. Y.; Horatio Seymour Papers, N. Y. State Library and Barlow Collection in HL; John Sherman Papers, LC; W. T. Sherman Papers, HL, LC; Kirby-Smith Papers, UNC; Clara E. Solomon Diary, La. State Univ.; Edwin M. Stanton Papers, LC, and two letterbooks, Univ. of Va. Library; Alexander H. Stephens Papers, Manhattanville College of the Sacred Heart, Purchase, N. Y.; LC, Duke Univ.; see prefatory note to Rudolph Von Abele, *Alexander H. Stephens: A Biography;* Thaddeus Stevens Papers, LC; see information on other sources in Fawn M. Brodie, *Thaddeus Stevens, Scourge of the South,* pp. 13-4; William H. Stiles, UNC; George Templeton Strong MS Diary, photostat copy, CU (the author edited the Civil War volume, but material of value remains unprinted in the MS); Charles Sumner Papers, Harvard Univ., LC, HL.

Robert Taggard, MS Diary, Pa. State Hist. Soc.; Joseph Terry Papers, UNC; Samuel J. Tilden Papers, NYPL; J. H. Tomb MS Memoirs, So. Caroliniana Library; Lyman Trumbull Papers, IHS, LC; John Randolph Tucker Papers, UNC.

United States Sanitary Commission Records, NYPL.

Clement L. Vallandigham Papers, UNC, Ohio State Hist. Soc.

Ben Wade Papers, LC; Elihu Washburne Papers, LC; Thurlow Weed Papers, Univ. of Rochester; David A. Wells Papers, NYPL; Gideon Welles Papers, LC; Horace White Papers, IHS; Louis T. Wigfall Papers, Univ. of Texas; J. L. Worden Papers, Lincoln Memorial University.

Benjamin C. Yancey Papers, Duke Univ.

NEWSPAPERS

Baton Rouge *State-Times;* Boston *Journal;* Boston *Transcript;* Cincinnati *Commercial* quoted in Providence *Journal;* Cincinnati *Enquirer;* Columbia, Mo., *Statesman;* Charleston *Courier;* Chicago *Morning Post;* Cleveland *Leader;* Cleveland *Enquirer;* Frankfort, Ky., *Commonwealth;* Lexington, Ky., *Observer and Reporter;* Lexington, Ky., *Observer and Courier;* London *Times;* London *Daily News;* London *Morning Post;* London *Punch;* London *Record;* London *Illustrated News;* London *Morning Star;* Manchester *Examiner;* Middletown, Conn., *Sentinel;* New Orleans *Daily Picayune;* New York *Tribune;* New York *Times;* New York *Evening Post;* New York *World;* New York *Herald;* New York *Shipping and Commercial List;* [New York] *Harper's Weekly;* Philadelphia *Evening Journal;* Philadelphia *North American;* Philadelphia *Press;* Philadelphia *Inquirer;* St. Louis *Republican;* Sacramento *Bee;* Springfield *Republican;* Washington *Star;* Washington *National Intelligencer;* Washington *National Republican.*

BOOKS

Adams, Charles Francis, *Richard Henry Dana 1815-1822* (2 vols., Boston, 1890-1); Alexander, D. S., *Political History of New York, 1774-1822* (3 vols., New York, 1906-3; Allan, William, *The Army of Northern Virginia in 1862* (Boston, 1892); Andrew, J. Cutler, *The North Reports the Civil War* (Pittsburgh, 1955); Arnold, Isaac N., *Life of Abraham Lincoln* (Chicago, 1887).

Badeau, Adam, *Military History of U. S. Grant* (3 vols., 1868-81); Ballard, Colin R., *The Military Genius of Abraham Lincoln* (New York, 1952); Bates, David H., *Lincoln in the Telegraph Office* (New York, 1907); Beck, Warren A., "Lincoln and Negro Colonization in Central America," *Abraham Lincoln Quarterly,* VI (Sept., 1950), 162-83; Beldon, Thomas G. and Marva R., *So Fell the Angels* (Boston, 1956); Bell, Herbert C., *Lord Palmerston* (New York, 1936); Beloff, Max, "Great Britain and the American Civil War," *History,* N. S., XXXVII (Feb., 1952), 40-8; Bettersworth, John K., *Confederate Mississippi:*

People and Policies of a Cotton State in Wartime (Baton Rouge, 1943); Beymer, William G., *On Hazardous Service* (New York, 1912); Bigelow, John, *France and the Confederate Navy* (New York, 1888); *Retrospections of an Active Life* (5 vols., New York, 1909–13); Blackford, Lieut. Col. W. W., *War Years with Jeb Stuart* (New York, 1945); Blackwell, Sarah Ellen, *A Military Genius, Anna Ella Carroll of Maryland* (Washington, D. C., 1891); von Borcke, Heros, *Memoirs of the Confederate War for Independence* (2 vols., New York, 1938); Boynton, C. B., *The Navy during the Rebellion* (1867); Brigham, Johnson, *James Harlan* (Iowa City, 1913); Brinkerhoff, Gen. Roeliff, *Recollections of a Lifetime* (Cincinnati, 1900); Brodie, Fawn M., *Thaddeus Stevens, Scourge of the South* (New York, 1959); Brown, E. F., *Raymond of the Times* (New York, 1951); Brown, L. A., *The Story of Maps* (Boston, 1949); Brownell, Henry H., *War Lyrics and Other Poems* (Boston, 1866); Brownlee, Richard S., *Gray Ghosts of the Confederacy: Guerrilla Warfare in the West 1861–5* (Baton Rouge, 1958); Bryan, T. Conn, *Confederate Georgia* (Athens, 1953); Bryan, Wilhelmus B., *A History of the National Capital* (2 vols., New York, 1914–16); Burton, Theodore E., *John Sherman* (Boston, 1906); Butler, Benjamin F., *Autobiography (Butler's Book)*, (Boston, 1892); *Private and Official Correspondence* (5 vols., Norwood, Mass., 1917).

Cadwallader, Sylvanus, *Three Years with Grant*, ed. by Benjamin P. Thomas (New York, 1955); Callahan, J. M., *A Diplomatic History of the Southern Confederacy* (New York, 1901); Capers, Gerald M., *Biography of a River Town: Memphis, Its Heroic Age* (Chapel Hill, 1939); Carpenter, Francis B., *Six Months at the White House with Abraham Lincoln* (Boston, 1866); Carr, Lucien, *Missouri: A Bone of Contention* (Boston, 1894); Case, L. M., ed., *French Opinion in the United States and Mexico 1860–67* (New York, 1936); Catton, Bruce, *Glory Road* (Garden City, 1952); *Grant Moves South* (Boston, 1960); *Mr. Lincoln's Army* (Garden City, 1951); Chandler, Peleg W., "Chandler's Memoir of Governor Andrew," *Nation*, XXXIII (July 28, 1881), 77–8; Chase, Salmon P., *Diary and Correspondence of Salmon P. Chase*, Annual *Report* of A. H. A. (1902), (Washington, 1903); Chetlain, Gen. A. L., *Recollections of Seventy Years* (Galena, Ill., 1899); Church, William C., *The Life of John Ericsson* (2 vols., New York, 1890); Cist, Henry Martin, *Army of the Cumberland* (New York, 1882); Clapp, Margaret A., *Forgotten First Citizen: John Bigelow* (New York, 1947); Cleaves, Freeman, *Rock of Chickamauga: the Life of Gen. George H. Thomas* (Norman, Okla., 1948); Clemens, Samuel, *Life on the Mississippi* (New York, 1923); Cleven, N. Andrew, "Some Plans for Colonizing Liberated Negro Slaves in Hispanic America," *Journal of Negro History*, XI (January, 1926), 35–49; Collyer, C., "Gladstone and the American Civil War," *Proceedings*, Leeds Philosophical Society, VI, pt. 8 (May, 1951), 583–94; Commager, H. S., *The Blue and the Gray* (2 vols., 1950); [Confederate States of America] *Correspondence between the President, War Dept. and Gov. T. O. Moore* (Richmond, 1863), *Correspondence between the War Department and Gen. Lovell* (Richmond, 1862); Confederate Tract Society, "The Confederate Hero and his Heroic Father," pamphlet No. 57; Conger, Col. Arthur L., "The Military Education of Grant as a General," *Wisconsin Magazine of History*, IV (March, 1921), 239–62; *The Rise of U. S. Grant* (New York, 1931); Connolly, James A., *Three Years in the Army of the Cumberland* (Bloomington, Indiana, 1959); Conrad, H. C., *History of the State of Delaware* (3 vols., Wilmington, 1908); Cook, Sir Edward T., *Delane of the Times* (New York, 1916); *Autobiography of T. Jefferson Coolidge 1831–1920* (Boston, 1923); Cornish, Dudley Taylor, *The Sable Arm: Negro Troops in the Union Army* (New York, 1956); Cortissoz, Royal, *The Life of Whitelaw Reid* (2 vols., New York, 1921); Coulter, E. M., *William G. Brownlow* (Chapel Hill, 1937); *The Confederate States of America, 1861–1865* (Baton Rouge, 1950); Cox, Jacob D., *Second Battle of Bull Run as Connected with the Fitz-John Porter Case* (Cincinnati, 1882); Crane, Mary Powell, *Life of James R. Powell* (New York, 1930), valuable for reprint of Caleb Huse's "The Supplies of the Confederate Army," (1904); Crozier, Emmet, *Yankee Reporters 1861–5* (New York, 1956); Culmer, F. A., *A New History of Missouri* (Mexico City, 1938); Current, Richard N., *The Lincoln*

Nobody Knows (New York, 1958); Curtis, Newton Martin, *From Bull Run to Chancellorsville* (New York, 1906).

Daly, Louise Haskell, *Alexander Cheves Haskell* (Norwood, Mass., 1924); Dana, Charles A., *Recollections of the Civil War* (New York, 1898); Davenport, Alfred, *Camp and Field Life of the Fifth New York Volunteer Infantry* (New York, 1879); Davis, Burke, *Gray Fox: Robert E. Lee and the Civil War* (New York, 1956); *Jeb Stuart: The Last Cavalier* (New York, 1957); Davis, Stanton L., *Pennsylvania Politics 1860-3* (Cleveland, 1935); Davis, Jefferson, *Rise and Fall of the Confederate Government* (2 vols., New York, 1881); *Letters, Papers, and Speeches,* Ed. by Dunbar Rowland (10 vols., Jackson, Miss., 1923); Dawes, Anna Laurens, *Charles Sumner* (New York, 1892); Detroyat, Léonce, *L'Intervention Française au Mexique* . . . (Paris, 1868); Dillahunty, Albert, *Shiloh National Military Park, Tennessee* (Washington, D.C., 1951); Dodd, Ira S., *The Song of the Rappahannock* (New York, 1898); Dodge, Grenville M., *Personal Recollections of President Abraham Lincoln, Gen. Ulysses S. Grant, Gen. William T. Sherman* (Glendale, California, 1914); Donald, Henderson H., *The Negro Freedman* (New York, 1952); Dorris, J. T., "President Lincoln's Treatment of Kentuckians," *Filson Club History Quarterly,* XXVIII (January, 1954), 3-20; Dorsey, Sarah A., *Recollections of Henry Watkins Allen* (New York, 1866); Douglas, Henry Kyd, *I Rode with Stonewall* (Chapel Hill, 1940); Dowdey, Clifford, *Experiment in Rebellion* (New York, 1946); Dubois, James T. and Gertrude Matthews, *Galusha A. Grow, Father of the Homestead Act* (Boston, 1917); Duer, William H., "The New Opposition Party," *Atlantic Monthly,* X (September, 1862), 377-80; Duke, Basil W., *Morgan's Cavalry* (New York, 1906); DuPont, H. A., *Rear Admiral Samuel Francis Du Pont* (New York, 1926); Durden, Robert Franklin, *James Shepherd Pike: Republicanism and the American Negro* (Durham, 1957); Dwight, Wilder, *Life and Letters* (Boston, 1868); Dyer, John P., *"Fightin Joe" Wheeler* (Baton Rouge, 1941).

Eaton, John, *Grant, Lincoln and the Freedmen* (New York, 1907); Eckenrode, H. J., and Conrad, Bryan, *George B. McClellan* (Chapel Hill, 1941); Eggleston, George Carey, *A Rebel's Recollections* (Indianapolis, 1958); Eisenschiml, Otto, *The Celebrated Case of Fitz-John Porter: An American Dreyfus Affair* (Indianapolis, 1950); *The Story of Shiloh* (Chicago, 1946); Elliott, Maud Howe, *Uncle Sam Ward and His Circle* (New York, 1938).

Fahrney, Ralph Ray, *Horace Greeley and the Tribune in the Civil War* (Cedar Rapids, Iowa, 1936); Fish, Carl Russell, *The American Civil War* (New York, 1937); Foote, Shelby, *The Civil War from Fort Sumter to Perryville* (New York, 1958); Force, Manning F., *From Fort Henry to Corinth* (New York, 1881); Franklin, John Hope, *From Slavery to Freedom: A History of the American Negro* (New York, 1950); Freeman, Douglas Southall, *R. E. Lee* (4 vols., New York, 1934); *Lee's Lieutenants: A Study in Command* (3 vols., New York, 1942-44); *A Calendar of Confederate Papers* (Richmond, 1908); *Lee's Dispatches* . . . *to Jefferson Davis, 1862-65* with Grady McWhinney (New York, 1957); Fremantle, Lieut. Col. A. J. L., *Three Months in the Southern States, April-June, 1863* (New York, 1864); Freidel, Frank, *Francis Lieber: Nineteenth Century Liberal* (Baton Rouge, 1947); Fritz, John, *Autobiography* (New York, 1912); Fry, James B., *Military Miscellanies* (New York, 1889); Fuess, Claude M., *The Life of Caleb Cushing* (2 vols., New York, 1923); Fuller, J. C. F., *The Generalship of Ulysses S. Grant* (London, 1929); *Grant and Lee: A Study in Personality and Generalship* (Bloomington, 1957).

Gambrell, Herbert P., "Rams and Gunboats," *Southwest Review,* XXIII (October, 1937), 46-78; Garland, Hamlin, *Grant, His Life and Character* (New York, 1920); Gates, Theodore B., *The "Ulster Guard" (20th N. Y. Militia) and the War of the Rebellion* . . . (New York, 1879); Gertz, Elmer, *Joe Medill's War* (Chicago, 1945); Gilmore, James R., *Personal Recollections of Abraham Lincoln and the Civil War* (Boston, 1898); Gooch, G. P., ed., *Later Correspondence of Lord John Russell, 1840-1878* (London, 1925); Gorgas, Gen. Josiah, *Civil War Diary,* ed. by Frank E. Vandiver (Tuscaloosa, 1947); Gorham, George C., *Edwin M. Stanton, Life and Public Services* (2 vols., Boston, 1899); Govan, G. E. and

Livingood, J. W., *A Different Valor: The Story of Joseph E. Johnston* (Indianapolis, 1956); Grant, U. S., *Personal Memoirs* (2 vols., New York, 1885); Grattan, Thomas C., "England and the Disrupted States of America," (a pamphlet, London, 1861); Greeley, Horace, *The American Conflict* (2 vols., Hartford, 1864); Greenbie, Sydney and Marjorie B., *Anna Ella Carroll and Abraham Lincoln: A Biography* (Tampa, 1952); Guedalla, Philip, *Palmerston, 1784-1865* (New York, 1927).

Hale, William Harlan, *Horace Greeley, Voice of the People* (New York, 1950); Hall, Clifton, *Andrew Johnson: Military Governor of Tennessee* (Princeton, 1916); Hart, B. H. Liddell, *Sherman: Soldier, Realist, American* (New York, 1929); Hartley, J. W., *Marcellus Hartley* (New York, 1903); Hartley, Marcellus, *A Brief Memoir*, privately printed (New York, 1903); Haupt, Herman, *Reminiscences* (Milwaukee, 1901); Hebert, Walter H., *Fighting Joe Hooker* (Indianapolis, 1944); Henderson, Lieut. Col. G. F. R., *Stonewall Jackson and the American Civil War* (2 vols., New York, 1898); Henderson, W. O., *The Lancashire Cotton Famine, 1861-5* (Manchester, England, 1934); Hendrick, Burton J., *The Lees of Virginia* (Boston, 1935); Henry, Robert Selph, *The Story of the Confederacy* (Indianapolis, 1931); Hesseltine, William B., *Lincoln and the War Governors* (New York, 1948); Higginson, Thomas Wentworth, *Army Life in a Black Regiment* (Boston, 1869); Hill, Lawrence F., *Diplomatic Relations between the United States and Brazil* (Durham, 1932); Hitchcock, Ethan Allen, *Fifty Years in Camp and Field* (New York, 1909); Hooker, Joseph, *Dedication of the Equestrian Statue to . . .* (Boston, 1903); Howe, M. A. DeWolfe, ed., *Some Letters of Gen. Sherman* (New York, 1909); Hulbert, Archer Butler, *The Paths of Inland Commerce; A Chronicle of Trail, Road and Waterway* (New Haven, 1920); Hunt, Gaillard, *Israel, Elihu and Cadwallader Washburn* (New York, 1925); Hunter, Louis C., *Steamboats on Western Rivers* (Cambridge, Mass., 1949).

Irwin, Richard B., *History of the 19th Army Corps* (New York, 1892).

James, A. P., "Strategy of Concentration of the Confederate Forces," A.H.A. Annual *Report*, (1919); Johnston, William Preston, *Life of Albert Sydney Johnston* (New York, 1878); Joinville, Francois Ferdinand, le prince de, *Campagne de l'Armée du Potomac (mars-juillet, 1862)* (New York, 1862); Jones, Virgil Carrington, *Ranger Mosby* (Chapel Hill, 1944); Julian, George W., *The Life of Joshua R. Giddings* (Chicago, 1892); *Political Recollections 1840-72* (Chicago, 1884).

Kamm, Samuel R., *The Civil War Career of Thomas A. Scott* (Philadelphia, 1940); Kelley, William D., *Lincoln and Hamlin* (New York, 1885); Knox, Dudley, W., *A History of the United States Navy* (New York, 1948); Knox, Thomas W., *Camp-Fire and Cotton-Field: Southern Adventure in Time of War . . .* (New York, 1865); Kreutzer, William, *Notes and Observations Made During Four Years of Service with the 98th N. Y. Volunteers in the War of 1861* (Philadelphia, 1878).

Langeluttig, Albert G., *The Department of Justice of the United States* (Wash., D. C., 1927); Lanman, Charles, *Haphazard Personalities* (Boston, 1885); Larson, Henrietta M., *Jay Cooke, Private Banker* (Cambridge, 1936); Lathers, Richard, *Reminiscences. . . .* (New York, 1907); Lawrence, William, *Life of Amos A. Lawrence* (Boston, 1888); Lee, Capt. Robert E., *Recollections and Letters of General Lee* (Garden City, N. Y., 1904); Leland, Edwin A., "Origin and Administration of the Louisiana Army During the Civil War," M. A. Thesis, Louisiana State University, 1938; Lerwill, Leonard L., *The Personal Replacement System in the United States Army* (Washington, D. C., 1954); Lewis, Charles Lee, *David Glasgow Farragut: Our First Admiral* (2 vols., Annapolis, 1941-3); *Admiral Franklin Buchanan* (Baltimore, 1929); Lindsey, David, "*Sunset Cox*," *Irrepressible Democrat* (Detroit, 1959); Livermore, Mary A., *The Story of My Life* (Hartford, 1897); Livermore, Thomas L., *Numbers and Losses in the Civil War* (Boston, 1900); Logan, Mrs. John A., *Reminiscences of a Soldier's Wife* (New York, 1916); Lusk, William T., *War Letters 1861-3* (New York, 1911); Lytle, Andrew Nelson, *Bedford Forrest and his Critter Company* (New York, 1931).

Mackay, Charles, *Life and Liberty in America* . . . (New York, 1859); *Through the Long Day* (London, 1887); Mahan, Alfred Thayer, *The Gulf and Inland Waters* (New York, 1883); Mahony, Dennis A., *The Prisoner of State* (New York, 1863); Maurice, Sir Frederick, *An Aide-de-Camp of Lee: the Papers of Colonel Charles Marshall* (Boston, 1927); *Robert E. Lee, the Soldier* (Boston, 1925); *Statesmen and Soldiers of the Civil War* (Boston, 1926); Meade, R. O., *Judah P. Benjamin* (New York, 1943); Mearns, David C., *The Lincoln Papers* (2 vols., New York, 1948); Michie, Peter S., *General McClellan* (New York, 1901); Military History Society of Massachusetts, *Campaigns in Kentucky and Virginia; Campaigns in Virginia, 1861-2; Virginia Campaigns of 1862 under Pope* (Boston, 1895 ff.); Milton, George Fort, *Lincoln and the Fifth Column* (New York, 1942); Mitchell, Stewart, *Horatio Seymour of New York* (Cambridge, Mass., 1938); Monaghan, Jay, *Civil War on the Western Border 1855-65* (Boston, 1955); Moors, J. F., *History of the 52nd Regiment, Mass. Volunteers, by the Chaplain* (Boston, 1893); Morison, Stanley, *History of the [London] Times* (5 vols., London, 1935-); Mosby, John Singleton, *Memoirs* ed. by Charles Wells Russell (Bloomington, Indiana, 1959); Munroe, James Phinney, *A Life of Francis Amasa Walker* (New York, 1923).

McCordock, Robert S., *The Yankee Cheese Box* (Philadelphia, 1938); McIlwaine, Shields, *Memphis, Down in Dixie* (New York, 1948); McKinstry, Justin, "Vindication of General McKinstry," undated pamphlet in NYPL; McRaven, Henry, *Nashville, Athens of the South* (Chapel Hill, 1949).

Nevins, Allan, *Frémont* (New York, 1955); *Abram S. Hewitt* (New York, 1935); Nicolay, Helen, "Lincoln's Cabinet," *Abraham Lincoln Quarterly*, V (March, 1949), 255-92; Nicolay, John G., and Hay, John, *Abraham Lincoln: A History* (10 vols., New York, 1890).

Oberholtzer, Ellis P., *Jay Cooke, Financier of the Civil War* (2 vols., Philadelphia, 1907); Owsley, Frank L., *State Rights in the Confederacy* (Chicago, 1925).

Page, Charles A., *Letters of a War Correspondent* (Boston, 1899); Palfrey, Francis Winthrop, *Memoir of William F. Bartlett* (Boston, 1878); Palmer, George Thomas, *A Conscientious Turncoat: The Story of John M. Palmer 1817-1900* (New Haven, 1941); Palmer, John M., *Personal Recollections* (Cincinnati, 1901); Palmer, John Williamson, *Stonewall Jackson's Way* (Cedar Rapids, 1915); Palmer, Gen. William J., *Letters 1853-68* (Philadelphia, 1906); Parks, Joseph H., *General Kirby Smith, C.S.A.* (Baton Rouge, 1954); Patrick, Rembert W., *Jefferson Davis and His Cabinet* (Baton Rouge, 1944); Paul, Herbert, *A History of Modern England* (New York, 1904-06); Pellet, Elias P., *A History of the 114th Regiment, N. Y. State Volunteers* (Norwich, N. Y., 1866); Phelan, Sister Mary Cortona, *Manton Marble of the New York World* (Washington, D. C., 1957); Phillips, Philip Lee, *Virginia Cartography: A Bibliographical Description* (Washington, D. C., 1896); Piatt, Donn, *Memories of Men Who Saved the Union* (Chicago, 1887); Plum, W. R., *The Military Telegraph During the Civil War* (Chicago, 1882); Polk, W. M., *Leonidas Polk, Bishop and General* (2 vols., rev. ed., New York, 1915); Pollard, Edward A., *The Lost Cause* . . . (New York, 1867); Porter, David D., *Incidents and Anecdotes of the Civil War* (New York, 1885); Pratt, Fletcher, *Ordeal by Fire: An Informal History of the Civil War* (New York, 1948).

Randall, James G., *Constitutional Problems under Lincoln* (rev. ed., New York, 1951); *Lincoln and the South* (Baton Rouge, 1946); *Lincoln, the Liberal Statesman* (New York, 1947); Read, T. B., "The Siege of Cincinnati," *Atlantic Monthly*, XI (February, 1863), 229-34; Reed, H. Clay, ed., *Delaware; A History of the First State* (3 vols., New York, 1947); "Lincoln's Compensated Emancipation Plan," in *Delaware Notes* (1931); Rhodes, James Ford, *History of the U.S. From the Compromise of 1850* (vols. 1-5, 1892-1904); Richardson, Elmo R. and Farley, Allen W., *John Palmer Usher: Lincoln's Secretary of the Interior* (Lawrence, Kansas, 1960); Robinson, W. S., *"Warrington" Pen Portraits* (Boston, 1877); Ropes, John Codman, *The Army under Pope* (New York, 1882); *The Story of the*

Civil War (2 vols., New York, 1894–1898); Rossetti, William Michael, "English Opinion on the American War," *Atlantic Monthly*, XVII (February, 1866), 129–49; Rowland, Dunbar, ed., *Jefferson Davis, Constitutionalist: His Letters, Papers and Speeches* (10 vols., Jackson, 1923); Russell, Lord John, *Recollections and Suggestions 1813–1873* (Boston, 1875).

Sandburg, Carl, *Abraham Lincoln: The War Years* (4 vols., New York, 1939); *Lincoln Collector: The Story of Oliver R. Barrett's Great Private Collection* (New York, 1950); Scharf, J. T., *History of Delaware 1609–1888* (2 vols., Philadelphia, 1888); Schley, W. S., *Forty-Five Years under the Flag* (New York, 1904); Sherman, John, *Recollections* (2 vols., Chicago, 1895); Sherman, William T., "General Sherman's Opinion of General Grant," *Century Magazine*, N. S., XXXI (April, 1897), 821; *Memoirs* (2 vols., New York, 1891); *The Sherman Letters*, ed. by Rachel Thorndike (New York, 1894); Sievers, Harry, *Benjamin Harrison, Hoosier Warrior 1833–1865* (Chicago, 1952); Smith, Theodore C., *The Life and Letters of James Abram Garfield* (2 vols., New Haven, 1925); Stampp, Kenneth M., *Indiana Politics during the Civil War* (Indianapolis, 1949); Stanton, H. B., *Random Recollections* (New York, 1887); Starr, Louis, *Bohemian Brigade* (New York, 1954); Stephenson, W. H., *Political Career of Gen. James H. Lane*, Kansas State Historical Publications, III (Topeka, 1930); Stiles, Major Robert, *Four Years Under Marse Robert* (New York, 1904); Strode, Hudson, *Jefferson Davis, Confederate President* (New York, 1959); Sumner, Charles, *Works* (15 vols., Boston, 1870–83).

Taylor, Richard, *Destruction and Reconstruction: Personal Experiences of the Late War* (New York, 1900); Tharp, Louise Hall, *Three Saints and a Sinner* (Boston, 1956); Thorndike, Rachel S., ed., *The Sherman Letters* (New York, 1894); Tilden, Samuel J., *Letters and Literary Memorials* (New York, 1908); Townsend, George Alfred, *Campaign of a Non-Combatant* (New York, 1866); Trexler, Harrison A., "The Confederate Navy Department and the Fall of New Orleans," *Southwest Review*, XIX (Autumn, 1933), 88–102; *Slavery in Missouri, 1804–65* (Baltimore, 1914); Trobriand, Regis de, *Four Years with the Army of the Potomac* (Boston, 1889); *Life and Memoirs*, ed. by Marie Caroline Post (New York, 1910).

Walker, Francis A., *History of the Second Army Corps* (New York, 1891); Warden, Robert B., *Account of the Private Life and Public Services of Salmon Portland Chase* (Cincinnati, 1874); Watts, John, *The Facts of the Cotton Famine* (London, 1866); Webb, Alexander, *The Peninsula* (New York, 1882); Weeden, William B., *War Government, Federal and State, 1861–5* (Boston, 1906); White, Ruth, *Yankee from Sweden* (New York, 1960); Williams, Kenneth P., "The Tennessee River Campaign and Anna Ella Carroll," *Indiana Magazine of History*, XLVI, No. 3 (September, 1950), 221–48; *Lincoln Finds a General* (5 vols., New York, 1949–1959); Williams, Harry T., "Investigation—1862," *American Heritage*, VI (December, 1954), 16–21; *Lincoln and His Generals* (New York, 1952); *Lincoln and the Radicals* (Madison, Wis., 1941); Willson, Beckles, *John Slidell and the Confederates in Paris* (New York, 1932); Wilson, Henry, "Edwin M. Stanton," *Atlantic Monthly*, XXV (February, 1870), 234–46; Wilson, H. W., *Ironclads in Action: A Sketch of Naval Warfare from 1855 to 1895* (Boston, 1898); Wilson, James H., *Life of Charles A. Dana* (New York, 1907); Wood, William, *Captains of the Civil War: A Chronicle of the Blue and the Gray* (New Haven, 1921); Wright, Gordon, "Economic Conditions in the Confederacy as seen by the French Consuls," *Journal of Southern History*, VII (May, 1941), 195 ff.; Wyeth, John Allen, *With Sabre and Scalpel, the Autobiography of a Soldier and Surgeon* (New York, 1914); *Life of General Nathan Bedford Forrest* (New York, 1901).

Younger, Edward, *Inside the Confederate Government: the Diary of Robert Garlick Hill Kean, Head of the Bureau of War* (New York, 1957).

APPENDIX I

Reporters After Shiloh

One of the dubious distinctions of Shiloh is that of being a battle in which a few press reporters boldly invented eyewitness accounts, and others used their pens to serve favorite commanders rather than truth. The contemptuous phrase "Cairo war correspondent" arose when men found that some of the reporters who sent "vivid" descriptions of down-river combats had stirred no farther than the Illinois river port. However, several good observers who were on the field at Shiloh wrote accounts which deserve scrutiny, with special attention to the kind and degree of bias they exhibit.

The two first full records to reach Northern readers appeared respectively in the New York *Herald* on April 9 and the Cincinnati *Gazette* on April 14, and were in such serious conflict that they seemed to present different battles. The *Herald* reporter was long thought to be one Frank Chapman, for George Alfred Townsend, in a series of articles in the San Francisco *Chronicle* in 1882, stated (or guessed) he was the author. Actually the writer was W. C. Carroll of New York, who wrote a frank statement of his exploit to Elihu Washburne under date of December 24, 1862. The writer of the *Gazette* story was Whitelaw Reid.

Of Carroll we know almost nothing beyond his own assertion that he had briefly served Grant as volunteer aide in Cairo. But Reid, though not yet twenty-five, was recognized as a gifted and responsible journalist. He had graduated from Miami University in Ohio, had taken active part in Frémont's presidential campaign, had been legislative correspondent for several papers in Columbus, Ohio, and had become city editor of the *Gazette*. He left this post to follow the war, and in 1861 had been volunteer aide to General Thomas A. Morris in the West Virginia campaign. Later, of course, he was to succeed Horace Greeley as owner and principal editor of the New York *Tribune*, was to run for the Vice-Presidency with Harrison in 1892, and was to be minister to France and ambassador to Great Britain.

Carroll tells in his letter to Washburne exactly how he came to write his report. After the battle he kept his ears open. "I discovered the bitterness of feeling and jealousy of Gen. Buell and his officers towards Gen. Grant and the Illinois troops, it being evident to me that no effort would be spared on their part to bring them into disrepute by a series of false and slanderous reports." He determined to defeat the Buell partisans. Without disclosing his intentions, he got permission to catch one of the numerous boats descending the Tennessee. On board it he discovered reporters for Cincinnati papers who were friends of Buell and were profuse in their denunciation of Grant. They had their stories ready written, he asserts; and "to overcome this disadvantage I got off the steamer at Fort Henry, the first telegraph station, and there secured the line and sent my account to the New York *Herald*, which was received in advance of all the Government and other dispatches—forwarded to the President, Senate and House, and then transmitted to all the leading newspapers of the United States."

This is a clear admission of bias; and though Carroll assured Washburne that his account was truthful and impartial, it was actually inaccurate, exaggerated, and partisan. He used sensational language: "The bloodiest battle of modern times just closed. . . . Slaughter on both sides immense. . . . [Federals] eighteen to twenty thousand; that of the enemy is estimated from thirty-five to forty thousand. . . ." He gave Grant unbounded praise, writing that on the afternoon of the 7th the general personally led an infantry assault, brandishing his sword and waving his men on to victory, "while cannon balls were falling like hail around him." His narrative produced a great effect. Later he went on to Washington, where Washburne took him to the White House, and he told Lincoln, as he put it, "all about the Illinois troops."

Reid's account of Shiloh had faults, but was a superior piece of work. His description of the combat was extraordinarily comprehensive in view of the chaotic nature of the fighting. He used moderate language, but wrote with color, and studded his narrative with episodes that gave it dramatic force. Some of the information he received from participants was incorrect; his tale of soldiers shot and bayoneted in the initial assault while trying to surrender is not supported. But by and large his report carried confidence. He ascribed blame to Grant and Sherman where blame seemed due. That is, he declared that the high command was responsible for lack of precautions, bad placing of picket lines, want of protection for the batteries, the location of Grant's headquarters some miles downstream, and once the battle began, the apparent confusion of orders to Lew Wallace. Reid believed that the army had been surprised, and was in danger of defeat when Buell's reinforcements began to arrive. But no personal antagonism to Grant marred his report. Instead, he wrote of seeing Grant calm and resolute in the worst of the fighting, and extolled his confidence in victory once reinforcements arrived.

Both Carroll's and Reid's reports were widely copied, compared, and commented upon. The Cincinnati *Commercial*, edited by Murat Halstead, condemned the New York *Herald* story as a piece of "enormous puffery." It declared that the battle had caused deep uneasiness in the West. "It is certain that at least for some days after the battle the troops under Gen. Grant's immediate command had lost faith in him. The surprise which so nearly proved fatal. . . . is a fact that cannot pass unnoticed." When the Chicago *Tribune* published Reid's story with sharp disapproval of Grant, Elihu Washburne gave the editors a lashing for using "the infamous and slanderous article," and failing to defend the home-State general "who has done the only fighting that has been done in this war." Joseph Medill rejected this criticism. Meanwhile, as hospital ships with wounded men reached Northern towns, and letters from soldiers pictured the horrors of the field, feeling against the commanders grew. A correspondent of the Cincinnati *Times* related how a multitude of wounded "lay, without a surgeon or attendant, without a mouthful to eat or drink, until Wednesday morning." The New York *World* correspondent called the field "the most awful spectacle of human suffering which even the horrors of a battlefield can exhibit." And the correspondent of the St. Louis *Republican* gave a still more horrifying picture of agony left unrelieved, ebbing lives left unsaved. He said the army had been "completely surprised."

The debate at once spread into Congress. John Sherman of Ohio vigorously defended the troops of his State, but admitted that Colonel J. J. Appler of the Fifty-third Ohio ran away, and quoted a letter of Colonel R. S. Buckland, commanding the Fourth Brigade of William Tecumseh Sherman's own division, who stated: "It is true that we were taken by surprise, and had hardly time to form into line of battle and advance about thirty rods when we met the enemy, and opened fire upon him." Senator James Harlan of Iowa was stingingly severe upon Grant, blaming him for horrible loss of life. He read a letter from a district judge of Iowa who spent several days on the battlefield just after it ended, and talked with officers and men. "There is no use," the judge wrote, "in trying to disguise or cover up the fact that our army was badly surprised on Sunday morning." The fieriest defense of Grant in Congress, as stated in the text, was by Elihu Washburne, who maintained that with 40,000 men he had withstood 80,000.

Controversy on the question of surprise was obviously idle until men agreed on a definition of the word. The two best summations by reporters were perhaps those of Henry Villard, a free-lance unconnected at the moment with any paper, and A. D. Richardson of the New York *Tribune*. Villard arrived on the field with Buell, was in the thick of the second day's fighting, and talked with many officers. He concluded that Grant and Sherman had not felt the remotest suspicion that the whole rebel army was within artillery range, that the disconnected position of Grant's six divisions was not such as a vigilant commander would have allowed, that Sherman's brigades were spread out over too much ground, that the approaches from Corinth were not properly guarded, that the failure to entrench was culpable, and that it was an error to place a number of wholly raw regiments in the very front divisions. He calls Grant's subsequent report "about as poor a production as the Rebellion brought forth in that line on the Northern side."

As for Richardson, he arrived after the battle on a boat crowded with Sanitary Commission workers, and scoured every part of the field with participating officers. On April 16 he wrote his managing editor, Sydney Howard Gay: "There is great feeling in Buell's army against Grant's, and a disposition to give Grant no credit whatever. The truth is, it was very bad that Grant had no heavier picket lines out, and so was partially surprised; but after the battle had fairly commenced, Grant and all his division commanders did admirably; and in spite of the skulkers, the tenacity and obstinacy with which his army contested every inch of the ground, and covered it with dead, during all that terrible Sunday before Buell came up, is deserving of all praise."

W. C. Carroll, Dec. 24, 1862, to Elihu Washburne, Washburne Papers, LC; Washington *National Republican*, April 24, July 22, 1862 (summaries of reports of Shiloh in other papers); St. Louis *Republican*, April 12, New York *Tribune*, April 12, Cincinnati *Commercial*, April 14, 15, 1862; W. R. Rowley, Grant's Headquarters, April 19, 1862, to Elihu Washburne, Washburne Papers, LC; Villard, Memoirs, I, 244–262; Richardson, *The Field, The Dungeon, and the Escape*, 236–242; Richardson, Pittsburgh Landing, April 16, 1862, Gay Papers, CU; Starr, *Bohemian Brigade*, 100–104; Crozier, *Yankee Reporters, 1861–1865*, pp. 208–225.

APPENDIX II

The Invasions by Lee and Bragg

One piece of evidence that Confederate leaders in the summer of 1862 planned the invasion of Maryland, the invasion of Kentucky, and a drive for British recognition as a grand coordinated piece of strategy is to be found in the London *Times*, September 5, 1862. It is a public statement by the audacious George N. Sanders, whilom leader of the "Young America" movement and President Pierce's unconfirmed consul in London, who had just arrived in England by way of Canada. He came as agent for the Confederacy, bearing information which he implied was officially entrusted to him by Jefferson Davis immediately on the discovery that McClellan would evacuate his army from the James.

Sanders announced that Lee in August had an army of 200,000 infantry, 400 guns, and 11,000 superior cavalry, ready to march on the North and confident of victory. In the West, meanwhile, Bragg, Hardee, Price, and Kirby-Smith were leading forces which aggregated 150,000 to the flanks and rear of Grant and Buell, equally confident of defeating them. In southeastern Kentucky General Humphrey Marshall was advancing to effect a junction with Kirby-Smith, while farther west Generals T. H. Holmes and T. C. Hindman were about to roll into Missouri with 30,000 men, and there enlist numerous recruits. Altogether, a grand sweep was under way, and Sanders expected British sympathizers to rally to the Southern cause.

From the moment of his arrival Sanders labored to produce an atmosphere favorable to a British offer of mediation. He came authorized to raise money on bonds secured by cotton, and to let contracts for ships to enter the Confederate navy (Owsley, *King Cotton Diplomacy*, 387). At once he saw William S. Lindsay, the largest British shipowner, member of Parliament, and Confederate sympathizer. Within a fortnight after the *Times* printed his statement, Russell and Palmerston exchanged letters asking whether the moment would not soon be auspicious for an offer of good services in ending the war (E. D. Adams, II, 38; Spencer Walpole, *Russell*, II, 349). These leaders were moved primarily by news of military events in America, but they had probably read Sanders's statement.

Index

Index